A Practical Introduction to Literary Theory and Criticism

D0431217

M[illegible] Booker
Un[illegible]sity of Arkansas

Longman Publishers USA

A Practical Introduction to Literary Theory and Criticism

Copyright © 1996 by Longman Publishers USA.
All rights reserved.
No part of this publication may be reproduced,
stored in a retrieval system, or transmitted
in any form or by any means, electronic, mechanical,
photocopying, recording, or otherwise,
without the prior permission of the publisher.

Longman, 10 Bank Street, White Plains, N.Y. 10606

Associated companies:
Longman Group Ltd., London
Longman Cheshire Pty., Melbourne
Longman Paul Pty., Auckland
Copp Clark Longman Ltd., Toronto

Acquisitions editor: Virginia L. Blanford
Assistant editor: Chris Konnari
Production editor: Linda Moser/Professional Book Center
Cover design: Betty L. Sokol
Production supervisor: Winston Sukhnanand
Compositor: ExecuStaff
Text credits appear on p. 496.

Library of Congress Cataloging-in-Publication Data
Booker, M. Keith.
A practical introduction to literary theory and criticism / M. Keith Booker.
p. cm.
Part 3: Introduction to criticism in practice contains various essays by various authors.
Includes bibliographical references and index.
ISBN 0-8013-1765-7
1. Criticism. 2. Literature, Modern—History and criticism—Theory, etc. I. Title.
PN81.B57 1996
801'.95—dc20 95-20852
CIP

1 2 3 4 5 6 7 8 9 10-MA-9998979695

For Dubravka

Contents

Preface *xi*

INTRODUCTION **1**

PART 1 INTRODUCTION TO THEORETICAL APPROACHES TO LITERATURE **11**

CHAPTER 1 **THE NEW CRITICISM** **13**

Bibliography *23*

CHAPTER 2 **PSYCHOANALYTIC LITERARY CRITICISM** **27**

Bibliography *38*

CHAPTER 3 **READER-RESPONSE LITERARY CRITICISM** **41**

Bibliography *51*

CHAPTER 4 **DECONSTRUCTIVE LITERARY CRITICISM** **55**

Bibliography *66*

CHAPTER 5 **MARXIST LITERARY CRITICISM** **71**

Bibliography *85*

CHAPTER 6 **FEMINIST LITERARY CRITICISM** **89**

Bibliography *99*

CHAPTER 7 **BAKHTINIAN LITERARY CRITICISM** **103**

Bibliography *114*

CHAPTER 8 **FOUCAULDIAN LITERARY CRITICISM** **119**

Bibliography *130*

CHAPTER 9 **NEW HISTORICIST LITERARY CRITICISM** **135**

Bibliography *145*

CHAPTER 10 **MULTICULTURAL LITERARY CRITICISM** **149**

Bibliography *159*

PART 2 INTRODUCTION TO THE APPLICATION OF LITERARY THEORY **165**

CHAPTER 11 **APPROACHES TO *THE TEMPEST*, BY WILLIAM SHAKESPEARE** **167**

Reader-Response Criticism *167*
Works Cited 173

Deconstructive Criticism *174*
Works Cited 180
New Historicist Criticism *181*
Works Cited 186
Multicultural Criticism *187*
Works Cited 193
Selected Bibliography *193*

CHAPTER 12 **APPROACHES TO *HEART OF DARKNESS,* BY JOSEPH CONRAD 199**

Psychoanalytic Criticism *200*
Works Cited 205
Bakhtinian Criticism *205*
Works Cited 211
New Historicist Criticism *212*
Works Cited 218
Multicultural Criticism *219*
Works Cited 225
Selected Bibliography *225*

CHAPTER 13 **APPROACHES TO *DEVIL ON THE CROSS,* BY NGUGI WA THIONG'O 229**

Reader-Response Criticism *230*
Works Cited 235
Marxist Criticism *236*
Works Cited 242
Feminist Criticism *242*
Works Cited 248
Foucauldian Criticism *248*
Works Cited 254
Selected Bibliography *254*

CHAPTER 14 **APPROACHES TO *THE HANDMAID'S TALE,* BY MARGARET ATWOOD 257**

The New Criticism *257*
Works Cited 263
Deconstructive Criticism *263*
Works Cited 268

Bakhtinian Criticism *269*
Works Cited 275
Foucauldian Criticism *275*
Works Cited 281
Selected Bibliography *281*

CHAPTER 15 **APPROACHES TO *BELOVED*, BY TONI MORRISON 285**

The New Criticism *286*
Works Cited 291
Psychoanalytic Criticism *291*
Works Cited 297
Marxist Criticism *297*
Works Cited 304
Feminist Criticism *305*
Works Cited 311
Selected Bibliography *312*

PART 3 INTRODUCTION TO CRITICISM IN PRACTICE 317

CHAPTER 16 **ESSAYS ON *THE TEMPEST*, BY WILLIAM SHAKESPEARE 319**

"Learning to Curse: Aspects of Linguistic Colonialism in the Sixteenth Century," Stephen J. Greenblatt 319

Notes 333

"Nymphs and Reapers Heavily Vanish: The Discursive Contexts of* The Tempest,*" Francis Barker and Peter Hulme 338

I *338*
II *339*
III *341*
IV *342*
V *343*

VI *348*
Notes *349*
References *350*

CHAPTER 17 **ESSAYS ON *HEART OF DARKNESS*, BY JOSEPH CONRAD** **353**

"Heart of Darkness: *Geography as Apocalypse*," *Patrick Parrinder* ***353***

Notes *364*

"'Rebarbarizing Civilization': Conrad's African Fiction and Spencerian Sociology," Brian W. Shaffer ***366***

Conrad and Spencer at the Fin de Siècle *367*
Spencer's "Militant-Industrial" Distinction in *Heart of Darkness* *368*
Spencer's "Rebarbarized" Civilization in *Heart of Darkness* *373*
Beyond Spencer: The Military-Industrial Complex in *Heart of Darkness* *375*
From Progress to Parody: Spencer's "Law" and Conrad's "Outpost" *377*
Notes *380*
Works Cited *383*

CHAPTER 18 **ESSAYS ON *DEVIL ON THE CROSS*, BY NGUGI WA THIONG'O** **387**

"The Strength of the Rhetoric of Oral Tradition in Ngugi wa Thiong'o's* Devil on the Cross," *Sam A. Adewoye ***387***

Notes *394*
Works Cited *394*

"Language, Oral Tradition, and Social Vision in Ngugi's* Devil on the Cross," *Bayo Ogunjimi ***394***

An Elegy for the Homestead *396*
A Mock-Epic of Capitalism *398*
Arts for Heart's Sake *401*
Notes *406*

CHAPTER 19 **ESSAYS ON *THE HANDMAID'S TALE*, BY MARGARET ATWOOD** **409**

"The World as It Will Be? Female Satire and the Technology of Power in* The Handmaid's Tale,*" Stephanie Barbé Hammer 409

Notes 418

"Margaret Atwood's* The Handmaid's Tale *and the Dystopian Tradition," Amin Malak 419

Notes 425

CHAPTER 20 **ESSAYS ON *BELOVED*, BY TONI MORRISON** **427**

"Giving Body to the Word: The Maternal Symbolic in Toni Morrison's* Beloved,*" Jean Wyatt 427

The Maternal Body in Language: A Discourse of Presence *428*
Who Is Beloved? *434*
A Maternal Symbolic *438*
Notes 441
Works Cited 446

"Daughters Signifyin(g) History: The Example of Toni Morrison's* Beloved,*" Ashraf H. A. Rushdy 448

Raising *Beloved:* A Requiem that Is a Resurrection *449*
Towards *Beloved:* Margaret Garner *452*
Signifiyin(g) on History *454*
Reading *Beloved* *455*
Hearing *Beloved* *463*
Notes 468

Glossary 473

Index 491

Preface

I wrote this book largely because I have often wished that I had such a book for use as a text in my own teaching, though the genesis probably goes back to my own student days when I myself could have profited greatly from such a text. In this book I seek to provide an up-to-date and comprehensive introduction to literary theory that is accessible and that takes into account the needs of beginning students without shying away from difficult topics or concepts. I also provide clear explanations of the ways this theory can be put into practice to enrich the reading of literary texts. The descriptions of theories and their applications are supplemented by extensive bibliographies for students who wish to read further on their own. Thus while intended primarily as a textbook for use in undergraduate surveys of literary theory and criticism, the book should be of use to any students (undergraduate or graduate) who feel the need for an introduction to the sometimes intimidating field of literary theory.

The book has three principal parts. The first part is a sort of handbook of literary theory. It comprises ten chapters, each of which provides a general introduction to one major theoretical school. The approaches described include the New Criticism, psychoanalytic criticism, reader-response criticism, poststructuralist criticism, Marxist criticism, feminist criticism, the new historicism, and multicultural or postcolonial criticism. Also described are the critical schools built around the theoretical work of Mikhail Bakhtin and Michel Foucault. The second part discusses the applicability of various theoretical methods to specific works of literature: William Shakespeare's *The Tempest,* Joseph Conrad's *Heart of Darkness,* Ngugi wa Thiong'o's *Devil on the Cross,* Margaret Atwood's *The Handmaid's Tale,* and Toni Morrison's *Beloved.* The third part contains a selection of previously published essays on these five works to provide students with an introduction to what professional critics actually write. These three parts are supplemented by a brief glossary that conveniently reviews many of the most important terms used in the rest of the book.

Recent literary theory teaches us that all texts are collective efforts, whether we realize it or not. This book is certainly no exception; it necessarily grows out of the work of the innumerable theorists and critics whose contributions are discussed in its pages. In addition, the book grows directly out of my own experiences in teaching theory and criticism to both undergraduate and graduate students at the University of Arkansas. My students are thus the principal inspiration for both the design and execution of this book. Given that this book represents a summation in introductory form of what I myself have learned about literary theory and criticism over the course of my own studies, I wish to thank my former teachers. Allen Dunn of the University of Tennessee provided a lively first introduction to literary theory. I also learned a great deal about theory and criticism from my professors during my doctoral studies at the University of Florida, especially Brandon Kershner, R. A. Shoaf, and Norman Holland.

I also want to thank those who have contributed directly to the development of this project into a finished book. James R. Bennett, a colleague at the University of Arkansas, read and commented on portions of the manuscript, and John Locke, another colleague, read and commented on most of the manuscript and tried out much of it in his own teaching. I thank Virginia Blanford and the staff at Longman Publishers USA for their help and support in transforming the manuscript into a final product, as well as the book's reviewers: Vincent Pecora, University of California at Los Angeles; David Blakesley, Southern Illinois University; Michael Sexson, Montana State University; William Geiger Jr., Whittier College; David Herman, North Carolina State University; and Patti White, Ball State University.

Most of all, I thank Dubravka Juraga for her comments, advice, and everything else.

Introduction

The last quarter century has been widely described as the age of "theory" in American literary criticism. And it is certainly true that beginning in the late 1960s, American literary critics began to think more self-consciously about the theoretical basis of their work. Central to this phenomenon was a sharp increase in the frequency with which American critics employed the ideas of European literary theorists, but it is also true that events in America in the late 1960s contributed quite directly to the rise of theory in American literary studies. The 1960s established an atmosphere in which the traditional practices of many disciplines were challenged, and literary criticism was no exception. In fact, the increase in interest in European theory can be at least partially attributed to the fact that American literary criticism (which for nearly two decades had been dominated by the ideas of the New Criticism) was actively looking for new sources of inspiration. Most directly, the political turmoil of the 1960s eventually led to a much greater emphasis on politics, society, and history in American literary criticism, and this emphasis has often been accompanied by an appeal to theoretical models of history and society.

It would be a mistake, however, to think that literary theory is itself a new phenomenon. Literary theory is probably nearly as old as literature itself. The ancient Greeks certainly devoted a great deal of theoretical reflection to literature, and works such as Aristotle's *Poetics* remain among the most important founding texts of literary theory. Medieval philosophers, among them Saint Thomas Aquinas, paid a great deal of attention to art and literature in their work, and Renaissance writers, Sir Philip Sidney for one, thought quite carefully about the theoretical implications of their literary efforts. In point of fact, all literary criticism (and, for that matter, all reading) is informed by theory. It would be impossible to understand literature at all without having some prior idea of what it is and how it functions.

By the time American students reach college age, they have already been exposed to a fair amount of literature. They have generally experienced a massive amount of other cultural material as well, whether it be in the form of music, film, or television. As a result, American college students have generally acquired a highly sophisticated array of interpretive techniques, though they may not generally be aware that they are employing these techniques. Even small children seem to be able to make sense of the narratives they see in television cartoons or have read to them from children's books, though the interpretive conversion of television images or written words into understandable "stories" is far from trivial. Meanwhile network series television (so often criticized as banal and "mind-numbing") is actually quite complex. The programming on commercial television is often criticized as "formulaic," meaning that the plots, characterization, and themes of such programs follow highly predictable formulas from which they show little creative deviation. But such formulas seem banal only if the viewer is quite familiar with them. A viewer entirely unfamiliar with commercial television might find the programming there highly complex and interesting, if not downright confusing. For example, a viewer who had never seen MTV might interpret the fragmentary form of a program such as *Beavis and Butt-head* (in which the "main" narrative is frequently interrupted by the intrusion of music videos that the title characters watch and comment on) as a sophisticated—and perhaps confusing—strategy intended to challenge our conventional notions of linear narrative or even call into question traditional models of history as a continual process of change. Similarly a viewer who had absolutely no knowledge of network television would no doubt be highly perplexed by the periodic intrusion of commercials into network programs. Such a viewer might attempt to make sense of these commercial interruptions by interpreting them as a subversive strategy to break up the linear narrative of the main program and thereby remind us that life itself does not always flow so smoothly.

Such an interpretation would not be uninteresting, but it would ignore a great deal of important information that is obvious to the more experienced viewer. Experienced MTV viewers tend to regard *Beavis and Butt-head* as somewhat mindless fun, and they can interpret the program so easily that there is probably little chance that any of their long-held ideas will be threatened or challenged. The same is true for viewers of network series television. Clearly, then, it is valuable to approach cultural artifacts, whether they be poems, novels, or television programs, with at least a minimal understanding of the way those artifacts function. This understanding can, of course, be acquired without conscious theoretical reflection. In the case of television, it almost always is: We generally acquire our knowledge of television not from reading articles about television theory but simply from watching television.

Until fairly recently, it has likewise been the case that most readers—even college students of literature—developed their understanding of the workings of literature simply from reading literary works. That a reader does not consciously approach literature from any particular theoretical perspective does not, however, necessarily mean that she is not using theory. Indeed we all employ theory when we read literature, whether we realize it or not. From this perspective, the rise of theory in literary studies consists largely of a rise in the self-consciousness with which texts are read and interpreted. The choice between "theoretical" and "nontheoretical" approaches to literature thus turns out to be a false one: A reader uses theory in any case, and the real choice is between doing so blindly and unconsciously or doing so with full critical awareness.

Given these alternatives, most of us would agree that the second option seems likely to yield more detailed and sophisticated readings. But all of this is not to say that critical or theoretical styles do not change with time. Clearly they do. Literary studies in the first part of the twentieth century were dominated by what are now sometimes called "traditional" approaches. These often involve little more than a report by an intelligent reader of his personal experience with the text in question—typically in a highly impressionistic mode. More scholarly traditional approaches include biographical studies (in which a work is illuminated through a discussion of the experiences and opinions of its author), philosophical studies (in which the ideas expressed in a literary text are compared to well-known philosophical concepts—and often judged in relation to the critic's own moral or philosophical stance), and textual studies (in which the historical record is carefully sifted in an attempt to determine the precisely correct rendering of important literary texts, especially those produced in the period before large-scale mechanical printing of literary texts). Probably the most successful traditional approach to literature is the so-called historical approach, in which literary works are illuminated by a close and careful study of the historical context in which they were written, thus presumably allowing the works to be understood much in the way they would have been understood by their original audiences.

All of these traditional approaches to literature are thus forms of what the American New Critics would later come to call "extrinsic" approaches to literature. That is, they focus on understanding literary works by bringing external information to bear on them rather than by close and careful consideration of what is already expressed in the work itself. Of course, to a certain extent *all* approaches to literature are by definition extrinsic because a reader must have certain basic information at hand to read a literary work at all. At the very least, a reader must know the language in which the work is written and must possess a certain basic amount of cultural knowledge. The reader who knows nothing about the institution of the monarchy or about the structure of the typical Western family would, for example, be hard-pressed to understand the issues at stake in a play such as *Hamlet.* Moreover a reader must have at least a minimal understanding of the conventions of literature to process the content of a literary work in any coherent way. For example, in Henry Fielding's novel *Tom Jones* the naive Partridge attends a performance of *Hamlet* but seems unable to distinguish the fiction on the stage from reality and is consequently plagued by nightmares about the play's ghost for nights to come.

We might compare the use of external information to aid in the interpretation of a literary text to the activities of a scientist who interprets a particular natural phenomenon by putting to use her overall knowledge of the workings of nature. Granted, we can appreciate the beauty of the stars at night without being an expert in astronomy, but even the most seemingly naive appreciation of the beauty of nature probably involves a complex process of cultural conditioning. To appreciate the beauty of the stars, for example, we must have acquired a basic concept of beauty, not to mention we must have learned to recognize a star. Moreover, matching the concepts "star" and "beauty" probably requires a certain amount of cultural conditioning. In our culture, we are accustomed to thinking of the nighttime sky and other natural objects as beautiful, but it is not at all obvious that someone from a culture without such a tradition would describe a star as beautiful. Meanwhile there are surely many things about stars that can be appreciated and understood only by a trained astronomer. There are simply aspects of celestial phenomena that are visible to the trained eyes of scientists but not visible to the untrained eyes of amateurs. Moreover a scientific appreciation of astronomical processes most likely enhances, rather than diminishes, a person's ability to appreciate the beauty of stars and other objects in the heavens. Most astronomers, after all, admire stars a great deal.

Literary theories are somewhat analogous to scientific theories (as the name perhaps already implies), and we could compare the astronomer who observes a star within the framework of detailed training in the functioning of stars to the reader who reads literary texts within the framework of one or more specific literary theories. The reader who enjoys fiction or poetry but does not have a theoretical understanding of literature would then be comparable to the nature lover who enjoys the sky at night without any scientific knowledge of celestial phenomena. Both this naive reader and this naive lover of nature actually bring a great deal of knowledge to their experience of books or stars, but this knowledge is not organized in a systematic way. Nor is either individual likely to be very aware of the amount of information that he is bringing to the appreciation of literature or nature.

This similarity between science and traditional approaches to literature is probably not accidental: The authority of science in Western culture in the early twentieth century served as a model for the development of traditional critical techniques. It is thus probably not surprising that the New Criticism, which made its first appearance in American literary studies in the 1930s, was so strongly opposed to traditional methods, especially historicism (which for years was the main rival of the New Criticism for dominance in academic literary studies). The New Criticism was formulated, after all, in direct opposition to the power of science in modern thought and was largely an attempt to restore culture to the position of social prominence that it had once held but that had now been taken by science. Contrary to the extrinsic focus of traditional methods, the New Critics insisted on the preeminence of the text itself, arguing that it was the job of the literary critic to read literary texts closely and carefully, attending primarily to their strictly literary properties.

Despite the antiquity of literary theory, professional literary study in the United States is a relatively new phenomenon. Literary studies as a major academic discipline certainly go back no further than the years after World War I. Thus traditional methods of literary scholarship were only traditional for thirty years or so. By the early 1950s, they had been thoroughly supplanted in the American academy by the New Criticism. Meanwhile the dominance of the New Criticism would itself be broken within about twenty years by the rise of newer forms of theory, many of which took their inspiration from developments in European philosophy, history, and human sciences. "Theory" of various kinds has now reigned supreme for more than twenty years. In short, the "new" theory is no longer all that new: It has been a prominent shaping force in American literary studies for as long as the New Criticism maintained its dominance and for almost as long as the traditional methods remained standard practice in American criticism.

Theory is therefore no passing fad—at least no more so than the New Criticism that preceded it or the traditional methods that preceded the New Criticism. Indeed the traditional methods and the New Criticism were themselves theories, and it is not inaccurate to suggest that "theory" is really a synonym for any perceptive, educated approach to literature. But it is also true that the theory that has caused such an uproar in the American academy in the last quarter century differs significantly from its predecessors in both self-consciousness and sophistication. This difference can be attributed partly to the importation of European theoretical models. It is also partly due to a simple understanding that literature is rich and complex enough to repay sophisticated analysis—an understanding that itself derives largely from the work of the New Critics, who (paradoxically) were to a large extent supplanted by the new theories. Meanwhile theory itself is a large and complex field, and there are many types of theory with distinctively different theoretical assumptions and goals.

Theory can help us not only better understand literature but also use literature better to understand the world outside of literature. Nevertheless literary theory, however fascinating in its own right, does not function independently of literature itself. It is designed not to replace literature as a field of study but to provide tools for the appreciation and understanding of the richness and evocative power of literature. Theoretical reflection is, in fact, a highly practical tool that greatly enriches our ability to understand literature and to derive the maximum amount of pleasure and enlightenment from it. Consider, for example, William Carlos Williams's 1923 poem "The Red Wheelbarrow," which at first glance seems so simple as to make sophisticated critical commentary almost pointless:

so much depends
upon

a red wheel
barrow

glazed with rain
water

beside the white
chickens.

But the very sparseness of this poem (one of Williams's most famous) seems to cry out for interpretation. If nothing else, given the typical expectations that we tend to have of poetry, we begin to suspect that there is more to this poem than meets the eye. As it turns out, this seemingly minimal poetic utterance can respond to a wide variety of critical approaches in rich and productive ways. Indeed this poem yields far more on sophisticated reading than we might ever suspect from a quick overview of it.

The New Criticism tends to place a great deal of emphasis on the difference between literary, or poetic, language and the language we typically encounter in the world at large. A New Critic, then, might first approach "The Red Wheelbarrow" by looking for ways in which the seemingly ordinary language of the poem is in fact quite different from, say, what a real farmer might say about a real wheelbarrow. Such a critic might observe that the poem, seemingly almost random in its structure, is in fact meticulously structured. For example, it consists of four stanzas of four words each, and each of these stanzas consists of a three-word line followed by a one-word line. And the rhythms of these lines are quite regular as well: All of the single-word lines have two syllables, while the three-word lines consist primarily of one-syllable words. This level of structure suggests that the words in the poem are packed with more significance than we might find in ordinary speech, where words are seldom so carefully organized. This very indication of significance, then, suggests that we should meditate carefully on the meaning of the poem, and the very fact that such meditations can produce a number of different readings indicates just how rich poetic language can be. If nothing else, by formulating this straightforward statement about a prosaic farm tool as a poem, the poet transforms the simple (and seemingly ordinary) experience of observing a red wheelbarrow into a special event that carries powerful psychological and spiritual resonances. The wheelbarrow *must* be important, or else why would there be a poem about it?

Of course, the production of such readings depends on the reader's familiarity with certain conventions for the close reading of poetry. That is, it requires that the reader bring a certain specialized knowledge and experience to the poem. A reader-response critic might focus on this requirement. Such a critic might also choose to focus carefully on the experience of the reader as he moves through this poem. Such a reader might, for example, be arrested by certain odd moments in the poem. That the first letter of the poem is not capitalized could provide such a moment, suggesting that the poem begins in the middle of a sentence—or of a thought. This reader might also stop to meditate on the significance of the break in the word *wheelbarrow* between the third and fourth lines. Is, for example, the wheelbarrow in the poem literally broken, and is that why it has been left out in the rain, sitting beside chickens rather than being used to do work? Was it the breakdown of the wheelbarrow that caused the speaker (perhaps its owner) suddenly to appreciate just how important the wheelbarrow had been?

If the wheelbarrow has been rendered useless, then in a sense nothing at all depends on it any longer, and the poem's initial expression of the importance of the wheelbarrow is rendered ironic. Such potential reversals would be of particular interest to deconstructionist critics, who typically seek in their readings of literature to locate moments when the meaning of language becomes unstable, potentially pointing toward interpretations that differ radically from the one that is most obviously intended. The paradoxical richness of "The Red Wheelbarrow" lends itself quite well to such readings because the meaning of this poem greatly exceeds the simple denotative statement of which it seems to consist. For example, we could easily read "The Red Wheelbarrow" as a poem about poetry, indeed as a parodic mockery of poetic convention. On this reading, the presentation of a simple and straightforward statement as a poem (or, for that matter, the construction of a meticulous poem about a lowly farm implement) becomes an extended joke, but one with potentially serious implications. The poem, despite its content (or lack of content), is clearly identified as a poem; it therefore asks to be read against the entire tradition of lyric poetry. But if the poem is nothing more than an elaborate leg pull, a demonstration that gullible readers can be convinced to jump through all sorts of interpretive hoops simply by being told that something is a poem (especially one by a "great" poet), then there is also a clear implication that more traditional poems may be informed by a certain pretentiousness as well. The joke may even be at the expense of these earlier poems, which concentrate on idealized notions rather than on the things (like wheelbarrows) that are truly important to human life.

This potential joke at the expense of the "high" art of poetry does not necessarily contradict the straightforward meaning of the poem in that the joke tends to reinforce the notion that common, everyday objects (red wheelbarrows) should not be devalued at the expense of loftier pursuits (poetry). Williams's poetry quite often focuses on common objects and scenes, suggesting his own belief in the importance of such seemingly trivial things. A Marxist critic might thus focus on this motif to read Williams's focus on the red wheelbarrow as an assertion of the primacy of the material over the ideal. That the red wheelbarrow seems to be located on a farm also associates it with the production of food, thus aligning it with Karl Marx's observation that all human society begins in a perceived need for cooperation in acquiring basic necessities such as food. The poem's suggestion that a lot depends on a red wheelbarrow can thus be taken as a suggestion that a lot depends on the production of food or on farmwork in general. The poem then indirectly becomes a reminder that even the richest and most powerful business magnate cannot live without food but that food cannot be produced without the labor of the farmers who use tools such as wheelbarrows.

Other critics might focus on the fact that the poem seems to present a direct opposition between the wheelbarrow, a humanmade technological implement, and the chickens, which can be taken (as can the rain) to represent nature. Such "culture versus nature" oppositions are often evoked in literary criticism, though critics with different theoretical perspectives might draw different conclusions about the significance of this opposition. A postcolonial critic, for example, might see the wheelbarrow as a symbol of European technology and the chickens as representative of the less technologically advanced postcolonial world. In that case, the "so much" that depends on the wheelbarrow might have very negative connotations, suggesting the crucial role played by technology in European and North American imperial (and later economic) domination of most of the rest of the globe. In a similar vein, a feminist critic might see the wheelbarrow as a symbol of masculine power as opposed to the clearly feminine chickens. The centrality of the wheelbarrow in the poem can thus be read as an indication of the traditional dominance of masculine attitudes in Western culture.

These brief examples are intended to give just a hint of the richness that well-defined theoretical perspectives can add to the interpretation of literary works. The rest of this book represents an attempt to present (in a manner accessible to undergraduate students) an introduction to some of the major trends in contemporary literary theory and criticism. Part 1 introduces the major features and concerns of some of the most important recent theoretical approaches to literature, beginning (by way of setting the stage for later discussions) with the New Criticism, then extending in turn through psychoanalytic criticism, reader-response criticism, deconstructionist criticism, Marxist criticism, and feminist criticism. It then presents a discussion of the work and influence of Mikhail Bakhtin and Michel Foucault, two extremely important individual theorists whose work is difficult to fit into any of the preceding categories. This part proceeds with a discussion of the new historicism, one of the most exciting and dynamic critical approaches of the 1990s. It then concludes with a discussion of what (for lack of a better term) might loosely be called "multicultural criticism"—that is, criticism that has taken its inspiration from an understanding and appreciation of a close and careful attention to cultural perspectives (such as African-American or postcolonial ones) that may differ in important ways from the mainstream traditions of (white) European and North American culture. These chapters also include extensive bibliographies, though in each case a small number of works are designated as good beginning points for introductory reading. The chapters may be profitably read in any sequence or combination, though they are designed to be *read* and not merely consulted as a reference.

Given the sheer amount of information in this first part of the text, this handbooklike approach provides students with a convenient source of information on specific literary theories. But this chapter-by-chapter separation of theories into individual categories is somewhat artificial. For one thing, though the chapters in this part are arranged roughly in chronological order according to when the theory discussed first became prominent in American literary studies, this arrangement may obscure the historical development of theory. Students should be encouraged to recognize this historicity. They may, in fact, want to consult other texts (for example, Terry Eagleton's excellent *Literary Theory*) that provide a more historical perspective but that lack the comprehensive coverage of the present text. Students also need to recognize that there is a great deal of cross-fertilization among theories in actual critical practice. Some of the interrelationships between theoretical approaches are discussed in the chapters in the first part of this book, as in the use of the work of Lacan or Foucault by feminist critics. But students should be aware that professional critics quite regularly combine different theoretical approaches in their work and that it is relatively rare to find a "pure" example of most of the theories discussed in this book.

Part 2 supplements the introductory information of part 1 by providing discussions of the applicability of various theoretical methods to specific works of literature: Shakespeare's *The Tempest,* Conrad's *Heart of Darkness,* Ngugi wa Thiong'o's *Devil on the Cross,* Atwood's *The Handmaid's Tale,* and Morrison's *Beloved.* Together the chapters in this part provide two discussions of each of the ten approaches introduced in part 1. An extensive annotated bibliography of criticism on each text is also included to introduce students to the actual critical literature on each text. The chapters in this second part should not be read as exemplary critical essays but as discussions of the ways literary theory might be used to help generate critical essays. They are intended to supplement the introductions of the first part by giving students concrete examples of the somewhat abstract material presented therein. These chapters are also written to stand alone and can be read profitably in any sequence or combination.

Part 3 includes some actual previously published critical essays on these same literary works. These essays are selected not because they exemplify specific theoretical perspectives (though they are generally theoretically informed), but because they exemplify real-world critical practice. All of these essays are referred to in the discussions of part 2, and their inclusion here gives students a convenient opportunity to read further about the texts treated in part 2 as well as to experience firsthand some professional examples of literary criticism. Together, then, the three parts of this book provide students with a basic introduction both to contemporary literary theory and to the application of that theory to the reading of literary texts. This material, together with the glossary of major terms at the end of text, should help students gain at least a preliminary grasp of the major ideas of the theoretical approaches and begin using these theories to enrich their own reading of and writing about literature.

part 1

Introduction to Theoretical Approaches to Literature

chapter 1

The New Criticism

The "New Criticism" is by now a somewhat misleading term for what is in fact the oldest systematic theoretical approach to literature in American criticism. This approach, which involves the close and careful reading and interpretation of individual literary texts, has its roots in the 1930s; the label *New Criticism* itself derives from the title of a 1941 book by John Crowe Ransom, one of the leading founders of the movement. The New Criticism was the dominant mode of American literary criticism throughout the 1950s and 1960s. But with the advent of a number of competing theoretical approaches in the late 1960s and 1970s, the New Criticism began to lose this dominance. In fact, the New Criticism has now fallen somewhat into disrepute for both political and technical reasons. Nevertheless, certain basic assumptions of the New Criticism have been so central to American approaches to literature for so long that they have become naturalized and seem almost like common sense. Indeed during the years of New Criticism dominance, many of the assumptions and techniques of the method became almost synonymous with criticism itself; characteristics such as close reading and detailed interpretation of specific texts were eventually broadly perceived as central to the critical enterprise.

As Louis D. Rubin Jr. puts the matter, we are now in a post-New Critical age only in the sense that the New Criticism "has become simply criticism" (106). Indeed Rubin's own rather sanguine acceptance of this situation serves to verify his remark. Many college students are essentially New Critics without even knowing it, and the same might be said for many of their teachers. Thus as William E. Cain notes, the New Criticism may now seem powerless "only because its power is so pervasive that we are ordinarily not even aware of it" (105). Finally even critics who recognize this power and assiduously attempt to escape it in their own criticism often find themselves slipping into New Critical practices in their teaching because such practices are so well suited to the classroom environment.

The New Criticism is a "formalist" approach to literature—that is, it pays close and careful attention to the language, form, and structure of literary texts while regarding individual texts (rather than historical context or broad generic trends) as the principal object of critical investigation. In the course of the 1950s, the formalism of the New Criticism thoroughly supplanted the historical methods of scholarship that had been dominant in America in the 1930s and 1940s. These methods sought to illuminate literary texts largely by exploring their historical background in terms of both the biographical details of the author's life and the kinds of issues and attitudes that were prevalent during the period in which he wrote the work. A historical scholar, for example, might seek to enhance our understanding of William Shakespeare's *Hamlet* by discussing the widespread fascination with the phenomenon of melancholia in Shakespeare's Elizabethan England. To an extent, historical scholarship attempts to restore literary texts to their original context, allowing us to react to those texts as their original audiences did.

The New Critics, in contrast, argued that the meaning of literary texts resides primarily in the texts themselves rather than in their historical context. They argued that historical scholarship tended to miss the point of literature by failing to recognize the aspects of literary language and technique that make literature unique, thus reducing literature to the same status as sociological or historical texts. The New Critics insisted that literature has to be read in special ways because style, form, and technique play roles in literary texts that are different from (and more important than) the roles they play in ordinary discursive texts. Moreover, these critics developed detailed and highly sophisticated techniques for the reading of literature. Indeed one of the central demands of the New Critics was that criticism be professionalized and that literary texts be interpreted according to certain well-defined and objective criteria rather than simply according to the impressionistic and subjective responses of the individual critic.

Because of a polemical relationship to other forms of literary study, the New Critics are in some ways best known for what they opposed than for what they espoused. In addition to their rejection of historical scholarship, they are closely associated with the notion of the "heresy of paraphrase," a term coined by Cleanth Brooks to indicate the impossibility of capturing the essence of a work of literature merely by summarizing its content. Two other key targets of the New Critics were the "intentional fallacy" and the "affective fallacy," terms coined by W. K. Wimsatt and Monroe Beardsley to describe the practices of equating the meaning of a literary work with the original expressive intention of the author and with the emotional response of the reader, respectively. In this way, the New Critics sought to shift attention away from the activities of both writer and reader and onto the text itself as a "verbal icon."

The New Criticism was the first systematic formalist movement in American literary criticism, though it had a number of important predecessors among

Anglo-American critics, of whom I. A. Richards and T. S. Eliot were probably the most important. The New Criticism was also importantly preceded in Europe by Russian formalism, which dominated Russian literary criticism in the decade before the 1917 revolution and remained influential after it, though more socially and political engaged forms of criticism would eventually become dominant in the Soviet state. The Russian formalists paid particular attention to literary language and to the differences between literary language and ordinary everyday language. In particular, they argued that the central strategy of literature was "defamiliarization," or the presentation of reality in new ways that can lead to a fresh perception of the world. Of course, for this process to continue functioning, literature itself must remain fresh and surprising. The Russian formalists thus emphasized that the process of renewal through defamiliarization applies to literature itself, with innovative literary texts continually changing our expectations of the kinds of linguistic strategies to be found in literature. This renewal of literature is accomplished through self-conscious strategies, such as parody, through which works of art "bare[d] the device" and reveal their own workings as aesthetic artifacts. Thus in one of the best-known Russian formalist essays, Viktor Shklovsky argues that Laurence Sterne's *Tristram Shandy*—precisely because it seems so odd and violates virtually all of the conventions of the eighteenth-century novel—may be "the most typical novel in world literature" (57).

By the 1930s, the political situation in the Stalinist USSR had effectively eliminated Russian formalism as an intellectual force in the Soviet Union. It is perhaps not surprising, then, that the New Critics often identified Marxism (and especially Stalinism) as one of their major ideological foes. The New Critical insistence that literature is a special realm to be distinguished from the social and political world clearly stands in direct opposition to the Marxist belief that literature cannot be understood apart from its historical context. However, the New Criticism, despite its seeming attempt to divorce literature from politics and despite the fact that many of its eventual practitioners had little or no sense of political engagement, grew out of a highly political project on the part of its founders. The New Criticism had its genesis in the "Fugitive" club, a conservative discussion group founded at Vanderbilt University in 1919 and dominated by Ransom, Donald Davidson, and Allen Tate. By the early 1930s, this club, with the Vanderbilt group now reinforced by Brooks and Robert Penn Warren at Louisiana State University, had evolved into the group known as the "Southern Agrarians" because of their vigorous advocacy of southern culture and agrarian modes of life. The politics of the Agrarians was avowedly conservative, an orientation that was further enhanced by their own conservative Christian religious attitudes.

In particular, the Agrarians contrasted life in the antebellum South, which they associated with harmonious relationships between man and God, culture and nature, and the individual and society, with the radical condition of alienation that they associated with life in the twentieth century under industrial capitalism. Brooks, for example, argued that "modern society was sick and that literature offered a diagnosis of its problems. Most particularly, society was said to have lost a sense of community. Individuals lacked any shared set of values through which they could relate to one another" (Jancovich 19). Society in the nineteenth-century South, in contrast, was informed by a strong sense of community, which continued to a certain extent even into the present, given that vestiges of traditional southern communal culture had yet to be eradicated by the growth of capitalism. And the Agrarians actively sought to draw on southern cultural traditions in an effort to transform what they saw as a fallen and degraded modern American society. Ransom, for example, felt that "industrial capitalism had produced a degraded form of culture which could only be changed through a social and economic reorganization of society, and the establishment of social relations which were fundamentally different from those of industrial capitalism, social relations which he identified with the Agrarian society" (Jancovich 24).

The Agrarian critique of industrial capitalism no doubt had much to do with the movement's roots in the Great Depression of the 1930s, when capitalism as a system seemed to have failed. Meanwhile this critique often focused specifically on science, whose dominance in modern society Brooks and Ransom, among others, identified as a central element in the dehumanization of life. The New Critics have often been described as attempting to bring scientific precision to the practice of reading poetry, but they consistently align themselves with poetry and against science. As Terry Eagleton points out, the New Criticism's "battery of critical instruments was a way of competing with hard sciences on their own terms, in a society where such science was the dominant criterion of knowledge" (49). I. A. Richards, in this and many other respects a forerunner of the New Critics, embodies this seemingly paradoxical attitude in his book *Science and Poetry,* which seems to be an attempt to provide a scientific method for reading poetry while at the same time asserting that, in its use of language, "poetry is just the reverse of science" (33). Indeed Gerald Graff is correct when he argues that, though the New Critics seemed to adopt scientific or technological styles of reading and argument, they actually did so to combat the "ruthlessly acquisitive and manipulative will-to-power" that they associated with science (*Literature* 136).

In the course of the 1930s, the Southern Agrarians evolved into the New Critics proper, shifting their emphasis from social critique to literary criticism. Meanwhile they moved away from the earlier Agrarian emphasis on southern culture, especially as key figures such as Ransom and Tate left the south to accept teaching positions elsewhere. This disavowal of strict regionalism no doubt played an important role in the subsequent institutionalization of the New Criticism as the principal academic approach to literature all over America. But this move did not represent a turn away from the political concerns of the Agrarians so much as a change in strategy resulting from the developing belief among the New Critics that literary criticism could help them achieve their political goals. For example, the New Critics held up the humanizing potential of poetry against what they saw as the dehumanizing consequences of the hegemony of science and technology in modern capitalist society. By this time, however, a number of other important critics (R. P. Blackmur, Kenneth Burke, Yvor Winters) were employing formalist critical techniques that in many ways resembled those of the New Critics, though the personal philosophies of the later group often differed dramatically from the Southern Agrarian heritage of Ransom, Brooks, Tate, and Warren.

Continuing the Agrarian tradition, the New Critics consistently argued that literary language, because of its richness and complexity, is superior to scientific language as an expression of the human condition. In particular, they felt that scientific language operates almost purely by denotation, that is, by direct expression of literal meaning, whereas literary language generates meaning through both denotation and connotation, or the implied suggestion of alternative or peripheral meanings. The central emphasis of the New Criticism, in fact, is a close and careful analysis of the techniques and strategies through which literature generates meanings that go beyond the direct denotation that the New Critics associated with science. It is perhaps not surprising, then, that they showed a particular affinity for the extremely rich, complex, and multiple texts of literary modernism. Indeed the institutionalization of the New Criticism occurred concurrently with the canonization of modernism as the official "high" culture of twentieth-century Western civilization. This canonization itself was clearly related to the political climate of the cold war, with the ultrasophisticated texts of modernism providing ample ammunition for those who wanted to argue that Western culture was somehow more advanced than Soviet culture, with its emphasis on the relatively simple works of socialist realism. That the New Critics focused almost entirely on American and British literature also worked to their advantage in this sense.

The difficulty and complexity of modernist works made necessary sophisticated explications like those espoused by the New Critics, helping in the process to justify the use of such techniques to interpret other kinds of literature as well. Conversely the availability of New Critical methods made it much easier to approach the complexities of modernist works for purposes of both criticism and pedagogy. There is thus a close historical relationship between the New Criticism and modernism, and New Critical readings directly set the standard for the interpretation of modernist literature at least from about 1950 to 1970. Furthermore the impact of the New Criticism on our perceptions of modernism was so profound that many later critics, working from perspectives very different from that of the New Critics, continued to treat modernism and the New Criticism as virtually indistinguishable. As Alan Wilde points out in a text published in 1981, "Modernist literature is by now virtually inextricable from the shape modernist criticism has imposed upon it" (20).

Much of this identification of modernism with the New Criticism arises from the tendencies of the New Critics themselves. Leading New Critics such as Ransom and Tate were also important poets, and the New Critics in general seemed to accept Eliot's judgment that in any given period "there is a significant relation between the best poetry and the best criticism of the same period" (20). Furthermore the New Critics consistently sought verification for their own social and political agenda in the literature they read, attributing their own ideas and attitudes (particularly a thoroughgoing aversion to the modern world) to works as diverse as *Oedipus Rex,* "The Fall of the House of Usher," and *Finnegans Wake.* This tendency was especially true in the case of modernist works, which the New Critics typically saw as informed by the same revulsion toward modern society that motivated their own work. In an early response to *Finnegans Wake,* for example, Ransom saw the chaotic and seemingly irrational form of the book as a commentary on the fragmentation and decay of modern society. In particular, he read the book's radical technique as a demonstration of the fact that "the intention of art is in reaction against the processes of science, and that it wants to set up an object which is different in metaphysical kind from the objects scrutinized by science" ("Aesthetics" 428). Indeed the New Criticism was new precisely in its departure from the tendency of previous teachers and scholars of literature to focus on the "great" texts of the past. As Walter J. Ong points out, the preoccupation of the New Critics with contemporary literature was unprecedented in the history of criticism (30).

The New Critics engaged in an active program of promoting their ideas and trying to have them accepted as the standard for critical practice and for the teaching of literature at the college level. In addition to major theoretical and critical texts such as Ransom's *The New Criticism* and *The World's Body* and Brooks's *The Well-Wrought Urn* and *Modern Poetry and the Tradition,* the New Critics produced a number of important textbooks that were widely adopted at universities all over America. The most prominent of these was *Understanding Poetry,* by Brooks and Warren, first published in 1938 and issued in a total of four editions through 1976. As John R. Willingham notes, this text effectively urges students to adopt what was essentially the practice of the New Critics themselves: "To pay closer attention to the language of literary texts; to form habits of identifying and justifying their identifications of tone, mood, voice, metaphors and symbols; to perceive how formalizing principles unify content and meaning; to share the creative process that brought the work into existence; and to celebrate the organic wholeness when it was discovered" (30–31).

Subsequent texts on fiction by Brooks and Warren (*Understanding Fiction,* 1943) and on drama by Brooks and Robert B. Heilman (*Understanding Drama,* 1948) were somewhat less successful, perhaps because the strategies of close reading followed by the New Critics are more easily applicable to poetry than to fiction or drama. One of the most important expressions of New Critical principles occurs in the 1942 *Theory of Literature,* by René Wellek and Austin Warren, which was widely adopted as a textbook for graduate classes in English but was also widely used by professional scholars as a kind of critical handbook. Although not among the founders of the New Criticism (and not identifying the book's approach specifically as New Critical), Wellek and Warren present a systematic and persuasive argument for what is essentially a New Critical program. They begin with a detailed attempt to define literature, thus specifying the object of their inquiry much in the mode of a scientific investigation. This definition turns out to be complex and difficult, but Wellek and Warren essentially conclude that literature is most importantly distinguished from other modes of discourse by the special operations of literary language, which differs from "scientific" and "everyday" language both in its complexity and richness and in its self-referential emphasis on its own operation. They finally conclude that it is "best to consider as literature only works in which the aesthetic function is dominant" (25). Furthermore they specify several distinctive characteristics of literature, including a drive to impose order, organization, and unity on the literary text through the self-conscious use of aesthetic strategies.

Wellek and Warren then go on to present an extensive review of existing theories of literary criticism, which they separate into two principal categories. "Extrinsic" approaches are those that depend centrally on information or theoretical frameworks outside the text, whereas "intrinsic" approaches are those that focus their attention on the text itself. Not surprisingly, Wellek and Warren prefer the latter. They review a number of the former, including those that relate literature to the author's biography, to theories of psychology, to social and political theories, to philosophical ideas, and to the other arts. While granting that external information can be valuable for reading and understanding literature, Wellek and Warren ultimately find all of these approaches lacking because they fail adequately to consider the elements of form and style that differentiate literature from other kinds of language use. For example, they reject psychological approaches to literature because "psychological truth is an artistic value only if it enhances coherence and complexity—if, in short, it is art" (93). They are most dismissive of social and political approaches to literature (especially Marxist ones), arguing that these tend to see literature as a mere reflection of society and thus fail to take into account the relative independence of art from its social context. Wellek and Warren adamantly reject the notion that "literature is primarily an 'imitation' of life as it is and of social life in particular" because "literature is no substitute for sociology or politics. It has its own justification and aim" (109).

Meanwhile Wellek and Warren openly embrace intrinsic (that is, formalist) approaches to literature. They review in detail how these approaches can attend to the special characteristics of literary language, especially in poetry. Intrinsic interpretation can pay close attention to such elements as rhythm, rhyme, and meter and to the way these aspects of the sound of literary language influence the overall impression of the literary work of art. Similarly such approaches can attend to the participation of images, metaphors, symbols, and myth in the "totality, the integrity, of the literary work" (211). Wellek and Warren also devote a chapter to the study of style, which they see as inseparable from a consideration of the content of a literary work. In particular, their emphasis on stylistic analysis is closely related to their insistence on attention to the organic unity of the work of art, that is, to the way the different parts of a work of art combine to make a coherent whole. They thus argue that "stylistic analysis seems most profitable to literary study when it can establish some unifying principle, some general aesthetic aim pervasive of a whole work" (182).

Wellek and Warren tellingly spend three chapters on poetry and only one on fiction and drama combined. Moreover their discussions of fiction are far less specific than those of poetry, dealing largely with what they see as the necessity of distinguishing between "great novels" (which they regard as legitimate literature) and lighter novels (which they regard as mere entertainment). They also argue that a novel must not be read as a "document or case history" but as a work of art, with attention to the details of its literary language and technique (212). Wellek and Warren thus reveal a tendency toward the kind of aestheticism and cultural elitism with which the New Critics have often been charged—but which their defenders have vigorously denied. They also show a typical New Critical preference for modern literature, arguing that modernist novels are more like poetry than are the novels of previous historical periods (235).

Wellek and Warren follow their discussion of fiction with comments on the "evaluation" of literature—on the kinds of judgments that critics should rightfully make concerning the quality of literature. Critics, they conclude, have a responsibility to make judgments about the quality and effectiveness of works of art. These judgments ought to involve valuing literature "for what it is"; that is, "they ought to evaluate it in terms and in degrees of literary values" (238). Wellek and Warren also comment on the nature of "literary values," arguing in particular that such values should not involve the various elements of a work of literature so much as the way those elements are put together to make an organic whole. They conclude that the central issue in aesthetic theory involves a confrontation between the belief that art is a realm relatively independent of the social and political world and the belief that art is simply a reflection of the external world (239). Wellek and Warren, of course, opt for the former position.

Their continual focus on the organic unity of the work of art and on the relative independence of art from the social and political world is typical of the New Critical project as a whole. Indeed for the New Critics, a successful work of literature is always that which employs a number of complex literary strategies to indicate a multiplicity of possible meanings but then resolves these multiple possibilities through the close integration of the various elements of the work into a coherent whole. Thus Brooks and Warren conclude in *Understanding Fiction* that the successful story is one that "is a unity," which occurs when "its elements are so related that we feel an expressive interpenetration among them, a set of vital relationships" (xviii). The New Critics tend to emphasize certain key terms in their discussion of the literary drive toward unity through multiplicity. In addition to specific devices such as metaphor and symbol, the New Critics continually call attention to the importance of broad concepts such as irony and ambiguity. Both concepts involve the simultaneous generation of multiple meanings, creating poetic energy through the resultant contrasts, or "tensions," between competing meanings. Robert Penn Warren, for example, argues that successful poems must achieve their effects in such a way that their "motion" generates its own "resistance," which is then overcome in the course of the poem. And this resistance can occur at a variety of levels, arising not simply from the expression of contradictory ideas but also from contrasts like that between the literary language of the poem and the language of everyday life or between various formal elements of the poem itself.

Brooks's *The Well-Wrought Urn,* one of the most representative works of the New Criticism, provides some excellent examples of the way this emphasis on the richness of literary language was often opposed to the poverty of scientific language. For Brooks, science thrives on precision, whereas poetry thrives on paradox: "It is the scientist whose truth requires a language purged of every trace of paradox; apparently the truth which the poet utters can be approached only in terms of paradox" (3). Brooks sees the precision of science as impoverishing and the paradox and ambiguity of poetry as vivifying and enriching: "The tendency of science," Brooks writes, "is necessarily to stabilize terms, to freeze them into strict denotations; the poet's tendency is by contrast disruptive. The terms are continually modifying each other, and thus violating their dictionary meanings" (9). In an example the more general implications of which are rather clear, he suggests that the lovers in works such as John Donne's "The Canonization" or Shakespeare's *Romeo and Juliet* derive their humanity from their poetic presentation, whereas if viewed "scientifically," they would become mere "animals" (17).

In this emphasis on the ability of literary language to produce a variety of meanings, the New Critics seem to anticipate recent developments in post-structuralist criticism, which emphasizes the unruly and unpredictable ability of language to generate meanings that go beyond the conscious intention of the author. But whereas poststructuralist critics often celebrate this multiplicity of meaning in its own right—sometimes in ways with powerful antiauthoritarian (and especially antitheological) political implications—the conservative Christian ideology of the New Critics remains thoroughly inscribed in their treatment of literary language. Key New Critical terms such as *paradox, irony, complexity, ambiguity, contrast,* and *tension*—all of which evoke the richness and diversity of literary language—are ultimately emphasized in the interest not of pluralism but of organic unity. Poems may gain energy from the creation of conflicts and tensions, but for the New Critics these conflicts and tensions in a successful poem are finally resolved. Irony and ambiguity may delay the final resolution of the interpretive process, but they do not prevent it. Brooks and Warren (speaking of themselves in third person) thus defend their emphasis on irony: "They would not endorse an irony which precluded resolution but they would endorse an irony which forced resolution to take stock of as full a context as possible. The reader wants resolution, but he does not want it too easy or too soon. He wants to see the knockout, but he does not want to see it until the fifteenth round" (*Understanding Fiction* xix).

The neatness with which contradictions and conflicts are typically resolved in New Critical readings (especially of poetry) meant that, among other things, the technique was extremely well suited to application in the classroom, where students found such neat solutions comforting. Indeed the obvious advantages of the New Criticism for classroom applications had a great deal to do with the widespread success of the method in the 1950s. The success of the New Criticism (like the success of most things) was largely the result of its being adequate to its particular historical moment. As the first truly professional literary scholars, the New Critics were able to take advantage of a perceived need for such professionalism (a perception they themselves helped create), especially in the context of an American society in which professional expertise traditionally carried a great deal of cultural prestige: "The New Criticism was the product of the first age when thousands of persons became intent on academic, and ultimately scholarly, analysis" (Ong 33). We might recall here Ransom's suggestion that critics in search of professionalism could consider themselves employees of "Criticism, Inc." (*World's* 329). More important, the convenience with which the professional insights of the New Criticism could be packaged for classroom use was an inestimable advantage in a 1950s environment informed in general by burgeoning college enrollments and in particular by a clear need for a fast and efficient method of literary education in a nation in which such education had not previously been emphasized. The emergence of the United States as a world power after World War II generated a newly perceived need for increased emphasis on culture to counter the supposed philistinism of the Soviet Union—which nevertheless had long emphasized culture and cultural education.

New Critical techniques, then, allowed a generation of English professors to define their work in ways that were well suited to the politics of the cold war and that furthermore made that work seem sufficiently technical and complex to satisfy the American fascination with specialized expertise. After all, the best efforts of critics such as Ransom or Tate or Brooks produced dazzling results that required a subtlety and a virtuosity that no mere amateurs (or, presumably, benighted Soviet professionals) could hope to match. Yet the New Criticism nevertheless provided a tool kit that made it relatively easy for teachers to produce interesting-sounding commentary on literary works and to expound on those works in ways that their students would find both comprehensible and convincing. Although the leading New Critics were themselves highly knowledgeable, the New Criticism allowed—even encouraged—critical approaches that required very little knowledge of historical backgrounds or of disciplines other than literature. New Critical readings were thus accessible to students who might lack such knowledge. Meanwhile the New Criticism was a boon both to professors who wished an opportunity to demonstrate their critical dexterity and creativity and to those who were too overwhelmed with expanding duties to acquire the kinds of knowledge required to interpret and teach literature effectively using historical or interdisciplinary methods. Indeed this ability of the New Criticism to function on a relatively small fund of cultural knowledge may have contributed substantially to the loss of "cultural literacy" bemoaned by certain observers in recent years.

The New Criticism, then, was effective at producing critical and pedagogical discourse that sounded sophisticated enough to justify the existence of professional literary scholars, who could in turn successfully do their work with relatively little actual scholarship. Most important of all, the New Criticism produced results that were politically safe in the hazardous and repressive climate of McCarthyism and its aftermath. The intellectualism of the New Critics themselves might have run against the McCarthyite grain, but that very intellectualism served effectively to divorce the New Critics (and their version of modernism) from American political reality, thus safely inscribing both the New Criticism and modernism within a harmless aesthetic realm. In this sense, the New Critical project can be seen as the culmination of the movement toward separation of the social and the aesthetic that numerous critics (especially with Marxist orientations) have seen as central to nineteenth-century bourgeois society.

At the same time, the unholy alliance of intellectualism and agrarianism that constituted a major part of the ideology of the New Criticism was not only highly political but also ran directly counter to the mainstream ideology of bourgeois society, especially in its American figuration. Thus Cain, while acknowledging that the New Criticism was "in a general way" well suited to the American political climate during the cold war, concludes that "it seems misleading to brand the New Critics as servants of the capitalist state when nearly all of them, in their Agrarian phase, assailed capitalism in the most severe terms" (4). But in some ways nothing serves the purposes of the capitalist state better than the assailing of capitalism, at least as long as that assault is not accompanied by any real threat, especially by any support for a genuine (for example, Marxist) alternative. Indeed the New Critical alternative to modern capitalism (basically a return to an idealized notion of the bucolic life of the South before the Civil War) was so patently untenable that even John Crowe Ransom dismissed it as an impossible fantasy late in his career. From this perspective, the naughtily antibourgeois stance of the New Critics was a point very much in their favor, their professional success with this stance providing an image of American tolerance for oppositional thought even as those who really opposed the system (or who were even *suspected* of opposing the system) were being brutally squelched in the McCarthyite purges and their aftermath. The cantankerous New Critics thus became academic reincarnations of the rebellious individual hero of the Wild West—and shining examples of a purported American tolerance standing in opposition to a Soviet system that allowed its citizens no such aberrant behavior, intellectual or otherwise.

BIBLIOGRAPHY

Introductory Works

Brooks, Cleanth. "My Credo: Formalist Critics." *Kenyon Review* 13 (1951): 72-81.
A brief presentation of some of the major ideas of the New Criticism.

———. *The Well-Wrought Urn: Studies in the Structure of Poetry*. 1943. Rev. ed. London: Dobson, 1968.
One of the classic works of New Criticism and one of the best examples of New Critical method.

Warren, Robert Penn. "Pure and Impure Poetry." *Kenyon Review* 5 (Spring 1943): 228-254.
A good representative statement of the New Critical view of poetry as a self-contained realm.

Wellek, René. "The New Criticism: Pro and Contra." *Critical Inquiry* 4 (Summer 1978): 611-624.

An excellent review of arguments for and against the New Critical method.

Selected Other Works

Bagwell, J. Timothy. *American Formalism and the Problem of Interpretation*. Houston: Rice UP, 1986.

Bennett, James R. "The New Criticism and the Corporate State." *CEA Critic* (forthcoming).

Brooks, Cleanth. *Modern Poetry and the Tradition*. New York: Oxford UP, 1965.

Brooks, Cleanth, and Robert B. Heilman. *Understanding Drama: Twelve Plays*. New York: Holt, 1948.

Brooks, Cleanth, and Robert Penn Warren. *Understanding Fiction*. 2d ed. New York: Appleton-Century-Crofts, 1960.

———. *Understanding Poetry*. 1938. 4th ed. New York: Holt, Rinehart and Winston, 1976.

Cain, William E. *The Crisis in Criticism: Theory, Literature, and Reform in English Studies*. Baltimore, Md.: Johns Hopkins UP, 1984.

Eagleton, Terry. *Literary Theory: An Introduction*. Minneapolis: U of Minnesota P, 1983.

Eliot, T. S. *The Use of Poetry and the Use of Criticism*. Cambridge, Mass.: Harvard UP, 1933.

Erlich, Victor. *Russian Formalism: History, Doctrine*. 3d ed. New Haven, Conn.: Yale UP, 1981.

Graff, Gerald. *Literature Against Itself: Literary Ideas in Modern Society*. Chicago: U of Chicago P, 1979.

———. *Poetic Statement and Critical Dogma*. Chicago: U of Chicago P, 1970.

Handy, William J. *Kant and the Southern New Critics*. Austin: U of Texas P, 1963.

Jancovich, Mark. *The Cultural Politics of the New Criticism*. Cambridge: Cambridge UP, 1993.

Krieger, Murray. *The New Apologists for Poetry*. Minneapolis: U of Minnesota P, 1956.

Lemon, Lee, and Marion Reis, eds. *Russian Formalist Criticism: Four Essays*. Lincoln: U of Nebraska P, 1965.

Ong, Walter J. *In the Human Grain*. New York: Macmillan, 1967.

Patnaik, J. N. *The Aesthetics of the New Criticism*. New Delhi: Intellectual Publishing House, 1982.

Ransom, John Crowe. "The Aesthetics of *Finnegans Wake*." *Kenyon Review* 1 (Autumn 1939): 424-428.

———. *Beating the Bushes: Selected Essays, 1941-1970*. New York: New Directions, 1972.

———. *The New Criticism*. New York: New Directions, 1941.

———. *The World's Body*. 1938. Baton Rouge: Louisiana State UP, 1968.

Richards, I. A. *Science and Poetry*. London: Kegan Paul, Trench, Trubner, 1926.

Richmond, H. M. "The Dead Albatross: 'New Criticism' as a Humanist Fallacy." *College English* 33.5 (1972): 515-531.

Rubin, Louis D., Jr. "Tory Formalists, New York Intellectuals, and the New Historical Science of Criticism." *Sewanee Review* 88 (Fall 1980): 674-683.

Shklovsky, Victor. "Sterne's *Tristram Shandy*: Stylistic Commentary." In *Russian Formalist Criticism: Four Essays,* ed. Lee Lemon and Marion Reis, 25-57. Lincoln: U of Nebraska P, 1965.

Thompson, E. M. *Russian Formalism and Anglo-American New Criticism*. The Hague: Mouton, 1971.

Walhout, Mark. "The New Criticism and the Crisis of American Liberalism: The Poetics of the Cold War." *College English* 49.8 (1987): 861-872.

Wellek, René, and Austin Warren. *Theory of Literature*. 1942. San Diego: Harcourt Brace Jovanovich, 1977.

Wilde, Alan. *Horizons of Assent: Modernism, Postmodernism, and the Ironic Imagination*. Baltimore, Md.: Johns Hopkins UP, 1981.

Willingham, John R. "The New Criticism: Then and Now." *Contemporary Literary Theory*, ed. G. Douglas Atkins and Laura Morrow, 24-41. Amherst: U of Massachusetts P, 1989.

Wimsatt, W. K., Jr. *The Verbal Icon: Studies in the Meaning of Poetry*. Lexington: U of Kentucky P, 1954.

Wimsatt, W. K., Jr., and Monroe Beardsley. "The Affective Fallacy." In *The Verbal Icon: Studies in the Meaning of Poetry*, ed. W. K. Wimsatt Jr., 21-39. Lexington: U of Kentucky P, 1954.

———. "The Intentional Fallacy." In *The Verbal Icon: Studies in the Meaning of Poetry*, ed. W. K. Wimsatt Jr., 3-18. Lexington: U of Kentucky P, 1954.

Wimsatt, W. K., Jr., and Cleanth Brooks. *Literary Criticism: A Short History*. New York: Knopf, 1957.

chapter 2

Psychoanalytic Literary Criticism

Psychoanalytic literary criticism has its roots in the work of Sigmund Freud (1856–1936) and the various thinkers who have been influenced by his work. Freud produced many important ideas in his long and prolific career, most of which are associated with his status as the founder of psychoanalysis. Strictly speaking, psychoanalysis is a medical technique, a method of therapy for the treatment of mentally ill or distressed patients that helps them understand the source of their symptoms. But there are a number of reasons the techniques and ideas of psychoanalysis are of special interest for the study of literature. For one thing, in its emphasis on discovery of the source of symptoms, psychoanalysis is first and foremost a method of interpretation. Moreover this interpretation is often of a rather literary kind. In a typical psychoanalytic session, the analyst listens carefully for subtle linguistic clues that will help her read beyond the literal meaning. In addition, an analyst often places considerable emphasis on the interpretation of the complex symbol systems embodied in dreams to gain access to the workings of the unconscious mind.

Freud himself quite frequently turned to examples from literature to illustrate his ideas. The most famous instance of this phenomenon was Freud's use of the Greek myth of Oedipus (especially as portrayed in the play *Oedipus Rex,* by Sophocles) to illustrate what psychoanalysis regards as the most crucial formative experience in the development of the human psyche. In Sophocles's play, the title character unwittingly kills his father and marries his mother, a situation that closely parallels the universal human experience that Freud describes as the "Oedipal drama." For Freud, a young infant (male or female) has a natural erotic attachment to the mother. As the infant grows older, however, he gradually comes to realize that the mother is not sexually available because she is already erotically attached to the father. According to Freud, the father at this point becomes for the boy infant a sexual rival—to the point that the child entertains fantasies of killing the father so that he can possess the mother. But the boy also comes to understand that the father's power is far greater than his own. In particular, the boy develops fears of castration at the hands of the father and comes to see the father as the source of all authority and all limitation on the realization of desire. In a successful negotiation of the Oedipal crisis, the young boy begins to identify with the father so that he can eventually partake of the power and authority associated with the paternal position. Unsuccessful negotiation of the crisis can lead to lifelong bitterness, mental instability, and difficulties in relationships with authority of all kinds.

For the girl infant, the situation is somewhat more complex, though Freud tends to treat the feminine position merely as an aberrant version of the masculine one. The baby girl also begins with an erotic attachment to the mother that cannot be realized because of the presence of the father. However rather than fear castration at the hands of the father, the baby girl feels that she is already in a sense castrated because of her lack of a penis. This feeling of lack is then attributed to a failure on the part of the mother to provide a penis to the baby girl, who then directs her erotic energies away from the mother and toward the father. In particular, the young girl desires to bear a child for the father as a means of compensating for her lack of a penis. The Oedipal situation is thus reversed, and it is now the mother who stands in the way of the girl child's erotic attachment to the father. As a result, successful negotiation of the Oedipal crisis is less well defined for the girl because she cannot identify with the authority of the father in the same way as the young boy can. Indeed Freud never provides a lucid description of the process through which the young girl overcomes her rivalry with the mother and gains a stable sense of feminine identity, and he even suggests at times that women inherently have a less stable sense of identity than do men.

Freud's depiction of the Oedipal drama as the experience through which the young child learns to accept the limitations represented by external authority is even more clear in his alternative description of this process in terms of the conflict between the "pleasure principle" and the "reality principle." According to this narrative, the infant knows only desire (of a primarily erotic variety, though the erotic for Freud goes well beyond conventional notions of the sexual) and is entirely ruled by the pleasure principle. As the child grows older, he gradually learns to recognize that desires cannot necessarily be fulfilled because of limitations imposed by society, thus accepting the rule of the reality principle.

Oedipus Rex may be a special case, but the crucial importance of the Oedipal drama to the subsequent development of the human psyche implies that we might expect to find resonances of Oedipal themes in virtually all literary works. And psychoanalytic critics do typically pay a great deal of attention to this motif. For example, one of the important early texts in the development of psychoanalytic criticism was *Hamlet and Oedipus,* a study by Freud's student and disciple Ernest Jones first published in 1910 and further elaborated in a book-length edition in 1949. In this study, Jones sees the predicament of Hamlet as a classic case of an unresolved Oedipal crisis in which the young prince is still beset by the desire to possess his mother sexually and resentment at not being able to do so because of the presence first of his father, then of his uncle Claudius. In addition, Jones tries to draw certain conclusions about the psychological makeup of Shakespeare himself by suggesting that Hamlet's psychological problems may be projections of Shakespeare's own.

In any case, the Oedipal drama is the central event in the development of what will eventually be the structure of the adult psyche. Freud at various points in his career provided a number of different descriptions of this structure, the best known of which is the spatial, or "topographical," model that he put forth fairly late (1923) in his career. According to this "tripartite" model, the human psyche is not a single integrated entity but in fact consists of three very different parts ("id," "superego," "ego"), essentially three different minds, which have different goals and desires and operate according to different principles. The id is for Freud the site of natural drives; it is a dark area of seething passion that knows only desire and has no sense of moderation or limitation. The superego is an internalized representation of the authority of the father and of society, authority that establishes strict limitations on the fulfillment of the unrestrained desires residing in the id. The ego moderates between the authoritarian demands of the superego and the unmitigated desires of the id. Essentially equivalent to the conscious, thinking mind, the ego is also the principal interface between the psyche and the outside world.

Freud's tripartite model of the psyche has been applied directly to literature by critics who have sought analogies to the relationship among id, ego, and superego in the workings of various aspects of the literary text. A good example of this approach is Henry A. Murray's famous essay on Herman Melville's *Moby Dick,* "In Nomine Diaboli." Murray argues that Moby Dick himself is a symbol of the repressive conscience of New England Puritanism and as such can be seen as a projection of Melville's superego. Meanwhile Captain Ahab, in his uncontrolled compulsion to destroy the whale, is analogous to the unrestrained drives of the id. Murray sees the reliable first mate Starbuck, who attempts to mediate between reality and Ahab's driving passion, as analogous to the ego.

The relationship between the Oedipal drama and Freud's tripartite model of the psyche is clear and quite direct. The infantile mind is essentially the source of the id; the authority of the father, which triggers the Oedipal crisis, becomes the principal source of the superego by limiting the id-based desire for the mother. Successful resolution of the Oedipal crisis is thus equivalent to the development of a stable and viable ego. The tripartite model of the psyche leads Freud to a number of conclusions that are directly relevant to the study of art and literature. Most important among these is Freud's notion of repression, or the process through which desires and urges deemed unacceptable by the ego are kept out of the conscious mind by being forced to remain in the unconscious realm of the id. But (in a typical use of images and ideas from physical science) Freud suggests that this process leads to a buildup of energy, or pressure in the id, which must be released in some way. For example, psychoanalysts often seek to detect the "return of the repressed" in the language, behavior, or dreams of their patients—thus the well-known phenomenon of the "Freudian slip," when an individual "accidentally" misspeaks in a way that may reveal unconscious desires or motivations. Healthy individuals can relieve the psychic pressure caused by repression through the process of "sublimation"—that is, by redirecting the energies associated with their unacceptable desires into acceptable activities. Unhealthy individuals tend not to sublimate effectively. In this case, repressed energies surface as symptoms of neurosis or even psychosis.

One of the most important ways in which repressed desires emerge is in dreams, which Freud sees as a kind of "safety valve" for allowing discharge of energy from the unconscious. Dreams have a special importance in psychoanalysis because they represent a leaking of the unconscious mind into consciousness, providing a potential window onto the normally inaccessible id. The interpretation of dreams is quite complicated, however, because unconscious desires are transformed in the dream through a process of dream "censorship" that makes them more palatable to consciousness. Freud suggests the existence of two basic "psychic forces" in the production of dreams, one of which forms the wish expressed in the dream, the other of which exercises censorship over this wish, causing a distortion. The psychoanalyst then must undertake a complex process of decoding to unravel the distortions caused by this censorship and thereby reveal the true meaning of the dream.

Freud's early work *The Interpretation of Dreams* (1895) remains the classic text of psychoanalytic dream interpretation. It is also a key text for psychoanalytic critics because Freud's techniques for interpreting dreams seem highly applicable to the interpretation of literary texts. Freud himself often interprets dreams by adopting methods and terminology from art and literature, and to literary critics Freud's discussions of dreams may be as useful for their demonstrations of interpretive technique as they are for their theoretical content. Among other things, Freud repeatedly insists that the content of dreams is so rich and complex that no dream can ever be completely interpreted, much in the way that literary scholars have often emphasized that no single interpretation of a work of literature can ever be final or complete. In a direct analogy to the production of works of art, Freud refers to the process of dream production as the construction of a "dream-work." Freud suggests that the dream-work is constructed through the operation of four basic processes: condensation, or the compression of larger unconscious content into the abbreviated content of the manifest dream; displacement, or the replacement of elements in the unconscious by other elements in the manifest dream for purposes of disguise; considerations of representability, or the transformation of unconscious content (which may be highly abstract) into dream images; and secondary elaboration, or a kind of last-minute editing and revision of the dream to emphasize or further disguise certain elements.

Clearly all of the processes that Freud relates to the construction of the dream-work have analogies in the construction of a work of literature. Literary works are notoriously condensed, and much of the work of the literary critic involves unfolding the rich and multiple implications of the content of the literary work. Literary works also tend to rely a great deal on figurative language that in various ways (metaphor, metonymy, symbol, allegory) displaces meaning. Much of the work of the literary artist involves a search for images and motifs with which to produce a comprehensible representation of complex and abstract ideas and emotions. And the literary artist must obviously be concerned with revision and editing in putting his work into final form. Moreover language itself is central both to the writing of literature and to the construction of the dream-work, and Freud places a great deal of emphasis on the role of language and wordplay in dreams. For example, Freud notes that in dreams processes such as condensation and displacement are often applied directly to words rather than to things and ideas. The process of condensation is thus often highly linguistic, with various words being combined, sometimes resulting in "comical and bizarre word-formations" (*Basic* 330). Words are also often displaced by other words by various techniques of association, including "klang association," in which a word replaces another with a similar sound, though a very different meaning. This technique frequently generates a sort of "double-talk" in which a single sentence (or even a single word) suggests two different meanings that may be in conflict, generating a tension in the language. For example, one meaning might be brash and profane; the other, sanctimonious and pure. For Freud, the dream-work crucially relies on the inherent ambiguity of language, which lends itself to the distortion and indirect representation that are characteristic of the dream-work.

The parallels between literary works and Freud's notion of the dream-work are not merely accidental. For Freud, the creation of art, like dreaming, is largely a mechanism for the release of unconscious psychic energies. The phenomena of repression and sublimation are particularly crucial to psychoanalytic criticism because Freud suggests that artistic creativity arises largely from the special ability of artists to sublimate their frustrated erotic energies into the production of art. In his classic study of Leonardo da Vinci, for example, Freud locates Leonardo's impressive artistic and scientific creativity in the process of sublimation. According to Freud, Leonardo converted his sexual desires first into a drive to produce art, then later into a thirst for knowledge (*Leonardo* 24). Freud thus concludes that "Leonardo has denied the unhappiness of his erotic life and has triumphed over it in his art" (68). In a classic example of psychoanalytic textual interpretation, Freud analyzes Leonardo's reputed homosexuality and tendency toward sublimation in terms of his being born illegitimate, initially cared for by his mother alone, then later removed to the care of his father and stepmother. Freud (who tended to see homosexuality as a sort of illness, or at least arrested development) suggests some general mechanisms for the development of homosexuality in terms of overly intense erotic attachment to the mother in early childhood. He concludes that Leonardo's mother "took her little son in place of her husband, and by the too early maturing of his eroticism robbed him of a part of his masculinity" (67).

Freud's use of Leonardo's art as a crucial key to the mind of the artist anticipates a later tendency by psychoanalytic critics to draw conclusions about the psychological makeup of various artists through an analysis of their art. For example, Freud's view of artistic creativity as arising from the unconscious mind has led to a great deal of discussion of possible links between art and madness. Freud's own views on art were probably influenced by the Romantic notion of the Coleridgean mad poet with flashing eyes and floating hair, and the notion that artistic creativity is somehow associated with madness is as old as Western civilization itself. It can be found, for example, in the discussion of the poet's blind frenzy in Plato's *Phaedrus.* But psychoanalytic critics have often drawn more specific links between writing and madness, attempting to diagnose specific symptoms in writers by reading their work. Carl Jung, for example, believes that the radical writing practice of James Joyce arises from Joyce's tendency toward schizophrenia and that Joyce is able to prevent an actual schizophrenic breakdown because he effectively releases psychic pressures in his writing.

Perhaps the classic case of such criticism is Marie Bonaparte's book-length study of Edgar Allan Poe; in it she uses Poe's stories to draw extensive conclusions about his psychological makeup. Bonaparte's own explanation of her method can stand as a summary of the premises on which this kind of criticism is based: "Works of art or literature reveal their creator's psychology and, as Freud has shown, their construction resembles that of our dreams. The same mechanisms which, in dreams and nightmares, govern the manner in which our strongest, though most carefully concealed desires are elaborated, desires which often are the most repugnant to consciousness, also govern the elaborations of a work of art" (209).

In recent years, such attempts to psychoanalyze authors on the basis of their texts have fallen somewhat into disrepute because they tend to be reductive in their assumption that literary texts somehow represent pure expressions of the unconscious drives of the artist while paying little attention to the role of conscious intervention on the part of the artist. But more sophisticated versions of such attempts to psychoanalyze authors (such as Harold Bloom's model of literary history as driven by the Oedipal relations between authors and their most important predecessors) have remained influential. Suggesting, however, that Shakespeare had an unresolved Oedipal complex because he depicted a character who appeared to have such a problem is not all that different from saying that Freud must have talked so much about Oedipal crises because he had not successfully negotiated his own. This problem, of course, is especially critical with modern writers, who are quite often familiar with Freud's theories and intentionally introduce aspects of them into their work. Indeed Freud's work has been a major influence on twentieth-century literature as numerous artists have employed such techniques as stream of consciousness to probe the workings of the human mind using Freud's work as an important guide. In discussing the phenomenon of literary modernism, Harry T. Moore argues that "no influence on modern literature has been so direct as that of Freud" (100). But discovering a classic Freudian complex in a literary character may not mean that the character's author had this complex, only that the author had read Freud's discussion of this complex and decided to use it in her work. The classic case of this situation is the work of Russian-American novelist Vladimir Nabokov, who was contemptuous of psychoanalytic modes of reading and often mocked such reading by introducing parodies of class Freudian images and situations into his fiction.

Some critics have also attempted to use Freud's work to explain the unconscious motivations of literary characters without then extending these diagnoses to the author. This technique unfortunately has an obvious drawback: Literary characters do not actually have minds. They are fictional creations of their author, and as such they have no id, ego, and superego, and they have experienced no Oedipal drama. As a result, it is not clear what the psychoanalysis of a literary character is really analyzing. More successful have been the attempts of other critics to use psychoanalysis as a framework within which to understand the reactions of readers to literary works. This kind of psychoanalytic criticism, most notably associated with the work of Norman Holland, is discussed in the introduction to reader-response criticism in chapter 3.

Many of the most successful psychoanalytic critics have simply employed Freud's work as a gloss, reading literary texts and comparing the images and motifs in those works to those discussed by Freud without making any attempt to draw conclusions about the psychological condition of authors, characters, or readers. Such critics often seek in literary texts the kinds of symbols (usually associated with some aspect of sexuality) that Freud tends to discuss in relation to dreams and other manifestations of the unconscious mind. Or these critics may simply look to Freud's discussions of such manifestations as a model of interpretive practice. We might say that such critics are psychoanalyzing the text itself. Psychoanalytic critics may draw only very loosely on Freud's descriptions of the human mind without employing any of his ideas in detail. Note, for example, Albert J. Guerard's reading of Joseph Conrad's *Heart of Darkness* as the story of Marlow's search for his own identity. For Guerard, Marlow's trip into the heart of Africa is a mere metaphor for his search in the dark recesses of his unconscious mind.

Some critics who might still be categorized as psychoanalytic have departed quite substantially from Freud's work, drawing not directly on Freud but on neo-Freudian thinkers. For example, numerous critics have been influenced by "object-relations" theorists such as Melanie Klein and D. W. Winnicott, whose work is concerned principally with the impact on psychological development of relations between the young child and certain kinds of external objects. Object-relations psychology focuses on the role played by external objects in the young child's development of a sense of self as an individuated entity apart from the mother and from the external world. Especially suggestive for literary critics has been Klein's notion of "part-objects," items that an adult would perceive as part of a larger object but that small children often invest with powerful emotional content by constructing fantasies about them. Klein argues that to develop in an emotionally healthy way, the child must learn to manage this powerful fantasy content through a process of symbolization. In a conclusion with obvious relevance for the study of literature, Klein suggests that the child can learn to cope adequately with reality only by learning first to cope with fantasy through the use of symbols. Winnicott, meanwhile, focuses his work on "transitional objects," which come into play when the young child is in the intermediate phase between the infantile sense of fusion with the world and the later sense of differentiation of the self from the world. Winnicott finds that play with such transitional objects helps the young child cope with her growing sense of separation from the mother, and his discussions of play and illusion in relation to transitional objects have proved useful to critics who have noted certain parallels with the way readers relate to literary texts. French psychoanalyst André Green, for example, employs a modified form of Winnicott's theories to explain the emotional impact of tragic drama.

The theories of Carl Jung—who began as a disciple of Freud but later differed substantially from his former teacher on major points, such as the centrality of sexuality to the human psyche—have been particularly important to literary critics. Jung developed the idea that the unconscious mind is not merely a place of individual fantasies and desires but also includes a "collective unconscious," or a repository of shared primordial desires and impressions common to the entire human race. Residing in this collective unconscious, according to Jung, are a number of fundamental images and motifs, or "archetypes." Jung derives his notion of the collective unconscious largely from cultural studies in which he finds that certain central images (related to such fundamental human experiences as birth, death, and the coming of the four seasons) tend to reappear over and over in myths and legends from various cultures around the world. Jung argues that these myths are powerful because they appeal to unconscious desires and fantasies and that they are common to different cultures because they arise not from individual experience but from primal material inherited by all members of the human race: "The fact of this inheritance explains the truly amazing phenomenon that certain motifs from myths and legends repeat themselves the world over in identical forms" (*Two Essays* 65).

The potential applications of Jung's ideas to literature are fairly obvious. We might expect, for example, that the archetypes appearing in myths and legends would also frequently appear in literary works. Thus critics such as Maud Bodkin have sought to recover archetypal patterns in literature and assess the significance of the appearance of such patterns. Presenting her study *Archetypal Patterns in Poetry* specifically as a "testing" of Jung's hypotheses, Bodkin concludes that *Hamlet, Paradise Lost, The Rime of the Ancient Mariner,* and "Kubla Khan," among other works, do indeed gain their power from their use of archetypal images that appeal to readers at a fundamental emotional level. Probably the most important critic to be significantly influenced by Jung's work is Northrop Frye, who develops a system of mythic criticism that incorporates elements of Jung's work on myths and archetypes into a systematic approach to literature reminiscent of structuralism. Frye maintains a view of literature as a realm relatively independent of the social world in a manner reminiscent of the New Criticism, from which his work ostensibly represents an important departure. In *The Anatomy of Criticism,* his most important work, Frye proposes an elaborate system for the classification of literary works and for the description of literary history that attempts to comprehend all of literature within a single mythic framework. For Frye, literary history is essentially unrelated to social and political history but instead proceeds cyclically through a series of sequential phases (comedy, romance, tragedy, and antiromance) that correspond to the four seasons of the year. Frye then categorizes various literary genres, styles, and strategies in terms of their relation to these fundamental phases.

Frye's attempt to divorce literature from the social world accorded well with the political climate of the cold war, so it is perhaps not surprising that his work was extremely influential in the late 1950s and early 1960s. Indeed mythic and archetypal criticism became far more prominent than more conventional Freudian psychoanalytic approaches in literary studies in America at that time. By the 1970s, however, psychoanalytic criticism had been greatly reenergized, largely through the impact of the work of the French neo-Freudian psychoanalyst Jacques Lacan. Lacan reread Freud's theories from the perspective of structuralist theory, placing central emphasis on the role of language in structuring both the conscious and unconscious mind. Lacan consistently described himself as a "Freudian," but his work departs from Freud's in several crucial ways, the most important of which is his view of the unconscious mind not as a dark and seething place of anarchic passions and drives but as a structure very much like language and therefore potentially available to far more systematic analysis than Freud himself had imagined.

Like Freud, Lacan develops a tripartite model of the human mind. He sees the mind as functioning through the operations of three different "orders," which he labels "Imaginary," "Symbolic," and "Real." Lacan's exposition of these three separate but interacting orders is complex and difficult to summarize. To a first approximation, however, the Imaginary Order, loosely related to Freud's notion of the pleasure principle, can be described as the realm dominated by a preverbal infantile stage of joyful fusion with the mother's body. It is the primary locus of fantasies and images and is thus of obvious importance for the study of literature. The Symbolic Order, loosely related to Freud's notion of the reality principle, is associated with the use of symbols and symbolic systems. It is the realm of language-as-representation. The Real Order is concerned with fundamental and emotionally powerful experiences such as death and sexuality. It is in a sense the "deepest" and most inaccessible of the realms, available to consciousness only in extremely brief and fleeting moments of joy and terror that Lacan describes as *jouissance.*

For Lacan, human subjectivity is not established simultaneously with birth. When a baby is born, her first period of life is one in which she does not distinguish herself from the rest of the world. There is a blissful fusion with the mother and with the world in which the infant lives—much like the "oceanic feeling" described by Freud in *Civilization and Its Discontents.* This first stage of human life is preverbal; images and rhythms are the dominant means of perceiving the world. At this time, the infant's mind is governed by the Imaginary Order. During this period before the constitution of the infant as a speaking subject in language, identity is inherently fluid, and strict boundaries between self and other have yet to be established.

At the age of about six to eighteen months, the infant enters into what Lacan calls the "mirror stage." During this stage the infant begins to gain a sense of her own existence as a separate entity and to establish an awareness of the boundaries of her own body through its literal mirror image or through outside objects—notably mother:

> At a certain point . . . and presumably when the perceptual apparatus has reached a certain stage of development, the infant becomes aware, through seeing his image in the mirror, of his own body as a totality, a total form of *Gestalt*. The mirror image is held together, it can come and go with a slight change of the infant's position, and his mastery of the image fills him with triumph and joy. (Benvenuto and Kennedy 55)

True to his structuralist method, Lacan figures the development of an infantile sense of selfhood principally as a process of differentiation: The infant gains of sense of what he is through a gradually increasing understanding of what he is not. Certain key objects (such as the mother's breast, the mother's voice, the child's own feces and urinary flow, and the sounds produced by the infant's own vocal apparatus) that were formerly experienced as parts of the infant's own self come in the mirror stage to be recognized as being separate from that self. These key objects (the Lacanian *objet a*) function as symbols of primordial lack, and even at this early prelinguistic stage the selfhood of the infant becomes intimately bound up in the sense of the lack of these objects. After the entry into the Symbolic Order of language, this feeling of lack will continue to function, and the striving for subjective wholeness will involve a fundamental (and unquenchable) desire for these key lost objects.

Having begun to establish a separate sense of self, the infant next undergoes the Oedipal drama from which he emerges (if successful) as a genuine subject. For Lacan, the subject is an artifact of language, so the assumption of a subjective position is tantamount to entry into the Symbolic Order of language. Moreover for the structuralist Lacan, language is based on difference. In particular, to Lacan the entry into the Symbolic Order (and the subsequent assumption of a subjective identity) is inextricably intertwined with the fundamental acknowledgement of difference that occurs in the taking on of a gender identity. The Symbolic Order for Lacan is closely associated with the Law of the Father; it is a masculine realm. As a result, entry into the Symbolic Order is a fundamentally different experience for boys (who both accept and identify with the father's law) and girls (who cannot directly assume the father's power).

As gender identity is based on difference, on division and loss, then it follows that identity itself is irrevocably divided as well. Thus "the distinction between the sexes brought about by the castration complex and the different positions that must subsequently be taken up, confirms that the subject is split and the object is lost" (Mitchell 25). Entry into the Symbolic Order is primarily an experience of loss and acceptance of a child's own limitations. For the young boy, it is an acknowledgement of the Law of the Father, interrupting the boy's sexual desire for his mother, which arises from a desire to recover the bliss of preverbal Imaginary Order fusion. For the young girl, entry into the Symbolic Order to a certain extent requires an acceptance of masculine authority and superiority in that order. In return, however, the girl may retain more access to the Imaginary Order than does the boy. In either case, however, the child to a certain extent has to give up the original happiness of the blissful fusion with the mother in the preOedipal phase to enter the Symbolic Order of language. Regarding this experience of loss, Lacan refers to entry into the Symbolic Order (for both genders) as "castration." For Lacan, castration is not a physical experience but a symbolic one, embodying the introduction to language and the acceptance of the rules and regulations according to which society functions.

This absence at the heart of human existence places the subject within an ongoing dynamic of impossible longing, with all apparent objects of desire in the life of the subject being merely metaphoric stand-ins for the true object of desire, which is the always lost and irreducibly anterior *objet a.* Thus the subject is consigned to a perpetual metonymic movement from one object of desire to another in search of a satisfaction that can never come: "In a lifetime individuals continually change objects and goals in their Desiring quest. . . . But no object—be it person, thing, sexual activity, or belief—will finally and permanently quell Desire. It is sorrowful, Lacan has said, that the loved person onto whom one projects Desire and narcissism serves to give proof of the image and pathos of existence" (Ragland-Sullivan, *Jacques* 81).

To Lacan, then, desire is driven by a sense of fragmentation of the self (and even of the physical body) and by a longing for a return to a primordial condition of wholeness in which the infant felt fused with the *objet a.* Lacan's work thus has a special relevance to literature not only because of his central emphasis on language but also because of the possibility that art and literature may offer some satisfaction of the desire for recovery of Imaginary Order (and sometimes, briefly, even Real Order) experience. Like Freud, Lacan himself frequently appeals to examples from literature to illustrate his theses, and two of his best-known essays are those on *Hamlet* and on Poe's "The Purloined Letter." Lacan had a particularly long and intense involvement with the texts of James Joyce, teaching a number of seminars on Joyce in the period 1971–1976. For Lacan, Joyce's writing gains its special power from an unusual ability to reflect pressure from the Real Order. The recent collection *Joyce avec Lacan* (edited by Jacques Aubert) contains much of Lacan's commentary on Joyce as well as related essays by other commentators. Lacan's work has also influenced a large number of literary critics in the last twenty-five years, providing important new insights into narrative technique and the role of language in literature. Lacan's discussion of gender identity as a linguistic construct has also proved inspirational for a number of feminist literary critics, despite Lacan's own seemingly masculinist biases.

BIBLIOGRAPHY

Introductory Works

Benvenuto, Bice, and Roger Kennedy. *The Works of Jacques Lacan: An Introduction*. New York: St. Martin's, 1986.
Probably the most accessible general introduction to Lacan's difficult work.

Paris, Bernard J. *A Psychological Approach to Fiction: Studies in Thackeray, Stendhal, George Eliot, and Dostoevsky, and Conrad*. Bloomington: Indiana UP, 1974.
A good example of psychoanalytic criticism in practice.

Wright, Elizabeth. *Psychoanalytic Criticism: Theory in Practice*. London: Methuen, 1984.
An excellent broad introduction to psychoanalytic criticism.

Selected Other Works

Arieti, Silvano. *Creativity: The Magic Synthesis*. New York: Basic Books, 1976.

Aubert, Jacques, ed. *Joyce avec Lacan*. Paris: Navarin, 1987.

Bloom, Harold. *The Anxiety of Influence: A Theory of Poetry*. New York: Oxford UP, 1973.

Bodkin, Maud. *Archetypal Patterns in Poetry: Psychological Studies of Imagination*. 1934. London: Oxford UP, 1963.

Bonaparte, Marie. *The Life and Works of Edgar Allan Poe*. Trans. John Rodker. London: Imago, 1949.

Crews, Frederick C. *Out of My System: Psychoanalysis, Ideology, and Critical Methods*. New York: Oxford UP, 1975.

Davis, Robert Con, ed. *Lacan and Narration: The Psychoanalytic Difference in Narrative Theory*. Baltimore, Md.: Johns Hopkins UP, 1983.

Feder, Lillian. *Madness in Literature*. Princeton, N.J.: Princeton UP, 1980.

Felman, Shoshana. *Jacques Lacan and the Adventure of Insight: Psychoanalysis in Contemporary Culture*. Cambridge, Mass.: Harvard UP, 1987.

———. *Writing and Madness (Literature/Philosophy/Psychoanalysis)*. Trans. Martha Noel Evans and Shoshana Felman. Ithaca, N.Y.: Cornell UP, 1985.

———, ed. *Literature and Psychoanalysis: The Question of Reading: Otherwise*. Baltimore, Md.: Johns Hopkins UP, 1982.

Freud, Sigmund. *The Basic Writings of Sigmund Freud*. Trans. and ed. A. A. Brill. New York: Modern Library, 1938. (Includes *Psychopathology of Everyday Life, The Interpretation of Dreams, Three Contributions to the Theory of Sex, Wit and Its Relation to the Unconscious, Totem and Taboo*)

———. *Beyond the Pleasure Principle*. Trans. James Strachey. New York: Norton, 1961.

———. *Civilization and Its Discontents*. Trans. James Strachey. New York: Norton, 1961.
Love, and Religion. Ed. Benjamin Nelson. New York: Harper and Row, 1958.

———. *The Future of an Illusion*. Trans. James Strachey. New York: Norton, 1989.

———. *A General Introduction to Psychoanalysis*. Trans. Joan Riviere. New York: Pocket Books, 1953.

———. *Group Psychology and the Analysis of the Ego*. Trans. James Strachey. New York: Norton, 1990.

———. *Leonardo da Vinci and a Memory of His Childhood*. Trans. Alan Tyson. New York: Norton, 1964.

———. *On Creativity and the Unconscious: Papers on the Psychology of Art, Literature,*

Frye, Northrop. *The Anatomy of Criticism: Four Essays.* Princeton, N.J.: Princeton UP, 1957.

Gilman, Sandor. *Reading Freud's Reading.* New York: New York UP, 1994.

Green, André. *The Tragic Effect.* Cambridge: Cambridge UP, 1979.

Guerard, Albert J. *Conrad the Novelist.* Cambridge, Mass.: Harvard UP, 1958.

Hoffman, Frederick J. *Freudianism and the Literary Mind.* Baton Rouge: Louisiana State UP, 1945.

Hogan, Patrick Colm, and Lalita Pandit, eds. *Criticism and Lacan: Essays and Dialogue on Language, Structure, and the Unconscious.* Athens: U of Georgia P, 1990.

Jones, Ernest. *Hamlet and Oedipus.* New York: Norton, 1949.

Jung, Carl. *The Archetypes and the Collective Unconscious.* Vol. 9, Part 1 of *Collected Works.* 2d ed. Trans. R. F. C. Hull. Princeton, N.J.: Princeton UP, 1968.

———. *Two Essays on Analytical Psychology.* Princeton, N.J.: Princeton UP, 1972.

Klein, Melanie. *"Envy and Gratitude" and Other Works, 1946–1963.* New York: Delacorte, 1975.

———. *"Love, Guilt, and Reparation" and Other Works, 1921–1945.* New York: Delacorte, 1975.

Knapp, Bettina Liebowitz. *A Jungian Approach to Literature.* Carbondale: Southern Illinois UP, 1984.

Kurzweil, Edith, and William Phillips, eds. *Literature and Psychoanalysis.* New York: Columbia UP, 1983.

Lacan, Jacques. "Desire and the Interpretation of Desire in *Hamlet.*" Ed. Jacques-Alain Miller. Trans. James Hulbert. In *Literature and Psychoanalysis: The Question of Reading: Otherwise,* ed. Shoshana Felman, 11–52. Baltimore, Md.: Johns Hopkins UP, 1982.

———. *Écrits: A Selection.* Trans. Alan Sheridan. New York: Norton, 1977.

———. *Feminine Sexuality: Jacques Lacan and the École Freudienne.* Ed. Juliet Mitchell and Jacqueline Rose. Trans. Jacqueline Rose. New York: Norton, 1982.

———. *The Four Fundamental Concepts of Psycho-Analysis.* Ed. Jacques-Alain Miller. Trans. Alan Sheridan. New York: Norton, 1978.

Meisel, Perry, ed. *Freud: A Collection of Critical Essays.* Englewood Cliffs, N.J.: Prentice-Hall, 1981.

Mitchell, Juliet. "Introduction—I." In *Feminine Sexuality: Jacques Lacan and the École Freudienne.* Ed. Juliet Mitchell and Jacqueline Rose. Trans. Jacqueline Rose. 1–26. New York: Norton, 1982.

Moore, Harry T. "Age of the Modern." In *Age of the Modern and Other Literary Essays,* 94–118. Carbondale: Southern Illinois UP, 1971.

Muller, John P., and William J. Richardson. *The Purloined Poe: Lacan, Derrida, and Psychoanalytic Reading.* Baltimore, Md.: Johns Hopkins UP, 1988.

Murray, Henry A. "In Nomine Diaboli." *New England Quarterly* 24 (1951): 435–452.

Ragland-Sullivan, Ellie. *Jacques Lacan and the Philosophy of Psychoanalysis.* Urbana: University of Illinois Press, 1986.

———. "Lacan, Language, and Literary Criticism." *Literary Review* 24.4 (1981): 562–577.

Segal, Hannah. *Introduction to the Work of Melanie Klein.* London: Hogarth and the Institute of Psycho-Analysis, 1973.

Skura, Meredith. *The Literary Use of the Psychoanalytic Process.* New Haven, Conn.: Yale UP, 1981.

Winnicott, D. W. *The Maturational Processes and the Facilitating Environment.* New York: International UP, 1965.

———. *Playing and Reality*. Harmondsworth, England: Penguin, 1977.

Wollheim, Richard. *Freud*. New York: Viking, 1971.

Wyatt, Jean. *Reconstructing Desire: The Role of the Unconscious in Women's Reading and Writing*. Chapel Hill: U of North Carolina P, 1990.

chapter 3

Reader-Response Literary Criticism

New Criticism focuses principally on the text, and psychoanalytic criticism often focuses on the psychology of the author. Reader-response criticism completes the circle by focusing on the third term in the reading experience: the reader. To the extent that all critics are readers who are responding to literary texts, we might say that all criticism is reader-response criticism. But the methods and techniques generally associated with reader-response criticism are special in the extent to which they focus on descriptions of the reader's activity during the process of reading. These methods often grant the reader a major responsibility for the creative production of the text in the process of reading and see the written text not as an end in itself but as a trigger for the creative activity of the reader. Reader-response criticism (in America, at least) arises in direct opposition to the dominance of the New Criticism, especially its articulation of the affective fallacy. But unlike the New Critics, reader-response critics do not represent an organized group with a specific critical (and political) agenda to promote. Indeed there are a wide number of reader-response approaches, some of which vary dramatically in their emphasis, particularly in the relative importance they grant to the text and to the reader in the reading process.

One of the most important early reader-response approaches was Stanley Fish's notion of "affective stylistics" (a direct response to the affective fallacy of Wimsatt and Beardsley), developed through his readings of John Milton and other seventeenth-century poets in *Surprised by Sin: The Reader in "Paradise Lost"* (1967) and *Self-Consuming Artifacts: The Experience of Seventeenth-Century Literature* (1972). In the first of these books, Fish responds to A. J. A. Waldock's influential argument that Milton's poem is flawed by a contradiction between the author's avowed intention to praise God and condemn Satan and the result of the poem—in which Satan often seems a far more attractive figure than God or Christ. But for Fish, Milton's depiction of Satan's charm, courage, and energy is entirely intentional, serving as a lesson for readers in just how seductive Satan can be. In Fish's view, Milton means for readers to be drawn to Satan, reenacting in their own minds the drama of the Fall depicted in the poem and presumably learning thereby to resist Satan in a fallen world. Moreover Fish's focus on the experiences of the readers goes beyond this general observation to include sometimes detailed descriptions of the reactions that might be expected from readers as they move through Milton's poem. Fish notes that critics conventionally discuss the meaning of Milton's poem (or even of his individual sentences) after they have read the entire poem and contemplated its significance. In particular, Fish argues that New Critical formalist analyses, because they are performed retrospectively, cannot adequately account for the various provisional interpretations that may be formulated and then discarded in the actual course of reading. Readers in fact make their ways through a poem (and its sentences) in linear, sequential fashion, encountering various stylistic devices and reacting by continually updating their interpretation of the poem. Fish illustrates the importance of this observation by discussing numerous examples in the poetry of Milton in which the progressive formulation and rejection of interpretations are crucial to the impact of a given poem. At such points, the poem builds certain expectations in the reader, who then finds in reading further that "the expectation and anticipation are disappointed, and the realization of that disappointment will be inseparable from the making of a new (and less comforting) sense" (*Is* 164).

Typical of Fish's technique of affective stylistics is his discussion of the lines in Book III of *Paradise Lost* that describe Satan landing on the sun:

> There lands the Fiend, a spot like which perhaps
> Astronomer in the Sun's lucent Orb
> Through his glaz'd optic Tube yet never saw.
> (588–590)

According to Fish, the first two and one-half lines of this segment invite the reader to compare the appearance of Satan on the sun to the sunspots recently observed by seventeenth-century astronomers such as Galileo, but the ending of the third line undermines this comparison by suddenly declaring that Satan's appearance did *not* resemble a sunspot. Fish then argues that this reversal can make a powerful point about the unreliability of human sensual perception of the world and about the inability of the new science epitomized by Galileo fully to understand the world by mere observation and gathering of data (*Surprised* 27–28).

Fish also places considerable emphasis on the ways poems utilize poetic conventions to achieve their effects. In a later reading of Milton's *Lycidas,* Fish cites the following lines:

> He must not float upon his wat'ry bier
> Unwept . . .
> (13–14)

Here Fish focuses on the importance of the expectation of some interpretive closure at the end of a line of poem; he argues that readers will tend to read the first of these lines as a self-contained unit, as a call to action, perhaps even as a "rescue mission" to prevent Lycidas from drowning. But the next line then undercuts this hope that Lycidas might be saved, urging readers instead to mourn his death. This experience of anticipation and disappointment is for Fish crucial to the working of these lines of poetry, and any interpretation that ignores this sequential process cannot capture the impact of the poem (*Is* 164–166).

For Fish, it is such sequences of anticipations, disappointments, and revaluations on the part of the reader that constitute the most important object of critical inquiry into Milton's poem. Critics should thus focus not so much on interpreting the meaning of *Paradise Lost* (or of any other literary work) as on describing the reading experience. In short, they should concentrate not on what works *mean* but on what they *do.* For Fish, the text, and even the individual sentence, "is no longer an object, a thing-in-itself, but an *event,* something that *happens* to, and with the participation of, the reader" (25). Thus despite his focus on the activities of the reader, Fish continues to grant a great deal of importance to authorial intention and the role of the text in provoking the reader's responses. For this reason, affective stylistics is sometimes referred to as a "text-active" approach to reader-response criticism.

Fish's reminder that readers initially experience poems in sequential fashion rather than all at once is important, and his suggestion that critics attend carefully to this process was widely influential, especially as it provides a fairly well-developed method for reading texts. Essentially Fish recommends that critics move through a poem (or other literary work) in sequential fashion, looking for points at which unusual uses of language might provoke reactions on the parts of readers that go beyond the simple meaning of the sentences being read. They then examine how this modification in meaning affects the overall impact of the work. But Fish's description of the reader's responses to *Paradise Lost* clearly points toward one of the crucial problems for reader-response criticism: the identification of the "reader" being described. As Fish points out, "My reader is a construct, an ideal or idealized reader . . . or to use a term of my own *the* reader is the *informed* reader" (48).

Fish and other critics employing his method must thus somehow place themselves in the position of this ideal reader to describe her experience: "The critic has the responsibility of becoming not one but a number of informed readers, each of whom will be identified by a matrix of political, cultural, and literary determinants" (87). But a critic like Fish, knowing as much as he does about Milton's work, cannot successfully ignore that knowledge and place himself in the position of the reader who is experiencing Milton's text for the first time. Few actual readers will be as informed as Fish's ideal reader (or as Fish himself), and there is a serious question whether most readers (lacking Fish's critical experience and literary knowledge) would necessarily even notice some of the devices he considers decisive in their reading experience. In the case of the example just cited, Fish is certainly correct that Milton's poem invites readers to compare Satan on the sun to a sunspot, then undermines this comparison. But whether ordinary readers will follow Fish in seeing this reversal as a criticism of science and as a comment on the vanity of human attempts to understand the world without help from God seems highly debatable.

A similar criticism might be leveled at the work of Wolfgang Iser, who describes the activities of the "implied" reader who works his way through a text, gradually constructing a response to the text in the process. Iser and his fellow theorist Hans Robert Jauss are the major figures in the German movement known as "reception aesthetics," though of the two Iser's work has been far more influential in America. His work grows out of the phenomenological theories of the philosopher Roman Ingarden, who seeks to define the literary text as a product of the interaction between the objective existence of literary texts and the subjective consciousnesses of their readers. Ingarden grants the literary text an objective existence of its own. He argues, however, that literary texts are filled with indeterminacies and gaps that must be filled in by readers to complete the work. Ingarden refers to this process as the "concretization" of the literary text.

This concretization is guided to a certain extent by the written text, but it also depends in significant ways on the skill, inclinations, and knowledge of the reader. Building on Ingarden's analysis, Iser develops a reader-response approach that, like Fish's affective stylistics, focuses on the experiences of the reader as he moves through the text participating in this process of concretization. In particular, Iser notes that the reader can never grasp the text as a whole but must develop partial and provisional attitudes toward the text, which he then continually updates and revises as his "horizons of expectation" change while reading. For Iser, then, the reader is like "a traveler in a stagecoach who has to make the often difficult journey through the novel, gazing out from his moving viewpoint. Naturally, he combines all that he sees within his memory and establishes a pattern of consistency, the nature and reliability of which will depend partly on the degree of attention he has paid during each phase of the journey. At no time, however, can he have a total view of that journey" (*Act* 16).

For Iser, as for Fish, the text presents instructions to the reader for its interpretation. Iser also resembles Fish in believing that these instructions are received and acted on sequentially as reading proceeds rather than received all at once. In short, both Iser and Fish produce what Jonathan Culler has called "stories of reading," narratives of the experiences of readers as they move through texts. But these narratives are not simple and straightforward. Iser emphasizes that literary texts tend to set up certain expectations in the reader, only to frustrate these expectations as reading proceeds, causing the reader continually to revise her interpretation of the text. Moreover Iser emphasizes that the instructions given readers by a text are necessarily incomplete, filled with blanks and indeterminacies, or "gaps," which the reader must complete according to his own knowledge, experience, and disposition. The completion of these gaps is a process of communication between the reader and the text, but at such moments the text is considerably less in control of the reader's response than in Fish's characterization of the reading process. Iser thus grants the reader a more creative role in the realization of the text than does Fish's affective stylistics, even as he continues to believe that the text as written provides guidance for and places limitations on possibilities for its own interpretation. Iser's approach, then, might be referred to as "biactive" in that it provides for an active participation on the part of both text and reader in the creation of meaning.

Iser's model is very much based on the notion of communication between the reader and the text. This communication is furthered, he argues, through the inclusion in the text of a stock of familiar cultural material that helps readers orient themselves within the text. Iser refers to this stock of familiar material imported from both the "real world" and the world of literature as the "repertoire" of the text: "The repertoire consists of all the familiar territory within the text. This may be in the form of references to earlier works, or to social and historical norms, or to the whole culture from which the text has emerged—in brief, to what the Prague structuralists have called the 'extratextual' reality" (*Act* 69).

This repertoire helps establish a common basis for understanding between text and reader and give the text a certain air of relevance to the reader's own experience so that she may relate more fully to the text. The reader then supplements this basic material by supplying information and attitudes from her own experience at points in the text where such supplemental information is required. Among other things, Iser's focus on gaps in the text implies that there can be no single correct or final interpretation of any literary work, as these gaps can be filled in many different ways depending on the interests, inclinations, and prior experiences of the reader. But if the reader can thus contribute to the realization of texts, the process of reading can make an important contribution to the ethical development of the reader. In particular, Iser suggests that the process of formulating, then revising various interpretations of a literary text can potentially make the reader more open-minded and flexible in her reactions to the world at large. Although the repertoire provides familiar and comfortable material that the reader can use to establish initial contact with the text, one function of literature is to surprise and unsettle the reader and present her with new perspectives from which to view not only literature but also the world.

Iser's reading of Samuel Beckett's "French Trilogy" (*Molloy, Malone Dies,* and *The Unnamable*) is illustrative of this argument. Noting the tendency of Beckett's narrators to make statements, then immediately cancel them with counter-statements, Iser suggests that a "variable but ceaseless alternation between statement and negation remains the characteristic feature of the style in all three novels" (*Implied* 164). Iser argues that readers can learn from this stylistic movement in Beckett's work to eschew final interpretations of the world and to remain open to change. Noting that Beckett's narrators tend continually to formulate, then revise hypotheses about themselves, Iser suggests that readers undergo a similar experience and thereby can develop an ability to grow as individuals: "The novels show how it becomes increasingly impossible for their narrators to conceive themselves—i.e., to find their own identity; and yet at the same time it is precisely this impossibility that leads them to actually discover something of their own reality" (174).

For Iser, by continually causing readers to examine their own assumptions and expectations, literary works can expand the consciousnesses of their readers: "The efficacy of a literary text is brought about by the apparent evocation and subsequent negation of the familiar. What at first seemed to be an affirmation of our assumptions leads to our own rejection of them, thus tending to prepare us for a re-orientation. And it is only when we have outstripped our preconceptions and left the shelter of the familiar that we are in a position to gather new experiences" (290). In his latest work, Iser extends this notion to develop a theory of what he refers to as "literary anthropology," in which he sees literature as a form of play that helps individuals act out their potentials as human beings (*Prospecting*).

Iser emphasizes that literary texts engage readers in a sort of mind-expanding game, frustrating not only the expectations created by the texts themselves but also the preexisting expectations that readers may bring to texts. In particular, much like the Russian formalists, Iser suggests that literary texts often frustrate expectations by violating the conventions of literature itself, by refusing to provide the elements that readers familiar with the literary tradition might expect to find. Of course, this frustration of literary expectations can be effective only for readers who *have* such expectations—that is, only for readers with a certain amount of familiarity with the literary tradition:

> Now if a literary text does not fulfill its traditionally expected functions, but instead uses its techniques to transform expected functions into "minus functions"—which is the deliberate omission of a generic technique—in order to invoke their nonfulfillment in the conscious mind of the reader, anyone who is not familiar with these traditional functions will automatically miss the communicatory intention of this technique widely applied in modern literature. (*Act* 207-208)

Iser's "implied reader" thus has a great deal in common with Fish's "informed reader." Both critics place a great deal of emphasis on the surprises texts present to unsuspecting readers while simultaneously assuming a great deal of knowledge and experience on the part of readers.

Other reader-response approaches have attempted to avoid the pitfalls associated with discussions of such hypothetical readers by focusing on the reported experiences of actual readers. The forerunner of such studies is I. A. Richards's *Practical Criticism,* which follows a discussion of certain basic principles for the interpretation of literary texts with a report on the interpretations performed by some of Richards's students. Richards presents these students with a series of poems, the source and authorship of which he does not reveal. He then asks the students to "comment freely" on these poems. Richards analyzes these comments, concluding that the students on the whole performed poorly, ignoring important aspects of the poems in favor of a preoccupation with their own interests and sentiments.

Richards ultimately concludes that his test subjects failed to understand or appreciate the poems because of their own inexperience in reading poems and inadequate educational training in doing so. They were not, in short, "informed" readers, and here Richards's comments anticipate the demands placed on reader competence by both Fish and Iser. Indeed Fish himself (while criticizing many of Richards's assumptions about the availability of correct interpretations) has argued that "if *Practical Criticism* makes any case, it is a case for the desirability of my informed reader" (*Is* 56). But Richards's assumption that there are "proper" or "commonsense" interpretations of poems provides very little opportunity for readers to participate creatively in the generation of meaning. He grants that there is a place in the reading of poetry for personal reactions and individual emotional responses, but he demands that these conform to certain cultural standards: "That they are personal is nothing against them—all experience is personal—the only conditions are that they must be genuine and relevant, and must respect the liberty and autonomy of the poem" (277).

Of course "genuine and relevant" sounds suspiciously similar to "correct," and how these criteria would be applied is not exactly clear. These problems are surmounted in the work of Norman Holland, who follows Richards by conducting research into the responses of real readers to real texts, but who radically departs from Richards by refusing to measure these responses against an objective standard of appropriate interpretations. Indeed for Holland, all interpretations are subjective, produced not so much by the content of the text as by the particular psychological inclinations of the reader. In *The Dynamics of Literary Response* (1968), Holland draws extensively on Freudian psychoanalysis, postulating that readers bring their own "identity themes," or characteristic patterns of interpretation and reaction, to literary texts and that their responses to literary texts are largely determined by the nature of these identity themes, variations on which Holland (following the work of the ego psychologist Heinz Lichtenstein) sees the individual as living out much as a musician might play numerous variations on a single musical theme.

Holland's project is firmly rooted in Freudian ego psychology—indeed one of his most important books is entitled *The I.* The very notion of an identity theme assumes a stable and ongoing core to individual identity, which Holland defines as "the individual's awareness of the continuity of his existence in space and time and his recognition of others' awareness of his existence; more his awareness of the continuity in the style of his individuality and its existence and the coincidence of his personal style with his meaning for significant others in his immediate community" ("UNITY" 120). This ongoing identity determines the style with which the individual copes with her reality, especially how she interprets literary texts. Holland's approach is nevertheless "biactive"; he preserves an important role for the formal properties of the literary text. This attention to the formal properties of texts is sometimes highly reminiscent of the New Criticism. For Holland, then, the process of reading is a transaction between the reader and the text, and his model of the reading process centrally involves the activities of the ego in mediating between the reader's desire for pleasure and the necessity of coping with the limitations that reality (that is, the text) places on this desire. In short, for Holland "literature is an objective text, but also a subjective experience" (*Dynamics* 108).

In Holland's view, the content of literary texts corresponds to typical human fantasies, which he describes in terms of standard Freudian categories (oral, anal, phallic, and genital). Meanwhile the formal properties of literary texts correspond to various "defense mechanisms" or to the kinds of transformative censorship strategies that Freud describes in relation to the construction of the dream-work. Literary form, in short, transforms the often disturbing material of unconscious fantasy into a shape in which it can be encountered by the ego in a comfortable, even pleasurable way. This transformation is also partially the work of the reader, and its ultimate outcome will depend on the kinds of defense mechanisms and coping strategies typical of the personalities of individual readers.

Holland's reading of Shakespeare's *Hamlet* is illustrative of this approach. He suggests that the true value of the play is the way in which it allows the audience to "create" the work by projecting into it audience identity and concerns. "If you look at the volumes upon volumes of commentary on this tragedy, you will realize that, finally, each person has his own *Hamlet*" (*Hamlet* 420). Holland does grant that the individuality of interpretations of *Hamlet* is affected by certain characteristics of the play itself, particularly by the prevalence of verbal ambiguities that let the audience make its own meanings: "I find that my favorite lines make it possible for me to create and explore several grammatical and semantic possibilities within a single thought" (423). Holland also argues that much of the power of the play comes from verbal strategies such as the effective utilization of words to substitute for external events: "The greatness of *Hamlet* is not the plot alone, nor the character, but the way the thousands, or tens of thousands, of details make it possible for me to explore possibilities and yet master them, to escape reality and yet, in a way, master it, too, by turning the words" (425).

In *5 Readers Reading* (1975), Holland explores the ideas he put forth earlier in *The Dynamics of Literary Response* by examining the characteristic interpretive strategies employed by five actual readers when confronted with William Faulkner's story "A Rose for Emily." Much like Richards, Holland finds that the reactions of these readers seem idiosyncratic and that they vary substantially from his own highly informed psychoanalytic reading of the story. But rather than simply mark down the seemingly aberrant responses of his readers to their ignorance and inadequate education, Holland postulates that these variant responses arise from the various identity themes of the readers. He then analyzes the responses of these readers and develops interpretations of their identity themes based on the nature of these responses. In a sense, then, we might say that Holland eschews the New Critical call for a unifying interpretation of literary texts by displacing the demand for unity from the text onto individual readers. The responses of different readers to a given text may thus be highly variable, but the responses of a given reader to different texts are presumed to be highly consistent and even predictable.

Of course, the obvious objection to Holland's approach is that, by his own assumptions, a critic's interpretation of readers' identity themes will necessarily be determined in large measure by the critic's own identity theme. This approach thus potentially initiates an endless chain of interpretations that moves the focus of interpretation farther and farther from the text and ultimately provides no stable ground for textual interpretation. In his later work, Holland often eschews detailed readings of the identity themes of specific readers and simply explores literary texts based on his own identity theme, reading these texts while remaining highly self-conscious of his own reading strategies and commenting extensively on the aspects of his own experience and personality that might cause him to read as he does. In a recent reading of Joyce's *A Portrait of the Artist as a Young Man,* for example, Holland notes how his negative response to the sermons embedded in this text are conditioned by "my own childhood hours spent in church and Sunday school, as well as my present unbelief" (*"Portrait"* 282). Ultimately Holland concludes that his reaction to Joyce's text is determined by his own need to be in control and his feeling that he is struggling with Joyce for control of the interpretation of this text. In particular, Holland admits that he finds the power of Joyce's prose threatening and that his sometimes defensive reactions to the text respond to "the power of the artist over me, the power that is so immense in Joyce. It feels dangerous to me. I do not like the idea of another man controlling me" (293).

Such self-conscious ruminations can no doubt be extremely useful, and all of us are probably wise to examine why we respond the way we do to literary texts. But when Holland reads Joyce by reading Holland reading Joyce, he again potentially initiates an infinite chain of interpretations the final implications of which are difficult to determine. Holland reads his own psychology by assuming that this psychology conditions his reading of Joyce, but Holland's psychology conditions his reading of his own psychology, and so on. Moreover it is difficult to imagine reader-response methods based on psychological or subjective approaches that will not be prone to such problems. In some of his later work (for example, *The Brain of Robert Frost*), Holland tries to surmount such difficulties in subjective approaches with an appeal to more objective and scientific foundations in cognitive psychology and brain physiology. He is still forced to admit, however, that attempts to interpret human identity ultimately result in an "infinite regression," but (employing the electro-mechanical analogy of the feedback loop) he argues that this infinite regression need not prevent the development of useful interpretations (*Brain* 149–153).

A similar self-consciousness informs the later work of Fish, who in the book *Is There a Text in This Class?* compiles an interesting sequence of essays published over the course of his career, thus illustrating the sequential development of his ideas about literature and reading. This course essentially entails a gradual movement away from his early espousal of affective stylistics (with its New Critical–like emphasis on close reading of the subtleties of literary texts) toward a far more radical position in which he argues that texts, far from manipulating the reactions of readers in the manner he earlier described, are created by readers in the process of reading. In the later Fish, for example, formal devices such as line endings do not direct the reading experience but are created by it and by the whole panoply of expectations and conventions invoked in the process of reading. Despite this emphasis on the creative role of the reader, Fish eschews the subjectivity of Holland and shifts his attention to the social conditioning of the reading process. Readers, for Fish in this later phase, create texts, but they do not do so as independent agents. Interpretations are not a matter of personal psychology but of social education in the interpretation of texts. For the later Fish, the formal features of texts do not direct the process of reading but are created by that process, by the fact that readers expect to find such formal features. But these expectations are a matter of training and experience in reading, not of individual psychology. Rather than suggest that readers interpret texts according to their personal identity themes, Fish argues that the characteristic interpretive styles of readers arise from their participation in public "interpretive communities," made up of "those who share interpretive strategies not for reading but for writing texts, for constituting their properties. In other words these strategies exist prior to the act of reading and therefore determine the shape of what is read rather than, as is usually assumed, the other way around" (*Is* 14).

In reality, however, an interpretive community is not so much a collection of individuals as a recognized practice for the interpretation of texts, somewhat akin to what Michel Foucault refers to as a "discourse." Different interpretive communities may apply different strategies and criteria to texts, resulting in different interpretations. This does not mean, however, that any and all interpretations of literary texts are acceptable. In *5 Readers Reading,* Holland argues that, despite variations in the identity themes of readers, some interpretations are simply not appropriate. As an example, he suggests that it would be unacceptable to interpret "A Rose for Emily" as being about Eskimos, regardless of the reader's personal inclinations, because there is simply nothing in the text to endorse such a reading (12). Fish agrees that the Eskimo interpretation of Faulkner's story can be rejected as unacceptable. But Fish insists, contrary to Holland, that this unacceptability is not a property of Faulkner's text itself but arises simply because there does not yet exist an interpretive community that would endorse such a reading strategy. Moreover Fish also argues that it is possible to envision circumstances in which such a community might develop, making an Eskimo reading of "A Rose for Emily" entirely appropriate (*Is* 346). Thus for the later Fish, "while there are always mechanisms for ruling out readings, their source is not the text but the presently recognized interpretive strategies for producing the text. It follows, then, that no reading, however outlandish it might appear, is inherently an impossible one" (347).

For Fish, both texts and readers are to a large extent the product of interpretive communities. He thus differs dramatically from Holland by insisting that the ways we read are the products not of our individual psychologies but of the social practices in which we participate. Fish's later work thus has a great deal in common with poststructuralist theory in its belief that the individual human subject is a product of language and discourse rather than the other way around. But Fish's notion that interpretations are produced by interpretive communities differs radically from the typical poststructuralist emphasis on the free play of language. For Fish, the play of language is decidedly not free. It is, in fact, quite strictly determined by existing practices and conventions. Fish grants that interpretive communities develop and change with time, but he does not provide a satisfactory model for this historical process. With readers thoroughly inscribed in existing interpretive practices, it is not clear how new practices ever arise. Thus Elizabeth Freund complains that Fish does not adequately address the possibility that the authority of interpretive communities might become "grimly coercive": "The salutary curb on subjectivity, without a corresponding curb on the authority of consensual norms, remains troubling. The appeal to the imperialism of agreement can chill the spines of reader whose experience of the community is less happily benign than Fish assumes" (110–111).

Clearly Fish's model of interpretive communities has philosophical implications that go well beyond the reading of literary texts, suggesting that our perceptions of the world as a whole are also to a large extent produced not by objective reality but by social conventions and discourses. Similarly Holland's psychoanalytic approach implies that our interpretations of the world are largely conditioned by our personal identity; his work also suggests that studies of the process of reading can tell us a great deal about the general workings of the human psyche. Finally Iser's emphasis on the ethics of reading and on the potential for expansion of consciousness through the reading process clearly implies a link between the experience of reading and the practice of everyday life. The stakes involved in reader-response criticism are thus high indeed, so it is probably not surprising that leading reader-response critics such as Fish, Iser, and Holland have participated in spirited (and sometimes acrimonious) debates among themselves. But whatever their individual differences, all of these critics would agree that the act of reading—however it is envisioned—is never innocent and never involves a "pure" response to the text at hand. Readers bring a great deal of extratextual material to their reading of texts, and the outcome of the reading experience is powerfully affected by this material.

BIBLIOGRAPHY

Introductory Works

Fish, Stanley. *Is There a Text in This Class?: The Authority of Interpretive Communities.* Cambridge, Mass.: Harvard UP, 1980.

A collection of essays that spans Fish's career and indicates its outlines.

Freund, Elizabeth. *The Return of the Reader: Reader-Response Criticism.* London: Methuen, 1987.

An excellent general introduction to reader-response criticism.

Holland, Norman. *Poems in Persons: An Introduction to the Psychoanalysis of Literature.* New York: Norton, 1973.
A valuable introduction to Holland's distinctive applications of psychoanalysis within the framework of reader-response theory.

Holub, Robert C. *Reception Theory: A Critical Introduction.* London: Methuen, 1984.
An extremely useful introduction to German reception theory, focusing on the work of Jauss and Iser.

Selected Other Works

Beckett, Samuel. *Three Novels: "Molloy," "Malone Dies," and "The Unnamable."* New York: Grove, 1965.

Bleich, David. *Subjective Criticism.* Baltimore, Md.: Johns Hopkins UP, 1978.

Booth, Stephen. "On the Value of *Hamlet.*" In *Reinterpretations of Elizabethan Drama,* ed. Norman Rabkin, 77–99. New York: Columbia UP, 1969.

Culler, Jonathan. *On Deconstruction: Theory and Criticism after Structuralism.* Ithaca, N.Y.: Cornell UP, 1982.

Fish, Stanley. *Self-Consuming Artifacts: The Experience of Seventeenth-Century Literature.* Berkeley and Los Angeles: U of California P, 1972.

———. *Surprised by Sin: The Reader in "Paradise Lost."* New York: St. Martin's, 1967.

Holland, Norman. *The Brain of Robert Frost: A Cognitive Approach to Literature.* New York: Routledge, 1988.

———. *The Dynamics of Literary Response.* New York: Oxford UP, 1968.

———. *5 Readers Reading.* New Haven, Conn.: Yale UP, 1975.

———. "*Hamlet*—My Greatest Creation." *Journal of the American Academy of Psychoanalysis* 3 (1975): 419–427.

———. *The I.* New Haven, Conn.: Yale UP, 1985.

———. "A *Portrait* as Rebellion: A Reader-Response Perspective." In *"A Portrait of the Artist as a Young Man": Complete, Authoritative Text with Biographical and Historical Contexts, Critical History, and Essays from Five Contemporary Critical Perspectives,* ed. R. B. Kershner, 279–294. Boston: Bedford Books–St. Martin's, 1993.

———. "UNITY IDENTITY TEXT SELF." In *Reader-Response Criticism: From Formalism to Post-Structuralism,* ed. Jane Tompkins, 118–133. Baltimore, Md.: Johns Hopkins UP, 1980.

Ingarden, Roman. *The Cognition of the Literary Work of Art.* Trans. Ruth Ann Crowley and Kenneth Olson. Evanston, Ill.: Northwestern UP, 1973.

———. *The Literary Work of Art.* Trans. George G. Grabowicz. Evanston, Ill.: Northwestern UP, 1973.

Iser, Wolfgang. *The Act of Reading: A Theory of Aesthetic Response.* Baltimore, Md.: Johns Hopkins UP, 1978.

———. *The Implied Reader: Patterns of Communication in Prose Fiction from Bunyan to Beckett.* Baltimore, Md.: Johns Hopkins UP, 1974.

———. *Prospecting: From Reader Response to Literary Anthropology.* Baltimore, Md.: Johns Hopkins UP, 1989.

Jauss, Hans Robert. *Aesthetic Experience and Literary Hermeneutics.* Minneapolis: U of Minnesota P, 1982.

———. *Toward an Aesthetics of Reception.* Minneapolis: U of Minnesota P, 1982.

Lichtenstein, Heinz. *The Dilemma of Human Identity.* New York: Jason Aronson, 1977.

Mailloux, Steven. *Interpretive Conventions: The Reader in the Study of American Fiction.* Ithaca, N.Y.: Cornell UP, 1982.

Richards, I. A. *Practical Criticism.* New York: Harcourt Brace, 1929.

Steig, Michael. *Stories of Reading: Subjectivity and Literary Understanding.* Baltimore, Md.: Johns Hopkins UP, 1988.

Suleiman, Susan R., and Inge Crosman, eds. *The Reader in the Text: Essays on Audience and Interpretation.* Princeton, N.J.: Princeton UP, 1980.

Tompkins, Jane, ed. *Reader-Response Criticism: From Formalism to Post-Structuralism.* Baltimore, Md.: Johns Hopkins UP, 1980.

Waldock, A. J. A. *"Paradise Lost" and Its Critics.* Cambridge: Cambridge UP, 1947.

Wyatt, Jean. *Reconstructing Desire: The Role of the Unconscious in Women's Reading and Writing.* Chapel Hill: U of North Carolina P, 1990.

chapter 4

Deconstructive Literary Criticism

In 1873 a youthful Friedrich Nietzsche wrote a brief essay entitled "On Truth and Lies in the Nonmoral Sense." The essay was never published in Nietzsche's lifetime and was never even finished—it comes down to us in the form of two completed sections and preliminary notes toward several more. The essay deals, more or less, with the question of human knowing and especially with the fundamental role that language plays in the conceptualization of all knowledge:

> It is this way with all of us concerning language: we believe that we know something about the things themselves when we speak of trees, colors, snow, and flowers; and yet we possess nothing but metaphors for things—metaphors which correspond in no way to the original entities. . . . Thus the genesis of language does not proceed logically in any case, and all the material within which the man of truth, the scientist, and the philosopher later work and build, if not derived from never-never land, is at least not derived from the essence of things. (82–83)

To Nietzsche, all knowledge is indirect and metaphorical, and "reality" is nothing but "an X which remains inaccessible and undefinable for us" (83). Language does not refer to some external reality but only to itself, and the same can be said for all knowledge. Any link between language and reality is purely metaphorical. "Every concept arises from the equation of unequal things," Nietzsche writes (83). All knowledge arises in relation to other knowledge, and the resultant epistemological self-referentiality results in an infinite regression that can never hit bottom.

Nietzsche's essay suggests that the search for truth and the quest for centers and origins that underlie the epistemological investigations of post-Cartesian

Western philosophy are ultimately doomed to failure. This suggestion strongly resembles many of the proclamations of recent poststructuralist philosophers such as Jacques Derrida—and with good reason. As Sanford Schwartz points out, the "On Truth" essay has become a sort of "manifesto" of the poststructuralist movement (75). Nietzsche's radical questioning of the ultimate authenticity of all human knowledge also anticipates many later developments in literature, where numerous authors have launched similar demystifying assaults against the epistemological tradition of the Enlightenment.

The term *poststructuralist criticism* can refer to any one of a number of critical approaches that arose in the late 1960s and early 1970s in reaction to the dominance of structuralism in European intellectual endeavors of the previous two decades. As was the case with structuralism, poststructuralist techniques and assumptions have been applied not only to a variety of strategies for reading literature but also to a variety of disciplines. Poststructuralism has been an important influence in such fields as philosophy, psychology, linguists, history, and anthropology, in addition to literary criticism. To a first approximation, we can identify two major branches of poststructuralist literary criticism. The first of these, deriving most importantly from the work of Michel Foucault, concentrates its work on culture and society, on the institutions and practices that condition our reading of literature. Poststructuralist cultural criticism is discussed in a later chapter. The other important branch of poststructuralist criticism is identified most directly with the work of the French philosopher Jacques Derrida. It involves the critical strategy known as "deconstruction," an approach that gained immense popularity (and attracted violent opposition) in America in the 1970s. This chapter deals with that approach.

Deconstruction is essentially a formalist method of close reading, and for that reason it has often (especially in recent discussions) been compared to the New Criticism. For example, deconstruction closely resembles the New Criticism in its emphasis on careful attention to linguistic subtleties that might lead to irony, ambiguity, paradox, and other forms of multiple meanings. Deconstruction differs substantially from the New Criticism in its refusal to attempt a resolution of these paradoxes and ambiguities through any appeal to organic unity in the literary text. As J. Hillis Miller, one of the leading American practitioners of deconstructive criticism, puts it, "The new turn in criticism involves an interrogation of the notion of the self-enclosed literary work and of the idea that any work has a fixed, identifiable meaning" ("Stevens'" 333). Moreover the formalist emphasis on the text itself is significantly problematized in deconstructive criticism, for which textual boundaries are highly permeable and unstable, thus challenging conventional notions of just what constitutes a "text." Indeed deconstructionists do not distinguish between text and world in New Critical fashion because in their view everything is textual. That is, humans approach everything through language. In an oft-quoted statement, Derrida thus declares that "there is nothing outside of the text" (*Grammatology* 158).

Derrida's project grows out of a fundamental challenge to the traditions of Western philosophy. In particular, he argues that this philosophy is consistently informed by what he refers to as "logocentric" or "metaphysical" thinking—that is, the notion (derived from the monotheistic religions of the Judeo-Christian tradition) that there is an ultimate center and ground to philosophical truth. Derrida notes that logocentric logic sees language as a reflection of some preexisting meaning or reality, whereas he believes that meaning is created in language. This emphasis on the creative potential of language has obvious implications for literature, though its ramifications go well beyond literature as well. For example, Derrida's challenge to the Western tradition of logocentric thought involves a fundamental challenge to the long-cherished notion of the "transcendental subject"—that is, to the idea that individual human beings exist as stable entities identifiably separate from the world around them. But just as Derrida sees no clear boundary between text and context, he also sees no absolute distinction between subject and world. The transcendental subject (modeled on the God of monotheistic religions) uses language to express its feelings and thoughts about the world. For Derrida, however, the human subject is created in and through language rather than existing prior to and independently of language.

The poststructuralist view of language grows out of the structuralist belief in language as a self-referential system that operates according to its own rules and conventions rather than out of any direct relationship to reality. Structuralism crucially relies on the work of the Swiss linguist Ferdinand de Saussure, who developed a systematic approach to the description of language as a self-contained system. Saussure distinguishes between *la parole* (specific instances of actual language use) and *la langue* (the system of accepted rules and conventions that govern the use of language and render communication possible). Saussure's work focuses on the latter aspect of language and on the ways rules and conventions operate to allow the expression of meaning in intelligible ways. For Saussure, language consists of "signs" that allow users to relate linguistic expressions to reality. A sign for Saussure has two fundamental components: the "signifier" (a unit of sound, usually corresponding to a word) and the "signified" (a concept or meaning invoked by the signifier). Importantly, however, the signifier and signified are not linked in any natural or absolute way—as the names of things were synonymous with the things themselves in the biblical language of the mythical Adam. Instead the two parts of the sign are linked purely by arbitrary convention and by their participation in the entire system of language.

Saussure's approach points toward a detailed and systematic study of language. Moreover given the centrality of language to human social endeavors, it is not surprising that Saussure's insights were widely adopted by investigators in a number of human sciences in the course of the twentieth century. Thus Claude Lévi-Strauss applied structuralist insights to anthropology in an attempt to develop an understanding of the social practices of "primitive" cultures and of the functioning of such cultural artifacts as myths; Louis Althusser used structuralist methods to extend the work of Karl Marx to develop detailed models of the workings of ideology in capitalist society; Jacques Lacan updated Freudian psychoanalysis by employing structuralism to produce models of the structure of the human mind; the early Michel Foucault applied structuralist insights to analyze the workings of social institutions and the history of ideas.

Not surprisingly, structuralist techniques were particularly valuable in the study of literature, with critics Roland Barthes and Tzvetan Todorov, among others, performing extensive studies of the structural principles of literary works. In the important work *S/Z,* for example, Barthes conducts a detailed and systematic analysis of the construction of Honoré de Balzac's *Sarrasine* by performing a sequential reading that separates the text into 561 segments, or "lexias," and explores the function of each lexia in terms of five codes: hermeneutic (dealing with enigmas), semantic (signifying connotations), symbolic (signifying the ability of literary motifs to represent ideas beyond the scope of the text itself), proairetic (dealing with actions), and cultural (referring to knowledge or wisdom). Barthes precedes this analysis with comments on the plurality of texts and on "readerly" texts (which allow the reader to consume them passively) and "writerly" texts (which require the reader actively to participate in the generation of meaning) (4–5).

But structuralist literary criticism goes far beyond the study of narrative structures or of patterns of imagery. In particular, the structuralist emphasis on the system of language undercuts the Romantic notion of the author as the transcendental originator of his own texts, proposing instead that all texts arise within the systems of conventions and practices that constitute language and literature. Thus in a famous essay, "The Death of the Author," Barthes argues that the notion of the "author" is a modern product of the Renaissance emphasis on the individual but that in writing "it is language which speaks, not the author" (143). For Barthes, then, "a text is not a line of words releasing a single 'theological' meaning (the 'message' of the Author-God) but a multi-dimensional space in which a variety of writings, none of them original, blend and clash. The text is a tissue of quotations drawn from the innumerable centres of culture" (146). It is the task of the reader, especially of writerly texts, to assemble these textual fragments into meaningful form: "The reader is the space on which all the quotations that make up a writing are inscribed without any of them being lost; a text's unity lies not in its origin but in its destination" (148).

In this view, all texts are products of "intertextuality," of the sometimes subtle relationships among all texts: "Every text, being itself the intertext of another text, belongs to the intertextual, which must not be confused with a text's origins: to search for the 'sources of' and 'influence upon' a work is to satisfy the myth of filiation" ("Work" 77). In the course of his career, Barthes gradually moved to a more and more radical emphasis on the plurality and "play" of language in this intertextual process. In particular, he began to emphasize the "pleasure" of the text, distinguishing between the "text of pleasure," a conventional, "comfortable" text, and the "text of bliss: the text that imposes a state of loss, the text that discomforts (perhaps to the point of a certain boredom), unsettles the reader's historical, cultural, psychological assumptions, the consistency of his tastes, values, memories, brings to a crisis his relation with language" (*Pleasure* 14). Such emphases, however, begin to unsettle the rather scientific structuralist emphasis on system and structure. Indeed while building significantly on the structuralist focus on the centrality of language to human endeavor, poststructuralism arose in the late 1960s and early 1970s largely against what was perceived as an overly simplistic and ultimately impoverishing structuralist emphasis on stable structure and well-behaved form.

From an American perspective, Derrida became the leader of the post-structuralist assault on structuralist decorum when he burst onto the American scene in the late 1960s with the essay "Structure, Sign, and Play in the Discourse of the Human Sciences." In this essay, he suggests that a fundamental "rupture" in the history of the concept of structure occurred in the late nineteenth and early twentieth centuries. This rupture, exemplified in the Nietzschean critique of metaphysics and in the Freudian critique of the identity of consciousness, involved a new ability to conceive of structures based on principles of play, interpretation, and sign rather than on older notions of presence, truth, and an ultimate center to all structures (247–250). Derrida then points out that there are two directly opposed ways of reacting to this loss. The first involves a longing or nostalgia for the apparent security that such centers had always provided. Derrida associates this nostalgic rage for order with structuralism, particularly with the anthropological studies of Lévi-Strauss. The second potential reaction is that of Nietzsche, "the Nietzschean *affirmation*—the joyous affirmation of the freeplay of the world and without truth, without origin, offered to an active interpretation" (264).

Derrida's deconstructive program pursues the implications of this Nietzschean affirmation, especially for philosophy. In the process, Derrida undertakes the development of an alternative approach to philosophy that eschews many of the most cherished and fundamental assumptions of the Western philosophical tradition. Vincent B. Leitch provides a series of aphorisms that summarize many of the principal implications of Derridean deconstruction:

> The world is text. Nothing stands behind. . . . The concepts "being," "consciousness," "presence," and "self" are creations, fabrications, patchworks—interpretations. Functions not facts. Effects of language, not causes. . . . The text is not an autonomous or unified object, but a set of relations with other texts. . . . The "genealogy" of the text is necessarily an incomplete network of conscious and unconscious borrowed fragments. Manifested, tradition is a mess. Every text is intertext. (58–59)

Probably the most fundamental assumption of Western philosophy is Aristotle's principle of noncontradiction, which states that a thing cannot both have a property and not have a property. Derrida, following Nietzsche, argues that this principle leads to an "either-or" logic that leads directly to the habit of dualistic thinking (or division of all aspects of life into binary sets of opposed categories) that is central to Western thought. For Derrida, such dualistic thinking is impoverishing; it cannot encompass the complexity and richness of language and its products, which do not fall neatly into either-or categories. Furthermore, and perhaps more important, Derrida finds that dualistic thought inevitably leads to hierarchization, with one pole of a binary opposition being valued over the other. He therefore seeks to undermine, or deconstruct, binary oppositions throughout his work, typically by showing that the two poles are not diametrically opposed but mutually involved. There can be no concept of "bad," for instance, without a concept of "good"—and vice versa. Derrida thereby disrupts the traditional privileging of one pole over the other by showing that they cannot even be conceived of independently.

This project can be applied directly to literary texts, which are often constructed on the basis of binary oppositions. As Christopher Norris, a leading explicator of Derrida's work, points out, one of the essential features of a deconstructive reading is that it "consists, not merely in *reversing* or *subverting* some established hierarchical order, but in showing how its terms are indissociably entwined in a strictly undecidable exchange of values and priorities" (*Derrida* 56). Barbara Johnson, describing her own deconstructive critical practice, provides an excellent summary of the process of deconstruction of binary oppositions in the reading of literature:

> The starting point is often a binary difference that is subsequently shown to be an illusion created by the workings of differences much harder to pin down. The differences *between* entities (prose and poetry, man and woman, literature and theory, guilt and innocence) are shown to be based on a repression *within* entities, ways in which an entity differs from itself. . . . The "deconstruction" of a binary opposition is thus not an annihilation of all values or differences; it is an attempt to follow the subtle, powerful effects of differences already at work within the illusion of a binary opposition. (x–xi)

Many of the dualities central to Western thought (male versus female, white versus nonwhite) have clear social and political implications. Others have more subtle philosophical implications, and it is on the latter that Derrida himself concentrates. For example, his challenge to the notion of a distinct boundary between the inside and outside of texts undercuts the dualistic distinction between these regions while at the same time questioning the traditional formalist privileging of the text while paying little attention to historical context. Similarly Derrida extends the structuralist challenge to the notion of the autonomous self to undermine the dualistic opposition between subject and object, or individual and surrounding world, that is central to Western philosophical systems like that proposed by René Descartes. From the perspective of literary studies, one of Derrida's most important projects involves a challenge to the traditional distinction between philosophy (as the literal expression of truth about the world) and literature (as the metaphorical realm of fiction).

In particular, Derrida denies a dualistic distinction between literal and metaphorical language. Following Nietzsche, Derrida argues that language cannot escape from metaphors: "If one wished to conceive and class all the metaphorical possibilities of philosophy, one metaphor, at least, always would remain excluded, outside the system: the metaphor, at the very least, without which the concept of metaphor could not be constructed, or, to syncopate an entire chain of reasoning, the metaphor of metaphor" (*Margins* 219–220). Philosophical language, like literary language, is fundamentally metaphorical in nature, and as a result the traditional claim that philosophy provides a more direct expression of truth than literature does has no basis.

Derrida pursues this deconstruction of the distinction between philosophy and literature in a number of ways. For one thing, he often writes about literature, as in the essays collected in *Acts of Literature.* For example, Derrida has identified the writing of James Joyce as one of the major influences on this philosophy. Derrida also writes in a highly literary fashion, employing complex writing strategies that eschew the traditional philosophical drive for lucidity and instead embrace a playful, punning discourse in which the sounds of words can be as important as their meanings and style can be as important as content. The sometimes frustrating experience of reading Derrida's writing is described in an early review of the English translation of *Of Grammatology:*

> A reader feels that to raise one question will necessarily uncover a whole network of possible lines of investigation, until he finds himself almost entirely implicated in Derrida's text and its system of literary and philosophical allusions—perhaps without hope of exit. . . . After reading a text written, as Derrida would say, by his ironic discourse, therefore, the reader trained in the Anglo-American school of analytic philosophy is likely to be left with the impression of a man playing with the pieces of a jig-saw puzzle—the pieces being fragments largely drawn from texts of Nietzsche, Freud, and Heidegger. . . . Such a reader naturally expects the puzzle to be solved in the end, and is disappointed and bewildered when he finds instead that Derrida appears able only to play with the pieces. Perhaps the essential pieces are missing after all, or perhaps there are too many pieces to begin with. (O'Hara 363–365)

A great deal of Derrida's work is in fact concerned with the topic of writing. One of his central arguments involves the somewhat surprising conclusion that Western thought has consistently privileged spoken over written language because the former seems more directly linked to its originating speaker and thus more closely similar to the Word of God that supposedly spoke the universe into being. Although Derrida's critique of the privileging of speech over writing goes back to Plato, it focuses particularly on structuralism. For example, he argues that Saussure's emphasis on spoken language is a principal modern example of this long-term trend. Derrida also discusses the argument of Lévi-Strauss in *Tristes Tropiques* that his introduction of writing into an oral South American native culture resulted in a powerful imperialistic drive toward bureaucratization in that culture. Lévi-Strauss thus sees the native culture as being threatened with enslavement by the introduction of writing, and Derrida finds here an especially clear example of his argument that Western culture in general hates and fears the power of writing. In fact, Derrida calls this episode "the finest example of what I have called the 'metaphysics of presence'" (*Grammatology* 131). He then proceeds to argue that there is more than one way to interpret Lévi-Strauss's data concerning the effect of writing: "What is going to be called *enslavement* can equally legitimately be called *liberation*. And it is at the moment that this oscillation is *stopped* on the signification of enslavement that the discourse is frozen into a determined ideology" (131).

Derrida's conclusion here flies in the face of most analyses of encounters between European (written) culture and the oral traditions of American, Asian, and African native cultures. In particular, it ignores the many instances of imperial power and domination in which written language often played a central role. It is for such reasons that Derrida's work has often been criticized for a seeming disengagement from political reality, though politically conscious critics such as Michael Ryan have argued that Derrida's frequent radical challenges to accepted ideas have a great deal in common with emancipatory political projects such as Marxism.

In any case, for Derrida the traditional privileging of speech over writing has far-reaching implications. It is related, for instance, to the view of the human subject as the originator of meaning. As Terry Eagleton points out:

> We have become accustomed since Derrida to associating a traditional Western prejudice for "living speech" as against script with a potent metaphysic of the human subject, centred in the rich plenitude of its linguistic presence, the fount and origin of all sense. It is in this refusal of the materiality of the sign, this ineradicable nostalgia for a transcendental source of meaning anterior to and constitutive of all sign systems, that Derrida finds the Western tradition most deeply marked by idealism. (55)

Derrida's own emphasis on the materiality of language, and particularly of writing, leads him to a number of important observations about the nature of the writing process. Arguing that Saussure's treatment of the relationship between signifier and signified is informed by a traditional Western belief that meaning precedes language (that the signified exists prior to the signifier, which then simply represents it), Derrida points out that in the epoch of theology/metaphysics, signification (the creation of meaning through signs) is always belated. Signs exist as the secondary expressions of preexisting meaning, and signification points back to a place of origin: "Thus, within this epoch, reading and writing, the production or interpretation of signs, the text in general as a fabric of signs, allow themselves to be confined within secondariness. They are preceded by a truth, or a meaning already constituted by and within the element of the logos"(*Grammatology* 14).

Derrida, however, proposes a fundamentally different conception of the process of signification in which meaning is dynamically generated on the fly in the process of writing. One of his key terms is *différance,* a neologism combining the French verbs for "to differ" and "to defer" to show how language depends on differential systems to produce meaning while at the same time endlessly postponing a final end to this production. There is, then, a fundamental difference between traditional authorship and what Derrida calls "writing": The theological notion of authorship points backward (and inward) to a prior point of origin; writing is radically contemporary, pointing forward and outward, irreducibly caught up in the flow of history and in an explosive dissemination of multiple meanings. Derrida extends Barthes's structuralist notion of writing not as the expression of individual consciousness but as an assemblage of intertextual fragments, making it more radical:

> It is a question of producing a new concept of writing. This concept can be called *gram* or *différance*. . . . Whether in the order of spoken or written discourse, no element can function as a sign without referring to another element which itself is not simply present. This interweaving results in each "element"—phoneme or grapheme—being constituted on the basis of the trace within it of the other elements of the chain or system. This interweaving, this textile, is the *text* produced only in the transformation of another text. Nothing, neither among the elements nor within the system, is anywhere ever simply present or absent. There are only, everywhere, differences and traces. The gram, then, is the most general concept of semiology—which thus becomes grammatology. (*Positions* 26)

To Derrida, not only do all words bear the traces of their previous appearances in other texts (and even of their *future* appearances in other texts), but they also bear the traces of the other words in the text. In fact, the system of self-reference in literary language extends outward to encompass the entire linguistic structure. Thus each word bears the traces of all other words in the entire language: "Certain forces of association unite—at diverse distances, with different strengths and according to disparate paths—the words 'actually present' in a discourse with all the other words in the lexical system" (*Dissemination* 129-130). The intricate interrelationships among different parts of the linguistic system are beyond authorial control and often lead to results that authors neither intend nor anticipate. Because of such relationships, no author can produce a pure expression of her own thoughts, which in any case are themselves a product of language. For Derrida, "the writer writes *in* a language and *in* a logic whose proper system, laws, and life his discourse by definition cannot dominate absolutely. He uses them only by letting himself, after a fashion and up to a point, be governed by the system" (*Grammatology* 158).

Among other things, Derrida is aware that his own project cannot escape the heritage of the metaphysical tradition: "*There is no sense* in doing without the concepts of metaphysics in order to attack metaphysics. We have no language —no syntax and no lexicon—which is alien to this history; we cannot utter a single destructive proposition which has not already slipped into the form, the logic, and the implicit postulations of precisely what it seeks to contest" ("Structure" 250). But Derrida is not suggesting here that nothing can be done; he is merely indicating that any attack on metaphysics must be an attack from within and that such an attack must include self-referential meditations on its own terms and conditions.

For Derrida, all writing is a process of "grafting," or assembling preexisting fragments, regardless of whether the author is aware of this process. No text exists in isolation. Instead all texts are part of the intertextual system, so that "reading . . . cannot legitimately transgress the text toward something other than it, toward the referent (a reality that is metaphysical, historical, psychobiographical, etc.) or toward a signifier outside the text whose content could take place, could have taken place outside of language, that is to say, in the sense that we give here to that word, outside of writing in general. . . . There is nothing outside of the text" (*Grammatology* 158).

Derrida relates his vision of texts as the result of intertextual connections to the process referred to by Lévi-Strauss as *bricolage,* where the *bricoleur* is a sort of junk man who randomly collects odd bits and scraps without any particular plan and then uses those diverse materials as the need arises. Derrida himself often foregrounds the *bricolage* nature of his own writing by creating split texts composed of different elements differentiated by the use of different fonts, multiple columns, and so on. Texts such as "The Double Session" (*Dissemination* 173–286), "Living on," and (most important) *Glas* overtly enact the Derridean view of the construction of all texts. Indeed Derrida sometimes relates his own methods to those of the *bricoleur* and even suggests that, because of the "necessity of borrowing one's concepts from the text of a heritage which is more or less coherent or ruined, it must be said that every discourse is *bricoleur*" ("Structure" 255). As Gayatri Chakravorty Spivak puts it, echoing Julia Kristeva's reminder of the inescapability of intertextuality, Derrida's views on the limitations of knowledge imply that "the reason for *bricolage* is that there can be nothing else" (xix). In this vein, Derrida speaks of the way his own texts are quite literally "assembled": "I insist on the word 'assemblage' here. . . . The word 'assemblage' seems more apt for suggesting that the kind of bringing-together proposed here has the structure of an interlacing, a weaving, or a web, which would allow different threads and different lines of sense or force to bring others together" (*Speech* 132).

This vision of writing leads Derrida to be particularly critical of classical forms of writing (philosophical and otherwise) that seek to hide their textuality and present themselves as finished, seamless wholes. For example, he argues that a book, through its very nature as a bound unit, stands as a representation of the metaphysical ideal of wholeness and full presence that underlies the entire history of Western philosophy. Furthermore, for Derrida the idea of the book as a totality implies a view of language as being capable of expressing complete, self-contained meaning. In his essay "The End of the Book and the Beginning of Writing," Derrida warns against the illusions of closure and completeness that the book tends to encourage. Instead Derrida wants to emphasize the notion of writing as an ongoing and dynamic activity as opposed to the static nature of the book. The very notion of the book as the endpoint of writing acts to devalue the process in favor of the product, and the very notion of endpoints and closures indicates a belief in ultimate origins and truths:

> The idea of the book is the idea of a totality, finite or infinite, of the signifier; this totality of the signifier cannot be a totality, unless a totality constituted by the signified preexists it, supervises its inscriptions and its signs, and is independent of it in its ideality. The idea of the book, which always refers to a natural totality, is profoundly alien to the sense of writing. It is the encyclopedic protection of theology and of logocentrism against the disruption of writing, against its aphoristic energy, and . . . against difference in general. (*Grammatology* 18)

Indeed Derrida has suggested that this attack on the totality of the book is central to his entire early project. When asked by an interviewer to comment on his own books, he responded that "in what you call my books, what is first put into question is the unity of the book and the unity 'book' considered as a perfect totality, with all the implications of such a concept. And you know that these implications concern the entirety of our culture, directly or indirectly" (*Positions* 3). Derrida's books, then, are in fact antibooks. Much of this attack on totalization, or the development of all-encompassing ideas or systems (occurring in the late 1960s), obviously arises from the intellectual climate of the time and is specifically motivated by an opposition to the kinds of totalizing systems proposed by Derrida's structuralist predecessors. Such attacks on the illusory wholeness of the book are common in poststructuralist discourse, and it is no accident that poststructuralist critics prefer to speak in terms of "texts" rather than "books." Derrida explains the difference: "If I distinguish the text from the book, I shall say that the destruction of the book, as it is now under way in all domains, denudes the surface of the text. That necessary violence responds to a violence that was no less necessary" (*Grammatology* 18). In short, a principal difference is that the text lays bare its own mode of operation, exhibiting a self-conscious awareness of (and thereby shattering) the illusion of wholeness and completeness implied by the physical status of the book as a bound volume.

It is in this opposition to ideas of wholeness, completeness, and unity that deconstruction differs most radically from the ideas of the New Critics. Derrida's own project radically resists reduction to the status of a well-defined system. For example, Rodolphe Gasché notes the importance of the ultimate undecidability of so many of Derrida's positions: "This plural nature, or openness, of Derrida's philosophy makes it thoroughly impossible to conceive of his work in terms of orthodoxy . . . primarily because it resists any possible closure, and thus doctrinal rigidity, for essential reasons" (8). Critics such as Richard Rorty have argued that Derrida's work depends so crucially on a direct confrontation with the Western philosophical tradition that Derrida's project is itself in danger of hardening into a system. Meanwhile the widespread popularity of Derrida's ideas among literary critics in America in the 1970s led to an institutionalization of deconstruction as a "method" that some (including Derrida himself) have seen as contrary to the antisystematic nature of his own project.

A number of important American critics (including Paul de Man, J. Hillis Miller, Geoffrey Hartman, Harold Bloom, Barbara Johnson, Shoshana Felman, and Joseph Riddel) have pursued deconstructionist methods of literary criticism that are importantly influenced by Derrida's work. Such criticism typically involves close and careful reading of literary texts to seek points at which they rely on metaphysical assumptions, dualistic thinking, or logocentric thought. Deconstructive critics then attempt to show how texts at such points contradict or undermine themselves, leading to the generation of meanings that may go beyond, or even directly oppose, those apparently intended by the author. When done well, deconstructive criticism makes important and fundamental statements about the nature of literary texts and of language itself. It can also be intellectually challenging, even exhilarating in the play of its language and the force of its ideas.

The radical challenge to closure and completeness that is so crucial to deconstruction has provoked a great deal of opposition from more conventional critics, who see the denial of firm meaning in deconstructive analysis as a form of interpretive anarchy. Such critics (M. H. Abrams, Robert Alter, Gerald Graff, John M. Ellis, Denis Donoghue, and E. D. Hirsch are among the more prominent) have also charged that deconstructive analyses, especially when performed by critics who may be less adept than leading practitioners such as Miller or de Man, tend to produce a tedious and formulaic sameness, predictably reducing all texts to a demonstration of the inherent instability and ambiguity of language. Indeed for some critics, deconstruction is not radical *enough,* amounting to little more than a reworking of the New Criticism with a French accent. For such reasons, and for difficulties in engaging with real-world political issues, deconstruction has become less popular in American literary criticism since the mid-1980s. Many of its proponents, however, believe that this loss in popularity may ultimately be a positive development, allowing an escape from trendiness that will encourage more serious and fundamental exploration of the implications of deconstruction.

BIBLIOGRAPHY

Introductory Works

Anderson, Danny J. "Deconstruction: Critical Strategy/Strategic Criticism." In *Contemporary Literary Theory,* ed. G. Douglas Atkins and Laura Morrow, 137–157. Amherst: U of Massachusetts P, 1989.

A good (brief) introduction to some of the major ideas of deconstruction.

Atkins, G. Douglas. *Reading Deconstruction, Deconstructive Reading.* Lexington: UP of Kentucky, 1983.
One of the more accessible general introductions to deconstruction. Includes both discussions of deconstructive theory and illustrative applications.

Culler, Jonathan. *On Deconstruction: Theory and Criticism after Structuralism.* Ithaca, N.Y.: Cornell UP, 1982.
A good general introduction to deconstruction that places it clearly in the transition from structuralist to poststructuralist theory.

Leitch, Vincent B. *Deconstructive Criticism: An Advanced Introduction.* New York: Columbia UP, 1983.
An excellent, though somewhat advanced, introduction to deconstruction.

Norris, Christopher. *Deconstruction: Theory and Practice.* London: Methuen, 1982.
A solid introduction to deconstruction and especially to the work of Derrida.

Selected Other Works

Abrams, M. H. "The Deconstructive Angel." *Critical Inquiry* 3 (1977): 425-438.

Alter, Robert. *The Pleasures of Reading in an Ideological Age.* New York: Simon, 1989.

Arac, Jonathan, Wallace Martin, and Wlad Godzich, eds. *The Yale Critics: Deconstruction in America.* Minneapolis: U of Minnesota P, 1983.

Barthes, Roland. "The Death of the Author." In *Image—Music—Text.* Trans. Stephen Heath. 142-148. London: Collins, 1977.

———. "From Work to Text." In *Textual Strategies: Perspectives in Post-Structuralist Criticism,* ed. Joshué Harari, 73-81. Ithaca, N.Y.: Cornell UP, 1979.

———. *The Pleasure of the Text.* Trans. Richard Miller. New York: Hill and Wang, 1975.

———. *S/Z.* New York: Hill and Wang, 1974.

———. "Theory of the Text." In *Untying the Text: A Post-Structuralist Reader,* ed. Robert Young, 31-47. London: Routledge and Kegan Paul, 1981.

Belsey, Catherine. *Critical Practice.* London: Methuen, 1980.

Berman, Art. *From the New Criticism to Deconstruction: The Reception of Structuralism and Post-Structuralism.* Urbana: U of Illinois P, 1988.

Bloom, Harold et al. *Deconstruction and Criticism.* New York: Seabury, 1979.

Carroll, David. *Paraesthetics: Foucault, Lyotard, Derrida.* London: Methuen, 1987.

Culler, Jonathan. *Structuralist Poetics.* Ithaca, N.Y.: Cornell UP, 1975.

de Man, Paul. *Allegories of Reading: Figural Language in Rousseau, Nietzsche, Rilke, and Proust.* New Haven, Conn.: Yale UP, 1979.

———. *Blindness and Insight.* 2d ed. Minneapolis: U of Minnesota P, 1983.

Derrida, Jacques. *Acts of Literature.* Ed. Derek Attridge. New York: Routledge, 1992.

———. *Dissemination.* Trans. Barbara Johnson. Chicago: U of Chicago P, 1981.

———. *Glas.* Trans. John P. Leavey, Jr. and Richard Rand. Lincoln: U of Nebraska P, 1986.

———. "Living on: Border Lines." In *Deconstruction and Criticism,* by Harold Bloom et al. 75-175. New York: Seabury, 1979.

———. *Margins of Philosophy.* Chicago: U of Chicago P, 1982.

———. *Of Grammatology.* Trans. Gayatri Chakravorty Spivak. Baltimore, Md.: Johns Hopkins UP, 1976.

———. *Positions.* Trans. Alan Bass. Chicago: U of Chicago P, 1981.

———. *Speech and Phenomena.* Trans. David B. Allison. Evanston, Ill.: Northwestern UP, 1973.

———. "Structure, Sign, and Play in the Discourse of the Human Sciences." In *The Structuralist Controversy: The Languages of Criticism and the Sciences of Man,* ed. Richard Macksey and Eugenio Donato. 247-265. Baltimore, Md.: Johns Hopkins UP, 1970.

———. *The Truth in Painting.* Trans. Geoff Bennington and Ian McLeod. Chicago: U of Chicago P, 1987.

———. *Writing and Difference.* Trans. Alan Bass. Chicago: U of Chicago P, 1978.

Donoghue, Denis. *Ferocious Alphabets.* New York: Columbia UP, 1984.

Eagleton, Terry. "Écriture and Eighteenth-Century Fiction." In *Literature, Society, and the Sociology of Literature,* 55-58. Proceedings of the conference held at the University of Essex, July 1976. Ed. Francis Barker et al. N.p.: N.p., n.d.

Ellis, John M. *Against Deconstruction.* Princeton, N.J.: Princeton UP, 1988.

Esch, Deborah. "Deconstruction." In *Redrawing the Boundaries: The Transformation of English and American Literary Studies,* ed. Stephen Greenblatt and Giles Gunn, 374-391. New York: Modern Language Association, 1992.

Felman, Shoshana. *Writing and Madness (Literature/Philosophy/Psychoanalysis).* Trans. Martha Noel Evans and Shoshana Felman. Ithaca, N.Y.: Cornell UP.

Gasché, Rodolphe. *The Tain of the Mirror: Derrida and the Philosophy of Reflection.* Cambridge, Mass.: Harvard UP, 1986.

Graff, Gerald. *Literature Against Itself: Literary Ideas in Modern Society.* Chicago: U of Chicago P, 1979.

Harari, Joshué, ed. *Textual Strategies: Perspectives in Post-Structuralist Criticism.* Ithaca, N.Y.: Cornell UP, 1979.

Hartman, Geoffrey. *Criticism in the Wilderness: The Study of Literature Today.* New Haven, Conn.: Yale UP, 1980.

———. *The Fate of Reading and Other Essays.* Chicago: U of Chicago P, 1975.

———. *Saving the Text: Literature/Derrida/Philosophy.* Baltimore, Md.: Johns Hopkins UP, 1981.

Hirsch, E. D. *The Aims of Interpretation.* Chicago: U of Chicago P, 1976.

———. *Validity in Interpretation.* New Haven: Yale UP, 1974.

Johnson, Barbara. *The Critical Difference: Essays in the Contemporary Rhetoric of Reading.* Baltimore, Md.: Johns Hopkins UP, 1980.

Kristeva, Julia. *Desire in Language: A Semiotic Approach to Literature and Art.* Ed. Leon S. Roudiez. Trans. Thomas Gora, Alice Jardine, and Leon S. Roudiez. New York: Columbia UP, 1980.

Lévi-Strauss, Claude. *Tristes Tropiques.* Trans. John and Doreen Weightman. New York: Atheneum, 1974.

Megill, Allan. *Prophets of Extremity: Nietzsche, Heidegger, Foucault, Derrida.* Berkeley and Los Angeles: U of California P, 1985.

Miller, J. Hillis. *The Linguistic Moment: From Wordsworth to Stevens.* Princeton, N.J.: Princeton UP, 1985.

———. "Narrative and History." *ELH* 41 (1974): 455-473.

———. "Stevens' Rock and Criticism as Cure, II." *Georgia Review* 30 (1976): 330-348.

———. *Theory Now and Then.* Durham, N.C.: Duke UP, 1991.

Nietzsche, Friedrich. "On Truth and Lies in a Nonmoral Sense." In *Philosophy and Truth: Selections from Nietzsche's Notebooks of the Early 1870's.* Trans. and ed. Daniel Breazeale. 79-97. Atlantic Highlands, N.J.: Humanities, 1979.

Norris, Christopher. *Deconstruction and the Interests of Theory.* London: Pinter, 1988.
———. *Derrida.* Cambridge, Mass.: Harvard UP, 1987.
———. *Paul de Man: Deconstruction and the Critique of Aesthetic Ideology.* New York: Methuen, 1988.
O'Hara, Daniel. Review of *Of Grammatology. Journal of Aesthetics and Art Criticism* 36 (1978): 361-365.
Riddel, Joseph N. *The Inverted Bell: Modern and the Counterpoetics of William Carlos Williams.* Baton Rouge: Louisiana State UP, 1974.
Rorty, Richard. *Consequences of Pragmatism.* Minneapolis: U of Minnesota P, 1982.
Ryan, Michael. *Marxism and Deconstruction: A Critical Articulation.* Baltimore, Md.: Johns Hopkins UP, 1982.
Saussure, Ferdinand de. *Course in General Linguistics.* New York: McGraw-Hill, 1966.
———. *Course in General Linguistics.* Ed. Charles Bally and Albert Reidlinger. Trans. Wade Baskin. New York: Philosophical Library, 1959.
Schwartz, Sanford. *The Matrix of Modernism: Pound, Eliot, and Twentieth-Century Thought.* Princeton, N.J.: Princeton UP, 1985.
Spivak, Gayatri Chakravorty. Translator's preface to *Of Grammatology,* by Jacques Derrida, ix-lxxxvii. Baltimore, Md.: Johns Hopkins UP, 1976.
Todorov, Tzvetan. *The Fantastic: A Structural Approach to a Literary Genre.* Trans. Richard Howard. Ithaca, N.Y.: Cornell UP, 1975.
———. *The Poetics of Prose.* Trans. Richard Howard. Ithaca, N.Y.: Cornell UP, 1977.
Ulmer, Gregory L. *Applied Grammatology: Post(e)-Pedagogy from Jacques Derrida to Joseph Beuys.* Baltimore, Md.: Johns Hopkins UP, 1985.
Young, Robert, ed. *Untying the Text: A Post-Structuralist Reader.* London: Routledge and Kegan Paul, 1981.

chapter 5

Marxist Literary Criticism

Marxist literary criticism takes its principal inspiration from the work of the German philosopher and economist Karl Marx (1818-1883). As opposed to the tradition of philosophical idealism that had dominated Western thought from Plato to G. W. F. Hegel, Marx's thought is thoroughly materialistic. That is, rather than base his philosophical system on abstract, ideal concepts (such as truth or beauty), Marx bases his system on physical reality. Stated otherwise, Marx believes—in contrast to René Descartes's idealist dictum "I think, therefore I am"—that material conditions in the world are prior to and play a determining role in human thought about the world. As Marx puts this view in a famous passage in *The German Ideology,* "Life is not determined by consciousness, but consciousness by life" (155).[1] This fundamental orientation leads Marx to a number of important conclusions about the nature of human society. For one thing, Marx's materialist stance implies that a change in material conditions can lead to changes in the way humans think and therefore to important and sweeping social and political change. For another, Marx's emphasis on material conditions leads him to the conclusion that the economic system is the most fundamental aspect, or "base," of any society, while all other aspects of society (culture, politics, religion, and so on) are parts of a "superstructure" whose characteristics are at least to some extent dependent on the nature of the base.

Marx begins his elaboration of a materialist philosophy with the very basic assumption of the existence of living human individuals who must acquire certain necessities to live: "Life involves before all else eating and drinking, a habitation, clothing, and many other things. The first historical act is thus the production of the means to satisfy these needs" (156). Human society then develops as

[1] All quotations from Marx are taken from the Tucker anthology.

individual human beings band together to obtain the basic necessities of life more efficiently. Such organization, however, has historically led to a "division of labor" in which different individuals are assigned different kinds of tasks. This division of labor leads to the development of class society, in which the population of a society is divided into separate classes whose needs and desires may be fundamentally at odds. For Marx, nineteenth-century capitalism is the ultimate result of this process, with most of the material wealth of Western society lying in the hands of a small, elite class of bourgeois owners who gain this wealth through exploitation of the labor of the working-class masses, or the proletariat. Marx acknowledges that capitalism (relative to feudalism, its immediate predecessor) represents a revolutionary increase in economic efficiency that has allowed the bourgeoisie to accomplish unprecedented feats of productivity. But he also points out the fundamental unfairness of the capitalist system: Its productivity benefits the bourgeoisie at the expense of the workers. Because of this fundamental unfairness and because of certain aspects of the capitalist economic system itself, Marx argues that capitalism contains the seeds of its own destruction and that it will eventually collapse as part of the natural historical process. This process is for Marx a *dialectical* one in that he envisions history as proceeding through a series of conflicts between opposing ideas, the resolution of which leads to the development of a new historical stage. Indeed, dialectical thought is so central to Marx's work that his overall approach is often referred to as *dialectical materialism.* The dialectical oppositions that drive history forward are particularly associated with the conflicting needs of different social classes. As one famous passage puts it, "The history of all hitherto existing society is the history of class struggles" (473).

Marx envisions the end of capitalism in a coming proletarian revolution that will lead to the establishment of a socialist society that (by dispensing with class distinctions) will do away once and for all with the inequities that have characterized human societies throughout history. As a result, the new classless society will lack the class conflict of previous ones, resulting in the end of the dialectical movement of history and the permanent establishment of socialism. Marx's vision of a coming proletarian revolution is spelled out most succinctly in the *Manifesto of the Communist Party,* coauthored with Friedrich Engels and published in the heady days of 1848, when insurrections against the ruling regimes were threatening to sweep across Europe. Most of these revolts later were crushed, but many of the specific recommendations for the transformation of society put forth by Marx and Engels would be implemented in the late nineteenth century as capitalism sought to modify itself to avoid the collapse predicted by Marx and seemingly signaled by a serious worldwide economic depression in the last decades of that century.

Marx's work, while focusing on history, philosophy, and economics, has proved of special interest to critics of literature and culture. Indeed as Perry Anderson details, twentieth-century "Western" Marxists (those working outside the Soviet Union and its sphere of political influence) have tended to place great emphasis on the aesthetic as a realm of both capitalist oppression and potential resistance. This emphasis occurs for a number of reasons. For one thing, Marx and Engels often refer to art and literature in their discussions of capitalist society (because culture plays a crucial role in their description of capitalism). Thus Terry Eagleton notes "Marx's impressively erudite allusions to world literature" (*Ideology* 1). For another, Marx's model of human society suggests that culture reflects economic, political, and social conditions in society as a whole. A careful study of culture thus potentially yields important information about these other areas as well.

Certain key Marxist concepts have proved particularly useful to critics of literature and culture. For example, in describing the phenomenon of "alienation," Marx notes that the division of labor in society leads to a separation between individuals, who become distanced from each other by virtue of the differences in their everyday activities. Individuals become estranged from society as a whole because they participate only in a small portion of it as a result of their specialized work activities. In the factory system of nineteenth-century capitalism, this alienation becomes particularly radical as work becomes more and more specialized and fragmented. During the feudal period, a shoemaker would typically own his own shop. He would acquire raw materials, manufacture complete products (shoes) through application of his craft, and then market those products to consumers, who had probably ordered the shoes custom-made. The shoemaker would therefore be intimately involved in every step of the shoemaking process, even though the division of labor would dictate that he would not participate in the work of other professions. In a nineteenth-century factory, however, a worker would be involved only in a small part of the manufacturing process. She would never see the finished product and have no contact with potential consumers. She would thus become distanced from the products of her own labor, becoming alienated not only from others but also even from herself.

Closely aligned with the process of alienation is the phenomenon of "commodification." For Marx, a "commodity" is an article that is produced not for use but for exchange within the market system of capitalism. Because commodities are intended for sale rather than use, they are valued not for their function but for the price they can bring on the open market. In other words, they are judged not according to their "use value" but according to their "exchange value." Commodities, though they may be physical articles such as shoes, hats, or candlesticks, have a decidedly abstract quality: They are valued not for their own genuine characteristics but for their ability to participate in a money economy the workings of which are inscrutable to most individuals. The commodity thus represents the embodiment of powerful and mysterious hidden forces, which in some cases endows the commodity with an almost mystical quality and leads individuals to become enthralled with the commodity, thus making the commodity a fetish, or the object of an intense emotional attachment. The gradual shift to a commodity economy under capitalism thus contributes to the progressive estrangement from material reality that for Marx is a central effect of capitalism. Furthermore the nature of a capitalist economy, which treats the labor of individuals as a source of commodities, eventually leads to the treatment of human beings as abstract economic quantities, again valued not for their own individual characteristics but for their economic function. In short, it leads to the commodification of human beings, a phenomenon closely associated with their alienation and most directly represented in the treatment of factory workers as mere pieces of manufacturing machinery.

The rich tradition of twentieth-century Marxist cultural critique has given rise to a number of important insights into literature and its relation to society as a whole. To a first approximation, twentieth-century Marxist critics can be divided into two basic groups. The first, for which the Hungarian Marxist theorist Georg Lukács can be taken as a founding figure, emphasizes the primacy of the economic base and grows directly out of Marx's discussion of alienation and commodification, exploring the implications of that discussion for modern society and culture. The second, for which the Italian Marxist thinker Antonio Gramsci can be taken as a founding figure, focuses on the superstructure and on the social institutions and practices through which bourgeois ideology establishes its dominance to provide support to the economic base.

Lukács, especially in his important work *History and Class Consciousness* (first published in 1923), pays a great deal of attention to the phenomenon that he calls "reification," or the conversion of all aspects of human life (including abstract concepts, social relations, and even humans themselves) into "things." Reification is clearly related to commodification. But whereas the notion of commodification emphasizes the participation of commodities in a single overarching economic system, Lukács's discussion of reification focuses on the flip side of this process, in which the separation into discrete things implies that human life is radically fragmented, individuals losing all sense that the different aspects of life fit into a coherent whole. Moreover reification is also closely related to process of alienation, especially to the effacement in capitalist society of all traces of the actual production of commodities, leading to a further separation between production and consumption of goods. This aspect of reification has become particularly important to Marxist critics in recent years, when consumers in "first world" countries such as the United States so often buy and use goods that were manufactured in the distant "third world." Reification thus becomes a sort of repression through which citizens of rich countries can enjoy their luxury products without thinking about the lives of the workers who produced those products under the most oppressive of conditions.

Meanwhile Lukács further argues that individual perception in a capitalist society is limited by class consciousness, which enables members of a certain class to understand the world only in ways allowed by their class position. For example, he argues that the bourgeois are by definition incapable of seeing through the process of reification; concerned only with the manipulation of commodities, the bourgeois owner acts essentially as a consumer of commodities with no real access to or understanding of the details of their production. Proletarians, by contrast, are intimately involved in production. As a result, despite their alienated condition, they can potentially develop a revolutionary class consciousness that will allow them to see through the mystifications of the commodity and gain access to the idea of society as a totality.

For Lukács, literature can play an important role in the development of this new proletarian consciousness of totality. In this view, the greatest artists are those who can effectively represent the totality of human life. The most effective mode for this representation is literary realism, which for Lukács reflects reality much in the mode that the Marxist superstructure reflects the base. Indeed in works such as *The Historical Novel,* Lukács sees realism as the only literary mode capable of representing the totality of society by revealing through its narrative form the underlying movement of history. Characterization is important to this project as well. The best literature involves characters that have a realistic individuality while at the same time incarnating larger historical forces; these characters thus become typical of their historical epoch. Lukács believes that the greatest realist literature, by embodying the forces in an epoch that enable historical change, is always progressive, regardless of the political leanings of the authors themselves.

Lukács's privileging of early-nineteenth-century realism, a fundamentally bourgeois mode of literature, has to do with his appreciation of the European bourgeoisie as a successful revolutionary class that had recently supplanted the aristocracy as the ruling class in Europe. For Lukács, the great bourgeois historical novels cohere because they narrate the grand historical process (sometimes referred to as the bourgeois cultural revolution) through which the bourgeoisie gained this power. Such novels thus become the official literature of the only genuine successful class revolution in history. This literature is thus valuable for study by socialist artists and critics interested in contributing to a similar revolution in which bourgeois rule would be supplanted by socialism and then communism.

Lukács sees nineteenth-century capitalism resulting in a growing fragmentation in life; he also believes that literature and culture undergo a corresponding tendency toward fragmentation and loss of totality. As the nineteenth century proceeds, the bourgeoisie, now firmly in power, becomes a reactionary, rather than a revolutionary, class, and its literature consequently begins to decline in quality. For example, Lukács characterizes the transition from realism to naturalism in European literature (epitomized by the movement from Honoré de Balzac to Émile Zola in France) as a process of decay, naturalism being a distortion and deterioration of realism into abstraction. But Lukács's harshest criticism is reserved for modernist literature. In essence, he believes that the formal fragmentation of modernist texts participates in the process of reification that is itself central to the fragmentation of social life under capitalism. Lukács sees in the dazzling verbal constructions of modernist writers a reflection of this process. He argues that modernist writers such as James Joyce and Franz Kafka make technique an end in itself, without regard for the human realities that this technique is supposed to convey. This "negation of outward reality" is a central project of modernist writing, which represents a turning away from the world and a retreat into an aesthetic realm divorced from social reality. And this disengagement is in direct complicity with the main cultural thrust of bourgeois society, which seeks to isolate art in a separate realm and thus deprive it of any potentially subversive political force. Modernist texts are thus for Lukács not progressive documents interacting with history in a positive and productive way. Instead they are sterile artifacts divorced from history and totally caught up in the inexorable drive of capitalist society to convert all it touches into mere commodities.

In his important essay "The Ideology of Modernism," Lukács grants that modernist texts can contain a great deal of realistic detail, but he argues that these details are intended not as representations of typical elements of reality but as mere allegorical stand-ins for abstract ideas: "Modernist literature thus replaces concrete typicality with abstract particularity" (*Realism* 43). The consistently allegorical quality of modernist literature implies that, despite the importation of abundant and vivid details from contemporary life into modernist texts, those texts are not "about" contemporary reality at all but about some generalized abstract city with no genuine relevance to the concrete specifics of human life on the streets of any real city: "Joyce uses Dublin, Kafka and Musil the Hapsburg Monarchy, as the locus of their masterpieces. But the locus they lovingly depict is little more than a backcloth; it is not basic to their artistic intention" (21). In a similar vein, Lukács criticizes the failure of modernist art to address the "typicalities" of the human condition. He suggests that modernism is informed by an "obsession with the pathological," which he compares to a similar fascination in Freudian psychoanalysis (30). Lukács offers Robert Musil's Moosbrugger—"a mentally-retarded sexual pervert with homicidal tendencies"—as his principal example of this obsession, but he hints that Joyce's focus on the streams of consciousness of his individual characters bespeaks a similar fascination with the aberrant (*Realism* 31).

A concern with issues of wholeness and fragmentation, along with a focus on the material aspects of cultural media, identifies an important area of contact between the work of the German Marxist theorist and cultural critic Walter Benjamin and that of Lukács. In the important essay "The Storyteller," Benjamin argues in a mode reminiscent of Lukács's narrative of gradual historical fragmentation that in the modern world the ability to tell meaningful stories is rapidly becoming a lost art. Storytelling for Benjamin is first and foremost a means of conveying advice for dealing with "real" life, but he suggests, writing in the tumultuous days of post–World War I Germany, that the modern world no longer makes sense. "Reality" itself is thus increasingly problematic, and there is no longer any meaningful advice to give. "The art of storytelling," he writes, "is reaching its end because the epic side of truth, wisdom, is dying out" (*Illuminations* 87). Benjamin suggests that events in the modern world (particularly World War I) have led to a general devaluation of human experience: "For never has experience been contradicted more thoroughly than strategic experience by tactical warfare, economic experience by inflation, bodily experience by mechanical warfare, moral experience by those in power" (84). And if experience is no longer meaningful, then it follows that the exchange of experiences in meaningful ways (the fundamental requirement of effective storytelling) is no longer possible.

This loss of the ability to convey experience is clearly related to the concepts of alienation and reification. Moreover Benjamin (like Marx and Lukács) sees the devaluation of experience in the modern world as the consequence of a long historical process. His discussions of this devaluation provide a poignant evocation of the modern condition, but he emphasizes that such devaluation is no sudden development of the twentieth century, arguing that "nothing would be more fatuous than to want to see in it merely a 'symptom of decay,' let alone a 'modern' symptom" (87). Always concerned with the relationship between works of art and the physical technology available to produce and distribute those works, Benjamin suggests that the demise of storytelling begins with the invention of the printing press and occurs as part of the shift from oral to print culture (and from stories to novels) that has characterized Western society for the past four centuries: "The earliest symptom of a process whose end is the decline of storytelling is the rise of the novel at the beginning of modern times. What distinguishes the novel from the story (and from the epic in the narrower sense) is its essential dependence on the book. The dissemination of the novel became possible only with the invention of printing" (87).

Benjamin particularly emphasizes the contribution that the rise of the novel makes to the decline in the ability of individuals to relate to others, much in the way that the early Lukács (in *The Theory of the Novel*) sees the novel as the genre of a modern world that has lost the sense of wholeness characteristic of the earlier world of the epic. In contrast to the communal activity of telling (and listening to) stories, both the reading and the writing of novels are for Benjamin solitary activities: "The storyteller takes what he tells from experience—his own or that reported by others. And he in turn makes it the experience of those who are listening to his tale. The novelist has isolated himself. The birthplace of the novel is the solitary individual" (87).

Benjamin's suggestion that print technology has impeded, rather than enhanced, human communication echoes the concern of early commentators such as Jonathan Swift and Alexander Pope, who felt that the new print technology would result in a degraded and impersonal form of communication that would disrupt the role of humanity as a special creation of God, given language is imitation of the Divine Word. However despite a pervading nostalgic tone, Benjamin differs markedly from conservatives like Swift in that he does not necessarily see the breakdown of traditional forms of communication as an entirely negative development. For Benjamin, though modern technology has destroyed the traditional quasi-religious wholeness, or "aura," of the work of art [a development he discusses in detail in "The Work of Art in the Age of Mechanical Reproduction," (Illuminations)], this destruction leads to a changed mode of aesthetic reception that produces a new kind of emancipated reader, free of the quasi-religious enthrallment associated with art in earlier eras and thus able to resist the authority of received ideas and read in challenging and critical ways.

Benjamin thus differs substantially from Lukács in this belief that formal fragmentation in art can potentially have progressive consequences. He resembles Lukács in his critique of the deterioration of the knowledge conveyed by traditional narrative into the ephemeral and fragmented kind of information conveyed by the modern newspaper. Moreover in making this distinction between genuine knowledge and mere information, Benjamin anticipates the critique of Enlightenment science carried out by the "Frankfurt School" theorists Max Horkheimer and Theodor W. Adorno in *The Dialectic of Enlightenment.* Noting the Enlightenment "motto" that "knowledge is power," Horkheimer and Adorno suggest that the scientific impetus of the Enlightenment is informed by a quest not for a liberating truth but for a power that ultimately enslaves. They suggest that the emphasis on the power of the individual in Enlightenment thought is related to a drive to dominate nature, a drive that inevitably turns back on itself and leads to the formation of individuals who are internally repressed and of societies that consist of individual subjects who strive for domination of each other. Horkheimer and Adorno do not oppose science itself but merely the mechanical application of science. Enlightenment science, they argue, seeks not knowledge but information, not understanding but practical application. Such science thus does not yield genuine enlightenment but simply a new myth of the power of technology: "With the abandonment of thought, which in its reified form of mathematics, machine, and organization avenges itself on the men who have forgotten it, enlightenment has relinquished its own realization" (41).

This emphasis on reification again identifies a Lukácsian strain in the work of Horkheimer and Adorno, though the powerful influence of Friedrich Nietzsche on their work leads to a number of differences from Lukács. Adorno, though far more pessimistic than Marx about the possibilities of a coming socialist utopia, finds in modernist art a potentially powerful and progressive counter to the oppressive overemphasis on reason and rationality that he sees as central to the Enlightenment. As Albrecht Wellmer notes, this suspicion of Enlightenment rationality also causes Adorno to look away from rational argument in search of a locus of genuine reason, finding a potential for such a locus in art: "Through the configuration of its elements the work of art *reveals* the irrational and false character of existing reality and, at the same time, by way of its aesthetic synthesis, it *prefigures* an order of reconciliation" (48).

Despite Adorno's notorious pessimism, his turn to art as an alternative to Enlightenment science and rationality suggests that he still harbors certain utopian urges, even if he believes that utopian goals will not naturally evolve from the progress of history but only through some radical rupture in the existing order. Indeed critic Terry Eagleton charges that Adorno places too much emphasis on modernist art, concluding that for Adorno such art is a "sphere largely disconnected from the major social forces of a given power-structure." Eagleton therefore concludes that Adorno displays a "bad" escapist utopianism (*Ideology* 407).

The recent work of Jürgen Habermas, the Frankfurt School successor of Horkheimer and Adorno, is even more directly related to that of Lukács, particularly in his emphasis on the fragmentation in social life as a major negative consequence of capitalism. For Habermas (following the work of Max Weber), modern thought has become separated into the distinct and noncommunicating spheres of science, morality, and art. What is needed for social progress, he argues, is the development of effective forms of communication among these realms that can reunite them as part of the reestablishment of a social totality. Moreover Habermas differs from Horkheimer and Adorno in his continuing faith that rationality can play a central and positive role in this project. In particular, Habermas sees a positive value in the Enlightenment that should not be lightly tossed aside. He thus criticizes the antirationalism of post-Nietzschean thinkers such as Michel Foucault and Jacques Derrida as "neoconservative" and as leading back to modernism rather than forward to a new historical era. Habermas consistently argues that any solution to our modern social and cultural problems will require rational communication among different groups and that we should learn from the mistakes of the Enlightenment rather than simply rejecting its values out of hand. For example, Habermas agrees with Foucault that knowledge is always to a certain extent informed by human interests, but he believes that emancipation from power can be one of the most important of these interests (*Knowledge* 287).

Like Benjamin and Adorno, Habermas is particularly concerned with the phenomenon of "modernity," or the complex of cultural and philosophical changes that seem to make the twentieth century distinctively different from earlier periods in history. Habermas has suggested that the idea of being "modern" as we know it—especially as reflected in modern art—began with the rise of a new science in the seventeenth century. In particular, modernity for Habermas begins when this science opens exciting new possibilities and inspires a belief in "the infinite progress of knowledge and in the infinite advance towards social and moral betterment" (4). For Habermas, the modern age thus begins in the seventeenth century, but this expectation of rapid and continual change becomes particularly central to twentieth-century culture. Paradoxically, however, this narrative of unlimited progress contributes to Habermas's belief in the loss of any genuine sense of history in the mind-set of aesthetic modernity. He grants that avant-garde artistic movements such as surrealism sought to destroy the autonomous institution of art and thereby give it a new political power and a new relevance to the everyday praxis of life. But he concludes that such attempts were "nonsense projects" that actually "served to bring back to life, and to illuminate all the more glaringly, exactly those structures of art which they were meant to dissolve" (10). In short, Habermas believes that avant-garde art merely increases the separation of modern culture into separate spheres, thereby contributing to a general cultural impoverishment.

Habermas argues that a denial of history is central to modernity itself. He further suggests that the emphasis on innovation in modern art is informed by an "exaltation of the present" in which "the new value placed on the transitory, the elusive, and the ephemeral, the very celebration of dynamism, discloses the longing for an undefiled, an immaculate and stable present" (5). The modern urge for continual, even radical change may in fact reveal a quest for stability and stasis. And this phenomenon would be entirely consistent with Marx's analyses of capitalism, which he sees as striving for continual, seemingly radical innovation and change as a means of solidifying the fundamental status quo. For Habermas, then, the fragmentation of modern life has a particular temporal element, the modern emphasis on the present leading to a separation of time into a series of discrete moments with no sense of historical connection.

This notion of temporal fragmentation in Habermas's work resembles that associated by Fredric Jameson with "late capitalism," or the current stage of multinational capitalism (as first delineated by the Frankfurt School). For Jameson, however, the loss of historical sense detailed by Habermas occurs not during modernism but during postmodernism. According to Jameson, postmodern reality is radically fragmented, discontinuous, and multiple; the plurality of overlapping realities that we face in postmodern society is aptly figured in the phenomenon of cable television channel switching. Moreover the fragmentation of reality in postmodern society is for Jameson a direct consequence of the alienating effects of capitalism. Indeed he views postmodernism as an "apotheosis of capitalism" ("Postmodernism" 77), as being fully in complicity with late capitalism and as thereby lacking any real critical force. He does, however, see more critical potential in modernism's reaction against commodification and consumer capitalism. Jameson indicates a strong link between the technical brilliance of modernist art and its supposed emphasis on individual psychology with his suggestion that the distinctive personal "styles" of the various modernist artists themselves function as evidence that within the modernist cultural milieu the concept of a distinctive self still had meaning.

Jameson's attention to fragmentation often integrates a consideration of art and literature with traditionally mainstream Marxist social critique. For example, in *The Political Unconscious* he relates the bourgeois attitude toward art as separate from social reality directly to the ideology of bourgeois individualism. This ideology leads to the perception that private life is sharply distinguished from the public world of politics in a way that parallels the bourgeois tendency to treat art as a self-enclosed realm separate from the social and political world. But this perception of art does not elevate it as somehow superior to everyday reality; instead it merely renders art irrelevant, diminishing its function in life. Similarly Jameson insists that the ostensible privileging of the private over the public that is central to bourgeois individualism actually impoverishes private life by obscuring the domination of the individual by capitalism and creating a false illusion of individual autonomy. Far from creating the strong, independent individuals mythologized by bourgeois ideology, capitalism "maims our existence as individual subjects and paralyzes our thinking" (20).

To oppose this tendency, Jameson elaborates an interpretive practice (based to some extent on Sigmund Freud's methods for reading the contents of the unconscious mind) that allows critics to detect the presence of a "political unconscious," or underlying ideological content, in literary texts. At the same time, Jameson insists on the need for critical self-consciousness and for critics (in the process he calls "metacommentary") to meditate on the ideological conditioning of their own work. Jameson thus proposes a model for a Marxist critical practice, which (along with his own large and impressive body of criticism) has been of special importance to the reemergence of Marxist critique in the United States after several decades of silence imposed on it by the political climate of the cold war. Jameson's 1971 book *Marxism and Form* can in many ways be taken as the founding text of contemporary American Marxist criticism. In this work, a critical introduction to the thought of a number of important Marxist thinkers (including Adorno, Benjamin, and Lukács), Jameson introduces a number of the key concepts that have since remained central to his career, including a Lukácsian concern with cultural and psychic fragmentation in the modern world, an emphasis on the importance of historical vision in cultural criticism, a firm belief that literature and culture cannot be separated from their social and political context, careful attention to both form and content in elaborating the political significance of cultural artifacts, and a strong commitment to the necessity for a utopian element (in the Marxist, scientific sense rather than in the idealistic sense) in critical thought. Jameson's work is marked by a sophisticated use of concepts from poststructuralist, psychoanalytic, and other forms of critical thought, but it remains firmly rooted in the Marxist tradition. It also provides an important methodological model in its insistence on the importance of a metacritical approach—that is, on criticism that not only discusses its object but also performs self-conscious critical examinations of the grounds of its own inquiry. Jameson's work has been tremendously influential for American Marxist critics and for other American critics interested in exploring the social and political dimensions of literature and culture.

Jameson's most important debt to Lukács may reside in the central emphasis of both critics on history as the basic fabric of human existence. In particular, Jameson follows Lukács in placing great emphasis on the way literature reflects the Marxist notion of history as class conflict. Thus in a recent essay, Jameson declares that history in the modern sense is an invention of the European bourgeoisie designed to tell the story of the cultural revolution through which it rose to hegemony in Europe. The story of "the transition from feudalism to capitalism," suggests Jameson, "is what is secretly (or more deeply) being told in most contemporary historiography, whatever its ostensible content." Furthermore, Jameson argues, this view of history makes the bourgeois cultural revolution "the only true Event of history" (*Signatures* 226–227).

Jameson's work, while owing a special debt to Lukács, also incorporates elements of the modern Marxist tradition of ideological critique that can be traced back to Gramsci's work, which is principally represented in a series of notebooks he wrote while in an Italian fascist prison (for his left-wing political activities) from 1927 until his death in 1937. Gramsci focuses on the way the European bourgeoisie gained and maintained its power through a complex of political and cultural practices that convinced the more numerous lower classes to accede willingly to bourgeois authority. Thus bourgeois power resides principally in what Gramsci calls "hegemony," in the ability of the bourgeoisie to obtain the "'spontaneous' consent given by the great masses of the population to the general direction imposed on social life by the dominant fundamental group; this consent is 'historically' caused by the prestige (and consequent confidence) which the dominant group enjoys because of its position and function in the world of production" (12). If absolutely necessary, this consensual obedience can be supplemented by "the apparatus of state coercive power," that is, by institutions, such as the police and the army, that use physical force to impose "discipline on those groups who do not 'consent' either actively or passively. This apparatus is, however, constituted for the whole of society in anticipation of moments of crisis of command and direction when spontaneous consent has failed" (12).

Because Gramsci's ideas are elaborated principally in notebooks, his work is necessarily somewhat fragmentary, but his focus on politics and culture (rather than economics) has proved extremely influential for a number of subsequent Marxist critics. The most important of these Gramscian Marxist critics is probably Louis Althusser, whose extensive body of work is particularly distinguished by his attempt to integrate Marxist thought with the structuralist methods of analysis that were dominant in France during the 1950s and 1960s. This project centrally involves art and culture, and Althusser is especially concerned with delineating the complex relationship between art and ideology. From this point of view, Althusser's most important concept is probably the notion of "interpellation," or the "hailing of the subject"—the process through which individuals are formed as subjects by powerful forces working in the interest of the prevailing ideology of a given society. For Althusser, we do not form our attitudes so much as they form us, and "the category of the subject is only constitutive of all ideology insofar as all ideology has the function (which defines it) of 'constituting' concrete individuals as subjects" (*Lenin* 171).

Echoing Gramsci, Althusser emphasizes that the process of interpellation allows the existing power structure of capitalist society to maintain its domination over the general population without resorting to violence or force. Interpellation occurs in subtle ways through the workings of what Althusser calls "Ideological State Apparatuses," including official culture and such specific institutions as churches and schools, though it is constantly backed up by the physical force represented by the "Repressive State Apparatus" of the police and the military. Althusser's focus on ideology as a shaping factor in the development of individual identity participates in a long Marxist tradition of the critique of ideology as false consciousness. At the same time, Althusser identifies ideology not simply as an illusion that hides the truth of social practices but as the material context within which those practices are necessarily carried out. Althusser's goal, then, is not to avoid or overcome ideology (which would be impossible) but to understand and delineate its workings so that individual subjects can interact with ideology in more critical and productive ways.

Nevertheless Althusser's discussion of interpellation has much in common with the frequent arguments of Marxist critics that ideological manipulation of individual psyches lies at the heart of the bourgeois conception of the free autonomous individual, a conception that turns out to be nothing more than a ruse to hide the fact that individuals are largely determined not by their own choices but by the needs of the economic and political systems in which they live. Indeed Althusser directly contrasts ideology (as knowledge thoroughly conditioned by politics) with science (as direct objective knowledge). This opposition leads to a special emphasis on culture and literature, which for Althusser is situated somewhere between the poles of science and ideology. Moreover in Althusser's view art plays a privileged role in ideological critique because the workings of ideology can be detected in art in ways that they cannot in society at large.

Althusser's distinctively structuralist style of Marxist thought and his central emphasis on the relationship between ideology and culture have made his work important for a number of subsequent cultural critics, especially those with a particular interest in the political dimensions of art. Althusser's most important protégé is Pierre Macherey, whose focus on the production of literary texts within the cultural context of official ideologies suggests important ways that literature might oppose the process of interpellation by revealing the ideological illusions on which official society is based. For example, Macherey notes that literary language is influenced by the other discourses (scientific, theoretical, everyday speech) that surround it in the historical moment. For him, much of the ideological power of literature comes from the way its language is able to mimic and parody these other discourses: "Mingling the real uses of language in an endless confrontation, it concludes by *revealing* their truth. Experimenting with language rather than inventing it, the literary work is both the analogy of a knowledge and a caricature of customary ideology" (59). Literary discourse is not about "reality," then, so much as it is about language itself; it is "a contestation of language rather than a representation of reality" (61). In short, literary language makes visible ideological orientations within language that might remain hidden in the discourse of the everyday world. However in his later work (perhaps influenced by the turn from structuralism to poststructuralism as a dominant mode in French intellectual life), Macherey departs somewhat from Althusser's identification of art as a special practice situated somewhere between science and ideology. Macherey begins to emphasize the participation of literature in its social context in ways that make it impossible to identify literature as a discourse distinct from others.

The Gramscian vein of Marxist ideological critique has also been central to the tradition of British cultural materialism. A key founding figure in this tradition is Raymond Williams, whose work grows directly out of the strong British tradition of socialist and working-class culture. Especially later in his career, Williams also draws extensively on the continental Marxist tradition of thinkers such as Althusser. Emphasizing the important role played by literature and culture in the development of society as a whole, Williams employs analysis of cultural artifacts as part of a project to develop a general vision of British socialism. In *The Country and the City*, he presents nothing less than a Marxist revision of the entire history of British literature from the Renaissance forward. But

Williams's work, perhaps influenced by his own working-class background, is marked by a distinctive emphasis on the creative potential of ordinary people. He pays serious attention not only to traditional "high" culture but also to popular culture, and his work on such popular media as television has been extremely influential for cultural critics in recent years. Williams's view of culture as the embodiment of the mutually lived experience of ordinary people and therefore as a source of organic unity has struck many contemporary Marxist critics as somewhat nostalgic and idealized. Nevertheless his insistence on attention to the needs and experiences of common people as a necessary element of cultural criticism has provided a positive example for many subsequent critics.

Terry Eagleton is probably the leading contemporary practitioner of British cultural materialism, though Eagleton's particular form of Marxism is distinguished by a broad perspective that includes strong influences not only from Williams and Althusser but also from other important Marxist thinkers, including Benjamin. For example, Eagleton sometimes resembles Jameson in his belief that both modernism and postmodernism are symptoms of the commodification of culture in capitalist society, except that Eagleton is suspicious of *both* modernism and postmodernism as consequences of commodification. For Eagleton, modernist art resists commodification as exchange only to fall prey to commodification as fetish, whereas postmodernist art has been completely absorbed in the phenomenon of commodification as exchange.

The breadth of Eagleton's work, which combines theoretical sophistication with a traditional Marxist class consciousness, can also be seen in the variety of his major works, which move from introductory texts on literary theory, to complex discussions of Marxist theory, to detailed criticism of specific literary texts. *Marxism and Literary Criticism,* for example, is an excellent basic introduction to the subject; *Literary Theory* provides a critical survey from a Marxist perspective of some of the more important bourgeois approaches to literary theory. *The Rape of Clarissa* draws on Marxist and feminist perspectives in an extended critical treatment of the fiction of Samuel Richardson; *Exiles and Emigrés* investigates the prominence of twentieth-century emigré writers by reading a number of their works. *Criticism and Ideology* combines critical discussion of specific texts with metacritical meditations on the social and political responsibilities of the literary critic; *Walter Benjamin* mixes a complex critical treatment of the work of Benjamin with an attempt to delineate a general project for revolutionary criticism.

Eagleton's recent *The Ideology of the Aesthetic* is indicative of the range of his thought. A sweeping history of Western aesthetic philosophy from David Hume to Michel Foucault, this work emphasizes the central role played by such philosophy in the evolution of bourgeois society. Eagleton reminds us that the very notion of the aesthetic as we know it arose in conjunction with the rise of the bourgeoisie. For Eagleton, many of our conceptions of the nature of the work of art (especially those having to do with organic unity) emerge in close complicity with the rise of the autonomous bourgeois individual as the principal paradigm of human subjectivity. Eagleton suggests that the work of art functions as an object of imaginary identification through which the bourgeois subject develops a fantasy of its own wholeness and autonomy in a process much like the Lacanian mirror stage (*Ideology* 87). However this process is not an entirely simple one. In a discussion of Immanuel Kant, for example, Eagleton notes the double movement of the key aesthetic concepts of the "beautiful" and the "sublime" in Kantian aesthetics. The beautiful, Eagleton suggests, supports this imaginary identification, shoring up the subject and giving it the confidence it needs to compete in a free market, whereas the sublime performs a humbling function, reminding the subject that, free or not, there are limits that are not to be crossed. This double movement is for Eagleton essential to the ideology of bourgeois society: "For one problem of all humanist ideology is how its centring and consoling of the subject is to be made compatible with a certain essential reverence and submissiveness on the subject's part" (90).

Indeed much of the point of Eagleton's survey is to suggest that, despite the fact that the aesthetic is a thoroughly bourgeois concept whose very purpose is the perpetuation of bourgeois ideology, there is something inherently uncontrollable in the aesthetic that still gives it a considerable subversive potential: "The aesthetic as custom, sentiment, spontaneous impulse may consort well enough with political domination; but these phenomena border embarrassingly on passion, imagination, sensuality, which are not always so easily incorporable" (28). This emphasis on the potential subversive power of art provides an important reminder of the central role that art has played in the thought of so many modern Marxist thinkers, just as Eagleton's extensive body of work provides an important contemporary model for politically committed critics and theorists.

BIBLIOGRAPHY

Introductory Works

Ahearn, Edward J. *Marx and Modern Fiction.* New Haven, Conn.: Yale UP, 1989.

A good example of the application of Marxist theory to the reading of some specific modern texts.

Eagleton, Terry. *Marxism and Literary Criticism.* Berkeley and Los Angeles: U of California P, 1976.

An excellent brief overview of the relevance of Marxist theory to literary criticism.

Gottlieb, Roger S., ed. *An Anthology of Western Marxism: From Lukács and Gramsci to Socialist-Feminism.* New York: Oxford UP, 1989.

An excellent anthology of some of the major statements by Marxist theorists and critics in the twentieth century.

Mulhern, Francis, ed. *Contemporary Marxist Literary Criticism.* London: Longman, 1992.

A collection of essays (some of which are quite difficult) that encompasses major contemporary trends in Marxist criticism.

Williams, Raymond. *Marxism and Literature.* Oxford: Oxford UP, 1977.

An excellent general discussion of the use of Marxist theory to illuminate literature.

Selected Other Works

Adorno, Theodor W. *Aesthetic Theory.* Trans. C. Lenhardt. Ed. Gretel Adorno and Rolf Tiedemann. London: Routledge and Kegan Paul, 1984.

———. *Minima Moralia: Reflections from a Damaged Life.* Trans. E. F. N. Jephcott. London: NLB, 1974.

———. *Negative Dialectics.* Trans. E. B. Ashton. New York: Seabury Press, 1973.

———. *Prisms: Cultural Criticism and Society.* Trans. Samuel Weber and Shierry Weber. Cambridge, Mass.: MIT P, 1972.

Althusser, Louis. *Lenin and Philosophy and Other Essays.* Trans. Ben Brewster. 170-183. London: Monthly Review, 1971.

———. *For Marx.* Harmondsworth, England: Allen Lane, 1969.

——— et al. *Reading Capital.* Trans. Ben Brewster. London: NLB, 1970.

Anderson, Perry. *Considerations on Western Marxism.* London: Routledge, Chapman and Hall, 1976.

Balibar, Etienne, and Pierre Macherey. "On Literature as an Ideological Form." Trans. Ian McLeod, John Whitehead, and Ann Wordsworth. In *Untying the Text: A Post-Structuralist Reader,* ed. Robert Young, 79-99. London: Routledge and Kegan Paul.

Benjamin, Walter. *Illuminations.* Trans. Harry Zohn. Ed. Hannah Arendt. New York: Harcourt, Brace and World, 1955.

———. *The Origin of German Tragic Drama.* Trans. John Osborne. London: NLB, 1977.

———. *Reflections: Essays, Aphorisms, Autobiographical Writings.* Trans. Edmund Jephcott. Ed. Peter Demetz. New York: Harcourt Brace Jovanovich, 1978.

———. *Understanding Brecht.* Trans. Anna Bostock. London: NLB, 1973.

Eagleton, Terry. "Capitalism, Modernism, and Postmodernism." *New Left Review* 152 (1985): 60-72.

———. *Criticism and Ideology: A Study in Marxist Literary Theory.* London: NLB, 1976.

———. *Exiles and Emigrés: Studies in Modern Literature.* New York: Schocken, 1970.

———. *The Ideology of the Aesthetic.* Oxford: Basil Blackwell, 1990.

———. *Literary Theory: An Introduction.* Minneapolis: U of Minnesota P, 1983.

———. *The Rape of Clarissa: Writing, Sexuality, and Class Struggle in Samuel Richardson.* Minneapolis: U of Minnesota P, 1982.

———. *Walter Benjamin, or Towards a Revolutionary Criticism.* London: Verso, 1981.

———, ed. *Raymond Williams: Critical Perspectives.* Boston: Northeastern UP, 1989.

Gramsci, Antonio. *Selections from the Prison Notebooks.* Ed. Quintin Hoare and Geoffrey Nowell Smith. New York: International Publishers, 1971.

Habermas, Jürgen. *Knowledge and Human Interests.* Trans. Jeremy J. Shapiro. Boston: Beacon, 1971.

———. "Modernity Versus Postmodernity." *New German Critique* 22 (1981): 3-14.

Horkheimer, Max, and Theodor W. Adorno. *The Dialectic of Enlightenment.* Trans. John Cumming. New York: Seabury, 1972.

Jameson, Fredric. *Late Marxism: Adorno, or, The Persistence of the Dialectic.* London: Verso, 1990.

———. *Marxism and Form: Twentieth-Century Dialectical Theories of Literature.* Princeton, N.J.: Princeton UP, 1971.

———. *The Political Unconscious: Narrative as a Socially Symbolic Act.* Ithaca, N.Y.: Cornell UP, 1981.

———. *Postmodernism, or, the Cultural Logic of Late Capitalism.* Durham, N.C.: Duke UP, 1991.

———. "Postmodernism or the Cultural Logic of Late Capitalism." *New Left Review* 145 (1984): 53–91.
———. *Signatures of the Visible.* New York: Routledge, 1992.
Lukács, Georg. *Essays on Realism.* Ed. Rodney Livingstone. Trans. David Fernbach. Cambridge, Mass.: MIT P, 1981.
———. *The Historical Novel.* Trans. Hannah Mitchell and Stanley Mitchell. Lincoln: U of Nebraska P, 1983.
———. *History and Class Consciousness: Studies in Marxist Dialectics.* Trans. Rodney Livingstone. Cambridge, Mass.: MIT P, 1971.
———. *Realism in Our Time: Literature and the Class Struggle.* Trans. John Mander and Necke Mander. New York: Harper and Row, 1964.
Macherey, Pierre. *A Theory of Literary Production.* Trans. Geoffrey Wall. London: Routledge and Kegan Paul, 1985.
Prawer, S. S. *Karl Marx and World Literature.* Oxford: Oxford UP, 1978.
Tucker, Robert C., ed. *The Marx-Engels Reader.* 2d ed. New York: Norton, 1978.
Weber, Max. *From Max Weber: Essays in Socialism.* Ed. H. H. Gerth and C. Wright Mills. New York: Oxford UP, 1958.
———. *Max Weber on Capitalism, Bureaucracy, and Religion: A Selection of Texts.* Ed. Stanislav Andreski. Boston: Allen and Unwin, 1983.
Wellmer, Albrecht. "Reason, Utopia, and the *Dialectic of Enlightenment.*" In *Habermas and Modernity,* ed. Richard J. Bernstein, 35–66. Cambridge, Mass.: MIT P, 1985.
Williams, Raymond. *The Country and the City.* New York: Oxford UP, 1973.
———. *Culture and Society.* New York: Columbia UP, 1958.
———. *Television: Technology and Cultural Form.* New York: Schocken, 1975.

chapter 6

Feminist Literary Criticism

Modern feminist criticism seeks to challenge the traditions and conventions of "patriarchal" society, or society that is based on the premise of masculine authority as embodied in the notion of the father as the head of the family. Feminist literary criticism focuses on the relationship between literature and patriarchal biases in society and on the potential role that literature can play in overcoming such biases. Many feminist critics have persuasively argued that literature plays a central role in the development of social attitudes toward women and of women's attitudes toward themselves. It comes as no surprise, then, that many of the leading figures in the feminist movement have been literary critics, literary artists, or both. To some extent, the prominence of feminist literary criticism and the political prominence of feminism as a whole in the past quarter century can be traced to the antiauthoritarian energies of the oppositional political movements of the 1960s. But contemporary feminist criticism has roots that go back well before the 1960s.

In the important 1929 book *A Room of One's Own,* Virginia Woolf attempts to explain why the Western literature tradition had until that time been thoroughly dominated by male writers. In answer to this central question, Woolf poses two basic kinds of answers, which foreshadow in their orientations the later development of Anglo-American and French feminist literary criticism respectively. On the one hand, like many later American and British feminist critics, Woolf attributes much of the paucity of women's writing to social and economic conditions that have historically made it difficult for women to write. Woolf argues that women, denied the financial opportunities accorded to men, have not typically been able to obtain either the time or the privacy to write. The title of her book refers to her envisioned solution to this problem: A woman writer needs to have an independent annual income to support herself and a room of her own in which to write without interruption. On the other hand, Woolf anticipates later French feminist critics by suggesting that the traditional masculine dominance of literature is related to a masculine dominance of language itself. Describing the difficulty of expression that faced the great nineteenth-century women novelists, Woolf notes in a now-famous passage that the very form of the sentence that has traditionally been considered acceptable by society has been an encumbrance to women writers. The acceptable sentence was "a man's sentence; behind it one can see Johnson, Gibbon and the rest. It was a sentence that was unsuited for a woman's use" (79-80).

In response to this traditional man's sentence, Woolf envisions the development of a more distinctively feminine mode of writing through the development of a "woman's sentence," though she also emphasizes the need to combine masculine and feminine elements in writing. This attempt to describe (and produce) a new form of feminine discourse directly anticipates the later work of French feminist theorists Hélène Cixous, Luce Irigaray, and Julia Kristeva, among others, whose work in the late 1960s and onward reflects a general emphasis on language in recent French literary theory and shows the strong influence of male theorists such as Jacques Derrida and Jacques Lacan. However French feminists have frequently challenged the authority of their masculine theoretical sources. They have particularly emphasized the necessity of new feminine forms of expression, as Irigaray explains: "If we continue to speak the same language to each other, we will reproduce the same story. Begin the same stories all over again. Don't you feel it? Listen: men and women around us all sound the same. Same arguments, same quarrels, same scenes. Same attractions and separations. Same difficulties, the impossibility of reaching each other" ("When" 69).

Xaviére Gauthier continues this theme, emphasizing that to enact social change, women must find a way to speak that exceeds and eludes traditional male language:

> Women are, in fact, caught in a very real contradiction. Throughout the course of history, they have been mute, and it is doubtless by virtue of this mutism that men have been able to speak and write. As long as women remain silent, they will be outside the historical process. But, if they begin to speak and write *as men do,* they will enter history subdued and alienated; it is a history that, logically speaking, their speech should disrupt. (162-163)

The French feminists have suggested two basic modes in which women might speak in the disruptive way for which Gauthier here calls. Both modes have their roots in Lacanian psychoanalysis and in the recognition that traditional male discourse arises from the Symbolic Order articulated by Lacan. To speak within the Symbolic Order requires that a person accept symbolic castration and submit herself to the Law of the Father. Thus writers such as Cixous (with her notion of *l'écriture féminine,* or women's writing) and Irigaray (in her notion of *le parler femme,* or women's speech) seek to resist this submission to patriarchal law by exploring a different mode of discourse that arises not from the Symbolic but from the Imaginary Order, from that preverbal infantile stage of joyful fusion with the mother's body. Kristeva, however, accepts the fact that we are all, women and men alike, constrained to speak and write from within the Symbolic Order. But she argues that this "symbolic" language can be disrupted from within through the eruption of "semiotic" modes of language, which are themselves in many ways related to Lacan's Imaginary Order.

In an attempt to avoid essentialist views of gender as informed by certain natural, predefined characteristics, French feminist theorists such as Cixous and Kristeva have typically insisted that feminine or semiotic language is related not to biological gender but to certain antipatriarchal modes of thought. Indeed many of the authors they have cited as exemplars of the new kinds of feminine writing they describe are male. Authors such as James Joyce, Stéphane Mallarmé, Antonin Artaud, Lautréamont, and Jean Genet figure prominently in these discussions. This emphasis on male writers can be traced in part to the importance of Lacanian psychoanalysis as a model for French feminist theorists. According to Lacan, male and female infants share a similar Imaginary Order experience. However recent work by such investigators as Nancy Chodorow has also shown that the preverbal infantile stage is not in fact entirely symmetrical because mothers tend to respond differently to baby daughters than to baby sons. Indeed for Lacan, the entry into the Symbolic Order problematizes access to the earlier Imaginary Order experience for the male child in a way that it does not for the female. As Francette Pacteau explains, "The little boy's passage from polymorphous sexuality to an adult sexual organization is doubly determined. Were he to turn his back he would lose his penis; but if he goes ahead he will gain the power which his organ has come to signify. Such deterrent and incentive are absent from the little girl's sexual development" (81).

Pacteau's analysis is entirely consistent with Cixous's comments on the special "generosity" available to the woman writer because of her lack of castration anxiety. Within a Lacanian framework, however, gender identity is determined not by biological "nature" but by linguistic construct. To gain the power and security offered to holders of the phallus by the male Symbolic Order, male writers must undergo Lacanian "castration," relinquishing access to the *jouissance* of infantile fusion with the mother. But it is possible for male writers (such as Joyce, Mallarmé, or Artaud) to resist this process. By refusing "castration," they can thereby become "women" writers. This refusal is generally evidenced by a radical opposition to traditional authority of all kinds. Ann Rosalind Jones notes the importance of writers such as Joyce, Mallarmé, and Artaud, who "rather than giving up their blissful infantile fusion with their mothers, their orality and anality, reexperience such *jouissances* subconsciously and set them into play by constructing texts against the rules and regularities of conventional language" (363).

As a result, feminine writing has a powerful political potential. Cixous (herself both a novelist and literary critic) optimistically proclaims the subversive potential of feminist literature when she declares: "A feminine text cannot fail to be more than subversive. It is volcanic; as it is written it brings about an upheaval of the old property crust, carrier of masculine investments; there's no other way" ("Laugh" 258). Cixous herself has perhaps done more than anyone to define (and to enact in her own practice) just what a new explicitly feminine way of speaking and writing might entail. She projects a utopian vision of a means of expression that is closely linked to a woman's special relationship to her body, with echoes of oral fantasies dating from a prelinguistic time of infantile Imaginary Order fusion with the mother. Because of this link to the prelinguistic Imaginary Order, Cixous's model for feminine speech is itself somewhat nonlinguistic, seeking to evade the masculine strictures of the Law of the Father associated with the Symbolic Order realm of language-as-representation. In particular, Cixous emphasizes the rhythmic and liberating element of song: "In women's speech, as in their writing, that element which never stops resonating, which, once we've been permeated by it, profoundly and imperceptibly touched by it, retains the power of moving us—that element is the song: first music from the first voice of love which is alive in every woman" (251).

This first music, alive in every woman, has a universal, rather than an individual, quality. The voice of the woman not only is her own but also springs from the deepest layers of her psyche as the echo of a primeval song she once heard, as the incarnation of the "first music of the voice of love, which every woman keeps alive. . . . Within each woman the first, nameless love is singing" (*Newly Born* 93). This voice is related to the voice of the mother that dominates the pre-Oedipal Imaginary Order fantasies of the infant.

This emphasis on "nameless love" indicates the element of selflessness and anonymity that informs Cixous's notion of feminine discourse. To Cixous, the masculine emphasis on ownership, related to a fear of castration, results in a libidinal economy of give-and-take in which giving is always associated with debt and nothing is to be given without the expectation of something in return. The consequence of this economic model is a masculine discomfort with both giving and receiving: "For the moment you receive something you are effectively 'open' to the other, and if you are a man you have only one wish, and that is hastily to return the gift, to break the circuit of an exchange that could have no end" ("Castration" 48).

Similarly the male author insists on having his name attached to his text, on receiving credit for his work, because "if a man spends and is spent, it's on condition that his power returns" (50). Women, in contrast, lack the typical masculine castration anxiety and can therefore be comfortable with generosity and anonymity:

> Unlike man, who holds so dearly to his title and his titles . . . woman couldn't care less about the fear of decapitation (or castration), adventuring, without the masculine temerity, into *anonymity,* which she can merge with, without annihilating herself: because she's a giver. . . . If there is a "propriety of woman," it is paradoxically her capacity to depropriate unselfishly, body without end, without appendage, without

principal "parts." Her libido is cosmic, just as her unconscious is worldwide. ("Laugh" 259; my emphasis)

Kristeva, like Cixous, has been highly concerned with the ways language itself can become a tool for the revolutionary enactment of social change. But Kristeva has shown considerable skepticism toward the notion of a separate woman's language. Working from a theoretical perspective influenced by both Lacan and Mikhail Bakhtin, she argues instead that the subversive potential of marginal discourse can arise only from within the existing system of language. To Kristeva, all language use must to some extent remain within this system, which, after Lacan, she refers to as the "symbolic." But at key points, especially in poetic language, another order of communication emerges, which she refers to as the "semiotic." Kristeva's semiotic, like Cixous's entire conception of a woman's language, is closely linked to the Imaginary Order experiences of the preverbal infant. During this period before constitution of the infant as a speaking subject in language, identity is inherently fluid, and strict boundaries between self and other have yet to be established. At this stage, the world of the infant consists of an endless flow of "rhythmic pulsions" that Kristeva calls the *chora*—"an essentially mobile and extremely provisional articulation constituted by movements and their ephemeral stases" (*Revolution* 25).

On the entry into Lacan's mirror stage, in which the infant first begins to learn how to differentiate between self and other, the child (of either sex) enters a new phase of development that Kristeva labels the "thetic." In this stage, the wholeness of the *chora* is disrupted, and the concept of difference, on which language depends, first enters the infant's world. In the process that Lacan calls "castration," this thetic phase is completed as the young child enters the Symbolic Order of language, boundaries between self and other are put in place, and the child becomes capable of assuming a fixed identity as speaker, as well as assuming a gender identity as either masculine or feminine. The semiotic elements are thus repressed, but they do not disappear entirely. Rather the *chora* continues to occur (for it is more a process than a thing) beneath the surface of language, always maintaining the potential to break through that surface at key moments with the disruptive force of the semiotic.

This potential is particularly strong in art, where semiotic elements such as sound, rhythm, and melody disrupt the stability of the symbolic order. "Art—this semiotization of the symbolic—thus represents the flow of *jouissance* into language" (79). Indeed to Kristeva, semiotic elements are absolutely essential for the creative use of language: "Though absolutely necessary, the thetic is not exclusive: the semiotic, which also precedes it, constantly tears it open, and this transgression brings about all the various transformations of the signifying practice that are called 'creation'" (62).

This emergence of the semiotic calls into question the fundamental assumptions on which the symbolic is based. In particular, the traditional notion of a static, autonomous subject is replaced by a more fluid and multiple conception of the subject, the Kristevan subject "in process/on trial." And this change can have a powerful political force because the assumption of a single, fixed identity underlies existing social and political systems in a fundamental way. "The text is a practice that could be compared to political revolution: the one brings about in the subject what the other introduces into society" (17).

For Kristeva, music may be purely semiotic, but language will always contain both symbolic and semiotic elements. Normally, especially in authoritarian discourse, symbolic elements will dominate language use, but the semiotic potential is always there. The obvious analogy here would be to Sigmund Freud's model of the psyche, in which the subject speaks from the conscious mind but in which unconscious elements can erupt at unexpected moments, such as in Freudian slips. Kristeva herself makes this connection, noting that "our positing of the semiotic is obviously inseparable from a theory of the subject that takes into account the Freudian positing of the unconscious" (30).

Kristeva ultimately suggests that women as well as men write largely in a symbolic mode, and her own writing practice has been criticized for conforming too closely to traditional patriarchal models of scholarship—Josette Féral's comment that "perhaps Kristeva's discourse lets itself be trapped by a language still marked by phallocratism" is a typical one (13). But to Kristeva there is no other choice. Toril Moi summarizes Kristeva's position: "There is no *other space* from which we can speak: if we are able to speak at all, it will have to be within the framework of symbolic language" (170). Certainly Irigaray and Cixous seem to pursue writing strategies that are more radical than that of Kristeva. But the difference here may be more of degree than of kind. Moreover it could also be argued that the attempt to explore a feminine discourse that arises from within the Imaginary simply cedes the Symbolic to masculine discourse and thereby plays directly into the hands of the patriarchy. As Moi points out, "It is, after all, patriarchy, not feminism, that insists on labelling women as emotional, intuitive and imaginative, while jealously converting reason and rationality into an exclusively male preserve" (123).

If Kristeva is skeptical toward the possibility of an entirely feminine mode of discourse, other feminists have been even more critical of the notion of a woman's language. To Cixous, the voice of the woman, raised loudly enough, threatens to shatter the patriarchal tradition, but other commentators have noted that this tradition is not so fragile. Susan Rubin Suleiman describes the ability of the patriarchal establishment to absorb and defuse challenges to its authority: "Like modern capitalism, modern patriarchy has a way of assimilating any number of subversive gestures into the 'mainstream,' where whatever subversive energy they may have possessed becomes neutralized" (11). Indeed Cixous herself has often been cited as a prime example of the dangers of this kind of assimilation, with any number of commentators observing that *l'écriture féminine* remains thoroughly inscribed within traditional male views of the feminine.

The important French Marxist-feminist critic Monique Wittig argues quite vigorously against the notion of a separate woman's language, opting instead to challenge the patriarchal literary tradition head-on. In both her criticism and her fiction, Wittig subverts the patriarchal tradition through a variety of techniques, including direct parody. She also frequently criticizes Cixous and other proponents of feminine writing for perpetuating male stereotypes of the feminine. Thus Hélène Vivienne Wenzel, defending the value of Wittig's position, argues that "far from being a subversive discourse as Cixous would have us believe, *écriture féminine* perpetuates and recreates long-held stereotypes and myths about woman as natural, sexual, biological, and corporal by celebrating her essences" (272).

American feminist critics have been particularly suspicious of French attempts to envision a new feminine mode of writing. Instead they have typically preferred to focus on readings of specific texts and on studies of the historical conditions under which gender stereotypes have been produced and sustained. Mary Jacobus expresses a typical American skepticism toward theories of feminine language: "Utopian attempts to define the specificity of women's writing—desired or hypothetical, but rarely empirically observed—either founder on the rock of essentialism (the text as body), gesture toward an avant-garde practice which turns out not to be specific to women, or, like Hélène Cixous in 'The Laugh of the Medusa,' do both" (37).

This dilemma illustrates that women are necessarily linguistically situated within patriarchal society, though it does not preclude the possibility of active linguistic subversion. I am reminded here of Judith Fetterley's argument that American literature presents only male perspectives, so that to read at all, women have traditionally been forced to adopt that perspective: "American literature is male. To read the canon of what is currently considered classic American literature is perforce to be identified as male" (xii). Fetterley suggests that in response women should become "resisting readers," that they should read against the grain of the traditional male canon and challenge the negative attitudes toward women embodied in that canon.

A similar project was central to a number of key texts published in the late 1960s and early 1970s that provided the initial impetus for the rise of feminist literary criticism to prominence in American intellectual life. One of the most important early influences on American feminism, however, was a French text, Simone de Beauvoir's 1949 *The Second Sex*. Here de Beauvoir addresses the traditional masculine stereotyping of women that would become a central target of American feminist critics. In particular, de Beauvoir focuses on the Western tendency to accept a duality of mind and body and to privilege the former. De Beauvoir notes that Western myth and literature tend to associate the mental side of this duality with the masculine while associating women with the physical aspects of life: "The uncleanness of birth is reflected upon the mother. . . . And if the little boy remains in early childhood sensually attached to the maternal flesh, when he grows older, becomes socialized, and takes note of his individual existence, this same flesh frightens him . . . calls him back from those realms of immanence whence he would fly" (136). This association of women with the flesh reflects a disdain for the animality of human corporeality. The male thus opposes himself as "spirit" to the woman as flesh, as "the Other, who limits and denies him" (129).

De Beauvoir supports her arguments by demonstrating the prevalence of such stereotyping in the work of male writers such as Stendhal and D. H. Lawrence. She thus directly anticipates such later American feminist texts as Mary Ellmann's *Thinking about Women* (1968), a witty and ironic survey of the stereotyping of women in patriarchal society, especially as conveyed through literature. Ellmann's main thesis is that Western culture is saturated with the phenomenon of "thought by sexual analogy," a general tendency to "comprehend all phenomena, however shifting, in terms of our original and simple sexual differences; and . . . classify almost all experience by means of sexual analogy" (6). She presents a catalog of eleven major stereotypes of the feminine that are typically found in the work of male writers and critics, including the prevalence of the figures of the Witch and the Shrew in descriptions of women, as well as the attribution to women of formlessness, passivity, instability, confinement, piety, materiality, spirituality, irrationality, and compliancy, among other characteristics. Ellmann discusses the work of such women writers as Dorothy Richardson, Ivy Compton-Burnett, and Nathalie Sarrault in an attempt to explore the ways women might challenge these traditional stereotypes.

Another important founding text of American feminist criticism is Kate Millett's *Sexual Politics,* a 1969 book that deals largely with the negative treatment of women by male writers such as D. H. Lawrence, Henry Miller, and Norman Mailer. Millett suggests an oppositional mode of reading in which a perspective other than that of the author is posited, then shows that the resulting conflict between the reader and the author/text can expose the underlying assumptions of the work. These assumptions, in the cases of Lawrence, Miller, and Mailer, usually have to do with the negative stereotyping of women. Somewhat in the mode of the French feminists, Millett also finds positive elements in some male writers. For example, she concludes that Joyce stereotypically relates women to "nature," "unspoiled primeval understanding," or "the eternal feminine" but argues that Joyce's stereotyping is less hostile to women than that found in contemporaries such as Lawrence (285). Millett finds particularly positive potential in the writing of the French male homosexual writer Jean Genet because his work usefully challenges conventional notions of gender roles.

Millett's focus on male writers has sometimes been criticized, but it is fairly typical of much early feminist criticism. Recognizing that the traditional canon of Western literature had until that time consisted almost entirely of texts written by (usually white) men, feminist critics were understandably concerned with exploring the potential for this situation to perpetuate stereotypical visions of women. After all, the ideas expressed in texts that have been included in the canon and thus acknowledged as "great literature" seem to bear the endorsement of society. But as Ellmann's work shows, American feminist critics turned quite early on to the complementary project of giving literature written by women the kind of serious critical attention it had long been denied by male critics. This vein of feminist criticism (which Elaine Showalter has labeled *gynocritics*) has ultimately proved to be extremely rich.

For one thing, work in this area has revealed that that there is a far richer tradition of women's writing than most critics had realized but that many women writers had simply been forgotten because masculine biases had made it difficult for the lasting value of their work to be recognized. One of the key texts in this project of historical recovery of women's writing is Elaine Showalter's 1977 *A Literature of Their Own,* which surveys the work of nineteenth-century British women novelists, discussing not only the work of such well-known writers as the Brontës but also forgotten writers. Showalter's book contains numerous useful insights into the feminine literary tradition, noting, for example, that women writers have sometimes achieved literary fame during their lifetimes but that this fame tends to fade away soon after their deaths: "Thus each generation of women writers has found itself, in a sense, without a history, forced to discover the past anew, forging again and again the consciousness of their sex. Given this perpetual disruption and also the self-hatred that has alienated women writers from a sense of collective identity, it does not seem possible to speak of a 'movement' " (11–12).

Another important text of historical recovery is *The Madwoman in the Attic,* Sandra M. Gilbert and Susan Gubar's sweeping 1979 study of nineteenth-century (mostly American and British) women writers. Like Showalter, Gilbert and Gubar seek to resurrect the work of forgotten women writers. They also emphasize the difficulties faced by women writers in a patriarchal society: "Since both patriarchy and its texts subordinate and imprison women, before women can even attempt that pen which is so rigorously kept from them they must escape just those male texts which, defining them as 'Cyphers,' deny them the autonomy to formulate alternatives to the authority that has imprisoned them and kept them from attempting the pen" (13). Gilbert and Gubar particularly note the centrality to masculine literature of the stereotype of the "eternal feminine" as a vision of angelic beauty and sweetness from Dante's Beatrice to Patmore's "Angel in the House." They also emphasize the stereotype of the "madwoman" as typical of masculine literary representations of women in the nineteenth century.

With all of these patriarchal definitions imposed on the woman writer, she faced a formidable task in finding her own literary voice or indeed in writing at all. Yet Gilbert and Gubar find that nineteenth-century women writers produced an impressive body of work nevertheless, often by slyly appearing to conform to patriarchal standards while actually subverting them:

> Women from Jane Austen and Mary Shelley to Emily Brontë and Emily Dickinson produced literary works that are in some sense palimpsestic, works whose surface designs conceal or obscure deeper, less accessible (and less socially acceptable) levels of meaning. Thus these authors managed the difficult task of achieving true female literary authority by simultaneously conforming to and subverting patriarchal literary standards. (59)

The work of many of these feminist critics is informed by a relatively conventional liberal humanist vision. Unlike their French counterparts, such critics do not tend to draw extensively on recent developments in literary theory; indeed they are often openly hostile to theory as an extension of patriarchal modes of thought. But their work does represent an important departure from the American New Critical tradition in its insistence on attention to the political implications of literature. In this sense, American feminist criticism clearly parallels other forms of criticism that have increasingly acknowledged the importance of history and politics in literary study.

In recent years, feminist critics have continued their attempts to recover the feminine literary tradition and to explore the differences between literature written by women and that written by men. Such projects have led to a considerable reconsideration of the literary canon and to a sharp increase in the number of texts written by women that receive serious critical attention and are taught in college literature classrooms. Meanwhile, as a recent anthology edited by Robyn R. Warhol and Diane Price Herndl demonstrates, the feminist critical project has expanded in a number of directions. For example, many recent American feminist critics have been concerned with the broad phenomenon of "culture," as opposed to a focus on literature. This project includes paying serious attention to the genres normally associated with "popular" culture; feminist studies in the theory and criticism of film have been particularly valuable. Such studies have also tended to show a high level of theoretical sophistication, drawing extensively on the work of Lacan and other theorists. Indeed recent developments in feminist theory and criticism have included a number of specifically feminist adaptations of Marxism and psychoanalysis and of the work of literary theorists such as Bakhtin and Michel Foucault. Recent American feminist criticism has also expanded beyond the relatively traditional liberal humanism of Showalter and Gilbert and Gubar via the important contributions of black, lesbian, and third-world feminist critics, whose challenges to the existing order are often far more radical than those of their more mainstream predecessors.

Important among these recent critics is Gayatri Chakravorty Spivak, who combines a sophisticated poststructuralist theoretical perspective with a strong neo-Marxist political commitment arising from Spivak's own position as a postcolonial subject. Her work thus provides important reminders that any politically effective feminist project must consider matters of class and race in addition to matters of sexuality and gender. Also central to recent developments in feminist criticism is the careful interrogation of the very notion of gender as a complex and historically determined social phenomenon. In this project, American and French feminist criticism tend to converge, as do feminist criticism and gay and lesbian criticism. Much recent American work in gender studies is very much in accord with French theoretical attempts to explore the notion of gender as a social and political construct, very much in the vein indicated by Wittig, who emphasizes the subversive potential of lesbian approaches to literature and describes the political function of traditional gender roles: "Heterosexuality is a cultural construct designed to justify the whole system of social domination based on the obligatory reproductive function of women and the appropriation of that reproduction" (115).

Foucault's *The History of Sexuality* has been a particularly important founding text in the development of such gender studies, though Foucault himself (with his focus on male homosexuality) pays notoriously little attention to *feminine* sexuality in his work. Foucault's work does, however, convincingly argue that sexuality is more social than natural and that the traditional privileging of heterosexuality in the West has its basis in matters not of biology but of social and political power. American gender critics such as Eve Kosofsky Sedgwick have built significantly on Foucault's work. For example, in her recent *Epistemology of the Closet,* Sedgwick follows Foucault in exploring the centrality of conceptual contradictions arising from issues related to definitions of male homosexuality and heterosexuality to the development of the entire Western epistemological tradition. At the same time, such critics have expanded the relevance of Foucault's work while challenging some of its more problematic assumptions.

Taken together, the work of French feminist critics, American feminist critics, third-world critics, and gender critics indicates the extremely broad range that feminist criticism has taken in the last quarter century, a range that has been made both possible and necessary by the central importance of gender to literature and the related institutions of modern society. Moreover it is clear that feminist criticism will continue to expand in exciting new directions in the coming years and to establish exciting new dialogues with criticism focused on race, class, and other issues.

BIBLIOGRAPHY

Introductory Works

Kolodny, Annette. "Dancing through the Minefield: Some Observations on the Theory, Practice, and Politics of a Feminist Literary Criticism." *Feminist Studies* 6.1 (1980): 1-25.
A good discussion of many of the major concerns of feminist criticism.

Moi, Toril. *Sexual/Textual Politics: Feminist Literary Theory.* London: Methuen, 1985.
Still one of the best general introductions to feminist criticism, though with a decided bias toward French feminism (especially the work of Kristeva).

Showalter, Elaine. *A Literature of Their Own: British Women Novelists from Brontë to Lessing.* Princeton, N.J.: Princeton UP, 1977.
An excellent example of Showalter's conception of gynocritics.

Warhol, Robyn R., and Diane Price Herndl, eds. *Feminisms: An Anthology of Literary Theory and Criticism.* New Brunswick, N.J.: Rutgers UP, 1991.
An extremely useful compilation of some of the latest work in feminist literary studies.

Woolf, Virginia. *A Room of One's Own.* New York: Harcourt Brace Jovanovich, 1929.
One of the founding texts of feminist literary study. Still very valuable.

Selected Other Works

Abel, Elizabeth, ed. *Writing and Sexual Difference.* Chicago: U of Chicago P, 1982.

Bauer, Dale M. *Feminist Dialogics: A Theory of Failed Community.* Albany: State U of New York P, 1988.

Beauvoir, Simone de. *The Second Sex.* 1949. Trans. and ed. H. M. Parshley. New York: Bantam, 1961.

Butler, Judith. *Gender Trouble: Feminism and the Subversion of Identity.* New York: Routledge, 1989.
Carby, Hazel V. *Reconstructing Womanhood: The Emergence of the Afro-American Woman Novelist.* New York: Oxford UP, 1987.
Castle, Terry. *The Apparitional Lesbian: Female Homosexuality and Modern Culture.* New York: Columbia UP, 1993.
Chodorow, Nancy. *The Reproduction of Mothering: Psychoanalysis and the Sociology of Gender.* Berkeley and Los Angeles: U of California P, 1978.
Cixous, Hélène. "Castration or Decapitation?" Trans. Annette Kuhn. *Signs* 7 (1981): 41-55.
———. "The Character of 'Character.' " *New Literary History* 5 (1974): 383-402.
———. "The Laugh of the Medusa." In *New French Feminisms,* ed. Elaine Marks and Isabelle Courtivron, 245-264. New York: Schocker, 1981.
———. "Rethinking Differences." In *Homosexuality and French Literature,* ed. George Stambolian and Elaine Marks, 70-86. Ithaca, N.Y.: Cornell UP, 1979.
Cixous, Hélène, and Catherine Clément. *The Newly Born Woman.* Trans. Betsy Wing. Minneapolis: U of Minnesota P, 1986.
Diamond, Irene, and Lee Quinby, eds. *Feminism and Foucault: Reflections on Resistance.* Boston: Northeastern UP, 1988.
Ellmann, Mary. *Thinking about Women.* New York: Harcourt Brace Jovanovich, 1968.
Féral, Josette. "Antigone or the Irony of the Tribe." *Diacritics* 8 (1978): 2-14.
Fetterley, Judith. *The Resisting Reader: A Feminist Approach to American Fiction.* Bloomington: Indiana UP, 1981.
Flynn, Elizabeth A., and Patrocinio Schweickart, eds. *Gender and Reading: Essays on Readers, Texts, and Contexts.* Baltimore, Md.: Johns Hopkins UP, 1986.
Foucault, Michel. *The History of Sexuality.* Vol. 1, *An Introduction.* Trans. Robert Hurley. New York: Vintage, 1980.
Gallop, Jane. *The Daughter's Seduction: Feminism and Psychoanalysis.* Ithaca, N.Y.: Cornell UP, 1982.
Gauthier, Xaviére. "Is There Such a Thing as Women's Writing?" In *New French Feminisms,* ed. Elaine Marks and Isabelle de Courtivron, 161-164. New York: Schocken, 1981.
Gilbert, Sandra M., and Susan Gubar. *The Madwoman in the Attic: The Woman Writer and the Nineteenth-Century Literary Imagination.* New Haven, Conn: Yale UP, 1979.
———. *No Man's Land: The Place of the Woman Writer in the Twentieth Century.* Vol.1, *The War of the Words.* New Haven, Conn.: Yale UP, 1988.
———. *No Man's Land: The Place of the Woman Writer in the Twentieth Century.* Vol. 2, *Sexchanges.* New Haven, Conn.: Yale UP, 1988.
Heilbrun, Carolyn G. *Toward a Recognition of Androgyny.* 1964. New York: Norton, 1982.
Herrmann, Anne. *The Dialogic and Difference: "An/Other Woman" in Virginia Woolf and Christa Wolf.* New York: Columbia UP, 1989.
Irigaray, Luce. "When Our Lips Speak Together." Trans. Carolyn Burke. *Signs* 6 (1980): 69-79.
———. *This Sex Which Is Not One.* Trans. Catherine Porter with Carolyn Burke. Ithaca, N.Y.: Cornell UP, 1985.
Jacobus, Mary. "The Question of Language: Men of Maxims and *The Mill on the Floss.*" In *Writing and Sexual Difference,* ed. Elizabeth Abel, 37-52. Chicago: U of Chicago P, 1982.
Jehlen, Myra. "Archimedes and the Paradox of Feminist Criticism." *Signs* 6 (1981): 575-601.
Jones, Ann Rosalind. "Writing the Body: Toward an Understanding of *l'Écriture Féminine.*" In *The New Feminist Criticism: Essays on Women, Literature, and Theory,* ed. Elaine Showalter, 361-377. New York: Pantheon, 1985.

Kristeva, Julia. *Desire in Language: A Semiotic Approach to Literature and Art.* Trans. Thomas Gora, Alice Jardine, and Leon S. Roudiez. Ed. Leon S. Roudiez. New York: Columbia UP, 1980.

———. "Oscillation between Power and Denial." In *New French Feminisms,* ed. Elaine Marks and Isabelle de Courtivron, 165–167. New York: Schocken, 1981.

———. *Powers of Horror: An Essay in Abjection.* Trans. Leon S. Roudiez. New York: Columbia UP, 1982.

———. *Revolution in Poetic Language.* Trans. Margaret Waller. New York: Columbia UP, 1984.

Lauretis, Teresa de. *Technologies of Gender: Essays on Theory, Film, and Fiction.* Bloomington: Indiana UP, 1987.

———, ed. *Feminist Studies/Critical Studies.* Bloomington: Indiana UP, 1986.

Looser, Devoney. "Feminist Theory and Foucault: A Bibliographical Essay." *Style* 26.4 (1992): 593–603.

Marks, Elaine, and Isabelle de Courtivron, eds. *New French Feminisms.* New York: Schocken, 1981.

Millett, Kate. *Sexual Politics.* Garden City, N.Y.: Doubleday, 1970.

Molinaro, Nina L. *Foucault, Feminism, and Power: Reader Esther Tusquets.* Lewisburg, Penn.: Bucknell UP, 1991.

Mulvey, Laura. *Visual and Other Pleasures.* Bloomington: Indiana UP, 1989.

Pacteau, Francette. "The Impossible Referent: Representations of the Androgyne." In *Formations of Fantasy,* ed. Victor Burgin, James Donald, and Cora Kaplan, 62–84. London: Methuen, 1986.

Sawicki, Jana. *Disciplining Foucault: Feminism, Power, and the Body.* New York: Routledge, 1991.

Sedgwick, Eve Kosofsky. *Between Men: English Literature and Male Homosocial Desire.* New York: Columbia UP, 1985.

———. *Epistemology of the Closet.* Berkeley and Los Angeles: U of California P, 1990.

Showalter, Elaine. "Feminist Criticism in the Wilderness." In *Writing and Sexual Difference,* ed. Elizabeth Abel, 9–35. Chicago: U of Chicago P, 1982.

———. *Sexual Anarchy: Gender and Culture at the Fin de Siècle.* New York: Viking-Penguin, 1990.

———, ed. *The New Feminist Criticism: Essays on Women, Literature, and Theory.* New York: Pantheon, 1985.

Silverman, Kaja. *The Acoustic Mirror: The Female Voice in Psychoanalysis and Cinema.* Bloomington: Indiana UP, 1988.

Spivak, Gayatri Chakravorty. *In Other Worlds: Essays in Cultural Politics.* New York: Routledge, 1988.

Stambolian, George, and Elaine Marks, eds. *Homosexualities and French Literature.* Ithaca, N.Y.: Cornell UP, 1979.

Suleiman, Susan Rubin. "(Re)writing the Body: The Politics and Poetics of Female Eroticism." In *The Female Body in Western Culture,* ed. Susan Rubin Suleiman, 7–29. Cambridge, Mass.: Harvard UP, 1986.

Vance, Carole S., ed. *Pleasure and Danger: Exploring Female Sexuality.* Boston: Routledge, 1984.

Waugh, Patricia. *Feminine Fictions: Revisiting the Postmodern.* New York: Routledge, 1989.

Wenzel, Hélène Vivienne. "The Text as Body/Politics: An Appreciation of Monique Wittig's Writings in Context." *Feminist Studies* 7 (1981): 264–287.

Wittig, Monique. "Paradigm." In *Homosexualities and French Literature,* ed. George Stambolian and Elaine Marks, 114–121. Ithaca, N.Y.: Cornell UP, 1979.

Wyatt, Jean. *Reconstructing Desire: The Role of the Unconscious in Women's Reading and Writing.* Chapel Hill: U of North Carolina P, 1990.

Yaeger, Patricia. *Honey-Mad Women: Emancipatory Strategies in Women's Writing.* New York: Columbia UP, 1988.

chapter 7

Bakhtinian Literary Criticism

The work of the Russian thinker Mikhail Bakhtin has been one of the major inspirations for the explosion in concern with theory that has informed American literary criticism in the last quarter century. Bakhtin's body of work, performed under adverse circumstances in the Soviet Union from the 1920s to the 1960s, is nevertheless large and diverse. David Lodge describes Bakhtin's career as "an extraordinary story of outstanding intellectual achievement in the teeth of every imaginable obstacle and discouragement" (3). Bakhtin's work includes meditations on history, sociology, philosophy, psychology, linguistics, and literature; his writings (as translated into English) include important book-length literary studies such as *Problems of Dostoevsky's Poetics* and *Rabelais and His World* as well as collections of essays on philosophy and ethics (*Art and Answerability*) and literary theory and language (*The Dialogic Imagination, Speech Genres and Other Late Essays*). In addition, works associated with Bakhtin include a group of "disputed" texts on psychology, language, and literature, including *Freudianism, Marxism and the Philosophy of Language,* and *The Formal Method in Literary Scholarship.* Critics Katerina Clark and Michael Holquist argue that Bakhtin in fact authored these texts, though when published they were attributed to Bakhtin associates Pavel Medvedev and V. N. Voloshinov. Critics I. R. Titunik and Gary Saul Morson and Caryl Emerson, however, vigorously argue that these texts were, in fact, written by the authors to whom they were originally attributed.

Bakhtin first became known in the West in the late 1960s when French structuralist and poststructuralist critics discovered in his work on the dialogic character of language a useful enrichment of their own thoughts on textuality and language. For Bakhtin, as for many structuralist and poststructuralist theorists, language is fundamentally multiple in its meaning. He characterizes this multiplicity as dialogic because in his view these multiple meanings arise from the fact that any utterance carries the traces of other utterances that have preceded it and that might come after it in response. In this sense, he clearly anticipates the figuration by such theorists as Roland Barthes and Jacques Derrida of all uses of language as intertextual constructs. Indeed Julia Kristeva, who is generally credited with having coined the important term *intertextuality,* directly attributes her thoughts on this subject to an insight derived from the work of Bakhtin. Meanwhile Bakhtin's work in genre theory, and particularly his commentary on the novel, has provided an important impetus to theoretical studies of fiction and narrative, leading Paul de Man to suggest that Bakhtin is a justified candidate for the role of "hero" in the modern development of the theory of narrative, particularly as it concerns the novel (106–107). Bakhtin's work has been so widely influential in recent years that a virtual "Bakhtin industry" of criticism and commentary has sprung up. Important general surveys of Bakhtin's work include a critical biography by Clark and Holquist and critical studies by Tzvetan Todorov, Morson and Emerson, and Holquist. Numerous collections of essays on Bakhtin have also appeared, including those edited by Morson, Morson and Emerson, and Ken Hirschkop.

Western critics who have employed Bakhtin's theories have typically emphasized two central aspects of his thought—dialogism and carnival. Thus R. B. Kershner, in a Bakhtinian study of the early fiction of James Joyce, introduces Bakhtin by noting that "Bakhtin's importance rests on two key concepts, *dialogism* . . . and *carnivalization*" (15). Elsewhere Michael Holquist has suggested dialogism as Bakhtin's master concept (*Dialogism*). But as Holquist emphasizes, Bakhtin's notion of dialogism is an extremely complex and subtle concept that involves an interconnecting network of ideas about language, epistemology, and human existence in general. In an influential critical biography of Bakhtin, Holquist and Clark argue for Bakhtin's consistent, lifelong focus on the ethical implications of dialogic relations between self and other, a focus that already takes shape in his early "architectonics of answerability" project of the 1920s. Morson and Emerson have challenged this rather static view of Bakhtin's ethical and intellectual concerns. In their excellent recent survey of Bakhtin's work, they argue that Bakhtin's ideas and interests change dramatically from one period to another in his long intellectual career. Morson and Emerson do suggest that there are certain "global concepts" that are of central importance to his work. These concepts include not only dialogism but also "prosaics" (in the sense both of a concern with prose as a literary form and an emphasis on the common details of everyday life) and "unfinalizability," or a nonteleological historical vision based on continual change and evolution.

Bakhtin's concern with history can be seen in his own description of his project as an attempt to develop a "historical poetics." Nevertheless his work is extremely diverse, and any attempt to summarize that work succinctly is in danger not only of oversimplifying Bakhtin's thought but also of doing considerable violence to the complex and avowedly nonsystematic nature of his project. Even Clark and Holquist, who have been criticized (particularly by Morson and Emerson) for trying to fit all of Bakhtin's work into a single mold, insist that Bakhtin's own emphasis on multiplicity implies that "to claim that any version of him is the correct one would be to straitjacket the philosopher of variety, to 'monologize' the singer of 'polyphony'" (4). Similarly they approvingly cite a speech made by L. E. Pinsky in a memorial service after Bakhtin's death, in which Pinsky stated that "Bakhtin's work is exciting precisely because of its contradictoriness and ability to spark different and unexpected interpretations, and that one should thus be careful not to assign his writings any single, authoritative interpretation" (344).

This warning is particularly crucial given that Bakhtin himself practices what he preaches, writing in a dialogic (and often parodic) mode that makes it impossible to appreciate the significance of his statements unless they are read in conjunction with other statements to which they respond and with potential responses that they themselves might be expected to invoke. The very heart of dialogism is a movement beyond monological modes of either-or logic, which demand that a given interpretation of a text (or of the world) be either accepted or rejected. Similarly the most important aspect of the spirit of carnival is its ambivalence and its refusal to allow simple choices between opposing alternatives. Bakhtin's historical vision crucially relies on a sense of continual becoming, which requires that final conclusions and interpretations be perpetually deferred in favor of an ongoing potentiality.

In addition, interpretations of Bakhtin's work are always complicated by the fact that, writing within the context of the Stalinist Soviet Union, Bakhtin was not necessarily free to say or write what he wanted. In reading Bakhtin, then, we must remain alert to absences that might have been caused by the exigencies of political reality in the Soviet Union. Moreover it is almost certain that what Bakhtin *does* say is distorted by this reality, both because some of his points must be made obliquely to skirt controversy and because many of his points are in fact subtly subversive commentaries on Stalinism itself. For example, it is now widely accepted among Bakhtin scholars that the description of the rigid, humorless, and authoritarian practices of the medieval Catholic Church put forth by Bakhtin in *Rabelais and His World* is at least partially a veiled comment on Stalinism. In the prologue to the English translation of the book, Holquist directs us to consider the "obvious parallels between Bakhtin's scathing references to the Catholic church in the sixteenth century and Stalinism in the twentieth" (xv). In the double-voiced mode that he himself praises in the work of writers such as François Rabelais and Fyodor Dostoevsky, Bakhtin's description of a sterile, monological society in *Rabelais and His World* thus refers simultaneously to a medieval world of the distant past and to a Soviet world of his own Stalinist present. A great deal of Bakhtin's more general commentary on the intrinsic multiplicity and ideological diversity of language and on the evolutionary nature of history can also be read as responses to Stalinist totalitarian utopianism.

Bakhtin made his most important initial impact on Anglo-American criticism through his commentary in *Rabelais and His World* on the transgressive energies of the medieval carnival. For example, in the important study *The Politics and Poetics of Transgression,* Peter Stallybrass and Allon White acknowledge their debt to Bakhtin's theories of the carnivalesque, noting that Bakhtin has in fact been the major figure in a widespread fascination with the notion of carnival among Western critics in the latter decades of the twentieth century. Bakhtin's book on Rabelais, Stallybrass and White suggest, "catalysed the interest of Western scholars . . . around the notion of carnival" (6).

There are a number of reasons for the enthusiastic reception of Bakhtin's presentation of the transgressive potential of carnivalesque imagery. Probably the most important of these reasons (especially if viewed in the light of Bakhtin's own continual insistence on the importance of historical context) is the ability of *Rabelais and His World* to respond so well to the needs and interests of Western critics when it was first introduced to them in the 1970s. In particular, the exuberant, exorbitant, transgressive, emancipatory rhetoric and imagery that most critics have associated with Bakhtin's readings of Rabelais closely parallel those that informed the oppositional political movements of the 1960s, movements that themselves had a major formative influence on Western literary critics in subsequent decades. Of course, as M. Keith Booker and Dubravka Juraga emphasize, we should keep in mind that the carnivalesque energies in Bakhtin's own work derive not from the 1960s but from the tumultuous political and cultural climate of the postrevolutionary Soviet Union in the 1920s. And Bakhtin's comments on the carnival are also to a certain extent a response to the decidedly noncarnivalesque turn taken by Soviet society in the Stalinist 1930s. Many Western critics, by ignoring Bakhtin's relation to his historical context, may miss some aspects of the coding of Bakhtin's discussion of the carnival as a time of radical transgression of hierarchies and of a general challenge to authority and rules of all kinds.

On the surface, at least, Bakhtin's carnival is a time of festive and exuberant celebration when normal social boundaries collapse and groups from different social classes and backgrounds meet and mingle freely in a mood of irreverence that runs directly counter to the cold, sterile, and humorless world of official medieval Catholicism. The carnival is a time when normal rules and hierarchies are suspended, when boundaries are transgressed, and when the energies of life erupt without regard for conventional decorum. Moreover Bakhtin argues that the energies of the carnival inform the writing of Rabelais—with its extravagant linguistic strategies and its heavy use of sexual and excremental imagery and of the fantastic—in important and potentially powerful ways.

Bakhtin pays particular attention to Rabelais's treatment of the "grotesque" body, of the aspects of human life (such as sex and excrement) associated with the "material bodily lower stratum" that call attention to the status of human beings as physical creatures living in a physical world. Bakhtin notes traditional attempts to view the body as a seamless classical whole by denying excremental, sexual, and other processes that emphasize the dynamic interaction between body and world; he then suggests that these attempts represent a denial of history. But the "unfinished and open body (dying, bringing forth and being born) is not separated from the world by clearly defined boundaries; it is blended with the world, with animals, with objects" (*Rabelais* 26–27). Moreover the dynamic nature of this blending and of the carnivalesque representation of body functions thrusts the subject directly into the contemporaneous flow of history: "The material bodily lower stratum and the entire system of degradation, turnovers, and travesties presented this essential relation to time and to social and historical transformation" (81). In short, the transfer of physical material from the interior of the body into the outside world (and vice versa) provides a graphic reminder that human beings are part of that world and undermines the Kantian duality of subject and object that underlies conventional Western approaches to the relationship between individuals and their surroundings. Such physical processes also provide reminders that human beings are biological creatures who live (and die) in time.

In addition, Bakhtin suggests that traditional attempts to taxonomize the body into "high" and "low" segments stand as a figure for the oppression of marginal social groups by dominant ones in class society. According to Bakhtin, Rabelais's explicit focus on the material lower bodily stratum undermines this movement with its transgressive challenge to the usual hierarchical privileging of the high parts of the body over the low. Stallybrass and White, following Bakhtin, note that hierarchical systems of classifying both bodily functions and literary works participate in a general trend toward social domination of oppressed groups by ruling ones: "The ranking of literary genres or authors in a hierarchy analogous to social classes is a particularly clear example of a much broader and more complex cultural process whereby the human body, psychic forms, geographical space, and the social formation are all constructed within interrelating and dependent hierarchies of high and low" (2). Bakhtin's carnival, by disrupting these hierarchies, thus potentially provides a metaphor for political revolution. Holquist concludes that "Bakhtin's carnival . . . is revolution itself" (Prologue xviii).

Numerous critics of Bakhtin, however, have seen the medieval carnival as a highly unsatisfactory metaphor for revolution because the carnival was in fact an officially sanctioned event whose very purpose was to release potentially subversive energies in politically harmless ways and thus *prevent* revolution. Terry Eagleton, for example, expresses a strong skepticism toward the subversive potential of Bakhtin's notion of the carnival, pointing out that carnival is "a *licensed* affair in every sense, a permissible rupture of hegemony, a contained popular blow-off as disturbing and relatively ineffectual as a revolutionary work of art" (*Walter* 148). In addition, Bakhtin's apparent treatment of the carnival as an unequivocal image of emancipation seems to ignore the important fact that carnivalesque violence was often directly not at official authority but precisely at the kinds of oppressed and marginal groups that would presumably be liberated by carnivalesque subversion of authority. Michael André Bernstein warns against the potential dark side of the Bakhtinian carnival.

Bakhtin's discussion of the carnival and frequent references to the anti-authoritarian power inherent in language itself have led many critics to charge him with an unwarranted, even naive, optimism concerning the possibility of radical political change. Michael Gardiner, for example, argues that Bakhtin "projects an almost entirely positive—indeed, utopian—image of carnival and related folk-festive practices" (181). Gardiner sees a similar utopian optimism in Bakhtin's discussion of the novel, concluding that the "central shortcoming" of Bakhtin's thought is that he "seriously overestimates the capacity of dialogic literature and popular culture to effect the liberation of human consciousness from the grip of monologism" (176). In contrast, Morson and Emerson argue that visions of Bakhtin as a radically emancipatory thinker on the order of his Russian predecessor Mikhail Bakunin seriously distort Bakhtin's thought, which is often centrally concerned with constraints and the difficulty of radical and sudden change. They specifically seek to downplay the importance of the carnivalesque in Bakhtin's thought, believing that this aspect of Bakhtin's work represents something of an anomaly that has probably been overemphasized, especially by Western critics. Booker and Juraga agree, arguing that Bakhtin's actual attitude toward the carnival is extremely complex and ambivalent, impossible to read without close and careful consideration of Bakhtin's relation to his Stalinist context.

Regardless of the complexities of Bakhtin's actual position, numerous literary and cultural critics have drawn on Bakhtin's discussion of the carnival in their work. Such uses of Bakhtin's concept of the carnivalesque include Jon Cook's readings of Geoffrey Chaucer, Michael Bristol's discussion of Renaissance drama, the focus by Stallybrass and White on eighteenth-century literature, the feminist criticism of Patricia Yaeger, and the film criticism of Robert Stam. Despite Bakhtin's own lack of commentary on twentieth-century literature (a lack that can be at least partially attributed to the limitations placed on him by Stalinist censorship), his discussion of the carnivalesque has been especially widely used by critics of modern and contemporary literature. Zack Bowen, for example, makes use of Bakhtin's descriptions of the carnivalesque aspects of the work of Rabelais to argue the essentially comic nature of James Joyce's project in *Ulysses;* Robert H. Bell draws extensively on Bakhtin's readings of Rabelais (and other aspects of Bakhtin's work as well) in a study of the comic dimension of Joyce's work. In *Techniques of Subversion in Modern Literature,* Booker employs Bakhtin's notion of the carnival to study the transgressive energies found in works by writers ranging from Chaucer to postmodernist writers Thomas Pynchon, Salman Rushdie, John Fowles, and Angela Carter. Booker then later uses Bakhtin's discussion of the carnival to illuminate the work of the Peruvian writer Mario Vargas Llosa within the context of postmodernism.

Max Nänny has related both T. S. Eliot's *The Waste Land* and Ezra Pound's *Cantos* to Bakhtin's discussions of Menippean satire and of the carnivalization of literature. Moreover Nänny suggests that such carnivalization is central to modernist literature as a whole:

> It may even be said that one of the major thrusts of 20th century literature (and art) seems to have been toward a kind of recarnivalization in Joyce's and Eliot's wake. . . . The chief modernist works, Joyce's *Ulysses,* Eliot's *The Waste Land,* and Pound's *Cantos* as well as so much post-modern writing may hence be seen as literary expressions of a

> pervasive carnivalization of 20th century consciousness and culture, expressions whose strongly ludic character demands an active participation in their carnivalesque games. ("*Waste*" 534–535)

Nänny's suggestion that a resurgence in carnivalesque energies is central to developments in postmodernist as well as modernist literature is echoed by William Spanos, who includes lengthy citations from Bakhtin to illustrate his argument that postmodernism participates not only in our contemporary historical moment but also in a long carnivalesque literary tradition. For Spanos, postmodernism is the latest incarnation of "a certain marginalized (or colonized) literature informed by the polyglotic 'parodic-travestying' impulse of the lowly folk imagination, a literature that, in the name of contemporaneity . . . has existed from the beginnings of Western civilization" ("Postmodern" 193–194).

Bakhtin's notion of the carnivalesque is intimately connected with his studies of genre. In particular (in his important study of Dostoevsky), Bakhtin associates carnivalesque energies particularly with the genre of Menippean satire. For Bakhtin, Menippean satire contains by its very nature a diverse collection of competing styles and voices, it tends to interrogate and satirize various philosophical ideas (usually in a highly irreverent way), and it is centrally informed by the energies that he refers to as "carnivalesque." The first and most fundamental characteristic of the carnival (and therefore of Menippean satire) is its ambivalence—different viewpoints, different worlds, may be mutually and simultaneously present without any privileging of one over the other so that the different worlds can comment on each other in a dialogic way. Bakhtin's emphasis on ambivalence in the carnival and in Menippean satire is highly appropriate given that his own highly dialogic writing style is informed by a consistent ambivalence. But this ambivalence is not evidence of simple indecision on Bakhtin's part. Philosophically dialogism implies a fundamental rejection of the either-or logic of the Aristotelian tradition in favor of a richly multiple reconceptualization of the notion of truth itself. This new notion of truth implies, among other things, that we should avoid coming to final conclusions about Bakhtin's work; faced with a choice of competing interpretations, we must always choose both, as difficult and unsatisfying as that might be to our monological habits of thought.

Of course, the complex nature of Bakhtin's own dialogic discourse sometimes leads to conflicting interpretations of his work, especially by critics who do not sufficiently appreciate the "both-and" nature of dialogic thought. Discussions of Bakhtin's relationship to Marxism (usefully reviewed by Robert Young and by Don Bialostosky) are illustrative of this phenomenon, with some critics reading Bakhtin as an essentially Marxist thinker and others seeing him as a fundamentally anti-Marxist thinker. Marxist critics such as Fredric Jameson, Tony Bennett, and Raymond Williams have openly endorsed at least some aspects of Bakhtin's work and have attempted to appropriate it for their own work. Marxist critics such as Eagleton have been more ambivalent toward Bakhtin's work, whereas critics such as Lodge and Todorov have figured Bakhtin as liberal bourgeois thinker.

David Patterson and Clark and Holquist see Bakhtin as a fundamentally religious (and anti-Marxist) thinker, whereas Morson and Emerson insist that Bakhtin's thought is far too complex to be assimilated under any single rubric. This issue is complicated by the fact that the disputed texts are clearly more Marxist in their orientation than are the other texts in the Bakhtin canon, but Bakhtin's uneasy relationship with Stalinism and the double-sided nature of all of his thought add to the complication.

Bakhtin's own account of literary history identifies Menippean satire—as exemplified in the work of Rabelais and others—as the major generic site of carnivalesque energies in literature only until the eighteenth century, when this role shifts to the emerging novel. But Bakhtin's work on Menippean satire is inseparable from his work on the novel because the types of novels he privileges are still centrally informed by Menippean energies. For him, the novel is a special genre, unique in its contemporaneity, its contact with everyday life, its close connection with extraliterary genres. Bakhtin's theory of the novel is founded on language; he argues that the distinguishing feature of the novel as a genre is the way it incorporates the various "languages" of society into its own discourse: "Diversity of voices and heteroglossia enter the novel and organize themselves within it into a structured artistic system. This constitutes the distinguishing feature of the novel as a genre" (*Dialogic* 300). But the languages in a novel have specific sociopolitical connotations as well, each language representing an entire world view. Bakhtin's key concept of heteroglossia refers not just to the words used by different groups in society but to the entire social, cultural, and ideological context of the novel. In the novel, the languages interact in a dynamic way, typically with the development of an opposition between "high" languages and "low." The dialogue in the novel thus dramatizes ideological struggles in the society as a whole.

Bakhtin defines two different lines of "stylistic development" in the history of the novel. He associates the "First Line" novel with attempts to suppress heteroglossia and to establish a unified and monological literary voice. The "Second Line" novel openly embraces heteroglossia and draws its most important energies directly from the diversity of styles, discourses, and ideologies that inform society as a whole. The Second Line novel, related to Menippean satire, strives for "generic, encyclopedic comprehensiveness," including the heavy use of inserted genres, which "serve the basic purpose of introducing heteroglossia *into* the novel, of introducing an era's many and diverse languages." This kind of novel embodies the view that "the novel must be a full and comprehensive reflection of its era. . . . The novel must represent all the social and ideological voices of its era, that is, all the era's languages that have any claim to being significant; the novel must be a microcosm of heteroglossia" (110–111).

It is this ability to incorporate heteroglossia—which places the Second Line novel in close contact with contemporary reality—that gives the novel its special ability to grow and evolve in time, responding to and participating in processes of historical change. Rather than functioning according to rigidly defined principles, the novel by its very nature challenges its own principles and thereby remains ever new, ever in touch with contemporary reality. To maintain this dynamic adaptive ability, the novel must continually challenge predefined notions of what it should be. It is therefore an inherently antiauthoritarian genre, "a genre that is ever questing, ever examining itself and subjecting its established forms to review. Such, indeed, is the only possibility open to a genre that structures itself in a zone of direct contact with developing reality" (39). The novel as a genre is "both critical and self-critical, one fated to revise the fundamental concepts of literariness and poeticalness dominant at the time" (10).

Bakhtin's understanding of dialogism extends to his vision of the human self as a dialogic phenomenon. This vision often recurs in Bakhtin's work, though it is probably presented most explicitly by Voloshinov in the disputed texts *Marxism and the Philosophy of Language* and *Freudianism.* In the latter, an extended neo-Marxist polemic against Freudian psychoanalysis, Voloshinov describes the Freudian psyche as a sort of formalist self-contained entity and opposes to that notion a model in which subjectivity is generated through social experiences with language. Voloshinov dispenses with Freud's vision of psychological depth, replacing the notion of separate conscious and unconscious minds with that of a continuum of "official" and "unofficial" consciousnesses, both operating according to similar linguistic principles. Official consciousness is reflected in outward speech, whereas unofficial consciousness expresses itself through "inner speech," which is still a thoroughly social phenomenon: "Every utterance is *the product of the interaction between speakers* and the product of the broader context of the whole complex *social situation* in which the utterance emerges. . . . Nothing changes at all if, instead of outward speech, we are dealing with inner speech. Inner speech, too, assumes a listener and is oriented in its constitution toward that listener" (79).

This dialogic model of selfhood thus posits a model in which speech is irreducibly social and subjectivity is meaningless apart from intersubjectivity: "Consciousness becomes consciousness only once it has been filled with ideological (semiotic) content, consequently, only in the process of social interaction" (*Marxism* 11). The psyche is not a *thing* that exists internally in an individual so much as an *event* that occurs in the process of intersubjective relations: "By its very existential nature, the subjective psyche is to be localized somewhere between the organism and the outside world, on the *borderline* separating these two spheres of reality" (26). Voloshinov's notion of "inner speech" recalls the psycholinguistic theories of Lev Vygotsky. In fact, the models of subjectivity of Vygotsky and of the Bakhtin circle converge at many points. Emerson outlines some of the similarities between the two thinkers and suggests that Vygotsky's *Thought and Language* "can be read as an important predecessor and perhaps even as clinical underpinning to Bakhtin's philosophy of language" (27).

This vision of subjectivity as a social phenomenon is often reflected in Bakhtin's discussions of characterization in the novel, especially in *Problems of Dostoevsky's Poetics.* According to Bakhtin, in a sense Dostoevsky's characters have virtually no psychological depth, despite his reputation as a psychological novelist. Rather than attempt to probe the psychological depths of his characters,

Dostoevsky stays on the surface, showing us the self-conscious images of his characters as they believe others perceive them externally. With a Dostoevsky character, "we see not who he is, but *how* he is conscious of himself; our act of artistic visualization occurs not before the reality of the hero, but before a pure function of his awareness of that reality" (49). What we see of any Dostoevsky character is determined at least partially by the Other: Dostoevsky does not create and describe fully formed and finalized characters; instead he lets those characters evolve in dialogue with their author and with the other characters. Dostoevsky's novels are thus "polyphonic" because they are so fundamentally informed by dialogues among multiple consciousnesses.

Bakhtin's theories of the dialogic nature of language (and especially of dialogism in the novel) have been applied by numerous critics to a wide variety of literature. Not surprisingly, some of the best Bakhtin-inspired studies of the novel have involved work on nineteenth-century Russian literature, as in Holquist's important *Dostoevsky and the Novel* and Morson's *Hidden in Plain View,* on Tolstoy. Again, however, Bakhtin's work has proved especially important to scholars of modern literature. Booker and Juraga, for example, read modern and contemporary Russian fiction from a Bakhtinian perspective. Ann Herrmann, meanwhile, employs Bakhtin's notion of dialogism to read the work of the modernist Virginia Woolf and the postmodernist Christa Wolf from a feminist perspective; critics such as Aaron Fogel and Mark A. Wollaeger use Bakhtin to illuminate the work of Joseph Conrad. David Lodge uses Bakhtin to read contemporary writers such as Fay Weldon and Martin Amis, as well as modern writers such as D. H. Lawrence and James Joyce. Indeed Bakhtin's work has proved especially suggestive for reading the work of Joyce, with its complex mixtures of discourses and intertextual references. R. B. Kershner uses Bakhtin to read the dialogic relationship between Joyce's early work and his contemporary popular culture, whereas Michael Patrick Gillespie uses Bakhtin's theories of dialogism and polyphony to describe the multiplicity of voices in Joyce's fiction, especially the participation of the reader in the creation of that polyvocality.

In *Joyce, Bakhtin, and the Literary Tradition,* Booker employs Bakhtin's notion of dialogism to explore the relationship between Joyce's texts and a number of important literary predecessors ranging from Homer to Dostoevsky. This use of Bakhtin's work in a study of literary history indicates the way that Bakhtin's conception of the novel is centrally informed by his understanding of the fundamental historicity of all language use, a historicity that the novel, as an ever-evolving genre, draws on in unique ways. Bakhtin's attempts to establish a historical poetics are centrally informed by a strong recognition that all uses of language are inevitably colored by textual traces from the past, meaning that all language has been used before and continues to carry the resonances of former use, so any utterance involves a dialogic mixture of meanings and intentions. Only the biblical Adam spoke a language untainted by the speech of others because he had no predecessors. Henceforth "our speech, that is, all our utterances (including creative works), is filled with others' words, varying degrees of otherness or varying degrees of 'our-own-ness,' varying degrees of awareness and detachment. These words of others carry with them their own expression, their own evaluative tone, which we assimilate, rework, and re-accentuate" (*Speech* 89).

But despite his consistent emphasis on the historicity of language, Bakhtin appears to show very different attitudes toward time and history at different points in his career. In *Rabelais and His World,* he depicts the carnival as a kind of time-out from history, a suspension of the normal flow of events in which the strange and marvelous temporarily become the rule of the day. It is largely for this reason that Morson and Emerson see the book as an aberration in Bakhtin's career—the bulk of his work is concerned with placing humanity in time and history, whereas the Rabelais book involves a removal, however momentary, from history. In short, *Rabelais* is to Bakhtin's career very much what the carnival itself is to history—a sudden disruption in the ordinary course of affairs. But for Bakhtin, the disjunctive nature of time in the Rabelaisian carnival actually shows an engagement with history because it corresponds to an intense sense of cultural crisis in Rabelais's early Renaissance historical context. Thus Bakhtin suggests that the removal from history implied in his discussion of the carnival in *Rabelais* is intended to provide a perspective from which history can be understood and engaged more profoundly. Similarly we could argue that the very different treatment of time and history in *Rabelais* provides an important perspective from which to view the treatment of these issues in his other work.

In point of fact, each of Bakhtin's major treatments of literature describes a very different vision of time and history. In *Rabelais,* Bakhtin emphasizes the carnival as a temporary and atypical removal from normal historical time. In *Problems of Dostoevsky's Poetics,* Bakhtin insists on the powerfully dynamic nature of the Dostoevskian text, in which the reader is propelled forward by an intense sense of temporal movement. But this temporal flow is jerky, moving forward discontinuously by starts and stops as one moment of crisis leads unpredictably to another. Dostoevsky, according to Bakhtin, visualizes history not as a smooth progression but as a series of stages, each of which is the "cross-section of a single moment" (28). What we have of Bakhtin's work on Johann Goethe shows still another vision of history and temporality. In Goethe's texts, according to Bakhtin, time flows smoothly and continuously, with change occurring gradually and steadily. Of all authors, in fact, it is Goethe who has the most profound sense of history and of the mutual involvement of time and space in human events:

> Everything—from an abstract idea to a piece of rock on the bank of a stream—bears the stamp of time, is saturated with time, and assumes its form and meaning in time. Therefore, everything is intensive in Goethe's world; it contains no inanimate, immobile, petrified places, no immutable background that does not participate in action and emergence (in events), no decorations or sets. On the other hand, this time, in all its essential aspects, is localized in concrete space, imprinted on it. In Goethe's world there are no events, plots, or temporal motifs that are not related in an essential way to the particular spatial place of their occurrence. (*Speech* 42)

A central element of Bakhtin's focus on history involves his notion of the "chronotope" of a literary work—literally, the sense of time and space (and their relation) that informs the work. Like all of Bakhtin's key terms, the chronotope is not merely a formal literary device but also a reflection of deep-seated attitudes in the society at large. For Bakhtin, the most fundamental characteristic of a society is the way it thinks about space and time, and this characteristic is inevitably reflected in one way or another in that society's literature. Of course, some writers have a stronger chronotopic sense than others—Goethe's imagination is, for example, unusually chronotopic.

Bakhtin's emphasis on the chronotope is closely related to his emphasis on genre: "The chronotope in literature has an intrinsic *generic* significance. It can even be said that it is precisely the chronotope that defines genre and generic distinctions" (*Dialogic* 84-85). Bakhtin notes that the chronotope is of obvious importance to narrative structure. Chronotopes are, he argues, "the organizing centers for the fundamental narrative events of the novel. The chronotope is the place where the knots of narrative are tied and untied" (250). At the same time, Bakhtin emphasizes that multiple chronotopes can inform a single work and that these can interact dialogically. Such mixtures of chronotopes are especially obvious in works (like the best novels) that openly incorporate different genres that might themselves typically be characterized by very different chronotopes.

As of yet, Bakhtin's notion of the chronotope—and his meditations on history in general—has been less widely used by literary critics than have his theories of dialogism and the carnivalesque. Nevertheless Clark draws on Bakhtin's discussion of the chronotope to illuminate important elements of socialist realism; Booker and Juraga rely extensively on Bakhtin's thoughts on history and the chronotope in their discussions of modern Russian fiction. Moreover this aspect of Bakhtin's work promises to receive more attention in the future, and we can expect more critics to look to Bakhtin's discussions of historicity to illuminate the work of specific authors and to meditate on fundamental questions of literary history and the relationship between that history and the social and political history in which it is embedded. Meanwhile Bakhtin's entire corpus of work remains influential for a wide spectrum of critics, who continue to use Bakhtin's work to generate valuable new insights into literature, language, and culture, even as they attempt to come to grips with the complex, dialogic nature of Bakhtin's thought.

BIBLIOGRAPHY

Introductory Works

Clark, Katerina, and Michael Holquist. *Mikhail Bakhtin.* Cambridge, Mass.: Belknap, 1984. An extremely informative critical biography that includes discussions of Bakhtin's major works as well as an outline of his life.

Holquist, Michael. *Dialogism: Bakhtin and His World.* London: Routledge, 1990.
A useful discussion of Bakhtin's major concept of dialogism.

Morson, Gary Saul, and Caryl Emerson. *Mikhail Bakhtin: Creation of a Prosaics.* Stanford, Calif.: Stanford UP, 1990.
Probably the best critical overview of Bakhtin's work.

Stam, Robert. *Subversive Pleasures: Bakhtin, Cultural Criticism, and Film.* Baltimore, Md.: Johns Hopkins UP, 1989.
An interesting application of Bakhtin's theories, especially the notion of the carnival. Includes a useful introductory survey of Bakhtin's work.

Selected Other Works

Bakhtin, M. M. *Art and Answerability: Early Philosophical Essays.* Ed. Michael Holquist and Vadim Liapunov. Trans. Vadim Liapunov and Kenneth Brostrum. Austin: U of Texas P, 1990.

———. *The Dialogic Imagination.* Ed. Michael Holquist. Trans. Caryl Emerson and Michael Holquist. Austin: U of Texas P, 1981.

———. *Problems of Dostoevsky's Poetics.* Trans. and ed. Caryl Emerson. Minneapolis: U of Minnesota P, 1984.

———. *Rabelais and His World.* Trans. Helene Iswolsky. Bloominton: Indiana UP, 1984.

———. Preface to *Resurrection,* by Leo Tolstoy. Trans. Caryl Emerson. Reprinted in *Rethinking Bakhtin: Extensions and Challenges,* ed. Gary Saul Morson and Caryl Emerson, 237-257. Evanston, Ill.: Northwestern UP, 1989.

———. *Speech Genres and Other Late Essays.* Trans. Vern W. McGhee. Ed. Caryl Emerson and Michael Holquist. Austin: U of Texas P, 1986.

Bakhtin, M. M./P. N. Medvedev. *The Formal Method in Literary Scholarship: A Critical Introduction to Sociological Poetics.* Trans. Albert J. Wehrle. Cambridge, Mass.: Harvard UP, 1985.

Bell, Robert H. *Jocoserious Joyce: The Fate of Folly in "Ulysses."* Ithaca, N.Y.: Cornell UP, 1991.

Bennett, Tony. *Formalism and Marxism.* London: Methuen, 1979.

Bernstein, Michael André. *Bitter Carnival: Ressentiment and the Abject Hero.* Princeton, N.J.: Princeton UP, 1992.

Berrong, Richard M. *Rabelais and Bakhtin: Popular Culture in "Gargantua and Pantagruel."* Lincoln: U of Nebraska P, 1986.

Bialostosky, Don. "Dialogic Criticism." In *Contemporary Literary Theory,* ed. G. Douglas Atkins and Laura Morrow, 214-228. Amherst: U of Massachusetts P, 1989.

Booker, M. Keith. *Joyce, Bakhtin, and the Literary Tradition: Toward a Comparative Cultural Poetics.* Ann Arbor: U of Michigan P, forthcoming.

———. *Techniques of Subversion in Modern Literature: Transgression, Abjection, and the Carnivalesque.* Gainesville: U of Florida P, 1991.

———. *Vargas Llosa among the Postmodernists: Commitment and Ambivalence.* Gainesville: UP of Florida, 1994.

Booker, M. Keith, and Dubravka Juraga. *Bakhtin, Stalin, and Modern Russian Fiction: Carnival, Dialogism, and History.* Westport, Conn.: Greenwood, forthcoming.

Bristol, Michael. *Carnival and Theatre: Plebeian Culture and the Structure of Authority in Renaissance England.* London: Methuen, 1985.

Clark, Katerina. "Political History and Literary Chronotope: Some Soviet Case Studies." In *Literature and History: Theoretical Problems and Russian Case Studies,* ed. Gary Saul Morson, 230-246. Stanford, Calif.: Stanford UP, 1986.

Cook, Jon. "Carnival and The Canterbury Tales." In *Medieval Literature: Criticism, Ideology, and History,* ed. David Aers, 169-191. Brighton: Harvester P, 1986.

de Man, Paul. *The Resistance to Theory.* Minneapolis: U of Minnesota P, 1986.

Eagleton, Terry. *Walter Benjamin: Towards a Revolutionary Criticism.* London: Verso, 1981.

———. "Wittgenstein's Friends." *New Left Review* 135 (1982): 64-90.

Emerson, Caryl. "The Outer Word and Inner Speech: Bakhtin, Vygotsky, and the Internalization of Language." In *Bakhtin: Essays and Dialogues on His Work,* ed. Gary Saul Morson, 21-40. Chicago: U of Chicago P, 1986.

Fogel, Aaron. *Coercion to Speak: Conrad's Poetics of Dialogue.* Cambridge, Mass.: Harvard UP, 1985.

Gardiner, Michael. *The Dialogics of Critique: M. M. Bakhtin and the Theory of Ideology.* London: Routledge, 1992.

Herrmann, Anne. *The Dialogic and Difference: "An/Other Woman" in Virginia Woolf and Christa Wolf.* New York: Columbia UP, 1989.

Hirschkop, Ken, ed. *Bakhtin and Cultural Theory.* Manchester: Manchester UP, 1989.

Holquist, Michael. *Dostoevsky and the Novel.* Princeton, N.J.: Princeton UP, 1977.

———. Prologue to *Rabelais and His World,* by Mikhail Bakhtin, xiii-xxiii. Bloomington: Indiana UP, 1984.

Jameson, Fredric. *The Political Unconscious: Narrative as a Socially Symbolic Act.* Ithaca, N.Y.: Cornell UP, 1981.

Kershner, R. B. *Joyce, Bakhtin, and Popular Literature: Chronicles of Disorder.* Chapel Hill: U of North Carolina P, 1989.

Kinser, Samuel. *Rabelais's Carnival: Text, Context, and Metatext.* Berkeley and Los Angeles: U of California P, 1990.

Kristeva, Julia. *Desire in Language: A Semiotic Approach to Literature and Art.* New York: Columbia UP, 1980.

Lodge, David. *After Bakhtin: Essays on Fiction and Criticism.* London: Routledge, 1990.

Morson, Gary Saul. *Hidden in Plain View: Narrative and Creative Potentials in "War and Peace."* Stanford, Calif.: Stanford UP, 1987.

Nänny, Max. "Ezra Pound and the Menippean Tradition." *Paideuma* 11 (1982): 395-405.

———. "*The Waste Land:* A Menippean Satire?" *English Studies* 66 (1985): 526-535.

Patterson, David. *Literature and Spirit: Essays on Bakhtin and His Contemporaries.* Lexington: UP of Kentucky, 1988.

Spanos, William V. "Postmodern Literature and Its Occasion: Retrieving the Preterite Middle." In *Repetitions: The Postmodern Occasion in Literature and Culture,* 189-276. Baton Rouge: Louisiana State UP, 1987.

Stallybrass, Peter, and Allon White. *The Politics and Poetics of Transgression.* Ithaca, N.Y.: Cornell UP, 1986.

Titunik, I. R. "The Baxtin Problem: Concerning Katerina Clark and Michael Holquist's *Mikhail Bakhtin." Slavic and East European Journal* 30.1 (1986): 91-95.

Todorov, Tzvetan. *Mikhail Bakhtin: The Dialogical Principle.* Trans. Wlad Godzich. Minneapolis: U of Minnesota P, 1984.

Voloshinov, V. N. *Freudianism: A Critical Sketch.* Trans. I. R. Titunik. Ed. I. R. Titunik and Neal H. Bruss. Bloomington: Indiana UP, 1987.

———. *Marxism and the Philosophy of Language.* Trans. Ladislav Matejka and I. R. Titunik. Cambridge, Mass.: Harvard UP, 1986.

Vygotsky, Lev. *Thought and Language.* Trans. Alex Kozulin. Cambridge, Mass.: MIT P, 1986.

Williams, Raymond. *Marxism and Literature.* Oxford: Oxford UP, 1977.

Wollaeger, Mark A. *Joseph Conrad and the Fictions of Skepticism.* Stanford, Calif.: Stanford UP, 1990.

Yaeger, Patricia. *Honey-Mad Women: Emancipatory Strategies in Women's Writing.* New York: Columbia UP, 1988.

Young, Robert. "Back to Bakhtin." *Cultural Critique* 2 (Winter 1985–1986): 71–92.

chapter **8**

Foucauldian Literary Criticism

The French thinker Michel Foucault (1926–1984) has emerged in the decade of the 1990s as one of the most influential (if controversial) figures in American intellectual life. Foucault made important contributions in a number of fields, including psychology, history, sociology, linguistics, and philosophy, in addition to literary theory and criticism. And his work has been widely influential on other workers in all of these fields, partly because Foucault was a brilliant and controversial thinker who frequently mounted radical challenges to accepted ideas in all of these areas, but perhaps even more because Foucault's approach was an exemplary of way of doing "intellectual work." Indeed the widespread fascination with Foucault's life and work can be seen in the fact that no less than three full-length biographies appeared in English in the early 1990s.

Foucault's understanding of society as a complex field in which various discourses compete for power has important implications for a number of disciplines, not the least of which is literary studies, for which Foucault's work has provided important insights into the relationship between literature and society. The range of Foucault's influence can be gauged by the number of otherwise quite diverse literary scholars who have turned to his work for inspiration. Foucault's influence on literary studies is most clear in the recent turn from criticism of specific texts to "cultural studies," or the examination of the participation of various kinds of texts in the broad phenomenon of culture. Particularly prominent in this turn to cultural studies is the recent rise of the new historicism, an approach to literature as a cultural practice that is described in the next chapter of this book.

But Foucault's influence goes well beyond new historicist critics. William Cain, after condemning most recent literary theory for failing to get beyond the basic assumptions of the New Criticism, suggests that we seek a radically new critical practice that can get beyond those assumptions. For Cain, Foucault's focus on "systems of thought" and "discursive practices" rather than individual texts or accepted canons can provide "guidance and inspiration," in this project (256). Even Terry Eagleton, who has sometimes been highly critical of Foucault and who works from the committed perspective of Marxism, with which Foucault had an uneasy and sometimes antagonistic relationship, ultimately identifies Foucault's work as an important model for literary scholars. He thus concludes his *Literary Theory* with a call for "political criticism." This criticism should begin with the recognition that "literature," far from involving a special, transcendent kind of language use that sets it apart from the social and political world, is in fact simply a name for "certain kinds of writing within the whole field of what Michel Foucault has called 'discursive practices,' and that if anything is to be an object of study it is this whole field of practices rather than just those sometimes rather obscurely labelled 'literature'" (205). A similar conclusion is reached from the very different poststructuralist perspective of Catherine Belsey, who in *Critical Practice* elaborates an approach to literature that draws extensively on such thinkers as Roland Barthes and Jacques Derrida but that ultimately concludes with the very Foucauldian insight that "criticism can no longer be isolated from other areas of knowledge" (144). Gerald Graff, who earlier was highly critical of textualist approaches such as Belsey's, nevertheless comes to base his later work on a similar insight. In *Professing Literature* (an institutional history of literary criticism and pedagogy that recalls Foucault's work but from a more conventional liberal humanist perspective), Graff acknowledges Foucault's influence on his conception of his project: "I echo Foucault in looking at the way seemingly neutral, disciplinary classifications and boundaries actually constitute the fields they organize" (11).

Foucault's approach is radically unconventional, and much of his work can be described as an extended criticism of the conformism and vulgarity of the French bourgeoisie. To a first approximation, his project can be described as the development of a highly self-conscious history of thought involving a study not only of the evolution of various ideas but also of the constitution of those ideas by complex social and institutional forces—and by the work of historians like himself. Foucault's characteristic practice involves an exploration of the historical development of ideas or concepts that have come to be taken as common sense or absolute fact in which he demonstrates that these ideas or concepts in fact arose in response to specific historical circumstances. Importantly influenced by both the innovative French historians known as the "*Annales* school" (epitomized by the work of Fernand Braudel) and the histories of science produced by French thinkers such as Gaston Bachelard and Georges Canguilhem, Foucault's historical research reflects a distinctively nonnarrative vision of history that eschews the development of linear cause-effect explanations of historical processes. Instead Foucault pursues what he himself refers to as "archaeology" or "genealogy." As Karlis Racevskis notes, the archaeology metaphor is appropriate because Foucault is similar to an archaeologist in the way he digs through materials from the past in search of clues that lie beneath the surface appearance of history, thus seeking to "reconstruct the processes through which human subjects have made themselves into objects of knowledge ("Genealogical" 230). Meanwhile genealogy (derived from Friedrich Nietzsche's *Genealogy of Morals*) refers to Foucault's realization that the present is a product of history and that to understand the present, we need to know as much as possible about the past that has shaped us. Without establishing narrative connections, Foucault thus explores the historical antecedents of ideas and discourses from the present, much as a genealogist traces the lineage of a family.

In *Madness and Civilization* (an abridged translation of *Histoire de la folie,* first published in 1961), Foucault looks at the distinction between madness and reason and concludes that this distinction, at least as we know it, is the product of specific historical occurrences in seventeenth-century Europe. Foucault argues here that societies historically tend to define "proper" or accepted ideas or behavior through opposition to excluded images of Otherness. The central image of this Otherness in the Middle Ages, he argues, was the leper, whose abject physical afflictions provided a stark contrast to the notion of spiritual escape from physicality that was central to the ideology of medieval Catholicism. In the seventeenth century, however, leprosy became less widespread as a health problem, while the focus of official power in general began to shift from the bodies to the minds of the subject population. With the beginnings of Enlightenment science, reason and rationality came to replace spiritual purity as the central paradigms of European society. As a result, the madman came to replace the leper as the chief image of Otherness in the popular European imagination, with the institution of the insane asylum arising to supplant the leper colony as the locus of containment of the excluded Other.

Madness and Civilization thus demonstrates the historical circumstances in which the opposition between reason and madness came to be accepted as one of the fundamental dichotomies of Western civilization. Foucault further argues that this opposition is not nearly as simple as it is generally thought to be. For example, he notes that an excessive emphasis on reason may contain many of the elements of madness and that madness frequently seems informed by entirely rigorous structures of logic that simply happen to be different from the structures that inform Enlightenment science (95-96). Indeed for Foucault, the very insistence on a strict polar opposition between madness and reason is evidence that Enlightenment thinkers remained troubled by the continuing existence of madness as an alien force in the Age of Reason, an existence that reminded them of "the precariousness of a reason that can at any moment be compromised, and definitively, by madness" (211).

If the rejection of madness as irreducibly alien to rational experience is, as Foucault suggests, a central means by which rationality defines itself, then the suggestion that rationality and madness are not in fact easily distinguished undermines one of the principal foundations of official modern Western civilization. In *The Birth of the Clinic* (a translation of *Naissance de la clinique,* 1963), Foucault continues his assault on some of the most cherished institutions of the Enlightenment tradition. Where *Madness and Civilization* argues that mental illness is constituted by specific historically conditioned discourses, *The Birth of the Clinic* does the same for physical illness, charting the ways in which the Enlightenment science of the eighteenth century created many of our conceptions about disease—and indeed about the nature of the human body itself. A fairly technical book that has thus far appealed mostly to historians of medicine, *The Birth of the Clinic* nevertheless displays Foucault's typical iconoclastic style by challenging the belief that the history of medical science is the story of a constant and monotonic progress toward better and better understanding of the "truth" of the human body. Instead Foucault shows that the eighteenth-century turn to visions of the body as a physical machine subject to visual inspection and mapping is conditioned by that century's general fascination with scientific observation, classification, and mapping. Moreover he argues that the findings of modern medicine are greatly determined by the discourse of rationality in which we describe the body and its ailments. Indeed the development of eighteenth-century science is part of a quite general Enlightenment shift from religion to science as the principal locus of knowledge and truth in the modern consciousness: "The locus in which knowledge is formed is no longer the pathological garden where God distributed the species, but a generalized medical consciousness, diffused in time and space, open and mobile, linked to each individual existence, as well as to the collective life of the nation, ever alert to the endless domain in which illness betrays, in its various aspects, its great, solid form" (31).

Foucault himself describes *The Birth of the Clinic* as "an attempt to apply a method in the confused, under-structured, and ill-structured domain of the history if ideas" (195). In *The Order of Things* (a translation of *Les Mots et les choses,* 1966), Foucault broadens this attempt to describe the discursive conditioning of knowledge, studying the conditioning of thought in linguistics, natural history, and economics from the Renaissance to the present. In this book, which first propelled Foucault to prominence in French intellectual circles, Foucault essentially seeks to develop a full-scale structuralist model of history, despite the fact that structuralism is typically seen as applicable only to the study of systems at a given point in time ("synchronic" systems), not to the description of systems that change with time ("diachronic" systems). Foucault attempts to solve this dilemma by separating history into different periods, or phases, each of which can then be treated separately by structuralist methods. Each of these periods, Foucault suggests, is governed by a common prevailing *episteme,* or characteristic attitude toward knowledge and the ways it is obtained. Within a given *episteme,* only certain kinds of thought and activity consistent with that *episteme* are generally conceivable, though historical developments (which Foucault does not attempt to describe) will eventually lead to a change in the *episteme* itself, thus initiating a new era in the history of knowledge.

Foucault argues in *The Order of Things* that during the rule of the *episteme* that prevailed during the Renaissance (through the sixteenth century), all knowledge is conditioned by a belief in the fundamental interconnectedness and resemblance of all aspects of creation—because everything is created by the same God and is therefore endowed with the same fundamental defining spirit. In the case of linguistics, for example, words and things are connected in the direct, mystical way suggested by the Christian notion of the Word of God. Foucault argues that Western thinkers from the Stoics to the sixteenth century accepted a ternary model of the sign in which signifier and signified are held together by a third element, or "conjuncture," that effects a connection between words and things based on resemblance (42). This conception of language—coming after the punishment inflicted at Babel—lacks the absolute connection between words and things envisioned in the biblical story of Adam, though Foucault does suggest that modern Hebrew still "contains, as if in the form of fragments, the marks of the original name-giving" (36). But the separation between words and things becomes more radical in the subsequent "classical" *episteme,* which involves a shift to the notion of "taxonomy," or categorization, as the fundamental technique of knowledge. In linguistics, this shift involves a further movement away from the Adamic language, a change (in the seventeenth century) to a binary conception of signification in which words and things are divorced and language represents—but is not mystically connected to—reality. What Foucault sees as the "modern" *episteme* involves a nineteenth-century shift toward history as the fundamental context within which all knowledge is produced, leading in linguistics to a shift from representation to signification in which language takes on a life of its own apart from its representational functions. Importantly, however, Foucault finds that these changes in the discursive conditioning of linguistic thought are paralleled by very similar changes in the fields of economics and natural history, leading him to conclude that the discursive conditioning of knowledge in any given *episteme* is quite broad and applies to a wide range of disciplines.

Foucault ends *The Order of Things* with a discussion of the way changes in *episteme* have conditioned our fundamental understanding of what it means to be human. Of course, if radical changes in *episteme* have occurred in the past, then they may occur in the future as well. Foucault thus suggests (in one of his most famous, if not notorious, proclamations) that the very concept of "man" may soon become obsolete. This concept, he argues, is a relatively recent invention, a product of habits of thinking that are central to the modern *episteme* but that may now be drawing to a close with the coming of a new era. Building on Nietzsche's announcement of the death of God, Foucault proposes that we may now be on the brink of a new *episteme* that will bring the death of man as well by ending the historical "arrangements" that made the concept of man appear: "If those arrangements were to disappear as they appeared, if some event of which we can at the moment do no more than sense the possibility—without knowing either what its form will be or what it promises—were to cause them to crumble, as the ground of Classical thought did, at the end of the eighteenth century, then one can certainly wager that man would be erased, a face drawn in sand at the edge of the sea" (387).

To some extent, Foucault's apocalyptic announcement of the end of man simply participates in a decentering of the self that is common to all structuralist thought. In fact, all of Foucault's work through *The Order of Things* is clearly informed by the structuralist methods that were so dominant in French thought at the time, even though Foucault himself consistently insisted that his work had little in common with structuralism. For one thing, even Foucault's earliest work is importantly influenced by the antisystematic philosophy of Nietzsche, an influence that already problematizes Foucault's relation to conventional structuralism. And the extravagantly irreverent Nietzschean rhetoric of passages such as the ending of *The Order of Things* stands in stark contrast to the typically placid, scientific tone of structuralism. Indeed this text can be taken as a sort of limit text that (by confronting structuralism directly with its nemesis, history) marks the beginning of the end of the era of structuralism.

In his next major theoretical text, *The Archaeology of Knowledge* (translated from *L'Archéologie du savoir,* 1969), Foucault produces what is essentially a detailed methodological analysis of his own techniques of historical research. On the surface, *The Archaeology of Knowledge* appears to be Foucault's most technical and systematic work. But several aspects of the text act to destabilize this systematic surface and reveal the book to be the first major text of Foucault's poststructuralist period. *The Archaeology of Knowledge* launches some of Foucault's most trenchant assaults on the Western preoccupation with individualism, a preoccupation he relates directly to the proclivity for continuous, linear narratives of history. In contrast, he describes his own project as an attempt to disrupt such sanguine visions of history by creating historical labyrinths and "opening up underground passages" in history, "finding overhangs that reduce and deform its itinerary" (17). Foucault also rejects subjectivism, ending his introduction to the book with a now-famous declaration of anonymity and repudiation of conventional morality. He writes, he proclaims, "in order to have no face. Do not ask who I am and do not ask me to remain the same: leave it to our bureaucrats and our police to see that our papers are in order. At least spare us their morality when we write" (17).

Paradoxically, however, *The Archaeology of Knowledge,* by focusing largely on discussions of Foucault's own previous work, would seem to be his most subjective text. But these discussions are often highly critical as Foucault seeks to problematize some of the structuralist assumptions of his early work by elaborating his notion of archaeology in a way that radically departs from conventional notions of history and tradition. Perhaps most important, Foucault substantially complicates his earlier treatment of the *episteme* in *The Order of Things* by insisting that the culture of a given period is far too complex to be encompassed by any single conceptual framework: "Nothing would be more false than to see in this analysis of discursive formations an attempt at totalitarian periodization, whereby from a certain moment and for a certain time, everyone would think in the same way, in spite of surface differences, say the same thing, through a polymorphous vocabulary, and produce a sort of great discourse that one could travel over in any direction" (148).

To some extent, Foucault here shows the influence of Louis Althusser's rejection in texts such as *Reading Capital* of conventional "historicism" and especially of the notion of "expressive causality," or the treatment of the cultural phenomena of a given period as expressions of a dominant "spirit of the age." But *The Archaeology of Knowledge* also clearly announces Foucault's turn to poststructuralism in thought and postmodernism in style. Allan Megill suggests, for example, that *The Archaeology of Knowledge* can be read as a sort of parody of René Descartes's *Discourse on Method* (228). Thus "for all its quasi-scientific manner, the work is an attack on science, on the whole idea of an objective knowing. . . . [Foucault] is concerned with an essentially Dionysian project—that of smashing science altogether" (231).

The subsequent texts of Foucault's career, while making important statements about history and society, often continue this parodic mode, and it is generally impossible to appreciate the full thrust of Foucault's later arguments without taking into account both the highly literary nature of his style and the parodic dialogues that he establishes with the texts of important predecessors such as Karl Marx and Sigmund Freud. Foucault's next major text, *Discipline and Punish* (translated from *Surveiller et punir,* 1975), clearly departs from the typical decorum of "scholarly" works by beginning with an extended graphic description of the 1757 public execution of a regicide by drawing and quartering. Foucault then proceeds to describe the historical movement through which such spectacular physical punishments were replaced with more subtle (and seemingly more humane) techniques, especially incarceration. For Foucault, this shift represents not so much a turn toward great humanity as toward greater sufficiency in the control of the general population. He argues that in the modern world power is not less pervasive, but more so. It is, however, more subtle and less visible. Meanwhile the focus on offical power in *Discipline and Punish* announces Foucault's turn from primarily philosophical and epistemological issues to concerns more directly related to politics. Foucault emphasizes, however, from this point on in his career that knowledge and power are inseparable, that "power and knowledge directly imply one another; that there is no power relation without the correlative constitution of a field of knowledge, nor any knowledge that does not presuppose and constitute at the same time power relations" (27).

A key image of *Discipline and Punish,* which is essentially an exploration of the genealogy of the modern prison, involves Jeremy Bentham's Panopticon, an experimental nineteenth-century prison design in which inmates could be kept under observation at all times. For Foucault, this design is symptomatic of a general tendency in modern society in which official power depends more and more on the ability to acquire a constant flow of information about the activities of the subjects of that power. This knowledge-based administration of power finds its model in the medieval Inquisition but reaches new levels through the capabilities of modern technology. With so many modern institutions deriving from this same emphasis on the gathering of knowledge about individuals, Foucault suggests that modern "prisons resemble factories, schools, barracks, hospitals, which all resemble prisons" (228). For Foucault, modern society itself is carceral (that is, prison-like) in nature, and the difference between life inside a prison and that outside is not so large as might first appear. Moreover he suggests that the modern prison system is not designed to eliminate crime but merely to establish a well-identified population of "delinquents" whose crimes can thus be monitored and kept within the limits of acts that are "politically harmless and economically negligible" (278). Among other things, these delinquents provide a marginal group against which society can define itself by exclusion, much along the lines discussed by Foucault in relation to the insane in *Madness and Civilization* or in relation to homosexuals in the later *The History of Sexuality.*

This use of delinquency, or "controlled illegality," is part of a shift in the object of official power from the bodies to the minds of individual subjects, a change from physical force to knowledge as the crucial technique through which such power is exercised. Central to this movement is surveillance, which produces the knowledge necessary for the administration of modern techniques of power. For Foucault, the typical citizen is constantly under surveillance in a way that differs very little in its fundamental nature from the plight of the inmate of the Panopticon. In this sense, Foucault's vision of the modern carceral society recalls dystopian visions such as George Orwell's *1984.* Indeed M. Keith Booker has outlined numerous points of contact between the work of Foucault and the modern dystopian fiction of writers such as Orwell, Yevgeny Zamyatin, and Aldous Huxley. However Foucault differs substantially from most dystopian critics of official power, who tend to describe that power purely in negative, or repressive, terms. That is, they focus on the activities and attitudes that are prevented or made impossible by official power. Foucault, in contrast, emphasizes the productive aspects of power: "We must cease once and for all to describe the effects of power in negative terms: it 'excludes,' it 'represses,' it 'censors,' it 'abstracts,' it 'masks,' it 'conceals.' In fact, power produces; it produces reality; it produces domains of objects and rituals of truth. The individual and the knowledge that may be gained of him belong to this production" (194).

In the carceral, or disciplinary, society of *Discipline and Punish,* individuals are controlled, even produced, by large, invisible structures of official power. Foucault's meditations on the ubiquity of power (reminiscent of Althusser's comments on ideology) are also central to the introductory volume of *The History of Sexuality* (translated from *La Volonté de savoir,* 1976). In this book Foucault continues his meditation on the productive aspects of power. He directly challenges Freud's notion that societies solidify their power by repressing sexual energies, thus tending to make sexuality itself an inherently subversive topic. Foucault argues, pace Freud, that modern society seeks not to repress or even extirpate sexuality but instead to produce and administer sexuality and thus to turn sexual energies to its own advantage. In short, sexuality does not necessarily stand in direct opposition to official power and may in fact stand in direct support of it: "Pleasure and power do not cancel or turn back against one another; they seek out, overlap, and reinforce one another" (48).

For Foucault, sexuality is not so much a matter of natural instinctive impulses as of socially and discursively conditioned responses. He describes sexuality as "an especially dense transfer point for relations of power" (103). In particular, sexuality functions as a focal point for an entire array of discursive practices through which modern society has attempted to constitute the individual as a subject of administrative control. Foucault explores the way discourses such as psychoanalysis participate in a quite general fascination with sexuality as the locus of epistemological inquiry in the late nineteenth century. Such discourses are all informed by the common conviction that sexuality is somehow "harboring a fundamental secret," that it is a dark and hidden area that contains the key to the true self (69). Sexuality, then, is a prime locus for epistemological inquiry into the nature of the self, resulting in an obsession with the sexual that participates in the general Western epistemological drive that Foucault refers to as the "will to knowledge." This will—as with the Enlightenment science of Max Horkheimer and Theodor W. Adorno—consists of an urge to master reality by understanding, ordering, and circumscribing it within the confines of well-behaved human concepts. Knowledge and sexuality are, for Foucault, intimately related, and the will to knowledge involves highly erotic pleasures: "Pleasure in the truth of pleasure, the pleasure of knowing that truth, of discovering and exposing it, the fascination of seeing it and telling it, of captivating and capturing others by it, of confiding it in secret, of luring it out in the open—the specific pleasure of the true discourse on pleasure" (71).

Among other things, this intense concentration on the study of sexuality leads to the development of a discourse of "perversion" through which "perverts" (like the "delinquents" of *Discipline and Punish*) can be identified, thereby making it possible for those exhibiting what have come to be classified as "perverse" sexual behaviors (especially homosexuality) to occupy the position of designated Other formerly reserved for the general category of madness. Like madness, however, homosexuality proved to be a troubling concept against which to define the "normal." Freud's own conclusion that all human beings are to a certain extent bisexual (with "normal" heterosexual genital desire merely representing a more mature stage than "infantile" behaviors such as homosexuality) indicates that the boundary between "normal" heterosexual conduct and "deviant" homosexual behavior was always recognized as permeable and problematic.

In this way, Foucault takes a step toward understanding the prevalence of revulsion toward homosexuality in modern society. He takes still another step in *The Use of Pleasure* (the second volume of *The History of Sexuality,* translated from *L'Usage des plaisirs,* 1984) when he turns to an analysis of the ancient Greeks, an analysis that must be read at least partially as a sort of fable about modern society. This text continues what Foucault would come to call his study of "technologies of the self," or the practices through which human beings are constituted as individuals. In *The Use of Pleasure,* Foucault focuses on the function of sexuality in ancient Greece, arguing that for the Greeks sexuality served as one of several practices through which individuals could exercise a creative freedom in constituting themselves as ethically admirable subjects, "by offering oneself as an example, or by seeking to give one's personal life a form that answers to criteria of brilliance, beauty, nobility, or perfection" (27). In short, Foucault sees the principal goal of Greek life as the making of a life into a masterful work of art for appreciation, admiration, and potential emulation by others, and he sees sexual behavior as a principal means by which this goal might be achieved.

If this figuration of sexuality as a realm of aesthetic practice seems to contradict Foucault's earlier notion of sexuality as a "transfer point for power relations," it is also true that power remains very much at the center of sexuality in his discussion of the Greeks. Foucault emphasizes that an important criteria for judging sexual "style" involved the notion of *enkrateia,* a process of self-mastery in which a person demonstrates control of pleasures and desires through "domination of oneself by oneself" (65). Sexuality thus becomes not a domain of unrestrained passion but a means of demonstrating, through the exercise of moderation and restraint, that a person's passions are under control. Having argued that mastery and control (beginning with self-mastery) were central to the Greek deployment of sexuality, Foucault concludes that for the Greeks "sexual relations—always conceived in terms of the model act of penetration, assuming a polarity that opposed activity and passivity—were seen as being of the same type as the relationship between a superior and a subordinate, an individual who dominates and one who is dominated, one who commands and one who complies, one who vanquishes and one who is vanquished" (215).

One corollary to this attitude is that the freedom actively to author the self as a sort of artistic or literary work belongs only to free males, who define themselves largely in relation to passive groups such as women and slaves. Moreover this model of sexuality as a realm of domination implies that Foucault's model of self-mastery in ancient Greece is closely involved with a notion of mastery of others. Indeed Foucault implies that the Greeks were constantly concerned with questions of power and control, feeling extremely uncomfortable with any situation, political or personal, in which power relations were not clearly defined. The mastery exerted over the self in sexual conduct was viewed as a mirror of the kind of mastery required to govern successfully a household or even a city-state. Sexual relations in which neither partner was clearly dominant were thus metaphorically similar to households or (especially) states with no clear leader. For this reason, homosexuality was a topic of great anxiety for the Greeks, even if homosexuality in ancient Greece lacked the associations with perversion, immorality, and madness that it would later acquire. In a heterosexual relationship, the respective identities of the penetrating and penetrated (and thus the dominating and dominated) partners were presumably given. In a homosexual relationship, however, the relative positions of the two partners were less clear, leading to the development among the Greeks of an entire complex of texts and discourses attempting to establish guidelines according to which such relations could be pursued so that the identity of the dominant partner could remain clear. For example, a typical ancient Greek homosexual partnership would involve an older man (playing the dominant "masculine" role) and a young boy (occupying the passive "female" position).

The element of domination of the Other that thus inheres even in Foucault's seemingly idealized depiction of aesthetic self-constitution in ancient Greece illustrates the highly complex nature of the technologies of the self described by Foucault in his late work. In particular, if the process of creative self-constitution is largely a quest for self-mastery, then this process will always be in danger of degenerating into the short-cut approach of achieving a sense of mastery through the domination of some weaker Other. Conversely the subject in quest of mastery will constantly be in danger of becoming the object of domination by other questing subjects or by more impersonal forces such as institutions and conventions. And the subject who is too successful in dominating himself through self-mastery will paradoxically experience a limitation on his ability to seek mastery by imposing overly rigid constraints on his own behavior.

Terry Eagleton charges Foucault with idealizing the technologies of the self he describes among the ancient Greeks. Eagleton finds this idealization inappropriate, arguing that Foucault attempts to aestheticize social life in ways that obscure the potentially troubling implications of his discussion of intersubjectivity principally as a matter of domination and submission. In Foucault's description of the Greeks, Eagleton charges, "what is gratifying and productive about power, its discipline and dominativeness, is salvaged from political oppressiveness and installed within the self" (*Ideology* 392). It is not at all clear that Foucault idealizes the behavior of the ancient Greeks as Eagleton charges. But Foucault does, in *The Use of Pleasure,* displace power relations from the political to the subjective. In this sense, Foucault repeats a central mechanism of bourgeois society itself, so it is perhaps no surprise that a Marxist such as Eagleton would find this displacement objectionable. But given the frequency with which Foucault writes in a parodic mode, it is possible to see in Foucault's discussion of self-mastery in the Greeks a critical parody of the phenomenon of bourgeois individualism, with its concomitant effacement of mass political action. By this reading, Foucault's overt link between individualism and domination makes clear a process that is typically obscured in bourgeois society.

This reading is also supported by the fact that *The Use of Pleasure* is the second volume of a continuing work. The third volume, *The Care of the Self* (translated from *Le Souci de soi,* 1984), traces the development of many of the ideas from *The Use of Pleasure* into the early Christian period. In Foucault's model, the essentially internal nature of the struggle for self-mastery makes mastery an ethical and aesthetic concept for the ancient Greeks, as opposed to Christianity, in which the focus on Satan leads to a new conception of mastery as defeat of an external enemy. There are obvious political implications in this Christian emphasis on mastery of the Other. In Christianity itself, it leads to an oppressive code-oriented morality based on strict rules of prohibition of certain activities, rules that act to limit and constrain the creativity of the process of self-constitution. And in Western society in general, the notion that personal mastery is to be gained through domination not of oneself but of the Other clearly contributes in an obvious way to the kinds of ideologies of domination that underlie such nineteenth-century practices as imperialism.

Unfortunately Foucault died in 1984 before he could complete *The History of Sexuality* project, which would presumably have traced the development of sexuality at least back to his starting point, in the introductory volume, in Western Europe in the late nineteenth century. But given that Foucault begins his history with bourgeois society at its height, we could reasonably expect Foucault's discussions of the Greeks to have relevance to bourgeois society. We can, in fact, discern a number of similarities between Foucault's description of sexuality as a locus of domination in the ancient Greeks and as a transfer point for power relations in the Victorians. Among other things, Foucault's figuration of Greek self-fashioning as a matter of power and domination, combined with his reminder that Victorian technologies of power involved an intense focus on the inner psychologies of individuals, suggests that bourgeois individualism, far from representing the liberation of the individual from political oppression, actually disguises a process of enslavement. If, as Eagleton believes, Foucault privileges the practices of the Greeks over those of the Victorians, it may well be because he uses the Greeks largely as a foil with which to expose and critique the strategies of domination that are central to the operation of modern bourgeois society.

In addition to his obvious thematic and methodological influence on the development of the new historicism, Foucault's work has been a central inspiration for a number of trends in contemporary criticism. For example, Foucault's emphasis on power relations has been inspirational for a number of critics who have focused on areas (such as postcolonial and African-American culture) where such relations are particularly crucial. Edward Said's *Orientalism,* one of the founding texts in postcolonial studies, draws extensively on Foucault's description of discourses in its delineation of the ideological conditioning of academic knowledge of the Middle East. As outlined in a collection edited by Irene Diamond and Lee Quinby and as shown in studies by Jana Sawicki and by Nina L. Molinaro, Foucault's work proves important for a number of feminist critics. Gender critics such as Eve Kosofsky Sedgwick draw significantly on Foucault's studies of the social construction of sexuality. And studies of American culture and society like those by Quinby and by Daniel O'Hara and studies of popular culture like that by Toby Miller and a collection edited by Chandra Mukerji and Michael Schudson centrally rely on Foucault's work, which remains one of the most vital sources of inspiration for new modes of critical inquiry as the twentieth century draws to a close.

BIBLIOGRAPHY

Introductory Works

Foucault, Michel. *The Foucault Reader.* Ed. Paul Rabinow. New York: Pantheon, 1984.
A useful selection of texts by Foucault, with a good overview of Foucault's thought in Rabinow's introduction.

Gutting, Gary, ed. *The Cambridge Companion to Foucault.* Cambridge: Cambridge UP, 1994.
An excellent anthology of essays on various aspects of Foucault's work.

Racevskis, Karlis. "Genealogical Critique: Michel Foucault and the Systems of Thought." In *Contemporary Literary Theory,* ed. G. Douglas Atkins and Laura Morrow, 229–245. Amherst: U of Massachusetts P, 1989.
A good introduction to the methodology of archaeology and genealogy.

Smart, Barry. *Michel Foucault.* London: Routledge, 1988.
A good (and reasonably accessible) discussion of Foucault's work.

Selected Other Works

Althusser, Louis et al. *Reading Capital.* Trans. Ben Brewster. London: New Left Books, 1970.

Arac, Jonathan, ed. *After Foucault: Humanistic Knowledge, Postmodern Challenges.* New Brunswick, N.J.: Rutgers UP, 1988.

Barrett, Michelle. *The Politics of Truth: From Marx to Foucault.* Stanford, Calif.: Stanford UP, 1991.

Belsey, Catherine. *Critical Practice.* London: Methuen, 1980.

Bernauer, James, and David Rasmusson, eds. *The Final Foucault.* Cambridge, Mass.: MIT P, 1988.

Booker, M. Keith. *The Dystopian Impulse in Modern Literature: Fiction as Social Criticism.* Westport, Conn.: Greenwood, 1994.

Cain, William E. *The Crisis in Criticism: Theory, Literature, and Reform in English Studies.* Baltimore, Md.: Johns Hopkins UP, 1984.

Carroll, David. *Paraesthetics: Foucault, Lyotard, Derrida.* London: Methuen, 1987.

Clark, Michael. *Michel Foucault, an Annotated Bibliography: Tool Kit for a New Age.* New York: Garland, 1983.

Cousins, Mark, and Athar Hussain. *Michel Foucault.* London: Macmillan, 1984.

Eribon, Didier. *Michel Foucault.* Trans. Betsy Wing. Cambridge, Mass.: Harvard UP, 1991.

Deleuze, Gilles. *Foucault.* Minneapolis: U of Minnesota P, 1988.

Dews, Peter. "Foucault and the French Tradition of Historical Epistemology." *History of European Ideas* 14.3 (1992): 347–363.

Diamond, Irene, and Lee Quinby, eds. *Feminism and Foucault: Reflections on Resistance.* Boston: Northeastern UP, 1988.

Docherty, Thomas. "Criticism, History, Foucault." *History of European Ideas* 14.3 (1992): 365–378.

Dreyfus, Hubert L., and Paul Rabinow. *Michel Foucault: Beyond Structuralism and Hermeneutics.* 2d ed. Chicago: U of Chicago P, 1983.

Eagleton, Terry. *The Ideology of the Aesthetic.* Oxford: Basil Blackwell, 1990.

———. *Literary Theory: An Introduction.* Minneapolis: U of Minnesota P, 1983.

Foucault, Michel. *The Archaeology of Knowledge and the Discourse on Language.* Trans. A. M. Sheridan Smith. New York: Pantheon, 1972.

———. *The Birth of the Clinic: An Archaeology of Medical Perception.* Trans. A. M. Sheridan Smith. New York: Vintage, 1994.

———. *The Care of the Self.* Vol. 3 of *The History of Sexuality.* Trans. Robert Hurley. New York: Vintage, 1988.

———. *Death and the Labyrinth: The World of Raymond Roussel.* 1963. Trans. Charles Ruas. Berkeley and Los Angeles: U of California P, 1987.

———. *Discipline and Punish: The Birth of the Prison.* Trans. Alan Sheridan. New York: Vintage, 1979.

———. *The History of Sexuality.* Vol. 1, *An Introduction.* Trans. Robert Hurley. New York: Vintage, 1980.

———. *Language, Counter-Memory, Practice.* Ed. Donald F. Bouchard. Trans. Donald F. Bouchard and Sherry Simon. Ithaca, N.Y.: Cornell UP, 1977.

———. *Madness and Civilization.* Trans. Richard Howard. New York: Vintage, 1973.

———. *The Order of Things: An Archaeology of the Human Sciences.* Trans. Anonymous. New York: Pantheon, 1970.

———. *Politics, Philosophy, Culture: Interviews and Other Writings, 1977-1984.* Trans. Alan Sheridan et al. Ed. Lawrence D. Kritzman. New York: Routledge, 1988.

———. *Power/Knowledge: Selected Interviews and Other Writings, 1972-1977.* Trans. Colin Gordon et al. Ed. Colin Gordon. New York: Pantheon, 1980.

———. *The Use of Pleasure.* Vol. 2 of *The History of Sexuality.* Trans Robert Hurley. New York: Vintage, 1986.

Graff, Gerald. *Professing Literature: An Institutional History.* Chicago: U of Chicago P, 1987.

Grossberg, Lawrence, Cary Nelson, and Paula Treichler, eds. *Cultural Studies.* New York: Routledge, 1991.

Gutting, Gary. *Michel Foucault's Archaeology of Scientific Reason.* Cambridge: Cambridge UP, 1989.

Horkheimer, Max, and Theodor W. Adorno. *Dialectic of Enlightment.* Trans. John Cumming. New York: Seabury, 1972.

Hoy, David Cousins, ed. *Foucault: A Critical Reader.* Oxford: Basil Blackwell, 1986.

Lecourt, Dominique. *Marxism and Epistemology: Bachelard, Canguilhem, and Foucault.* Trans. Ben Brewster. London: New Left Books, 1975.

Lemert, Charles C., and Garth Gillan. *Michel Foucault: Social Theory and Transgression.* New York: Columbia UP, 1982.

Lentricchia, Frank. *Ariel and the Police: Michel Foucault, William James, Wallace Stevens.* Madison: U of Wisconsin P, 1988.

Looser, Devoney. "Feminist Theory and Foucault: A Bibliographical Essay." *Style* 26.4 (1992): 593-603.

Macey, David. *The Lives of Michel Foucault.* New York: Pantheon, 1993.

Martin, Rux, Huck Gutman, and Patrick H. Hutton. *Technologies of the Self: A Seminar with Michel Foucault.* Amherst: U of Massachusetts P, 1988.

Megill, Allan. *Prophets of Extremity: Nietzsche, Heidegger, Foucault, Derrida.* Berkeley and Los Angeles: U of California P, 1985.

Miller, James. *The Passion of Michel Foucault.* New York: Simon and Schuster, 1993.

Miller, Toby. *The Well-Tempered Self: Citizenship, Culture, and the Postmodern Subject.* Baltimore, Md.: Johns Hopkins UP, 1993.

Molinaro, Nina L. *Foucault, Feminism, and Power: Reader Esther Tusquets.* Lewisburg, Penn.: Bucknell UP, 1991.

Mukerji, Chandra, and Michael Schudson, eds. *Rethinking Popular Culture: Contemporary Perspectives in Cultural Studies.* Berkeley and Los Angeles: U of California P, 1991.

Nietzsche, Friedrich. *On the Genealogy of Morals.* In *Basic Writings of Nietzsche,* trans. and ed. Walter Kaufmann, 439-599. New York: Modern Library, 1968.

O'Hara, Daniel. *Radical Parody: American Culture and Critical Agency after Foucault.* New York: Columbia UP, 1992.

Poster, Mark. *Foucault, Marxism, and History: Mode of Production versus Mode of Information.* Cambridge: Polity, 1984.

Quinby, Lee. *Freedom, Foucault, and the Subject of America.* Boston: Northeastern UP, 1991.

Racevskis, Karlis. *Michel Foucault and the Subversion of Intellect.* Ithaca, N.Y.: Cornell UP, 1983.

Radhakrishnan, R. "Toward an Effective Intellectual: Foucault or Gramsci?" In *Intellectuals: Aesthetics, Politics, Academics,* ed. Bruce Robbins, 57–99. Minneapolis: U of Minnesota P, 1990.

Rajchman, John. *Michel Foucault: The Freedom of Philosophy.* New York: Columbia UP, 1985.

Said, Edward. *Orientalism.* New York: Vintage, 1979.

Sawicki, Jana. *Disciplining Foucault: Feminism, Power, and the Body.* New York: Routledge, 1991.

Sedgwick, Eve Kosofsky. *Between Men: English Literature and Male Homosocial Desire.* New York: Columbia UP, 1985.

———. *Epistemology of the Closet.* Berkeley and Los Angeles: U of California P, 1990.

Shapiro, Michael J. "Michel Foucault and the Analysis of Discursive Practices." In *Language and Political Understanding: The Politics of Discursive Practices,* 127–164. New Haven, Conn.: Yale UP, 1981.

Sheridan, Alan. *Michel Foucault: The Will to Truth.* London: Tavistock, 1980.

Smart, Barry. *Foucault, Marxism, and Critique.* London: Routledge, 1983.

White, Hayden. "Michel Foucault." In *Structuralism and Since: From Lévi-Strauss to Derrida,* 81–115. Oxford: Oxford UP, 1979.

chapter 9

New Historicist Literary Criticism

New historicist criticism represents one of the most important trends in literary study in the past decade. Like traditional historical scholars, new historicists accept the basic importance of historical context in the reading of literary works. But the new historicism departs from traditional historical scholarship in important and crucial ways. Jeffrey N. Cox and Larry J. Reynolds summarize the essence of these differences: "For the most part, new historicism can be distinguished from 'old' historicism by its lack of faith in 'objectivity' and 'permanence' and its stress not upon the direct recreation of the past, but rather the processes by which the past is constructed or invented" ("Historicist" 4).

Building on the insights of recent poststructuralist theory, new historicists are intensely aware of the fundamental *textuality* of history. In particular, new historicists understand that no amount of historical scholarship can uncover the ultimate "truth" of history. All historical accounts are partial, and all are conditioned by the terms of inquiry. It is important, a new historicist critic would argue, to read William Shakespeare within the context of the culture of Elizabethan England. But cultures are extremely complex entities, and "Elizabethan England" cannot be simply described. Despite the large amount of available material, historical information is necessarily incomplete; we can never know everything there is to know about our own society, much less a society from hundreds of years in the past about which much detailed information will always have been lost. Meanwhile the amount of historical information available about Elizabethan England is vast; any historian investigating the period must focus on specific aspects of Elizabethan society while making certain choices about which information and documents to include in her analysis and which material to disregard. New historicist scholars are intensely aware that their own decisions concerning the focus of their investigations and the kinds of information to employ in pursuing their conclusions have a powerful impact on the resulting historical visions they produce. They also extend their recognition of the importance of historical context to their own activities, understanding that their own situation in contemporary culture exerts a powerful influence on the ways they view cultures from the past. A new historicist scholar in the 1990s knows that he cannot produce a "pure" picture of Elizabethan culture; he can only produce a partial picture of certain aspects of Elizabethan culture as seen through the eyes (and prejudices) of an inhabitant of the 1990s.

New historicist criticism derives from a number of important influences and participates in a quite broad turn toward social, political, and historical concerns in recent literary criticism. The new historicist emphasis on material practices in society bears obvious affinities to the historical materialism of Karl Marx, and new historicist analysis in general often recalls the cultural criticism of neo-Marxists such as Raymond Williams. At the same time, new historicism is importantly informed by "textualist" models of history and society deriving from the philosophy of Friedrich Nietzsche and particularly recalling the more recent poststructuralist criticism of Paul de Man. Stephen Greenblatt, probably the most influential practitioner of the new historicism (and the person often credited with having coined the term—though he tends to refer to his own project as "cultural poetics" rather than new historicism), thus suggests that "an openness to the theoretical ferment of the last few years is precisely what distinguishes the new historicism from the positivist historical scholarship of the early twentieth century" ("Towards" 1). In a famous formulation, Louis Montrose summarizes the distinctive combination of cultural materialism and poststructuralist textualism that informs the new historicism as

> a reciprocal concern with the historicity of texts and the textuality of history. By *the historicity of texts,* I mean to suggest the cultural specificity, the social embedment, of all modes of writing. . . . By *the textuality of history,* I mean to suggest, firstly, that we can have no access to a full and authentic past, a lived material existence, whose survival we cannot assume to be merely contingent but must rather presume to be at least partially consequent upon complex and subtle social processes of preservation and effacement; and secondly, that those textual traces are themselves subject to subsequent textual mediations when they are construed as the "documents" upon which historians ground their own texts. ("Professing" 20)

Probably the most important theoretical inspiration for the new historicism is provided by the work of Michel Foucault. Foucault's impressive body of work (described in more detail in chapter 8) includes a number of historical studies that have pointed the way for new historicist critics. In works such as *Madness and Civilization, The Birth of the Clinic, The Order of Things, Discipline and Punish,* and *The History of Sexuality,* Foucault utilizes massive amounts of historical research to develop detailed descriptions of the history of various social institutions and practices and various habits of thought. Foucault is, however, quite well aware that his own habits of thought shape the outcome of these investigations. Viewing society as the product of a complex network of interacting discourses, the relationships among which are conditioned by questions of power, Foucault attempts to read specific discourses and to draw conclusions about the power relationships that inform them. At the same time, he insists that these relationships are too complex to be understood completely and that the events of history are driven by interrelationships far too complicated to be described in terms of simple cause-effect sequences. He thus eschews the grand historical narratives often produced by traditional historians, insisting that we cannot "understand events in terms of . . . some great evolutionary process" (*Discipline* 129).

Foucault's reminders of the necessary limitations of historical descriptions, together with the models provided by his own intellectual practice, have inspired new historicist critics. Another important source of new historical method is the work of cultural anthropologists such as Victor Turner and Clifford Geertz, whose studies of cultural rituals and theatrical traditions in various cultures provide important procedural models. Geertz, for example, performs extensive field work in which he collects large amounts of data about the cultures he is studying—much like many traditional anthropologists. However he eschews the tendencies of traditional social science to dehumanize foreign cultures by viewing them through totalizing theories or reducing them to a mere set of data for analysis by quantitative scientific techniques. Geertz's "symbolic anthropology" focuses on "culture," which for Geertz means "an historically transmitted pattern of meanings embodied in symbols, a system of inherited conceptions expressed in symbolic forms by means of which men communicate, perpetuate, and develop their knowledge about and attitudes toward life" (*Interpretation* 89).

Somewhat in the mode of the structuralist anthropology of Claude Lévi-Strauss, Geertz views culture largely as a system of signs and codes that govern behavior and allow different individuals to communicate. Unlike Lévi-Strauss, however, Geertz does not attempt to develop overall models for the functioning of these codes in a given culture, in the manner of Ferdinand de Saussure's study of *la langue,* the system of codes and conventions by which languages operate. Instead Geertz focuses on a cultural version of Saussure's *parole,* paying close and careful attention to specific cultural practices but refusing to draw general conclusions about a culture from these specific studies. Instead Geertz seeks to find individual events, performances, or practices that he can interpret in great detail, developing "local knowledge" of this specific phenomenon rather than "global knowledge" of the culture as a whole. Geertz refers to his technique as "thick description" of culture, and his focus on very specific and local aspects of culture can be seen as a cultural version of the close reading strategies of the New Critics. Indeed Geertz himself has suggested that his approach is "like that of the literary critic" (9).

Geertz's own comparison of his work to the interpretation of literary texts suggests the relevance of his anthropological writings to literary study. Indeed coming at a time when decades of New Critical dominance had in the view of some virtually exhausted the interpretation of most canonical texts, Geertz's work proved inspirational to literary scholars in its demonstration of the constant availability of new interpretations. Geertz's frequent emphasis on marginal cultural events and institutions also suggested that important knowledge could be gained from the interpretation of marginal literary texts and thus added impetus to the attempts of many literary scholars to expand the scope of their work beyond the traditional canon. Geertz's technique is well illustrated in his influential essay "Deep Play: Notes on the Balinese Cockfight" (*Interpretation* 412-453). Noting that Bali has been well studied by a number of traditional anthropological scholars, Geertz demonstrates that it is still possible to derive new and important insights into Balinese society. He develops these insights by focusing on the cockfight, a seemingly marginal element of Balinese culture. Through close observation and extensive interpretation, Geertz convincingly reveals aspects of Balinese social life that had escaped the attention of traditional scholars, with their emphasis on more "important" mainstream aspects of Balinese society.

Applied to literature, the new historical methods inspired by the work of thinkers such as Foucault and Geertz produce not only a distinctive style of literary criticism but also a distinctive vision of the relationship between literary and society. Much in the vein of poststructuralists such as Roland Barthes and Jacques Derrida, new historicists see literary texts as the product of complex intertextual relationships rather than of the individual creative genius of the author. But where Barthes and Derrida locate intertextuality primarily in the realm of language itself, new historicists (influenced by Foucault's vision of social forces as the productive interaction of various discourses) locate intertextuality in culture and society. Contrary to the New Critical insistence on the autonomy of literary texts and on the importance of reading such texts "intrinsically," new historicists believe that it makes no sense to separate literary texts from the social context around them because such texts are the product of complex social "exchanges" or "negotiations." There is, in fact, no such thing as an intrinsic approach to literature, both because literary texts come into existence through a close involvement with the context around them and because literary critics (and all readers) necessarily bring an entire array of extrinsic knowledge, assumptions, and preoccupations with them when they read literary texts, no matter how formalist their style of interpretation might appear. For new historicists, we can thus understand the real significance of literary texts only by paying close and careful attention to the nature and implications of the cultural exchanges and negotiations that bring these texts into being, while also remaining aware that the process of reading is itself a culturally situated exchange.

New historicist readings of cultural negotiations and exchanges are necessarily partial and contingent, both because these readings are themselves cultural negotiations and because culture is far too complex and multiple to be encompassed within any single vision. Different new historicist critics emphasize different aspects of culture and therefore achieve different results with their new historical readings. Montrose thus entitles an important essay on the approach

"New Historicisms" to indicate the multiplicity of the field. And Jerome McGann, an important new historicist critic importantly influenced by Mikhail Bakhtin as well as Foucault, has made pluralism a central part of his own political and critical project. The flexibility of new historical methods is one of the great strengths of the approach, though it has also led to a certain amount of confusion over just what the approach entails and just what ideological position it occupies. But despite this multiplicity, certain basic assumptions are common to new historical critics, regardless of their ideological orientation. For H. Aram Veeser, for example, new historicist critics can be identified by the presence of the following basic assumptions in their work:

1. That every expressive act is embedded in a network of material practices;
2. That every act of unmasking, critique, and opposition uses the tools it condemns and risks falling prey to the practice it exposes;
3. That literary and non-literary "texts" circulate inseparably;
4. That no discourse, imaginative or archival, gives access to unchanging truths nor expresses inalterable human nature;
5. . . . That a critical method and a language adequate to describe culture under capitalism participate in the economy they describe. (xi)

One of the important early works of the new historicism is Greenblatt's *Renaissance Self-Fashioning* (1980), a book that was both influenced by the work of Foucault and itself influenced the later stages of Foucault's technologies of the self project. Here Greenblatt examines the work of English Renaissance writers such as Sir Thomas More, William Tyndale, Sir Thomas Wyatt, Edmund Spenser, Christopher Marlowe, and William Shakespeare to look at the ways these writers attempt, through their writing, to fashion their personal identities amid the cultural context of Renaissance England. While Greenblatt sees a strong aesthetic component to this self-fashioning, he also insists that the social and cultural contexts in which these writers lived and worked placed strict limitations on the kinds of selves they could fashion. Indeed Greenblatt argues that "there may well have been less *autonomy* in self-fashioning in the sixteenth century than before, that family, state, and religious institutions impose a more rigid and far-reaching discipline upon their middle-class and aristocratic subjects" (1). In addition, Greenblatt points the way for much subsequent new historical criticism by supplementing his readings of the texts of major writers with readings of a number of more marginal contemporary documents and anecdotes. He also acknowledges that his interpretation of the self-fashioning of writers from More to Shakespeare is conditioned by his own project of self-fashioning in the late twentieth century.

Greenblatt ultimately concludes that most of these writers shape identities for themselves within the context of submission to some outside authority: "God, a sacred book, an institution such as church, court, colonial or military administration" (9). In the course of his readings, Greenblatt develops a detailed description of the complex interrelationship among religion, sexuality, politics, literature, and other discourses within the context of sixteenth-century England. He finds that all of the writers he studies ultimately fashion their identities through their relationships to official power (religious or secular). More and Tyndale, for example, largely fashion their identities through radical opposition to the state and the church, respectively, yet both authors do so within the context of a search for a higher power that will replace the authority of the one they challenge. Spenser thoroughly aligns himself with both secular and religious authority and against alien threats to that authority. Marlowe fashions his identity through opposition to official power of all kinds and through "a subversive identification with the alien" (203).

Greenblatt's model thus posits Marlowe as the most antiauthoritarian of sixteenth-century writers, with Spenser as the poet most supportive of authority. Spenser and Marlowe are thus "mighty opposites, poised in antagonism as radical as that of More and Tyndale in the 1530s. If Spenser sees human identity as conferred by loving service to legitimate authority, to the yoke power of God and the state, Marlowe sees identity established at those moments in which order—political theological, sexual—is violated" (222). But for Greenblatt, the terms of Marlowe's rebellion against authority are strictly set by the powers against which he rebels, and Marlowe is in some ways as much a product of official power as is Spenser. Greenblatt thus argues that Marlowe's plays are populated by rebels who, like Marlowe himself, "imagine themselves set in diametrical opposition to their society where in fact they have unwittingly accepted its crucial structural elements" (209).

Although critics have seen Greenblatt's emphasis on the conditioning of art by social and cultural power as "demystifying" the traditional critical respect for the greatness of English Renaissance literature, he continues to show a great deal of admiration for that literature in his work. Moreover he comes to the rather unrevolutionary conclusion that Shakespeare is probably the richest of English Renaissance writers because his relation to official power is the most complex. In particular, Shakespeare ultimately functions for Greenblatt as a combination of Marlowe and Spenser, paying obedient homage to official power while radically challenging that power through the uniquely complex and paradoxical nature of his drama: "If there are intimations in Shakespeare of a release from the complex narrative orders in which everyone is inscribed, these intimations do not arise from bristling resistance or strident denunciation. . . . They arise paradoxically from a peculiarly intense *submission* whose downright violence undermines everything it was meant to shore up" (254).

Shakespeare, then, is in a sense not the most unusual of Renaissance dramatists but the most conventional, displaying in his drama a conventionality so extreme that it ultimately undermines convention. But for Greenblatt, this paradoxical movement tells us less about Shakespeare's mind and talent than about the contradictory and paradoxical nature of the Elizabethan society that Shakespeare so strikingly reflects. Greenblatt extends this analysis in the later *Shakespearean Negotiations* (1988), perhaps the single most influential work of literary criticism to have been produced by a new historicist scholar. In this book, Greenblatt produces a number of important new insights into literature by examining the work of Shakespeare, the most thoroughly researched and interpreted writer in all of literature. Greenblatt thus demonstrates that the interpretation of literary texts is always incomplete and that new interpretations can always be produced. He also convincingly demonstrates the special ability of the new historicism to generate such new interpretations. In *Shakespearean Negotiations,* Greenblatt also perfects his own distinctive critical style, which has come to be considered by many as paradigmatic of the new historicism. Seizing on very specific moments in particular Shakespearean plays, Greenblatt discusses at length the relationship between these moments and larger phenomena in Elizabethan culture as a whole. He focuses his attention not on close and careful reading of Shakespeare's texts and their language but on reading of (sometimes seemingly marginal) contemporary cultural texts (diaries, chronicles, church and municipal records) that illuminate Shakespeare's plays in important ways. Greenblatt is thus able to show that Elizabethan England was a time of great crisis and uncertainty over fundamental issues such as religion, political power, and gender and that this unusual state of crisis energizes Shakespeare's plays.

In the opening chapter of *Shakespearean Negotiations,* Greenblatt provides a convenient list of rules that inform his reading of Shakespeare, and this list (similar on many points to that provided by Veeser) can be taken as indicative of the rules followed by new historicist scholars as a whole:

1. There can be no appeals to genius as the sole origin of the energies of great art.
2. There can be no motiveless creation.
3. There can be no transcendent or timeless or unchanging representation.
4. There can be no autonomous artifacts.
5. There can be no expression without an origin and an object, a *from* and a *for.*
6. There can be no art without social energy.
7. There can be no spontaneous generation of social energy. (12)

Greenblatt accompanies these negative commandments with a list of "generative principles," including the assumption that literary texts can be read as a sort of "cultural capital" that is produced by "negotiation and exchange." Much in the vein of Foucault's description of power as an immanent field that precedes any notion of human agency, Greenblatt insists that these negotiations and exchanges, while often involving individuals, are ultimately the product of larger social forces. Indeed he insists that "individuals are themselves the products of collective exchange" (12).

Shakespearean Negotiations employs a significantly more sophisticated and complex model of culture and society than had *Renaissance Self-Fashioning,* in which Greenblatt's figuration of Elizabethan society tended to reduce to dualistic oppositions between official power and opposition to that power—with official power always tending to come out on top. In the later book, however,

Greenblatt puts his emphasis on the complexity of Elizabethan society, arguing extensively that it is indeed the multifaceted and sometimes contradictory nature of this society that gives Shakespeare's work its distinctive quality. For Greenblatt, Shakespeare is not a unique and transcendent genius whose greatness lies in his ability to escape his historical situation and to express universal and timeless human truths. On the contrary, Shakespeare's work is great because of his singular ability to draw on the energies generated by the conflicts in his contemporary society. Shakespeare, in short, is special neither because his works reflect universal human truths nor because he writes in a time of unparalleled cultural greatness and integration. Shakespeare's works have a special energy precisely because they are so firmly embedded in their own historical context and because that context was a time of conflict, crisis, and fragmentation.

Greenblatt emphasizes again and again that Elizabethan cultural wholeness and grandeur have been exaggerated not only in the historical record but also during Elizabeth's reign. Elizabethan England was a time of famine, pestilence, and political violence, the true nature of which was obscured at the time (and for generations of historians) by a Renaissance version of the Big Lie, by an intentional strategy of pretending to cultural and political greatness. Assuming the throne in a time of chaotic social and political fragmentation, Elizabeth was able to hold that throne by patching together a makeshift political alliance of various noblemen and aristocrats. And she did so largely through sheer theater, through the production of spectacles that made her *seem* a grand and powerful ruler, even if she was not. Queen Elizabeth was "a ruler without a standing army, without a highly developed bureaucracy, without an extensive police force, a ruler whose power is constituted in theatrical celebrations of royal glory and theatrical violence visited upon the enemies of that glory" (64).

History attests to the success of Elizabeth's attempts to simulate power through official theater. Greenblatt also emphasizes that the spectacular surface of Elizabethan politics obscures what was in fact a time of intense social and political crisis when powerful competing forces were already creating the rifts that would within a few decades explode in revolution and civil war. The work of other scholars supports this vision of Elizabethan society. In *The Illusion of Power* (1975), Stephen Orgel precedes Greenblatt with an extensive exploration of the theatricality of power in Elizabethan England. Jeffrey Knapp's recent *An Empire Nowhere* (1992) is a wide-ranging examination of Elizabethan society that demonstrates that the Elizabethan period was not the time of burgeoning English power and prestige that popular stereotypes would have it be. In fact, looking at literary works from More to Shakespeare and drawing on a number of Elizabethan historical and documents as well, Knapp concludes that the worldwide extent of England's political domination and influence was actually *decreasing* during most of Elizabeth's reign.

The work of such scholars suggests a considerable revaluation of historical accounts of Renaissance England, which often functions as a utopian golden age in the modern imagination. This grand vision of the Renaissance has been especially prominent in literary studies, where Elizabethan England (dominated by the towering figure of Shakespeare as the "greatest genius" of the English literary tradition) has often figured as the high point of English cultural productivity and creativity, a time of cultural wholeness from which subsequent English literary history represents a decline into fragmentation and confusion. Numerous modern artists, for example, have responded to the seeming chaos of twentieth-century history by contrasting the modern world to the seemingly more tranquil and stable world of the Elizabethans. Thus artists otherwise as different in their ideologies as T. S. Eliot and Virginia Woolf have both envisioned Renaissance England as a period of ideal wholeness and integration as opposed to the cultural and psychic fragmentation that for them informs the modern world. New historical studies of the contradictions of Elizabethan society obviously challenge this vision of the English Renaissance. The rereadings of Shakespeare and other Renaissance writers by new historicist critics are important not only for what they tell us about Elizabethan literature and culture but also for what they tell us about modern literature and culture—and about the institution of literature as a whole. A dual temporal focus—on the historical contexts of the author and of the critic—is central to new historical method.

Renaissance England remains (under the impetus of the work of Montrose, Greenblatt, Orgel, Knapp, and others) in many ways the center of the new historical project, though new historicist critics tend to prefer the term *early modern period* to *Renaissance,* partially to avoid the glorification traditionally associated with the latter term. The success of the new historical method in early modern studies has attracted critics working in other periods as well. Even scholars of modern and contemporary literature, to which the method is least obviously applicable, have taken important turns toward new historical analysis in recent years. Walter Benn Michaels applies new historicist methods to American naturalism; Vincent Pecora reads Joseph Conrad's *Heart of Darkness* and James Joyce's story "The Dead" through contemporary historical documents and issues; and Cheryl Herr, R. B. Kershner, and Jennifer A. Wicke, among others, extensively explore the relationship between Joyce and his contemporary Irish social and cultural context. And Alan Sinfield's cultural materialist readings of contemporary British literature and culture have a great deal in common with new historicist studies.

In short, the new historicism has been extremely successful in the past decade as more and more critics have turned to the method to find new ways to extend our understanding of literary texts. For example, a recent anthology on the latest trends in literary study published by the Modern Language Association includes a striking (if not surprising, given that the book is edited by Greenblatt and Giles Gunn) emphasis on new historical techniques and insights. Indeed the success of the method has become so widespread that many of its original practitioners are concerned that it may be in danger of losing its critical force. Montrose thus worries that the new historicism is "on its way to becoming the latest academic orthodoxy—not so much a critique as a subject of ideological appropriation" ("Renaissance" 7 n4).

Meanwhile despite its popularity, the method has also been highly controversial and has come in for a significant amount of opposition. Somewhat like deconstruction, the new historicism has been seen by some critics as too dependent on the interpretive and stylistic virtuosity of individual practitioners. Greenblatt's extremely well-written essays tend to be entertaining, informative, and insightful, but they depend on extremely perceptive readings of cultural documents. It is not clear whether in the hands of less talented critics the new historicism will be able to produce such impressive results. Some critics feel that the emphasis on cultural context in the new historicism puts the method in danger of losing sight of the aesthetic properties of literary texts, whereas others argue just the opposite: that the conclusions reached in new historical readings of texts (such as Greenblatt's emphasis on paradox in Shakespeare) often sound suspiciously similar to the characteristic conclusions of the New Criticism.

Criticisms of the political implications of the new historicism are similarly double-edged. Some critics have seen the political flexibility of the new historicism as evidence of confusion and lack of commitment while viewing the frequent new historical emphasis on contradictions in culture and society as symptomatic of contradictions within the new historicism itself. The relationship of the new historicism to politically informed critical approaches such as Marxism and feminism has been particularly vexed, especially as it appears that new historical methods can be used equally well either by Marxists and feminists or by critics with little interest in (or even antipathy toward) Marxism and feminism. Catherine Gallagher summarizes the complex attitude taken toward the new historicism by its political critics:

> Critics of the "new historicism" have given wildly different accounts of its political implications, but they generally agree that its politics are obnoxious. Charged on the one hand with being a crude version of Marxism and on the other with being a formalist equivalent of colonialism, the new historicism attracts an unusual amount of specifically political criticism for a criticism whose politics are so difficult to specify. ("Marxism" 37)

The complex combination of historicism and poststructuralism that gives the new historicism much of its distinctive character has also brought the method in for considerable criticism from opposing perspectives. Brook Thomas, for example, argues that the new historicism is not poststructuralist *enough* and that in the final analysis it tends to reduce to conventional "old" historicism. Thomas sees poststructuralism as a reaction against the tradition of historicism, concluding that the new historicism remains too rooted in the historical tradition to be genuinely poststructuralist. He argues that the impulse toward historicism is a central characteristic of modernity, with its consistent privileging of the new. Modern historians, claims Thomas, always tend to assume that "history will always be made new. As a result, the history of historicism is marked by perpetual claims to newness" ("New" 189). Moreover Thomas goes on to argue that historians have long acknowledged that they "do not objectively and scientifically recover the past but construct it from a present perspective" (195). Thomas does see promise in new historical method but urges that new historicist critics draw on poststructuralism to develop more fundamental and radical challenges to their historicist assumptions.

If for Thomas new historicist critics sometimes miss the point of poststructuralism by relying too much on historicist assumptions, Elizabeth Fox-Genovese argues that new historicists miss the point of historicism by relying too much on poststructuralist assumptions. For Fox-Genovese, the central conviction of the new historicism is that "we think, exist, know, only through text—that extratextual considerations defy proof and, accordingly, relevance" (218). But it is these extratextual considerations that allow historians to deal with the material reality of history, something she sees new historicists as unable to do. "Notwithstanding some notable exceptions," Fox-Genovese concludes of the new historicism, "it is not very historical" (214). Indeed such charges of ahistoricism are probably the most common complaints against the new historicism, many critics of which feel that the emphasis on thick descriptions of specific times and places leaves new historicists with no way to deal with historical process and change. Moreover the new historical emphasis on the embeddedness of individuals within networks of official power seems for some critics to leave no room for effective opposition to that power. For example, because of the seeming conclusion that official power is ultimately inescapable and that any attempts at subversion are liable to appropriation in the interests of official power, Greenblatt's vision of Elizabethan society in *Renaissance Self-Fashioning* has been criticized by some as overly pessimistic and as leading to political quietism.

Despite such criticisms, there can be little doubt that the new historicism has been a tremendous energizing force in recent literary criticism because of both its development of new insights into the work of major authors and its demonstration of procedural models for the development of such insights. Meanwhile the method is still developing, and promises to continue to do so for some time, in response to its antagonists and to the self-criticisms of its practitioners, who consistently meditate on the limitations of the method even as they practice it. The controversy and criticism produced by new historical scholarship—even from sources outside the academy—are themselves a potentially positive result of the method. As Montrose puts it, the sometimes hostile reactions to the new historicism are valuable because they confirm that "the academy is perceived as a site for contestation as well as for reproduction of ideological dominants; that there may be something important at stake in our reading, teaching, and revision of the literary canon; and that, if we suddenly discover ourselves to be culturally and institutionally empowered, we are now compelled to choose if, when, and how to employ that power" ("New" 416).

BIBLIOGRAPHY

Introductory Works

Cox, Jeffrey N., and Larry J. Reynolds, eds. *New Historical Literary Study: Essays on Reproducing Texts, Representing History.* Princeton, N.J.: Princeton UP, 1993.
An extremely useful compilation of new historicist critical essays, with a good survey of the "historicist enterprise" in the introduction.

Greenblatt, Stephen. *Shakespearean Negotiations: The Circulation of Social Energy in Renaissance England.* Berkeley and Los Angeles: U of California P, 1988.
Perhaps the most important work of new historicist criticism.

Veeser, H. Aram., ed. *The New Historicism.* New York: Routledge, 1989.
An extremely useful compilation of essays about the new historicism.

Selected Other Works

Foucault, Michel. *Discipline and Punish: The Birth of the Prison.* Trans. Alan Sheridan. New York: Vintage, 1979.

Fox-Genovese, Elizabeth. "Literary Criticism and the Politics of the New Historicism." In *The New Historicism,* ed. H. Aram Veeser, 213-224. New York: Routledge, 1989.

Gallagher, Catherine. *The Industrial Reformation of English Fiction, 1832-1867.* Chicago: U of Chicago P, 1985.

———. "Marxism and the New Historicism." In *The New Historicism,* ed. H. Aram Veeser, 37-48. New York: Routledge, 1989.

Geertz, Clifford. *The Interpretation of Cultures: Selected Essays.* New York: Basic Books, 1973.

———. *Local Knowledge: Further Essays in Interpretive Anthropology.* New York: Basic Books, 1983.

———. *Negara: The Theatre State of Nineteenth-Century Bali.* Princeton, N.J.: Princeton UP, 1980.

Greenblatt, Stephen. *Learning to Curse: Essays in Early Modern Culture.* New York: Routledge, 1991.

———. *Marvelous Possessions: The Wonder of the New World.* Chicago: U of Chicago P, 1991.

———. *Renaissance Self-Fashioning: From More to Shakespeare.* Chicago: U of Chicago P, 1980.

———. "Towards a Poetics of Culture." In *The New Historicism,* ed. H. Aram Veeser, 1-14. New York: Routledge, 1989.

Greenblatt, Stephen and Giles Gunn, eds. *Redrawing the Boundaries: The Transformation of English and American Literary Studies.* New York: Modern Language Association, 1992.

Herr, Cheryl. *Joyce's Anatomy of Culture.* Urbana: U of Illinois P, 1986.

Howard, Jean. "The New Historicism in Renaissance Studies." *English Literary Renaissance* 16 (1986): 13-43.

Hunt, Lynn, ed. *The New Cultural History.* Berkeley and Los Angeles: U of California P, 1989.

Kershner, R. B., Jr. *Joyce, Bakhtin, and Popular Literature: Chronicles of Disorder.* Chapel Hill: U of North Carolina P, 1989.

Knapp, Jeffrey. *An Empire Nowhere: England, America, and Literature from "Utopia" to "The Tempest."* Berkeley and Los Angeles: U of California P, 1992.

McGann, Jerome. *The Beauty of Inflections: Literary Investigations in Historical Method and Theory.* Oxford: Clarendon-Oxford UP, 1985.

———. *Historical Studies and Literary Criticism.* Madison: U of Wisconsin P, 1985.

Michaels, Walter Benn. *The Gold Standard and the Logic of Naturalism: American Literature at the Turn of the Century.* Berkeley and Los Angeles: U of California P, 1987.

Montrose, Louis. "New Historicisms." In *Redrawing the Boundaries: The Transformation of English and American Literary Studies,* ed. Stephen Greenblatt and Giles Gunn, 392-418. New York: Modern Language Association, 1992.

———. "Professing the Renaissance: The Poetics and Politics of Culture." In *The New Historicism,* ed. H. Aram Veeser, 15-36. New York: Routledge, 1989.

———. "Renaissance Literary Studies and the Subject of History." *English Literary Renaissance* 16 (1986): 5-12.

Orgel, Stephen. *The Illusion of Power: Political Theater in the English Renaissance.* Berkeley and Los Angeles: U of California P, 1975.

Pecora, Vincent. *Self and Form in Modern Narrative.* Baltimore, Md.: Johns Hopkins UP, 1989.

Sinfield, Alan. *Literature, Politics, and Culture in Postwar Britain.* Berkeley and Los Angeles: U of California P, 1989.

Thomas, Brook. "The New Historicism and Other Old-Fashioned Topics." In *The New Historicism,* ed. H. Aram Veeser, 182-203. New York: Routledge, 1989.

———. *The New Historicism and Other Old-Fashioned Topics.* Princeton, N.J.: Princeton UP, 1991.

Turner, Victor. *Celebration: Studies in Festivity and Ritual.* Washington, D.C.: Smithsonian Institution, 1982.

———. *The Forest of Symbols: Aspects of Ndembu Ritual.* Ithaca, N.Y.: Cornell UP, 1967.

Veeser, H. Aram. Introduction to *The New Historicism,* ed. H. Aram Veeser, ix-xvi. New York: Routledge, 1989.

Wicke, Jennifer A. *Advertising Fictions: Literature, Advertisement, and Social Reading.* New York: Columbia UP, 1988.

Williams, Raymond. *The Country and the City.* New York: Oxford UP, 1973.

———. *Marxism and Literature.* Oxford.: Oxford UP, 1977.

chapter **10**

Multicultural Literary Criticism

Toni Morrison's winning of the Nobel Prize for Literature in 1993 highlighted the great prominence that African-American writing (especially writing by African-American women such as Morrison, Alice Walker, and Gloria Naylor) has gained in American literature in recent decades. Meanwhile a number of important works by Native American writers (such as N. Scott Momaday's Pulitzer Prize-winning *House Made of Dawn*) have recently received serious critical attention and made their way into college syllabi. Chicano literature is a burgeoning cultural force in America as well, and in general works by authors outside the white Protestant mainstream have been among the most important and exciting sources of literary and cultural energy in America in the past few decades. A similar phenomenon is at work worldwide. Latin American literature, propelled by the work of young novelists such as Gabriel García Márquez, Carlos Fuentes, and Mario Vargas Llosa in the "boom" of the 1960s, has for some time been recognized as one of the world's richest and most exciting cultural forces. And recent decades have also seen a worldwide explosion of literary production in the postcolonial societies of areas in Africa and Asia that were once ruled by European empires, especially the British and the French. The Nigerian Wole Soyinka and the Egyptian Naguib Mahfouz are also recent winners of the Nobel Prize, and Britain's prestigious Booker Prize (awarded annually to the best work of fiction by a writer from the British Commonwealth) has recently been won by writers from Ireland, Nigeria, New Zealand, and Australia, indicating a powerful decentering of "English" literature from the former metropolitan center of England.

In short, writers working outside the long dominant white European cultural tradition have become a major force—for many, *the* major force—in contemporary world literature. Much of the excitement over this new literature has to do with its obvious relevance to real-world problems: Postcolonial and minority writers are involved in serious efforts to develop viable cultural identities to replace those thrust on them by the culture of their former colonial masters, and the stakes in these efforts are clearly high. Moreover the "marginal" cultural positions of such writers—sometimes referred to as "subaltern" positions after Antonio Gramsci's term for classes other than the one in hegemonic control of culture—often produce new perspectives that allow us to see the dominant culture in different ways. Thus the work of such writers has been an important inspiration for literary theorists seeking to understand literature in ways that escape the mystifications created by the complex cultural forces in which all literature participates. At the same time, literary theory, no matter how iconoclastic, remains dominated by white male Europeans and North Americans, creating a disjunction between the cultural positions of critics and theorists and those of the subaltern writers to whom they often turn for inspiration. Although the recent increase in critical attention to works by subaltern writers is potentially a very positive development, it also raises a number of vexing issues, including the question of whether such critics and theorists are not themselves enacting a sort of intellectual imperialism by conscripting multicultural texts in the interest of their own professional endeavors.

In a recent review, W. J. T. Mitchell summarizes this phenomenon, focusing especially on postcolonial literature: "The commonplace is simply this: the most important literature is now emerging from the former colonies of the Western empires—from (for instance) Africa, South America, Australia, New Zealand; the most provocative new criticism is emanating from research universities in the advanced industrial democracies, that is, from the former centers of the 'Western empires'—Europe and the United States" (14). For Mitchell, postcolonial literature and contemporary Western criticism are in a sense natural allies, given that both tend to situate themselves in opposition to the official ideology of the Western tradition. Moreover he argues that we should resist the temptation to read this alliance as a scholarly recreation of "the traditional economic relations of imperial centers and colonial periphery," especially given that the work of so many postcolonial writers is informed by a high degree of theoretical sophistication (17).

But Mitchell also warns that Western critics engaged in deconstructive attempts to challenge and destabilize long-dominant cultural traditions are not necessarily in the best position to understand the constructive attempts of postcolonial writers to contribute to the development of a viable culture. Critics should be wary of the pitfalls of bringing "an imperial theory of culture into a situation that resists any conceptual totality" (17). In short, the insights of Western literary theory can provide extremely useful approaches to the criticism of multicultural literature, but critics should remain vigilantly aware that Western theory and multicultural literature arise from fundamentally different cultural positions. Special problems must therefore be considered in relation to the criticism of multicultural literature, and indeed special theoretical approaches have recently evolved to deal with these problems.

Multicultural theory has much in common with feminist theory in the way it poses fundamental challenges to traditional literary canons and traditional modes of literary interpretation. As in the case of feminism, these challenges are of various types. Multicultural theorists have demonstrated the historical complicity of the canon and of literary studies in racism, imperialism, and the general cultural domination by Western Europe and North America of most of the rest of the world. Until very recently, virtually every text in the Western literary canon was authored by a white male from Western Europe or the United States. Moreover recent rereadings of major canonical authors have concluded that many of the major texts of the canon are informed by racist biases and stereotypes. In a famous reading of Joseph Conrad's *Heart of Darkness,* the Nigerian novelist Chinua Achebe concludes that Conrad's text, one of the most frequently taught in American college literature courses, is fundamentally driven by racist impulses. Similarly recent criticism of Shakespeare's *The Tempest* has centered on the play's apparent endorsement of British colonial expansion. Indeed critics such as Malcolm Evans have argued that a complicity with the ideologies of racism and imperialism lies at the very center of Shakespeare's vision as a writer.

Perhaps the most important work in the development of multicultural "stereotype" criticism was Edward Said's *Orientalism* (1978), which argues that nineteenth-century Europeans often justified their imperial expansion into the rest of the world through a belief in "Orientalist" stereotypes that envisioned non-Europeans as lazy, irresponsible, irrational, and sexually promiscuous. Importantly the major purveyors of these Orientalist stereotypes were not politicians but scholars, the anthropologists and ethnologists charged with generating "knowledge" about the Orient. Said's work suggests, however, that these Orientalist scholars were not a unique phenomenon. He argues that all human knowledge is filtered through ideological discourses and that "all cultures impose corrections upon raw reality, changing it from free-floating objects into units of knowledge" (67). These corrections occur even (and maybe especially) in the most academic of disciplines: "Fields of learning, as much as works of even the most eccentric artist, are constrained and acted upon by society, by cultural traditions, by worldly circumstance, and by stabilizing influences like schools, libraries, and governments" (201). As a result, according to Said, the findings of "a 'science' like Orientalism in its academic form are less objectively true than we often like to think" (202). Said's findings are, of course, highly relevant to literary theory and criticism. His work may be especially important for literary scholars, who historically have often regarded their work as particularly free of political and ideological distortion.

Recent historical studies have revealed that literature and literary studies have often played a direct role in the domination of subaltern cultures by the metropolitan centers of Europe and America. Gauri Viswanathan, for example, demonstrates that the whole notion of academic study of English literature began as part of a strategy of British colonial domination in India. As Viswanathan points out, the British had concluded by the early nineteenth century that education was crucial to the maintenance of their power in India. By the 1820s, they had made English literature central to the curriculum of British schools in India—at a time when the classical curriculum still held sway in England itself. Faced with the task of inculcating good "British" values in Indian subjects, the British rejected the direct teaching of Christianity as liable to trigger a revolt on the part of their Hindu and Muslim subjects. They also rejected the teaching of science as too radically inconsistent with the presumably irrational minds of Indians. What remained was literature: "The history of education in British India shows that certain humanistic functions traditionally associated with literature—for example, the shaping of character or the development of the aesthetic sense or the disciplines of ethical thinking—were considered essential to the processes of sociopolitical control by the guardians of the same tradition" (3).

Much of the groundwork for recent African-American literary theory and criticism was laid by pioneering demonstrations of the traditional complicity between the literary canon and white cultural dominance in America. For example, an important (and exceedingly controversial) 1979 anthology edited by Leslie Fiedler and Houston A. Baker Jr. sought to demonstrate the highly political nature of traditional assumptions about the glories of English as a sort of universal language of literary expression. Baker's introduction to the book declares that "the conception of English as a 'world language' is rooted in Western economic history" and that scholars working in the academy must be aware of the relationship between "the economic ascendancy of English and the historical correlation between this academy and the process of modern thought" (xiii). Baker then suggests the cultural imperialism inherent in the widespread use of English as a literary language in Africa, thus introducing into his argument what has become one of the most heated issues in contemporary debates over postcolonial culture. The Indian-British novelist Salman Rushdie, for example, argues that writers from the former British colonies should seek to adapt English to their particular situations and thereby "decolonise" the language. The Kenyan novelist Ngugi wa Thiong'o, in contrast, is quite adamant in texts such as *Decolonising the Mind* about the responsibility of African writers to reject the languages inherited from their former imperial oppressors. Language, he argues, is central to an individual's cultural identity, and Africans will never be able to establish a strong sense of self as long as they continue to express their deepest thoughts in European languages: "The choice of language and the use of to which language is put is central to a people's definition of themselves in relation to their natural and social environment, indeed in relation to the entire universe. Hence language has always been at the heart of the two contending social forces in the Africa of the twentieth century" (4).

For Ngugi, these two contending forces are, on the one hand, the neo-colonialists who would continue the tradition of African imperial subjugation (and who would thus support the use of European languages in "African" literature) and, on the other, those who would resist and oppose that subjugation (and who would thus demand the use of African languages for African literary expression). The battle lines for Ngugi are clear, and he (seeking to reach an audience among the poor and dispossessed in his native Kenya) has insisted since the late 1970s on the importance of writing in his native Kikuyu, a very common language of Kenyan workers and peasants, who can thus better be reached by his work. At the same time, Ngugi does not demand an end to all congress with European culture. He demonstrates in *Decolonising the Mind* a near-encyclopedic knowledge of Western literature, and he remains willing to translate his texts into English to communicate with a Western audience.

Ngugi seeks to break free of the cultural domination of the colonial past not only through critiques of Western culture but also through active participation in the development of a vibrant new postcolonial African culture. Part of the latter project involves the expansion of traditional Western literary canons to include multicultural perspectives. Thus multicultural critics have gone well beyond challenges to the traditional canon, drawing on the rich body of work by African-American and postcolonial writers to explore the possibilities for alternative cultural traditions. Indeed multicultural criticism and theory tend to be characterized by an openness to alternatives. For example, although such theory has tended to focus on the work of African-American and postcolonial writers, some of the important contributions in the area deal with the work of white European writers. Gilles Deleuze and Félix Guattari read Franz Kafka as a writer of "minor literature"; that is, as a writer who writes in the language of a major European culture but who himself occupies a subaltern position within that culture. Recent criticism of James Joyce has emphasized his status as an Irish writer working largely in opposition to the cultural hegemony of Britain. Joyce is, in fact, a postcolonial writer, and such recent criticism of his work (along with the Deleuze/Guattari notion of minor literature) has obvious relevance to postcolonial and African-American writing.

The plurality of multicultural theory is further enhanced by the fact that postcolonial literature and theory both arise in a cultural context informed by the attempt to build a new hybrid culture that transcends the past but still draws on the vestigial echoes of precolonial culture, the remnants of the colonial culture, and the continuing legacy of traditions of anticolonial resistance. African-American literature inhabits a similarly complex cultural terrain. Postcolonial theory thus draws extensively on Western theory, modified with insights gained from an array of recent historical, sociological, psychological, and political meditations on subaltern cultures and societies. Frantz Fanon, one of the most important founding thinkers of multicultural theory, can be taken as a marker of this hybridity. Born in Martinique of a black father and white mother, Fanon was trained in France as a psychoanalyst. He later drew extensively on Marxist theory (in many ways the antithesis of psychoanalytic theory) in his efforts to work for the end of French colonial domination of Algeria while he lived there as a practicing psychiatrist during the fight for independence in the 1950s.

Fanon died prematurely in 1961, very early in the postcolonial moment. But his work remains powerfully relevant to the postcolonial condition more than thirty years after his death. A fierce advocate of independence, he nevertheless eschewed the utopian rhetoric of African nationalism and warned that in an era of global capitalism it was necessary to continue the fight against cultural and economic colonialism even after independence: "We should flatly refuse the situation to which Western countries wish to condemn us. Colonialism and imperialism have not paid their score even when they draw their flags and their police forces from our territories. For centuries the capitalists have behaved in the underdeveloped world like nothing more than criminals" (*Wretched* 101). In particular, Fanon warned against the possibility of continuing neocolonial oppression in postcolonial nations dominated by a ruling class modeled on the European bourgeoisie and by a national consciousness modeled on European nationalism. He was thus the first major theorist to recognize that the nationalist spirit of independence in the colonial world did not necessarily stand in direct opposition to foreign imperial domination but might in fact extend that domination in more subtle ways. As Said puts it, Fanon "more dramatically and decisively than anyone . . . expresses the immense cultural shift from the terrain of nationalist independence to the theoretical domain of liberation" (*Culture* 268).

Fanon's attempt to delineate a means by which postcolonial peoples could pursue the development of viable personal and cultural identities free of domination by the colonial past, along with his radically adversarial stance toward the traditional domination of white Western culture, has proved inspirational to insurgent political movements around the globe, including American Black Power advocates in the 1960s. Although Fanon's concern is direct political intervention, and although he wrote very little about literature per se, his analyses of the negative consequences of the fictional stereotypes produced by Western discourses have numerous implications for literary criticism and theory. Indeed Fanon's meditations on the psychology of colonialism and on the effects of colonialism on African politics and society have provided an important theoretical framework for postcolonial writers such as Ngugi and the Senegalese Sembéne Ousmane. Fanon's body of work, with its distinctively multicultural adaptation of psychoanalytic and Marxist theory and its fiercely dedicated political opposition to continuing domination of the postcolonial world by Western theory and thought, also remains among the founding texts of postcolonial literary theory.

Many of the most important contributions in multicultural theory take Fanon's work as their starting point, whereas many of the fiercest debates in the field involve disagreements over the interpretation of his sometimes complex and difficult writing. But like Fanon himself, multicultural theorists influenced by his work tend to draw on a number of Western theoretical perspectives. For example, Homi K. Bhabha, whose work is characterized by sophisticated applications of Lacanian and Derridean theory to the postcolonial situation (especially in India), also draws on Fanon, whom he tends to read as a precursor of poststructuralism by seeking to deconstruct the strict dual opposition that Fanon appears to posit between colonizer and the colonized. Abdul R. JanMohamed, who has been critical of Bhabha's readings of Fanon, makes extensive use of Jacques Lacan and of the Marxist theorist Fredric Jameson in his work. Gayatri Chakravorty Spivak regards Fanon as an important precursor to her own project, which involves sophisticated applications of Derridean, Marxist, and feminist theory to the postcolonial situation. Spivak is joined by postcolonial Indian historians such as Ranajit Guha and Partha Chatterjee, who employ a number of theoretical perspectives (drawing especially on Antonio Gramsci and Michel Foucault) to focus attention on formerly silenced subaltern voices in Indian history (especially peasant revolts) long ignored by colonialist historians. These Indian scholars, incidentally, publish much of their work in a series of volumes entitled *Subaltern Studies* and collectively are primarily responsible for the use of the term *subaltern* to describe the cultural positions of postcolonial and other "marginal" subjects. And Said, probably the most influential American critic who writes from a multicultural perspective, draws on numerous Western theorists (perhaps most importantly Foucault) but still sees Fanon as an essential figure in the attempts of multicultural peoples to develop viable cultural and personal identities for themselves.

The poststructuralist orientation of postcolonial critics such as Bhabha and Spivak often includes an emphasis on language and representation that points to an important focus in multicultural theory on the possibility that signification may operate according to fundamentally different principles in multicultural texts than in texts of the Western tradition. Indeed an entire field of "colonial discourse theory" (usefully reviewed by Benita Parry) has arisen to study this possibility. Fredric Jameson, for example, suggests that all "third-world texts"—and particularly the major characters in those texts—must necessarily be read as "national allegories." For Jameson, the allegorical nature of such texts arises from the fundamental nature of third-world (postcolonial) societies, in which the lack of the clear separation between public and private realms typical of Western societies effaces the boundary between individual characters and the societies in which they live, leading to a situation in which "*the story of a private individual destiny is always an allegory of the embattled situation of the public third-world culture and society*" (69).

Jameson remarks that postcolonial texts should be read as allegorical "particularly when their forms develop out of predominantly western machineries of representation, such as the novel" (69). In these cases, Western readers, believing that they are encountering a familiar literary form, might be especially tempted to read postcolonial literature as if it operates according to Western principles of literary signification, one of the most ingrained of which (particularly in the novel) is the tendency to think of characters as representing individual human beings. In a similar way, Bhabha has warned against readings of third-world literature that approach "the problem of representing the colonial subject at this mimetic level" ("Representation" 95). Bhabha, however, situates his analysis at a deeper level than does Jameson, arguing not simply for a shift in reading modes but for an "unseating [of] the Transcendental subject" (98). Indeed from the point of view of Bhabha's analysis, Jameson's sweeping claim for the allegorical functioning of third-world literary texts seems to come dangerously close to a safe reinscription of the Otherness of the third world within a preexisting Western analytical category. As Aijaz Ahmad points out, Jameson's vision of the third world tends to cast that world as the passive product of the clash between the active "first" and "second" worlds, and his emphasis on national allegory tends to place too much emphasis on the fundamentally Western concept of nationalism as the only available third-world response to the legacy of colonialism and imperialism: "Politically we are Calibans, all. Formally, we are fated to be in the poststructuralist world of repetition with difference; the same allegory, the nationalist one, re-written, over and over again, until the end of time" ("Jameson's" 9).

Sara Suleri, in contrast, argues that both Jameson and Ahmad accept all too easily the distinction between the third-world and the first-world "West," whether that distinction involves Jameson's identification of national allegory as a literary strategy with the third world or Ahmad's identification of nationalism. Both Jameson and Ahmad, for Suleri, are in danger of falling into the kind of "alteritist" readings of texts from the colonial and postcolonial world that emphasize the foreignness of that world and that, despite their attempt to respect Otherness, are thus in danger simply of routing that Otherness into the Orientalist category of the exotic (12). Moreover a close look at the highly allegorical nature of British colonial texts by such writers as Rudyard Kipling, E. M. Forster, George Orwell, and Sir Walter Scott suggests that, far from representing a radically other mode of literary representation, the allegorical strategy Jameson identifies as crucial to postcolonial writers may often simply repeat the practice of their European colonial predecessors.

Jameson sees a consistent attempt in third-world texts to contribute to the development of national cultural identities in postcolonial states by creating coherent images of such identities in literary texts. But this process, so seemingly similar to the literarization of colonial reality in the work of British writers from Kipling to Scott, clearly resembles the process of textualization of the Orient that Said describes in *Orientalism* as a crucial strategy of European visions of the East. Said demonstrates that stereotypical Orientalist European depictions of the East are consistently textual in nature. Orientalists, he concludes, do not study and describe the Orient in the direct ways that their Western Enlightenment ideologies would like to claim. Instead they generate highly stylized textual representations of the Orient, thereby creating Oriental cultural identities via imperial allegories that serve as clear predecessors of the national allegories Jameson identifies in the work of postcolonial writers.

The differences between the self-generation of cultural identities in postcolonial national allegories and the imposition of cultural identities through Orientalist imperial allegories are obvious. Nevertheless postcolonial writers engaged in the work of helping build cultural identities for their new societies would probably do well to keep in mind the structural similarities between their projects and the former (and current, for that matter) strategies of the imperial West. Jameson himself grants that the very concept of a single unified "national culture" is problematic. Indeed he insists that the kind of allegory he has in mind in relation to third-world literature is considerably more complex than a Bunyanesque "one-to-one table of equivalences." In particular, he invokes an "allegorical spirit" that is "profoundly discontinuous, a matter of breaks and heterogeneities" (73). But this understanding of allegory (partially derived from the work of Walter

Benjamin) grows largely out of the centrality of collage and other techniques of fragmentation to the twentieth-century European avant-garde, suggesting that Jameson's readings of the difference of third-world allegory may once again involve a mapping of Western concepts onto non-Western literature. Jameson, of course, is perfectly aware of the potential drift toward Orientalist stereotyping embodied in his totalizing analysis of third-world literature. He argues that "*any* articulation of radical difference . . . is susceptible to appropriation by that strategy of otherness which Edward Said, in the context of the Middle East, called 'orientalism'" (77). At the same time, Jameson concludes that the potential pitfalls of such an appeal to cultural otherness are preferable to what he sees as the only alternative: a "liberal and humanistic universalism" that would fail to respect the alterity of third-world cultures.

Whether an Orientalist emphasis on difference and a universalist insistence on similarity are the only two alternative approach to postcolonial literature is debatable, however. Bhabha, exploring these two alternatives, suggests what he sees as a preferable third course: to approach postcolonial texts through a mode of Althusserian ideological analysis. For Bhabha, ideological analysis provides an alternative to reading strategies based strictly on interpretation of a text's meaning as the representation of some preexisting reality and allows an interrogation of the historical situation in which that text was produced. This mode of reading thus potentially allows a comprehension of the different signifying practices at work in colonial texts rather than merely projecting Western modes of representation onto non-Western writing. In the particular case of the colonial situation, this interrogation potentially results in fundamental challenges to the Western notion of the transcendental self and to the aligned concepts of authority and intention. It is for this reason, according to Bhabha, that uncanny scenes of colonial abyss like that in Forster's Marabar Caves or that encompassed by the "horror" of Joseph Conrad's Kurtz can be so powerfully unsettling.

We could argue, of course, that in his appeal to Althusser (as in his appeals to various forms of poststructuralist theory elsewhere in his work), Bhabha—like Jameson—is in danger of inscribing third-world literature within first-world theoretical categories. In their different ways, Bhabha and Jameson illustrate the tremendous difficulty faced by any critic who attempts to approach third-world texts through a critical vocabulary that will make them accessible to a first-world audience. Bhabha himself addresses the charge that the application of Western theory to non-Western literature involves a kind of critical imperialism, arguing that the rejection of theory on the basis of this assumption is "damaging and self-defeating" (*Location* 19). For Bhabha, avoidance of Western theory deprives the critic of third-world literature of potentially powerful tools with which to explicate and galvanize the cultural energies of that literature. Bhabha concludes that the very notion of a strict separation between first-world theory and third-world literature is the "mirror image" of the nineteenth-century Orientalist polarity between East and West.

Central to Bhabha's critical project is a rather Derridean deconstruction of the opposition between the cultures of the colonizers and of the colonized. He thus insists that a complexly ambivalent cultural hybridity—on both sides—is the inevitable consequence of all colonial encounters. Bhabha has in mind a subtle mutual implication of the discourses of colonizer and colonized (especially of England and India), and this colonial hybridity of British culture is especially strong given the overt ambivalence of the British imperial project in India, a project informed by fascination and fear, confidence and insecurity, responsibility and guilt. JanMohamed takes Bhabha to task for what he sees as an overly sanguine deconstruction of the polar opposition between colonizer and colonized. JanMohamed argues that Bhabha's poststructuralist perspective ultimately ignores the real point of Fanon's discussion of binary oppositions, thus effacing politics and the realities of domination in the colonial situation (78–79).

Debates like that between JanMohamed and Bhabha indicate the complexity of the issues involved in multicultural literary theory and criticism. They also indicate the high level of engagement, even passion, that often informs this criticism and theory, the real-world importance of which is quite direct. But as Henry Louis Gates Jr. points out in a review of conflicting readings of Fanon's work by theorists such as Said, Bhabha, JanMohamed, Spivak, and Parry, postcolonial theorists should be content to accept that "our own theoretical reflections must be as provisional, reactive, and local as the texts we reflect upon" (470). For Gates, the rejection of imperialism by multicultural theory also implies the rejection of "the imperial agenda of global theory." Multicultural theorists are thus not forced to choose between conflicting views but should remain open to all possible perspectives.

Gates's own criticism, which extends colonial discourse theories to the African-American context, is marked by a similar openmindedness. His capacious vision, theoretical sophistication, and gracefully lucid prose have combined in the last few years to make him probably the most important critic and theorist of African-American literature and culture. In texts such as *Figures in Black* (1987), *The Signifying Monkey* (1988), and *Loose Canons* (1992), Gates employs techniques and ideas from literature, history, and other disciplines to explore a number of important social and cultural issues. His work combines a sophisticated understanding of "white" theory with important elements from the black folk tradition to produce a complex hybrid approach to African-American culture. *Figures in Black,* for example, takes as its starting point a number of poststructuralist literary theories, then explores the application of those theories to black literature. In *The Signifying Monkey,* Gates takes his principal theoretical cues from the vernacular tradition of African-American culture. Here Gates examines the work of important African-American writers such as Zora Neale Hurston, Richard Wright, Ralph Ellison, Ismael Reed, and Alice Walker to explore the relation between African-American literature and the black vernacular tradition. In the process, Gates concludes that the African-American literary tradition is to an important extent shaped by a theory of criticism that is already embedded in the black vernacular tradition. In particular, Gates turns to the folk tradition of the trickster figure, showing how trickster myths often imply a theory of language use and interpretation that significantly departs from traditional Western views but that well describes the working of language in African-American texts. *Loose Canons* meditates not only on the inherently political nature of the notion of literary canons but also on the relevance of recent debates over the canon to issues in society as a whole. Gates counters recent conservative reactions against the growth of multiculturalism in American literary studies by arguing that the richness provided by multicultural perspectives "represents the very best hope for us, collectively, to forge a new, and vital, common American culture in the twenty-first century" (xvii).

For Gates, African-American literature is inherently double-voiced, drawing on energies from both white and black cultural traditions to produce the complex mode of discourse that he refers to as "Signifyin(g)." He believes that theory and criticism should strive for the same kind of richness, and his own work is characterized by a productive combination of energies from metropolitan theory and multicultural countertheory. He describes the challenges facing critics and theorists of African-American literature and culture in a statement that can be taken as a description of his own project:

> We must redefine "theory" itself from within our own black cultures, refusing to grant the premise that theory is something that white people do, so that we are doomed to imitate our white colleagues, like reverse black minstrel critics done up in white face. We are all heirs to critical theory, but we black critics are heir to the black vernacular critical tradition as well. Our task now is to invent and employ our own critical theory, to assume our own propositions, and to stand within the academy as politically responsible and responsive parts of a social and cultural African-American whole. ("Authority" 344)

Gates's appeal for critics of African-American literature to draw on the cultural energies of the African-American tradition while still learning as much as possible from white European and North American traditions can also be taken as a manifesto for multicultural critics as a whole. The resultant exciting combination of cultural energies that characterizes postcolonial and African-American theory and criticism promises to help keep both at the forefront of new developments in literary and cultural studies as we near the end of the twentieth century. As Gates puts it, "The future of theory, in the remainder of this century, is black, indeed" (346).

BIBLIOGRAPHY

Introductory Works

Ashcroft, Bill, Gareth Griffiths, and Helen Tiffin. *The Empire Writes Back: Theory and Practice in Post-Colonial Literatures.* London: Routledge, 1989.

A useful survey of the issues confronting postcolonial criticism, though with surprisingly little emphasis on Africa.

Fanon, Frantz. *The Wretched of the Earth.* Trans. Constance Farrington. New York: Grove, 1968.
Probably the most important founding text of postcolonial theory.

Gates, Henry Louis Jr. *The Signifying Monkey: A Theory of African-American Literary Criticism.* New York: Oxford UP, 1988.
An impressive elaboration of a distinctively African-American theory of literature and criticism.

JanMohamed, Abdul R. *Manichean Aesthetics: The Politics of Literature in Colonial Africa.* Amherst: U of Massachusetts P, 1983.
One of the best available studies of African literature (read against European colonial fictions about Africa).

Said, Edward. *Orientalism.* New York: Vintage, 1979.
A study of negative European stereotypes of the Middle East; perhaps the most widely influential text of American multicultural theory.

Selected Other Works

Achebe, Chinua. "An Image of Africa: Racism in Conrad's *Heart of Darkness.*" *The Massachusetts Review* 18 (1977): 782-794.

Afzal-Khan, Fawzia. *Cultural Imperialism and the Indo-English Novel: Genre and Ideology in R. K. Narayan, Anita Desai, Kamala Markandaya, and Salman Rushdie.* University Park: Pennsylvania State UP, 1993.

Ahmad, Aijaz. "Jameson's Rhetoric of Otherness and the 'National Allegory.'" *Social Text* 17 (Fall 1987): 3-25.

———. *In Theory: Nations, Classes, Literatures.* London: Verso, 1994.

Appiah, Kwame Anthony. *In My Father's House: Africa in the Philosophy of Culture.* New York: Oxford UP, 1992.

Baker, Houston A. Jr. *Afro-American Poetics: Revisions of Harlem and the Black Aesthetic.* Madison: U of Wisconsin P, 1988.

———. *Blues, Ideology, and Afro-American Literature: A Vernacular Theory.* Chicago: U of Chicago P, 1984.

———. *Modernism and the Harlem Renaissance.* Chicago: U of Chicago P, 1987.

———. *Workings of the Spirit: The Poetics of Afro-American Women's Writing.* Chicago: U of Chicago P, 1990.

Bates, Robert H., V. Y. Mudimbe, and Jean O'Barr, eds. *Africa and the Disciplines: The Contributions of Research in Africa to the Social Sciences and Humanities.* Chicago: U of Chicago P, 1993.

Benjamin, Walter. *The Origin of German Tragic Drama.* Trans. John Osborne. London: NLB, 1977.

Bhabha, Homi K. *The Location of Culture.* London: Routledge, 1994.

———. "Postcolonial Criticism." In *Redrawing the Boundaries: The Transformation of English and American Literary Studies,* ed. Stephen Greenblatt and Giles Gunn, 437-465. New York: Modern Language Association, 1992.

Brennan, Timothy. *Salman Rushdie and the Third World: Myths of the Nation.* New York: St. Martin's, 1989.

Brewer, Anthony. *Marxist Theories of Imperialism: A Critical Survey.* London: Routledge and Kegan Paul, 1980.

Carby, Hazel V. *Reconstructing Womanhood: The Emergence of the Afro-American Woman Novelist.* New York: Oxford UP, 1987.

Chatterjee, Partha. "More on Modes of Power and the Peasantry." In *Selected Subaltern Studies,* ed. Ranajit Guha and Gayatri Chakravorty Spivak, 351-390. New York: Oxford UP, 1988.

———. *The Nation and Its Fragments: Colonial and Postcolonial Histories.* Princeton, N.J.: Princeton UP, 1993.

Cheyfitz, Eric. *The Poetics of Imperialism: Translation and Colonization from "The Tempest" to "Tarzan."* New York: Oxford UP, 1991.

Chinweizu, Onwuchekwa Jemie, and Ihechukwu Madubuike. *Toward the Decolonization of African Literature.* Vol. 1, *African Fiction and Poetry and Their Critics.* Washington, D.C.: Howard UP, 1983.

Cooke, Michael G. *Afro-American Literature in the Twentieth Century: The Achievement of Intimacy.* New Haven, Conn.: Yale UP, 1984.

Davidson, Basil. *The Black Man's Burden: Africa and the Curse of the Nation-State.* New York: Random House, 1992.

Davis, Angela Y. *Women, Race, and Class.* 1981. New York: Vintage, 1983.

Deleuze, Gilles, and Félix Guattari. *Kafka: Toward a Minor Literature.* 1975. Trans. Dana Polan. Minneapolis: U of Minnesota P, 1986.

Du Bois, W. E. B. *The Souls of Black Folk.* 1903. New York: Penguin, 1989.

During, Simon. "Postmodernism or Post-Colonialism Today." *Textual Practice* 1.1 (1987): 32-47.

Evans, Malcolm. *Signifying Nothing: Truth's True Contents in Shakespeare's Text.* Athens: U of Georgia P, 1986.

Fanon, Frantz. *Black Skin, White Masks.* Trans. Charles Lam Markmann. New York: Grove, 1967.

———. *A Dying Colonialism.* Trans. Haakon Chevalier. New York: Grove, 1965.

———. *Toward the African Revolution: Political Essays.* Trans. Haakon Chevalier. New York: Grove, 1967.

Fiedler, Leslie, and Houston A. Baker Jr. *Opening up the Canon: Selected Papers from the English Institute.* 1979. Baltimore, Md.: Johns Hopkins UP, 1981.

Gates, Henry Louis Jr. "Authority, (White) Power, and the (Black) Critic; or, It's All Greek to Me." In *The Future of Literary Theory,* ed. Ralph Cohen, 324-346. New York: Routledge, 1989.

———. "Critical Fanonism." *Critical Inquiry* 17.3 (1991): 457-470.

———. *Figures in Black: Words, Signs, and the "Racial" Self.* New York: Oxford UP, 1987.

———. *Loose Canons: Notes on the Culture Wars.* New York: Oxford UP, 1992.

———, ed. *Black Literature and Literary Theory.* New York; Methuen, 1984.

———, ed. *"Race," Writing, and Difference.* Chicago: U of Chicago P, 1986.

Giddings, Robert, ed. *Literature and Imperialism.* New York: St. Martin's, 1991.

Gramsci, Antonio. *Selections from the Prison Notebooks.* Ed. Quintin Hoare and Geoffrey Nowell Smith. New York: International Publishers, 1971.

Gugelberger, Georg M., ed. *Marxism and African Literature.* London: James Currey, 1985.

Guha, Ranajit. "Dominance Without Hegemony and Its Historiography." In *Subaltern Studies: Writings on South Asian History and Society,* Vol. 6, ed. Ranajit Guha, 210-309. Delhi: Oxford UP, 1989.

Guha, Ranajit, and Gayatri Chakravorty Spivak, eds. *Selected Subaltern Studies.* New York: Oxford UP, 1988.

Henry, Charles P. *Culture and African American Politics.* Bloomington: Indiana UP, 1990.

Irele, Abiola. *The African Experience in Literature and Ideology.* London: Heinemann, 1981.

Jameson, Fredric. "Third-World Literature in the Era of Multinational Capitalism." *Social Text* 15 (1986): 65-88.

King, Bruce, ed. *West Indian Literature.* London: Macmillan, 1979.

Krupat, Arnold. *Ethnocriticism: Ethnography, History, Literature.* Berkeley and Los Angeles: U of California P, 1991.

Lamming, George. *The Pleasures of Exile.* London: Michael Joseph, 1960.

Lazarus, Neil. *Resistance in Postcolonial African Fiction.* New Haven, Conn.: Yale UP, 1990.

Lincoln, Kenneth. *Native American Renaissance.* Berkeley and Los Angeles: U of California P, 1983.

Mbalia, Dorothea Drummond. *Toni Morrison's Developing Class Consciousness.* London: Associated UP, 1991.

Memmi, Albert. *The Colonizer and the Colonized.* New York: Orion, 1965.

Miller, Christopher L. *Blank Darkness: Africanist Discourse in French.* Chicago: U of Chicago P, 1985.

———. *Theories of Africans: Francophone Literature and Anthropology in Africa.* Chicago: U of Chicago P, 1990.

Mitchell, W. J. T. "Postcolonial Culture, Postimperial Criticism." *Transition* 56 (1992): 11-19.

Morrison, Toni. *Playing in the Dark: Whiteness and the Literary Imagination.* Cambridge, Mass.: Harvard UP, 1992.

Mudimbe, V. Y. *The Invention of Africa: Gnosis, Philosophy, and the Order of Knowledge.* Bloomington: Indiana UP, 1988.

Murray, David. *Forked Tongues: Speech, Writing, and Representation in North American Indian Texts.* Bloomington: Indiana UP, 1991.

Ngara, Emmanuel. *Art and Ideology in the African Novel: A Study of the Influence of Marxism on African Writing.* London: Heinemann, 1985.

Ngugi wa Thiong'o. *Decolonising the Mind: The Politics of Language in African Literature.* London: James Currey, 1986.

———. *Moving the Centre: The Struggle for Cultural Freedoms.* London: James Currey, 1993.

Nirajani, Tejaswini. *Siting Translation: History, Poststructuralism, and the Colonial Context.* Berkeley and Los Angeles: U of California P, 1992.

Nkrumah, Kwame. *Class Struggle in Africa.* New York: International Publishers, 1970.

Obiechina, Emmanuel N. *Language and Theme: Essays on African Literature.* Washington, D.C.: Howard UP, 1990.

Owomoyela, Oyekan, ed. *A History of Twentieth-Century African Literatures.* Lincoln: U of Nebraska P, 1993.

Parry, Benita. *Delusions and Discoveries: Studies on India in the British Imagination, 1880-1930.* Berkeley and Los Angeles: U of California P, 1972.

———. "Problems in Current Theories of Colonial Discourse." *Oxford Literary Review* 9.1-2 (1987): 27-58.

Richards, Thomas. *The Imperial Archive: Knowledge and the Fantasy of Empire.* London: Verso, 1993.

Robinson, Ronald E., and John A. Gallagher, with Alice Denny. *Africa and the Victorians: The Official Mind of Imperialism.* London: Macmillan, 1961.

Rodney, Walter. *How Europe Underdeveloped Africa.* Dar es Salaam: Tanzania Publishing House, 1972.
Rushdie, Salman. "The Empire Writes Back with a Vengeance." *London Times* (July 3, 1982): 8.
Said, Edward. *Culture and Imperialism.* New York: Knopf, 1993.
Schipper, Mineke. *Beyond the Boundaries: African Literature and Literary Theory.* London: Allison and Busby, 1989.
Soyinka, Wole. *Art, Dialogue and Outrage: Essays on Literature and Culture.* Ibadan, Nigeria: New Horn, 1988.
Spivak, Gayatri Chakravorty. "Can the Subaltern Speak?" In *Marxism and the Interpretation of Culture,* ed. Cary Nelson and Lawrence Grossberg, 271–313. Urbana: U of Illinois P, 1988.
———. *In Other Worlds: Essays in Cultural Politics.* New York: Routledge, 1988.
———. *The Post-Colonial Critic: Interviews, Strategies, Dialogues.* Ed. Sarah Harasym. New York: Routledge, 1990.
———. "Subaltern Studies: Deconstructing Historiography." In *Subaltern Studies: Writings on South Asian History and Society,* Vol. 4, ed. Ranajit Guha, 330–363. Delhi: Oxford UP, 1985.
Stampp, Kenneth. *The Peculiar Institution: Slavery in the Ante-Bellum South.* New York: Random House, 1956.
Stuckey, Sterling. *Slave Culture: Nationalist Theory and the Foundations of Black America.* New York: Oxford UP, 1987.
Suleri, Sarah. *The Rhetoric of English India.* Chicago: U of Chicago P, 1992.
Sundquist, Eric J. *To Wake the Nations: Race in the Making of American Literature.* Cambridge, Mass.: Belknap, 1993.
Thiam, Awa. *Speak Out, Black Sisters: Feminism and Oppression in Black Africa.* London: Pluto, 1986.
Viswanathan, Gauri. *Masks of Conquest: Literary Study and British Rule in India.* New York: Columbia UP, 1989.
Vizenor, Gerald, ed. *Narrative Chance: Postmodern Discourse on Native American Indian Literatures.* Albuquerque: U of New Mexico P, 1989.
Wolf, Eric R. *Europe and the People without History.* Berkeley and Los Angeles: U of California P, 1982.
Zahar, Renate. *Frantz Fanon: Colonialism and Alienation.* New York: Monthly Review, 1974.

Introduction to the Application of Literary Theory

chapter **11**

Approaches to *The Tempest*, by William Shakespeare

The Tempest, probably written in 1611, is generally accepted as Shakespeare's last play. It has also long been one of Shakespeare's most popular, partially because it has special status as his last play and partially because so many critics have envisioned the character Prospero as an image of Shakespeare himself, thus making *The Tempest* a sort of emblem of Shakespeare's entire artistic practice. In recent years, however, *The Tempest* has gained renewed attention from critics, largely because the content of the play (which deals directly with the contemporary European colonization of the Americas) corresponds directly with the focus on political issues that has characterized the most important recent critical work on Renaissance literature as a whole. As a result, all of the following discussions focus somewhat on the issue of colonialism in *The Tempest,* though they approach this issue in different ways. The theoretical approaches discussed in this section comprise reader-response criticism, deconstruction, the new historicism, and multicultural criticism. Other approaches could have been used as well. For example, the treatment of Miranda in the play has received a great deal of attention from feminist critics in recent years, and the motif of power and domination that clearly informs many of the relationships among the play's characters (especially that between Prospero and Caliban) offers a number of opportunities for application of the work of Foucault.

READER-RESPONSE CRITICISM

As Stephen Greenblatt points out at the end of *Shakespearean Negotiations,* William Shakespeare's work now survives more as printed literature than as live theater. That is, Shakespeare's plays are far more often read (especially in college literature classes) than they are seen in performance. This shift of Shakespeare's plays from the stage to the book has a number of important implications, one of the most obvious of which pertains to reader-response criticism. Reading a play like *The Tempest,* for example, is a far different proposition than seeing that same play in performance, even if the reader attempts to imagine in her mind how the play might be presented on stage. In the case of *The Tempest,* this gap between *reader* response and *audience* response is particularly large given that the play contains so many fantastic elements that are clearly difficult to represent in performance but that can quite easily be imagined by readers.

As Anthony B. Dawson notes, one of the biggest problems with *The Tempest* is that the play includes so many elements of magic that it is almost impossible to stage adequately:

> An obvious problem with producing the play is that actors swaying and lurching on an adamantly stationary stage floor are unlikely to persuade us of the storm at sea—despite the help of gauze and scrim, creaking rigging, or screaming winds over which the actors have to shout their inconsequential and usually inaudible lines. And the same goes for the other spectacles of the play—the disappearing banquet, the wedding masque, even the "discovery" of Miranda and Ferdinand—it is all so disconcertingly stagy. (67)

Moreover, Dawson goes on to echo Lytton Strachey's famous condemnation of *The Tempest* as a tedious and poorly constructed play, concluding that the technical problems in staging combine with various predictably unsuccessful conspiracies and wearisome attempts at comedy to make the play just plain boring. Dawson does acknowledge, however, that numerous performances of *The Tempest* have apparently been rousingly successful and that most Shakespeare buffs can claim at one time or another to have seen a "great" production of the play.

For Dawson, the success of these performances has more to do with the fact that audiences simply expect Shakespeare's plays to be great than with any greatness in *The Tempest* itself. Indeed he suggests that Shakespeare aficionados have such a personal investment in Shakespeare's greatness that they cannot afford to see the flaws in his work. The experience of viewing *The Tempest,* in short, is as much a product of the desires and expectations of the audience as of the play itself, an insight that suggests that reader-response (or audience-response) approaches to the play should be particularly fruitful. Of course, Shakespeare's plays often present technical problems in performance (the storm in *King Lear* is a notorious example), and as a rule his plays require a great deal of what Samuel Taylor Coleridge calls a "willing suspension of disbelief." That is, Shakespeare's audiences typically must agree to forget the obvious fact that what they are watching is merely a play so that they can become more intimately engaged in the action.

The Tempest is a particularly good example of this phenomenon, with numerous aspects of the play being realizable on stage only with the willing imaginative complicity of the audience, a complicity that Shakespeare's reputation for greatness helps secure. Beginning with the unstageable storm in the opening scene, the play continually asks the audience to grant its magical premises and to believe that the events unfolding on the stage are actually occurring on an enchanted island as the characters describe them. Representation of characters such as Ariel and Caliban is particularly problematic. Ariel, for example, must be played by an actor whose humanity is all too obvious to the audience, but he must nevertheless be envisioned as a spritelike creature of air. In particular, there are numerous scenes in which Ariel is supposedly invisible, even though the audience can clearly see him on the stage. Caliban, meanwhile, is the very figure of ambiguity, sometimes seeming human, sometimes animal-like, but all the while a creature of such strange otherness that his representation by a human actor is well-nigh impossible without a boost from a complicitous audience. Trinculo's reaction on first seeing Caliban can be taken as indicative of Caliban's ambiguous status: "What have we here? A man or a fish? Dead or alive? A fish! He smells like a fish; a very ancient and fishlike smell. . . . Legged like a man! And his fins like arms! . . . This is no fish, but an islander, that hath lately suffered by a thunderbolt" (II.ii.25–38).

Caliban, in fact, is one of the most enigmatic characters in all of Shakespeare's work. His description in the play is not only vague but also contradictory, leaving directors and actors a great deal of room for their own imaginative intervention in his representation. But this interpretive freedom tends to be undercut by the fact that he remains "almost impossible to put convincingly on stage" (Hulme 107). Thus Morton Luce, summing up the wide variety of Calibans who have appeared on stages throughout the centuries, concludes that "if all the suggestions as to Caliban's form and feature and endowments that are thrown out in the play are collected, it will be found that the one half renders the other half impossible" (quoted in Hulme 107).

Peter Hulme, however, concludes that Caliban's ambiguity is an effective enhancement of his status as alien Other to the play's European characters: "The difficulty in visualizing Caliban cannot be put down to a failure of clarity in the text. Caliban, as a compromise formation, can exist only within discourse: he is fundamentally and essentially beyond the bounds of representation" (108). Hulme reads the play within the context of early-seventeenth-century colonialism and sees Caliban as a representation of the seeming strangeness of the Native Americans encountered by the Europeans in their first travels in the New World. Indeed Hulme's work participates in a quite general trend in recent criticism of *The Tempest* that emphasizes the play's complicity in the colonialist discourse of its contemporary Jacobean England. But even though Hulme (like Greenblatt, Paul Brown, Michael Dobson, and others) seeks to read the play against the grain and thereby to reveal its own colonialist and racist biases, he does so in such a way that leaves the aesthetic greatness of the play unchallenged. Of course, this interpretation of Caliban's complexity nicely serves the projects of critics like Hulme and Greenblatt, for whom an appreciation of Shakespeare's fundamental complexity is crucial to an adequate understanding of the relationship of his plays to their contemporary social and historical context—and to an adequate appreciation of the work of Hulme and Greenblatt. Thus as Dawson notes, where conventional formalist critics once praised *The Tempest* because of its harmonies, reconciliations, and ultimate organic unities, more recent new historicist, poststructuralist, and neo-Marxist critics have praised the play precisely because its lack of unity helps reveal contradictions in its own ideology. In short, critics have typically found in *The Tempest* what they hoped and expected to find, and their reactions to the play are largely conditioned by the requirements of the criticism they pursue. Or, as Stanley Fish would have it, their readings of the play are produced by their participation in particular interpretive communities.

The phenomenon of varying interpretations of *The Tempest* is especially clear in reactions to the figure of Caliban. For some, Caliban has served as a marker of savagery and subhuman evil, whereas for others his resistance to Prospero's cruel oppression makes him a heroic model for oppressed minorities everywhere. It is certainly clear that Prospero dominates *The Tempest,* just as he dominates his slaves Ariel and Caliban. And audiences throughout the centuries have tended to identify and sympathize with Prospero's position, seeing him as the play's "hero" and regarding his restoration to his "rightful" place as the duke of Milan as the major movement of the play's romance plot. This tendency to sympathize with Prospero is further enhanced by the long-standing tradition of identifying Prospero with Shakespeare himself. Prospero's illusion-producing magic thus becomes a figure of Shakespeare's art and the drowning of Prospero's books at the end of the play an announcement of Shakespeare's retirement as a dramatist.

Recent critics, however, have tended to emphasize Prospero's ill temper and his despotic treatment of Ariel and Caliban. And recent audiences, especially those that view the play from the perspective of Africans, Native Americans, and other postcolonial peoples (for whom Prospero's imperial domination of Caliban's island has historical resonances that are only too familiar), have sometimes seen Prospero as the villain of the play. Such audiences identify with Caliban instead. This tendency to identify with Caliban is perhaps strongest of all in the Caribbean, where important writers such as Aimé Césaire and George Lamming have adopted Caliban as a figure of their own marginality to the European cultural tradition. In a similar way, recent feminist critics such as Lorie Jerrell Leininger have identified with Miranda's position, emphasizing Prospero's domination of his daughter and his use of her as a pawn in his own political maneuvering. Readings that treat Prospero as a villain and identify instead with Caliban or Miranda appear to arise from the specific political positions of subaltern or feminist audiences, that is, from the interpretive communities to which those audiences belong. Moreover we might attribute such readings to changes in historical perspective that make available responses to the play that would presumably not have occurred to Shakespeare's contemporary audience in Jacobean London. Thus Alden T. Vaughan and Virginia Mason Vaughan suggest that their historical study of reactions to Caliban also produces a study of cultural history as a whole: "Caliban's history is cultural history, or at least a significant strand of it, in microcosm. Changing interpretations of Caliban provide a window on cultural trends, just as those trends simultaneously determine Caliban's changing characteristics" (xi).

In short, the way we view Caliban may reflect our own attitudes and preoccupations more than anything that exists in *The Tempest,* providing an exemplary illustration of a point often made by such reader-response critics as Fish. In a very real sense, the play has changed with history. Thus as Hulme puts it, recent readings of the play within the context of colonialism have made it a "much more complex play than it used to be" (106). But Curt Breight has recently argued that Prospero's tyranny is so obvious and extreme that even contemporary audiences would have been likely to react against him. Moreover Breight argues that such audiences would have identified Prospero's political maneuvers with the operations of official power in Jacobean England, so that the negative depiction of Prospero would also have been received as a negative commentary on King James and other contemporary figures of official power.

Breight further argues that the overt fictionality of *The Tempest* (what Dawson characterizes as the play's "staginess") is a key element making this subversive response to the play available. He concludes that by making Prospero's various machinations seem so blatantly artificial, the play also exposes the artificiality of the official strategies of power (especially those involving a contemporary official obsession with treason and conspiracy) with which Prospero would have been identified by the audience. For Breight, most of the characters in the play are firmly in the thrall of Prospero's magic, but

> the audience exists *outside* Prospero's manipulation of characters and situations and is thereby enabled to perceive Shakespeare's clever demystification of various official strategies within the discourse of treason. The audience is allowed to see that conspiracy is often a fiction, or a construct, or a real yet wholly containable piece of social theatre. The play can thus be viewed within a sphere of oppositional discourse that arose against official discourse in this period. (1)

We could argue, of course, that Breight's reading of Jacobean audiences is conditioned by his own contemporary view, but his suggestion that Jacobean audiences would not necessarily have unquestioningly identified with Prospero is probably a good one. Meanwhile Breight's suggestion that the play's overt artificiality is actually a virtue aligns his reading with those of other critics who have attempted to recuperate that aspect of the play under the rubric of "metadrama." By this reading, *The Tempest* is about theater (in the world of politics as well as in the world of the theater proper), and its staginess comes about because the play seeks to call attention to its own workings as a theatrical production. The audience again plays a crucial role in such readings because one of the most important metadramatic aspects of the play concerns the way in which Prospero constantly stages theatrical events for the benefit of the other characters, who become audiences for his productions. The audience of *The*

Tempest thus becomes a "meta-audience" that observes this audience while it observes Prospero's spectacles.

This "play-within-a-play" effect is, of course, one of the most frequent devices through which Shakespeare's plays seem openly to invite audience participation. Perhaps the most famous example of this phenomenon is the "Mousetrap" play that is staged within *Hamlet,* and it may be no coincidence that this play has been a favorite of reader-response critics. Norman Holland, for example, suggests that the character of Hamlet is largely a projection of the identity themes of the audience, though Holland also concludes that this phenomenon is encouraged by certain verbal aspects of the play. Stephen Booth similarly concludes that the structure of *Hamlet* encourages audience identification with the events of the play. For Booth (sounding somewhat like Wolfgang Iser), the play invites the audience to follow Polonius in expecting that events will proceed in a logical and predictable way, only to have this attitude revealed as foolish as one expectation after another fails to develop. The audience thus learns the valuable lesson that "truth is bigger than any one system of knowing it, and *Hamlet* is bigger than any of the frames of reference it inhabits. *Hamlet* allows us to comprehend—hold on to—all the contradictions it contains. *Hamlet* refuses to cradle its audience's mind in a closed generic framework, or otherwise limit the ideological context of its actions. In *Hamlet* the mind is cradled in nothing more than the fabric of the play" (175).

The power of this lesson depends on audience members granting authority to the play and not simply concluding that the play's failure to meet their expectations is the result of poor construction. Indeed the response of Shakespeare's audiences is in general powerfully conditioned by the strength of his reputation as the world's "greatest" dramatist, a reputation that obviously affects the expectations that audiences bring to his plays. Thus contradictions and inconsistencies that might be regarded as flaws in the work of "lesser" figures tend in the case of Shakespeare to be interpreted as brilliant strategies that add richness, complexity, and ambiguity to his work. This is especially the case with *The Tempest,* which historical studies have established as the last of Shakespeare's plays. It is thus conventional to regard the play as Shakespeare's most mature work and as the culmination of his development as a dramatist, resulting in a tendency among audiences and critics to assume that Skakespeare was fully in control of his art in this play and that any apparent anomalies in it were put there intentionally.

Of course, Shakespeare's reputation had to come from somewhere in the first place, and it has long been conventional to assume that his exalted reputation is attributable to the simple fact that he deserves it. In this view, the tendency to see apparent flaws in Shakespeare's plays as intentional complications is entirely appropriate. According to virtually all conventional aesthetic criteria, of course, Shakespeare *is* a great writer. But aesthetic criteria are neither absolute nor innocent, and the development of the criteria by which Shakespeare has been judged great is itself the product of specific social and historical complexes—that is, of interpretive communities. A number of recent critics have challenged the traditional assumptions of Shakespeare's unique genius, stopping seriously to ask just how we know he is the greatest writer in English and, indeed, in world literature. In an extensive review of Shakespeare's critical reputation, Gary Taylor concludes that there is no objective justification within Shakespeare's writing for his unique reputation and that this reputation is largely a result of practices within the institution of Shakespeare criticism. As Taylor points out, "Shakespeare cannot claim any unique command of theatrical resources, longevity or reach of reputation, depth or range of style, universality or comprehensiveness" (395). What Shakespeare can claim is a unique level of attention from modern critics, who participate in an interpretive community that is professionally invested in perpetuating his reputation.

Meanwhile the political effects on Shakespeare's reputation go beyond the institutional politics of literary criticism. He has long stood, for example, as an icon of British nationalism. Thus Michael Dobson notes that Shakespeare's reputation was enhanced in the seventeenth and eighteenth centuries when English nationalism "conscripted him extensively in the service of imperial expansion" (191). In the eighteenth century, for example, there were several cases in which delegations of leaders of various Native American tribes were treated to performances of Shakespeare's plays, apparently to impress them with the glories of English culture. The Native Americans, not surprisingly, were unimpressed, but their failure to appreciate Shakespeare was simply taken by the British as further evidence of Native American cultural inferiority. Meanwhile as tensions between England and its American colonies grew, Shakespeare came to stand for the English as a reminder of their superiority to the coarse white colonists in America. Tellingly *The Tempest* (with Prospero standing as a marker of British imperial power) was the most frequently performed Shakespeare play in late-eighteenth-century America, and revolutionary leaders such as George Washington were perfectly well aware that "the British Empire, Prospero, and Shakespeare are inextricably linked" (Dobson 197). Shakespeare continued to serve as an icon of British culture in the great nineteenth-century era of imperial expansion as well, and (as Dobson notes) he would eventually be adopted in America as a marker of the supposed superiority of Western culture in general. The politics of interpretation involved in the legacy of Shakespeare's reputation as a unique individual genius thus provide a striking example of the production of texts by reader expectations, for which Prospero's suggestion at the end of *The Tempest* that the audience is now in charge of his fate can stand as a striking announcement.

Works Cited

Booth, Stephen. "On the Value of *Hamlet.*" In *Reinterpretations of Elizabethan Drama,* ed. Norman Rabkin, 77-99. New York: Columbia UP, 1969.

Breight, Curt. "'Treason Doth Never Prosper': *The Tempest* and the Discourse of Treason." *Shakespeare Quarterly* 41.1 (1990): 1-28.

Brown, Paul. "'This Thing of Darkness I Acknowledge Mine': *The Tempest* and the Discourse of Colonialism." In *Political Shakespeare: New Essays in Cultural Materialism,* ed. Jonathan Dollimore and Alan Sinfield, 48-71. Ithaca, N.Y.: Cornell UP, 1985.

Césaire, Aimé. *Un Tempête.* Paris: Seuil, 1969.
Dawson, Anthony B. "*Tempest* in a Teapot: Critics, Evaluation, Ideology." In *"Bad" Shakespeare: Revaluations of the Shakespeare Canon,* ed. Maurice Charney, 61-73. Rutherford, N.J.: Fairleigh Dickinson UP, 1988.
Dobson, Michael. "Fairly Brave New World: Shakespeare, the American Colonies, and the American Revolution." *Renaissance Drama* 23 (1992): 189-207.
Fish, Stanley. *Is There a Text in This Class?: The Authority of Interpretive Communities.* Cambridge, Mass.: Harvard UP, 1980.
Greenblatt, Stephen. *Shakespearean Negotiations: The Circulation of Social Energy in Renaissance England.* Berkeley and Los Angeles: U of California P, 1988.
Holland, Norman. "*Hamlet*—My Greatest Creation." *Journal of the American Academy of Psychoanalysis* 3 (1975): 419-427.
Hulme, Peter. *Colonial Encounters: Europe and the Native Caribbean, 1492-1797.* London: Methuen, 1986.
Lamming, George. *The Pleasures of Exile.* London: Michael Joseph, 1960.
Leininger, Lorie Jerrell. "The Miranda Trap: Sexism and Racism in Shakespeare's *The Tempest.*" In *The Woman's Part: Feminist Criticism of Shakespeare,* ed. Carolyn R. S. Lenz, Gayle Green, and Carol T. Neely, 285-294. Urbana: U of Illinois P, 1980.
Shakespeare, William. *The Tempest.* New York: Signet-New American Library, 1964.
Taylor, Gary. *Reinventing Shakespeare: A Cultural History, from the Restoration to the Present.* New York: Weidenfield and Nicolson, 1989.
Vaughan, Alden T., and Virginia Mason Vaughan. *Shakespeare's Caliban: A Cultural History.* Cambridge: Cambridge UP, 1991.

DECONSTRUCTIVE CRITICISM

The most important trend in criticism of *The Tempest* in the last quarter century has argued that the play is intimately concerned with English colonial expansion into the Americas in the early seventeenth century. The structure of the play would thus be expected to display especially strong tendencies toward binary oppositions of the kind that deconstructive criticism often seeks to undermine. After all, such oppositions are crucial to the ideology of colonialism. Fundamental to the colonial enterprise is the firm belief that the colonizer (that is, the English) is fundamentally different from (and superior to) the colonized (in this case, the Native American). Indeed Ronald Takaki has convincingly argued that the very notion of strict racial differences is largely a product of early European exploration of the Americas. For centuries the English had regarded themselves as the epitome of civilization and thus as radically superior to their most important Others, the "primitive" and "barbaric" Irish. Prior to the seventeenth century, the English had regarded these differences as largely cultural rather than biological and had assumed that the Irish could be civilized by proper acculturation. Contacts with Native Americans in the early seventeenth century, however, eventually led the English to believe that their differences from Native Americans were racial and could not be overcome by culture. This development, Takaki argues, was largely related to religion and had centrally to do with the growing tendency of the New England Puritans to identify the native inhabitants of that region as unredeemable minions of Satan: "To the colonists, the Indians were not merely a wayward people: They personified something fearful within Puritan society itself. Like Caliban, a 'born devil'" (908).

As the reference to Caliban here shows, Takaki regards *The Tempest* as an important marker of this "racialization of savagery" in the early seventeenth century. In particular, he notes that the structural oppositions inherent in the play mirror those that the English settlers saw between themselves and the Native Americans from whom they sought so desperately to differentiate themselves. Takaki suggests that Shakespeare's contemporary audiences would have had no trouble recognizing Caliban as a representation of the irrationality and debased sexuality that were already being projected onto Native Americans, while Prospero would have clearly stood as a marker of European reason and triumph of the mind over the body: "To be civilized, they believed, required denial of wholeness—the repression of the instinctual forces of human nature. Prospero, personification of civilized man, identified himself as mind rather than body. His epistemology relied on the visual rather than the tactile and on the linear knowledge of books rather than the polymorphous knowledge of experience" (899).

Takaki's identification of the roots of seventeenth-century racism in the Puritan obsession with Satan clearly recalls Michel Foucault's argument that the Western habit of defining identity in opposition to an alien Other (who is rejected as evil and inferior) arises from the emphasis on Satan in Christianity. But Takaki's discussion of the polar oppositions at work in the sexual and epistemological structure of *The Tempest* also recalls Jacques Derrida's deconstructive assault on binary oppositions in the Western philosophical tradition as a whole. A closer look at the play reveals the operation of an entire array of such oppositions. At the level of specific content and imagery, the disorder of the storm underlines the potential utopian order of Prospero's island; the exotic enchanted island is contrasted with the everyday world of Europe; Ariel's airiness opposes Caliban's gross physicality; Caliban's supposed lechery opposes Miranda's chastity; Prospero's knowledge is highlighted by the ignorance of Caliban and his coconspirators Stephano and Trinculo. Literary and aesthetic oppositions inform *The Tempest* as well. The play's generic structure sets tragedy against comedy, while its language contrasts prose with poetry and puns and wordplay with serious statement.

The play is underwritten by a number of larger and more abstract social and philosophical oppositions. In addition to an anticipation of the fundamental Cartesian duality of mind and body, truth and reality stand against appearance and illusion, while wisdom, knowledge, and reason oppose folly, ignorance, and madness. And fundamental oppositions between masculine and feminine, obedience and treason, and master and slave suggest a structure of social stability of which the opposition between the civilized Europeans and the "savage" Caliban is the most obvious marker but of which the strict class differentiation between the play's aristocrats (Prospero, Antonio, Alonso, Sebastian, Ferdinand) and its commoners (Trinculo, Stephano, the crew of the "wrecked" ship) stand as reminders that European society (and the white race) is itself informed by fundamental divisions. Moreover the clearly defined class structure of the island's societal microcosm is typical of the strictly hierarchial nature of all of the play's binary oppositions.

Catherine Belsey notes how both linguistic and social stability rely on the kinds of binary oppositions around which *The Tempest* seems to be structured:

> Meaning depends on difference, and the fixing of meaning is the fixing of difference as opposition. It is precisely this identification of difference as polarity which Derrida defines as *metaphysical*. . . . This process of fixing meaning provides us with a series of polarities which define what is. These definitions are also values. In the oppositions "I/you," "individual/society," "truth/fiction," "masculine/feminine" one term is always privileged, and one is always other, always what is *not* the thing itself. (177)

Of course, we could see the unusual prevalence of binary oppositions in *The Tempest* as evidence of a complacent confidence in the stability of an order based on such images. Belsey claims that the insistence on stable binary oppositions, which leads to a view of meaning as "single, fixed, and given," is generally "a way of reaffirming existing values" (178–179). But we might follow the famous suggestion of a character in another well-known Shakespeare play and suspect that *The Tempest* doth protest too much in its seeming insistence on the reliability of binary oppositions as a structural principle and in its almost hysterical attempt to reaffirm existing social values. In this case, the remarkable number of such oppositions that informs the play can be taken as evidence of a fundamental anxiety and insecurity over existing values, particularly over the stability and validity of the binary oppositions on which those values are based.

There are, in fact, good historical reasons to adopt this reading. As Belsey goes on to note, Shakespeare's England was in a state of almost perpetual crisis; he lived in a period in which many of his society's most fundamental assumptions were being radically challenged, in a Renaissance era that had seen the breakdown of centuries of almost universal Catholic hegemony throughout Europe but that had not seen this old order replaced by anything comparable as a source of authority and security. For Belsey, the famous plurality of meaning that informs Shakespeare's writing can be taken as a marker of this crisis, as can certain fundamental uncertainties over the validity of the major polar oppositions that provide the structural scaffolding for Jacobean society. In particular, Belsey notes how Shakespeare's plays feature a remarkable number of challenges to conventional gender boundaries. The young woman disguised as a man is a stock Shakespeare character, and the uncertainties suggested by this figure are made all the more unsettling by the contemporary practice of having female characters played by young male actors.

There are no such overt transgressions of gender boundaries in *The Tempest,* but numerous elements of the play do suggest that the anxieties about gender described by Belsey were made all the more powerful through the European encounter with the Otherness of the New World. In particular, the binary oppositions that inform *The Tempest* can be highly unstable, and a close look at them reveals that the structure and language of the play often undermine such oppositions even as they strive to establish them. For example, the relationship between Prospero and Caliban seems to be strictly defined by binary oppositions: master versus slave, European versus Native American, culture versus nature. But the relationship between these two characters might not be quite as clear as it seems. Prospero, for example, seems to depend on Caliban's labor for food, firewood, and other necessities, just as the early English settlers in America were often dependent on the local native inhabitants. Yet Prospero seems at times to have almost unlimited magical powers, making us wonder exactly why Caliban's services would be necessary. One explanation, of course, might have to do with the nature of Prospero's magic, which at times seems to be principally an art of illusion. He seems able to manipulate the perceptions that human beings have of their material surroundings, but whether he can actually change those surroundings or produce material objects like food and wood is not entirely clear. But, material needs aside, it is also clear that Prospero needs Caliban for the simple reason that to be lord of the island, Prospero needs subjects. As Eric Cheyfitz puts it, "No amount of technology, no amount of eloquence can make Prospero a noble. For that he needs others to play the role of the lower classes" (84). In the same way, Prospero cannot be a master without slaves, and he cannot occupy a position of superior civilization and sophistication without someone to occupy the position labeled as uncivilized and unsophisticated.

In short, Prospero's position as lord and master is structurally dependent on Caliban's position as subject and slave. They occupy positions that are not diametrically opposed but that are in fact mutually dependent, part of the same phenomenon. Even the two most radically opposed characters in the entire play—Caliban and Miranda—turn out to be mutually dependent on each other for their identities. The sweet, gentle, and (above all) virginal Miranda is the very paragon of young womanhood in Renaissance Europe. Meanwhile the supposedly brutish Caliban seems to represent uncontrolled masculine sexual desire of the kind often associated by the early English settlers with the "Satanic" character of Native Americans. But Caliban's desire needs an object, which Miranda provides, and Miranda's virginity needs the foil provided by Caliban's lust. But if Caliban and Miranda are vividly characterized by their differences, then their characters must also be interdependent.

The binary opposition of Caliban and Miranda is further undermined by the fact that the two actually have a great deal in common. For example, both serve as important objects of Prospero's power, and both help define by contrast Prospero's role as patriarchal master of the island. Moreover both have grown up on the island, far from any contact with European civilization other than that provided by Prospero's domination of them. Both are therefore characterized by a remarkable innocence and lack of experience. For example, the strength of Miranda's initial attraction to Ferdinand is at least partially due to the fact that he is the only man she has ever seen other than her father, Prospero, and

Caliban—though this attraction is also due to Prospero's manipulation of her responses. Indeed at first she suspects that Ferdinand is a god: "I might call him/A thing divine; for nothing natural/I ever saw so noble (I.ii.418–420). Prospero, meanwhile, seeks to impede Miranda's enthrallment to Ferdinand and thereby presumably to make the attraction all the stronger. He assures her, therefore, that in the larger world of Europe Ferdinand is nothing special:

> Thou think'st there is no more such shapes as he,
> Having seen but him and Caliban. Foolish wench!
> To th' most of men this is a Caliban,
> And they to him are angels.
>
> *(I.ii.479–482)*

Prospero's juxtaposition here of Ferdinand and Caliban (another of the play's binary oppositions) is a mere ploy, of course, but it does tend to destabilize the opposition between the two. Indeed Prospero will then set Ferdinand to work gathering wood, a task formerly reserved for Caliban. Meanwhile Caliban's initial assumption that the lowly Stephano is a god descended from heaven, however comic it is intended to be, clearly parallels Miranda's reaction to Ferdinand and arises from a similar lack of experience. We wonder, in fact, if Miranda might have reacted the same way to Stephano had she seen him before Ferdinand. Moreover Caliban's apparently irresistible attraction to Miranda precisely parallels Miranda's to Ferdinand. Caliban himself describes the position of innocence from which he regards Miranda:

> I never saw a woman
> But only Sycorax my dam and she;
> But she as far surpasseth Sycorax
> As great'st does the least.
>
> *(III.ii.104–107)*

We wonder, then, if Caliban's alleged attempt to rape Miranda did not simply arise from his own innocence or indeed if this "rape" was anything more than a well-meaning attempt at courtship.

Of course, within the context of the play we are apparently meant to regard Caliban and Miranda quite differently. His inexperience is a mark of inadequate acculturation; it helps identify him as a savage creature driven by animalistic desires and impulses untempered by the restraint that would presumably be introduced by civilization. Miranda's innocence is presented as a virtue; her chastity and virginity represent precisely the feminine characteristics valued most by the European civilization from which she has been separated. It is Miranda's virginity that furthers the reintegration of herself and Prospero into European society: As a virgin she remains eligible to marry the princely Ferdinand, thus sealing a political alliance between Prospero and Ferdinand's father, Alonso, the king of Naples, that enables Prospero to resume his former role as duke of Milan. Thus Prospero's insistence on Miranda's continuing chastity, an insistence presumably made necessary by the fact that her lack of experience would render her incapable of resisting any sexual advances made by Ferdinand, is politically motivated.

Caliban's attraction to Miranda is also partially political, and he appears to recognize that a liaison with her would help him regain sovereignty over the island he had ruled before Prospero's arrival (I.ii.349–351). When Caliban later encourages Stephano to try unseating Prospero, he offers Miranda as a potential bride for Stephano (III.ii.108–109). Caliban's "lustful" attitude toward Miranda, in short, is not very different from Prospero's: Both regard her largely as a political pawn, her value enhanced by her virginity. Indeed Caliban has learned this attitude toward Miranda from observing Prospero. Caliban, of course, is also a virgin, but he is separated from Miranda by differences in race and gender that supposedly give his virginity a very different meaning. A close deconstructive look at the play, however, raises serious questions about the opposition between Miranda and Caliban, suggesting the artificiality of this opposition.

The very language of *The Tempest* also suggests, yet simultaneously undermines, a number of binary oppositions. As Maurice Hunt notes, the play (like most of Shakespeare's plays) contains numerous examples of puns and wordplay. Moreover Hunt argues that these puns are often highly significant, the use of puns by characters such as Sebastian and Antonio indicating their treacherous and conniving natures, and the use of puns by characters such as Stephano and Trinculo indicating their coarseness and lack of culture. Puns are by nature multiple in meaning, and by employing puns, a character is in danger of losing control over the interpretation of his statements. For Hunt, this control is crucial, as "a character's knowledge of his purpose is conferred mainly by his ability to formulate it distinctly in words" (67). This ability belongs supremely to Prospero, and it is largely a mastery of language that gives Prospero his power.

The distinction between proper and improper uses of language is thus central to the opposition between proper and improper conduct in *The Tempest.* Yet a close look at the play shows that this linguistic distinction tends to break down. For example, even supposedly positive characters frequently employ language that can be interpreted in multiple ways. Ferdinand tends to use Hamletesque bawdy puns in reference to the virginal Miranda. For example, when he initially asks if she is a "maid," he is asking both if she is human (as opposed to supernatural) and if she is a virgin (I.ii.428). Later he assures Prospero that he will respect Miranda's virginity until after their wedding so as to increase the "edge of that day's celebration" IV.i.28). "Edge" here seems to refer innocently to the keenness of Ferdinand's enjoyment of the wedding festival, but in Renaissance English edge also refers to a male erection, as when Hamlet warns Ophelia that it will cost her a "groaning" to "take off" his "edge."

Of course, once we begin to seek sexual innuendos in language, we can find them almost everywhere. Moreover the sexual suggestiveness that infects so much of the language of *The Tempest* is part of a larger phenomenon that indicates that the ultimate interpretation of language can always potentially escape the intentions of the original speaker. For example, we would normally expect proper names to involve extremely stable and straightforward language use. After all, a proper name is presumably an unambiguous label that points directly to the designated person. In *The Tempest,* however, even proper naming can be complicated, and proper names can suggest meanings that go far beyond simple labeling. Numerous critics, for example, have noted that Caliban's name appears to be an anagram of "cannibal," itself apparently derived from the same root as "Caribbean." Caliban's name thus identifies him as an allegorical stand-in for all native inhabitants of the Caribbean. It also involves him in the complex discourse surrounding cannibalism that grew up in the early years of European colonial expansion in the Americas and that was clearly designed to associate Native Americans with subhuman brutality, thus helping justify European colonization of America even when that colonization involved genocide of the native inhabitants. For Europeans, a complex discourse surrounding the notion of cannibalism thus became "part of a diverse arsenal of rhetorical weapons used to distinguish what they conceive of as their 'civilized' selves from certain 'savage' others, principally Native Americans and Africans" (Cheyfitz 42).

Prospero's name carries clearly economic resonances that help identify the profit motive that lay behind most early colonial adventures in the Americas. Indeed Shakespeare directly plays on this association, making Prospero's name itself a pun. Thus one sign that the treacherous Sebastian is not properly in control of his language occurs when he sarcastically suggests that he and his traveling companions "prosper well" on their return from Africa, thus making an inadvertent pun on the name of Prospero, who (unbeknownst to Sebastian) has engineered their emergency landing on the island (II.i.75–76). But if even names can be puns, then it is not clear that the meaning of language can ever be stable and predictable. Despite the fact that Shakespeare seems consistently to offer reassurances regarding the stability of language—and political authority—in his contemporary England, numerous elements of *The Tempest* serve to demonstrate precisely the lack of stability that informed the social, political, and linguistic structure of Shakespeare's troubled times.

Works Cited

Belsey, Catherine. "Disrupting Sexual Difference: Meaning and Gender in the Comedies." In *Alternative Shakespeares,* ed. John Drakakis, 166–190. London: Methuen, 1985.

Cheyfitz, Eric. *The Poetics of Imperialism: Translation and Colonization from "The Tempest" to "Tarzan."* New York: Oxford UP, 1991.

Hunt, Maurice. "'The Backward Voice': Puns and the Comic Subplot of *The Tempest.*" *Modern Language Studies* 12.4 (1982): 64–74.

Shakespeare, William. *The Tempest.* New York: Signet-New American Library, 1964.

Takaki, Ronald. "*The Tempest* in the Wilderness: The Racialization of Savagery." *Journal of American History* 79.3 (1992): 892–912.

NEW HISTORICIST CRITICISM

In a now-notorious article in the April 22, 1991, issue of *Newsweek,* conservative commentator George Will bemoans the turn to politics in recent literary criticism and claims that the politicization of literary studies represents a serious threat to the traditional American way of life. By seeking to explore the political ramifications of literary texts (rather than simply seeking to glorify canonical texts and impart to students a reverence for the greatness of such texts), English professors, according to Will, are mounting an all-out assault on the Western cultural tradition. Moreover Will claims that this assault is more dangerous to the continuation of traditional values than any military threat that might be mounted by foes such as Saddam Hussein. As one central example of the supposedly ridiculous extremes to which literary criticism has now gone, Will adduces the case of *The Tempest,* which he mocks critics for reading as a cultural text informed by "the imperialist rape of the Third World" when anyone in his right mind knows that William Shakespeare's play transcends history and should be read for the beauty of its language and the timeless universality of its human themes.

Will's article is typical of the wave of conservative reaction against the growing awareness of social and political concerns in American literary studies in the last two decades. As Aijaz Ahmad points out, numerous conservative commentators have recently joined an effort to depict any and all attempts to dissent against prevailing mainstream American cultural views as "mad attacks on Western civilization and 'family values,' and as outright degenerations against which 'the American mind' . . . needs to defend itself" (65). (We might wonder about the desirability of preserving values informed by such intolerance.) Will's choice of *The Tempest* as an example is highly appropriate given the historically close association between Shakespeare's plays and the kinds of official cultural values that Will seeks to defend. And Will is certainly right that critics have emphasized the motif of imperialism in recent readings of *The Tempest.* But Will's use of *The Tempest* is particularly problematic given that critics have known for centuries that the play was directly inspired by the accounts of English colonial expansion in America. As Stephen Greenblatt notes in a response to Will's article, "This is a curious example—since it is very difficult to argue that *The Tempest* is *not* about imperialism" ("Best" B1).

Greenblatt, of course, has been exceedingly influential in detailing the close relationship between *The Tempest* and early English colonization in the Americas. His new historicist discussions of the play have convincingly demonstrated that many contemporary Jacobean cultural documents—some of which were quite overtly associated with colonialism in the New World—expressed ideas similar to those in *The Tempest.* As Charles Frey notes, however, critics have been relating elements of Shakespeare's play to the exploration and colonization of the Americas at least since the eighteenth century, when it was demonstrated that the mention of "Setebos" in the play apparently referred to a god worshipped by the native inhabitants of South America as reported in Richard Eden's account of the voyage of Magellan past the southern tip of the continent. Perhaps more important, Edmond Malone argued as early as 1808 that Shakespeare derived the title and numerous incidents in his play from accounts of a 1609 storm that caused the shipwreck in the Bermudas of a British expedition headed for the Jamestown colony.

Critics ever since Malone have explored Shakespeare's use of accounts of the shipwreck of the *Sea Venture,* discovering numerous verbal echoes that indicate that Shakespeare adapted much of his play quite directly from those accounts. There were numerous accounts of this shipwreck and of the subsequent experiences of the company in the Bermudas and of its later safe passage to Virginia. These accounts include at least three that seem to have been read by Shakespeare before writing *The Tempest* in 1611: a letter sent in July 1610 to a noblewoman in England by William Strachey, one of the passengers on the wrecked ship; an account written by another passenger, William Jourdain, entitled *A Discovery of the Bermudas* and published in October 1610; and a pamphlet commissioned by the Council of Virginia entitled *A True Declaration of the Estate of the Colonie in Virginia,* published in November 1610.

Recent new historicist suggestions that *The Tempest* derives in important ways from accounts of the voyage and wreck of the *Sea Venture* thus build on a long critical heritage. What is different about new historicist readings of this relationship is that they go beyond the simple demonstration of Shakespeare's borrowings from specific contemporary texts to explore in considerable detail the implications not only of these direct borrowings but also of similarities between *The Tempest* and numerous other contemporary documents dealing with the colonial experience. In *The Poetics of Imperialism,* Eric Cheyfitz notes how the rhetorical strategies employed in various accounts of the wreck of the *Sea Venture* show ideological affinities with *The Tempest. A True Declaration,* for example, is structured by the common Renaissance metaphor of the "ship of state," a metaphor that clearly informs Shakespeare's play. Cheyfitz then shows that a recognition of the significance of this metaphor sheds light on Shakespeare's treatment of questions of authority and of the motif of translation. Cheyfitz also shows that attitudes toward gender in *A True Declaration* and in Strachey's letter are similar to those in *The Tempest,* a recognition that aids greatly in understanding the figuration of Miranda in Shakespeare's play. For example, Cheyfitz shows how these attitudes toward gender are centrally related to European attitudes toward the New World, as when Strachey describes Virginia as a fallen woman whose honor the *Sea Venture* expedition (bringing, among other things, a new governor for the colony) is intended to restore. Miranda, Cheyfitz notes, might best be read not as an individual character in the conventional sense but as an allegorical figure around which typical Renaissance discourses concerning gender and sexuality—and colonization of the New World—circulate in the play. "Miranda" thus becomes "a figure or name that articulates a complex of masculine attitudes toward the British settlement of the New World" (71).

In a similar way, Peter Hulme shows that *The Tempest* draws inspiration for its various depictions of political conspiracies from accounts of such conspiracies among the passengers of the *Sea Venture* while stranded in the Bermudas. In both cases, the focus on conspiracies indicates an anxiety over the status of official authority that constituted an important element of the Jacobean world view. Hulme also shows that the storm motif in *The Tempest* corresponds to a contemporary European fascination with hurricanes in the Caribbean, noting that "no phenomenon—not even the natives themselves—characterized so well the novelty of the New World for Europeans; and as a result no natural phenomenon was more open to the interpretive skills of the age" (94). Hulme notes, however, that this fascination with the power of hurricanes is symptomatic of a much larger interest in the strangeness and exoticism of the New World, an interest that extended to that world's human inhabitants in ways that allowed them to be regarded as dangerous, uncivilized, and not worthy of treatment as equals. In particular, Hulme suggests an ideological commonality between Renaissance discourse on the savage weather represented by hurricanes and that on the savage perversion of humanity represented by the presumed cannibalism of Native Americans. Both discourses are represented in *The Tempest,* which thus takes much of its famed ambiguity from the tension between terror and desire that informed all aspects of the European attitude toward the newly colonized Americas.

Greenblatt's new historicist discussions of *The Tempest* similarly go well beyond the simple demonstration that Shakespeare drew on accounts of colonial voyages to write his play. In *Learning to Curse,* for example, Greenblatt argues that the treatment of language in *The Tempest* addresses general concerns over the linguistic status of Native Americans similar to those in any number of other cultural texts of the period. Greenblatt also argues that Shakespeare's depiction of Caliban derives from more than a simple attempt to dramatize any descriptions that Shakespeare might have read of Native Americans. Caliban also draws on the European tradition of the "Wild Man," which goes back to the Middle Ages and seems to arise from deep-seated anxieties about the sexual, political, and economic assumptions of Christian society (21).

Of course, the tradition of the Wild Man and contemporary accounts of Native Americans are not entirely independent, and Greenblatt is able to show that European descriptions of Native Americans quite frequently draw on the Wild Man tradition for their details. Indeed the Wild Man tradition is quite central to European fantasies and fears over the New World as a whole: "The figure of the Wild Man, and the Indians identified as Wild Men, serve as a screen onto which Renaissance Europeans, bound by their institutions, project their darkest and yet most compelling fantasies" (22). The earliest known English tract on America contains the fantasies of bestiality, sexual wantonness, and cannibalism that would come to inhabit the popular European imagination in regard to Native Americans:

> The people of this land have no king nor lord nor their god. But all things is common/this people go all naked. . . . The folks live like beasts without any reasonableness and the woman be also as common. And

> the men have conversation with the women/who that they been or who they first meet/is she his sister/his mother/his daughter/or any other kindred. And the women be very hot and disposed to lechery. And they eat also one another. (Quoted on 22; spelling modernization added.)

Moreover Greenblatt argues that Shakespeare's depiction of Caliban participates quite directly in this discursive phenomenon: "Shakespeare does not shrink from the darkest European fantasies of the Wild Man; indeed he exaggerates them: Caliban is deformed, lecherous, evil-smelling, idle, treacherous, naive, drunken, rebellious, violent, and devil-worshipping" (26).

Greenblatt's impressive discussion of *The Tempest* in *Shakespearean Negotiations* is even more representative of new historicist critical practice. Here in the course of discussing Shakespeare's play, Greenblatt predictably draws on Strachey's narrative of the voyage of the *Sea Venture,* but he also brings in more peripheral texts, such as a 1552 sermon by Hugh Latimer, Dudley Carleton's account of an abortive execution in 1603, and H. M. Stanley's recollections of having been saved by a volume of Shakespeare's works in an encounter with Moa tribesmen in central Africa in 1877. Greenblatt spends most of his time discussing this diverse array of auxiliary texts rather than *The Tempest* itself, but he eventually uses Shakespeare's play to pull all of the other materials together. Indeed Greenblatt's major point is that *The Tempest* reflects a number of multiple and even contradictory points of view and that this complexity is indicative of the powerful tensions that informed Shakespeare's society as a whole, especially with regard to its attitude toward official authority and toward the New World.

The title of Greenblatt's article "Martial Law in the Land of Cockaigne" reflects the diversity of ideas and discourses he finds relevant to a reading of *The Tempest.* "Cockaigne" in the medieval tradition is a mythical land of plenty, an abundant utopia, and the notion of Cockaigne well expresses the expectations that many Europeans had of the New World. But the "martial law" portion of his title reflects the strong strain of political domination that constituted the dark side of the European presence in America. Most specifically, the contrast between the ideal of Cockaigne and the reality of martial law reflects what occurred in the Bermudas when the passengers and crew of the *Sea Venture* found a rich tropical land so different from Europe that the leaders of the expedition had difficulty maintaining their rule over the rest of the group, which to many seemed illegitimate in this radically new setting. The relevance of this tension between utopia and domination to *The Tempest* is clear. The play is very centrally concerned with questions of political authority and challenges to the legitimacy of that authority. And the island of the play is quite explicitly presented as a possible Cockaigne, most directly in Gonzalo's description of his vision of a utopian society that might be established on the island. Gonzalo proposes that this new society be founded on principals radically different from those on which European society is based. He appears to reject virtually all of the political and economic activities that make European society what it is:

I' th' commonwealth I would by contraries
Execute all things. For no kind of traffic
Would I admit; no name of magistrate;
Letters should not be known; riches, poverty,
And use of service, none; contract, succession,
Bourn, bound of land, tilth, vineyard, none;
No use of metal, corn, or wine, or oil;
No occupation; all men idle, all;
And women too, but innocent and pure;
No sovereignty.

(II.i.152-161)

Gonzalo's speech here gains force from its resonance with what by 1611 was already a well-established discourse concerning the utopian potential of America. For example, Sir Thomas More, nearly one hundred years earlier, had located the island society described in his *Utopia* in the New World. But More's early-sixteenth-century text is already highly complex; in many ways his description of an island utopia is not a literal attempt to envision a perfect society so much as an occasion to satirize certain social and political ills obtaining in his contemporary Europe. In the same way, Gonzalo's vision of a society that would reject most of the values of his European society (except, perhaps, the glorification of "innocence" in women) suggests a powerful condemnation of that society.

Gonzalo, however, is hardly a revolutionary figure, and he later seems to mock his own utopian rhetoric. He is also at the very center of much of the interrogation of political authority in *The Tempest.* As Paul Yachnin points out, Prospero seems to respect Gonzalo as a wise and loyal counselor and greatly appreciate the fact that Gonzalo provided him with books and provisions while arranging (on the orders of Antonio and Alonso) to have Prospero and Miranda set adrift in a rickety boat. That Prospero seems oblivious to the fact that Gonzalo was still working in league with his treacherous bosses serves for Yachnin as potential evidence of Prospero's lack of judgment and wisdom. In any case, Gonzalo occupies a potentially enigmatic position, and his figuration for Yachnin serves to bring into the play a number of the political "contradictions" that informed Shakespeare's contemporary society. Yachnin grants that *The Tempest* is fundamentally royalist in its politics and that it openly recommends obedience to legitimately constituted authority. But he also suggests that the play, by offering possibilities for multiple interpretations (as when audiences may regard Gonzalo as a figure of either obedience or treachery), presents a number of opportunities for audiences that may harbor antiroyalist sympathies to find support for their positions.

Greenblatt's careful new historicist reading of a number of cultural documents from Renaissance England reveals that a similar doubleness in attitudes toward authority can be found in those documents as well, which suggests that the social fabric of Shakespeare's England was pervaded by a deep sense of crisis and uncertainty with regard to the status of official power. For Greenblatt, uncertainties in reactions to the colonization of the New World served only to exacerbate this English crisis in authority. Indeed Jeffrey Knapp argues that the doubleness of *The Tempest* has largely to do with anxieties over the racial Otherness of Native Americans, anxieties related to the insistence of English colonists on "keeping their Englishness virginal, unmixed" (242). Yachnin's readings, however, place the political anxieties of the play within a more European context. In particular, Yachnin reads the anxieties over obedience and authority in *The Tempest* against contemporary documents and concludes that these anxieties arise not so much from fears of racial contamination by Native Americans, or even of a rebellion of England's lower classes against their rulers, as from fears of an invasion from abroad. For Yachnin, these fears are closely associated with England's sense of itself as an embattled Protestant nation surrounded by powerful Catholic enemies. That Prospero has been unseated from his dukedom by the intervention of a foreign power (Alonso's Naples) and that Caliban is inspired to rebel against Prospero by the arrival of the foreigners Stephano and Trinculo both serve for Yachnin as reflections of English fears that a foreign power like Spain might incite dissatisfied elements in the English populace to rebellion: "*The Tempest*'s endorsement of political obedience constitutes, in the broadest terms, a nationalist reaction to a threat which was seen to be primarily foreign rather than primarily domestic, in particular the danger of Spanish Catholic subornation of disaffected elements within the English Protestant commonwealth" (16).

The different emphases of the new historicist readings of Greenblatt, Knapp, and Yachnin should not be construed as mutually exclusive. Instead the availability of such differing readings only serves to reinforce the central new historicist point that societies and texts are extremely complex and that no one reading can encompass all the nuances of either a society or the texts it produces. These readings, together with *The Tempest* itself, illustrate the tremendous multiplicity and complexity of the political climate that informed Shakespeare's England.

Works Cited

Ahmad, Aijaz. *In Theory: Nations, Classes, Literatures.* London: Verso, 1994.

Cheyfitz, Eric. *The Poetics of Imperialism: Translation and Colonization from "The Tempest" to "Tarzan."* New York: Oxford UP, 1991.

Frey, Charles H. *Experiencing Shakespeare: Essays on Text, Classroom, and Performance.* Columbia: U of Missouri P, 1988.

Greenblatt, Stephen. "The Best Way to Kill Our Literary Inheritance Is to Turn It into a Decorous Celebration of the New World Order." *Chronicle of Higher Education* (June 12, 1991): B1, B3.

———. *Learning to Curse: Essays in Early Modern Culture.* New York: Routledge, 1990.

———. *Shakespearean Negotiations: The Circulation of Social Energy in Renaissance England.* Berkeley and Los Angeles: U of California P, 1988.

Hulme, Peter. *Colonial Encounters: Europe and the Native Caribbean, 1492–1797.* London: Methuen, 1986.

Knapp, Jeffrey. *An Empire Nowhere: England, America, and Literature from "Utopia" to "The Tempest."* Berkeley and Los Angeles: U of California P, 1992.
More, Sir Thomas. *Utopia.* Norton critical ed. Ed. Robert M. Adams. New York: Norton, 1992.
Shakespeare, William. *The Tempest.* New York: Signet-New American Library, 1964.
Will, George. "Literary Politics: 'The Tempest'? It's 'Really' about Imperialism. Emily Dickinson's Poetry? Masturbation." *Newsweek* (April 22, 1991): 72.
Yachnin, Paul. "Shakespeare and the Idea of Obedience: Gonzalo in *The Tempest.*" *Mosaic* 24.2 (1991): 1-18.

MULTICULTURAL CRITICISM

The novel *A Grain of Wheat,* by the Kenyan writer Ngugi wa Thiong'o, tells the story of the coming of Kenya's independence from British colonial rule in 1963. It also relates how this independence was gained through years of fierce, sometimes bloody Kenyan resistance to colonial domination, a resistance that the British unsuccessfully attempted to squelch with the application of overwhelming force and overt terror tactics. In the so-called Emergency of the 1950s, when Kenyan Mau Mau guerrilla fighters mounted a furious assault on the British system of colonial rule, the British responded with a full-scale military invasion. They also imprisoned, without trial, thousands of Kenyans in concentration camps, where they were routinely beaten, tortured, or even killed. One of the major characters in *A Grain of Wheat* is John Thompson, a British colonial officer who is placed in command of one of these concentration camps, which he rules with such brutality that it calls international attention to British abuses, thus ruining Thompson's once-promising career.

That career, interestingly enough, is intimately related to Thompson's reading of *The Tempest.* As a young man, Thompson becomes enthralled by the idea of "the British mission in the world," an idea he understands largely through his reading of British literature (53). Central to this reading is *The Tempest,* and when he later goes off to Africa, he envisions himself as a Prospero figure, bringing peace and prosperity to benighted Africa through the glorious civilizing effects of British culture. He begins to write a book—which he entitles *Prospero in Africa*—to describe his mission: "In it he argued that to be English was basically an attitude of mind: it was a way of looking at life, at human relationship, at the just ordering of human society. Was it not possible to reorientate people into this way of life by altering their social and cultural environments?" (54).

Thompson's attitudes, simplistic though they may appear, are typical of the history of British imperialism: The British, well aware that they lacked the power directly to enforce their control of their far-flung empire, sought instead to elicit the cooperation of their colonial subjects by more subtle techniques of cultural domination—reinforced by the selective application of localized violence. But Thompson's later disillusionment and turn to brutality (recalling Kurtz's turn in Joseph Conrad's *Heart of Darkness* from an initial claim to idealistic concern for Africans to a final call to "exterminate the brutes") serve as a reminder of the domination and exploitation that lay at the heart of European imperialism, even when it purported to be bringing civilization and salvation to the "dark places" of the earth.

The British often employed English literature—which they regarded as a central example of their cultural superiority to their colonial subjects—as a central tool in their attempts to teach their subjects to accept British values. As Gauri Viswanathan convincingly demonstrates, the whole notion of teaching British literature began as part of the British effort to endow Indian subjects with properly British attitudes and opinions. And William Shakespeare, as the principal icon of the greatness of British culture, was at the very center of this imperial project. It is no accident, for example, that when the protagonist of Conrad's *Lord Jim* goes off to become the lord of Patusan, somewhere in the distant and exotic East, he takes with him on his journey two crucial tools of nineteenth-century European imperial expansion. One tool, a revolver, is a predictable reminder of the contribution of superior European military technology to the establishment of dominion over other peoples. Perhaps even more indicative of British imperial strategies, however, is the other tool—a volume of the complete works of Shakespeare. Conrad thus provides a reminder of the important supplement provided by European culture to European military might in the building of the great nineteenth-century empires. Jim's book suggests the central role played by Shakespeare and other icons of European cultural "superiority" in a two-pronged effort to justify imperial domination at home (by assuring the Europeans that they were bringing enlightenment to their colonies) and to reinforce European rule in the colonies (by convincing colonized peoples of the superiority of European culture).

Ngugi's choice in *A Grain of Wheat* of Shakespeare as a marker of British cultural imperialism is thus highly appropriate. Especially appropriate is his invocation of *The Tempest.* Thomas Cartelli notes the importance of the colonial resonances in this play for postcolonial Africa; the choice of Prospero as a role model for Ngugi's John Thompson in his attempts to "civilize" Africa is a good one. That generations of critics have tended to identify Prospero with Shakespeare himself only makes Thompson's identification with Prospero more powerful by suggesting the central role that Shakespeare's work has played as a tool of British imperial expansion around the world. Terence Hawkes, in fact, argues that Shakespeare's creation of Prospero might have been partially inspired by his perception of a resemblance between the roles of playwright and colonist: "A colonist acts essentially as a dramatist. He imposes the 'shape' of his own culture, embodied in his speech, on the new world, and makes that world recognizable, habitable, 'natural,' able to speak his language" (211). Meanwhile the dramatist metaphorically resembles a colonist in that "his art penetrates new areas of experience, his language expands the boundaries of our culture, and makes the new territory over in its own image" (212).

In any case, critics have been aware since early in the nineteenth century that *The Tempest* was largely inspired from reports of British expeditions to the new colonies in America, and recent critical discussions of *The Tempest* have focused on the parallels between the European conquest of the Americas and Prospero's domination of the island that once belonged to Caliban. That Shakespeare seems untroubled by the implications of this conquest is, of course, not surprising. After all, Shakespeare was a man very much of his time, and few people in his contemporary England were concerned that their American colonies had been gained at the expense of the native inhabitants, who were typically regarded as subhuman and therefore not worthy of dominion over the rich and promising lands that the Europeans found awaiting them in America. That Shakespeare's work appears to endorse European imperial domination of the rest of the world becomes highly significant in the light of the fact that this work occupies the very center of the Western literary canon, which has so often been held up as universal and as the grandest expression of the greatest thoughts ever conceived by the human race.

But as multicultural critics have pointed out in recent years, in the history of imperialism "universal" is synonymous with the mainstream white culture of Western Europe and North America. Shakespeare is certainly no exception, and the attention paid by multicultural critics to Shakespeare's work in recent years is an important part of their project to demonstrate that the Western literary canon is shot through with racial, sexual, and cultural biases and that the respect typically paid to canonical works tends subtly to endorse these biases. Virtually all of the various forms of oppression that inform the modern world can already be located within *The Tempest.* There is, for example, a clear class structure in the play, embodied not only in the relationship between the crewmen of the "wrecked" ship and their aristocratic passengers, but also in the very plot structure of the play, which consists of parallel stories of attempted "coups" by the aristocrats Sebastian and Antonio (against Alonso, king of Naples) and by Trinculo and Stephano (against Prospero, at the urging of Caliban). Both conspiracies mirror the earlier overthrow of Prospero by Antonio as the duke of Milan. The structure of power reflected in the play is also strongly patriarchal. Miranda is the only female character, and she remains thoroughly under the domination of her powerful father, who in the course of the play cedes her to Ferdinand like a piece of property to further his own political purposes.

Shakespeare himself shows little overt sympathy with any of the victims of oppression represented in the play. Prospero's treatment of Miranda goes entirely unchallenged, and any potentially subversive energies activated by the boatswain's insubordination to his aristocratic bosses at the beginning of the play are safely contained by the eventual revelation that these bosses have themselves transgressed against the legitimate structure of authority in their society. And even Caliban, the play's most central oppressed character, eventually seems to acknowledge and accept Prospero's dominion over him. Caliban's ultimate fate is left unclear at the end of the play, however, and multicultural critics have frequently found Caliban's character an important source of inspiration, Shakespeare's own apparent lack of sympathy for him notwithstanding. For such critics, the relationship between Prospero and Caliban stands as the very prototype of relations between the dominant culture of Western Europe and North America and the subjugated cultures of Africa, Asia, and Latin America. Prospero, after all, is a European aristocrat who comes to a remote island already occupied by Caliban. He then, by a combination of force and deceit, wrests control of the island from Caliban and makes Caliban his slave. Prospero's treatment of Caliban, in short, can be read not only as an allegory of the European conquest of the Americas but also as a striking anticipation of the later European imperial domination of most of the rest of the globe.

Caliban's own description of his initial seduction and subsequent enslavement by Prospero reads very much like an allegory of American colonialism, where European settlers often ingratiated themselves with Native Americans, gaining their trust, only later to betray, exploit, and even slaughter them, taking their land and destroying their former way of life. Among other things, Caliban clearly understands the importance of the subtle techniques of power that would later become central to the imperial project:

> When thou cam'st first,
> Thou strok'st me and made much of me; wouldst give me
> Water with berries in't; and teach me how
> To name the bigger light, and how the less,
> That burn by day and night. And then I loved thee
> And showed thee all the qualities o' th' isle,
> The fresh springs, brine pits, barren place and fertile.
> Cursed be I that did so! All the charms
> Of Sycorax—toads, beetles, bats, lights on you!
> For I am all the subjects that you have,
> Which first was mine own king; and here you sty me
> In this hard rock, whiles you do keep from me
> The rest o' th' island.
>
> *(I.ii.332-344)*

Caliban knows very well that Prospero's attempts to educate him (and especially to teach him language) arise not from any sort of generosity but from Prospero's understanding that his domination of Caliban requires that the two have some common basis for communication. In this Caliban anticipates the central role that education would come to play in the British imperial project for the next three and one-half centuries. For example, one of the most notorious monuments to the project of British cultural domination in India is Thomas Babington Macaulay's 1835 "Minute on Indian Education." Here Macaulay proudly proclaims the superiority of Western literature, stating that no Orientalist "could deny that a single shelf of a good European library was worth the whole native literature of India and Arabia" (722). For Macaulay, the British in India must convey to their Indian subjects this "superiority" of European culture, presumably thereby teaching them to accept English rule as being in their own best interests.

Macaulay's emphasis on the importance of education to the British project in India echoes a British colonial policy that can be traced all the way back to the early colonization of North America: The London Council of the Virginia Company instructed Sir Thomas Gates, prospective governor of its Virginia colony, to emphasize the education of the native inhabitants in English manners, language, and values so that "their people will easily obey you and become in time Civill and Christian" (quoted in Vaughan 59). Caliban in *The Tempest* already seems to understand this project and to reject it. Partly because of his clear understanding of Prospero's imperial intrusion and partly because of his continuing defiance despite Prospero's clearly superior power, Caliban has been seen by postcolonial critics as an admirable, heroic figure. His refusal fully to submit to Prospero's rule thus becomes a sign not of savage animality but of a courageous insistence on his right to live free of domination by a foreign interloper who neither understands nor appreciates his culture and way of life.

Caliban has served as a particularly important model of resistance for postcolonial critics and writers from the Caribbean, which was, after all, the location of the real-world shipwreck that helped inspire Shakespeare's fanciful play. Fernández Retamar sums up this Caribbean view of Caliban as hero, with Prospero as villain:

> This is something that we, the *mestizo* inhabitants of these same isles where Caliban lived, see with particular clarity: Prospero invaded the islands, killed our ancestors, enslaved Caliban, and taught him his language to make himself understood. What else can Caliban do but use that same language—today he has no other—to curse him, to wish that the "red plague" would fall on him? I know no other metaphor more expressive of our cultural situation, of our reality. . . . What is our history, what is our culture, if not the history and culture of Caliban? (Quoted in Vaughan and Vaughan 156)

As Retamar's emphasis on the role of language in *The Tempest* indicates, the issue of language is one of the most important ways the play resonates with contemporary debates in multicultural criticism. For example, when Miranda complains that Caliban has not shown the proper gratitude for her attempts to teach him her language, Caliban responds with an expression of bitter resentment: "You taught me language, and my profit on't/Is, I know how to curse. The red plague rid you/For learning me your language!" (I.ii.363-365). Caliban here shows an understanding of language as colonial oppression that foreshadows Ngugi's insistence that for African writers to continue working in the languages of their former colonial rulers only serves to perpetuate the cultural domination of Africa by Europe. But language was already a crucial issue in European colonialism even in Shakespeare's day. As Stephen Greenblatt notes, a great deal of the early European reaction to the native inhabitants of the Americas had to do with the question of language. As early as Christopher Columbus, teaching Native Americans "to speak" was considered a crucial element of the attempt to establish European dominion in the Americas, and European language was deemed a great gift being brought to the Americas by the European conquerors.

But the early European reaction to Native American languages was paradoxically double. On the one hand, much European commentary seemed to assume that Native American languages differed very little from European ones and that communication between Europeans and Native Americans should therefore be relatively straightforward. On the other hand, perhaps the most common European reaction was to assume that Native American languages were hardly languages at all and that Native American culture was virtually nonexistent.

Greenblatt emphasizes that either attitude works to the disadvantage of Native Americans. In the first case, Europeans simply assumed that "reality was one and universal, constituted identically for all men at all times and in all places" (28). But "universal" meant "European," and their assumption that they could communicate with Native Americans was based on a confident belief that Native Americans could not possibly see language and the world differently than did Europeans. In the second case, Europeans assumed that Native Americans were subhuman and that their perspectives, however different, were not worthy of serious consideration. In either case, Europeans dismissed Native American language either by "denying its existence or by dismissing its significance as an obstacle to communication between peoples" (32).

As Greenblatt points out, *The Tempest* is "perhaps the profoundest literary exploration of these themes in the Renaissance" (23). In particular, Caliban seems to epitomize the notion of the Native American as a subhuman savage possessing little or no language. Miranda, for example, describes Caliban as being able to do little more than make animal-like noises before she taught him language:

> I pitied thee
> Took pains to make thee speak, taught thee each hour
> One thing or another. When thou didst not, savage,
> Know thine own meaning, but wouldst gabble like
> A thing most brutish, I endowed thy purposes
> With words that made them known.
>
> *(I.ii.353-358)*

Prospero, meanwhile, is the paradigm of the articulate and cultured European who is accomplished in the use of spoken language *and* written language, for Renaissance Europeans a key marker of acculturation. It is thus significant that Prospero's power appears to emanate largely from his books, which Caliban knows must be destroyed to unseat Prospero as ruler of the island (III.ii.95-99).

Caliban's insurrection does not succeed, of course. Indeed it is dismissed as an object of mockery, the very idea of Caliban mounting a serious threat to Prospero's rule serving merely as the occasion for the play's comic subplot. In *The Tempest,* the lines of power are clear—as they were in the European conquest of the New World. And Caliban himself is treated by Shakespeare via the kinds of racist stereotypes that would provide ideological support for centuries of European and North American imperial conquests, from the decimation of the Aztecs by Spanish conquistadors in the sixteenth century to the high-tech massacre of more than 100,000 Iraqi soldiers and civilians in the 1991 U.S.-led invasion of Iraq. That such stereotypes inform a text by the central author in the Western literary canon should make us seriously reconsider the implications of an unquestioned reverence for the works of that canon. At the same time, that multicultural critics have found an important source of inspiration in the "lowly" Caliban demonstrates the ability of oppositional criticism to activate energies in literary texts that might run counter to the ideologies of the texts themselves.

Works Cited

Cartelli, Thomas. "Prospero in Africa: *The Tempest* as Colonialist Text and Pretext." In *Shakespeare Reproduced: The Text in History and Ideology,* ed. Jean E. Howard and Marion F. O'Connor, 99–115. London: Methuen, 1987.

Conrad, Joseph. *Lord Jim.* New York: Signet-New American Library, 1961.

———. *Heart of Darkness.* Norton critical ed. 3d ed. New York: Norton, 1988.

Greenblatt, Stephen. *Learning to Curse: Essays in Early Modern Culture.* New York: Routledge, 1991.

Hawkes, Terence. *Shakespeare's Talking Animals: Language and Drama in Society.* London: Edward Arnold, 1973.

Macaulay, Thomas Babington. *Macaulay: Prose and Poetry.* Ed. G. M. Young. Cambridge, Mass.: Harvard UP, 1952.

Ngugi wa Thiong'o. *A Grain of Wheat.* 1967. Rev./Ed. London: Heinemann, 1986.

Shakespeare, William. *The Tempest.* New York: Signet-New American Library, 1964.

Vaughan, Alden T. *American Genesis: Captain John Smith and the Founding of Virginia.* Boston: Little, Brown, 1975.

Vaughan, Alden T., and Virginia Mason Vaughan. *Shakespeare's Caliban: A Cultural History.* Cambridge: Cambridge UP, 1991.

Viswanathan, Gauri. *Masks of Conquest: Literary Study and British Rule in India.* New York: Columbia UP, 1989.

SELECTED BIBLIOGRAPHY

Barker, Francis, and Peter Hulme. "'Nymphs and Reapers Heavily Vanish': The Discursive Contexts of *The Tempest.*" In *Alternative Shakespeares,* ed. John Drakakis, 191–205. London: Methuen, 1985.

Proposes an intertextual reading of *The Tempest* based on Foucault's notion of discourses. Focuses on the participation of the play in the contemporary discourse of English colonialism. Notes how this participation illuminates the anxiety over domination and resistance embedded in the play.

Breight, Curt. "'Treason Doth Never Prosper': *The Tempest* and the Discourse of Treason." *Shakespeare Quarterly* 41.1 (1990): 1–28.

Reads *The Tempest* within the context of a contemporary fascination with treason and conspiracy, arguing that the play undermines official strategies in the discourse of treason by its revelation of the workings of official power. Enhances the view of Prospero as a tyrant by reading his treatment of Caliban within the context of contemporary descriptions of torture. Argues, however, that this motif would have made Prospero's tyranny obvious to a contemporary audience and that the play is therefore subversive because that audience would also have identified Prospero with official power.

Brown, Paul. "'This Thing of Darkness I Acknowledge Mine': *The Tempest* and the Discourse of Colonialism." In *Political Shakespeare: New Essays in Cultural Materialism,* ed. Jonathan Dollimore and Alan Sinfield, 48-71. Ithaca, N.Y.: Cornell UP, 1985.
Extends the colonialist context of *The Tempest* to include Ireland as well as America and argues that the play provides conservative support for the English colonial project in both countries. Sees Caliban as a hybrid figure, neither Irish nor Native American, but a generalized figure of the savage Other against whom the English sought to identify themselves.

Cartelli, Thomas. "Prospero in Africa: *The Tempest* as Colonialist Text and Pretext." In *Shakespeare Reproduced: The Text in History and Ideology,* ed. Jean E. Howard and Marion F. O'Connor, 99-115. London: Methuen, 1987.
Reviews recent literature on the theme of colonialism in *The Tempest,* focusing especially on the play's relevance to the context of colonial Africa and on the resultant treatment of the play in Ngugi's *A Grain of Wheat.*

Cheyfitz, Eric. *The Poetics of Imperialism: Translation and Colonization from "The Tempest" to "Tarzan."* New York: Oxford UP, 1991.
Studies the role of language and translation as techniques of imperial power. Discusses at some length the importance of this motif in *The Tempest,* emphasizing the ways the treatment of language in the play reinforces Caliban's status as both racially and socially inferior to Prospero. Usefully outlines the relationship of *The Tempest* to accounts of the wreck of the English colonial ship *Sea Venture* in the Bermudas in 1609.

Corfield, Cosmo. "Why Does Prospero Abjure His 'Rough Magic'?" *Shakespeare Quarterly* 36.1 (1985): 31-48.
Reads *The Tempest* as the story of Prospero's failure as a neoplatonic theurgist seeking to transcend his human nature, which is represented symbolically in the play by Caliban.

Dawson, Anthony B. "*Tempest* in a Teapot: Critics, Evaluation, Ideology." In *"Bad" Shakespeare: Revaluations of the Shakespeare Canon,* ed. Maurice Charney, 61-73. Rutherford, N.J.: Fairleigh Dickinson UP, 1988.
Suggests that *The Tempest* is a rather weak play that is extremely difficult to stage adequately. Concludes that the play's critical reputation is based not so much on aesthetic merit as on its ability to serve the purposes of critics with various theoretical and ideological orientations.

Dobson, Michael. "Fairly Brave New World: Shakespeare, the American Colonies, and the American Revolution." *Renaissance Drama* 23 (1992): 189-207.
Discusses the role of *The Tempest* in British attempts to use Shakespeare as an icon of their cultural superiority over Americans before and during the American Revolution. Notes how the subsequent American appropriation of Shakespeare and *The Tempest* after the success of the revolution prefigured America's later growth as an imperial power.

Frey, Charles H. *Experiencing Shakespeare: Essays on Text, Classroom, and Performance.* Columbia: U of Missouri P, 1988.
Offers, in "*The Tempest* and the New World," a somewhat simplistic but good introduction to other critical discussions of the importance of New World materials in *The Tempest.*

Greenblatt, Stephen J. "Learning to Curse." In *Learning to Curse: Essays in Early Modern Culture,* 16-39. New York: Routledge, 1990.

Reads *The Tempest* as a profound literary exploration of the clash between written and oral cultures that centrally informed early colonial encounters in the Americas. Notes the appropriateness of Caliban's rejection of Prospero's language as a form of domination.

Greenblatt, Stephen. *Shakespearean Negotiations: The Circulation of Social Energy in Renaissance England.* Berkeley and Los Angeles: U of California P, 1988.
Offers new historicist essays on Shakespeare's relationship to his contemporary social context. Discusses *The Tempest*'s relation to Strachey's account of the wreck of the *Sea Venture.* Notes how the texts of both Strachey and Shakespeare reflect anxieties over a crisis in authority in Jacobean England.

Hillman, Richard. "*The Tempest* as Romance and Anti-Romance." *University of Toronto Quarterly* 55.2 (1985-1986): 141-160.
Notes the elements of romance in *The Tempest,* but also argues that numerous aspects of the play ultimately undermine the comfortable resolution usually associated with the romance genre. Concludes that *The Tempest* is "in its basic terms, a play of confinements, contortions, problems" (141).

Hulme, Peter. *Colonial Encounters: Europe and the Native Caribbean, 1492-1797.* London: Methuen, 1986.
Includes an extensive chapter on *The Tempest* and on its participation in many of the same issues as contemporary European colonial texts about America. Parallels the play's treatment of Prospero's magic to the functioning of European technology in the colonial Americas. Includes a discussion of the critical history of the play and of the ways recent recognition of the importance of the colonial subtext has complicated critical responses to the play.

Hunt, Maurice. "'The Backward Voice': Puns and the Comic Subplot of *The Tempest.*" *Modern Language Studies* 12.4 (1982): 64-74.
Discusses the role of puns and wordplay in *The Tempest,* arguing that Shakespeare employs puns in the play as signs of a character's lack of understanding and inability to communicate. Argues that by rejecting the jester Trinculo, Caliban shows a readiness to move beyond his animal-like condition and receive "fresh grace" (71).

Kermode, Frank. Introduction to *The Tempest,* by William Shakespeare, xi-lxxxviii. Arden ed. Ed. Frank Kermode. Cambridge, Mass.: Harvard UP, 1954.
Gives a classic general account of the play that acknowledges its use of New World sources but that places little emphasis on the link to colonialism.

Knight, G. Wilson. *The Crown of Life.* 1947. New York: Barnes and Noble, 1966.
Discusses *The Tempest* as a demonstration of the glories of imperialism, concluding with the now-astonishing claim that Prospero represents the spirit of England's "colonizing, especially her will to raise savage peoples from superstition and blood-sacrifice, taboos and witchcraft and the attendant fears and slaveries, to a more enlightened existence" (255).

Knox, Bernard. "*The Tempest* and the Ancient Comic Tradition." In *English Stage Comedy,* ed. W. K. Wimsatt, 52-73. New York: Columbia UP, 1955.
Attempts to situate *The Tempest* in relation to classical comedy as exemplified in the plays of Terence, Plautus, and Menander. Notes numerous similarities between the typical plot and the scenario of these plays and those of *The Tempest.*

Lamming, George. *The Pleasures of Exile.* London: Michael Joseph, 1960.

Challenges, in "A Monster, a Child, a Slave," the hierarchy of the Prospero/Caliban relationship and reads Caliban not as a monster but as a human being who has been robbed of his humanity by the European insistence that only those occupying a European position can be fully human. Notes many of the affinities between Miranda and Caliban. Represents the critical movement toward appreciation of colonialism as a major motif in the play.

Leininger, Lorie Jerrell. "The Miranda Trap: Sexism and Racism in Shakespeare's *The Tempest.*" In *The Woman's Part: Feminist Criticism of Shakespeare,* ed. Carolyn R. S. Lenz, Gayle Green, and Carol T. Neely, 285-294. Urbana: U of Illinois P, 1980.
Discusses parallels between the marriage of Miranda and Ferdinand in the play and that of King James's daughter Elizabeth to Frederick the Elector Palatine, at which the play was performed. Notes how Miranda and Caliban both function as objects for Prospero's domination and how this situation parallels the historical oppression of women and slaves.

Magnusson, A. Lynne. "Interruption in *The Tempest.*" *Shakespeare Quarterly* 37.1 (1986): 52-65.
Argues that the various interruptions of scenes and speeches in *The Tempest* are designed by Shakespeare to show that art expresses a human need to establish order and coherence amid the chaos of reality.

Mannoni, O. *Prospero and Caliban: The Psychology of Colonization.* 1950. Trans. Pamela Powesland. Ann Arbor: U of Michigan P, 1990.
Attempts to develop a theory of the psychology of colonialism based on the need of "primitive" colonized peoples to be dominated by strong rulers (Mannoni's famous "dependency complex") and the need of European colonizers to compensate for their own feelings of inadequacy by dominating others. Uses *The Tempest,* albeit briefly, as a major demonstration of this situation. Offers one of the first discussions of the colonial politics implicit in the play.

Maus, Katharine Eisaman. "Arcadia Lost: Politics and Revision in the Restoration *Tempest.*" *Renaissance Drama* 13 (1982): 189-209.
Notes that many of Shakespeare's plays were rewritten during the English Restoration to make them more appropriate to the time. Discusses the adaptation of *The Tempest* by John Dryden and William D'Avenant in 1667 and notes how that adaptation reflected the political climate (especially the growing anxiety over the legitimacy of the monarchy) of that time.

Schorin, Gerald. "Approaching the Genre of *The Tempest.*" In *Shakespeare's Late Plays,* ed. Richard C. Tobias and Paul G. Zolbrod, 166-184. Athens: Ohio UP, 1974.
Agrees with the conventional view that romance is the prevailing genre of the play, but notes the important presence of elements from tragedy and comedy as well.

Skura, Meredith Anne. "Discourse and the Individual: The Case of Colonialism in *The Tempest.*" *Shakespeare Quarterly* 40.1 (1989): 42-69.
Reviews—and acknowledges the usefulness of—recent readings of *The Tempest* within the context of colonialism. Warns, however, that an overly literal identification of the play with contemporary colonialist discourse might lose sight of the complexity of the play as a work of literature.

Takaki, Ronald. "*The Tempest* in the Wilderness: The Racialization of Savagery." *Journal of American History* 79.3 (1992): 892-912.
Notes how *The Tempest* reflects early English reactions to Native Americans and how it anticipates the later brutalization of Native Americans by the English and other

Europeans. Notes, in particular, how the play participates in the English discourse of savagery, which had long been seen as a cultural phenomenon when applied to the Irish, but which came to be seen as a racial characteristic when applied to Native Americans, especially by New England Puritans, who identified Native Americans with Satan.

Vaughan, Alden T., and Virginia Mason Vaughan. *Shakespeare's Caliban: A Cultural History.* Cambridge: Cambridge UP, 1991.
Surveys the reception of Caliban from Shakespeare's day to the present, noting how changing reactions to Caliban reflect larger trends in society.

Yachnin, Paul. "Shakespeare and the Idea of Obedience: Gonzalo in *The Tempest.*" *Mosaic* 24.2 (1991): 1-18.
Argues that the most important context of *The Tempest* is not colonialism but the domestic politics of Europe. Sees the play as a profoundly conservative demonstration of the importance of obedience to official royal power.

chapter 12

Approaches to *Heart of Darkness*, by Joseph Conrad

Heart of Darkness[1] is one of the central texts in the canon of modern British literature. Written in 1899 and published in its final form in 1902, the text is located precisely at the transition between the nineteenth and twentieth centuries. And the text is virtually unique in the extent to which (especially in such a brief work) it expresses many of the concerns and anxieties that were central to European thought during that crucial period. The stylistic and psychological complexities of *Heart of Darkness* made it a favorite text of critics and teachers of literature during the cold war years, when political readings of literature were rare in the United States. The turn to history and politics in recent literary criticism has stimulated new interest in Conrad's text, which is centrally concerned with imperialism and colonialism, key issues for many contemporary critics. In addition, *Heart of Darkness* addresses the crucial questions of race, class, and gender, which places it very much at the center of many critical debates in the 1990s. Critics now tend to treat Conrad's text with a considerable amount of skepticism; while still often admiring its language and structure, they see the book as an expression of certain attitudes toward race, class, gender, and colonialism that were typical of Conrad's time but that need to be challenged in our own historical moment. This section presents readings of *Heart of Darkness* from the points of view of psychoanalytic criticism, Bakhtinian criticism, the new historicism, and multicultural criticism, though Conrad's book has proved responsive to other critical approaches as well.

[1] Citations from *Heart of Darkness* include dual page numbers, the first referring to the Norton critical edition, the second to the Penguin edition.

PSYCHOANALYTIC CRITICISM

Joseph Conrad's Charlie Marlow, the protagonist of *Heart of Darkness,* recognizes that his trip up the Congo River in search of the mysterious Kurtz is in fact a quest for himself: "Droll thing life is—that mysterious arrangement of merciless logic for a futile purpose. The most you can hope from it is some knowledge of yourself" (69, 112). The value Marlow places on work derives largely from his belief that, through work, he can discover his true self: "I don't like work—no man does—but I like what is in the work—the chance to find yourself. Your own reality—for yourself—not for others—what no other man can ever know" (31, 59). Indeed for decades perhaps the most influential reading of *Heart of Darkness* was Albert J. Guerard's argument in his 1958 book *Conrad the Novelist* that Conrad's text is primarily a representation of Marlow's "voyage of self-discovery" (39).

The idea of the novel as the story of the hero's quest for identity is quite consistent with the psychoanalytic notion that true human identity resides in some deep, largely inaccessible, inner place hidden somewhere within the psyche. Given Marlow's own espousal of this model of identity, it is thus not surprising that psychoanalytic critics have often found much of interest in *Heart of Darkness.* During the 1950s and 1960s—when political readings had been almost entirely effaced from Anglo-American literary criticism—psychoanalysis came to the fore as the most prominent way of approaching Conrad's complex text.

Heart of Darkness invites psychoanalytic readings from any number of perspectives. For example, Guerard's reading sees the African jungle essentially as a metaphor for the unconscious mind and therefore Marlow's treacherous and nightmarish trip up the Congo as a metaphor for his attempt to probe the depths of his own unconscious mind. Guerard notes that Kurtz himself can be read as a dramatization of Marlow's unconscious desires, as "the Freudian id or the Jungian shadow or more vaguely the outlaw" (39). Such symbolic readings of Conrad's representation of Africa suggest a number of potential psychoanalytic approaches. For example, both the Congo River and the African jungle are described in *Heart of Darkness* as elements of primal human experience, a representation that clearly suggests the use of Carl Jung's notion of archetypes to explore the symbolic significance of these images. The highly symbolic atmosphere of the entire text (Conrad himself later expressed regret at perhaps having made the text, and especially the depiction of Kurtz, *too* symbolic) invites a number of such comparisons with Sigmund Freud's structural model of the psyche. Thus if the African jungle is the unconscious, or the id, then the entire system of European civilization, with its rules and its "police," is the super-ego. Marlow himself then might be the ego, attempting to negotiate between these extremes.

Guerard believes that Marlow's voyage of self-discovery is largely successful and that he returns to Europe a much-changed man. But readings by Frederick R. Karl and by Gary Adelman, among others, emphasize the pessimistic tone of the text and call the ultimate success of Marlow's voyage into question. There is a sense in the text that Marlow believes he will discover some ultimate and final secret—not only about himself but also about life in general—once he reaches the Inner Station and meets the incomparable Kurtz. No such revelation occurs, however; Kurtz leaves Marlow only with a final enigmatic invocation of "the horror." We might, then, see the text as an unfulfilled quest, a motif that within a psychoanalytic context recalls the work of Jacques Lacan. When read through Lacan, *Heart of Darkness* can be seen as the story of Marlow's attempt to restore in the African jungle a sense of subjective wholeness that he has lost as a result of his alienated life in Europe. The African jungle, which Marlow clearly regards as the primal home of the human race, is a symbol of the Imaginary Order world of infancy. Marlow's quest can therefore be read as an attempt to recover an Imaginary Order sense of fusion with the Lacanian *objet a.* Lacan, of course, would also predict the ultimate failure of this quest. For Lacan, all such quests fail—in the very process of assuming a human identity, we must irrevocably give up this wholeness in exchange for our entry into the Symbolic Order of language.

The problem with such readings, of course, is that they are clearly Eurocentric. For one thing, thinking of Africa as a mere symbol for certain aspects of the European mind tends to efface the historical reality of African life. *Heart of Darkness* is a fiction, but it is one about a real continent on which millions of Africans suffered and died as a result of European brutality during centuries of slave trading and colonization. And although the association of Africa with the primitive passion of the id would have been a commonplace at the end of the nineteenth century, when Conrad was writing *Heart of Darkness,* this association has racist implications that are impossible for any sensitive reader to miss at the end of the twentieth century. Psychoanalytic critics must always be extremely cautious when approaching texts that deal with other cultures or that were produced in other cultures. Psychoanalysis, despite its claims to universality, is a fundamentally European discourse. It is firmly rooted not only in Europe but also in *turn-of-the-century* Europe, and its insights must be carefully scrutinized within the context of its own origins.

With such cautions in mind, it is also true that Marlow himself almost seems directly to invite psychoanalytic readings of his story. For one thing, he frequently suggests that truth must be sought deep beneath the obscuring veil of surface appearance. His description of Brussels as a "whited sepulchre," for example, suggests that the true (dark) nature of the city is hidden by its shiny exterior (13, 35). And when he arrives in Africa, Marlow realizes that there must be more to the story of Kurtz than can be seen in a superficial examination: "The essentials of this affair lay deep under the surface, beyond my reach and beyond my power of meddling" (40, 72). This notion of epistemological depth is quite central to psychoanalysis, which assumes that the source of human psychological characteristics lies hidden deep within the unconscious mind and which attempts to extract the truth of this source through techniques of interpretive probing. The assumption of epistemological depth is also central to a number of European disciplines at the turn of the century, and it is not surprising that the assumption often informs modernist literature, which frequently seems designed to explore reality in more profound ways than did its realist predecessors. Moreover the depths explored by modernist texts are often psychological in nature, and one of the most distinctive features of modernist literature is its turn to techniques such as stream of consciousness that are designed specifically to allow the representation of the deep, inner recesses of characters' minds.

Heart of Darkness shows a strong skepticism toward the possibility of such representation, however. As a result, Conrad does not employ stream of consciousness or other devices designed to convey inner psychological experience. Instead he has Marlow express his doubts that such experience can ever be conveyed. This doubt itself arises from Marlow's belief that the truth of human experience lies so deep beneath the surface that it becomes virtually inaccessible. And Marlow's version of depth epistemology matches quite closely with Freud's in that Marlow quite consistently uses the metaphor of dreams to convey the inexpressible quality of his experience in Africa. Marlow emphasizes his ultimate inability to convey the truth of his experience to his listeners by comparing his narration to the telling of a dream: "It seems to me I am trying to tell you a dream—making a vain attempt, because no relation of a dream can convey the dream-sensation. . . . No, it is impossible; it is impossible to convey the life-sensation of any given epoch of one's existence—that which makes its truth, its meaning—its subtle and penetrating essence. It is impossible. We live, as we dream—alone" (30, 57).

In the same vein, Marlow mentions the "dream-sensation that pervaded all my days" in Africa (43, 76); and he describes Kurtz's words as having had "the terrific suggestiveness of words heard in dreams, of phrases spoken in nightmares" (65, 108). This suggestiveness is precisely what propels the Freudian interpretation of dreams, just as there is a clearly Freudian element in Marlow's consistent implication that it is in dreams that the real truth of human experience lies and that his difficulty in communication lies precisely in the difficulty of unraveling the content of dreams and expressing it in waking language. This attempt to unravel and express the truth of dreams, of course, is precisely the one undertaken by Freud.

Psychoanalytic critics of *Heart of Darkness* have, quite naturally, often focused on the motif of dreams in the text. In the essay "The Power of Darkness," Frederick Crews reads *Heart of Darkness* as an Oedipal fantasy that is propelled by Conrad's sexual insecurities but that also appeals to universal symbolic experiences. Crews argues that Marlow's narration is analogous to what might be recounted to a psychoanalyst by a patient. He further argues that the psychoanalytic interpretation of such a narration would be "beyond doubt":

> The exposed sinner at the heart of darkness would be an image of the father, accused of sexual "rites" with the mother. The dreamer is preoccupied with the primal scene, which he symbolically interrupts. The journey into the maternal body is both voyeuristic and incestuous, and the rescue of the father is more defiant and supplantive than tender

> and restitutive. The closing episode with the "phantom" woman in a sarcophagal setting would be the dreamer-son's squaring of accounts with his dead mother. (520)

In a less purely psychoanalytic way, Guerard also draws on the frequent references to dreams in *Heart of Darkness* to emphasize the dreamlike quality of the text. But Guerard goes well beyond a reading of Marlow's specific references to dreams, noting that the imagery and language of the text themselves have an inherently dreamlike quality. Thus for Guerard, the experience of reading *Heart of Darkness* is itself something like a dream, and Marlow's voyage of self-discovery resembles the reader's own. In a similar vein, Thomas Moser (working from a perspective clearly influenced by Guerard) argues that a fundamental defining characteristic of *Heart of Darkness* is its ability to provoke certain effects in its readers. Moser thus argues that "Conrad's masterly control of the reader's responses is one of the most significant results of his unorthodox methods" (24). Moser's reading of *Heart of Darkness* also remains strongly rooted in psychoanalytic theory. He contends that the fundamental impulse behind the text is Conrad's own deep-seated fear of sexual abandon, a fear embodied in his depiction of Kurtz's loss of civilized restraint. Moser believes, however, that (in contrast to the author's earlier novels) Conrad has been successful in *Heart of Darkness* in finding an artistic outlet for his anxieties: "For the first time Conrad has been able to use material potentially related to sex in such a way as not to ruin his story" (80). But Moser also believes that Conrad's success may ultimately be tempered by the final scene between Marlow and the Intended, where Marlow's lie shows a reemergence of the fear of women that informs much of Conrad's earlier fiction. Moser does, however, grant that this scene can be read as an "indictment of this woman, safe and ignorant in her complacent, Belgian bourgeois existence; she does not *deserve* to hear the truth" (81).

Other psychoanalytic critics have broadened their focus beyond attempts to relate *Heart of Darkness* to Conrad's personal psychological makeup. Gary Adelman, for example, agrees that the book is informed by a deep-seated sense of psychological disturbance but that this disturbance is located in turn-of-the-century European society rather than in Conrad's individual mind. For Adelman, *Heart of Darkness* is a profoundly pessimistic work that suggests that "the Victorian has had fostered within him a psychopathic craving for destruction, and that imperialism is an irremediable manifestation of this unconscious desire" (3). Adelman notes that certain aspects of the opposition between European civilization and African nature in *Heart of Darkness* can be usefully illuminated in terms of Freud's more sociologically oriented work, such as the discussion of the opposition between civilized restraint and natural aggression in *Civilization and Its Discontents* (47–48).

Frederick R. Karl's psychoanalytic reading of *Heart of Darkness* similarly looks beyond Conrad's psyche. Rather than see the text as an expression of Conrad's unconscious impulses, Karl views Conrad as a highly self-conscious artist who employs images analogous to those discussed by Freud to present a diagnosis of modern European society as fundamentally driven by irrational impulses. Karl notes, for example, Conrad's extensive use of "doubling" as a structural device, whether it includes the opposition of the peaceful Thames to the turbulent Congo, the European metropolis to the African jungle, or Kurtz's European fiancée to his African mistress (135). Drawing not only on Freud but also on Jung's notion of the collective unconscious and Nietzsche's concept of the will to power, Karl concludes that Conrad's central image of "darkness" is quite comparable to Freud's "unconscious" and that Conrad's presentation of the "Kurtz-Marlow polarity" is a "definition of our times" (136). "European history as well as the history of individual men can be read more clearly in the light of Conrad's art; for he tells us that the most dutiful of men, a Marlow, can be led to the brink of savagery and brutality if the will to power touches him; that the most idealistic of men, Kurtz, can become a sadistic murderer; that the dirty work of this world is carried out by men whose reputations are preserved by lies" (136). In addressing such issues, Karl concludes, *Heart of Darkness* is more a continental text than an English one, perhaps reflecting Conrad's Polish origins. For Karl, the literary tradition to which Conrad's text belongs is not that of British modernism but that of texts such as Fyodor Dostoevsky's *Notes from Underground,* Franz Kafka's *Metamorphosis,* Thomas Mann's *Death in Venice,* and Albert Camus's *The Stranger,* all fictions of "'underground' men, men who through force of character or artistic sensibility suffer in isolation or alienation, outside the mainstream of society" (135).

As Karl shows, it is possible to draw on many of the Freudian resonances in *Heart of Darkness* to produce readings of the text that do not strictly rely on a belief in Freud's theories. For one example, acceptance of the notion of *Heart of Darkness* as Marlow's voyage of self-discovery makes the book a central participant in the novelistic tradition, at least according to Georg Lukács's theory of the novel, which (written before he became a Marxist) emphasizes the "transcendental homelessness" of the questing hero in an alien world:

> The novel is the epic of an age in which the extensive totality of life is no longer directly given, in which the immanence of meaning in life has become a problem, yet which still thinks in terms of totality. . . . Thus the fundamental form-determining intention of the novel is objectivised as the psychology of the novel's heroes: they are seekers. . . . The content of the novel is the story of the soul that goes to find itself, that seeks adventures in order to be proved and tested by them, and, by proving itself, to find its own essence. (56, 60, 89)

For Lukács, the novel is the genre of a modern European society in which the status of human beings, once guaranteed by a religious faith in the place of humanity within a divine scheme of creation, is now uncertain. In this sense, we might read Conrad's text and Freud's nearly contemporaneous *Interpretation of Dreams* as a parallel symptom of a turn-of-the-century anxiety over the status of the self, once viewed as a stable and autonomous entity but now open to question in an era in which the authority of so many aspects of the Western tradition was beginning to crumble.

Certainly the central "story" of the book, the tale of the river journey into Africa, can very clearly be read as Marlow's quest to attain a vision of his own selfhood with which he can feel comfortable, but the dialogues with temporality, history, imperialism, and sexuality that are initiated by that journey address most of the psychological, political, and social issues that are involved in the human quest for selfhood in general. The seeming universality of the theme of a journey of self-discovery should not be allowed to obscure the very important historical specificity of Conrad's text. First published in 1899, *Heart of Darkness* participates in a number of important issues of its day. In particular, a turn-of-the-century European narrative that occurs mostly in Africa cannot be responsibly read apart from the historical reality of the European domination of Africa during that period.

Works Cited

Adelman, Gary. *"Heart of Darkness": Search for the Unconscious.* Boston: Twayne, 1987.

Conrad, Joseph. *Heart of Darkness.* 1902. Norton critical ed. 3d ed. Ed. Robert Kimbrough. New York: Norton, 1988.

———. *Heart of Darkness.* 1902. Ed. Paul O'Prey. London: Penguin, 1994.

Crews, Frederick. "The Power of Darkness." *Partisan Review* 34 (Fall 1967): 507-525.

Guerard, Albert J. *Conrad the Novelist.* Cambridge, Mass.: Harvard UP, 1958.

Karl, Frederick R. "Introduction to the *Danse Macabre:* Conrad's *Heart of Darkness.*" In *"Heart of Darkness": A Case Study in Contemporary Criticism*, ed. Ross C. Murfin, 123-138. New York: St. Martin's, 1989.

Lukács, Georg. *The Theory of the Novel.* 1920. Trans. Anna Bostock. Cambridge, Mass.: MIT P, 1985.

Moser, Thomas. *Joseph Conrad: Achievement and Decline.* Cambridge, Mass.: Harvard UP, 1957.

BAKHTINIAN CRITICISM

Numerous critics have turned in recent years to the theories of Mikhail Bakhtin in search of a framework within which to read the fiction of Joseph Conrad. Daphna Erdinast-Vulcan, for example, appeals to Bakhtin's readings of Dostoevsky to argue that Conrad's work resembles Dostoevsky's polyphonic novels in that "the mode of representation is entirely subjected to the consciousness of the protagonists themselves, and reality becomes a projection of the hero's perception" (8). Both Aaron Fogel and Mark A. Wollaeger argue that the distinctive feature of Conrad's novels is precisely their *lack* of polyphony. Thus Wollaeger argues that Conrad's novels tend to be dominated by the authorial voice, in contrast to Bakhtin's vision of the novels of Dostoevsky, in which the voices of various characters sound with an intensity and an authority equal to that of the author's. Fogel finds that, contrary to Bakhtin's idea of the polyphonic novel in which various voices freely sound, novels such as *Nostromo* present a plurality of voices that nevertheless "dramatizes the unequal and 'jerky' relations among them" (133). In particular, in the phenomenon that he refers to as "forced dialogue," Fogel argues that in Conrad different voices are not just *allowed* to speak but actually *forced* to speak. Fogel then notes the prevalence in Conrad's work of scenes in which one character interrogates another, attempting to force him to speak while he tries to remain silent. Fogel thus characterizes Conrad's view of social relations not as the free and open dialogue envisioned by Bakhtin but as scenes of domination and submission, with one participant usually clearly having power over the other.

Such critical disagreements over Conrad's work are, of course, not surprising. One of the most distinctive characteristics of his writing is its seeming ability to generate multiple, even contradictory, interpretations. We might say, then, that Conrad criticism is itself dialogic, a phenomenon related to the dialogic character of Conrad's texts. In the case of *Heart of Darkness,* there are a number of potential sources of this dialogism, the most obvious of which is the complex structure of the book's narration. The narrative voice of *Heart of Darkness* is inherently multiple. Rather than write the story in the authoritative voice of the nineteenth-century omniscient third-person narrator, Conrad decenters his narration by relaying accounts of events in a mode of hearsay. In the outer frame of the book, we are addressed by an anonymous first-person narrator who quickly gives way to Marlow, the narrator of most of the events in the story. And Marlow himself often relays events as they were told to him by still other narrators, such as the Russian sailor. The original narrator periodically intrudes into the narration to remind us that we are already listening secondhand to Marlow's account. This narrator also subtly undermines Marlow's authority with a variety of slyly subversive comments. For example, as Marlow begins his tale, the narrator bids us farewell with an ironic aside, noting that he and his comrades "knew we were fated . . . to hear about one of Marlow's inconclusive experiences" (11, 32). Already, then, we are warned that Marlow's account is not likely to achieve the neat closure of a classic nineteenth-century narrative, a warning that is particularly subversive given the especially goal-oriented nature of the quest motif that so clearly informs Marlow's story. And in the oh-no-not-again weariness of this remark (as in the later suggestions that most of the listeners may have fallen asleep), there is a hint that Marlow's stories may not be entirely enthralling or even believable.

Conrad's complex texts quite consistently evade closure. Fredric Jameson notes that "nothing is more alien to the windless closure of high naturalism than the works of Joseph Conrad" (206). In *Heart of Darkness,* numerous elements of Marlow's narrative work against any simple and final interpretation, dramatizing Bakhtin's notion of unfinalizability in interpretation. For example, Marlow further decenters his narrative by indicating that most of his impressions of Kurtz were derived from vague sensations arising from hearsay and that conveying these sensations to his audience is as impossible as fully explaining a dream: "It seems to me I am trying to tell you a dream—making a vain attempt, because no relation of a dream can convey the dream-sensation. . . . No, it is impossible; it is impossible to convey the life-sensation of any given epoch of one's existence—that which makes its truth, its meaning—its subtle and penetrating essence. It is impossible. We live, as we dream—alone" (30, 57). Marlow suggests that reality cannot finally be circumscribed within the confines of narrative. Yet he is, above all, a storyteller, and narrative is his principal means of ordering and mastering the flux of reality. His disavowal of narrative, like his later critiques of imperialism in general and of Kurtz in particular, seems to do little more than provide a thin disguise of an underlying complicity. Although Marlow indicates that any attempt to communicate his experiences in Africa will necessarily lose something in the telling, he then pauses and adds to his listeners: "Of course in this you fellows see more than I could then. You see me, whom you know" (30, 58). Paradoxically he now seems to be saying that something has been added in the telling and that his listeners will be better able to understand his experiences as narrated than he could while undergoing them.

Jeremy Hawthorn suggests that this turnabout is not really a contradiction, arguing that "Marlow, unable to express the 'inexpressible,' is able to express its inexpressibility" (28). Hawthorn is right to an extent, and his interpretation of this passage has the interesting effect of making Marlow's comment echo the final words of Kurtz. The contradiction can also be partially illuminated by the unusual character of all of Marlow's narratives, as the frame narrator explains: "Marlow was not typical. . . . To him the meaning of an episode was not inside like a kernel but outside, enveloping the tale which brought it out only as a glow brings out a haze, in the likeness of one of these misty halos that sometimes are made visible by the spectral illumination of moonshine" (9, 30).

This passage can be taken in many ways, but among other things it suggests a view of Marlow's narrative as inherently intertextual and as deriving its meaning from dialogues with other texts that are outside the actual body of the narrative. Moreover Marlow's suggestion that new meaning is created in the storytelling process indicates a productive intersubjective process that can be usefully illuminated by Bakhtin's key concept of dialogism. Peter Brooks has noted as much, suggesting that in *Heart of Darkness* meaning is "dialogic in nature, located in the interstices of story and frame, born of the relationship between tellers and listeners" (260).

This dialogism ultimately occurs more in the interaction between Conrad's text and the reader, not between Marlow and his audience on the *Nellie.* In the story itself, Marlow assumes the role of authoritarian master, dictating to his listeners, who are virtually invisible and almost entirely silent. The only dialogue between Marlow and his listeners once he begins his tale occurs when he describes their everyday bourgeois lives as a series of "monkey tricks," at which a disembodied voice growls, "Try to be civil, Marlow" (36, 67). Marlow thus strives to be a monological narrator of the type associated by Fogel and Wollaeger with Conrad's work in general. But Marlow's narration is dialogized, as it were, by the complex narrative structure of the final text, which removes him from an authoritative position and assures that he cannot get the last word. Moreover Marlow's statements themselves are frequently contradictory, setting up a kind of internal dialogue with themselves. Contradiction is, in fact, a central element of *Heart of Darkness.* Thus the suggestion that Marlow's meaning lies outside, rather than inside, his narrative proper contradicts Marlow's own continuing emphasis on penetrating to the heart of things, where presumably he will find meaning. And Marlow's critique of the reliability of narrative (reminiscent of the motif of criticism of its own discourse that Bakhtin describes in relation to the novel) assures that his own narrative cannot be reduced to a single, authoritative meaning. Indeed Marlow's statement within a narrative that the truth of narratives cannot be relied on recalls the famous liar paradox, in which a "Cretan liar" proclaims that "I always lie," thus presenting a radically unfinalizable statement: If he always lies, then he must be lying when he says he always lies, and so on.

Heart of Darkness also incorporates different social voices into the fabric of its own language. Probably the most important opposition initiated in the text is that between Europe and Africa. Among other things, this opposition can be usefully described via Bakhtin's notion of the chronotope. Spatially, for example, Marlow consistently figures Europe as "here," while portraying Africa as distant, dark, and mysterious. Europe is also treated as the locus of contemporaneity, while Africa is consistently described as ancient, even primeval. The spatial and temporal connotations of Europe and Africa are thus radically different; they are characterized through different chronotopes, which then interact in the text. But this interaction is not truly dialogic: The European position in the here and now is quite clearly privileged over the primitive and distant position of Africa. The same might also be said for the figuration of language in the text, which is thoroughly dominated by European perspectives. Africans, in fact, hardly speak at all, and when they do, they speak a broken pidgin English that enhances their representation in the text as primitive and lacking in the civilized attainment of Europeans.

We might argue that Marlow's descriptions of Africans attempting to speak English ultimately undermine the European position. After all, the Africans seem to speak European languages far better than the Europeans speak African ones, and as the Congo was a Belgian colony, French, not English, would likely be the European language that Marlow's African crewmen know best. Nevertheless the Russian sailor Marlow meets at the Inner Station seems to have no real trouble with English, even though he is hardly presented in a favorable light in the text. And Kurtz, who is only one-quarter English, is described as being brilliantly eloquent in English. In this case, then, *Heart of Darkness* appears to bear out the conclusions of critics such as Fogel that in Conrad's "dialogues" one participant tends to occupy a position of dominance relative to the other.

In *Heart of Darkness,* the most important example of the forced dialogue described by Fogel occurs in Marlow's final interview with the Intended. In this conversation, Marlow seems continually to demonstrate his position of superior linguistic power. He continually misleads the woman, telling her exactly what she wants to hear, but does so in such a way that every statement he utters can also be taken to mean almost precisely the opposite of what he knows she will think it means. Conrad thereby produces a complex form of dramatic irony in which Marlow, his audience on the *Nellie,* and we the readers have access to interpretive dimensions that are apparently barred to the Intended, who thus appears naive and linguistically powerless in comparison to Marlow's advanced ability to manipulate language. For example, asked if he had known Kurtz well, Marlow replies, "I knew him as well as it is possible for one man to know another" (73, 118). The Intended, as would anyone, takes this to mean that he knew Kurtz well indeed, but the context suggests that it means that he knew him not at all, that it is never possible for one man to know another. And when the Intended misinterprets Marlow's suggestion that Kurtz was "remarkable" to mean that it was impossible not to love him, Marlow rather viciously replies, "You knew him best" (73, 118).

Marlow's hostility seems to mount as the conversation continues, reaching its peak when the Intended raises her arms in a gesture that links her to the wild African woman, "resembling in this gesture another one, tragic also, and bedecked with powerless charms, stretching bare brown arms over the glitter of the infernal stream" (75, 120). When the Intended interrupts this troubling vision to note that Kurtz "died as he lived," her own statement becomes inadvertently double-voiced, meaning both that he died in the manner that he had lived and that he was already dying *while* he lived, mirroring the living dead who walk about the sepulchral city of Europe. Marlow then maliciously replies that Kurtz's end was "in every way worthy of his life," admitting to his later listeners that by this time there had been a "dull anger stirring in me" (75, 120). Even Marlow's climactic lie, in which he tells the Intended that Kurtz's last word had been her name, is not a simple falsehood; it can also be interpreted as Marlow's double-voiced suggestion that the Intended (with all that she represents in European culture) was indeed the "horror" to which Kurtz referred in the last words Marlow heard him speak (75, 121). And Johanna M. Smith may be entirely correct when she argues that Marlow effects this equation (of which the Intended is obviously unaware) as a means of humiliating her. Smith suggests that Marlow shows such hostility and such determination to dominate the Intended that this interview becomes a sort of verbal rape (193).

Normally to Bakhtin, a double-voiced discourse is employed by a member of a marginal group to parody and undermine the dominant group. This use of double-voiced discourse to reinforce the power of a member of a dominant social group (here, men) over a member of a marginal social group (here, women) provides an interesting twist on the Bakhtinian notion of dialogism. It also reinforces the notion that Conrad's fiction frequently attempts to overcome the inherent dialogism of language through the imposition of an authoritative discursive position. But dialogism is not so easy to overcome, and Marlow's final encounter with the Intended can be variously interpreted. We could read Marlow's final lie as a kind gesture, even if a somewhat condescending one. And we could even argue that it is the Intended who manipulates Marlow in this interview. After all, she seems consistently able to formulate her remarks in such a way as to receive from Marlow precisely the responses that she hopes for, whatever alternative hidden meanings these responses might carry.

Indeed virtually all of the statements and actions related in *Heart of Darkness* could be read in markedly different ways. Even the treatment of imperialism in the text, which so clearly privileges European over African perspectives, is dialogic in its treatment of the European position. Critics such as Benita Parry have pointed out that Conrad's treatment of imperialism tends to be highly ambivalent in all of his fiction, and *Heart of Darkness* is certainly no exception. Even though Marlow makes a number of negative remarks about imperialism as a whole and clearly disapproves of the brutalities being committed by Europeans against Africans in the Congo, neither Marlow nor the text in which he appears ever actually challenges the notion that Europe has a right, even a duty, to colonize Africa. Early in his narrative, Marlow supplies a succinct statement of the drive for mastery that underlies imperial conquests, noting that "for that you want only brute force—nothing to boast of, when you have it, since your strength is just an accident arising from the weakness of others." That this quest for strength is underwritten by racism is then indicated by his remark that the "conquest of the earth" mostly consists of "taking it away from those who have a different complexion or slightly flatter noses than ourselves" (10, 31-32). Later Marlow reinforces this picture of imperialism as an opportunity to display power for the sake of power in his depiction of the apparently inane shelling of unseen "enemies" on the African coast by a French warship (17, 40-41) and in the parallel pointless dynamiting of the cliff near the company station at which he disembarks (19, 42). Marlow links these examples of senseless violence with a vivid depiction of the treatment of a group of Africans suffering on a chain gang: "I could see every rib, the joints of their limbs were like knots in a rope; each had an iron collar on his neck, and all were connected together with a chain whose bights swung between them, rhythmically clinking. Another report from the cliff made me think of that ship I had seen firing into the continent. It was the same ominous voice; but these men could by no stretch of imagination be called enemies" (19, 43).

Marlow here shows a certain sympathy with the enchained blacks, though his oddly dehumanizing description of them—like his later description of his African helmsman as an "instrument" (51, 87)—tends to reduce them to objects. The depiction here of colonialism as an "ominous voice" will have important resonances with Marlow's later depiction of Kurtz, the embodiment of that imperialism, as a sort of Bakhtinian allegory, that is, as consisting primarily of a voice. Moreover though Marlow is certainly not above deceiving himself, here he shows that he has no illusions about the dynamics of imperial power. Suggestions that colonialism is pursued for the benefit of those colonized draw from him nothing but scorn, as shown by his encounter with his aunt: "There had been a lot of such rot let loose in print and talk just about that time, and the excellent woman, living right in the rush of all that humbug, got carried off her feet. She talked about 'weaning those ignorant millions from their horrid ways,' till, upon my word, she made me quite uncomfortable. I ventured to hint that the Company was run for profit" (15-16, 39).

Later Marlow further undermines the ideology of the "white man's burden" by noting that Kurtz had begun his work in Africa in a "benevolent" spirit very similar to that of the aunt. Kurtz's report for the "International Society for the Suppression of Savage Customs" is a perfect example of the printed "rot" that Marlow sees as a source of his aunt's unrealistic notions about imperialism. According to this report, Kurtz begins his mission with a desire to "exert a power for good practically unbounded" (50, 86-87). Yet he ends up in a compound decorated with the heads of slain enemies, and his last recommendation for the "suppression of savage customs" is to "exterminate all the brutes" (51, 87). One of the most important sources of potential dialogism in *Heart of Darkness* involves the incorporation into the novel of echoes from other texts and other genres, of which the contemporary rot of pro-imperial propaganda is one of the most important. From a Bakhtinian point of view, even the seemingly innocuous text *An Inquiry into some Points of Seamanship* has potentially powerful implications (39, 71). The sudden appearance of this text within Marlow's narrative is analogous to the incongruity with which this technical manual—with its intonations of European technology and scientific method—appears in the middle of the African jungle. In both cases, the textual intrusion suggests the foreignness and unnaturalness of the European presence in Africa.

Kurtz himself is a walking embodiment of the heteroglossia of contemporary European society. He is described as a "universal genius," and his talents and expertise seem to include an equal mixture of science, music, painting, poetry, journalism, politics, business, and any number of other fields (71, 115). Indeed the same might be said for *Heart of Darkness* itself: Science, literature, religion, business, politics, and other disciplines all contribute to the overall texture of the book. Bakhtin's theories provide a powerful tool with which to explore the complexity of this mixture of languages. Those theories also yield important new insights into the complexities and ambiguities of Conrad's book as a whole, suggesting how the interactions of different voices within the language of the book reflect the interactions among powerful social forces in Conrad's contemporary Europe.

Works Cited

Bakhtin, Mikhail. *Problems of Dostoevsky's Poetics.* Trans. and ed. Caryl Emerson. Minneapolis: U of Minnesota P, 1984.

Brooks, Peter. *Reading for the Plot: Design and Intention in Narrative.* New York: Vintage, 1985.

Conrad, Joseph. *Heart of Darkness.* 1902. Norton critical ed. 3d ed. Ed. Robert Kimbrough. New York: Norton, 1988.

———. *Heart of Darkness.* 1902. Ed. Paul O'Prey. London: Penguin, 1994.

Erdinast-Vulcan, Daphna. *Joseph Conrad and the Modern Temper.* Oxford, Clarendon-Oxford UP, 1991.

Fogel, Aaron. *Coercion to Speak: Conrad's Poetics of Dialogue.* Cambridge, Mass.: Harvard UP, 1985.
Hawthorn, Jeremy. *Joseph Conrad: Language and Fictional Self-Consciousness.* Lincoln: U of Nebraska P, 1979.
Jameson, Fredric. *The Political Unconscious: Narrative as a Socially Symbolic Act.* Ithaca, N.Y.: Cornell UP, 1981.
Parry, Benita. *Conrad and Imperialism: Ideological Boundaries and Visionary Frontiers.* London: Macmillan, 1983.
Smith, Johanna M. "'Too Beautiful Altogether': Patriarchal Ideology in *Heart of Darkness.*" In *"Heart of Darkness": A Case Study in Contemporary Criticism,* ed. Ross C. Murfin, 179–195. New York: St. Martin's, 1989.
Wollaeger, Mark A. *Joseph Conrad and the Fictions of Skepticism.* Stanford, Calif.: Stanford UP, 1990.

NEW HISTORICIST CRITICISM

Perhaps the most frequent critical observation made about the fiction of Joseph Conrad is the way his work displays a consistent ambivalence toward almost all of the major issues it addresses. Benita Parry, for example, notes that Conrad's work both undermines and supports the ideology of imperialism. Fredric Jameson remarks that Conrad's work includes many of the characteristics of both the sophisticated texts of modernism and the entertainment-oriented texts of popular culture. For Jameson, this doubleness derives from Conrad's historical location at a crucial point when modern culture itself was fragmenting into different currents, when there was a "coexistence of all these distinct but as yet imperfectly differentiated cultural 'spaces'" (208). Jameson's attribution of Conrad's ambivalence to his historical moment (rather than to his personal psychology) suggests that new historicist analysis should be able to locate other contemporary texts showing a similar doubleness. Such analysis of texts like *Heart of Darkness* is extremely valuable, both because it helps us understand the broader significance of Conrad's ambivalence and because it helps locate Conrad's treatment of a number of specific issues within contemporary discourses.

For example, the treatment of Africa in *Heart of Darkness* is quite typical of European discourses about that continent at the turn of the century. The important late-nineteenth- and early-twentieth-century black thinker E. W. Blyden (an influence on such later African thinkers as Kwame Nkrumah and Léopold Senghor and one of the forerunners of the *Négritude* movement in twentieth-century black literature) frequently complained that European scholars commenting on Africa fundamentally misunderstood the differences between Africa and Europe. In his 1888 book *Christianity, Islam, and the Negro Race,* for example, Blyden pointed out the tendency of Europeans to see Africans as undeveloped, even infantile, versions of themselves:

> The mistake which Europeans often make in considering questions of Negro improvement and the future of Africa, is in supposing that the

> Negro is the European in embryo—in the undeveloped stage—and that when, by and by, he shall enjoy the advantages of civilization and culture, he will become like the European; in other words, that the Negro is on the same line of progress, in the same groove, with the European, but infinitely in the rear. (276)

Blyden was accurate in his description of European scholarship. In a recent study, R. H. Lyons notes the consistency with which nineteenth-century European commentators regarded blacks as inferior to whites, quite often comparing the two along the lines of children versus adults: "Though they did disagree among themselves about which European 'races' were inferior to others, Western racial commentators generally agreed that Blacks were inferior to whites in moral fiber, cultural attainment, and mental ability; the African was, to many eyes, the child in the family of man, modern man in embryo" (86-87). As V. Y. Mudimbe points out, an entire array of nineteenth-century European discourses on Africa quite consistently tended to envision Africa as radically separated from Europe in terms of temporal development. European writers in fields such as botany, anthropology, and phrenology "attempted to prove that in Africa the physical environment, the flora and fauna, as well as the people, represent relics of a remote age of antiquity" (107). Powerful currents in nineteenth-century European thought, including a fascination with evolution, history, and social progress, all tended to envision the course of both nature and society as an ongoing forward movement in time. Such models tended to be global in scope, treating Africa and Europe as part of the same process, with Europe simply being farther along on the temporal scale. Africa came to be treated as the locus of primitivity in virtually all areas, thus serving as an anchor point against which the progressive development of Europe could be measured.

Probably the most important formulation of nineteenth-century narrative history was G. W. F. Hegel's scientific/rational version of providence, in which history is an inexorable movement toward the realization of an ultimate goal that is identified with God's plan for humanity: "That world history is governed by an absolute design, that it is a rational process—whose rationality is not that of a particular subject, but a divine and absolute reason—this is a proposition whose truth we must assume" (28). Hegel's view of the divine plan behind history leads him to the ethnocentric conclusion that his contemporary European culture is the culmination of that plan and to the nationalistic belief that his own Germany is supreme among the nations of the earth. In short, his model of history tends to provide a justification for European imperial conquest of Africa and other "undeveloped" regions because it envisions Europe as closer to the fulfillment of God's plan for all of humanity.

This vision of Europe's greater development can clearly be seen in the rhetoric that accompanied the colonization of Africa. For example, in the 1922 book *The Dual Mandate in British Tropical Africa,* the renowned British colonial administrator Lord Lugard, while admitting that European nations could certainly expect to profit from their African colonies, nevertheless maintains that this colonization also works for the benefit of Africans: "Europe is in Africa for the mutual benefit of her own industrial classes, and of the native races in their progress to a higher plane. . . . It is the aim and desire of civilised administration to fulfill this dual mandate. . . . In Africa to-day we are . . . bringing to the dark places of the earth . . . the torch of culture and progress, while ministering to the material needs of our own civilization" (quoted in Sicherman 148).

The vision of history as progress (of which Hegel's philosophy is the most important founding text) was one of the most critical determining forces in European thought in the nineteenth century. In one field after another, European thinkers of the time produced models based on a notion of forward temporal movement. The distinctive plot structure of the nineteenth-century realistic novel can be seen as a direct instance of this notion of history as progress. As J. Hillis Miller remarks, "The notions of narrative, of character, and of formal unity in fiction are all congruent with the system of concepts making up the Western idea of history" (461). Miller argues that the Hegelian model of rational history infects our view of fiction in a quite inclusive way:

> The assumptions about history which have been transferred to the traditional conception of the form of fiction . . . include the notions of origin and end ("archeology" and "teleology"); of unity and totality or "totalization"; of underlying "reason" or "ground" of selfhood, consciousness, or "human nature"; of the homogeneity, linearity, and continuity of time; of necessary progress; of "fate," "destiny," or "Providence"; of causality; of gradually emerging "meaning"; of representation and truth. (459-460)

In addition to Hegel, perhaps the most influential model of temporal progress in nineteenth-century Europe was Charles Darwin's theory of evolution, set forth in the 1859 volume *Origin of Species.* This theory proposes that plant and animal species evolve by a process of natural selection. For Darwin, however, evolution is a discontinuous and random process determined by chance mutations. If a genetic mutation happens to help the individual organism survive in its particular environment, then that mutation will tend to be passed on to future generations simply because the organism will be more likely to live long enough to reproduce. If a mutation is harmful, it will probably not be passed on because the organism bearing it probably will not live long enough to reproduce. Darwin's theory applies to all plant and animal species, though what captured the popular European imagination of the time was its implication that even human beings evolved from more primitive species. This idea spurred a number of visions of future evolution, of the advanced forms that human life might take. But the theory also created anxiety because it implied that humans were not fundamentally different from other animals, that they had not been specially created by God to rule the planet and ultimately to repopulate a heaven emptied out by the expulsion of Satan and his rebellious angels.

Darwin's model differs drastically from Hegel's in that, within the laws of natural selection, evolution proceeds by chance and is not determined by some overriding plan. But the nineteenth-century fascination with progress was such that the randomness of Darwinian evolution was virtually ignored in popular accounts. Evolution came instead to be viewed as a process of adaptation in which plants and animals somehow develop characteristics specifically because those characteristics help them survive: Birds need to be able to fly, so they develop wings, and so on. In short, evolution came to be viewed very much as another sort of progress. In the movement known as "social Darwinism," many models of social progress were fashioned on Darwin's theory of evolution. Thinkers such as Herbert Spencer argued that human societies advance through a process of natural selection analogous to that attributed to plants and animals by Darwin, presumably assuring that society will gradually progress to more and more efficient and sophisticated states.

These kinds of narratives are responsible for the remarkable emphasis on progress that characterized so much European thought in the nineteenth century, although the late Victorians were ambivalent toward even their most cherished notions. As Ian Watt remarked some time ago, Conrad's work is powerfully informed by a growing skepticism toward the notion of limitless progress. For example, Watt notes that the pessimistic tone of *Heart of Darkness* "is largely reflecting the much bleaker and more threatening ideological perspective on human life which followed from new developments in physical science, in evolutionary theory, and in political life, during the last half of the nineteenth century" (151).

The Darwinian vision of progress (with no divine plan to assure its forward movement) also triggered a growing anxiety over the possibility that evolution might somehow reverse itself and begin to proceed backward, with humans then becoming more and more primitive. Even Spencer's notion of social progress contributed to these anxieties. For Spencer, Victorian England was a unique society because it had the sophistication of advanced, or "industrial," societies but still maintained the raw energy and drive that he associated with primitive, or "militant," societies. But this hybrid vision of Victorian England implied that the Victorians maintained strong vestiges of their primitive past, reinforcing fears that these primitive characteristics might somehow come back to the fore.

Perhaps the central expression of nineteenth-century European anxieties over the possibility of "backward" evolution was Max Nordau's 1895 book *Degeneration,* an enormously popular work that helped fuel the widespread fascination with the concept of "degeneration" (or backward evolution to a primitive state) that swept across Europe in the last years of the nineteenth century. As R. B. Kershner notes, the concept of degeneration captured the populist imagination of the time perhaps more than any other. Nordau was a student of Cesare Lombroso, the physician and criminalist who had developed the concept of inborn criminal traits, which he believed could be detected through phrenological and other physical examination of would-be criminals. Nordau's book bears a clear relationship to Lombroso's work. It purports not only to describe the characteristics of "degenerate" types but also to elaborate on the opposing characteristics to be found in men of genius. (Late Victorian literature is filled with images of degeneration, of which Robert Louis Stevenson's *Dr. Jekyll and*

Mr. Hyde is perhaps the classic example. The doubleness of Stevenson's memorable character also displays a typical late Victorian ambivalence.)

The relevance of the work of men such as Lombroso and Nordau to *Heart of Darkness* is quite obvious. For example, although Lombroso is not mentioned by name, Conrad directly alludes to him early in the text when Marlow encounters a doctor in Brussels who is fascinated by Lombroso's theories and who asks if he can measure Marlow's skull (15, 37–38). Moreover Conrad's depiction of Kurtz seems a classic example of degeneration. Beginning with a sense of a civilizing mission that corresponds very closely to that espoused by Lord Lugard, Kurtz apparently descends into savagery once the primitive aspects of his nature are reactivated by his contact with the African jungle. As Susan J. Navarette observes, the physical appearance of the huge Kurtz, with his "lofty frontal bone," seems to match Nordau's description of the degenerate criminal type almost exactly, as do certain elements of Kurtz's behavior (309 n 21).

But Conrad (with his typical ambivalence) clearly does not intend Kurtz as a simple demonstration of the theories of Lombroso and Nordau. Marlow seems to present the doctor who wishes to examine him as a rather ridiculous figure. Moreover Kurtz the degenerate is also described as a universal genius. He is, as Ian Glenn points out, an intellectual and an artist. The depiction of Kurtz thus challenges the beliefs of Lombroso and Nordau that good and evil characteristics can be simply distinguished by physical measurement. But it is also true that Nordau himself describes how what Lombroso sees as "genius" might actually be evidence of "neurotic degeneration." In short, Nordau already undermines the genius-degenerate opposition, thus showing his own form of ambivalence.

Brian W. Shaffer demonstrates that Conrad's opposition between Europe and Africa in *Heart of Darkness* clearly echoes Spencer's contrast between primitive and advanced societies. But, as Shaffer notes, Conrad again complicates this opposition by attributing the book's greatest savagery to "sophisticated" Europeans. Thus "Conrad's African fictions inquire into Spencer's typology of civilization, both incorporating and criticizing it, both absorbing its rubrics and parodying its resolutions" (54). The dialogues with Lombroso, Nordau, and Spencer in *Heart of Darkness* form only a small part of the book's remarkable ability to address so many of the central concerns of its day. It is not surprising, then, that new historicist critics have shown a great interest in Conrad's work in recent years. Recent critical treatments of *Heart of Darkness* with a strong new historicist component include Patrick Parrinder's discussion of the book within the context of contemporary European fantasies of cannibalism and devil worship in Africa; Shaffer's description of Conrad's treatment of Africa in terms of Spencer's comparison between primitive and advanced societies; Ian Glenn's illumination of the text through a discussion of the role of intellectuals in Conrad's contemporary society; and Vince Pecora's materialist critique of Conrad's view of imperialism in terms of turn-of-the century capitalist expansion.

Situated exactly at the turn of the century, Conrad's text participates in its historical moment in several ways. For one thing, the book deals with issues such as imperialism, capitalism, race, and gender that were very much at the forefront of the turn-of-the-century European mind. For another, Conrad's ambivalent treatment of these issues is extremely representative of the way they were treated in any number of European discourses of the time. A new historicist comparison of *Heart of Darkness* with other contemporary cultural texts can thus go a long way toward providing illumination of Conrad's text while reinforcing that text's status as a striking example of turn-of-the-century thought in a number of areas.

Marlow, for example, consistently characterizes Africa as primitive, much in the mode described by Blyden and Mudimbe. The African jungle is the "primeval forest" (29, 56); traveling up the Congo is like going "back to the earliest beginnings of the world" (35, 66); and the "cannibals" in Marlow's crew "still belonged to the beginnings of time" (42, 75). And Kurtz's atrocities are clearly attributed to his return to primeval ways, to "the awakening of forgotten and brutal instincts" (65, 107). In light of the descriptions by Blyden and Lyons of the way Europeans of the time tended to see Africans as primitive and undeveloped versions of themselves, it is perhaps not surprising that Marlow sees Africans similarly. The comments of Blyden and Lyons also shed new light on Marlow's acknowledgement of a "remote kinship" with black Africans (38, 69). After all, to Marlow the remoteness of this kinship resides precisely in the fact that the Africans are remote from the Europeans in time and development. Marlow sees the black Africans as embodying a primeval truth of the human condition, a truth "stripped of the cloak of time" that still lies at the heart of the existence of the contemporary white European but that is now buried beneath the many layers of civilization that Europe has accumulated over those two thousand years (38, 69).

But Marlow's point is not that the Africans are equally capable of developing an advanced civilization. Rather he shows a typical turn-of-the-century European anxiety over the possibility of degeneration and suggests that European civilization is all that prevents Europeans from reverting to the condition of savages. His depiction of Africans as primitive versions of Europeans reveals an ideological bias in which the European perspective is always maintained as primary. Africans are not granted a genuine Otherness, an independent existence. Rather they are merely primitive versions of Europeans. Marlow asks his listeners to understand not the Africans but themselves, and his reminder of the fundamental similarities between the Europeans and the Africans is not a call for tolerance or better understanding. It is a call for distance, a suggestion that those layers of civilization be maintained at all costs to ward off the threat of a descent into savagery that hovers over us all and to which Kurtz succumbed.

Marlow, then, seems to accept the Hegelian notion of history as progress, with Europeans accompanying a position of superior development relative to Africans. But *Heart of Darkness* dramatically demonstrates the racist and imperialist ideology that lies at the heart of Hegelian history—and of progressive historicism in general. The novel undermines such teleological notions of history by its suggestion that the culmination of European history is not divine order but the diabolical Kurtz. As Marlow puts it, "All Europe contributed to the making of Kurtz" (50, 86). And Marlow's own "inconclusive" narrative seems radically to undermine the kinds of plot structures to which teleological history naturally leads. Although the quest structure of Conrad's basic plot seems highly teleological, the ultimate failure of Marlow's quest for truth conflicts with the notion of history as smooth progression toward a predefined goal. Conrad's modernist technique, with its interruptions, its hesitancies, and its unresolvable ambiguities, assures that his text can never reach a stable conclusion of the kind implied by Hegelian history and typically enacted in nineteenth-century realist narratives.

Conrad thus both incorporates and challenges major ideas of his day not only in the content of his book but also in the style. But this very doubleness is itself a quintessential late Victorian strategy. Virtually every aspect of *Heart of Darkness* is solidly rooted in its historical moment. An understanding of the specificity of the book's participation in the discourses of its time can add greatly to our understanding of the implications of many of Conrad's complex attitudes. It can also serve as a powerful reminder that we should not be too quick to declare *Heart of Darkness* (or any other "canonical" text) an expression of timeless, universal truths.

Works Cited

Blyden, E. W. *Christianity, Islam, and the Negro Race.* 1888. London: Edinburgh UP, 1967.

Conrad, Joseph. *Heart of Darkness.* 1902. Norton critical ed. 3d ed. Ed. Robert Kimbrough. New York: Norton, 1988.

———. *Heart of Darkness.* 1902. Ed. Paul O'Prey. London: Penguin, 1994.

Darwin, Charles. *The Origin of Species* and *The Descent of Man.* New York: Modern Library, n.d. (Originally published 1859 and 1971, respectively.)

Glenn, Ian. "Conrad's *Heart of Darkness:* A Sociological Reading." *Literature and History* 13.2 (1987): 238-256.

Hegel, G. W. F. *Lectures on the Philosophy of History.* Trans. H. B. Nisbet. Cambridge: Cambridge UP, 1975.

Jameson, Fredric. *The Political Unconscious: Narrative as a Socially Symbolic Act.* Ithaca, N.Y.: Cornell UP, 1981.

Kershner, R. B. Jr. "Degeneration: The Explanatory Nightmare." *Georgia Review* 40 (1986): 416-444.

Lyons, R. H. *To Wash an Aethiop White.* New York: Teachers College Press, 1975.

Miller, J. Hillis. "Narrative and History." *ELH* 41 (1974): 455-473.

Mudimbe, V. Y. *The Invention of Africa: Gnosis, Philosophy, and the Order of Knowledge.* Bloomington: Indiana UP, 1988.

Navarette, Susan J. "The Anatomy of Failure in Joseph Conrad's *Heart of Darkness.*" *Texas Studies in Literature and Language* 35.3 (1993): 279-315.

Nordau, Max. *Degeneration.* Trans. anon. New York: Appleton, 1905.

Parrinder, Patrick. "*Heart of Darkness:* Geography as Apocalypse." In *Fin de Siècle/Fin du Globe,* ed. John Stokes, 85-101. New York: St. Martin's, 1992.

Parry, Benita. *Conrad and Imperialism: Ideological Boundaries and Visionary Frontiers.* London: Macmillan, 1983.

Pecora, Vince. *Self and Form in Modern Narrative.* Baltimore, Md.: Johns Hopkins UP, 1989.

Shaffer, Brian W. "'Rebarbarizing Civilization': Conrad's African Fiction and Spencerian Sociology." *PMLA* 108.1 (1993): 45-58.
Sicherman, Carol. *Ngugi wa Thiong'o: The Making of a Rebel.* London: Hans Zell, 1990.
Watt, Ian. *Conrad in the Nineteenth Century.* Berkeley and Los Angeles: U of California P, 1979.

MULTICULTURAL CRITICISM

At the notorious Berlin Conference of 1885, the major European powers met to divide up the African continent into different areas of European control. After this conference, most of Africa came under the colonial rule of either England, Germany, or France. The huge Congo region of central Africa, however, was made the virtual private property of King Leopold of Belgium, though no one (of course) consulted the Congolese about this decision. From that point forward, the brutalization of Africans in the Congo was extreme even by European colonial standards, so much so that in 1903 the British government instructed Roger Casement, its consul in the Congo, to investigate the situation there and report back to Parliament. When Casement returned, he brought such stories of horror that it caused a public outcry, and Casement himself headed a campaign to demand an amelioration of current European practices in the Congo.

One of the British citizens who supported (though somewhat halfheartedly) Casement's efforts was Joseph Conrad, who contributed a letter for publication in which he decried the situation in the Congo. In the letter, Conrad points out that "in 1903, seventy five years or so after the abolition of the slave trade (because it was cruel) there exists in Africa a Congo State, created by the act of European powers where ruthless, systematic cruelty towards the blacks is the basis of administration, and bad faith towards all the other states the basis of commercial policy" (quoted in Hawkins, "Joseph" 70).

Conrad had maintained an interest in the Congo since his own trip there in 1890. In 1901, for example, he had published (along with Ford Madox Ford) a novel entitled *The Inheritors* that was largely a satire of Leopold's rule in the Congo. But Conrad's most famous and enduring comment on the Belgian Congo appears in his short novel *Heart of Darkness,* written in 1899 and first published in its final form in 1902. In *Heart of Darkness,* Conrad's Charlie Marlow is openly critical of much of the European activity that he observes in Africa, especially of the brutal treatment of many of the Africans by their European masters. Moreover many of Marlow's comments seem openly critical of the imperial project as a whole, as when he argues that the "conquest of the earth," which consists mostly of "the taking it away from those who have a different complexion or slightly flatter noses than ourselves, is not a pretty thing when you look into it too much" (10, 31-32). Indeed it is little more than "robbery with violence, aggravated murder on a great scale" (10, 31).

Marlow's attitude, however, is not quite so anti-imperial as it might first appear. For one thing, his characterization of imperialism as robbery and murder applies only to the Roman imperial conquest of England two thousand years earlier. He specifically contrasts Roman imperialism with the British variety, arguing that the efficiency of the latter, informed as it is by a central "idea" of bringing enlightenment to the dark places of the earth, might actually bring benefits to colonized peoples. Marlow's criticism of contemporary practices in the Congo applies to *Belgian* imperialism, not British, and even then his criticism pertains to specific abuses, not to the basic fact of European rule in the Congo. Marlow's attitude, in short, leaves a great deal of room for interpretation. It is therefore probably not surprising that the most important trend in the criticism of *Heart of Darkness* in recent years has been a growing focus on the issue of imperialism in the text, especially as we know from other sources that Marlow's complex attitude toward imperialism and colonialism seems to mirror Conrad's own ambivalence.

One of the key issues in recent critical discussions of the issue of imperialism in *Heart of Darkness* is the question of racism in the text. This issue became especially prominent in 1975 when the Nigerian novelist Chinua Achebe delivered a lecture (published in 1977) in which he argued that *Heart of Darkness,* perhaps more than any other work, is informed by a conventional European tendency to "set Africa up as a foil to Europe, as a place of negations at once remote and vaguely familiar, in comparison with which Europe's own state of spiritual grace will be manifest" (251-252). Achebe declares *Heart of Darkness* a racist text and supports his argument with specific examples in which Africans are depicted in terms of conventional racist stereotypes. Despite Marlow's occasional expressions of sentimental sympathy with the Africans he sees being beaten and starved by their European masters, the fact remains that this sympathy is extremely condescending and that the Africans themselves are consistently described as "cannibals," "niggers," and "savages," who are little more than animals. Marlow's description of the fireman on his steamer (the one African with whom he seems to have the most "sympathy") is telling:

> And between whiles I had to look after the savage who was my fireman. He was an improved specimen; he could fire up a vertical boiler. He was there below me and, upon my word, to look at him was as edifying as seeing a dog in breeches and a feather hat walking on his hind legs. A few months training had done for that really fine chap. He squinted at the steam-gauge and at the water-gauge with an evident effort of intrepidity—and he had filed his teeth, too, the poor devil, and the wool of his pate shaved into queer patterns, and three ornamental scars on each of his cheeks. He ought to have been clapping his hands and stamping his feet on the bank, instead of which he was hard at work, a thrall to strange witchcraft, full of improving knowledge. (38-39, 70)

Achebe concludes from such passages that "Joseph Conrad was a thoroughgoing racist" (257) and that *Heart of Darkness* is an "offensive and deplorable book": "I am talking about a book which parades in the most vulgar fashion prejudices and insults from which a section of mankind has suffered untold agonies and atrocities in the past and continues to do so in many ways and many places today" (259).

Achebe's charges, of course, are particularly troubling given the canonical status of Conrad's book, which is one of the most frequently taught texts in English courses in universities all over America. Achebe, in fact, goes on to question whether such a racist text should be endorsed as great literature or taught so widely as an example of such. Of course, we could argue that the racism of *Heart of Darkness* is precisely what makes it valuable as a teaching text if this racism is not effaced in the teaching process. Achebe's call to remove *Heart of Darkness* from college syllabi clearly has as much to do with how the text has traditionally been taught than with the text itself. Many instructors now teach *Heart of Darkness* in conjunction with Achebe's criticism of it and sometimes even alongside Achebe's own novels, a practice that has been described and recommended, for example, by Gerald Graff (25–33).

Other critics, following Achebe's lead, have explored the potential racist and colonialist biases of *Heart of Darkness.* The Indian critic Frances Singh argues that, despite the seeming critique of colonialism embedded in much of Marlow's narration, the most fundamental metaphor of the text, the "heart of darkness" of the title, suggests intonations of evil and savagery that the text associates not with the atrocities committed by Europeans against Africans but with the Africans themselves. For Singh, Marlow's anticolonialist rhetoric is seriously undermined by his seeming inability to regard Africans as fully human: "He may sympathize with the plight of blacks, he may be disgusted by the effects of economic colonialism, but because he has no desire to understand or appreciate people of any culture other than his own, he is not emancipated from the mentality of a colonizer" (272).

Other critics have come to the defense of Conrad and his text. They point out that no text can be understood apart from its historical context and that Conrad's attitude toward African blacks, though probably racist by the standards of the late twentieth century, was, if anything, unusually sympathetic by the standards of the time in which he wrote. Singh does grant that the limitations of Conrad's vision were not especially reactionary or racist in the context of turn-of-the-century England (280), but she argues that we must nevertheless face the fact that his text is racially and culturally biased. And it is especially crucial to recognize such biases in a text that is well established in the Western literary canon, which supposedly contains the greatest expressions of the West's cultural heritage. That *Heart of Darkness* is not unusually racist for its time only serves to call attention to the racism that is central to the Western cultural tradition. Moreover racism is despicable in any context, and a racist text is a racist text regardless of whether it is especially racist for its time. The fact that Conrad's racist attitudes are typical of his time only makes it all the more important to examine them closely and critically.

Other critics, however, have performed this examination and found that, on balance, Conrad's attitude is antiracist and anticolonialist. In "The Issue of Racism in *Heart of Darkness,*" Hunt Hawkins, for example, reviews the numerous attempts that have been made to defend Conrad against charges of racism. He admits that Conrad's depiction of Africans does not show a very subtle or profound understanding of them. Indeed Conrad's descriptions of Africans read almost like a catalog of superficial stereotypes. But, Hawkins points out, *Heart of Darkness* can potentially be defended on this score because it is not *about* Africans in the first place. It is about Europeans who simply happen to be in Africa. Hawkins, however, grants that this European focus does not in itself excuse Conrad's dehumanizing descriptions of Africans. Achebe regards Conrad's use of Africa as a stage setting for European adventure and his reduction of Africa "to the role of props for the break-up of one petty European mind" as particularly offensive elements of the text (257).

Hawkins then produces a "you too" argument in which he implies that Conrad's attitude is partially defensible because European atrocities in the Congo were no worse than the atrocities already being committed there among the Africans themselves. According to Hawkins, though the European colonial intrusions into Africa no doubt shattered the existing African tribal society, this life was hardly ideal in the first place. Hawkins then cites contemporary European sources to the effect that "cannibalism and human sacrifice were rife" in the Congo region during the time Conrad was there and that Conrad may have been influenced by this situation, though Hawkins grants that there is no actual evidence that Conrad observed any incidences of either cannibalism or human sacrifice ("Issue" 164–166).

The problem with this defense is that it requires us to accept the characterization of Africans as savage that Achebe and others have found so offensive in Conrad's work. But, in point of fact, European accounts of the savagery and cannibalism of Africans in the late nineteenth century appear to have been greatly exaggerated, if not fabricated outright. Patrick Parrinder notes that there is no evidence to support Conrad's description of Africans at several points in *Heart of Darkness* as devil worshippers, even if that characterization was typical of contemporary European fantasies. Parrinder even suggests that African religions of the time, viewed objectively, were no more savage or fetishistic than Christianity itself (98–99).

Parrinder grants that Conrad's emphasis on cannibalism in *Heart of Darkness* was typical of European discourse about Africa at the time but also points out that European reports of African cannibalism were highly unreliable and seldom (if ever) based on confirmed evidence. He notes that there were very few reports of cannibalism in central Africa during the four centuries of European contact with the region prior to the late nineteenth century, when a belief in the cannibalistic tendencies of Africans suddenly became extremely convenient as European missionaries fanned out across the continent in search of converts and European powers scrambled to gain control of their share of what only then came to be known as the "dark" continent. The characterization of Africans as cannibals (and thus as primitives in need of salvation) during this period helped make the European loss of life in "civilizing" the continent seem worthwhile,

while at the same time it justified European rule of Africa by demonstrating the superiority of Europeans to their primitive African counterparts. Parrinder also observes that when human flesh was used as a source of food in the Congo in the late nineteenth century, this occurred only because the Belgians and the Arabs were engaged in an all-out war for control of the region, a war the devastating effects of which led to widespread starvation and to desperate acts of cannibalism on both sides (91–92).

Conrad suppresses from his narrative any mention of these hostilities. In fact, he does not mention the presence of Arabs at all, an omission made more curious by Conrad's focus on Arabs in novels such as *Almayer's Folly* and *An Outcast of the Islands.* The effacement of Arabs from *Heart of Darkness,* according to Patrick Brantlinger, "has the effect of sharpening the light-and-dark dichotomies, the staple of racism. . . . Furthermore, because of the omission of the Arabs Conrad treats cannibalism not as a result of war but as an everyday custom of the Congolese" (263).

These criticisms notwithstanding, Hawkins defends *Heart of Darkness* on the basis of his reading of the text as a "powerful indictment of imperialism" ("Issue" 166). Here Hawkins focuses on the depiction of Kurtz in the text, arguing that the brutalities committed by Kurtz are not attributed to his having been corrupted by his contact with the "evil practices of the Africans." Instead for Hawkins, Kurtz represents the corruption brought to Africa from Europe. Hawkins then claims that Marlow's harshest descriptions of Africans have to do not with their own indigenous practices but with their cooperation with Kurtz and his specifically European form of evil. Hawkins then cites (and endorses) the suggestion by the Guyanese postcolonial novelist Wilson Harris (in direct response to Achebe) that *Heart of Darkness* is first and foremost an indictment of European liberalism itself. Harris regards the book as a "frontier novel" that points the way to more positive and productive literary representations of the third world, even though Conrad himself does not cross this frontier and achieve these representations (263). And this defense of Conrad is potentially a good one, though most readers have found Marlow's attribution of Kurtz's savagery to his having "gone native" quite clear. He describes Kurtz, for example, as having "taken a seat amongst the devils of the land" (49, 85).

Hawkins also suggests that Conrad can be defended on the simple basis that his representations of Africans are often quite positive, though the only examples Hawkins can produce are Marlow's description of "Kurtz's mistress" as "superb . . . magnificent . . . stately" (60, 101); his characterization of a group of blacks paddling a boat off the shore of Africa as working with "energy, vitality, natural dignity" (17, 40); and his description of the "cannibals" in his crew as "fine fellows . . . men one could work with" (36, 67). Hawkins further argues that Marlow, in the course of his journey, overcomes some of his initial prejudices against Africans and performs acts of kindness to them, such as offering a biscuit to the dying man in the "grove of death" (20, 45).

Unfortunately these examples are weak indeed. Marlow's description of the "superb" African woman includes "savage" and "ominous" in addition to the adjectives cited by Hawkins, and she serves in the text as an image of animal-like feminine sexual energy. Marlow also describes the "dignified" boat rowers as having "faces like grotesque masks" and as being visible from a distance because of the glistening whites of their eyeballs—in short, in the stock terms of the racist tradition. Marlow's description of his "cannibals" as "fine fellows" is clearly ironic, and the very fact that Conrad calls attention to their cannibalism is another example of his own acceptance of European racist stereotypes about Africa. And Marlow's "charity" to the dying man in the grove of death is precisely the sort of kindness he might have bestowed on a dying dog. In this very passage, he describes Africans in specifically dehumanizing ways: They are "black shadows," "moribund shapes," and "bundles of acute angles." And the man to whom he gives his biscuit is described in stereotypically racist terms as being of uncertain age ("with them it's hard to tell") and as wearing a pathetic string around his neck, which Marlow interprets as some sort of magical charm (20–21, 44–45).

Hawkins's final defense of Conrad is that Conrad himself openly and strongly opposed racism. To support this point, however, Hawkins must turn to Conrad's Malayan novels, where the black-and-white racial dichotomies are less clear than in Africa. In these novels, Hawkins concludes, Conrad shows scorn for Europeans who claim racial superiority to Asians, matching this scorn with a "sympathy and respect for Malayans" ("Issue" 169). However as Reynold Humphries points out, Conrad's critique of "self-satisfied Western superiority" in these novels is accompanied by a consideration of the European presence in Asia as not merely justified but entirely natural. In particular, Hawkins lists several portrayals of "admirable" Malayan characters in these novels, including the woman Jewel, the half-white native mistress of the title character of *Lord Jim.* Yet Jewel functions in that text as little more than a prop for Jim's romancelike rise to power in distant Patusan. She is a typical European fantasy of the obedient and sexually suppliant Oriental woman, perhaps made more acceptable by her European blood. Jewel is so subservient to Jim that she even begins to resemble him physically: "She lived so completely in his contemplation that she had acquired something of his outward aspect, something that recalled him in her movements, in the way she stretched her arm, turned her head, directed her glances. Her vigilant affection had an intensity that made it almost perceptible to the senses" (210). Humphries also notes that Conrad's positive representations of Malays are largely intended to set them apart from Arabs, whom he consistently portrays as sinister and conniving villains, much as described by Edward Said in *Orientalism* (119).

Hawkins concludes that Conrad may not have "been able to break entirely free from the racial biases and epithets of his age. But we should recognize his special status as one of the few writers of his period who struggled with the issue of race, and we should appreciate the remarkable fair-mindedness he achieved" (169). Whether Conrad's "fair-mindedness" was really so "remarkable" is debatable. Although Conrad's focus on issues such as imperialism and racism makes his book important as a cultural document, as readers we must approach his text with caution and suspicion rather than with the reverence sometimes accorded canonical texts. As Parrinder puts it, "That it took an 'Africanist' narrative, sensationally and unforgettably misrepresenting the history, geography and ethnography of the Congo, to set the scene for his vision of universal horror suggests that we now need to say (though we can only say it with Conradian irony) that *Heart of Darkness* is no idol of ours" (99).

Works Cited

Achebe, Chinua. "An Image of Africa: Racism in Conrad's *Heart of Darkness.*"

Brantlinger, Patrick. *Rule of Darkness: British Literature and Imperialism, 1830-1914.* Ithaca, N.Y.: Cornell UP, 1988.

Conrad, Joseph. *Almayer's Folly: A Story of an Eastern River.* Garden City, N.Y.: Doubleday, 1928.

———. *Heart of Darkness.* 1902. Norton critical ed. 3d ed. Ed. Robert Kimbrough. New York: Norton, 1988.

———. *Heart of Darkness.* 1902. Ed. Paul O'Prey. London: Penguin, 1994.

———. *Lord Jim.* New York: Signet-New American Library, 1981.

———. *An Outcast of the Islands.* London: Dent, 1949.

Conrad, Joseph, and Ford Maddox Ford. *The Inheritors.* New York: Carroll and Graf, 1985.

Graff, Gerald. *Beyond the Culture Wars: How Teaching the Conflicts Can Revitalize American Education.* New York: Norton, 1992.

Harris, Wilson. "The Frontier on which *Heart of Darkness* Stands." *Research on African Literatures* 12 (1981): 86-92. Citations from the reprint in Kimbrough 262-268.

Hawkins, Hunt. "The Issue of Racism in *Heart of Darkness.*" *Conradiana* 14.3 (1982): 163-171.

———. "Joseph Conrad, Roger Casement, and the Congo Reform Movement." *Journal of Modern Literature* 9.1 (1981-1982): 65-79.

Humphries, Reynold. "The Discourse of Colonialism: The Meaning and Relevance for Conrad's Fiction." *Conradiana* 21.2 (1989): 107-133.

Parrinder, Patrick. "*Heart of Darkness:* Geography as Apocalypse." In *Fin de Siècle/Fin du Globe,* ed. John Stokes, 85-101. New York: St. Martin's, 1992.

Said, Edward. *Orientalism.* New York: Vintage, 1979.

Singh, Frances. "The Colonialistic Bias of *Heart of Darkness.*" *Conradiana* 10 (1978): 41-54. Citations from the reprint in Kimbrough 268-280.

SELECTED BIBLIOGRAPHY

Achebe, Chinua. "An Image of Africa: Racism in Conrad's *Heart of Darkness.*" *Massachusetts Review* 18 (1977): 782-794.
Argues that Conrad's depiction of Africans in *Heart of Darkness* is profoundly racist and questions whether a work founded on such views is worthy of being considered great literature.

Adams, Richard. *Joseph Conrad: "Heart of Darkness."* London: Penguin, 1991.
Introduces *Heart of Darkness,* including a detailed step-by-step reading of the text.

Adelman, Gary. *"Heart of Darkness": Search for the Unconscious.* Boston: Twayne, 1987.
Provides a detailed reading of *Heart of Darkness* as well as extensive discussion of the book's historical background and Conrad's biographical background. Includes brief

descriptions of numerous previous critical treatments of the book. Suggests that the book is profoundly pessimistic and that it projects a belief that "the Victorian has had fostered within him a psychopathic craving for destruction, and that imperialism is an irremediable manifestation of this unconscious desire" (3).

Crews, Frederick. "The Power of Darkness." *Partisan Review* 34 (Fall 1967): 507–525.
Presents a somewhat strained psychoanalytic interpretation of *Heart of Darkness* as an Oedipal fantasy propelled by Conrad's sexual insecurities but appealing to universal symbolic experiences.

Erdinast-Vulcan, Daphna. *Joseph Conrad and the Modern Temper.* Oxford: Clarendon-Oxford UP, 1991.
Notes the tension between the "strong religious overtones" of Marlow's narration and the "explicit denial of the metaphysical which his story carries" (91). Suggests that the book's power derives from its defiance of negativity and from its eventual affirmation (97). Contends that "Marlow's lies are deliberate and willed attempts to redeem Kurtz by retrospectively investing his life and death with an ethical significance" (106).

Fogel, Aaron. *Coercion to Speak: Conrad's Poetics of Dialogue.* Cambridge, Mass.: Harvard UP, 1985.
Suggests a comic dimension to Kurtz's "the horror," noting that the repetition emphasizes Kurtz's narcissism and deflates expectations of something more profound (20).

Glenn, Ian. "Conrad's *Heart of Darkness:* A Sociological Reading." *Literature and History* 13.2 (1987): 238–256.
Draws on the work of Pierre Bourdieu and reads *Heart of Darkness* in terms of the position of intellectuals in turn-of-the-century class structure of British society. Includes an interesting reading of Kurtz as an embodiment of Conrad's fear of the negative potential of radical intellectuals. Argues that Conrad himself was a conservative intellectual who shows a strong antipathy toward upper-class British society in the book and that Marlow enacts Conrad's own class position.

Guerard, Albert J. *Conrad the Novelist.* Cambridge, Mass.: Harvard UP, 1958.
Includes an influential reading of *Heart of Darkness* as the story of Marlow's attempt to discover his true identity by journeying into his own unconscious mind. Argues that Marlow achieves a potentially healing self-knowledge by discovering the id, or "outlaw," within him—symbolized by Kurtz.

Hawkins, Hunt. "Conrad's Critique of Imperialism in *Heart of Darkness.*" *PMLA* 94.2 (1979): 286–299.
Reads *Heart of Darkness* as a powerful critique of imperialism that shows a fundamental respect for the African cultures being disrupted by the intrusions of European colonialism. Sees focus of the book as "the failure and subversiveness of the civilizing mission that presumed Africans had to be redeemed" (296).

Hawkins, Hunt. "The Issue of Racism in *Heart of Darkness.*" *Conradiana* 14.3 (1982): 163–171.
Defends Conrad against charges by Achebe and others that *Heart of Darkness* is a racist text. Argues that Conrad's attitude is complex but ultimately critical of racism and especially critical of European imperial activities in Africa.

Hawthorn, Jeremy. *Joseph Conrad: Language and Fictional Self-Consciousness.* Lincoln: U of Nebraska P, 1979.
Discusses from a Marxist perspective Conrad's attitude toward language, especially as it affects *Heart of Darkness.* Notes Conrad's linguistic skepticism and suspicion of "eloquence" and emphasizes the motif of "inexpressibility" in the text. Observes that

imperialism operates in a mode of distance and mediation that is highly relevant to the dreamlike existence of the people in the book (22). Suggests that the book shows that imperialism is supported by a structure of social lies.

Hay, Eloise Knapp. *The Political Novels of Joseph Conrad.* Chicago: U of Chicago P, 1963.
Characterizes *Heart of Darkness* as "a vehement denunciation of imperialism and racialism" (112). Includes a great deal of background information on Conrad's mixed attitude toward imperialism. Believes that in the final conversation with the Intended the irony is all Conrad's and that "Marlow behaves here, as before consistently, as a punctilious, well-meaning British conservative" (153 n).

McClure, John A. *Kipling and Conrad: The Colonial Fiction.* Cambridge, Mass.: Harvard UP, 1981.
Concludes that *Heart of Darkness* is a particularly enlightened critique of imperialism for its time. Argues that it treats Africans "with sympathy and respect" (137) and figures European civilization as "morally bankrupt" (13).

Moser, Thomas. *Joseph Conrad: Achievement and Decline.* Cambridge, Mass.: Harvard UP, 1957.
Argues that the fundamental impulse behind *Heart of Darkness* is Conrad's deep-seated fear of sexual abandon, a fear embodied in Kurtz. Believes, however, that in the book Conrad has been successful in finding an artistic outlet for his anxieties: "For the first time Conrad has been able to use material potentially related to sex in such a way as not to ruin his story" (80). Suggests that the final scene with the Intended shows Marlow's spitefulness and can be read as his "indictment of this woman, safe and ignorant in her complacent, Belgian bourgeois existence; she does not *deserve* to hear the truth" (81).

Navarette, Susan J. "The Anatomy of Failure in Joseph Conrad's *Heart of Darkness.*" *Texas Studies in Literature and Language* 35.3 (1993): 279-315.
Reads *Heart of Darkness* within the context of the fin de siècle literary phenomena of decadence and gothic horror stories, which are motivated by a similar horror of the possibility that life may be meaningless. Notes how images typical of decadence and the gothic appear in the text. But argues that the most profound reflection of the relationship between Conrad's text and these movements occurs at the level of style and that the book's sense of horror most centrally relates to the fear that language is inadequate genuinely to express human experience: "The horror of *Heart of Darkness* consists not in Conrad's oblique references to unnameable rites nor in the thinly veiled suggestions of midnight orgies, human sacrifices, and cannibalism, but rather in our confrontation with a text that, in its linguistic, stylistic, and thematic corruption, levels an assault on the reader" (290-291).

Parrinder, Patrick. "*Heart of Darkness:* Geography as Apocalypse." *Fin de Siècle/Fin du Globe,* ed. John Stokes, 85-101. New York: St. Martin's, 1992.
Discusses *Heart of Darkness* within the context of turn-of-the-century European attitudes toward Africa, including a fascination with cannibalism and devil worship. Notes how Conrad effaces many aspects of the political situation in Africa at the time, especially the all-out war between Belgian and Arab colonizers for control of the Congo. Concludes that Conrad's book propagates inaccurate racist stereotypes and therefore should be regarded with suspicion.

Parry, Benita. *Conrad and Imperialism: Ideological Boundaries and Visionary Frontiers.* London: Macmillan, 1983.
Argues that Conrad's engagement with imperialism in *Heart of Darkness* is highly complex and ambivalent. Notes Conrad's use of estranging devices to challenge the

world view of imperialism, but observes a constellation of images that conforms to colonialist theology, creating a strong tension (21). Grants that the book is "ultimately a public disavowal of imperialism's authorised lies" but notes that it also subtly confirms a number of elements of imperialist ideology (38–39).

Pittock, Murray. "Rider Haggard and *Heart of Darkness.*" *Conradiana* 19.3 (1987): 206–208.
Points out many similarities between *Heart of Darkness* and Haggard's *She* and argues that careful thought should be given to these similarities and to Haggard's possible influence on Conrad.

Sedlack, Valerie. "'A World of Their Own': Narrative Distortion and Fictive Exemplification in the Portrayal of Women in *Heart of Darkness.*" *CLA Journal* 32.4 (1989): 443–465.
Notes Marlow's negative attitude toward women in *Heart of Darkness,* but argues that the book undermines this attitude so thoroughly that an active criticism of Marlow's view of women is one of the central themes of the book.

Shaffer, Brian W. "'Rebarbarizing Civilization': Conrad's African Fiction and Spencerian Sociology." *PMLA* 108.1 (1993): 45–58.
Reads *Heart of Darkness* and "An Outpost of Progress" in the light of Spencer's nineteenth-century sociological theories. Notes that Conrad incorporates into his fiction Spencer's distinction between primitive "militant" societies and advanced "industrial" societies but ultimately undermines this dichotomy by showing industrial European society to be informed by many of the same militant characteristics as African society.

Smith, Johanna M. "'Too Beautiful Altogether': Patriarchal Ideology in *Heart of Darkness.*" In *"Heart of Darkness": A Case Study in Contemporary Criticism,* ed. Ross C. Murfin, 179–195. New York: St. Martin's, 1989.
Argues that in *Heart of Darkness* Marlow's helplessness before the "contradiction between experience and ideology" places him in "what Karen Klein calls the feminine predicament, a situation defined by a sense of physical and/or social powerlessness" (188). Suggests that Marlow's negative view of women is largely a response to this feeling of powerlessness and therefore that his subtle equation of the Intended with "the horror" in his final lie is a way of humiliating her and asserting his dominance (193). Notes that the "savage" woman in the text may not be Kurtz's mistress: "What if she is a woman warrior whose gestures and speech remained unreadable, giving her the power that 'a formidable silence' indicates?" (186).

Stewart, Garrett. "Lying as Dying in *Heart of Darkness.*" *PMLA* 95 (1980): 319–331.
Suggests that Conrad equates deceit with death: "Whether political, moral or psychological, mendacity is the most mortal of sins, against ourselves and others. Although Marlow equivocates, Conrad is there behind him to warn us that the lies of Western idealism mislead us to death" (319). Notes how Marlow's expectations of Kurtz's death are "fashioned by myth or literature or both" (324). Discusses the implications of Marlow's lie to the Intended but concludes that the most important lie in the book is that which undergirds imperialism.

Watt, Ian. *Conrad in the Nineteenth Century.* Berkeley and Los Angeles: U of California P, 1979.
Provides a wealth of information on the nineteenth-century historical and cultural background of Conrad's work, including an especially useful and extensive treatment of *Heart of Darkness.* Notes, for example, that the pessimistic tone of the book reflects a contemporary response to developments, both theoretical and actual, in late-nineteenth-century life (151).

chapter 13

Approaches to *Devil on the Cross*, by Ngugi wa Thiong'o

The artistic creativity and intense political commitment that mark the work of the Kenyan novelist Ngugi wa Thiong'o have made him a prominent literary and political figure worldwide. His writing is engaged in an attempt to create a viable cultural identity for modern Kenya and thereby makes Ngugi an important model for postcolonial writers around the world. *Devil on the Cross,* which draws on a rich combination of Kenyan and European cultural traditions, is one of Ngugi's most interesting and important works. Written while Ngugi was in a Kenyan prison for his political beliefs, *Devil on the Cross* nevertheless expresses those beliefs with courage and passion. The book describes a postcolonial Kenyan society that remains under the domination of foreign cultural and economic forces, even years after the nominal end of British colonial rule. Ngugi presents a blistering critique of this continuing aftermath of the colonial past and suggests from a Marxist perspective that true freedom for the Kenyan people can be obtained only after they free themselves of domination by both international capitalism and an indigenous elite working in league with that capitalism. The distinctive combination of brilliant formal inventiveness and clear political message that characterizes *Devil on the Cross* ensures for it a place as one of the most important works of contemporary world literature. The issues of race, class, gender, imperialism, and cultural identity raised by the book make it a rich object of study for modern literary criticism. Multicultural criticism is obviously relevant to *Devil on the Cross*—so much so that virtually any approach to the text has a multicultural aspect. This section discusses approaches to the book using reader-response criticism, Marxist criticism, feminist criticism, and Foucauldian criticism, all of which remain sensitive to Ngugi's particular cultural perspective.

READER-RESPONSE CRITICISM

There is an extremely interesting moment at the end of chapter 3 of Ngugi wa Thiong'o's *Devil on the Cross* when businessman Mwireri wa Mukiraai begins to recite the New Testament "Parable of the Talents" to his fellow passengers aboard Robin Mwaura's battered *matatu* as it makes its way toward Ilmorog, site of the Devil's Feast and Thieves' Competition that is the centerpiece of the book. The chapter ends with ellipses, but chapter 4 then begins on the next page (also with ellipses) and appears to continue the story. But as the story proceeds, it becomes clear that this Christian parable has become a capitalist one instead; it is now about the workings of capitalism and its inability to grow without exploiting the sweat and labor of workers. It is not, however, until four pages later that we realize that this modified parable is being related not by the businessman on the *matatu* but by the master of ceremonies at the Thieves' Competition, which is now under way.

At this point in Ngugi's text, then, the reader proceeds for several pages on the basis of one assumption, then has to rethink her entire reaction on the basis of new information that undermines that original assumption. In short, the experience of the reader here is very much that described by Stanley Fish in his elaboration of the notion of affective stylistics. Moreover, just as described by Fish, this experience of assumption and revision significantly modifies the reader's reaction to the text. It reinforces the close link between capitalism and Christianity suggested in numerous ways throughout the text. The reader who assumes he is about to hear one of the most famous of all Bible stories initially experiences confusion when the story turns out to be something different. At the same time, the story is close enough to the one the reader was expecting that for a few minutes of reading time the Christian parable and the story of capitalism are combined in the reader's mind. This combination then prepares the way for the coming performances of the various thieves in the competition, which will emphasize the complicity between capitalism and Christianity as modes of oppression in postcolonial Kenya.

Devil on the Cross includes twists and turns and sudden revelations that lead to similar reading experiences. And such passages help make the book amenable to reading not only through affective stylistics but also through reader-response approaches in general. But Ngugi's book raises some unique and interesting issues with regard to the relationship between texts and their readers. For one thing, Western readers must be willing to acknowledge that the text arises from a cultural tradition that differs from ours and must strain against the temptation to try reading the book as a Western novel. For another, we must remain aware that the principal "implied readers" of this book are not Westerners at all and that when we read the book in English, we are reading a translation across languages and cultures.

Devil on the Cross was a crucial turning point in Ngugi's career; it was the first novel he wrote in his native Gikuyu after he had already established a major reputation as an English-language novelist. *Devil on the Cross* also marked the point at which the choice of language became central to Ngugi's writing, making him one of the most important figures in the ongoing debate over this issue (see Westley). There are several reasons for Ngugi's shift to writing in Gikuyu, but one of the most important involves his attempt directly to address Kenyan peasants and workers, who are by and large not literate in English. Thus an overt declaration of the intended audience of *Devil on the Cross* is built into the book's language. Moreover the book draws extensively on Gikuyu oral culture, and its narrative is liberally punctuated with proverbs, songs, and other elements normally associated with oral performances rather than printed novels, establishing a further line of communication with Ngugi's anticipated audience. Critics such as Sam A. Adewoye, Bayo Ogunjimi, and Edward Sackey emphasize this link to the oral tradition as one of the most important characteristics of *Devil on the Cross.*

Actually the entire book is structured as an oral tale being delivered by a "Gĩcaandĩ player," a narrator who is introduced on the first page. This narrator becomes virtually invisible after his introduction, a disappearance that David Cook and Michael Okenimkpe regard as a "structural weakness" (128). We should keep in mind, however, that this narrator is lost only to an audience reading the printed book. In point of fact, Ngugi clearly envisions his novel as a kind of script for an oral performance that would be delivered by a reader before a live audience. The role of the frame narrator would then in essence be played by this live reader, who would be anything but invisible. In this sense, *Devil on the Cross* represents a brilliantly inventive solution to the seemingly insoluble dilemma faced by Ngugi in constructing the book. After all, if his Gikuyu audience cannot read English, most of them cannot read Gikuyu either, partially because the educational system of postcolonial Kenyan is dominated by Kiswahili and English (the central languages of the Kenyan upper classes) and partially because there is very little written in Gikuyu that they might read. Ngugi, then, has a complex and double problem: Like any author, he must reach a readership, but he must also teach that readership to read. Because the novel is structured according to the principles and conventions of Gikuyu oral culture, it can be read aloud and still understood. Thus *Devil on the Cross* is accessible to an audience that cannot read it directly. By producing important literature in the Gikuyu language, Ngugi hopes to stimulate literacy in that language by providing his audience with a reason to learn how to read Gikuyu. At the same time, Ngugi can provide a source of cultural pride and identity for a populace that has long been encouraged to regard its own culture as inferior to cultural models imported from the West. Before Ngugi, most Gikuyu peasants had never seen a book printed in Gikuyu, and the very existence of high-quality literature (printed professionally on high-quality paper) provides a powerful rejoinder to those who insist that Gikuyu is somehow more primitive than languages (such as English) with an established print tradition.

Devil on the Cross thus allows Ngugi effectively to challenge the myth of Western cultural superiority on its own terms. But the prominent use of elements from oral culture also allows Ngugi to mount this challenge without himself granting the Western premise that print is somehow more sophisticated and "advanced" than oral culture. Ngugi's use of Gikuyu oral culture and the Gikuyu language helps him establish a special rapport with his Gikuyu audience, a rapport that furthers a sense of solidarity between text and reader. This solidarity, together with the overtly political content of the book, makes *Devil on the Cross* an extremely powerful political statement. Moreover it establishes with a Gikuyu audience the kind of communication between reader and text emphasized by reader-response critics such as Wolfgang Iser. At the same time, *Devil on the Cross* provides a new and defamiliarizing perspective for Western readers, who encounter a text based on premises far different from those to which they are accustomed, thus potentially broadening their horizons in the manner discussed by Iser.

This engagement with the text by Western readers is facilitated by the fact that the text's "repertoire" (to use Iser's term) includes issues and literary motifs that such readers can easily recognize, thus helping them get their bearings. After all, Ngugi is no fanatic, and he does not demand an end to all congress with European culture. He himself demonstrates in *Decolonising the Mind* a vast knowledge of Western literature, and he remains willing to translate his texts into English to communicate with a Western audience—though he was careful to ensure that *Devil on the Cross* was published in English only after appearing in both Gikuyu and Kiswahili. Although the direct allusions to Western texts in English novels such as *Petals of Blood* become less frequent in Ngugi's later Gikuyu works, the influence of Western literary models remains clear. Even the peculiar mixture of fantasy and realism that informs the style of *Devil on the Cross* can be quite well described through appeal to familiar Western literary modes. To a certain extent, for example, the highly unusual texture of *Devil on the Cross* is achieved through a combination of magical realism and socialist realism, and in any case the book is identifiable as a novel, in many ways the most Western (and bourgeois) of genres.

If the unusual background of *Devil on the Cross* sheds important light on its relationship to Kenyan readers, this background poses a number of special questions for Western readers as well. That we can find recognizable cultural "road signs" in the text should not mislead us into thinking that we can recuperate Ngugi's novel merely as another work of Western literature, even though the book's satirical tone has much in common with that of such writers as Jonathan Swift and Alexander Pope, its ideology is highly reminiscent of the plays of Bertolt Brecht, and its fantastic elements can comfortably be understood within the category of magical realism. For one thing, as we read we should attempt to keep the book's frame in our minds, envisioning as we go the telling of the story by a live narrator to a live audience. We do have some experience with this kind of reading, as all of us are accustomed to reading written texts of dramas that were actually intended for live performance. But even in this case such an association is too direct. *Devil on the Cross* has much in common with the genre of drama, and reading the book within the tradition of drama with which we are familiar (especially that of Brecht, with which the book is especially closely related) can be quite helpful. But we should never forget that the dramatic tradition on which the book draws most importantly is that of various Gikuyu communal performances.

From Iser's point of view, such necessary cultural displacements can make us not only better readers but also better people, though the personal consciousness-raising envisioned by Iser will be available only to readers willing to work to understand the text on its own terms, a process that will require diligent reading, an active imagination, and some research into Kenyan history and culture. Moreover if the non-Western cultural background of *Devil on the Cross* presents special challenges for Western readers as a whole, it poses particularly vexing problems for reader-response critics. After all, reader-response, with its emphasis on the activities and inclinations of the individual reader, is among the most Western and most bourgeois of critical approaches. A reader attempting to discuss Ngugi's book within the framework of Norman Holland's notion of the identity theme would be faced not only with identity themes culturally inconsistent with those of Western readers, but also with the problem of reconciling a psychoanalytically based approach with a text whose cultural assumptions might be entirely different from those employed by Sigmund Freud and those who followed him.

Devil on the Cross also poses difficult questions to a radically reader-active approach such as Stanley Fish's notion of the interpretive community. After all, the interpretive community clearly intended by Ngugi is exceedingly different from those to which most Western readers and critics belong. According to Fish, a reader who is, say, an American college professor and literary critic (like Fish) and who reads "Ngugi's" novel is creating that novel in the process of reading based on that reader's experience and training with literature. This "version" of *Devil on the Cross* is thus very much an American novel in the sense that it is produced through the operations of conventions and expectations that are themselves American. In short, the reader rewrites Ngugi's African novel from an American perspective, thereby re-creating the typical movement through which imperialist powers dominated African culture during the century in which virtually all of Africa was colonized. Given that one of the major themes of *Devil on the Cross* is that the former British colonial oppression still continues in Kenya in subtler forms (and with the British largely supplanted by the Americans), the imperialist resonances in Fish's model of reading are troubling indeed. In fact, Fish's notion of interpretive communities implies to a large extent that we can never fully appreciate the Otherness of postcolonial texts because as citizens of the "advanced" West we can never transcend our own horizon in the process of reading. But we might argue that, rather than implying that we should give up on reading postcolonial literature (or any literature from cultures other than our own), this dilemma suggests that we should read as much of such literature as possible. If performed with an awareness of the possible cultural imperialism at stake in our encounter with such texts, reading them might help us change our own interpretive communities in positive and exciting ways.

Ngugi's work, with its intense awareness of the realities of neocolonial oppression, seems ideally suited for such a project, especially as he places such emphasis on language and literature as elements both of that oppression and any possible resistance to it. For example, Ngugi, more than almost any other postcolonial writer, has foregrounded the political dimensions of language itself, calling attention to the fact that the English language in which he first began to write novels (and which remains, along with French, perhaps the most frequently used language in African literature) is not only part of the British colonial heritage of Kenya, but also central to a system of neocolonial oppression that continues to this day and that is centrally informed by the status of English as the language of choice of the Kenyan ruling elite. Ngugi's emphasis on the role played by the English language in neocolonial oppression demonstrates just how subtle imperialism can be and should therefore be of great concern to anyone considering the relationship between Western readers and Ngugi's texts.

Ngugi's recognition of the particular positioning of the former colonial within the English language can enrich our reading of other texts as well. For example, Ngugi's view of language recalls the famous and oft-cited passage in Joyce's *A Portrait of the Artist as a Young Man* in which Stephen becomes intensely aware of the political orientation of language, comparing his own speech to that of the English dean of studies: "The language in which we are speaking is his before it is mine. How different are the words *home, Christ, ale, master,* on his lips and on mine! I cannot speak or write these words without unrest of spirit. His language, so familiar and so foreign, will always be for me an acquired speech" (189).

Joyce, of course, opted to write in English nevertheless, though his cultural situation was certainly far different from Ngugi's in that Ireland's native Gaelic had been a virtually dead language for many centuries by the time of Joyce, whereas Ngugi's Gikuyu is still the living, everyday language of a large part of the Kenyan population. In his attitude toward English, Ngugi might be more appropriately contrasted with the Indian-British novelist Salman Rushdie, who chooses to write in English, though most Indian literature is written in Indian languages. Rushdie, in fact, is a great lover of the English language, noting in a newspaper article that "I don't think there's another language large or flexible enough to include so many different realities." In this same article, Rushdie also shows a profound appreciation for the historicity and political embeddedness of language, arguing that the vestiges of empire are still to be found in the "cadences" of the English language itself. He also sees the political charge that inheres in language to be potentially energizing. Citing the great Irish writers Joyce, Samuel Beckett, and Flann O'Brien as predecessors, Rushdie argues that much "vitality and excitement" can be derived from attempts to "decolonise" the English language. He cites a number of contemporary writers such as Chinua Achebe and Ngugi who are resisting the history of imperialism that inheres within the language by "busily forging English into new shapes": "But of course a good deal more than formal, stylistic alteration is going on in this new fiction. And perhaps above all, what is going on is politics. . . . There are very few major writers in the new English literatures who do not place politics at the very centre of their art" (8).

Ngugi (though identified because of his early English-language novels by Rushdie as a leading decolonizer of English) has argued in response that attempts to explore new postcolonial uses of English simply lead to the enrichment of the English language at the expense of the impoverishment of the native languages of postcolonial nations. Ngugi has thus eschewed the use of English in his writing, preferring to write his later original texts in his native Gikuyu. Ngugi is, in fact, quite adamant in texts such as *Decolonising the Mind* about the responsibility of African writers to reject the languages inherited from their former imperial oppressors. Language, he argues, is central to cultural identity, and Africans will never be able to establish a strong sense of self as long as they continue to express their deepest thoughts in European languages:

> The choice of language and the use to which language is put is [sic] central to a people's definition of themselves in relation to their natural and social environment, indeed in relation to the entire universe. Hence language has always been at the heart of the two contending social forces in the Africa of the twentieth century. (4)

For Ngugi, these two contending forces are the neo-colonialists who would continue the tradition of African imperial subjugation and those who would resist and oppose that subjugation. The battle lines for Ngugi are clear, just as *Devil on the Cross* insists that, at least in certain situations, there is a clear distinction between good and evil. Close attention to our own attitudes and activities in reading Ngugi's might help us emerge on the right side of this opposition.

Works Cited

Adewoye, Sam A. "The Strength of the Rhetoric of Oral Tradition in Ngugi wa Thiong'o's *Devil on the Cross.*" *Commonwealth Literature in English* 5.1 (1992): 11-19.

Cook, David, and Michael Okenimpke. *Ngugi wa Thiong'o: An Exploration of His Writings.* London: Heineman, 1983.

Fish, Stanley. *Self-Consuming Artifacts: The Experience of Seventeenth-Century Literature.* Berkeley and Los Angeles: U of California P, 1972.

———. *Surprised by Sin: The Reader in "Paradise Lost."* New York: St. Martin's, 1967.

Holland, Norman. *The Dynamics of Literary Response.* New York: Oxford UP, 1968.

Iser, Wolfgang. *The Act of Reading: A Theory of Aesthetic Response.* Baltimore: Johns Hopkins UP, 1978.

Joyce, James. *"A Portrait of the Artist as a Young Man": Text, Criticism, and Notes.* Ed. Chester G. Anderson. New York: Viking, 1968.

Ngugi wa Thiong'o. *Decolonising the Mind: The Politics of Language in African Literature.* London: James Currey, 1986.

———. *Devil on the Cross.* Trans. Ngugi wa Thiong'o. London: Heinemann, 1982.

———. *The River Between.* London: Heinemann, 1965.

Ogunjimi, Bayo. "Language, Oral Tradition, and Social Vision in Ngugi's *Devil on the Cross.*" *Ufahamu* 14.1 (1984): 56-70.

Rushdie, Salman. "The Empire Writes Back with a Vengeance." *London Times* (July 3, 1982): 8.

Sackey, Edward. "Oral Tradition and the African Novel." *Modern Fiction Studies* 37.3 (1991): 389-407.

Westley, David. "Choice of Language and African Literature: A Bibliographic Essay." *Research in African Literatures* 23.1 (1992): 159-171.

MARXIST CRITICISM

In a sense, it is difficult to add much to Ngugi wa Thiong'o's *Devil on the Cross* via Marxist criticism because the novel itself is an avowedly Marxist text. But for this very reason we must be aware of some fundamental Marxist ideas in approaching Ngugi's book. We must also recognize that Ngugi's work is strongly tied to its context in postcolonial Kenya and that Marxism, however valid its claim to be a master narrative of all of human history, originated in Europe. Ngugi's Marxism, while quite true to the major ideas of Marx himself, is indeed of a distinctively African variety, and Ngugi's own turn to Marxism can be traced to his reading of Frantz Fanon's *The Wretched of the Earth,* one of the first works of African Marxism to be widely known in the West. Vladimir Ilich Lenin's *Imperialism: The Highest Stage of Capitalism* was also important in forming Ngugi's original understanding of the complicity between capitalism and imperialism (Sicherman 6).

Ngugi's career can be divided into two stages: Novels such as *The River Between* (written before his reading of Fanon and Lenin) seem to be informed by a relatively conventional liberal humanist ideology, whereas he begins to shift to a more Marxist orientation in *A Grain of Wheat* and becomes a full-blown Marxist writer in the works after that (Aborisade). Fanon himself was preceded by a long tradition of African Marxist thought. V. Y. Mudimbe notes that, even though African thought from the 1930s to the 1950s was informed by several important influences, Marxism was clearly the most important of these (90). Mudimbe further notes that (even though he himself works from a somewhat Foucauldian perspective) Marxism, along with a more general critique of imperialism, remains the most vital force in African philosophy to this day. Figures such as Aimé Césaire, Leopold Senghor, Kwame Nkrumah, and Julius Nyere all made important contributions in the attempt to adapt socialism to an African context, and Ngugi draws on the work of all of these thinkers in his fiction. Ngugi's use of Marxism in an African context is thus not an aberration; this use connects him to the mainstream of African anti-imperialist thought. As critics Emmanuel Ngara and Georg M. Gugelberger observe, Marxism has had an important influence not only on African philosophy and politics but also on African literature—which is inseparable from African philosophy and politics.

To an extent, *Devil on the Cross* can be read as a primer on Marxism written for uneducated Kenyan peasants and workers, who, unlike African philosophers, may not be very familiar with Marxist theory. In fact, this novel was the first that Ngugi wrote in the Gikuyu language, which is accessible to a large segment of the Kenyan poor, whereas the English in which he formerly wrote is generally known well in Kenya only to the upper classes. Given this purpose, it is not surprising that *Devil on the Cross* is so openly didactic and that it contains so many passages that are essentially little more than introductions to the Marxist critique of capitalism and imperialism. In this sense, the book resembles Jack London's *The Iron Heel,* a 1907 novel that was intended to introduce Marxist theory to an audience of workers and farmers (this time in America) who knew little of Marxism. *The Iron Heel* thus consists largely of lectures on Marxist theory by its protagonist, Ernest Everhard. The comparison to *The Iron Heel* (which falls flat as a novel, even if its lectures might be useful) also serves to highlight the immensity of Ngugi's achievement in *Devil on the Cross,* which manages to be so openly (even simplistically) didactic and yet succeeds brilliantly as a work of art. As G. D. Killam points out, this novel can be seen as a thoroughly successful enactment of the political and artistic program described in Ngugi's essays and prison diary. Killam announces that *Devil on the Cross* is aesthetically innovative but suggests that this artistic innovation is employed in the service of political statement. In the book, "Ngugi is not . . . concerned with finding new ways to be new; he is concerned with finding new ways to be effective" (142).

Ngugi's success in *Devil on the Cross* can be attributed to his ability to find a form appropriate to his message. Where London attempts to construct a dystopian narrative in a realistic narrative style, Ngugi eschews realism and produces a much more sophisticated work that is in many ways more a ritualized performance than a novel proper. In this sense, the best analogue for Ngugi's project in the tradition of Western leftist literature is not London's novel but the epic theater of Bertolt Brecht. Ngugi has much in common with Brecht in terms of both aesthetics and political philosophy. Moreover Ngugi greatly admires Brecht as an artist, quoting Brecht's work frequently in his own nonfiction writings. *Devil on the Cross* makes particularly prominent use of some of Brecht's favorite metaphors for the workings of capitalism. The central metaphor of *Devil on the Cross* is the very Brechtian notion that capitalism is little more than an organized system of thievery and corruption. The various competitors in the Thieves' Competition are thus not criminals in the normal sense (the one ordinary thief who shows up for the competition is quickly expelled as unworthy because of the meager level of his crimes) but businessmen who make their wealth by exploiting the workers of Kenya. Ngugi also gets a great deal of symbolic mileage in *Devil on the Cross* from the central Brechtian motifs of prostitution and cannibalism. Prostitutes feature prominently in Brecht's work, where they are used as especially obvious examples of the overt commodification of human beings and as images of the way even the most "personal" relationships under capitalism are converted into mere economic transactions. *Devil on the Cross* makes frequent reference to the fact that women, the most oppressed sector of the postcolonial Kenyan populace, are frequently forced to resort to prostitution (either directly or indirectly) to survive. Thus the protagonist Wariinga finds it virtually impossible to find employment without agreeing to grant sexual favors to her bosses. Ngugi also uses prostitution as a symbol of the foreign economic domination of Kenya. He includes in *Devil on the Cross* the story of an aged American tourist who comes to Kenya because his wealth can buy the sexual favors of young girls, whom he regards as just another example of the exotic indigenous species (like lions and elephants) that make Kenya so attractive to foreign tourists (70-71). Ngugi links tourism to prostitution by noting that more and more of Kenya is being converted into tourist facilities where foreigners can enjoy themselves and where Kenyans can service them in the demeaning roles of prostitutes, servants, and cooks (223).

Cannibalism, of course, is an even more overt example of the commodification of human beings, and Ngugi uses this motif throughout *Devil on the Cross* as a symbol of the way foreign business interests and their Kenyan collaborators are feeding off of the people of Kenya. Ngugi also links the motifs of prostitution and cannibalism. In her teenage years, Wariinga was once offered by the corrupt uncle with whom she lived to a rich acquaintance in return for his help in securing a bank loan and some land for the uncle. The element of prostitution in this transaction is clear, but Ngugi describes it in terms that smack of cannibalism as well by suggesting that the uncle regards Wariinga as a young chick whose tender flesh will provide "soft food for a toothless old man" (142). Ngugi also extends his use of cannibalism to reinforce his suggestion throughout *Devil on the Cross* of a close complicity between Christianity and the colonial and neocolonial oppression of Kenya, a suggestion that (as F. Odun Balogun notes) is a major element of the book. The Devil who appears to Wariinga in a vision and explains to her the workings of capitalism reminds her that a central ritual of Christianity involves eating the body and drinking the blood of Christ, thus paving the way for an ideological climate in which a more economic form of cannibalism is also deemed acceptable (190).

This Devil (who himself is an embodiment of capitalism) then reveals the plans of Kimeendeeri (one of the favorites in the Thieves' Competition) to develop a scientific research farm on which workers will be raised like cattle to be milked of their blood, sweat, and brains, which will then be shipped abroad for consumption by foreign industries. This ultimate form of commodification of the human body (the symbolic resonances of which are clear in a neocolonial context) echoes the references to prostitution that run throughout the text. These references also reinforce the striking (and hilarious) allegory of commodification introduced a few pages earlier when the thief Nditika wa Nguunji (who has made his wealth in smuggling and the black market) bemoans the fact that, despite his riches, the limitations of his human body mean that he can eat only so much food, wear only so many clothes, and have only so much sex. So (inspired by news from South Africa of Dr. Christiaan Barnard's successful experiments with heart transplants) he envisions the development of factories for human body parts, the installation of which will enable rich men to experience more physical pleasure and live forever, making death the province only of the poor (180-181).

Nditika (predictably) reacts with fury when his wife suggests that perhaps she should receive spare genitals as well. He thus reveals one limitation of his phallocentric plan. Moreover from a Marxist point of view, the fact that Nditika's plan would transform him into a monster suggests the fate that awaits capitalists in general; the fact that Nditika clearly regards his own bodily organs as mere commodities suggests that the dehumanizing consequences of alienation and commodification under a capitalist system extend to the capitalists themselves. Nevertheless Ngugi's sympathies for Kenya's capitalist bosses are meager, and *Devil on the Cross* constantly reminds us of the clear separation between capitalist and worker (or, to use the cannibalism metaphor that runs through the book, eater and eaten).

This insistence on the clear class distinction between worker and capitalist clearly participates in the Marxist vision of history as class warfare. Indeed Ngugi's description of the workings of capitalism in *Devil on the Cross* is an extremely conventional Marxist one, and textbook Marxist characterizations of capitalism as a system in which the few grow rich by unfairly exploiting the labor of the many are sprinkled liberally throughout the book. Muturi's observation that under capitalism there are two kinds of men—"he who lives by his own sweat and he who lives by the sweat of others"—is the major premise out of which all of the book's other observations grow (57). Ngugi, with his Kenyan background, places special emphasis on the role played by foreign business interests in the neocolonial capitalist system of Kenya. But even here he follows Marx in a fairly direct way: One of Marx's central insights into capitalism is that it is an inherently global system that by its very nature will expand and extend its dominion over the entire planet—before finally collapsing beneath its own weight.

The international flavor of capitalist domination in Kenya is perhaps captured most effectively in Mwireri wa Mukiraai's speech during the Thieves' Competition. Mwireri himself is an unscrupulous capitalist who has nothing against exploiting the poor of Kenya for his personal gain. His definition of capitalism thus comes from an insider's perspective: "The system is this: the masses cultivate; a select few . . . harvest. Five rich men grow roots in the flesh of fifty workers and peasants" (166). Mwireri argues, however, that Kenyan capitalists should keep the wealth of Kenya for themselves rather than allowing it to wind up in the pockets of foreign business interests: "Let us steal from among ourselves, so that the wealth of the country remains in the country, and so that in the flesh of ten million poor we can plant the roots of ten national millionaires" (167). But Mwireri's speech is met with great hostility; he is not only shouted off the stage at the competition but also later murdered because his attitude poses a serious threat to the foreign capitalists who dominate the economy of neocolonial Kenya. Ngugi's depiction of Mwireri thus serves to draw special attention to this foreign domination. At the same time, Ngugi makes it clear that the poor of Kenya would probably be no better off even if the policy advocated by Mwireri were adopted. True liberation in Kenya will require an end to foreign domination of the Kenyan economy and to capitalism itself.

Ngugi also pays a great deal of attention in *Devil on the Cross* to the complicity between capitalism and the postcolonial Kenyan government of Jomo Kenyatta. The book makes clear that the full force of the Kenyan police and military (what Althusser calls the Repressive State Apparatus) is always on call to support the interests of business and capital and crush any potential opposition to those interests by the Kenyan people. Ngugi also investigates more subtle forms of capitalist domination, such as the realms of education and culture and religion that Althusser refers to as Ideological State Apparatuses. For example, in describing the proposed program of Kimeendeeri, the Devil of Wariinga's vision notes that Kimeendeeri plans to assure the cooperation of the inhabitants of his "people farms" by building an elaborate system of prisons and law courts reinforced by heavily armed military units. But these coercive institutions will be employed only in emergencies. Kimeendeeri plans to rely mostly on less obvious forms of domination. He will thus build an extensive system of churches and mosques in which an army of priests will instruct the people in submission, assuring them that their exploitation has been ordained by God (188). Kimeendeeri also proposes to build a system of schools in which children will be taught that the current system of exploitation is the only one imaginable and that "drinking human blood and eating human flesh" have always been the way of human societies and always will be (188–189). Finally Kimeendeeri envisions the production of procapitalist poems, songs, plays, and films through which the full force of culture can be employed to "glorify the deeds, traditions and culture of the drinkers of human blood and the eaters of human flesh" and to teach the victims of this system that they are actually fortunate and happy (189).

Devil on the Cross presents an intentionally exaggerated and highly metaphorical description of capitalism as an unholy combination of cannibalism and crime. But what is probably most powerful about the book is that, on close inspection, these "exaggerated" depictions of capitalism (whatever their literary or symbolic elements) are not that far from reality. The Kenyan people have been woefully exploited throughout this century, first through colonization by the British and then through ongoing political oppression and foreign economic domination even after Kenya officially became independent of British rule in 1963. And this system has received the full support not only of the British colonial police and military (and later the Kenyan police and military) but also of the whole superstructural system of religion, education, and culture. *Devil on the Cross* produces a complex form of defamiliarization in which readers experience the shock of realizing that even the book's most seemingly fantastic and bizarre descriptions of capitalism are not that far off the mark. This shock effect thus counters the attempts of the capitalist cultural system to portray capitalism as a natural, commonsense way of ordering a society. Western readers would probably do well to ask themselves if much of Ngugi's commentary on the woeful results of capitalism in Kenya do not apply to their own more affluent (but equally alienated) situation.

Devil on the Cross—like all of Ngugi's work—is an attempt to meet subtle forms of procapitalist cultural domination head-on by creating an anticapitalist counterculture. Ngugi makes quite clear in *Devil on the Cross* his belief that Western cultural imperialism has played a major role in the political and economic subjugation of the Kenyan people. As the composer Gatuiria notes,

"Our culture has been dominated by the Western imperialist cultures. That is what in English we call cultural imperialism. Cultural imperialism is mother to the slavery of the mind and body" (58). To oppose this cultural imperialism, Gatuiria hopes to participate through his own work in the creation of a vital and active Kenyan culture free of domination by foreign influences. "I would like to compose music that expresses the soul and the aspirations and the dreams of our nation" (132). Gatuiria's music—with its central emphasis on "harmony in polyphony"—itself becomes a metaphor for the new Kenyan national culture that Ngugi himself hopes to help establish, a national culture in which all of Kenya's numerous and rich cultural traditions can participate (60).

Ngugi insists, however, that the development of Kenyan culture is in itself insufficient unless accompanied by fundamental, even revolutionary, political and economic changes. By the end of the book, Gatuiria has succeeded in composing his long-planned national oratorio, which he hopes will make a major contribution to the development of a viable Kenyan national culture. But the effectiveness of this oratorio is limited by Gatuiria's own lack of faith in revolutionary change and by his continuing reliance on foreign cultural models for many of his ideas—for example, he quotes the Russian composer Igor Stravinsky in support of his belief that art progresses not through revolutionary change but through gradual evolution (244). More important, Gatuiria is focused so exclusively on the world of music that he neglects the larger world of politics and history. "I am not a politician," he tells Wariinga in response to her (somewhat joking) suggestion that his music might start a revolution in Kenyan music (244).

In this sense, Ngugi's Gatuiria resembles Brecht's Galileo, who passes up a chance to provide leadership in a people's revolt so that he can be allowed to continue with his scientific research. For Brecht, this research is important, just as for Ngugi Gatuiria's music is important. Both science and culture can make fundamental contributions to a change in attitudes and modes of thought, but neither can bring about social justice unless accompanied by a larger program of political change. It comes as no surprise, then, that Gatuiria fails to come to Wariinga's aid at the end of the book when she turns to violence in her quest for justice. Gatuiria's ultimate commitment is not to the Kenyan people but to his own art, and in this he stands as an emblem of the Kenyan intelligentsia as a whole, which Ngugi frequently criticizes for its lack of commitment to revolutionary political change. The true exemplar of the Kenyan artist that emerges from *Devil on the Cross* is not Gatuiria but Ngugi himself. *Devil on the Cross,* written in the Gikuyu language and drawing extensively on Kenyan oral folk culture for its aesthetic inspiration, is a major contribution to the effort to develop a Kenyan national culture. That Ngugi, who had already established a major reputation as an English-language novelist, turned to this new form clearly indicates his willingness to sacrifice personal artistic ambitions in the interest of the larger cause of Kenyan national culture. And that he wrote the book while in prison for his criticism of the corrupt Kenyan government stands as eloquent testimony to his own courage and commitment to positive social and political change in Kenya.

Works Cited

Aborisade, P. A. "National and Revolutionary Consciousness: Two Phases of Ngugi's Artistic Praxis." *Ufahamu* 18 (1989–1990): 57–74.

Althusser, Louis. *Lenin and Philosophy and Other Essays,* 170–183. Trans. Ben Brewster. London: Monthly Review, 1971.

Balogun, F. Odun. "Ngugi's *Devil on the Cross:* The Novel as Hagiography of a Marxist." *Ufahamu* 16.2 (1988): 76–87.

Brecht, Bertolt. *Galileo.* Trans. Charles Laughton. New York: Grove, 1966.

Fanon, Frantz. *The Wretched of the Earth.* Trans. Constance Farrington. New York: Grove, 1968.

Gugelberger, Georg M., ed. *Marxism and African Literature.* London: James Currey, 1985.

Killam, G. D. "Ngugi wa Thiong'o." In *The Writing of East and Central Africa,* ed. G. D. Killam, 123–143. London: Heinemann, 1984.

Lenin, Vladimir Ilich. *Imperialism: The Highest Stage of Capitalism.* In *"Imperialism" and "The State and Revolution."* New York: Vanguard, 1926.

London, Jack. *The Iron Heel.* 1907. New York: Bantam, 1971.

Mudimbe, V. Y. *The Invention of Africa: Gnosis, Philosophy, and the Order of Knowledge.* Bloomington: Indiana UP, 1988.

Ngara, Emmanuel. *Art and Ideology in the African Novel: A Study of the Influence of Marxism on African Writing.* London: Heinemann, 1985.

Ngugi wa Thiong'o. *Devil on the Cross.* Trans. Ngugi wa Thiong'o. London: Heinemann, 1982.

———. *Petals of Blood.* London: Heinemann, 1977.

———. *The River Between.* London: Heinemann, 1965.

Sicherman, Carol. *Ngugi wa Thiong'o: The Making of a Rebel.* London: Hans Zell, 1990.

FEMINIST CRITICISM

African literature has received a great deal of critical attention in the West in recent years, and writers such as Chinua Achebe, Wole Soyinka, and Ngugi wa Thiong'o have developed major worldwide reputations as literary artists. Probably the most distinctive feature of African literature (and of postcolonial literature in general) is its inherently political character. Severe poverty, rampant political corruption, widespread civil strife (including a number of cataclysmic civil wars), and a strong tendency toward rule by oppressive dictatorships have been the order of the day in postcolonial Africa. These troubles can be attributed to a number of factors, most of which have to do with the general destruction of traditional African societies in the colonial period and with the radical mismatch between traditional African ways of life and the structure of the postcolonial nation-state, which is based on fundamentally European bourgeois models. African writers have played an important role in the attempt to diagnose and describe the ills of modern African society. In the meantime, African literature and culture are clearly central to any attempt to develop viable cultural identities that will help African nations escape the limitations of European social, political, and cultural models. We can sense in the work of these writers their own awareness of the important contributions that they can make in this effort.

At the same time, virtually all of the African writers who are well known in the West are male, yet women constitute the poorest and most oppressed sector of the African population. Moreover most of the best-known African literature deals with postcolonial political oppression or with the struggle against colonialism and its neocolonial aftermath; gender issues appear at best in a marginal way. Women writers such as Bessie Head, Grace Ogot, Flora Nwapa, Buchi Emecheta, Mariama Ba, and Tsitsi Dangarembga are beginning to change this situation and to work toward the establishment of an African women's literary tradition. In the meantime, more and more African male writers are beginning to pay attention to gender oppression as one of the fundamental injustices that must be corrected before African societies can be truly free. Ngugi's *Devil on the Cross,* with its feminine protagonist and its specific criticism of the special kinds of oppression suffered by women in postcolonial Kenya, is a major contribution to this effort. Indeed the double focus of *Devil on the Cross,* which presents both a bitter criticism of the current situation of women in Kenya and a positive alternative in its protagonist Wariinga, makes the book a very effective feminist statement.

Actually women characters have played major roles in Ngugi's work throughout his career. Nyambura in *The River Between,* Mumbi in *A Grain of Wheat,* and Wanja in *Petals of Blood* are all extremely important characters, though critics have observed that Ngugi fails to escape entirely the constraints of patriarchal thought in these books. Elleke Boehmer argues that Ngugi's thought maintains a "patriarchal cast," largely because of its emphasis on the importance of workers, who are almost invariably male (188). Women characters do, however, become more important in Ngugi's work as his career proceeds, and Wariinga in *Devil on the Cross* is a breakthrough in the sense that, by becoming an engineer and auto mechanic, she does become an effective member of the working class. Florence Stratton identifies *Devil on the Cross* as an important example of a recent turn toward more concern with gender issues in works by male writers. She concludes, however, that Ngugi's novel treats class as a more fundamental social category than gender, ultimately making gender little more than a metaphor for class. For Stratton, then, Ngugi's treatment of gender in *Devil on the Cross* operates finally "in the interest of preserving patriarchal relations" (160).

The criticisms of observers such as Boehmer and Stratton are surely fair in regard to Ngugi's consistent focus on Wariinga's sexual attractiveness. For example, when Wariinga is transformed through her education into a new woman with a greater sense of security and self-esteem, she undergoes a corresponding increase in her physical beauty, which she had diminished by straightening her hair and lightening her skin, both attempts to deny her nature. We are thus reminded that, to her fellow Kenyans, one of the most surprising aspects of her technical abilities is that they belong not just to a woman but to a *beautiful* woman. Ngugi's point, of course, is that black women can be beautiful without attempting to look like white women and that women who are educated and professionally competent can still be sexually attractive. Moreover this motif can be taken as a criticism of the obsession of Wariinga's fellow Kenyans with her beauty. After all, the narrator focuses more on Wariinga's other abilities than on her beauty, and it is only Wariinga's fiancé Gatuiria who seems to focus on her beauty, admiring her almost like one of his musical compositions. This focus can thus be taken as a suggestion of the limitation in Gatuiria's vision, paralleling the aestheticist focus on art that renders him incapable of taking firm political action at the end of the book.

In any case, Stratton's argument is more with Marxism itself than with Ngugi. A committed feminist, she believes that the unequal treatment of the genders is the principal source of inequality and injustice in modern African society. Ngugi, a committed Marxist, believes that the separation of society into different social classes (basically bourgeois bosses, on the one hand, and peasants and workers, on the other) is the principal source of social inequality and injustice. Feminist critics approaching Ngugi's work should certainly attend to Ngugi's basic assumption that class differences are more fundamental than gender differences in modern capitalist society. But this emphasis does not necessarily imply a lack of concern with the situation of women in modern society. Ngugi (like most Marxists) simply believes that the best way to improve the treatment of women is first to do away with class inequalities, which will then cause all other social inequalities (including those based on gender) to vanish as a matter of course.

Granted, part of the feminist focus of *Devil on the Cross* has to do with Ngugi's fairly conventional symbolic representation of Kenya as feminine and as a victim of rape by her neocolonial oppressors (194). But he also maintains an unwavering focus on the real difficulties experienced by Kenyan women in their everyday lives. It is, in fact, quite clear in *Devil on the Cross* that Ngugi believes the unequal treatment of women to be one of the greatest social ills in post-colonial Kenya. The story of Wariinga serves as an allegory of the injustices suffered by women in Kenyan society. A long section midway through the book relates her biography in some detail, beginning with her birth in the midst of the Emergency of the 1950s, when the British colonial rulers of Kenya imposed extremely repressive measures in their attempt to quell the Mau Mau forces that were waging a guerrilla war against British rule (138–153). Wariinga's parents, like thousands of Kenyans, are placed in detention camps for suspected complicity with the guerrillas, so Wariinga is sent to live with an aunt and uncle. As she grows older, Wariinga becomes a good student (especially at mathematics) and a dedicated Christian. She also becomes sexually attractive, at which point her corrupt uncle offers her as a sexual prize to a rich acquaintance of his in return for the rich man's help in securing a bank loan and buying some land. The innocent Wariinga, however, does not even realize that she is being sold like a piece of property. She becomes fascinated by the wealthy lifestyle of the Rich Old Man and is seduced by him; she loses interest in her studies and eventually becomes pregnant. At this point, the Rich Old Man casts her aside, accusing her of infidelity in the most demeaning of terms. Wariinga considers first an abortion, then suicide, but ultimately decides to have the baby and go on with her life.

At this point in Ngugi's text, the narrative of Wariinga's life breaks off. But we already know the rest of her story because she has related it earlier in the book, though casting it in terms of the story of "any girl in Nairobi," thus enhancing her function as a allegorical representation of the women of Kenya (17–26). She has the baby (a girl, named Wambui), whom she leaves with her parents. Wariinga then enrolls in secretarial college to prepare for a career. Afterward, however, she finds that prospective employers expect her to provide sexual favors in addition to typing and office work, though she resolutely maintains her integrity. She finally acquires both a job and a new boyfriend, a student who appears to have progressive views about women. Eventually, however, Wariinga's boss (a hypocrite who claims to be a devout Christian) fires her when she continues to refuse his sexual advances. Moreover now that she is without income, her boyfriend rejects her as well. To make matters worse, she is soon evicted from her rented room. It is at this point when the book opens, with Wariinga wandering, forlorn and homeless, so distracted that she nearly falls in front of a bus (12).

She is pulled away from the bus by a young student who gives her a card inviting her to a "Devil's Feast" featuring a competition for thieves and robbers in Ilmorog, her hometown. She decides to attend, and in the course of doing so she meets a poor woman, Wangari, who has suffered much of the same gender discrimination. Having lost her small farm to a bank repossession, Wangari could not find employment except as a prostitute. She was arrested as a vagrant and potential thief, released only because the police suspect that she could lead them to other criminals. Wariinga thus begins to realize that the misfortunes she has experienced go beyond her own life and extend to Kenyan women as a whole. As a young girl, Wangari worked to support the Mau Mau guerrillas by carrying guns and bullets to their forest hideouts. Wariinga becomes aware of the glorious tradition of Kenyan resistance to colonial oppression, a tradition that has been virtually extinguished in a postcolonial Kenya where the former guerrillas are treated not as national heroes but as criminals.

Wariinga's revolutionary consciousness is further raised when she meets the worker Muturi, a former Mau Mau who is now a dedicated socialist working for revolution in Kenya. She also meets the composer Gatuiria, who is trying to help build an indigenous Kenyan cultural tradition free of Western domination. He helps her recognize the importance of building a new Kenya free of foreign cultural domination.

Meanwhile Wariinga goes with her new acquaintances to the Thieves' Competition in Ilmorog. There she observes various "thieves and robbers" who proudly boast of their wickedness and corruption as businessmen working in league with foreign companies to exploit the Kenyan people. The oppression of women is quite central to these performances. It is not insignificant, for example, that all of the competitors are men and that the only women who "participate" in the event are scantily clad waitresses who serve drinks to the onlookers somewhat in the manner of the "bunnies" in American Playboy Clubs (92). Indeed one requirement of the competition is that the competitors must boast of the number of mistresses they have, just as they must catalogue the automobiles they own. The link is clear: Women in postcolonial Kenya are treated as possessions somewhat on the order of cars; their chief function is to provide pleasure and status for the men who "own" them.

The competitors, in fact, proudly brag of their exploitation of women. Gitutu wa Gataanguru announces that he is a pious Christian, an elder in the Thogoto Mission Church. Nevertheless he admits to having two mistresses in addition to his wife (99). Kihaahu wa Gatheeca admits that he has two wives, one he married while he was still poor and another he acquired after he became rich—because she spoke English and was more presentable at the cocktail parties of his rich foreign friends (109). He also admits to a penchant for adultery, arguing that the idle wives of his rich friends represent easy pickings, though sometimes he is forced to pay for their services like prostitutes (110). Mwireri wa Mukiraai, the only competitor who rejects foreign economic domination of Kenya, nevertheless smugly proclaims that he has no objection to foreign women. For him, "women belong to no age group, no clan, no country." Therefore women of all races and nationalities are equally acceptable as objects of exploitation (60). And Nditika wa Nguunji admits to having an insatiable weakness for women, so much so that he fantasizes being able to acquire a spare penis so that he can better fulfill his sexual appetites. But when his wife envisions the possibility of acquiring a spare set of genitals as well, he beats her savagely and proclaims that her idea is an outrageous violation of African cultural traditions (180-181).

To top off these performances, Wariinga has a vision in which the Devil (an incarnation of capitalism) openly confesses to her the true depths of evil and depravity to which the capitalist oppressors of Kenya have sunk. When Wariinga expresses shock that the poor people of Kenya allow themselves to be exploited in the manner described by the Devil, he reminds her that she has allowed men to exploit her all her life, thinking herself too weak to take action on her own and therefore waiting passively for a man to save her from exploitation by other men (191). Wariinga is here a clear allegorical stand-in for the Kenyan people, passively exploited by their neocolonial rulers. These events have a transforming effect on Wariinga, who finally realizes that the personal tragedies she has experienced are actually part of a much larger social phenomenon and that to have a successful and fulfilling life, she must work to change her fundamental social situation. She therefore abandons her earlier attitude (in which she hoped to achieve happiness by finding a man to love her and take care of her) and goes back to school to finish her engineering degree. By the end of the book, she has become a competent mechanical engineer and has gained the respect and admiration of her male coworkers. She is engaged to marry Gatuiria, but she does not rely on him for her sense of self-worth.

The new, independent Wariinga is a potentially powerful positive role model for Kenya as a whole, especially for Kenyan women, as the narrator of *Devil on the Cross* proclaims:

> People love to denigrate the intelligence and intellectual capacity of our women by saying that the only jobs a woman can do are to cook, to

> make beds and to spread their legs in the market of love. The Wariinga of today has rejected all that, reasoning that because her thighs are hers, her brain is hers, her hands are hers, and her body is hers, she must accord all her faculties their proper role and proper time and place and not let any one part be the sole ruler of her life. (218)

But Ngugi suggests that even Wariinga's newfound education and professional competence are not sufficient to ensure that she will be treated with dignity and respect in her society. After all, she still lives in a society dominated by neocolonial capitalism, and the women of Kenya are regarded as little more than prostitutes whose function is to provide sexual services not only to the men of Kenya but also to the foreign businessmen who come to Kenya in search of easy profits—and easy sex. For example, Ngugi tells the story of an aged American tourist who comes to Kenya because he has the wealth to buy the sexual favors of young girls, whom he regards as just another example of Kenya's exotic indigenous species (70-71).

Wariinga herself realizes that the problem goes deeper than the use of Kenyan women as bait to lure foreign investors. As she and Gatuiria drive to the home of his rich father for a reception in honor of their impending marriage, she responds to Gatuiria's criticism of the use of Kenyan women as "flowers to decorate the beds of foreign tourists" by reminding him that it is not only foreigners who treat Kenyan women like trinkets and sexual toys, despite the fact that women have played such a central role in the heroic tradition of resistance to colonial domination: "Even you, the Kenyan men, think that there is no job a woman can do other than cooking your food and massaging your bodies. The other day I told some young men that my ambition was to design and build a simple machine to ease the burden of rural women. . . . And you know, the men laughed! Why have people forgotten how Kenyan women used to make guns during the Mau Mau war against the British?" (245).

When Wariinga and Gatuiria arrive at the reception, she discovers to her great horror that Gatuiria's father is none other than the Rich Old Man who seduced and then abandoned her in her youth, the father of Wambui. When the Rich Old Man recognizes Wariinga, he insists that she not marry his son, as that would be almost a form of incest. He offers instead to resume their former relationship and again to make her his mistress. Wariinga suddenly realizes that no Kenyan woman—even one with her education and professional skills—can be free of sexual oppression as long as the country remains in the hands of Rich Old Men like this one. She takes out a gun and shoots the old man dead, thus declaring her intention to embark on a program of violent revolution against the prevailing order. As the book ends, Wariinga's fate is left undetermined, but it is clear that she can never again seek comfort merely in personal achievement. She has now committed herself to the revolutionary transformation of Kenyan society as a whole, and she has done so without the help or support of any man. Gatuiria stays behind with his slain father, unsure which side he should take. By the end of the book, therefore, Wariinga has grown from a frightened, passive, exploited woman into a proud, defiant, woman warrior. In this sense, *Devil on the Cross* appears to be one of the most effective feminist statements ever produced by an African male writer, despite its insistence that action against capitalism must precede any effective action against sexism.

Works Cited

Boehmer, Elleke. "The Master's Dance to the Master's Voice: Revolutionary Nationalism and the Representation of Women in the Writing of Ngugi wa Thiong'o." *Journal of Commonwealth Literature* 26.1 (1991): 188–197.

Ngugi wa Thiong'o. *Devil on the Cross.* Trans. Ngugi wa Thiong'o. London: Heinemann, 1982.

Stratton, Florence. *Contemporary African Literature and the Politics of Gender.* London: Routledge, 1994.

FOUCAULDIAN CRITICISM

In Ngugi wa Thiong'o's *Devil on the Cross,* the workers' leader Muturi is arrested for disturbing the peace after he organizes a demonstration to protest a meeting between international capitalist investors and corrupt Kenyan businessmen hoping to gain the support of the foreign investors for their own exploitative ventures in Kenya. That the police side with these unscrupulous and dishonest businessmen rather than the virtuous Muturi is itself a telling indictment of the legal system of postcolonial Kenya. What is in some ways even more telling, however, is the eventual outcome of Muturi's arrest. In the midst of his criminal trial, the authorities suddenly order that the charges be dropped and that he be released. But this order comes about only so that Muturi, rather than being sent to jail on a criminal charge, can be placed in detention as a dangerous political subversive. In Kenya, such detention is a far worse punishment than imprisonment for a crime because political detainees can be incarcerated indefinitely without a trial. They do not even have the solace of seeing the days tick off of their sentence as they languish in prison; they never know whether they are being detained for only a few hours or for much longer—even for life. Meanwhile the fate of these "subversives" can be used as a warning to keep the rest of the populace in line.

This episode can be usefully read through Michel Foucault's argument in *Discipline and Punish* that a major function of the modern prison system is the identification of a criminal population of "delinquents," who can then be subjected to especially careful surveillance while also being put to specific political and economic uses (277–281). Ngugi's understanding of this phenomenon comes not from theory but from all too real experience. He was detained for nearly a year (December 1977–December 1978) in Kenya's Kamiti Maximum Security Prison, once the site of mass hangings of Mau Mau guerrillas for their opposition to British colonial rule in Kenya in the 1950s. Ngugi was imprisoned in this facility without trial and for an indefinite period because his writing (especially in the play *Ngaahika Ndeenda* [English translation, *I Will Marry When I Want*] and the novel *Petals of Blood*) was judged dangerous to the Kenyan government. Ngugi's prison diary, *Detained,* describes the events of his year in prison, including his efforts to write the novel that would eventually become *Devil on the Cross.*

Foucauldian critical approaches generally do not limit themselves to the bounds of a given text but seek other related texts that will help develop an understanding of the particular discourses that inform the text in question. In the case of *Devil on the Cross,* a proper Foucauldian analysis would probably examine a number of British colonial texts (such as Richard Meinertzhagen's *Kenya Diary*) and a number of texts from the tradition of Kenyan anticolonial resistance (such as Josiah Mwangi Kariuki's *Mau Mau Detainee*). The results of these examinations could then be used to construct a model of the opposed discourses of colonialism and anticolonialism that provide the major tension in all of Ngugi's work. There is no room to perform such detailed examinations here, though it is worth looking at least at Ngugi's own *Detained,* which (because of its close relationship to *Devil on the Cross*) obviously offers opportunities to the Foucauldian critic. Both *Detained* and *Devil on the Cross* resonate with the work of Foucault in numerous ways, though the differences in cultural and political orientation between Ngugi the postcolonial socialist and Foucault the European poststructuralist should always be kept in mind.

Ngugi notes in *Detained* that his efforts to write in prison were seriously hampered by the fact that he was cut off from the outside world, from the everyday lives of the common people of Kenya from whom his work draws its central inspiration:

> Contrary to popular mythology, a novel is not a product of the imaginative feats of a single individual but the work of many hands and tongues. A writer just takes down notes dictated to him by life among the people, which he then arranges in this or that form. For me, in writing a novel, I love to hear the voices of the people working on the land, forging metal in a factory, telling anecdotes in crowded matatus and buses, gyrating their hips in a crowded bar before a jukebox or a live band, people playing games of love and hate and fear and glory in their struggle to live. (8)

For Ngugi, fiction does not arise from the individual imagination of the author but from the public discourses that constitute his social and political context. Indeed Ngugi suggests that he was able to succeed in his quest to write in prison only because he luckily came into contact with other prisoners who shared with him the specialized knowledge and viewpoints that he needed to enrich his writing. In a motif reminiscent of Foucault's discussion of productive power, the repressive measures that led to the imprisonment of a number of artists and intellectuals helped produce antirepressive discourse by bringing the various detainees together inside Kamiti Prison. Ngugi was able to draw on the resultant discursive energies to set them in opposition to the discourses of colonialism and capitalism in the writing of *Devil on the Cross* (*Detained* 9).

Ngugi's notion of authorship as the product of public discourses closely resembles that of Foucault. Indeed the unusual genesis of *Devil on the Cross* suggests a number of immediate points of contact between that novel and the work of Foucault, particularly his focus on the history of the modern prison system, in which he finds echoes of a gradual movement toward regimentation and control in society at large. *Devil on the Cross* was written in prison but also in an oppressive postcolonial Kenya that in many ways corresponds quite well to Foucault's notion of a carceral society. Ngugi's descriptions in *Detained* of the Kenyan prison have much in common with the European prisons described by Foucault. Ngugi, for example, comes early on to the Foucauldian recognition that the prison in which he is incarcerated is intended not as a means of punishment and rehabilitation of criminals but as a tool of political power: "The prison system is a repressive weapon in the hands of a ruling minority determined to ensure maximum security for its class dictatorship over the rest of the population" (4). The current government, Ngugi concludes, knows quite well that the full power of its police and military would never in the long run be able to subdue the forces of resistance in the Kenyan population by direct application of force. Therefore the government uses psychological techniques of persuasion and intimidation, including the imprisonment of a small minority, to deprive the opposition of leadership and to demonstrate the consequences of resistance to official authority. The imprisonment of the few, in short, is used as a technique of power against the many.

In another Foucauldian vein, Ngugi relates how he was kept in a small cell in which a 100-watt bulb burned around the clock so that he could be kept under constant surveillance, even while sleeping, defecating, and urinating (6–7). Ngugi also realizes (in the mode of Foucault's discussions in *Discipline and Punish* and the introductory volume of *The History of Sexuality* of confession as a central technique of power in the modern world) that what is wanted of him is a repentant confession, though he knows that he has done nothing more than speak the truth as he sees it and defend the rights of the Kenyan people in the process. Ngugi notes that Kamiti Prison had formerly been an insane asylum and that political prisoners were sometimes treated for mental instability to discredit them as madmen. He thus provides a link between the treatment of so-called madmen and the operations of the Kenyan penal system, very much along the lines of the similar link suggested by Foucault in his parallel studies of madness and the history of the modern prison. Ngugi reacts to this link in a highly Foucauldian vein, noting that madness is a relative condition and that in his contemporary Kenya "anybody who is not mad is mad" (120).

Perhaps the most ironic Foucauldian note in relation to *Devil on the Cross* concerns the fact that Ngugi succeeded in writing what may well be his most powerful novel while being detained precisely to silence him as a writer. His response was to continue writing while in prison, though he had to do so secretly. He employed a method he had learned from the autobiography of Kwame Nkrumah: writing the entire text of *Devil on the Cross* (actually of *Caitaani Mutharaba-ini,* the original Gikuyu title) on sheets of toilet paper that he smuggled into his cell. But as Foucault has emphasized, there is very little privacy in prison, and it was difficult to keep such a major project from the prison authorities. On Friday, September 22, 1978, a thorough prison search unearthed Ngugi's manuscript, which was then confiscated, much to Ngugi's horror.

He resolved, however, to continue his work and to re-create the entire manuscript. As it turned out, this re-creation was unnecessary. Three weeks later, the senior superintendent of the prison inexplicably returned Ngugi's manuscript to him and even offered to supply him with better paper onto which he could transcribe the book from its toilet-paper original. This paper was never actually supplied, but two months after the return of the manuscript Ngugi was released from detention. In 1980, Heinemann Educational Books published *Caitaani Mutharaba-ini,* the first novel that Ngugi (or anybody, for that matter) had written in the Gikuyu language. Translations in Kiswahili and English soon followed. As in Foucault's insistence that power can be productive as well as repressive, the attempts of state power to repress Ngugi's writing only served to produce more of it, just as the long history of state repression in Kenya has helped produce the heroic tradition of resistance in which Ngugi participates.

Devil on the Cross depicts a carceral Kenyan society in which ordinary Kenyan citizens are liable to imprisonment or even death at the whim of powerful neocolonial forces that operate largely under foreign economic and cultural domination. In this sense, the book clearly reflects Ngugi's own position in Kamiti Prison while also indicating his wish to suggest (much in the manner of Foucault) that the brutalization and humiliation to which he was subjected in prison were very much of a piece with life in Kenya, even outside of prison. In *Detained,* Ngugi (quoting William Shakespeare's Richard II) suggests that one of his major goals in writing *Devil on the Cross* was to compare "this prison where I live unto the world" (9). Elsewhere in *Detained,* Ngugi goes to great lengths to place his own situation in a larger historical context. The book is, as much as Ngugi's personal diary, a history of colonial and neocolonial oppression in Kenya. Importantly, however, it is also the story of resistance to that oppression, and its pages are filled with reminders of the heroic exploits of figures such as Waiyaki, leader of a campaign against the original British colonial occupation of Kenya; Koitalel, leader of the late-nineteenth-century Nandi uprising against British rule (murdered by Meinertzhagen, commander of the British occupation forces in Kenya at the time); Dedan Kimaathi, a Mau Mau leader whose imprisonment and hanging—for the seemingly minor charge of possession of a firearm—marked the virtual end of the Mau Mau movement in 1956; and Kariuki, another Mau Mau leader, who was imprisoned and tortured for seven years in the 1950s under British colonial rule, then imprisoned, tortured, and finally killed under the postcolonial government of Jomo Kenyatta in the 1970s.

Detained makes it clear, in fact, that a major inspiration for all of Ngugi's fiction is the long and heroic Kenyan tradition of resistance to foreign domination and oppression:

> It is the history of Kenyan people ceaselessly struggling against Arab feudalists and slave dealers; against Portuguese marauders who opened up Africa to her four-hundred years of devastating encounter with European domination, and later against British predators trying to embrace Kenya with claws and fangs of blood; yes, a history of Kenyan people waging a protracted guerrilla war against a British imperialist power that used to boast of its invincibility to man or God; the history of Kenyan people creating a resistance culture, a revolutionary culture of courage and patriotic heroism. The culture of the defiant Koitalel and Kimaathi. A fight-back, creative culture, unleashing tremendous energies among the Kenyan people. (64)

Ngugi notes that this glorious history has found expression in many areas, not the least of which is literature, where it has given rise to a rich array of patriotic songs, poems, plays, and dances. Numerous elements of this cultural tradition have been incorporated into *Devil on the Cross,* clearly identifying his novel with the cultural tradition of Kenyan resistance. Indeed all of Ngugi's fiction is closely related to Kenyan history, as a useful compilation by Carol Sicherman shows.

Devil on the Cross is clearly a product of the discourse (or, perhaps more properly, counterdiscourse) of Kenyan anticolonial resistance. The text can thus usefully be read within Foucault's description of the productive capabilities of discourses, especially as questions of power are so clearly and overtly at stake in the clash between the discourses of colonialism and anticolonialism. The characters in *Devil on the Cross* are not so much representations of individuals as of discursive positions. Muturi, for example, is an allegorization of the working classes of Kenya. The woman Wangari plays a similar role on the feminine side and is additionally identified with the Mau Mau tradition, in which she participated as a girl. The main protagonist, Wariinga, is an allegorical representative of the young women of Kenya, traditionally the most oppressed sector of the population, yet still a potentially powerful source of subversive energies. At the same time, that she eventually studies to become an engineer identifies Wariinga with the discourse of technology and with the need for Kenyans to become technologically independent of the West. The music student Gatuiria similarly represents two discourses. In his understanding of the important role that culture can play in furthering the development of a positive Kenyan national identity, he represents the discourse of art. In his final ambivalence and inability to take effective action against neocolonial oppression, he represents the generation of Kenyan postcolonial intellectuals who have sometimes mouthed patriotic slogans but have seldom acted with conviction to oppose the neocolonial enslavement of most of the Kenyan population. The status of the various thieves who perform at the Devil's Feast (along with that of the foreign investors for whom they perform) as allegorical representatives of the discourse of neo-colonialism is abundantly clear.

This allegorical mode of characterization can be related to the tradition of Kenyan oral culture from which it derives. But it can also be related to Ngugi's rejection of individualism and to his firm belief in the need for collective action against oppression in Kenya. This emphasis on the collective has roots in both African and Marxist traditions, though it might also be compared to Foucault's rejection of individualism and to his sense that individuals are not unique, autonomous entities but the products of social discourses. Ngugi's anti-individualistic characterization grows directly out of his own sense of his struggles against the Kenyan government as a battle not of individuals but of discourses. As he notes in the preface to *Detained,* those responsible for his imprisonment had no personal grudge against him. Instead they "saw themselves as representing certain social forces; and I as representing others" (xi).

Because of this allegorical mode of characterization, Ngugi is able, through his depiction of the interactions among these characters, to produce a narrative of the workings of power in postcolonial Kenya, workings that he finds suspiciously similar to (if more subtle than) the workings of power in *colonial* Kenya. In the days of British rule, Kenyan resistance was often met with brutality on a grand scale. For example, entire villages might be wiped out in retribution for the death of a single British soldier. The postcolonial government of Kenya is forced to be more subtle and to employ more psychological techniques of terror, but for Ngugi the direct genealogical relationship between the techniques of power once used by the British and those now used by the postcolonial government of Kenya is clear.

Here again, the work of Foucault can be useful. For Foucault, the "controlled illegality" that lies at the heart of the modern prison system is part of a general shift in the object of official power from the bodies to the minds of individual subjects. As a result, the modern world no longer sees the spectacular public tortures and executions that marked the workings of power in medieval Europe. Foucault warns, however, that we should not be deceived into believing that power is any less real or any less pervasive than it had formerly been. Indeed Foucault believes that the modern turn to less overt and psychological techniques of power allows that power to become even more pervasive, leading to a situation in which the various elements of our everyday lives are increasingly controlled and administered by official power.

Foucault's warnings of the increasingly carceral nature of modern society provide an interesting gloss on Ngugi's depiction of postcolonial Kenya as effectively no less oppressive than colonial Kenya had been. At the same time, Ngugi's faith in the eventual ability of the Kenyan people to defeat the forces of oppression remains strong, and his hopes for liberation ultimately seem far stronger than Foucault's. The forces of official power are still very much on the ascendent in Kenya at the end of *Devil on the Cross,* but the forces of resistance remain strong as well. Wariinga's future is, at best, uncertain as she goes forth after having killed the Rich Old Man. Yet it is a future ultimately laden with hope.

After all, Ngugi ends *Detained* by quoting a line from Bertolt Brecht that declares, "Those defeated today will be the victors tomorrow" (232).

Works Cited

Foucault, Michel. *Discipline and Punish: The Birth of the Prison.* Trans. Alan Sheridan. New York: Vintage, 1979.

———. *The History of Sexuality.* Vol. I, *An Introduction.* Trans. Robert Hurley. New York: Vintage, 1980.

Kariuki, Josiah Mwangi. *Mau Mau Detainee: The Account by a Kenyan African of His Experiences in Detention Camps, 1953-1960.* Harmondsworth, England: Penguin, 1964.

Meinertzhagen, Richard. *Kenya Diary (1902-1906).* 1957. New York: Hippocrene, 1983.

Ngugi wa Thiong'o. *Detained: A Writer's Prison Diary.* London: Heinemann, 1981.

———. *Devil on the Cross.* Trans. Ngugi wa Thiong'o. London: Heinemann, 1982.

———. *Petals of Blood.* London: Heinemann, 1977.

Ngugi wa Thiong'o and Ngugi wa Mirii. *I Will Marry When I Want.* Trans. by the authors. London: Heinemann, 1988.

Nkrumah, Kwame. *Ghana: The Autobiography of Kwame Nkrumah.* New York: International Publishers, 1971.

Sicherman, Carol. *Ngugi wa Thiong'o: The Making of a Rebel.* London: Hans Zell, 1990.

SELECTED BIBLIOGRAPHY

Aborisade, P. A. "National and Revolutionary Consciousness: Two Phases of Ngugi's Artistic Praxis." *Ufahamu* 18 (1989-1990): 57-74.

Argues that Ngugi's career passes through two phases: that of "national consciousness" and that of "revolutionary consciousness," with the latter corresponding to Ngugi's socialist phase, which is importantly influenced by his reading of Fanon, begins to appear in *A Grain of Wheat,* and is fully dominant in the novels after that. Notes Ngugi's strong commitment in this later phase to the working class as a source of revolutionary energy. Argues that in *Devil on the Cross* Ngugi seeks to "appropriate the novel form, rewrite it and, in a re-enactment of its origin, turn it into the form of what he considers the most progressive class of this epoch" (70).

Adewoye, Sam A. "The Strength of the Rhetoric of Oral Tradition in Ngugi wa Thiong'o's *Devil on the Cross.*" *Commonwealth Literature in English* 5.1 (1992): 11-19.

Argues that Ngugi effectively employs elements of oral tradition in *Devil on the Cross* to endow the novel with a specifically African cultural richness. Concludes that *Devil* effectively demonstrates the ability of the oral tradition to give voice to the aspirations of the African masses and that it "reveals the potential of the African novel to evolve" in a manner "totally distinct from the one we have inherited from the West" (18).

Balogun, F. Odun. "Ngugi's *Devil on the Cross:* The Novel as Hagiography of a Marxist." *Ufahamu* 16.2 (1988): 76-87.

Notes that the "anti-capitalist pro-marxist message" of *Devil on the Cross* is encoded in Christian language and symbology, but that this strategy is used to undermine Christianity, which is shown to work in complicity with capitalism in the continuing neocolonial oppression of Kenya.

Boehmer, Elleke. "The Master's Dance to the Master's Voice: Revolutionary Nationalism and the Representation of Women in the Writing of Ngugi wa Thiong'o." *Journal of Commonwealth Literature* 26.1 (1991): 188-197.
Notes the strong role played by women in Ngugi's fiction, a fact that makes him a pioneer in African fiction. Concludes, however, that Ngugi's thought maintains a "patriarchal cast" (188). Observes, for example, that workers in Ngugi are almost invariably male, though Wariinga in *Devil on the Cross* is an exception.

Cook, David, and Michael Okenimpke. *Ngugi wa Thiong'o: An Exploration of His Writings.* London: Heineman, 1983.
Studies Ngugi's work at length. Presents a useful reading of *Devil on the Cross,* outlining the roles of the major characters and detailing the use of several literary strategies and techniques. Discusses the book's relation both to European satirical traditions and African oral culture. Argues that the book's combination of a fantastic mode of satire with a realistic depiction of life in Kenya is a "technical triumph" (123).

Curtis, Lisa. "The Divergence of Art and Ideology in the Later Novels of Ngugi wa Thiong'o: A Critique." *Ufahamu* 13.2-3 (1984): 186-214.
Traces the development of Ngugi's career as a novelist in terms of his shift from an early liberal humanist ideology to a later (from *A Grain of Wheat* forward) commitment to socialism. Believes, however, that this movement represents a decline in his effectiveness as an artist. Argues, for example, that *Devil on the Cross* is informed by an "overbearing didacticism" that makes it a failure as a novel (210).

Killam, G. D. "Ngugi wa Thiong'o." In *The Writing of East and Central Africa,* ed. G. D. Killam, 123-143. London: Heinemann, 1984.
Offers a good general introduction to Ngugi's work. Emphasizes the satirical aspects of *Devil on the Cross* and compares Ngugi's satire to that of Swift and Pope. Considers Ngugi's satire powerful and effective and sees *Devil* as a successful enactment of the political and artistic program described in Ngugi's essays and prison diary. Sees *Devil* as aesthetically innovative, but believes that in the book "Ngugi is not . . . concerned with finding new ways to be new; he is concerned with finding new ways to be effective" (142).

Ngugi wa Thiong'o. *Decolonising the Mind: The Politics of Language in African Literature.* London: James Currey, 1986.
Collects Ngugi's essays, many of which focus on his commitment to writing in African languages, with "The Language of African Literature" containing perhaps his most important single statement on this issue.

Ngugi wa Thiong'o. *Detained: A Writer's Prison Diary.* London: Heinemann, 1981.
Describes the year (December 1977-December 1978) Ngugi spent without trial in a Kenyan prison because of his writing. Discusses, among other things, the writing of *Devil on the Cross* during that time.

Nwankwo, Chimalum. "Ngugi's *Devil on the Cross:* A Feminization of Chaos." *Commonwealth* 1 (Autumn 1987): 119-122.
Discusses the central importance of feminine energies in *Devil on the Cross,* emphasizing Wariinga's role late in the text as an image of positive social change. Notes, however, that by pairing the women Wariinga and Wangari with the men Gatuiria and Muturi, Ngugi implies that genuine change in Kenya will require cooperative action on the part of both men and women.

Ogunjimi, Bayo. "Language, Oral Tradition, and Social Vision in Ngugi's *Devil on the Cross.*" *Ufahamu* 14.1 (1984): 56-70.

Points out that *Devil on the Cross* combines the form of the authentic epic and that of the mock epic. Notes the engagement of *Devil* with African oral tradition and with the recent history of Kenya in Ngugi's attempt to "put art to the service of the oppressed class" (68).

Riemenschneider, Dieter. "Ngugi wa Thiong'o and the Question of Language and Literature in Kenya." *World Literature Written in English* 24.1 (1984): 78-87.

Describes Ngugi's attempts in various genres to explore a national culture for Kenya (81). Notes that *Petals of Blood* (written in English) employs many narrative techniques that would be familiar to European readers, whereas *Devil on the Cross* (written in Gikuyu) uses more traditional Gikuyu methods of storytelling (83-84). Observes how Ngugi's occasional use of English in the Gikuyu *Devil* shows his facility with the language and turns it against the dominance of English culture in Kenya: "There are numerous examples in which Ngugi satirizes those who feel that they need English in order to express themselves adequately" (86).

Sackey, Edward. "Oral Tradition and the African Novel." *Modern Fiction Studies* 37.3 (1991): 389-407.

Discusses the influence of African oral traditions on the African novel, focusing on the work of Ayi Kwei Armah, Ngugi, Ama Ata Aidoo, and Kofi Awoonor. Notes that *Devil on the Cross* manifests this oral tradition in important ways. Argues that *Devil* is "deeply rooted in the fertile soil of African folklore" and that it incorporates "song, dance, formal patterns of celebration, and mourning" (402).

Sicherman, Carol. *Ngugi wa Thiong'o: The Making of a Rebel.* London: Hans Zell, 1990.

Compiles historical information and original documents that provide an extremely useful background to all of Ngugi's work.

Sicherman, Carol. "Ngugi wa Thiong'o and the Writing of Kenyan History." *Research in African Literatures* 20.3 (1989): 347-370.

Discusses the relationship between Ngugi's fiction and the work of historians of Kenya.

Stratton, Florence. *Contemporary African Literature and the Politics of Gender.* London: Routledge, 1994.

Discusses *Devil on the Cross* as an important example of a recent turn toward more concern with gender issues in works by male writers. Describes *Devil* as "a female *bildungsroman* . . . written by a male author" (159). Concludes, however, that Ngugi's novel, by treating class as a more fundamental social category than gender, ultimately operates "in the interest of preserving patriarchal relations" (160). Argues, in fact, that gender in *Devil* becomes a mere metaphor for class.

Westley, David. "Choice of Language and African Literature: A Bibliographic Essay." *Research in African Literatures* 23.1 (1992): 159-171.

Surveys the important issue of language choice in the writing of African literature, an issue to which Ngugi's work has been quite central. Includes an extensive bibliography of sources on the subject.

chapter 14

Approaches to *The Handmaid's Tale*, by Margaret Atwood

Margaret Atwood is one of the best-known contemporary Canadian writers. A poet as well as a novelist, Atwood has a genuine gift for language. At the same time, her writing addresses a number of important contemporary political issues, especially relative to feminist concerns and to the special position of Canada as a nation seeking its identity in the shadow of a much richer and more powerful neighbor, the United States. *The Handmaid's Tale* is Atwood's best-known work. This text participates in a genre known as "dystopian fiction," which includes works that depict fictional societies (often in the distant future) to present warnings against the potential negative consequences of certain proposals for the reformulation of human societies. Dystopian fictions are usually directed toward specific trends in existing societies. In *The Handmaid's Tale,* Atwood's imaginative satirical creation of a future society ruled by authoritarian religious fanatics comments directly on the rise of right-wing religious fundamentalism as a political force in the United States in the 1980s. The novel also addresses more general issues having to do with the nature of fanaticism, of patriarchal societies, and of history. Feminist criticism is the most obvious way to approach *The Handmaid's Tale.* This section, however, presents approaches to the text using the New Criticism, deconstruction, Bakhtinian criticism, and Foucauldian criticism, all of which acknowledge the crucial importance of gender issues in the text.

THE NEW CRITICISM

Margaret Atwood's *The Handmaid's Tale* grows out of specific political developments in the United States in the Reaganite 1980s, especially the growing political power of Christian fundamentalism and a general shift to the right in

American politics. These changes brought about a number of reversals for feminist causes, the most obvious of which was the defeat of the Equal Rights Amendment, which would have guaranteed equal treatment under the law regardless of gender. In a satiric response to these developments, *The Handmaid's Tale* is an avowedly political work that seems to run directly counter to the insistence of the New Criticism that literary works should be read and judged according to strictly literary criteria without the intrusion of "extrinsic" (especially political) considerations. Moreover the political orientation of the book is powerfully opposed to the conservative Christian philosophy that underlay the work of the central New Critics. In a formal sense, however, *The Handmaid's Tale* responds quite well to New Critical readings. Atwood herself is an established poet, and her fiction often shows the close attention to language evident in her poetry. *The Handmaid's Tale* describes a starkly repressive dystopian America of the near future, but it does so through language that is richly figurative, often playful, and highly literary.

The Handmaid's Tale projects a nightmare future in which right-wing religious forces have established control of the government. Although pockets of rebel resistance remain, the United States has been replaced by the Republic of Gilead, in which the ideology of religious fundamentalism is imposed by brute force on a stupefied populace. Gilead is a police state, with the movements and activities of its citizens closely monitored and controlled. But the new government also attempts to gain the "voluntary" loyalty of its subjects through measures reminiscent both of religious tradition and the reinscriptions of religion in dystopian classics such as *We, Brave New World,* and *1984.*

Sexuality is a principal focus for the exercise of religious totalitarianism in Gilead. In the Christian theocracy of the Republic of Gilead, marriage is promoted as a social goal, though it is available only to those who have a reached a certain social status in this strongly stratified society. Wives are "issued" to successful males as rewards for loyal service to the community, demonstrating the thorough commodification of women in Gilead. Because there are few roles available to women in our own contemporary world, women in this society exist not as individuals but as members of well-defined groups corresponding almost to brand names. Among the upper classes, women function principally either as wives (who serve as domestic managers), domestic servants ("Marthas"), or handmaids (sexual surrogates). In the lower classes, however, "Econowives" have to play all of these roles. There are also "Aunts" (who serve to train and discipline the handmaids) and "Jezebels" (officially, though covertly, sanctioned prostitutes used to service foreign dignitaries and important government officials). Women who cannot or will not play one of these roles are labeled "Unwomen" and are exiled to the "colonies," where they are used for hazardous duties such as cleaning up toxic waste.

Atwood's book focuses on the handmaids, who are used strictly for breeding purposes. They are issued to important men ("Commanders") whose wives have proved unable to bear children so that those men might still have an opportunity to procreate. The narrator and title character of *The Handmaid's Tale* is labeled

"Offred," indicating her service to a Commander named "Fred," and we never learn her real name. She succinctly describes her role as handmaid (authorized by the biblical story of Jacob, Rachel, and Bilhah), noting that her sexual services are intended for breeding purposes only, with no hint of pleasure or affection: "We are two-legged wombs, that's all: sacred vessels, ambulatory chalices" (176).

This reference to vessels and chalices is clearly ironic, linking the traditional religious significance of such items with traditional social attitudes toward women, attitudes that have been spectacularly literalized in the society of Gilead. Such references are quite typical of Offred's narration, which often employs irony and wordplay to increase its effect. Very early in the narrative, for example, Offred describes the taste for old-fashioned home furnishings that characterizes Gilead and notes that this preference is part of the regime's general call for a return to "traditional values," such as those embodied in the epigram "Waste not want not" (9). Offred responds to this particular epigram by noting sardonically that she still feels a great deal of want, even though she is not being wasted. But surely Offred is here being intentionally perverse. She knows full well that in the repressive context of Gilead, such epigrams have been converted from advice to direct orders. This particular epigram no longer merely suggests that efficient use of resources leads to prosperity. Instead it is a command that the citizenry neither waste resources nor want anything more than they already have. Offred's linguistic play with the epigram suggests that such epigrams are perfect icons of Gilead. Like the traditional values espoused by the regime, these epigrams are things of the past that are out of place in the present. They originally expressed wisdom but have now become empty clichés, devoid of all real relevance except through their use as tools of official power. At the same time, Offred's wordplay reenergizes the epigram to a certain extent, using the inherent ironic potential of language to produce a meaning far different from that intended by the regime.

Offred quite frequently employs such linguistic play in her narrative, which also often resorts to highly poetic language. Jeanne Campbell Reesman notes the frequent use of metaphors in *The Handmaid's Tale* and compares Atwood's work in this respect to the poetry of Emily Dickinson (9–10). Reesman relates the metaphoricity of Atwood's language to the "hermeneutic" quality of her text—that is, to the ability of the text to provoke thought and conversation rather than to provide, in the mode of "epistemology," final answers to the questions it poses. In making this distinction between hermeneutic and epistemological texts, Reesman appeals to the work of the American philosopher Richard Rorty. Her approach is thus, strictly speaking, extrinsic. But within the context of the interpretation of literature, this distinction clearly resembles that made by the New Critics between poetry and science. Poetry, for the New Critics, provides an understanding of the world superior to that provided by science precisely because science insists on reducing all problems to final truths, whereas poetry opens up the possibility for multiple interpretations of phenomena.

This opposition is clearly central to the structure of *The Handmaid's Tale.* The book ostensibly consists of a diary left by Offred detailing her nightmarish experiences as a forced sexual surrogate in the fundamentalist Christian dictatorship of Gilead. Yet the book ends with an epilogue that reveals that what we have been reading is a text assembled and edited by one Professor James Darcy Pieixoto, working from a collection of audiotapes discovered two hundred years after the experiences related on them. We are thus, in a sense, reading two narratives at once, a situation well encompassed by Michele Lacombe's characterization of the text as a "palimpsest" in which Pieixoto's version of the story is written over Offred's, as it were (5). From a feminist perspective, that seems to be the most obvious way to read *The Handmaid's Tale;* the tension between these two narratives seems to be that between masculine and feminine perspectives. Offred's feminine tale is fluid, playful, and poetic, whereas Pieixoto's masculine reinscription of it seeks to reduce the story's ambiguities and deemphasize the personal aspects of Offred's experience in the interest of developing a detailed scholarly understanding of the Republic of Gilead, a historical phenomenon about which little seems to be known in Pieixoto's time. From the point of view of the New Criticism, however, it might be useful to regard Offred as a poet who tells her story using the techniques of poetry and to see the scholar Pieixoto as a scientist who seeks to reduce the historical past to a series of scientific facts at the expense of ignoring the subjective and emotional dimension of past events.

The contrast between the styles of Pieixoto and Offred is quite clear in the text. In his quest for historical knowledge, Pieixoto regards Offred's tapes as disappointing and inadequate. He thus somewhat disparagingly refers to the tapes as an "item," specifically suggesting that they do not deserve to be called a "document" (381). Rather than appreciate Offred's narrative for its own value, Pieixoto and his coworker, Professor Wade, seem to regard it as a curiosity that might lead them to other, more "authoritative" sources. They thus attempt to correlate the information contained in Offred's account with more conventional historical records. In so doing, Pieixoto bemoans the fact that these records are relatively sparse for the Gilead period because the revisionist Gileadean regime was given to destroying its own records periodically as its policies changed (385). As opposed to Offred's feminine spoken narrative, Pieixoto would really like to have the computer printouts of her male masters, thus providing him with the kind of information that he regards as reliable.

One reason for Pieixoto's disdain of Offred's narrative is its intensely subjective quality. Indeed Offred's narrative often has the feel of poetry rather than history. At one point, for example, she describes the changed sense of relationship to her own body that has been brought about by her experiences under the brutal Gileadean regime. Where she once regarded her body as a practical instrument that helped her perform various tasks and reach various goals, she is now estranged from it, regarding it as insubstantial and unreliable: "Now the flesh arranges itself differently. I'm a cloud, congealed around a central object, the shape of a pear, which is hard and more real than I am and glows red within its translucent wrapping. Inside it is a space, huge as the sky at night and dark and curved like that, though black-red rather than black. Pinpoints of light well, sparkle, burst and shrivel within it, countless as stars" (95). Such poetic passages indicate the relevance of New Critical readings to this novel, even though the New Criticism is widely recognized to be more effective as a technique for reading poetry than for interpreting fiction.

Pieixoto also employs wordplay. For example, the title of the text (actually suggested by Wade) is a pun on the words "tale" and "tail," indicating the use of Offred as a sexual object (381). The abusive nature of this sexist pun is one of the clearest indications of the different attitudes of Pieixoto and Offred toward language. When Pieixoto employs wordplay, it is at the expense of others and seems intended to demonstrate his power and superiority over them. When Offred employs wordplay, it is largely a matter of self-defense, part of an attempt to maintain a sense of her own self amid the brutal environment in which she must live as a handmaid in Gilead.

Pieixoto gets the last word in a literal sense, and the epilogue does cause most of the preceding narrative to appear in a somewhat different light than it had before. Nevertheless Offred's poetic perspective seems more powerful than Pieixoto's scientific one, as a New Critic would expect. After all, Offred's puns and various other plays with language still come through even in the text as edited by Pieixoto—no doubt much to his own frustration. Moreover the narrative leaves many questions unanswered, thus defeating Pieixoto's quest for precise, scientific knowledge of the past. In particular, as Offred leaves the Commander's residence in a van at the end of her narrative, we are not sure if she is being rescued and taken to safety or arrested by the secret police and taken to further torment. We also do not know how she was finally able to record her story or how the tapes were able to survive until discovered two centuries later. From Pieixoto's point of view, the most vexing uncertainties involve Gilead itself, and the text gives no indication of what happened to bring about the end of this apparently short-lived Christian dictatorship. As a result of all of these uncertainties and ambiguities, there is a great deal of irony in the fact that Pieixoto ends his presentation to his audience at the academic symposium of the epilogue by asking them if there are any questions. There are, of course, many questions, and there is thus a suggestion in this ending that scientific approaches like those employed by Pieixoto always leave important questions unanswered, despite their drive for a seemingly complete compilation and explanation of the "facts."

To an extent, then, *The Handmaid's Tale* can be read as a parable of the limitations of scientific inquiry and of the ultimate superiority of poetry over science as a means of understanding the human condition. At the same time, the opposition between poetic and scientific languages in the text has such clear political resonances that this very opposition seems to defeat the New Critical insistence on intrinsic readings. For example, the power of language is one of the book's central subjects, and it is no accident that some of the most repressive measures instituted by the government of the Republic of Gilead have to do with attempts to establish strict control of language itself. The regime in Gilead thus keeps a tight rein on the media, assuring that all potentially subversive discourse is suppressed. Even reading of the Bible is strictly controlled, for fear that variant interpretations of this complex document might further opposition to the extremist policies of the regime. Women in Gilead are subject to especially stringent linguistic controls. Except for the "Aunts" charged with training potential handmaids, they are forbidden either to read or write, thus making written language (and the power that goes with it) a strictly male preserve.

The totalitarian Christian government of Gilead can tolerate no opposition and no deviation from its own interpretation of reality. The attempts of the government to control language can then be taken as an indication of the potential ability of language to produce perceptions of reality. But language turns out not to be so easy to control. Indeed the official attempts to suppress unapproved language use in Gilead seem paradoxically to give language an additional subversive force, and it is probably not surprising that language is such a key resource for Offred in her attempts to resist the role thrust on her by the Gileadean regime. It is certainly no accident that Offred emphasizes the large collection of books she observes in her first secret unofficial visit to the Commander's study, thus linking books directly with this serious transgression of Gileadean law. It is also significant that during these illicit meetings with the Commander, Offred plays Scrabble and reads novels by banned authors such as Raymond Chandler and Charles Dickens. It is clear that Offred's own private attempts to maintain a mastery of language that goes beyond that alloted to women in Gilead represents her most important and successful form of resistance to the dehumanization that she experiences in her role as a handmaid.

In *The Handmaid's Tale,* even the most seemingly literary uses of language have significance that goes far beyond the realm of literature. Indeed dystopian texts such as *The Handmaid's Tale* tend to derive their most powerful energies from their direct relevance to reality. As M. Keith Booker notes, "Dystopian fictions are typically set in places or times far distant from the author's own, but it is usually clear that the real referents of dystopian fictions are generally quite concrete and near-at-hand" (19). In the case of *The Handmaid's Tale,* we cannot appreciate the significance of Offred's predicament in Gilead without understanding it as a thinly veiled satirical reinscription of the situation of real women in the real America of the 1980s. For example, the subjugated position of women in Gilead can be taken as a direct commentary on the failure of the Equal Rights Amendment, and the use of handmaids merely as vehicles for the production of children can be seen as a commentary on the "right to life" movement and its insistence that pregnant women be forced to bear children. Linda Kauffman argues that in *The Handmaid's Tale* Atwood has not created a purely fictional dystopia but has simply defamiliarized the America of the 1980s: "Whether one thinks of the trials of surrogate motherhood, or the Vatican's recent doctrinal edict against anything but married 'normal sexuality,' or of the AIDS epidemic and its attendant repressions, or the resurgence of racial and religious intolerance—the seeds of hatred, violence, and repression are already prepared" (241).

These links are established quite directly in the text, though they are sometimes more complex than we might expect. For example, Atwood warns against what she clearly sees as a dangerous trend in contemporary feminism by suggesting that the censorship policies of Gilead have roots in the attempts of feminists to suppress certain kinds of books and magazines (especially those labeled by them as "pornography") in the 1980s (50–51). It is Pieixoto, however, who expresses the links between Gilead and America most clearly when he insists that no historical phenomena come out of nowhere and that the policies of the regime in Gilead must have grown directly out of certain attitudes in the society that preceded Gilead (386–387).

Such connections between Gilead and America show that *The Handmaid's Tale* cannot be fully appreciated within a strictly literary context but must be related to the social issues and historical trends that the book is intended to address. The richly poetic language of the novel provides an ideal demonstration of the potential of New Critical close reading for the interpretation of fiction. At the same time, the intense political engagement of the book provides important reminders of the limitations of the New Critical insistence on formalist readings, an insistence that renders the method fundamentally inadequate for exploring the connections between literature and society.

Works Cited

Atwood, Margaret. *The Handmaid's Tale.* New York: Fawcett, 1987.

Booker, M. Keith. *The Dystopian Impulse in Modern Literature: Fiction as Social Criticism.* Westport, Conn.: Greenwood, 1994.

Kauffman, Linda. "Special Delivery: Twenty-First Century Epistolarity in *The Handmaid's Tale.*" In *Writing the Female Voice: Essays on Epistolary Literature,* ed. Elizabeth C. Goldsmith, 221–244. Boston: Northeastern UP, 1989.

Lacombe, Michele. "The Writing on the Wall: Amputated Speech in Margaret Atwood's *The Handmaid's Tale.*" *Wascana Review* 21.2 (1986): 2–12.

Reesman, Jeanne Campbell. "Dark Knowledge in *The Handmaid's Tale.*" *CEA Critic* 53.3 (1991): 6–22.

Rorty, Richard. *Consequences of Pragmatism.* Minneapolis: U of Minnesota P, 1982.

———. *Philosophy and the Mirror of Nature.* Princeton, N.J.: Princeton UP, 1979.

DECONSTRUCTIVE CRITICISM

The Handmaid's Tale is an overtly political work that describes a near-future dystopian America in which fundamentalist religious fanatics have gained control of the government and have forced their views on the entire population. The direct relevance of this theme to contemporary political issues in present-day America is obvious. At the same time, the book's highly complex and literary language offers many opportunities for useful commentary from the perspective of deconstruction. The Christian dictatorship of Gilead is based on an extreme form of the kind of logocentric thought that deconstruction is specifically intended to counter. And this logocentric thought leads to a society based on strict (but hierarchical) polar oppositions (especially male versus female) of precisely the kind associated by deconstructionist critics with such thought. Language itself is a major theme of *The Handmaid's Tale* in the way both that the regime uses language as a central tool of its power and that the narrator, Offred, uses language as a strategy of resistance, attempting to create for herself an identity in language that differs from the one forced on her by this oppressive society.

Drawing on the insights of feminist critics that the oppression of women in patriarchal society is embedded in the very languages used in such societies, writers of feminist utopian and dystopian fiction have frequently focused on language as an aspect of both the patriarchal traditions they oppose and the feminine alternatives they suggest. For example, writers such as Ursula K. LeGuin (in *The Dispossessed*) and Suzette Haden Elgin (in *Native Tongue*) have envisioned the development of entirely new languages based on premises more amenable to the fair treatment of women. In *The Handmaid's Tale,* Atwood imagines no such language, but she does emphasize that the brutal treatment of women in the Republic of Gilead is largely linguistic in nature. The handmaids in Atwood's dystopian Gilead have no identity except as potential childbearers; they are even stripped of their original names, which are replaced with possessive nominations such as "Ofglen," "Ofwayne," or "Ofwarren," indicating their status as mere property of their Commanders ("Glen" or "Fred" or "Warren"). Among other things, this linguistic domination through naming recalls Louis Althusser's argument that the interpellation of the subject begins even before birth in the complex of expectations that the family and society develop concerning the infant-to-be. In particular, "it is certain in advance that it will bear its Father's Name, and will therefore have an identity and be irreplaceable. Before its birth, the child is therefore always already a subject" (Althusser 176). In a similar way, Jacques Lacan suggests that naming is a paradigmatic enactment of the rule of the Law of the Father. Just as the handmaids are named by others without any input of their own, so too are we all generally named before we can speak, labeled in language before we can choose our own labels. As Lacan points out, "The subject, too, if he can appear to be the slave of language is all the more so of a discourse in the universal movement in which his place is already inscribed at birth, if only by virtue of his proper name" (148).

If the renaming of the handmaids appears to usurp the Name of the Father given them at birth, it is worth keeping in mind that this sort of renaming has gone on in Western civilization for centuries through the use of the designation "Mrs.," whereby women are transferred from the jurisdiction of the Father to that of the Husband (and presumed Father-to-be). Offred herself clearly finds this renaming a significant threat to her identity, and she jealously guards her former name (though it was given her by someone else) as an almost magical emblem of her former identity: "I tell myself it doesn't matter, your name is like your telephone number, useful only to others; but what I tell myself is wrong, it does matter. I keep the knowledge of this name like something hidden, some treasure I'll come back to dig up, one day. I think of this name as buried. This name has an aura around it, like an amulet" (108).

Lacan's general formulation of the subject as a "slave of language" takes on a special resonance when women are named specifically to indicate their domination by men, especially given feminist charges that Lacan sees the Symbolic Order of language (especially written language) as a predominately masculine realm. As Teresa de Lauretis notes, for Lacan

> writing is the masculine activity par excellence, because it exists in the order of the symbolic where language, the circulation of signifiers, and signification itself are subject to the name of the Father, to the structure of symbolic castration in which the phallus is the signifier of desire. Writing thus presupposes possession of the phallus—symbolically speaking, of course; and for a woman to write is to usurp a place, a discursive position, she does not have by nature or by culture. (80)

The Handmaid's Tale bears out this analysis; men in Gilead maintain an especially strong control over written language, and women are generally forbidden either to read or write. Atwood directly relates this motif to psychoanalysis; one of the mottos of the center where the handmaids are trained is "Pen Is Envy" (241).

Lacan's particular version of psychoanalysis (with its emphasis on the status of the subject as a product of language) has much in common with the work of poststructuralist critics such as Jacques Derrida. The insistence on the power of written language in *The Handmaid's Tale* recalls Derrida's important meditations on writing. Indeed a tension between spoken and written language turns out to be a central issue in *The Handmaid's Tale,* just as for Derrida the opposition between writing and speech is one of the central aspects of Western dualistic thinking. Offred's written text is, we learn in the epilogue, an artificial construction pieced together by the male Professors Pieixoto and Wade from audiotapes presumably recorded by Offred herself sometime after the events she relates on the tapes. By converting these recorded tapes into a written document, these professors are trying to construct a more authoritative record, reflecting the usual assumption that Western culture grants more authority to written than to spoken words. Nevertheless Offred's spoken text is primary, whereas the written text is a secondary reconstruction, probably modified by the assumptions made by the professors in their construction of the written document. To a certain extent, then, the text bears out Derrida's point that Western thought actually privileges the immediacy of speech over the seeming secondariness of writing, despite widespread perceptions to the contrary.

This privileging of Offred's voice over the written text constructed by the male professors can also be interpreted as a feminist gesture; Offred's play with language throughout her narration is an attempt to explore feminine alternatives to the subjective position offered Offred by her patriarchal society. But this link between subjectivity and speech is also central to Derrida's point about the

Western privileging of the latter: We traditionally tend to regard language as produced by stable transcendental subjects to express ideas or truths that are fully formulated before their expression in language. This view of language as anchored by the individual subject seems to be accepted by Pieixoto and Wade. In attempting to assess the authenticity of the tapes, for example, they try to ascertain that all of them were recorded by the same speaker. But the playfulness and multiplicity of Offred's language clearly indicate that meaning continues to be produced long after a particular statement is made, and the "immediacy" of Offred's spoken narrative is an illusion given that her tapes are discovered centuries after they were recorded.

Offred herself recognizes the possibility that the subject is a product of language rather than the other way around. The rulers of Gilead attempt strictly to control the subjectivity of women, as when the women of the society are divided into rigidly defined categories such as wives (domestic managers), domestic servants ("Marthas"), or handmaids (sexual surrogates). In the lower classes, however, "Econowives" perform all three roles. "Aunts" train and discipline the handmaids, and "Jezebels," officially, though covertly, are sanctioned prostitutes who service foreign VIPs and high-level government officials. Women who refuse these roles, or are unable to perform them, are labeled "Unwomen" and sent to the "colonies," where they clean up toxic waste and do other hazardous duties. These category labels are accompanied by strict codes of conduct and dress.

This separation into clearly designated groups (an exaggerated version of the Marxist concept of division of labor) is clearly intended not only to control the behavior of individual women but also to create divisions among different women that will prevent them from developing a sense of solidarity with others of their own gender. These group labels provide a central source of women's identities, and (like the naming of the handmaids) they participate in an extensive program of linguistic controls. The regime in Gilead enforces its own interpretation of reality by exercising a direct control over the language with which reality is described. In Gilead, "language thus defines reality, which is one reason that Offred spends so much time meditating about words, comparing their meanings before the coup and after, their arbitrariness and construction" (Kauffman 233). As a result of the official perception of the power of language, most women in Gilead are strictly forbidden to read or write. They also have very limited access to spoken language. Expected mechanically to occupy predetermined roles without deviation, they are also expected to speak in mechanical and predetermined ways. Thus when Offred meets her shopping partner Ofglen, the two respond to each other in thoroughly determined ways, speaking only in clichés such as "Blessed be the fruit" and "Praise be."

But as is often the case in dystopian fiction, language functions in *The Handmaid's Tale* as a potentially powerful locus of transgression. For one thing, the linguistic practices of Gilead are exposed in the book as the blatant attempts at domination that they are. For another, language specifically functions as a locus of subversive practice. When Offred is called to secret (and illegal) meetings with her Commander in his office, she expects that he will demand illicit sex, but instead they play Scrabble, a language game. He also also provides her with forbidden reading material, which allows her to exercise her literacy. And it is precisely to the plurality of language that Offred turns to rebel against the strict monologism of Gileadean society. She frequently employs puns and other wordplay in her narration, seeking thereby to demonstrate an ability to manipulate the complexities of language that goes far beyond the linguistic disenfranchisement legislated for her by this masculine society. She also demonstrates (much like Derrida in his own frequent use of puns) that language itself inherently eludes attempts at strict control. Musing on the openness of showers in men's locker rooms, Offred comments on the "public display of privates" (94). And when she thinks of her friend Moira, who escaped from the handmaid training center, she sardonically describes her as "a loose woman" (172).

This play with words shows an almost desperate attempt to create calming humor amid horror. But more important, it also represents an attempt by Offred to maintain an identity of her own apart from the one prescribed for her in this ultimate patriarchal society: "I sit in the chair and think about the word *chair.* It can also mean the leader of a meeting. It can also mean a mode of execution. It is the first syllable in *charity.* It is the French word for flesh. None of these facts has any connection with the others. These are the kinds of litanies I use, to compose myself" (140). The plurality of language embedded in the multiple meanings of the word *chair* comforts Offred with a reminder of alternatives to the strictly monological society of Gilead. And "compose" is itself here a pun, indicating Offred's attempts to calm herself but also suggesting her project of using language subversively to construct an independent sense of herself.

Offred's play with language also allows her to devise a record of her experiences that specifically refuses the logocentric assumptions of the Republic of Gilead. Her tone is often playful (sometimes in a rather bawdy way), clearly violating the mood of seriousness and sanctimoniousness that informs the official ideology of Gilead. As Karen F. Stein points out, Offred frequently "plays with and questions the limits of language and of storytelling. Even while telling her tale, she deconstructs it. This is accomplished within Offred's narrative by the use of word-play and metafictional interventions" (274). Moreover Offred's highly figurative language runs directly counter to the beliefs of Gilead's fundamentalist Christian rulers in a literal interpretation of the Bible. Offred (like Derrida) specifically denies that any such literal interpretation of language is ever possible. She consistently undermines (or deconstructs) her own narrative as she goes along, commenting on her narrative in ways that remind her audience that what she says can never be regarded as a strictly accurate and literal account of events: "It's impossible to say a thing exactly the way it was, because what you say can never be exact, you always have to leave something out, there are too many parts, sides, crosscurrents, nuances; too many gestures, which could mean this or that, too many shapes which can never be fully described, too many flavors, in the air or on the tongue, half-colors, too many" (173–174). *The Handmaid's Tale* is specifically constructed so that Offred herself cannot have the last word.

Not only does her very language invite multiple interpretations, but also her text as we read it has been altered and edited by Pieixoto and Wade in ways Offred could not have anticipated.

If the language of Offred's narrative recalls Derrida's emphasis on the multiplicity of all language, the formal structure of *The Handmaid's Tale* recalls Derrida's insistence that all texts are assembled from bits and pieces of pre-existing discourse rather than originating in the subjective consciousness of an author. Atwood, for example, constructs the text in two parts, one of which is presumably Offred's diary and one of which is a transcript of the proceedings of an academic conference that has been convened to study that diary as reconstructed by Pieixoto and Wade. This combination of very different genres within a single text directly recalls Derrida's notion of *bricolage.* It is, in fact, somewhat reminiscent of Derrida's own *Glas,* in which he combines commentaries on the very different work of the philosopher G. W. F. Hegel and the novelist and playwright Jean Genet in a single text but prints these commentaries in different columns to call attention to their roots in different realms of discourse. *The Handmaid's Tale* also has a *bricolage* character on the level of the narrative itself. The text is, after all, assembled from thirty or so audiotapes discovered hidden in a foot locker two hundred years after the events related on the tapes. The text thus calls attention to its assembled nature and reminds readers that it might have been assembled otherwise, again undermining the notion that it (or, by implication, any other text) can provide a final and unambiguous statement of truth.

Offred's ability to retain a facility with language beyond that dictated for her by the authorities in Gilead constitutes an important part of her attempt to maintain a connection with the pre-Gilead past, when conditions were less oppressive. The complex formal structure of *The Handmaid's Tale* directly opposes the insistence of the Gileadean regime on imposing its own logocentric views on reality. Atwood thus gives Derrida's vision of the inherent multiplicity of language a specifically political twist. Of course, Atwood's Gilead is in many ways a parodic extension of Western culture, in which women have always suffered from a certain amount of linguistic oppression, as feminist critics have often noted. Her text thus continues the critique of logocentrism begun by Derrida, drawing on similar insights into the nature of the Western philosophical tradition but adding specific resonances derived from contemporary historical events.

Works Cited

Althusser, Louis. *Lenin and Philosophy and Other Essays.* Trans. Ben Brewster. London: Monthly Review, 1971.

Atwood, Margaret. *The Handmaid's Tale.* New York: Fawcett, 1987.

de Lauretis, Teresa. *Technologies of Gender: Essays on Theory, Film, and Fiction.* Bloomington: Indiana UP, 1987.

Derrida, Jacques. *Glas.* Trans. John P. Leavey, Jr. and Richard Rand. Lincoln: U of Nebraska P, 1986.

Elgin, Suzette Haden. *Native Tongue.* New York: DAW, 1984.
Kauffman, Linda. "Special Delivery: Twenty-First Century Epistolarity in *The Handmaid's Tale.*" In *Writing the Female Voice: Essays on Epistolary Literature,* ed. Elizabeth C. Goldsmith, 221-244. Boston: Northeastern UP, 1989.
Lacan, Jacques. *Écrits: A Selection.* Trans. Alan Sheridan. New York: Norton, 1977.
Le Guin, Ursula K. *The Dispossessed: An Ambiguous Utopia.* New York: Harper, 1991.
Stein, Karen F. "Margaret Atwood's *The Handmaid's Tale:* Scheherazade in Dystopia." *University of Toronto Quarterly* 61.2 (1991-1992): 269-279.

BAKHTINIAN CRITICISM

The work of Mikhail Bakhtin can be used to illuminate Margaret Atwood's *The Handmaid's Tale* in a number of ways. The language of Atwood's book is highly dialogic both in the general tendency of the narrator Offred to use language that might be interpreted differently by different readers and in the specifically literary nature of Offred's narrative, which establishes a dialogic connection with a number of different literary genres. The text of *The Handmaid's Tale* is inherently dialogic in structure because it is actually a hybrid product of Offred's original narration and of the scholar Pieixoto's later editing of that narrative. In addition, the sometimes playful character of Offred's narration contrasts strikingly with the official seriousness of the religious regime in Gilead much in the way that François Rabelais's carnivalesque writing, for Bakhtin, stands in opposition to the sterility and seriousness of the Catholic power structure in medieval Europe. The element of academic satire in the epilogue (and in certain other elements) of *The Handmaid's Tale* places the book within the context of Bakhtin's discussions of Menippean satire, and this generic placement usefully explains several otherwise anomalous features of Atwood's text.

Numerous critics have focused on the dialogic interaction between the voices of Offred and Pieixoto in the published version of Offred's narrative. Michele Lacombe, for example, describes the text as a "palimpsest" in which Pieixoto's version of the story is written over Offred's but in which Offred's voice is nevertheless still audible underneath. There are thus always at least two different simultaneous narrative voices at work in *The Handmaid's Tale,* though readers are not aware of the nature of this doubleness until they reach the epilogue. In a sense, however, this retroactive double voicing actually increases the dialogic nature of the text. Pieixoto's reinscription of Offred's narrative is an excellent example of what Bakhtin refers to as "reaccentuation"—the process through which speakers and writers repeat the words of previous speakers and writers but modify the meaning and orientation of those words by adding their own intonations. Indeed there is a double reaccentuation at work in *The Handmaid's Tale:* Not only does Pieixoto reaccentuate Offred's tapes in the process of editing and transcribing them, but also the epilogue relating his activities reaccentuates the entire preceding text and powerfully transforms our understanding of it.

Bakhtin sees the process of reaccentuation as particularly important in the genre of the novel, which draws many of its energies from a reaccentuation of a wide range of materials, including other literary genres. The novel tends to incorporate many such materials, which are transformed by their reappearance in the new context of the novel but which continue to bear traces of their original contexts, thus creating complex dialogic interactions. In particular, discourse that may be relatively inert in its original context can be powerfully energized within the dialogic context of the novel. Such discourse may "under changed conditions . . . emit bright new rays, burning away the reifying crust that had grown up around it" (*Dialogic* 419). For Bakhtin, one of the most important ways such energizing reaccentuation can occur in the novel involves what he refers to as "authoritative" language, that is, language that can brook no questioning or disagreement but that demands acquiescence: "The authoritative word demands that we acknowledge it, that we make it our own; it binds us, quite independent of any power it might have to persuade us internally; we encounter it with its authority already fused to it" (342). But for Bakhtin, always seeking signs of hope, language itself is inherently inimical to such authori-tarianism. He argues that all language is dialogic to some extent and that no single group or attitude can ever dominate language entirely. In every society there will be a dominant discourse (actually, a family of discourses), but that discourse can define itself only in relation to other repressed discourses with which it maintains a dialogic tension. Thus the very nature of language itself indicates that there will always be a possibility that opposing voices can arise, even if they must do so through parodic manipulation of the language of authority.

This view of language is particularly relevant to dystopian fictions such as *The Handmaid's Tale* because the oppressive regimes depicted in such fictions quite frequently employ language as a means of social control. As part of a larger attempt at total social domination, the fundamentalist Christian regime in the Republic of Gilead strives mightily to control the ways language is used in society. The regime seeks to impose its own authoritative language, the principal model of which is the language of the Bible, which the powers that be see as the direct, literal, and unchanging word of God. An appreciation of the centrality of literal interpretations of the Bible to the ideology of the Republic of Gilead points toward one of the most important implications of Atwood's construction of *The Handmaid's Tale* not as the literal diary of Offred but as Pieixoto's rewriting of that diary. *The Handmaid's Tale* is constructed very much like the New Testament, especially the four Gospels. These varying accounts of the life of Christ were, after all, constructed in their final canonical form by historical scholars many years after the actual events recounted. Thus just as Pieixoto's editing makes it impossible for us to recover the story of Offred's life in pure form, the complex textual history of the New Testament makes it impossible to recover the story of the life of Christ in pure form without the distorting contributions of later editors. The Gileadean insistence on literal interpretation of the Bible is further problematized because the editors who compiled the Bible did so based on a theory that the book was a highly complex, multileveled allegory, not a simple and direct expression of divine truth.

The Gileadean view of biblical language as monologic and authoritative leads to the establishment of an entire society based (at least ostensibly) on a similar vision of single, eternal truth. Clearly, however, Bakhtin's vision of the novel as a continually evolving genre that opposes any sense of final perfection is fundamentally opposed to such utopian visions of final perfection. As Yurij Striedter points out, dystopian novels are especially well suited to the kind of antiauthoritarian autocriticism described by Bakhtin, which involves a rejection of utopian pretensions: "Unmasking political utopian pretensions by laying bare the utopian pretensions of the novelistic word destroys the utopian pretensions of the utopian novel itself. The history of the utopian novel leads to the antiutopian novel" (186).

The overtly dialogic texture of *The Handmaid's Tale* stands in direct opposition to the kinds of linguistic domination sought by the rulers of Gilead. For Bakhtin, the novel, as an inherently dialogic genre, is by nature opposed to authoritative language. Bakhtin argues that there can be no authoritative language in the novel and that one of the most powerfully subversive aspects of the novel is its tendency to expose the pretensions of any authoritative discourse brought into it. In Bakhtin's view, the novel does not simply use language to represent reality in a transparent way. On the contrary, language itself is an object of representation (and criticism) in the novel, and authoritative discourse is stripped of its authority when represented in this way because the inherently dialogic and multivoiced linguistic environment of the novel is by its very nature critical of such authority. The novel form is oriented toward the creation and depiction of a world, and in the utopian form this world is endowed with wholeness and perfection. But for Bakhtin, the novel undermines its own utopian impulses through the antiauthoritarian texture of its heteroglossic language. The novel as a genre thus inherently includes certain dystopian impulses, which are then particularly emphasized in dystopian novels.

In a critical biography of Bakhtin, Katerina Clark and Michael Holquist note that Bakhtin's continual emphasis on linguistic energy and diversity had special resonances in a Stalinist context that was characterized by official attempts to limit and control language: "The official language had become homogenized and dominated all aspects of public life. Most literature and literary scholarship were mere subfunctions of the official rhetoric and myths. Official pronouncements were absolutely authoritative and final" (267). This description of the language of Stalinism has a great deal in common with Bakhtin's figuration of Catholic linguistic control in medieval Europe. But it also closely resembles the use of language as a tool of monological power in Atwood's Protestant Republic of Gilead.

The Handmaid's Tale generates some of its most important dialogic energies by enacting confrontations between different styles of language and in particular between different genres. Most obviously, the book places itself directly within the tradition of dystopian fiction, which carries a number of specific ideological resonances. Atwood draws on these resonances to enhance her critique of the fundamentalist regime in Gilead, which is thus directly linked to regimes such as the One State of Zamyatin's *We* or the Oceania of Orwell's *1984*. But dystopian fiction has long been a traditionally masculine genre, with feminist imaginative fictions tending to be more utopian in their orientation. *The Handmaid's Tale* thus encourages readers to examine the potential masculine biases of previous dystopian fictions while also providing a direct commentary on political developments in the 1980s, which from a feminist perspective tend to undermine the utopian optimism that informed much American feminist thought in the 1970s. As Peter Fitting notes, feminist visions of the future tended in general to show a dark turn in the 1980s, due primarily to such political reverses as the defeat of the Equal Rights Amendment and the growing political power of the anti-feminist religious right: "More recent fictions no longer give us images of a radically different future, in which the values and ideals of feminism have been extended to much of the planet, but rather offer depressing images of a brutal reestablishment of capitalist patriarchy" (142).

The Handmaid's Tale also initiates dialogues of the genre of dystopian fiction with several other genres. Linda Kauffman's placement of the text within the tradition of epistolary fiction calls attention to Offred's frequent insistence that she views her narrative as a conversation with an imaginary reader. "You don't tell a story only to yourself," Offred insists. "There's always someone else" (52). In this way, *The Handmaid's Tale* recalls Bakhtin's indication of the potential for dialogic interaction between text and reader and particularly to Bakhtin's notion that all literary texts (and in fact all utterances) are produced with the expectation of a response from another. Moreover it is clear that Offred seeks desperately to imagine a reader of her tale as a means of establishing contact with a sympathetic Other and thus stabilizing her own sense of identity, recalling the arguments of Bakhtin and Voloshinov that the human subject is a product of social interaction.

Atwood's book initiates a direct confrontation with the genre of scholarly history, the parody of which in the epilogue powerfully questions the usual assumption that such scholarly discourses present truth, as opposed to the fictions of literature which do not. Within the context of the obvious religious satire of *The Handmaid's Tale,* this subversive dialogue with scholarly discourse suggests that scientific and scholarly inquiries (which generally seek to distance themselves from the kinds of myth and superstition that they typically associate with religion) are quite similar to religious thought in their insistence on single and unambiguous truth. Atwood's parody of the pretentiousness of both scholarly and religious discourse is further enhanced by her placement of both genres in opposition to the "lowly" genres of popular culture. It is significant, for example, that Offred's narrative is originally discovered on tapes that are labeled as recordings by Elvis Presley, Boy George, Mantovani, and Twisted Sister, among others, all producers of secular popular culture of the kind banned in the Republic of Gilead. That these tapes also include some labeled as "Folk Songs of Lithuania" links these figures of popular culture with the kinds of folk cultural energies that Bakhtin describes in *Rabelais and His World* as powerfully subversive of official discourse. As Sandra Tomc points out, such "tacky unreadable texts" of popular culture stand in direct opposition to Pieixoto's academic tyranny and therefore "signify the potential of resistance and hope" (82).

Numerous critics have also observed that *The Handmaid's Tale* seems modeled largely on the genre of the female romance. After all, Offred's story is to some extent typical of those of the heroines of such popular romances: She waits in relative passivity, dreaming of escape, until a dynamic and active male (in this case, Nick) comes along to rescue her. Some critics have seen this reliance on the paradigm of female romance as a serious flaw in Atwood's book that undermines its ostensibly feminist purpose. But Tomc argues that however unsatisfactory "drugstore" romances might appear as a counter to official power, Atwood's use of this highly marginal, feminine-oriented genre can be taken as a gesture of defiance of the authority of traditional masculine literary values. By drawing so centrally on a genre that is generally treated with contempt by literary scholars, Atwood announces her refusal to construct her text according to the vision of the "literary" endorsed by those scholars. The use of female romance in *The Handmaid's Tale* can also be taken as Atwood's response to feminist critics who dismiss such genres as harmful to women. In this sense, Atwood's use of romance paradigms can be taken as an attack on censorship of all kinds—after all, the rise of the fundamentalist regime in Gilead begins when feminists start supporting the suppression of texts they find offensive.

In the use of material from so many different genres, in the frank treatment of matters (such as sexuality) that are often considered improper for discussion in polite company, in the critical examination of utopian ideals, in the satire of specific topical issues, and in the appeal to an imaginative plot that does not necessarily remain within the bounds of verisimilitude, *The Handmaid's Tale* closely resembles Bakhtin's description of the genre of Menippean satire in *Problems of Dostoevsky's Poetics.* Bakhtin also argues there that Menippean satires tend to be centrally informed by carnivalesque energies, and such energies are indeed prominent in *The Handmaid's Tale.* For example, if we recall the argument by Peter Stallybrass and Allon White that the hierarchical ranking of literary genres participates in the same movement by which Western society has tended to hierarchize bodily functions, then Atwood's appeal to the "lowly" genre of female romance can be seen as an openly carnivalesque gesture. Offred's refusal to conform to the somber and tragic language we might expect her to use in her situation can be taken as a similar carnivalesque violation of literary propriety. Such carnivalesque gestures are particularly effective in *The Handmaid's Tale* because of their stark contrast with the official seriousness of the Christian dictatorship of Gilead, just as Bakhtin finds the carnivalesque elements of the writing of Rabelais particularly powerful because of their opposition to official high seriousness in Catholic medieval Europe.

There are a number of openly carnivalesque moments in *The Handmaid's Tale,* just as we would expect in a work of Menippean satire. In one passage, for example, Offred recalls a conversation with her friend Moira while they were in training as handmaids. Moira, whose resistance to the Gileadean regime eventually leads to her forced employment as a prostitute in a brothel secretly operated by the hypocritical government of Gilead, suggests that the dour "Aunt Lydia," one of the women in charge of their training, might be having lesbian relationships with some of her trainees. When Offred expresses shock, Moira explains that such visions are healthy and useful. Later Offred realizes that Moira was right because "there is something powerful in the whispering of obscenities, about those in power" (287). The echo here of Bakhtin's discussion of Rabelais is clear. Later Offred again recalls Moira when she herself experiences an insight that is even more openly Rabelaisian. Realizing that she finds toilets reassuring, Offred concludes that this reassurance comes about because toilets and what they represent run directly counter to the rigid hierarchy of power that defines the society of Gilead: "Bodily functions at least remain democratic. Everybody shits, as Moira would say" (327).

There is also a carnivalesque element in Atwood's parodies of academic scholarship in the epilogue. The implication that the male scholars Pieixoto and Wade may have modified Offred's tale considerable in their editing of it opens the possibility that the bawdy humor that sometimes informs Offred's narrative is their addition, in which case the "carnivalesque" jokes in Offred's narrative would be at her own expense. Pieixoto himself makes several bawdy jokes about women in the course of the epilogue, thus providing a reminder that seemingly carnivalesque images can be used in the interest of official power as well as against it. The medieval carnival was, after all, an officially sanctioned function, and the violence that often played an important role in such carnivals was generally directed at women, the poor, and other groups marginal to the patriarchal structure of official medieval power.

Scholars such as Michael André Bernstein have thus warned against the potential dark side of the Bakhtinian carnival. This side plays a prominent role in *The Handmaid's Tale* because the Republic of Gilead officially sponsors a number of public rituals that can be seen as dark inversions of the Bakhtinian carnival. These include "Salvagings" (public hangings of women criminals who are supposedly being "saved" through Christian charity from the effects of their sins) and "Particicutions" (brutal public mutilation and murder of male transgressors in which groups of women act as executioners). These rituals, like the medieval carnival, allow individuals to release pent-up frustrations and hostilities without doing damage to official power. In fact, they work in direct support of official power. These rituals also reveal the hypocrisy of the Gileadean regime. Thus they might work against official power, just as Offred's irreverent language might work in the interests of such power. But such is the nature of carnivalesque imagery, which for Bakhtin is always inherently ambivalent. Such doubleness is central to Atwood's highly dialogic text, which conducts a scathing assault on the antifeminist biases of Christian fundamentalism while at the same time excoriating feminists for their own failures. By leaving so many questions unanswered and so many issues open to debate, Atwood strikingly enacts Bakhtin's famous dictum that no human experience is ever totally completed and that there can never be a "last word" on any topic.

Works Cited

Atwood, Margaret. *The Handmaid's Tale.* New York: Fawcett, 1987.

Bakhtin, M. M. *The Dialogic Imagination.* Ed. Michael Holquist. Trans. Caryl Emerson and Michael Holquist. Austin: U of Texas P, 1981.

———. *Problems of Dostoevsky's Poetics.* Trans. and ed. Caryl Emerson. Minneapolis: U of Minnesota P, 1984.

———. *Rabelais and His World.* Trans. Helene Iswolsky. Bloomington: Indiana UP, 1984.

Bernstein, Michael André. *Bitter Carnival: Ressentiment and the Abject Hero.* Princeton, N.J.: Princeton UP, 1992.

Clark, Katerina, and Michael Holquist. *Mikhail Bakhtin.* Cambridge, Mass.: Belknap, 1984.

Fitting, Peter. "The Turn from Utopia in Recent Feminist Fiction." In *Feminism, Utopia, and Narrative,* ed. Libby Falk Jones and Sarah Webster Goodwin, 141-158. Knoxville: U of Tennessee P, 1990.

Kauffman, Linda. "Special Delivery: Twenty-First Century Epistolarity in *The Handmaid's Tale.*" In *Writing the Female Voice: Essays on Epistolary Literature,* ed. Elizabeth C. Goldsmith, 221-244. Boston: Northeastern UP, 1989.

Lacombe, Michele. "The Writing on the Wall: Amputated Speech in Margaret Atwood's *The Handmaid's Tale.*" *Wascana Review* 21.2 (1986): 2-12.

Orwell, George. *1984.* New York: New American Library, 1961.

Stallybrass, Peter, and Allon White. *The Politics and Poetics of Transgression.* Ithaca, N.Y.: Cornell UP, 1986.

Striedter, Yurij. "Three Postrevolutionary Russian Utopian Novels." In *The Russian Novel from Pushkin to Pasternak,* ed. John Garrard, 177-201. New Haven, Conn.: Yale UP, 1983.

Tomc, Sandra. "'The Missionary Position': Feminism and Nationalism in Margaret Atwood's *The Handmaid's Tale.*" *Canadian Literature* 138-139 (Fall-Winter 1993): 73-87.

Voloshinov, V. N. *Marxism and the Philosophy of Language.* Trans. Ladislav Matejka and I. R. Titunik. Cambridge, Mass: Harvard UP, 1986.

Zamyatin, Yevgeny. *We.* Trans. Mirra Ginsberg. New York: Avon, 1983.

FOUCAULDIAN CRITICISM

Beginning a discussion of *The Handmaid's Tale* with a quotation from Michel Foucault on the complex relationship between sexuality and power in modern society, Amin Malak suggests that any reader of Atwood's book "needs to recall Foucault's observation to contextualize the agonies of the narrator-protagonist" (9). *The Handmaid's Tale* serves in many ways as an exemplary literary dramatization of some of Foucault's major ideas. Atwood's book reacts directly to the growing political power of the American religious right in the 1980s, projecting a nightmare future in which the forces of religious fundamentalism have established control of the government. These forces then impose their ideology on the entire populace, seeking to dominate and control every aspect of the lives of individual citizens, much in the mode of Foucault's notion of the carceral society. As we might expect in a fundamentalist regime, official power in the Republic of Gilead is focused largely on the control and administration of sexuality, thus echoing

Foucault's important elaboration of the connection between sexuality and power in modern society.

It comes as no surprise, then, that critics such as Malak have often appealed to the work of Foucault in their discussions of the book. Stephanie Barbé Hammer, for example, notes the relative lack of conventional technology in Atwood's future society and suggests that this lack comes about because this society emphasizes the technology of power rather than of machinery, in the mode of Foucault's discussions of "discipline" (45). Hammer goes on to observe how techniques of surveillance and manipulation in Gilead respond quite closely to those described by Foucault. Linda Kauffman works from an explicitly Foucauldian perspective to conclude that in *The Handmaid's Tale,* "sex and politics are indistinguishable as transfer points of power and oppression in a society under siege" (226). Kauffman also relates the complete regimentation of life in Gilead to Foucault's notion of the carceral society. Not only are the citizens of Gilead slotted into rigidly defined roles in an overarching system of social controls, but also every movement made by individuals is carefully scheduled and then monitored to assure compliance with the schedule. For example, a system of bells (which the narrator Offred specifically compares to the bells formerly used in nunneries) is used to signal times for specific activities. Offred, as a "handmaid," occupies one of the most throughly controlled positions in the society of Gilead: She is even granted only a specific number of minutes in the bathroom each day. Kauffman also points out that the extreme regimentation of life in Gilead is reinforced by an elaborate technology of punishment.

A quick look at Foucault's description of the discursive production of sexuality in modern society shows the obvious relevance of his work to *The Handmaid's Tale.* As opposed to Sigmund Freud's "repressive hypothesis" that modern societies gain power through a repression of sexual energies, Foucault argues that modern society seeks not to repress or even destroy sexuality but instead to administer and use it to society's advantage. In short, sexuality, rather than opposing official power, may actually support it: "Pleasure and power do not cancel or turn back against one another; they seek out, overlap, and reinforce one another" (*History* 48). For Foucault, sexuality is not so much a matter of natural instinctive impulses as of socially and discursively conditioned responses. He describes sexuality as "an especially dense transfer point for relations of power" (103). In particular, sexuality functions as a focal point for an entire array of practices through which modern society has attempted to constitute the individual as a subject of administrative control.

Foucault's description of administered sexuality matches the practices of the Republic of Gilead quite closely. Offred's narrative in *The Handmaid's Tale* reveals quite clearly that the regime in Gilead, despite its puritanical aversion to sexual pleasure, does not seek to eradicate sexuality but simply to control and administer it. Indeed the entire society is to a large extent organized around sexuality, both in its emphasis on the family structure and in its implementation of the handmaid system as a means of producing offspring. Offred, like many fertile women living in Gilead, is thus forced into functioning in a role that is principally sexual in nature. As a result of deteriorating environmental conditions, most of the women (or at least most of the Caucasian women) in this near-future society are sterile—as probably are most of the men, though in Gilead the infertility of a couple is always attributed to the woman. Nevertheless the fundamentalist regime in Gilead strictly voids the use of any technological aid to the solution of the population crisis. Gilead's leaders insist, presumably on the authority of scripture, on strictly "natural" means of procreation, though the actual way they go about achieving such procreation within the framework of the traditional Western nuclear family is highly artificial. They establish the institution of the handmaids, whose function (authorized by the biblical story of Jacob, Rachel, and Bilhah) is to be impregnated by husbands while their (presumably infertile) wives look on during highly ritualized ceremonies that are supposedly sacred but that function somewhat like unpleasant medical procedures. This ceremony is obligatory for both the husband and the handmaid; it is strictly impersonal, and individual choice (like individual pleasure) plays no part.

The Handmaid's Tale derives from the diary of Offred, who succinctly describes her role as a handmaid, noting that her sexual services are intended for breeding purposes only, with no hint of pleasure or affection (176). But despite precautions to the contrary, a private connection of sorts does develop between Offred and the Commander, the husband who is assigned to impregnate her. He induces her to start meeting with him privately, and in these sessions they enact various transgressions, such as reading banned books and playing Scrabble, a game forbidden to women because it promotes literacy. In this way, the text seems to support Foucault's point that the will to knowledge is actually more fundamental in modern society than the desire for sex.

Meanwhile the Commander's wife (a former gospel singer whose stage name was "Serena Joy") suspects the Commander of being sterile, so she recruits Offred to engage in covert sexual relations with the chauffeur Nick in the hope that the handmaid will thereby become pregnant and bring increased status to the family. Offred herself then becomes emotionally attached to Nick, and the couple secretly begins its own private series of sexual liaisons in addition to those arranged by Serena Joy. Sexual energies that are ostensibly transgressive thus circulate rather freely in the text, despite the repressive environment. As opposed to the ritual nature of the handmaid ceremony, these "extracurricular" sexual activities are endowed with an aura of secrecy, corresponding to Foucault's observation that in modern society sexuality is consistently regarded as "harboring a fundamental secret" and that as a consequence sexuality is thought to be the locus of "the fragment of darkness that we each carry within us" (69).

Importantly, though, Offred's secret liaisons with the Commander are conducted strictly under his orders, and she remains a tool of his power. Similarly her relationship with Nick is, at least initially, authorized by Serena Joy. Despite the decidedly antierotic figuration of the handmaid's role in this puritanical society, even exotic sexual pleasure is secretly endorsed by the powers that be in Gilead in the form of the authorized brothels where the Jezebels ply their trade under strict government control and where the wildest fantasies of the clientele can be realized. Even lesbian relationships between Jezebels are openly condoned, though the society at large is violently homophobic. And when the Commander takes Offred to one of these brothels to have sexual intercourse with her outside the bounds of the impersonal ritual of the handmaid ceremony, she submits not out of private loyalty or feeling but merely out of her firm understanding of the workings of power that are involved. Even the relationship between Nick and Offred turns out to be highly political; he is apparently an agent of the "Mayday" underground, and his interest in Offred may be largely due to his understanding that she is in a position to extract useful information from the Commander. But he may also be an agent of the secret police charged with keeping the populace under constant surveillance. In any case, sexuality functions in the final analysis not as a counter to political power in Gilead but as one of the most effective tools through which that power is manifested (and opposed).

Sex in the Republic of Gilead is a matter not of emotion or biology but of pure political power. Indeed every aspect of this society functions as part of a total system of behavioral controls. The religious emphasis that centrally informs the society is concerned not with spiritual salvation but with political domination. Television programming in Gilead consists primarily of religious programs and of heavily biased news reports that are little more than official propaganda. And literature is even more strictly censored and controlled. Most women are not allowed to read at all; the signs in stores consist of pictorial symbols so that shopping will not require reading. Even the Bible is considered highly dangerous. In family groups such as the one around which *The Handmaid's Tale* is centered, the Bible can be read only by the Commander, though he does sometimes read passages aloud to his wife and female servants for their group edification. As Offred explains, "The Bible is kept locked up, the way people once kept tea locked up, so the servants wouldn't steal it. It is an incendiary device: who knows what we'd make of it, if we ever got our hands on it? We can be read to from it, by him, but we cannot read" (112).

This secrecy already hints that there may be something fraudulent about the religious ideology that rules Gilead, and indeed Atwood's text is full of such hints. The official policies of Gilead are invariably justified by biblical precedent, but as no one but the leaders of the "republic" have access to the Bible, they are able to claim biblical precedent for almost anything they want. The Gileadeans have in fact imported a number of bits of spurious Christian ideology, as when the distribution of women as sexual objects among men in the society is justified by a perversion of Karl Marx that is claimed to come from Saint Paul himself, in Acts: "From each according to her ability: to each according to his needs" (151).

Such "biblical" slogans, intended to evoke political obedience rather than spiritual elevation, are often chanted in the various communal ceremonies that Gilead uses as a central means of indoctrination of its citizens. These ceremonies mimic Christian rituals, but they often have a dark tone that strongly recalls the rituals of public torture and execution described by Foucault in relation to technologies of power prominent in Europe prior to the modern period. One such ceremony is the "Salvaging," the name of which carries hints of Christian salvation of those who have strayed but which is in reality nothing more than a public hanging of groups of subversives, who serve as a focus for mass hatred—and as a warning to potential opponents of the regime. This hatred surfaces most violently in the ritual of "Particicution," a chilling reinscription of medieval public executions in which groups of women servants act as executioners: They are whipped to a frenzy by incendiary rhetoric, turned loose on a convicted transgressor against society, and encouraged to beat the victim to death, thus gaining their full complicity in the enforcement of the rules of the state. Even "sinners" who are not publicly executed still have their bodies put on public display, hanging for days from hooks set in a wall as an abject reminder of the fate that awaits such sinners.

Atwood further emphasizes the lack of a true spiritual basis for the religiosity of Gilead in a number of ways, as when Offred describes the "Soul Scrolls" shop, where a person can order (for a fee) by telephone any one of five prefabricated prayers. These commodified prayers are then produced by machines, without human intervention: "There are no people inside the building: the machines run by themselves" (216). This shop serves as a fairly obvious symbol of the mechanical, dehumanized, and spiritually bankrupt nature of religion in Gilead, but this suggestion is made all the more powerful because of the way it closely parallels certain highly automated and commercialized religious activities (like dial-a-prayer telephone lines) that already exist in 1980s America. Although Atwood's book is a little vague about the mechanisms by which the theocracy of Gilead managed to supplant the U.S. government, her vision does gain energy from the fact that the seeds of her dystopia do exist in the contemporary efforts of the American religious right to enforce its beliefs through political power.

It is no accident that Foucault's analyses of the carceral elements in modern society correspond so well to Atwood's depiction of the Republic of Gilead. As Kauffman puts it, "Like Foucault, Atwood is writing a history of the present" (242). Both Foucault and Atwood are responding to phenomena already present in contemporary Western society, and the clear relevance of Foucault's work to Atwood's dystopian vision is of considerable help in illuminating the links between Atwood's projected future and practices already under way in the present. For example, Atwood calls attention to the fact that Gilead is not an entirely new departure for America and that an element of religious fundamentalism has always been present in American culture. Thus *The Handmaid's Tale* is partially dedicated to Mary Webster, one of Atwood's own ancestors who was publically hanged as a witch in Puritan New England, thus linking the Republic of Gilead to America's Puritan past. The numerous parallels between the practices of the Republic of Gilead and those of the medieval Inquisition suggest that the oppressive religious energies that inform Atwood's dystopia have been present in Western civilization for centuries. That a resurgence of these energies could occur reinforces Foucault's suggestion that official power has not diminished in modern Western society but has simply been routed in more subtle directions.

Atwood's delineation of the complex interrelationships among power, sexuality, and discipline in Gilead provides a striking dramatization of Foucault's ideas in these areas. *The Handmaid's Tale* also recalls Foucault in its satirical treatment of the work of historians in the epilogue. Professor Pieixoto, the keynote speaker at the academic conference of historians featured in the epilogue, is the kind of conventional historian that Foucault frequently criticizes in his work. Pieixoto seeks to find a single version of historical truth and to construct smooth, continuous narratives that precisely and unambiguously explain the course of history. He thus fails to appreciate Foucault's insistence that all historical accounts are necessarily partial and that many different accounts of history can be produced depending on the assumptions of the historians doing the producing. The scenario presented in the epilogue tends to support Foucault's, rather than Pieixoto's, vision of history. After all, the Republic of Gilead has long since passed from the scene, much in the mode of Foucault's vision of history as a sequence of distinct epochs, each of which can differ radically from the others. Atwood's text offers no explanation for the passing of Gilead, much as Foucault (believing that such processes are far too complex to be described in simple cause-effect terms) refuses to speculate on the specific causes of the shift from one epoch to another in the movement of history.

Atwood reinforces this element of academic satire by locating the capital of the Republic of Gilead in Cambridge, Massachusetts (one of the main centers of American academic life) and by dedicating her book partially to Perry Miller, a well-known literary and historical scholar whose work emphasizes the centrality of the Puritan heritage to American culture. Miller is especially well known for his two-volume work *The New England Mind* (1936, 1953), in which he attempts to depict the New England Puritans as tough, hardworking, independent, and energetic. In *The Handmaid's Tale,* Atwood clearly suggests that this energetic Puritan spirit, because of the rejection of difference that underlies it, can lead to tyranny and oppression rather than expansion and dynamism. And the Puritan rejection of difference derives precisely from a tendency to see the world in terms of polar dualities based on the God-Satan opposition, a phenomenon that Foucault in *The Care of the Self* describes as central to Christian thought in general.

Atwood's depiction of an academic conference in the epilogue and her dedication of *The Handmaid's Tale* to Perry Miller suggest that traditional modes of scholarship, with their dehumanizing insistence on single, authoritative versions of truth, are complicitous with the ideology of puritanism. As Sandra Tomc puts it, Atwood is criticizing "not just the persistence of a puritan strain in modern American culture but a tradition of American studies that celebrates Puritan intransigence as quintessentially representative of the American spirit" (80). Here again Atwood echoes Foucault and his memorable declaration that he should not be expected to adhere to the rules of conventional scholarship because it is the job not of scholars but of "our bureaucrats and our police to see that our papers are in order. At least spare us their morality when we write" (*Archaeology* 17). This rejection of conventional morality as a guide for historical scholarship is very much in the spirit of Atwood's academic satire in *The Handmaid's Tale,* just as the dystopian carceral society of Atwood's book corresponds closely to Foucault's warnings about the increasing regimentation of modern life.

Works Cited

Atwood, Margaret. *The Handmaid's Tale.* New York: Fawcett, 1987.

Foucault, Michel. *The Archaeology of Knowledge and the Discourse on Language.* Trans. A. M. Sheridan Smith. New York: Pantheon, 1972.

———. *The Care of the Self.* Vol. 3 of *The History of Sexuality.* Trans. Robert Hurley. New York: Vintage, 1988.

———. *The History of Sexuality.* Vol. 1, *An Introduction.* Trans. Robert Hurley. New York: Vintage, 1980.

Hammer, Stephanie Barbé. "The World as It Will Be? Female Satire and the Technology of Power in *The Handmaid's Tale.*" *Modern Language Studies* 20.2 (1990): 39-49.

Kauffman, Linda. "Special Delivery: Twenty-First Century Epistolarity in *The Handmaid's Tale.*" In *Writing the Female Voice: Essays on Epistolary Literature,* ed. Elizabeth C. Goldsmith, 221-244. Boston: Northeastern UP, 1989.

Malak, Amin. "Margaret Atwood's *The Handmaid's Tale* and the Dystopian Tradition." *Canadian Literature* 112 (1987): 9-16.

Miller, Perry. *The New England Mind.* (2 vols). Vol. 1: *The Seventeenth Century.* 1936. Vol. 2: *From Colony to Province.* 1953. Boston: Beacon, 1953.

Tomc, Sandra. "'The Missionary Position': Feminism and Nationalism in Margaret Atwood's *The Handmaid's Tale.*" *Canadian Literature* 138-139 (Fall-Winter 1993): 73-87.

SELECTED BIBLIOGRAPHY

Booker, M. Keith. *The Dystopian Impulse in Modern Literature: Fiction as Social Criticism.* Westport, Conn.: Greenwood, 1994.

Studies modern dystopian fiction and its relation to the work of literary and cultural critics such as Adorno, Benjamin, Foucault, and Bakhtin. Includes an extensive discussion of *The Handmaid's Tale* in this context, emphasizing the feminist implications of Atwood's critique of Christian fundamentalism, but also placing Atwood's book within the larger context of Western postmodernism.

Caldwell, Larry W. "Wells, Orwell, and Atwood: (EPI)Logic and Eu/Utopia." *Extrapolation* 33.4 (1992): 333-345.

Reads *The Handmaid's Tale* within the context of More's *Utopia,* Wells's *The Time Machine,* and Orwell's *1984.* Notes in particular how Atwood's book shares certain complex narrative structures with these other texts and how the epilogue of Atwood's book participates in a tradition of situating utopian and dystopian works within "pseudo-scholarly" frameworks.

Deer, Glenn. "Rhetorical Strategies in *The Handmaid's Tale:* Dystopia and the Paradoxes of Power." *English Studies in Canada* 18.2 (1992): 215-233.

Argues that the effectiveness of Atwood's satire in *The Handmaid's Tale* is com-promised by a "contradictory fascination" with the very horrors it criticizes. Notes in particular that Offred is a sophisticated and authoritarian narrator who manipulates her audience in ways reminiscent of the abuses of power that the book associates with the regime in Gilead. Does not acknowledge, however, that Offred's account has been edited by others.

Filipczak, Dorota. "'Is There No Balm in Gilead?': Biblical Intertext in *The Handmaid's Tale.*" *Journal of Literature and Theology* 7.2 (1993): 171-185.

Presents a detailed discussion of the appearances of the Gilead theme in the Bible and of their relevance to *The Handmaid's Tale.* Argues that the interpretive closure enforced by the fundamentalist regime in Gilead is inconsistent with the complexity of the Bible itself as a text, but that Atwood's book does not bring out this point.

Finnell, Susanna. "Unwriting the Quest: Margaret Atwood's Fiction and *The Handmaid's Tale.*" *Women and the Journey: The Female Travel Experience,* 199-215. Ed. Bonnie Frederick and Susan H. McLeod. Pullman: Washington State UP, 1993.

Discusses *The Handmaid's Tale* within the context of the masculine tradition of the quest narrative and notes how the text ultimately subverts this tradition by refusing to bring the quest to a conventional completion.

Foley, Michael. "Satiric Intent in the 'Historical Notes' Epilogue of Margaret Atwood's *The Handmaid's Tale.*" *Commonwealth* 11.2 (1989): 44-52.

Emphasizes the importance of the epilogue to the overall satirical message of *The Handmaid's Tale.* Argues that the epilogue shows how "intellectually and morally bankrupt" attitudes such as racism and sexism "can flourish in the temple of dispassionate thought and inquiry itself, the university" (51).

Freibert, Lucy M. "Control and Creativity: The Politics of Risk in Margaret Atwood's *The Handmaid's Tale.*" In *Critical Essays on Margaret Atwood,* ed. Judith McCombs, 280-291. Boston: G. K. Hall, 1988.

Discusses the ways *The Handmaid's Tale* "deconstructs Western phallocentrism and explores those aspects of French feminist theory that offer women a measure of hope" (280-281). Notes the relevance of Cixous's notion of *l'écriture féminine* to Atwood's demonstration of the ability of women to use language to escape conditioning and attempt to reclaim their own identities.

Hammer, Stephanie Barbé. "The World as It Will Be? Female Satire and the Technology of Power in *The Handmaid's Tale.*" *Modern Language Studies* 20.2 (1990): 39-49.

Reads *The Handmaid's Tale* within the context of satire, suggesting that the book is "at once a text-book example of modern fictional satire and at the same time a clever appropiration of a predominantly male literature for feminist purposes" (46). Focuses on the book's critique of subtle technologies of power and domination as implemented in Gilead—and in our own world.

Hansen, Elaine Tuttle. "Mothers Tomorrow and Mothers Yesterday, but Never Mothers Today: *Woman on the Edge of Time* and *The Handmaid's Tale.*" In *Narrating Mothers: Theorizing Maternal Subjectivities,* ed. Brenda O. Daly and Maureen T. Reddy, 21-43. Knoxville: U of Tennessee P, 1991.

Compares *The Handmaid's Tale* to Marge Piercy's *Woman on the Edge of Time* in terms of their treatment of motherhood, noting the complex relationship between motherhood and femininity and the difficulty of adequately representing this relationship in literature.

Jones, Dorothy. "Not Much Balm in Gilead." *Commonwealth* 11.2 (1989): 31-43.
Discusses the dystopian impact of *The Handmaid's Tale* by comparing the book's imagery to the utopian tradition, especially as embodied in biblical images of earthly paradise. Notes how the motif of enclosure often compromises utopian visions and effaces the boundary between utopia and dystopia. Sees the ending of Atwood's book as ultimately hopeful and optimistic.

Kauffman, Linda. "Special Delivery: Twenty-First Century Epistolarity in *The Handmaid's Tale*." In *Writing the Female Voice: Essays on Epistolary Literature*," ed. Elizabeth C. Goldsmith, 221-244. Boston: Northeastern UP, 1989.
Reads *The Handmaid's Tale* within the context of epistolary literature. Also provides a particularly useful treatment of the book within the framework of the theories of Foucault.

Ketterer, David. "Margaret Atwood's *The Handmaid's Tale:* A Contextual Dystopia." *Science-Fiction Studies* 16 (1989): 209-217.
Reads *The Handmaid's Tale* as a "contextual dystopia"—that is, as a dystopia that is concerned not only with the delineation of a nightmare future society but also with a treatment of society as it stands both before and after the particular dystopian period in question. Notes the sexism that still seems prevalent in the year 2195 in the epilogue.

Lacombe, Michele. "The Writing on the Wall: Amputated Speech in Margaret Atwood's *The Handmaid's Tale*." *Wascana Review* 21.2 (1986): 2-12.
Discusses the relationship between Offred's diary and Pieixoto's editing of it, describing the text as a palimpsest in which Pieixoto's version of the story is written over Offred's.

Malak, Amin. "Margaret Atwood's *The Handmaid's Tale* and the Dystopian Tradition." *Canadian Literature* 112 (1987): 9-16.
Indicates the importance of reading *The Handmaid's Tale* through the optic of Foucault's discussion of the relationship between sexuality and power. Discusses Atwood's book within the context of dystopian fictions such as *We, 1984*, and *Brave New World.*

Reesman, Jeanne Campbell. "Dark Knowledge in *The Handmaid's Tale*." *CEA Critic* 53.3 (1991): 6-22.
Suggests that Atwood writes in *The Handmaid's Tale* in a hermeneutic mode that leads to continuing dialogue rather than to final epistemological interpretation.

Stein, Karen F. "Margaret Atwood's *The Handmaid's Tale:* Scheherazade in Dystopia." *University of Toronto Quarterly* 61.2 (1991-1992): 269-279.
Emphasizes the relation between the narrator and the tale in *The Handmaid's Tale.* Notes that the text is importantly informed by a dialogue between Offred's original narrative and Pieixoto's editing of it.

Tomc, Sandra. "'The Missionary Position': Feminism and Nationalism in Margaret Atwood's *The Handmaid's Tale*." *Canadian Literature* 138-139 (Fall-Winter 1993): 73-87.
Reads *The Handmaid's Tale* within the context of Atwood's Canadian nationalist opposition to American cultural and economic domination. Discusses the importance of Atwood's dialogue with Perry Miller and American traditions of literary scholarship.

chapter **15**

Approaches to *Beloved*, by Toni Morrison

Toni Morrison, winner of the Nobel Prize for literature in 1993, is one of America's most respected living authors. Her work is also part of a broad phenomenon in which African-American literature (especially that produced African-American women writers) has come to be recognized as one of the most vital and exciting forces in contemporary American culture. Morrison's work is marked not only by its intense engagement with important social and political issues but also by its literary complexity and sophistication. *Beloved,* a work of genuine artistic brilliance that addresses some of the most profound (if unpleasant) issues in American history, is possibly Morrison's most important work to date. It is no surprise, then, that literary critics have shown a great deal of interest in *Beloved* and Morrison's other work or that recent criticism of Morrison's work has tended to be informed by a strong theoretical element. This section presents discussions of potential critical approaches to *Beloved* through the use of New Critical, psychoanalytic, Marxist, and feminist approaches. Multicultural criticism (perhaps the most obvious approach to *Beloved*) is not discussed per se, both because the applicability of multicultural criticism to Morrison's work is so obvious and because all of the discussions presented here are already informed by multicultural perspectives. Of course, other approaches could be used as well. For example, the issues of power and domination and the mixtures of different literary genres and modes that inform *Beloved* would be of great interest, respectively, to Foucauldian and Bakhtinian critics.

THE NEW CRITICISM

Beloved is an extremely complex work of art that employs a number of sophisticated, self-conscious literary strategies. These strategies powerfully interact with the content of the book to make a statement about slavery and its effects; the impact of this statement potentially exceeds any that might be achieved through a direct "scientific" account of the historical facts. In the depiction of Schoolteacher's attempts to construct a scientific description of the behavior of slaves, Morrison suggests a direct relationship between scientific uses of language and the ideology of domination that made slavery possible. Morrison's own highly literary language then serves as a counter to the dehumanizing scientific discourse employed by Schoolteacher and his pupils.

In many ways, then, *Beloved* seems ideally suited for analysis by the techniques of the New Criticism. Nevertheless Morrison's book directly challenges the most fundamental assumptions on which the New Critical approach is based. *Beloved,* whatever its formal brilliance, derives its power from the importance of its historical context and from its intense engagement with that context. Morrison's major project in the book is to provide reminders of the genuine horrors of slavery and of the immense human suffering that institution entailed. The significance of this project clearly cannot be appreciated by purely formalist analysis. Moreover Morrison's depiction of the human consequences of slavery radically undermines the New Critics' vision of the antebellum South as an idyllic paradise free of the alienation they associate with modern industrial capitalism.

Probably the most obvious literary strategy employed by Morrison in *Beloved* occurs in the construction of the plot of the book. Following a distinction made by the Russian formalists, the New Critics emphasize that there is a strict difference between a story—as a sequence of events in chronological order—and a plot, which is the "structure of the action *as presented* in a piece of fiction" (Brooks and Warren 80). This presentation may involve a great deal of artistic intervention and restructuring of the action in nonsequential order. The fictional story of Sethe and her children is based on the real historical experiences of Margaret Garner, a slave who escaped from a Kentucky farm in 1856 and crossed the Ohio River to take refuge in Cincinnati. Recaptured there by slave hunters, Garner cut the throat of her young daughter to prevent the child from being returned to slavery. In transforming these events into fiction, Morrison changes a number of the details to enhance the impact of her narrative. Perhaps most important, she relates the story not in chronological sequence, as might a conventional historian, but in a highly complex and nonlinear form. The plot functions as a kind of puzzle, with bits and pieces of the story gradually falling into place as the reader makes her way through the book. Rather than present the narrative from the single objective point of view typical of most conventional histories, Morrison narrates different parts of the story from the perspectives of different characters, allowing readers better to appreciate the human dimension of the events she is describing rather than simply seeing them as a sequence of "facts."

Morrison's complex narrative can sometimes be disorienting, or even confusing, but even this confusion serves a positive function. Morrison herself has suggested that the sudden shifts and changes that her readers must negotiate are intended to give them something of the flavor of the experience of the original slaves, snatched from their homes in Africa and then transported inexplicably into slavery in America ("Unspeakable" 228). In addition, Morrison's disavowal of chronological sequence challenges the linear models of history typical of Western culture. In that sense, her plot structure clearly shows the influence of alternative cultural perspectives, including both African and African-American oral storytelling traditions.

Nonlinear plots are also typical of the modernist literature that was so central to the work of the New Critics. Such plots were often employed by modernist authors precisely as challenges to rational Western models of linear history. One of the most striking aspects of *Beloved* is its effective combination of elements and techniques from the African-American oral tradition and from European and American modernism. The plot of *Beloved,* which is revealed to readers in nonlinear fashion, is particularly reminiscent of the work of William Faulkner, whose technique is sometimes referred to as "plotting by discovery." Peter Brooks describes the plot of Faulkner's *Absalom, Absalom!* (a text also very much concerned with both history and historiography) in a manner highly relevant to *Beloved:* "The novel becomes a kind of detective story where the object of investigation—the mystery—is the narrative design, or plot, itself" (294).

Morrison's echoes of European modernism (and especially of the white southerner Faulkner) may seem ironic, but it is not really surprising given that Morrison wrote her master's thesis at Cornell University on the work of Faulkner and Virginia Woolf. The complex plot structure of *Beloved* is also highly reminiscent of Robert Penn Warren's New Critical suggestion that a successful work of fiction should delay resolution of the plot as long as possible, gaining energy by forcing the reader to work through conflicts and contradictions to reach a final conclusion about the text. *Beloved* seems directly to verify the New Critical perception that an artistically constructed plot, with its various delays, digressions, and violations of chronological sequence, can ultimately make a far more powerful statement about human experience than can a mere retelling of facts in linear order.

In *Understanding Fiction,* Brooks and Warren (in typical New Critical fashion) insist on the importance of "the relation of plot to the resources of language which the writer uses" (84). Here again Morrison's text seems to respond well to New Critical analysis. She frequently uses figurative, connotative language, often taking particular advantage of the potential multiple meanings of language. For example, a key image that runs throughout the text is that of "possession," but Morrison carefully builds on the multiple meanings of this word. In *Beloved,* "possession" may mean ownership (especially the ownership of slaves), it may refer to the notion of possession by a ghost, or it may mean the kind of possession indicated by the term *self-possessed,* as in Baby Suggs's suggestion that white people simply "don't know when to stop" (104).

In a similar fashion, the last chapter of *Beloved* repeats three times the declaration that Beloved's story "was not a story to pass on" (274–275). At first glance, this declaration seems to mean that the story is too horrific to be retold, that Sethe, Paul D, Denver, and the others involved in it need to put it behind them once and for all to get on with their lives. Yet this meaning seems directly to contradict the whole project of Morrison's book, which is to assure that stories like this one are not forgotten. Moreover the triple repetition of this passage suggests that we should look at it with special care. A closer look reminds us that to "pass on" a story can also mean to decline to tell it or listen to: in short, to ignore it. The declaration can also mean that the story should not be allowed to expire or be forgotten because to "pass on" also means to die. Indeed early in the text Sethe suggests just this sort of meaning in relation to stories from the past when she tells her daughter Denver that some things from the past simply disappear from memory, or "pass on," while others can never be forgotten (35–36). The clear tension between the potential meanings of this final declaration—that Beloved's story should *not* be told and that it *must* be told—makes the declaration more powerful, even as it also evokes the entire history of slave narratives, which have traditionally revealed many of the conditions of slavery while repressing (through censorship, either overt or subtle) some of its more horrific aspects.

The impact of Morrison's text is often enhanced by literary uses of language that deviate significantly from ordinary "standard" language use. For example, Morrison often uses African-American dialects in depicting the speech of her African-American characters. She also links her narrative to African-American storytelling traditions through the use of colloquial language that flows in the text with oral, sometimes musical, rhythms. Numerous critics (Linda Krumholz, Ashraf H. A. Rushdy) have thus emphasized the importance of oral elements in the narration of *Beloved.* This technique is probably most obvious in the chapters directly narrated by the characters, as when Sethe begins her section: "Beloved, she my daughter. She mine. See. She come back to me of her own free will and I don't have to explain a thing" (200). Similarly the later section narrated by Beloved, with its broken syntax and lack of punctuation, reflects through the texture of its language the agony and confusion of the slave experience of which Beloved is an allegorical marker (210–213).

For the New Critics, metaphor is a crucial element of literary language, just as for the Russian formalists the use of striking metaphors can be an effective technique of defamiliarization. But one of Morrison's more interesting linguistic strategies involves a defamiliarization of metaphor itself. She sometimes reverses the normal relationship between literal and figurative language in *Beloved* when she employs in a literal sense words or expressions that are normally used metaphorically. For example, in the first encounter between Paul D and Sethe, he tenderly cups her breasts from behind, giving her a feeling of relief that, for once, "the responsibility for her breasts . . . was in somebody else's hands." She thus feels relieved of the "weight" of her breasts (18). Here both the phrase *in somebody else's hands* and the phrase *relieved of the weight* would normally be read as metaphors for a transfer of responsibility, yet the situation actually dictates literal readings: The physical weight of Sethe's breasts is indeed in Paul D's hands. Later as Beloved's attentions gradually drive Paul D to take up residence in one room, then another of the house at 124 Bluestone, we are told that "she moved him" (114). Again we would normally read this expression metaphorically as a suggestion that she had a strong emotional impact on Paul D. But in context, we learn that she literally and physically causes him to move about the house.

In such passages, Morrison renews worn and clichéd metaphors by causing us to look at them in new and different ways—as Jean Wyatt puts it, to do a "double take" (478). In this sense, Morrison's innovative play with the tension between metaphorical and literal language corresponds closely to the kinds of techniques typically privileged by the New Critics. Also of particular interest from a New Critical perspective is the way Morrison directly opposes the literary language of her text to the language of science. Schoolteacher's brutal humiliation of the slaves in his charge is presented very much as a matter of language, the notebooks in which he records his observations about slave behavior serving as a central image of his domination of the slaves. Schoolteacher himself is very well aware that his control of language and its "proper" use is a key to his control of the slaves on Sweet Home Farm. Thus Sethe, who had personally made the ink used by Schoolteacher for his notes, directly identifies his notetaking as a central element of his brutality. "I made the ink," she tells Paul D in their crucial encounter at the end of the book. "He couldn't have done it if I hadn't made the ink" (271). In a key scene, the slave Sixo cleverly defends his theft of a pig from the farm on the grounds that he needed the meat for his nutrition and therefore for the improvement of Schoolteacher's property, thus echoing an episode in *Narrative of the Life of Frederick Douglass* in which a slave wins emancipation by successfully defeating his master's argument for slavery (83). But in *Beloved,* freedom is not so easily won: Schoolteacher beats Sixo anyway, as a reminder that "definitions belonged to the definers—not the defined" (190). In response, the defiant Sixo turns away from the use of English altogether, refusing to endorse the language of his white masters.

Given the close New Critical association between science and modern industrial capitalism, we could read Schoolteacher's function as a New Critical allegory of southern history. From this point of view, Sweet Home Farm could be read as a utopian image of southern agrarian culture of the kind celebrated by the New Critics in their Southern Agrarian phase. Schoolteacher's arrival then brings science and modernization to the farm, bringing misery to the inhabitants. He disrupts the utopian setting of Sweet Home Farm much as (according to the New Critics) the coming of science and modern capitalism after the Civil War brought about the decline of traditional agrarian culture in the South. It is also clear that Morrison regards Schoolteacher not as the antithesis of the attitudes of the antebellum South but as their quintessential representative, and the overall thrust of the book provides a powerful rejoinder to the historical vision typical of the New Critics.

Morrison's opposition of metaphorical to literal language is central to the political oppositions that inform her book, something the New Critics could well appreciate. But for Morrison, this opposition has powerful political implications that contrast sharply with the political predilections of the New Critics. In particular, *Beloved* does not oppose the dominative language of science and modern capitalism to the more poetic and genteel language of traditional southern culture. These two poles are collapsed into one, subsumed under the general category of white male Western culture, which is then opposed in her more rhythmic and flexible language to alternative cultural perspectives associated with African and African-American cultures and with the particular perspectives of women within those cultures. And Morrison's choice of the opposition between literal and figurative language as the grounds on which to stage this confrontation is highly appropriate.

As Eric Cheyfitz points out, the opposition between literal and metaphorical language was quite central to the ideology of early European colonial expansion in the sixteenth and seventeenth centuries—and of American slavery up until the Civil War. Cheyfitz observes that the notion of the literal in that ideology privileges the written (European culture) over the oral cultures of Native Americans and Africans. Cheyfitz echoes Morrison's strategy of literalizing conventional metaphors when he argues that the literal and metaphorical poles of language cannot be separated and that one continually tends to spill over into the other. He also emphasizes that in the ideology of slavery and of colonial domination these poles were kept strictly separate, with clear cultural and political implications. Cheyfitz discusses the 1845 *Narrative of the Life of Frederick Douglass* to note how this opposition between linguistic poles functioned as a technique of domination of black American slaves: "The literal and the figurative aspects of language become hierarchized into absolute and oppositional entities, with the masters occupying the territory of the literal or proper and consigning the slaves to that of the figurative" (39). By challenging the strict polar opposition between metaphorical and literal language, and by using conventional metaphors to produce literal meanings, Morrison breaks out of the linguistic territory traditionally assigned to slaves and launches a direct assault on the linguistic domain of their white male masters.

In the final analysis, *Beloved* provides an emphatic rejoinder to the New Critical notion that genuine art must be informed by an "ironical ambivalence," that in the world of such art there is "neither black nor white, neither right nor wrong which can be defined with absolute certainty" (Brooks and Warren xviii–xix). Interestingly Cleanth Brooks and Robert Penn Warren follow this call for ambivalence with reminders that in Harriet Beecher Stowe's *Uncle Tom's Cabin,* an important antislavery text, one of the most reprehensible characters is Simon Legree, "a Yankee," and that what they regard as the greatest brutality in Ernest Hemingway's *For Whom the Bell Tolls* is committed not by fascist forces against the leftist loyalists but vice versa. Brooks and Warren characterize these examples as instances of irony that intensify the conflicts portrayed by Stowe and Hemingway, but these critics are also betraying their own political prejudices, which require them to suggest that, even in extreme situations such as slavery and fascism, southerners and right-wingers are not necessarily the villains.

But the examples provided by Brooks and Warren are themselves highly ironic, given that they call attention to American slavery and European fascism, probably the two most forceful historical arguments against the southern conservative ideology of the New Criticism. Of all the events in history, these two examples are among those in which the distinction between moral right and wrong is most clearly defined. For the millions of Jews (and numerous other "marginal" peoples) exterminated in the Nazi concentration camps and for the tens of millions of black Africans who died miserably on slave ships or who experienced, along with their descendants, almost unthinkable suffering and degradation as slaves in America, the New Critical argument against clear delineation of right and wrong in art rings hollow indeed. *Beloved* makes a powerful and unambiguous moral statement about the evils of slavery, even as it demonstrates (contrary to the arguments of the New Critics) that literature with such a clear moral and political message need not be simplistic or formulaic.

Works Cited

Brooks, Cleanth, and Robert Penn Warren. *Understanding Fiction.* 2d ed. New York: Appleton-Century-Crofts, 1960.

Brooks, Peter. *Reading for the Plot.* New York: Vintage, 1985.

Cheyfitz, Eric. *The Poetics of Imperialism: Translation and Colonization from "The Tempest" to "Tarzan."* New York: Oxford UP, 1991.

Douglass, Frederick. *Narrative of the Life of Frederick Douglass, an American Slave.* 1845. London: Penguin, 1982.

Faulkner, William. *Absalom, Absalom!* New York: Vintage, 1972.

Hemingway, Ernest. *For Whom the Bell Tolls.* New York: Scribner's, 1940.

Krumholz, Linda. "The Ghosts of Slavery: Historical Recovery in Toni Morrison's *Beloved.*" *African American Review* 26.3 (1992): 395–408.

Morrison, Toni. *Beloved.* New York: Plume-Penguin, 1988.

———. "Unspeakable Things Unspoken: The Afro-American Presence in American Literature." In *Modern Critical Views: Toni Morrison,* ed. Harold Bloom, 201–230. New York: Chelsea House, 1990.

Rushdy, Ashraf H. A. "Daughters Signifyin(g) History: The Example of Toni Morrison's *Beloved.*" *American Literature* 64.3 (1992): 567–597.

Stowe, Harriet Beecher. *Uncle Tom's Cabin, or, Life Among the Lowly.* Boston: Jewett, 1852.

Warren, Robert Penn. "Pure and Impure Poetry." *Kenyon Review* 5 (Spring 1943): 228–254.

Wyatt, Jean. "Giving Body to the Word: The Maternal Symbolic in Toni Morrison's *Beloved.*" *PMLA* 108.3 (1993): 474–488.

PSYCHOANALYTIC CRITICISM

Beloved deals more directly with the public world of politics and history than with the private world of individual psychology. Nevertheless one of the book's major points is that these two worlds are not necessarily separate. Morrison makes extensive use of parallels between personal memory and public history in constructing her account of the legacy of slavery in American society. Moreover she does so in a way that can be usefully illuminated, at least metaphorically, by Sigmund Freud's work. Just as Freud developed psychoanalysis as a means of probing unconscious memories to reveal the past sources of current psychological disturbances in his patients, Morrison explores the dark recesses of American history, bringing to light repressed aspects of American history that continue to have consequences in contemporary America. A major motivation for Morrison's text seems to be the rather Freudian insight that the wounds brought about by abject experiences in the past can be healed only after those experiences are acknowledged and directly confronted.

Mae G. Henderson notes that the "return of the repressed" can be seen as the "theme which preoccupies Morrison's novel" (74). Indeed the central metaphor of *Beloved* is the return of the repressed and on several different levels. At the level of the plot, the murder of the infant Beloved is the crucial event that determines the course of the future lives of the other characters, especially Sethe and Denver. Yet this event is never talked about in the family, which seeks to forget that it ever happened. At age seven, Denver is asked by one of her schoolmates about rumors that Sethe had been imprisoned for murder and that the baby Denver had lived in prison with her mother. In response, Denver ceases attending school so that she will not have to confront these rumors. And when her curiosity finally drives her to ask Sethe and Baby Suggs about the rumor, Denver experiences a sudden deafness that makes her unable to hear the answer (103). Denver's deafness thus becomes a metaphor for the repression of past experiences that are simply too unpleasant to be accepted by the conscious mind. She then remains deaf for two years, until she hears the ghost of the dead baby crawling up the stairs of the house at 124 Bluestone Road. The haunting of this house by the ghost can be read as a metaphor for the return of the repressed, a return that becomes complete when the reincarnated Beloved moves into the house in bodily form.

Although Freudian repression is not a conscious, intentional process per se, Denver does consciously continue to repress the past altogether and live only in the present. In a similar way, both Sethe and Paul D try to repress their memories of past sufferings under slavery. The latter, for example, often feels that his heart has been replaced by a "tobacco tin lodged in his chest" (113). And he actively seeks to lock away his more unpleasant memories in this tin, hoping thereby to be able to live his life free of the burdens of the past. Sethe (whose past trauma includes the killing of her child in addition to the humiliations she suffered as a slave) is constantly engaged in "keeping the past at bay" as a way of moving into the future (42); she feels that she must confront on a daily basis the "serious work of beating back the past" (73). But Paul D's arrival in Sethe's life brings about precisely a return of the repressed, causing her to remember "something she had forgotten she knew" (61). In the end, both Sethe and Paul D recognize that they cannot move successfully into the future without first confronting the past. They decide to face the past together, their shared memories of the time on Sweet Home Farm forming a crucial element in their relationship. At the same time, this confrontation allows them to avoid being obsessed with the past and to move forward. As Paul D tells Sethe in their crucial last scene, "Me and you, we got more yesterday than anybody. We need some kind of tomorrow" (273).

On another, and perhaps more important level, the entire text of *Beloved* represents a return of the repressed past history of slavery. Morrison suggests that American society—black and white—can successfully solve its current and future problems only by coming to terms with this national history, just as Sethe and Paul D must come to terms with their personal memories. By focusing on slavery as the subject matter of her text, Morrison calls attention to one of the ugliest episodes in American history, an episode so horrendous that many Americans have found it convenient to forget. We can think, for example, of the nostalgic visions of the New Critics of the pre-Civil War South as an ideal agrarian society, visions that fail to take into account the human suffering associated with slavery. As Henderson points out, "Slave narratives can be regarded as classic examples of the 'return of the repressed,' primarily because the events relating to violence and violation (which are self-censored or edited out) return again and again in 'veiled allusions'" (63). In *Beloved,* however, there is no such disguise. Morrison actively seeks to force her readers to confront the human reality of slavery by building her text around graphic accounts of sexual abuse, rape, torture, and death, accounts that have often been omitted from narratives of slavery, even those written by former slaves, who felt that such abject material would make their stories unpalatable to white audiences. She has described her task as trying to tear away "that veil drawn over 'proceedings too terrible to relate'" ("Site" 110).

In addition to this central metaphor of the repression and recovery of the past, numerous aspects of *Beloved* resemble classic situations described by Freud. Linda Krumholz, for example, suggests that Beloved herself, by forcing the other characters to confront their repressed memories, acts as a sort of Freudian analyst: "She pries open suppressed memories and emotions. In a sense she is like an analyst, the object of transference and cathexis that draws out the past, while at the same time she is that past. Countering traumatic repression, she makes the characters accept their past, their squelched memories, and their own hearts, as beloved" (400). Most particularly, Sethe's killing of Beloved and the attempted killings of her other children represent an enactment (with a change of gender) of the feared castration by the father so often discussed by Freud. It is not surprising that Sethe's other children remain frightened of her after this experience or that the boys Buglar and Howard run away from home as soon as they are old enough to survive on their own. Beloved's seduction of Sethe's lover Paul D has clear Oedipal resonances, and Beloved's later "pregnancy," though it may be simply symbolic of her growth at the expense of Sethe, can be taken as an enactment of Freud's notion that young girls fantasize about bearing children by their fathers. Finally Denver feels that she must warn the returned Beloved not to get too close to Sethe, lest she be endangered—

much in the way that emotional access to the mother is limited in the Freudian Oedipal drama.

Indeed Denver herself feels estranged from her mother by what seem to be classic fantasies of castration. Lying in bed at night, she envisions her mother cutting off her head as a normal maternal activity, like pulling out a splinter or removing a cinder from a child's eye (206). That Sethe is a mother rather than a father, and that her "castration" of Beloved occurs in defiance of the patriarchal authority of Schoolteacher rather than as an enforcement of paternal rule, can then be taken to indicate the distortions in normal human experience brought about by slavery. The warping of the Oedipal drama in *Beloved* also challenges the universality of Freud's narrative of infantile development, a narrative that was, after all, developed very much from a European white male perspective.

The resurrected Beloved, though now ostensibly about eighteen years old (as she would have been had she not been killed), retains many of the classic characteristic that Freud associates with the behavior of infants (as she was when she died). This is especially true of her relationship with her mother, Sethe, toward whom she feels excessively possessive and whose constant presence she desires. Psychoanalytic descriptions of mother-daughter relationships can usefully illuminate the link between Sethe and Beloved. Barbara Schapiro, for example, suggests that the significance of interpersonal relationships in *Beloved* can be usefully understood within the framework of the object-relations psychology of Melanie Klein and D. W. Winnicott. But Schapiro especially appeals to Jessica Benjamin's *The Bonds of Love,* a feminist psychoanalytic study that extends object-relations theory to a general consideration of relations among individuals and particularly the tendency in Western society of such relations to degenerate into a dynamic of domination and submission. According to Schapiro, Benjamin's theory concludes that the necessarily relational nature of selfhood implies that in some cases individuals become so attuned that their status as separate subjects is threatened, leading to a struggle for identity: "When the boundaries break down and the necessary tension between self and other dissolves, domination takes root. The search for recognition then becomes a struggle for power and control, and assertion turns into aggression" (196). Schapiro sees in the relationship between Sethe and the resurrected Beloved very much the kind of intersubjective situation that Benjamin notes with respect to mothers and children in general. Meanwhile Beloved's growing domination of Sethe corresponds to the tendency toward dominative relations that Benjamin describes.

Probably the most promising psychoanalytic approach suggested by the relation between Sethe and Beloved is that of Lacan, and numerous critics have seen Lacanian resonances in this situation. After all, Beloved was killed while still a one-year-old infant whose mind was dominated by the Imaginary Order and who had not reached the stage of subjective differentiation necessary for entry into the Symbolic Order. As a result, Beloved would not be expected to have a full sense of herself and her mother as separate entities. Beloved sometimes directly expresses this sense of fusion with her mother: "I am not separate from her there is no place where I stop her face is my own" (210).

Beloved is also typical of the young infant in the voracious possessiveness that she feels toward her mother. Beloved feels extremely anxious whenever Sethe is not in her presence. She is especially disturbed when Sethe leaves the house to go to work each day, and Beloved walks out each day to meet her mother on her return, indeed venturing farther and farther to meet her mother a little earlier each day (57). Here Beloved's attitude toward her mother echoes one of the most famous episodes in all of Freud's writing, an anecdote that he relates in *Beyond the Pleasure Principle* in relation to his own grandson Ernst. According to Freud, Ernst first began to learn language by playing a game in which he threw a wooden reel attached to a string, then drew it back to him, yelling, *"Fort! Da!"* (Gone! There!) in relation to the going and coming of the reel. Freud interprets this game as a symbolic reenactment of the leaving and returning of the boy's mother, Ernst's mastery of the alternating presence and absence of the reel compensating for his lack of ability to control the coming and going of his mother. The words *fort* and *da* become closely associated with this compensatory sense of control.

Ernst, in short, learns to use language to substititue for the lost ability fully to possess his mother, putting words in the place left vacant by the absence of the maternal body. His experience of loss of the object of desire and simultaneous acquisition of language is very similar to that described by Jacques Lacan as "castration," and it is not surprising that one of Lacan's most important essays draws on this Freudian anecdote. In "The Function and Field of Speech and Language in Psychoanalysis," Lacan notes that Freud's grandson displaces his desire from his mother into language itself and that this anecdote shows how language aids in individuation by distancing the child from the objects around him (30–113). Beloved, having undergone a form of physical castration when her throat was cut and she was nearly beheaded, did not live to undergo the symbolic castration of entry into the Symbolic Order described by Lacan. Therefore she is unable to cope with her mother's absence, and she eventually forces her mother to quit work altogether so that she will never have to be absent.

Interestingly, however, it is often Sethe, rather than Beloved, who expresses an Imaginary Order sense of merger with her daughter. She sometimes describes her children as parts of herself, which presumably explains why she feels she has the right to take their lives to prevent them from returning to slavery. This phenomenon is often observed in clinical situations, as in Alice Balint's description (from a perspective informed by the work of Winnicott) of the difficulty of differentiating between infantile and maternal interests in some cases: "Just as the child does not recognize the separate identity of the mother, so the mother looks upon her child as a part of herself whose interests are identical with her own" (quoted in Chodorow 85). But it is again Lacan who provides what is probably the most useful gloss on this phenomenon. Jean Wyatt notes, working from a Lacanian perspective, "Sethe is of course in the mother's position rather than the child's, but her physical connection with her nursing baby resembles the infant's initial radical dependency on the mother's body" (477). Moreover Sethe's sense of bodily connection with her children is accompanied by an uneasy relationship to language that also shows that she has not fully left the Imaginary Order behind her to enter the Symbolic Order of normal language use. Wyatt goes on to note that Sethe distrusts words and often hesitates to represent her feelings and memories in language—that is, she is unwilling (or unable) to substitute words for things in the manner normally associated with Symbolic Order language. From a purely Lacanian perspective, then, Sethe has not fully undergone the process of castration. From this point of view, her psyche may therefore have what Lacan calls a "psychotic structure," which would make her susceptible to episodes of psychosis.

It would clearly not be appropriate to interpret Sethe's killing of her baby daughter as the mere act of a madwoman—at least not without careful consideration of the factors involved in her madness. For one thing, we must remember that Sethe and Beloved are literary characters, not real people. Furthermore they are highly allegorical characters who represent large groups of people, not individuals. There is thus clearly a political dimension to Sethe's "madness." The Symbolic Order is the place not only of language but also of masculine authority, and *Beloved* reminds us that this authority is also inevitably white in the American tradition. Sethe is thus excluded from the Symbolic Order by both gender and race. Indeed if Lacanian castration is the process by which a young child becomes a human subject, Sethe's incomplete castration is easily understandable in a social system that refuses to deny her fully human status.

Images of madness run throughout the text of *Beloved,* one intention of which is clearly to challenge the simple distinction between "madness" (which in extreme cases may seem the only "sane" response) and sanity (which, taken as far as in the case of the hyperrational Schoolteacher, can be a form of madness). In this sense, Morrison's treatment of madness recalls Michel Foucault's work in *Madness and Civilization* more than the work of Freud or Lacan. Psychoanalytic theories may be useful to describe Sethe's situation, but those theories should be supplemented with an awareness of the importance of Sethe's social and historical context. The slave Sethe, after all, is not treated as a subject who uses language but as an object on which language is used, whether it be in the humiliated notes taken by Schoolteacher and his pupils or in the literal inscription of her subservience on Sethe's body in the form of her scarred back. As Jean Wyatt puts it, "Sethe's problematic relation to language results from her position as body not only in a maternal order but also in a social order that systematically denied the subject position to those it defined as objects of exchange" (478).

Of course, the only real user of language in *Beloved* is Morrison herself, and—although she challenges conventional language use in numerous ways—Morrison certainly demonstrates an exceptional adroitness with language in the book. This adroitness is itself significant given the traditional tendency of American society to see both African Americans and women as linguistically inferior to white men. This issue can be viewed in numerous ways, but Freud's famous *fort-da* anecdote might again prove useful. Jacques Derrida, in a reading of chapter 2 of *Beyond the Pleasure Principle,* observes that the famous episode involving Freud's grandchild functions as an internal image, or *mise en abyme,* of the book as a whole. Derrida notes that Freud seems to reject, then bring back the pleasure principle much as Ernst does the spool: "In every detail we can see the superposition of the subsequent description of the *fort/da* (on the grandson's side of the house of Freud) with the description of the speculative game, itself so assiduous and so repetitive, of the grandfather in writing *Beyond the Pleasure Principle*" (119). We might apply a similar procedure to *Beloved,* which centrally deals with elements of American history that have traditionally been pushed aside but that continually return. Morrison's book is itself a powerful contribution to the bringing back of this history. We might interpret Morrison's extremely skillful writing as a means of helping her cope with the painful subject matter of her book by using language to establish some control over it—much as Freud's grandson establishes a sense of control over the comings and goings of his mother by learning to use language to describe the phenomenon.

Works Cited

Benjamin, Jessica. *The Bonds of Love: Psychoanalysis, Feminism and the Problem of Domination.* New York: Pantheon, 1988.

Chodorow, Nancy. *The Reproduction of Mothering: Psychoanalysis and the Sociology of Gender.* Berkeley and Los Angeles: U of California P, 1978.

Derrida, Jacques. "Coming into One's Own." Trans. James Hulbert. In *Psychoanalysis and the Question of the Text,* ed. Geoffrey Hartman, 114-148. Baltimore, Md.: Johns Hopkins UP, 1978.

Foucault, Michel. *Madness and Civilization.* Trans. Richard Howard. New York: Vintage, 1973.

Freud, Sigmund. *Beyond the Pleasure Principle.* Trans. James Strachey. New York: Norton, 1961.

Henderson, Mae G. "Toni Morrison's *Beloved:* Re-membering the Body as Historical Text." In *Comparative American Identities: Race, Sex, and Nationality in the Modern Text,* ed. Hortense J. Spillers, 62-86. New York: Routledge, 1991.

Krumholz, Linda. "The Ghosts of Slavery: Historical Recovery in Toni Morrison's *Beloved.*" *African American Review* 26.3 (1992): 395-408.

Lacan, Jacques. *Écrits: A Selection.* Trans. Alan Sheridan. New York: Norton, 1977.

Morrison, Toni. "The Site of Memory." In *Inventing the Truth: The Art and Craft of Memoir,* ed. William Zinsser, 101-124. Boston: Houghton Mifflin, 1987.

———. *Beloved.* New York: Plume-Penguin, 1988.

Schapiro, Barbara. "The Bonds of Love and the Boundaries of the Self in Toni Morrison's *Beloved.*" *Contemporary Literature* 32.2 (1991): 194-210.

Wyatt, Jean. "Giving Body to the Word: The Maternal Symbolic in Toni Morrison's *Beloved.*" *PMLA* 108.3 (1993): 474-488.

MARXIST CRITICISM

Beloved centers on the phenomenon of slavery in the American South in the nineteenth century, and slavery was first and foremost an economic institution. But slavery constituted a noncapitalist (or, more accurately, precapitalist) economic system. Moreover, the social oppositions on which slavery was founded seem to be based on race rather than class in the Marxist sense. At first glance, then, Marxist analysis might not seem directly applicable to Morrison's book. But there are several reasons *Beloved* can be usefully approached from a Marxist perspective. For one thing, the book is carefully constructed to indicate that the techniques of oppression associated with slavery were not limited to the American South. The physical and psychological abuse suffered by Sethe and Paul D (and by the black Americans on whose real-life stories these characters are based) ends neither when they move spatially into the "free" North nor when they move temporally into the years after the "emancipation" of the slaves in the Civil War. For another thing, the race relations on which *Beloved* focuses may be more relevant to class relations than is immediately obvious, especially in the United States, where the complexities of class society are inseparable from the question of racial and ethnic differences and where, as Fredric Jameson points out, the system of class is complicated by "American social reality with its racial and ethnic groupings" (*Marxism* 401). Indeed the centrality of race in *Beloved* potentially makes a Marxist critique of the book all the more valuable, leading to analysis that might usefully address the special problems of American society.

Dorothea Drummond Mbalia notes the relevance to Morrison's work of the arguments by numerous scholars that slavery and capitalism are intimately related as historical phenomena (18–20). Contrary to the conventional belief that slavery was made possible by racism, Walter Rodney argues that racism was made thinkable merely by economic necessity and that racism was a product of slavery rather than the other way around: "Having been utterly dependent on African labour, Europeans at home and abroad found it necessary to rationalize that exploitation in racist terms as well" (99). Eric Williams emphasizes the economic motivation for slavery as a form of cheap labor and concludes that "racial differences made it easier to justify and rationalize Negro slavery" (18). African political leader Kwame Nkrumah argues that "it was only with the capitalist economic penetration that the master-servant relationship emerged, and with it, racism" (29). Nkrumah, moreover, goes on to suggest that the end of capitalism is necessary to end racism: "Race is inextricably linked with class exploitation; in a racist-capitalist power structure, capitalist exploitation and race oppression are complementary, the removal of one ensures the removal of the other" (27).

In any case, racism involves the overt oppression of one group in society for the economic benefit of another, so slavery and capitalism are related structurally, if in no other way. We should not forget the very real suffering of American slaves, who were subjected to confinement, torture, brutalization, and humiliation in their everyday lives. Even the most abject events in *Beloved* are based on historical reality. But the extension of the suffering of Morrison's characters beyond the spatial and temporal bounds of the slave South suggests that their experience may have broad, almost allegorical, relevance to American society as a whole. Morrison carefully extends the slavery motif beyond strictly racial bounds as well, introducing into the text a band of renegade Cherokee Indians (who help Paul D escape from imprisonment in Georgia) and the escaped white indentured servant Amy Denver (who crucially assists the escaped Sethe in childbirth, establishing an interracial bond that provides a direct reminder that many white workers lived in a condition of virtual slavery in the nineteenth century as well).

From a Marxist perspective, these suggestions of a broader relevance in Morrison's depiction of slavery acknowledge that the treatment of human beings as property in slavery makes it a particularly overt example of the commodification of human beings that occurs in more subtle ways in capitalist society. Indeed Morrison calls a great deal of attention to the way slaves were often regarded merely as aspects of the economic system, not only because their labor was crucial to the operation of the agricultural economy of the American South, but also because they were quite frequently bought and sold, used almost as a secondary form of currency. Slaves were, in short, valued for the uses to which they could be put as farm laborers and household servants and for their exchange value, for the price they could be expected to command on the open market.

In one crucial scene, Paul D and his friend Sixo attempt to escape from slavery on Sweet Home Farm but are recaptured by a group of white slave catchers. Sixo is brutally murdered because of his stubborn defiance of these captors, while Paul D is shackled and taken back into captivity. On the way, Paul D overhears the white men discussing his market price, and he understands for the first time that he is primarily valued by his white masters not for the work he can do on the farm but for the price he can command at sale. In a moment of realization of his status as a commodity, Paul D learns the "dollar value of his weight, his strength, his heart, his brain, his penis, and his future" (226). Moreover he learns that he will probably be sold soon (for about $900) so that the farm can use the money to purchase two younger slaves to rebuild the farm's "stock" after the recent escapes. Slaves, in short, are exchanged much in the mode of cattle, with no attention to their needs (or abilities) as individual human beings.

Beloved also emphasizes that slaves were often regarded as breeding stock, a woman slave often being treated merely as "a brood mare purchased to produce human capital" (Keenan 60). And this emphasis is quite true to history. As Hazel V. Carby points out, the slave woman's "reproductive destiny was bound to capital accumulation; black women gave birth to property and, directly, to capital itself in the form of slaves" (24–25). In this sense, the process of "labor" through which infant slaves come into the world becomes a sort of pun on the way capital in general is produced by the labor of workers. The sexuality of slave women is a mere mechanism for the production of capital rather than a potential source of genuine human relationship, contributing to their alienation in a radical way. Understanding this phenomenon well, the white neighbors scoff at the policies of Mr. Garner, the former master of Sweet Home, who allowed his slaves to marry rather than simply mating them like animals to produce the maximum number of new slaves (226).

Under these conditions, it is not surprising that the slaves in Morrison's book find it difficult to establish meaningful personal relationships among themselves. Indeed *Beloved* extensively explores the way the commodification of slaves contributes to their alienation. Knowing that they might be sold at any moment, slaves have trouble feeling at home anywhere. Moreover, they shy away from meaningful personal relationships because anyone to whom they become emotionally attached (including their own children) might be taken away from them, sold to a distant owner, and never seen or heard from again. Sethe's mother-in-law, Baby Suggs, thinks of her life as a game in which people she loves are moved around like checkers, subject to sudden and permanent removal from the board. She hardly remembers most of her eight children or their six different fathers, all of whom were merely temporary presences in her life: "Anybody Baby Suggs knew, let alone loved, who hadn't run off or been hanged, got rented out, loaned out, bought up, bought back, stored up, mortgaged, won, stolen, or seized" (23).

In a similar way, Paul D knows that it is dangerous in a slave economy to become too attached to anyone or anything. So he tries to love everyone and everything a little, but not so much that its removal will be too painful. This strategy of universal (if limited) love represents a potential gesture toward the kinds of communal relationships that informed the traditional African societies from which American slaves were originally removed. But for most of the book, the emphasis is not on the universality of Paul D's love but on its muted quality, on his inability to establish a genuinely meaningful connection with anyone. In this sense, the attempts of the reincarnated Beloved to seduce Paul D (and thus impede his connection with Sethe) can be read as an allegorical representation of the way the legacy of slavery continues to make personal relationships difficult for former slaves. The relationship that is nevertheless established between Paul D and Sethe in the course of the novel is particularly crucial because it suggests that the two former slaves, by learning to love and trust each other, have at least partially overcome the alienating effects of the past.

For Mbalia, in fact, "solidarity" is the major theme of *Beloved,* which details the possibilities for resistance to oppression through collective action by the African people (89). Morrison thus introduces into her text a number of positive images of interpersonal communication and cooperation as a counter to the alienation experienced by the slaves. These include the network of former slaves and sympathizers who work together to help Sethe and other slaves escape from the South and who later continue to function as a cooperative community in the Cincinnati area after the nominal end of slavery. A scene early in the book in which Paul D, Sethe, and Denver attend a carnival suggests a more private form of solidarity, as does a later scene in which Sethe, Beloved, and Denver function for once as a real family during an outing in which they go ice skating in "a moment of Utopian unity, of mythic resolution" (Keenan 76).

The central example of intersubjective contact in the book is the connection between mother and child, often powerful despite the fact that under slavery the two might be separated at any moment. Sethe, for example, describes her children as parts of herself, apparently feeling—in direct defiance of the alienating strategies of the slave system—that she has the right to take their lives because those lives are inseparable from her own. Here the book's central metaphor is breast-feeding; Sethe's urgent drive to get to Ohio so that she can bring her milk to the infant daughter who has preceded her there serves as an important example of quite literal and direct human contact. The material nature of this contact again suggests Karl Marx's analysis of human society and of the primacy of the need for necessities such as food in social relations. The brutal taking of Sethe's milk by Schoolteacher's pupils at Sweet Home Farm thus stands as the book's most powerful and direct image of the interference in communciation between slaves that is central to the system of slavery.

Of course, the alienation of individual slaves from each other can be seen as part of an intentional "divide-and-conquer" strategy on the part of their owners: By making it difficult for slaves to establish and maintain strong interpersonal ties, the white owners help assure that the slaves will not band together in revolt. It is for this reason that conditions on Sweet Home Farm under the regime of Mr. Garner are particularly horrifying to many of Garner's neighbors. By allowing slaves to marry and conduct other forms of close personal relationships, Garner potentially provides the slaves with a source of communal bonding that might lead to rebellion. Indeed the eventual mass escape from the farm seems to vindicate those who see Garner's ostensibly enlightened policies as leading inevitably to trouble.

The fragmentation in the communal lives of slaves brought about by the divide-and-conquer strategies of slavery corresponds to numerous other ways the lives of slaves were radically fragmented. For example, Barbara Omolade notes that a slave woman was often treated as a "fragmented commodity," the different parts of her body being assigned to different tasks: back and muscle for fieldwork, hands for more delicate service such as child rearing, and sexual organs for the sexual pleasure of the white master and as "his place of capital investment —the capital being the sex act and the resulting child the accumulated surplus, worth money on the slave market" (365). In *Beloved,* the most radical example of such bodily fragmentation occurs in a scene in which the reincarnated Beloved begins to feel that her body is literally flying apart and that one day she will wake up and "find herself in pieces" (133). But the ex-slave Sethe clearly experiences this sort of fragmentation as well, exacerbated in her case by the "scientific" attempts of Schoolteacher to measure and record the characteristics of the separate parts of her body. Again, however, Morrison provides a positive counter to this fragmentation of the bodies of slave women. In a crucial scene near the end of the text, Paul D offers to bathe Sethe, and she wonders if the parts of her body will hold together as he bathes them one by one. Paul D's reassurances then suggest that they will and that the connection between Sethe and Paul D will help Sethe reconnect the fragmented parts of her psyche as well (272–273).

The specifically economic terms of Omolade's description point to a direct parallel between the fragmentation in the lives of the slaves depicted by Morrison and the fragmentation of life that Marxist critics such as Georg Lukács and (more recently) Frederic Jameson have seen as central to the alienating effects of a capitalist economic system on the lives of those who live within it. Relevant here is Jameson's suggestion that "third-world" literature (including African) might function quite differently from "Western" literature because third-world societies lack the strong sense of separation of life into private and public spheres that is characteristic of Western capitalist societies ("Third"). African societies, according to this reading, might be expected to rely more centrally on communal activities than do Western societies, with their central ideology of bourgeois individualism. The intentional alienation of individual slaves by their white masters can thus be read as an attempt to separate the slaves from traditional African culture and to assure that African cultural traditions will be unavailable as a source of potentially subversive inspiration for the slaves. But this motif has a number of possible implications for Western capitalist society as well. For one thing, it points toward the way Western culture, by promoting the ideology of individualism, increases alienation and fragmentation rather than providing a source of communal feeling. For another, that the fragmentation of the slaves' lives leads to an almost total suppression of their private lives might point toward the way the separation of private and public life under capitalism, while seeming to glorify private life, in fact impoverishes it. The suppression of communal relations among the slaves leads not to the development of genuine individuals but to the suppression of genuine individuality, much in the way that Marxist critiques of the ideology of bourgeois individualism have frequently emphasized that this ideology prevents individuals from realizing their full potentials as human beings.

Fragmentation is also central to the historical turn from storytelling to the novel as detailed by Walter Benjamin, and *Beloved* might seem to embody this turn. Yet Morrison's novel contains so many elements of storytelling and oral culture that it can also be read as an attempt to resurrect, through the novel, the African-American tradition of storytelling as a means toward the establishment of community. In a similar way, *Beloved* appears to be implicated in Lukács's criticisms of modernism, especially as its allegorical mode is combined with radical textual fragmentation and a focus on the kinds of abject details that Lukács associates with the "pathology" of modernism. But the horrific events detailed in Morrison's book are typical of the historical epoch of slavery, and Jameson's comments on third-world literature suggest that Morrison's use of allegory is a sign of totality rather than reification. Finally it is clear that the textual fragmentation of *Beloved* is true to the slave experience and that the mixture of genres that constitutes one of the more interesting formal features of Morrison's text has highly positive political implications, suggesting a combination of different modes of accessing the world in opposition to the bouregeois tendency to treat such modes as separate and incommensurable.

Jameson's analysis of third-world literature supports the positive potential of Morrison's allegory. He suggests that all third-world texts—and particularly the major characters in those texts—must necessarily be read as "national allegories," as stories of the development of the new postcolonial nation in which they arise. For Jameson, the allegorical nature of such texts derives from the fundamental nature of third-world societies, in which the lack of the clear separation between public and private realms typical of Western societies effaces the boundary between individual characters and the societies in which they live, leading to a situation in which "*the story of a private individual destiny is always an allegory of the embattled situation of the public third-world culture and society*" ("Third" 69). In *Beloved,* the generic mixture of personal biography and public history suggests that the characters serve not as unique individuals in the bouregeois sense but as allegorical representations of black America as a whole.

The most obviously allegorical character in Morrison's text is Beloved herself, whose generic name suggests that she stands in as a representative of "all the loved ones lost through slavery, beginning with the Africans who died on the slave ships" (Wyatt 479). As a ghost returning from the dead in reincarnated form, Beloved also suggests the slave past in general, which continues to haunt Sethe, Paul D, and other former slaves long after the nominal end of slavery. Beloved's allegorical function seems clear throughout the text, though it becomes most forceful in the strange chapter late in the book when Beloved begins to narrate the text from a position in which she at one point merges with a woman on one of the early slave ships coming from Africa (210–213). This scene is rather confusing, and Morrison gives no explanation for the sudden shift in narrative voice, which also involves a radical textual fragmentation. But this fragmentation is less confusing if we read it as an attempt to represent the bewildering experience of Africans who were captured, sold into slavery, then taken halfway around the world on squalid and stifling slave ships to new lives that bore little relation to their former lives in Africa.

The white characters in *Beloved* play allegorical roles as well. Most obvious here is Morrison's treatment of "Schoolteacher," whose representation by a professional label rather than a personal name already suggests that he may stand in for larger phenomena. In particular, Schoolteacher can be taken to represent knowledge and education and the roles they play in slavery. His "scientific" studies of slave behavior—which are clearly designed to gather information about the slaves that might be useful in furthering their domination—can be read as a particularly overt example of the ideology of domination that Max Horkheimer and Theodor W. Adorno see as underlying Western Enlightenment science in general. Schoolteacher's studies are not driven by a genuine interest in the lives of slaves or by a search for genuine knowledge and understanding. His observations, which reduce slaves to objects of measurement and description, merely contribute to the dehumanization of slaves. Indeed the information he collects (like the parallel listing of "human" and "animal" characteristics of the slaves) is clearly based on the assumption that slaves are subhuman and on a desire to verify that assumption.

Morrison's indictment of science is especially appropriate given the crucial role played by European science and technology in the domination and colonization of Africa and America and in the establishment and maintenance of the institution of slavery. The depiction of Schoolteacher also suggests that the domination of slaves was achieved not only through the direct physical control provided by superior weapons technology, but also through the aid of science and other ideological discourses that were used to justify the institution of slavery to official white society and to endow the slaves themselves with a sense of inferiority and a tendency toward submissiveness. We might note here Stanley Elkins's influential (if often disputed) argument that the obedience of slaves was largely assured because the slaves, faced with a sense of the overwhelmingly superior power of their white masters, assumed a childlike and "feminine" submissiveness.

Regardless of whether we accept the specifics of Elkins's argument, his indication of the important role play by psychological—in addition to physical—domination in slavery is useful and accords well with Morrison's emphasis in *Beloved* on the psychic effects of slavery. As Barbara Schapiro notes, *Beloved* suggests that the "internal resonances" of slavery "are so profound that even if one is eventually freed from external bondage, the self will still be trapped in an inner world that prevents a genuine experience of freedom" (194). This internalization of the bondage of slavery can be compared to Louis Althusser's notion of interpellation. In this case, individual blacks are constructed by the ideology of slavery as subjects who are subjected to the domination of their white masters. They are exposed throughout their lives to a barrage of discourses that define them as slaves and provide them with no source of identity apart from servitude. As Sethe puts it after escaping into Ohio, "Freeing yourself was one thing; claiming ownership of that freed self was another" (95).

Clearly Marxist analysis can help illuminate many aspects of Morrison's complex novel. The fundamental Marxist concept of commodification is relevant to the treatment of slaves as property, and the concept of alienation pertains to the fragmentation of social relations and of individual selfhood experienced by slaves. In addition, *Beloved* indicates the important role played by the Western discourses of reason in the domination of slaves, a role that is usefully elucidated by the Horkheimer/Adorno critique of Enlightenment science. Finally Althusser's notion of interpellation provides a valuable framework within which to understand the important role played by psychological conditioning in the domination of slaves. Morrison's focus on the precapitalist phenomenon of slavery does not vitiate Marxist analysis. Indeed such an analysis makes an important contribution to more general discussions of the relationships among slavery, capitalism, racism, and gender oppression.

Works Cited

Althusser, Louis. *Lenin and Philosophy and Other Essays,* 170–183. Trans. Ben Brewster. London: Monthly Review, 1971.

Carby, Hazel V. *Reconstructing Womanhood: The Emergence of the Afro-American Woman Novelist.* New York: Oxford UP, 1987.

Elkins, Stanley. *Slavery: A Problem in American Institutional and Intellectual Life.* Chicago: U of Chicago P, 1968.

Horkheimer, Max, and Theodor W. Adorno. *Dialectic of Enlightenment.* Trans. John Cumming. New York: Seabury, 1972.

Jameson, Fredric. *Marxism and Form: Twentieth-Century Dialectical Theories of Literature.* Princeton, N.J.: Princeton UP, 1971.

———. "Third-World Literature in the Era of Multinational Capitalism." *Social Text* 15 (1986): 65-88.

Keenan, Sally. "'Four Hundred Years of Silence': Myth, History, and Motherhood in Toni Morrison's *Beloved.*" In *Recasting the World: Writing after Colonialism,* ed. Jonathan White, 45-81. Baltimore, Md.: Johns Hopkins UP, 1993.

Mbalia, Dorothea Drummond. *Toni Morrison's Developing Class Consciousness.* London: Associated UP, 1991.

Morrison, Toni. *Beloved.* New York: Plume-Penguin, 1988.

Nkrumah, Kwame. *Class Struggle in Africa.* New York: International Publishers, 1970.

Omolade, Barbara. "Hearts of Darkness." In *Desire: The Politics of Sexuality,* ed. A. Snitow, C. Stansell, and S. Thompson, 350-367. New York: Monthly Review, 1983.

Rodney, Walter. *How Europe Underdeveloped Africa.* Dar es Salaam: Tanzania Publishing House, 1972.

Schapiro, Barbara. "The Bonds of Love and the Boundaries of the Self in Toni Morrison's *Beloved.*" *Contemporary Literature* 32.2 (1991): 194-210.

Williams, Eric. *Capitalism and Slavery.* New York: Putnam, 1944.

Wyatt, Jean. "Giving Body to the Word: The Maternal Symbolic in Toni Morrison's *Beloved.*" *PMLA* 108.3 (1993): 474-488.

FEMINIST CRITICISM

Beloved focuses most obviously on issues related to race, but (as in all of Morrison's work) gender issues are central to the text as well. Morrison's treatment of slavery in the book concentrates on the special forms of oppression suffered by women slaves. By extension, Morrison also suggests the special difficulties encountered by black women in American society even outside the bounds of slavery. At the same time, Morrison indicates that prevailing stereotypes of masculinity pose special problems for black men. On the positive side, Morrison explores potential solutions to the problems she delineates in the novel, suggesting in particular the contribution that feminine energies can make to this project. Indeed Morrison's own text, which employs a number of modes of discourse that have been identified as feminine in recent feminist criticism, can itself be taken as a direct demonstration of the possibilities for feminine subversion of traditional patriarchal attitudes.

Morrison has specifically characterized her career as an attempt to explore the kinds of experience that black male writers have failed to encompass in their work. For example, she once said in an interview with a white male, "I always missed some intimacy, some direction, some voice. Ralph Ellison and Richard Wright—all of whose books I admire enormously—I didn't feel they were telling *me* something. I thought they were saying something about *it* or *us* that revealed something about *us* to *you,* to others, to white people, to men" (Ruas 218). In *Beloved,* Morrison seeks to uncover private and intimate aspects of slave life that have been suppressed (for various reasons) in both conventional histories and slave narratives such as Harriet Jacobs's *Incidents in the Life of a Slave Girl.*

And she does so partially by employing a mode of writing that has much in common with discussions of feminine language in the work of French feminists such as Héléne Cixous and Julia Kristeva.

Paralleling the identification by both Cixous and Kristeva of musical language as distinctively feminine, elements of song often creep into Morrison's text, as various characters recall songs that they have heard at earlier important periods in their lives. *Beloved* echoes the belief (articulated especially by Cixous) that feminine language is related to the special sense of connection that women have to their bodies, a sense that arises from primal memories of infantile Imaginary Order fantasies of fusion with the body of the mother. *Beloved* also emphasizes that these sorts of private psychological experiences cannot be separated from the social world. The book suggests that for slave women the experience of slavery might impede the easy acceptance of the physical body that Cixous identifies as quintessentially feminine and that the propagation of certain stereotypes about black women might perpetuate this alienation well beyond the nominal end of slavery.

In response, *Beloved* seeks to overcome this alienation. As Jean Wyatt notes, the book places a great deal of emphasis on forms of experience normally excluded from "Western cultural narratives," including the experiences of childbirth and nursing (474). Several passages in the book openly embrace the physicality of the feminine body. In one scene, Denver recalls the advice given her by her grandmother, Baby Suggs, to overcome the abusive expropriation of the feminine body that had been the lot of slave women: "Slaves not supposed to have pleasurable feelings on their own; their bodies not supposed to be like that, but they have to have as many children as they can to please whoever owned them. Still they were not supposed to have pleasure deep down. She said for me not to listen to all that. That I should always listen to my body and love it" (209).

The emphasis on feminine physicality in *Beloved* often focuses on bodily fluids, reinforcing an emphasis on images of water and other fluids that are central to the entire text. These images may involve the crucial Ohio River that Sethe and the slaves with her must cross to enter the free North or the breaking of Sethe's water as she is about to give birth to her daughter Denver while crossing that river. Indeed the text's images of water and other fluids (especially Sethe's breast milk and her daughter's blood) are quite often associated with the experience of motherhood. One of *Beloved*'s most important instances of water imagery occurs when Sethe first sees the reincarnated Beloved and then immediately produces a copious, uncontrollable flow of urine that the text specifically identifies as a symbolic reenactment of the release of amniotic fluids before childbirth: "Like flooding the boat when Denver was born. . . . But there was no stopping water breaking from a breaking womb and there was no stopping now" (51).

Morrison's extensive use of water imagery recalls Cixous's argument that water is a central feminine image. Cixous describes the woman's text as "a lively combination of flying colors, leaves, and rivers plunging into the sea. . . . We are ourselves sea, sand, coral, sea-weed, beaches, tides, swimmers, children, waves" (260). Such water imagery is common to Imaginary Order fantasies of the feminine. It is perhaps no accident that Sigmund Freud describes the experience of his "oral" stage (somewhat analogous to Jacques Lacan's Imaginary) as an "oceanic feeling." Water imagery is also prevalent in the brief but crucial chapter narrated late in *Beloved* by Beloved herself. Seeming to merge with an ancestor who came over from Africa on a slave ship, Beloved identifies the lack of water (despite the fact that the ship itself is in the midst of an ocean) as one of the more oppressive elements of the long sea journey. Images of floating in water are also prominent in this chapter, which involves a number of fantasies of fusion of the kind typically associated with Lacan's Imaginary Order. These fantasies are somewhat vague, and it is not always clear whether Beloved is fantasizing a fusion with her mother Sethe or with her symbolic ancestor on the slave ship, but then such generalized fantasies would be consistent with Beloved's allegorical role in the text.

Stylistically this chapter—with its lack of punctuation, its nonstandard syntax, and its flowing, musical rhythms—is the section of the book that corresponds most clearly to French feminist ideas of feminine writing. Indeed this section's appearance in the text might be described as an eruption of the semiotic of the kind discussed by Kristeva. But if the semiotic (or Cixous's *l'écriture féminine*) is related to a recovery of the infant's experience in the early stage dominated by the Imaginary Order, then we would expect Beloved's own discourse to correspond quite closely to these notions of feminine language. After all, Beloved was killed while she was still quite young. Her development was thus arrested while still in the Imaginary Order stage, and she would retain a special access to the feelings and experiences associated with that stage. Lorraine Liscio suggests that Morrison's text as a whole can be usefully comprehended within the context of Kristeva's notion of the revolutionary potential of semiotic language: "Morrison's focus on the preoedipal mother/infant daughter bond offers a subversive modality meant to disrupt the symbolic white schoolteacherly language that kills" (35).

French feminists such as Cixous and Kristeva might suggest that Morrison's experimental writing practice, with its numerous violations of traditional literary decorum, is automatically subversive of patriarchal authority. But Morrison supplements the subversive potential of her style through her focus on powerful feminist content. Much of the oppression described in *Beloved* is specifically related to gender and sexuality. Morrison emphasizes that slave women were valued more for their reproductive capabilities than for their work as servants or field laborers. Thus Paul D recognizes that Schoolteacher was willing to track the escaped Sethe all the way to Cincinnati because of the high value of slave women of child-bearing age: "Her price was greater than his; property that reproduced itself without cost" (228). The treatment of slave women as breeding stock is one of the central themes of *Beloved,* which calls attention to the dehumanization of slave women brought about by this practice.

In this sense, Morrison describes an element of slave life that has been extensively documented in slave narratives and conventional histories. But Morrison follows through on the implications of this motif in ways that most of her predecessors did not. Noting, for example, that the children produced by slave women were quite frequently fathered by their white masters, Morrison specifically calls attention to the fact that the sexuality of slave women added to their value not only because they could produce additional slaves but also because they could provide their white masters with sexual pleasure. It has long been conventional to describe the whole phenomenon of slavery as a metaphorical rape of the slave population. But Morrison forcefully points out in *Beloved* that quite literal rapes were an everyday occurrence in the lives of slave women. Morrison has emphasized to Marsha Darling in an interview that she wanted in the book to make sure that readers were forced to confront the horrors of slavery "in the flesh" rather than from the more comfortable distance of metaphor (5). *Beloved* contains numerous examples of the literal use of black women as sexual slaves. After the young Sethe observes the gruesome death of her mother by hanging, another slave woman reveals to the girl that the mother had earlier given birth to several children as a result of forced sex with numerous white men. The woman Ella recalls her earlier life in slavery when she was once kept locked in a room for more than a year by a white man and his son, who tortured and sexually brutalized her.

This sexual abuse of black women does not end with the nominal termination of slavery. For example, there are rumors in the contemporary (1873-1874) Cincinnati of the book that a black girl was recently held for years as a sexual slave by a local white man. And even when black women are not literally raped, they are often forced to submit to unwanted sexual advances to survive. Sethe's mother-in-law, Baby Suggs, once agreed to have sex with a farm boss for four months to be able to keep her latest child with her—only to have the child sold away the next year. In what is probably the book's most poignant example of this sort of sexual commodification, the destitute Sethe is forced to have sex with a stonecutter to pay him for carving the word "Beloved" on the headstone of her dead baby daughter.

Sethe remains traumatized by this experience, the memory of which remains "more alive, more pulsating than the baby blood that soaked her fingers like oil" (5). But for Sethe, the most painful memory of sexual abuse involves a crucial experience on Sweet Home Farm when, in a kind of rape, she is held down by one of Schoolteacher's "pupils" while the other nurses from her breasts, still flowing with milk for her infant daughter. Schoolteacher, meanwhile, looks on and takes notes on the event, making it all the more humiliating for Sethe. Humiliation is, of course, the very point of the taking of Sethe's milk, which is done in retribution for the recent attempted escape of several of the Sweet Home men. When Sethe complains to Mrs. Garner about this humiliation, she is beaten savagely by one of the pupils as a punishment for her "indiscretion," leaving her back permanently scarred.

The brutality of the rape of black women by white men in *Beloved* allows Morrison to counter the myth that slave women submitted quite willingly to sex with their white masters. As Hazel V. Carby points out, this myth of the sexual acquiescence of slave women (which still contributes to stereotypes about the sexual promiscuity of black women to this very day) can be attributed to male historians and sociologists being reluctant "to condemn as an act of rape what is conceived in patriarchal terms to be sexual compliance" (22). Morrison's text has a great deal in common with much feminist criticism in its focus on the deconstruction of negative representations of women. Thus Sally Keenan points out that *Beloved* makes a powerful statement against the traditional stereotyping of black women: "If black women have been historically captured between representations of themselves as lascivious whores and emasculating matriarchs, images that derive directly from the enslaved condition of their maternal ancestors, then Morrison's vision of the stories of mothers and daughters under slavery can be seen as undoing those deadly cultural myths" (53).

Morrison also counters the tendency to see women simply as passive victims of male violence. There are numerous examples of feminine resistance in the text. The taking of Sethe's milk and her subsequent beating do not humble her into submission. Instead they merely increase her resolve to escape and get her breast milk to her baby daughter, who has already been taken safely to Cincinnati. And the book's central event, Sethe's killing of that baby daughter to prevent her from being taken into slavery, is also clearly an act of resistance, however horrifying and morally ambiguous. Many of the examples of feminine resistance in *Beloved* echo Sethe's refusal to allow her children to be slaves. There are at least two examples of women who attempt to regain control of their own bodies by refusing to mother the children produced by forced sex in slavery. Sethe's mother "throws away" the babies fathered on her by white men, and Ella refuses to nurse the baby born after her year in captivity, allowing it to die. The girl held as a sexual slave in Cincinnati apparently kills her captor and escapes.

Morrison also explores the impact of sexual subjugation on black men. For one thing, men are also treated as sexual objects under slavery, frequently being ordered to couple with black women to produce offspring or even being rented out to stud on neighboring farms (140). Men are also sometimes subjected to rape, as when the black men on the chain gang with Paul D in Alfred, Georgia, are forced to perform oral sex on their white guards at gunpoint (108). In addition, Morrison suggests that black men feel sexually frustrated and humiliated not only by their own treatment by whites but also by the treatment of black women as sexual objects for the pleasure of white men. When Sethe's husband, Halle, observes the taking of her milk by Schoolteacher and his pupils, Halle himself is so shamed that he goes insane. Worse, black men sometimes take out their frustration and humiliation on the black women rather than on the white men. When Paul D proclaims that he has never mistreated a woman, Sethe responds that he is perhaps the only man in the world who can make such a claim (68).

Before the arrival of Schoolteacher, slave women on Sweet Home Farm are not sexually used by the master Mr. Garner, who also treats his slave men more humanely than most slave owners in the South. Among other things, Mr. Garner's relatively enlightened policies mean that his five young, unattached slave men are not put out to stud to produce more slaves. As a result, with no young women on the farm, they copulate with calves as the only outlet for their sexual impulses. This turn to bestiality seems quite natural given that the men themselves are essentially treated like cattle, despite Garner's supposed liberality. When the young Sethe first comes to Sweet Home Farm, all of the farm's slave men entertain fantasies of raping her, though they manage to resist this temptation (10–11). Dehumanized themselves and conditioned to think of black women as cattle, the men believe that "the jump . . . from a calf to a girl wasn't all that mighty" (26).

Beloved also notes that slave men often felt contempt for the slave women who were used for the sexual pleasure of white men. Late in the text, the old ex-slave Stamp Paid reveals to Paul D that during his days as a slave named Joshua, his wife, Vashti, was appropriated for nearly a year for use as a sexual object by the son of his white owner. During that time, Joshua had no sexual relations with his wife and hardly spoke to her. When Vashti returned after the son tired of her, Joshua, feeling his own manhood undermined, contemplated murdering her. Again, however, Morrison points toward potential forms of resistance to such impulses. Joshua channeled his anger in positive directions, changing his name to Stamp Paid (indicating that he has paid his dues) as a sort of declaration of independence, then gaining his freedom and working tirelessly to help other slaves escape to freedom as well.

Joshua's activities, crucial to the black community in Cincinnati, indicate the importance that Morrison places on communal solidarity among blacks as a response to the difficulties thrust on them by white society. Often this solidarity involves meaningful sexual relationships between men and women, as when the defiant slave Sixo feels the pieces of his fragmented selfhood being reassembled through the love of his "Thirty-Mile Woman" or when Paul D and Sethe resolve to face the future together and help each other overcome the wounds of the past. But cooperative relations among women are also crucial to Morrison's vision of communal solidarity. Sethe is able to give birth to her daughter Denver only with the help of escaped white indentured servant Amy Denver. And a key scene in the book occurs when Ella and the other black women in the Cincinnati community where Sethe lives band together to try freeing her from being haunted by Beloved's ghost.

Barbara Schapiro emphasizes the importance of community in *Beloved* and argues that Morrison's book suggests that human selfhood is defined only through relation to others: "The free, autonomous self, *Beloved* teaches, is an inherently social self, rooted in relationship and dependent at its core on the vital bond of mutual recognition" (209). Such visions of selfhood, or subjectivity, that emphasize the primary importance of relations between different subjects, or intersubjectivity, have been central to a number of feminist attempts to explore new feminine models of selfhood. Reviewing a number of feminist notions of the communal selfhood, Judith Kegan Gardiner observes, "Throughout women's lives, the self is defined through social relationships; issues of fusion and merger of the self with others are significant, and ego and body boundaries remain flexible" (182). Gardiner notes that feminine models of subjectivity, based on sharing and communication between individuals, differ markedly from traditional masculine models of the strong, independent individual. Drawing on the work of Nancy Chodorow, Gardiner concludes (in an analysis with clear relevance to the relationship between Morrison's Sethe and Beloved) that this difference arises from the fundamentally different nature of the infantile relationship to the mother: "The daughter acquires empathy and the capacity for symbiotic merger through her infantile identification with her mother" (186).

Of course, in *Beloved* the relationship between Sethe and Beloved has a dark side, and the "merger" between mother and daughter nearly results in the mother's death. This complication can be attributed to the complexity of Beloved's function in the text: She represents not merely an individual daughter but also the entire burden of black American history. In particular, Beloved represents the slave past, in which mother-daughter relations were routinely interrupted. In any case, Morrison's representation of communality is never simple or naive, and the text suggests that true solidarity is not easy to achieve. At times, for example, the threesome of Sethe, Denver, and Beloved seem on their way to a viable sense of community, especially during the scene in which they go ice skating. But there are ambiguities even in this scene: The three women do not have enough skates to go around, and they fall constantly on the ice. The attempts of Paul D and Sethe to build a life must overcome considerable difficulties as well; when Paul D first learns that Sethe killed her infant daughter eighteen years earlier, he is so appalled that he moves out of the house, and their relationship is seriously threatened. Finally the community of black women in Cincinnati is seriously disrupted when a communal feast conducted by Baby Suggs leads not to solidarity but to jealousy and strife (137). This disruption leads directly to the book's central tragedy when the community fails to warn Sethe of the approach of Schoolteacher when he comes to take her and her children back into slavery. In the end, however, Paul D and Sethe are together, and the black women of Cincinnati have again come together in Sethe's defense. *Beloved* is thus ultimately hopeful about the possibility of community even as it insists that the past can never be completely escaped. It is significant that the ghost of Beloved still roams the woods around 124 Bluestone, even as Sethe undertakes her new life.

Works Cited

Carby, Hazel V. *Reconstructing Womanhood: The Emergence of the Afro-American Woman Novelist.* New York: Oxford UP, 1987.

Cixous, Hélène. "The Laugh of the Medusa." In *New French Feminisms,* ed. Elaine Marks and Isabelle de Courtivron, 245-264. New York: Schocken, 1981.

Darling, Marsha. "In the Realm of Responsibility: A Conversation with Toni Morrison." *Women's Review of Books* (March 1988): 5-6.

Gardiner, Judith Kegan. "On Female Identity and Writing by Women." In *Writing and Sexual Difference,* ed. Elizabeth Abel, 177-191. Chicago: U of Chicago P, 1982.

Jacobs, Harriet. *Incidents in the Life of a Slave Girl, Written by Herself.* Ed. Jean Fagan Yellin. Cambridge, Mass.: Harvard UP, 1987.

Keenan, Sally. "'Four Hundred Years of Silence': Myth, History, and Motherhood in Toni Morrison's *Beloved.*" In *Recasting the World: Writing after Colonialism,* ed. Jonathan White, 45-81. Baltimore, Md.: Johns Hopkins UP, 1993.

Liscio, Lorraine. "*Beloved*'s Narrative: Writing Mother's Milk." *Tulsa Studies in Women's Literature* 11.1 (1992): 31-46.

Morrison, Toni. *Beloved.* New York: Plume-Penguin, 1988.

Ruas, Charles. *Conversations with American Writers.* New York: Knopf, 1985.

Schapiro, Barbara. "The Bonds of Love and the Boundaries of the Self in Toni Morrison's *Beloved.*" *Contemporary Literature* 32.2 (1991): 194-210.

Wyatt, Jean. "Giving Body to the Word: The Maternal Symbolic in Toni Morrison's *Beloved.*" *PMLA* 108.3 (1993): 474-488.

SELECTED BIBLIOGRAPHY

Corti, Lillian. "*Medea* and *Beloved:* Self-Definition and Abortive Nurturing in Literary Treatments of the Infanticidal Mother." In *Disorderly Eaters: Texts in Self-Empowerment,* ed. Lilian R. Furst and Peter W. Graham, 61-77. University Park: Pennsylvania State UP, 1992.

Compares *Beloved* to Euripides's *Medea* in their treatment of the theme of infanticide and suggests certain affinities between Morrison's fictional world and Greek tragedy. Notes in particular the prominence of eating disorders and of the theme of cannibalism in Morrison's text.

Ferguson, Rebecca. "History, Memory, and Language in Toni Morrison's *Beloved.*" In *Feminist Criticism: Theory and Practice,* ed. Susan Sellers, 109-127. Toronto: U of Toronto P, 1991.

Examines the role of language and writing in Morrison's treatment of the theme of history in *Beloved.* Looks at Morrison's writing practice within the context of post-modernism, but notes that the experimental technique of *Beloved* is crucially related to the historical events that form its basis.

Henderson, Mae G. "Toni Morrison's *Beloved:* Re-membering the Body as Historical Text." In *Comparative American Identities: Race, Sex, and Nationality in the Modern Text,* ed. Hortense J. Spillers, 62-86. New York: Routledge, 1991.

Examines Morrison's treatment of personal memory as a source of public history. Discusses the motifs of memory, narrative, and history in *Beloved* in the context of contemporary theories of history and narrativity. Also comments on these motifs from the point of view of psychoanalysis.

Keenan, Sally. "'Four Hundred Years of Silence': Myth, History, and Motherhood in Toni Morrison's *Beloved.*" In *Recasting the World: Writing after Colonialism,* ed. Jonathan White, 45-81. Baltimore, Md.: Johns Hopkins UP, 1993.

Discusses the tension between myth and history in *Beloved.* Examines Morrison's treatment of the themes of motherhood and feminine resistance to slavery within the context of a meditation on memory and the processes of historical representation. Concludes that in *Beloved* the complexities of the relationship between the slave mother and her children mirrors the complexities of the relationship between African Americans and their history.

Krumholz, Linda. "The Ghosts of Slavery: Historical Recovery in Toni Morrison's *Beloved.*" *African American Review* 26.3 (1992): 395–408.

Focuses on the recovery of history as a process of healing in *Beloved.* Notes how Morrison uses elements from both the European novel tradition and African-American oral and literary traditions in constructing the text. Discusses the book's "rituals of healing" in terms of Freud's notion of repression. Notes the importance of the folk tradition of the trickster tale in Morrison's text.

Liscio, Lorraine. "*Beloved*'s Narrative: Writing Mother's Milk." *Tulsa Studies in Women's Literature* 11.1 (1992): 31–46.

Discusses the themes of language and history in *Beloved* within the context of theories of women's writing such as Kristeva's notion of the symbolic and the semiotic. Notes the "trickster-like" use of language in slave narratives as a means of linguistic subversion of white domination and relates this use to Morrison's attempt to relate the unspoken history of slave women.

Mbalia, Dorothea Drummond. *Toni Morrison's Developing Class Consciousness.* London: Associated UP, 1991.

Discusses Morrison's novels from *The Bluest Eye* to *Beloved* in terms of the gradual development of Morrison's class consciousness and of her understanding that the true enemy of black people in America is capitalism. Sees *Beloved* as a positive exploration of the theme of solidarity and of the possibility for resistance to oppression though collective action: "Thus, the stress on shared relationships, community, and race responsibility—the traditional African principle of collectivism—is the dominant theme of the novel" (91).

Mobley, Marilyn Sanders. "A Different Remembering: Memory, History, and Meaning in Toni Morrison's *Beloved.*" In *Modern Critical Views: Toni Morrison,* ed. Harold Bloom, 189–199. New York: Chelsea House, 1990.

Discusses the background of *Beloved* in Morrison's work editing *The Black Book.* Notes how Morrison "uses the trope of memory to revise the genre of the slave narrative and thereby to make the slave experience it inscribes more accessible to contemporary readers" (191). Compares Morrison's retelling of history to Bakhtin's concept of reaccentuation.

Morrison, Toni. "Unspeakable Things Unspoken: The Afro-American Presence in American Literature." In *Modern Critical Views: Toni Morrison,* ed. Harold Bloom, 201–230. New York: Chelsea House, 1990.

Notes that literary canons are inherently political and discusses some of the specific political motivations for the domination of the American canon by white male writers. Suggests some of the ways the study of Afro-American literature can productively challenge this canon. Looks at the first lines of her novels in an effort to reveal the Afro-American presence in her own writing.

Owusu, Kofi. "Rethinking Canonicity: Toni Morrison and the (Non)Canonic 'Other.'" In *Rewriting the Dream: Reflections on the Changing American Literary Canon,* ed. W. M. Verhoeven, 60–74. Amsterdam: Rodopi, 1992.

Discusses the history of the American literary canon and its relationship to a politics of exclusion. Investigates several of Morrison's novels and suggests that her work importantly challenges the traditional politics of canon formation.

Park, Sue. "One Reader's Response to Toni Morrison's *Beloved.*" *Conference of College Teachers of English Studies* 56 (September 1991): 39–46.

Offers a personal response to the book, emphasizing unusual factors such as the title page design and the decorations on the first pages of the main sections.

Rushdy, Ashraf H. A. "Daughters Signifyin(g) History: The Example of Toni Morrison's *Beloved.*" *American Literature* 64.3 (1992): 567-597.
Reads *Beloved* within the larger context of the project to develop viable forms of African-American historiography that will enable the use of the past as a stimulus to positive action in the present. Includes a detailed discussion of the historical background of the book's main story line. Emphasizes the importance of elements of oral culture in *Beloved* and focuses on the doubleness of Morrison's vision in the book.

Samuels, Wilfred D., and Clenora Hudson-Weems. *Toni Morrison.* Boston: Twayne, 1990.
Looks at Morrison's novels from *The Bluest Eye* to *Beloved.* Reviews the historical background of *Beloved* and relates it to the tradition of slave narratives. Discusses the relationship between Sethe and Beloved from the point of view of Chodorow's studies of mother-daughter relations. Provides a useful review of the book's major characters and their roles in the text.

Schapiro, Barbara. "The Bonds of Love and the Boundaries of the Self in Toni Morrison's *Beloved.*" *Contemporary Literature* 32.2 (1991): 194-210.
Employs object-relations psychology to explore the psychic impact of slavery and the importance of intersubjective relations in *Beloved.* Notes the importance of such relations and of narrative to the development of personal identity. Concludes that for Morrison the self is essentially social and that a free, autonomous self is "rooted in relationship and dependent at its core on the vital bond of mutual recognition" (209).

Schmudde, Carol E. "Knowing When to Stop: A Reading of Toni Morrison's *Beloved.*" *CLA Journal* 37.2 (1993): 121-135.
Compares *Beloved* to Greek tragedy in terms of the moral ambiguity of Sethe's action in killing her child. Notes how the present action of the book unfolds as a result of events many years earlier, as in a Greek tragedy. Observes that the black community in the book functions in a manner reminiscent of the chorus in a Greek tragedy.

Scruggs, Charles. "The Invisible City in Toni Morrison's *Beloved.*" *Arizona Quarterly* 48.3 (1992): 95-132.
Focuses on the theme of community in *Beloved,* seeing the text as a meditation on "the origins of community and the integration of the individual within the community's life-sustaining body" (99). Notes how the movement toward a black community in the text counters the forces from the society at large that tend to lead toward fragmentation of the community and alienation of the individual. Discusses storytelling as one of the book's principal images of communal activity.

Stave, Shirley A. "Toni Morrison's *Beloved* and the Vindication of Lilith." *South Atlantic Review* 58.1 (1993): 49-66.
Notes the parallels between Morrison's narrative and the cabalistic myth of Lilith, Adam's first wife. Concludes that Morrison's use of the Lilith myth results in a subversive reconstruction of the biblical story of Eden that "sanctions female defiance of patriarchal authority at the same time that it allows an unsentimentalized view of motherhood" (65).

Todd, Richard. "Toni Morrison and Canonicity: Acceptance or Appropriation?" In *Rewriting the Dream: Reflections on the Changing American Literary Canon,* ed. W. M. Verhoeven, 43-59. Amsterdam: Rodopi, 1992.
Meditates on whether Morrison's newly canonical status represents long overdue recognition of writing by women and African Americans or appropriation of her writing in the interests of the existing establishment. Warns against arguing the importance of Morrison's work simply by comparing it to that of traditional canonical figures such as Shakespeare.

Travis, Molly Abel. "Speaking from the Silence of the Slave Narrative: *Beloved* and African-American Women's History." *Texas Review* 1-2 (Spring-Summer 1992): 69-81.
Notes how *Beloved* attempts to fill in the gaps in traditional slave narratives and compares Morrison's project of historical recovery to the work of feminist revisionist historians such as Gerda Lerner, Paula Gaddings, and Angela Davis.

Wyatt, Jean. "Giving Body to the Word: The Maternal Symbolic in Toni Morrison's *Beloved.*" *PMLA* 108.3 (1993): 474-488.
Approaches *Beloved* from a feminist perspective informed by Lacanian psychoanalysis. Discusses Morrison's attempts to find a language for giving voice to orders of experience that are typically excluded from conventional history, including childbirth and nursing from the mother's perspective, the desires of the preverbal infant, and the sufferings of those destroyed by slavery. Emphasizes Beloved's "collective identity" as a representative of the slave experience.

Introduction to Criticism in Practice

chapter **16**

Essays on *The Tempest*, by William Shakespeare

Learning to Curse: Aspects of Linguistic Colonialism in the Sixteenth Century

STEPHEN J. GREENBLATT

At the close of *Musophilus,* Samuel Daniel's brooding philosophical poem of 1599, the poet's spokesman, anxious and uncertain through much of the dialogue in the face of his opponent's skepticism, at last rises to a ringing defense of eloquence, and particularly English eloquence, culminating in a vision of its future possibilities:

> And who in time knowes whither we may vent
> The treasure of our tongue, to what strange shores
> This gaine of our best glorie shal be sent,
> T'inrich vnknowing Nations with our stores?
> What worlds in th'yet vnformed Occident
> May come refin'd with th'accents that are ours?[1]

For Daniel, the New World is a vast, rich field for the plantation of the English language. Deftly he reverses the conventional image and imagines argosies freighted with a cargo of priceless words, sailing west "T'inrich vnknowing Nations with our stores." There is another reversal of sorts here: the "best glorie" that the English voyagers will carry with them is not "the treasure of our faith" but "the treasure of our tongue." It is as if in place of the evangelical spirit, which in the early English voyages is but a small flame compared to the blazing mission of the Spanish friars, Daniel would substitute a linguistic mission, the propagation of English speech.

Linguistic colonialism is mentioned by continental writers as well but usually as a small part of the larger enterprise of conquest, conversion, and settlement. Thus Peter Martyr writes to Pope Leo X of the "large landes and many regyons whiche shal hereafter receaue owre nations, tounges, and maners: and therwith embrase owre relygion."[2] Occasionally, more substantial claims are made. In 1492, in the introduction to his *Gramática*, the first grammar of a modern European tongue, Antonio de Nebrija writes that language has always been the partner ("compañera") of empire. And in the ceremonial presentation of the volume to Queen Isabella, the bishop of Avila, speaking on the scholar's behalf, claimed a still more central role for language. When the queen asked flatly, "What is it for?" the bishop replied, "Your Majesty, language is the perfect instrument of empire."[3] But for Daniel, English is neither partner nor instrument; its expansion is virtually the goal of the whole enterprise.

Daniel does not consider the spread of English a conquest but rather a gift of inestimable value. He hasn't the slightest sense that the natives might be reluctant to abandon their own tongue; for him, the Occident is "yet unformed," its nations "unknowing." Or, as Peter Martyr puts it, the natives are a *tabula rasa* ready to take the imprint of European civilization: "For lyke as rased or vnpaynted tables, are apte to receaue what formes soo euer are fyrst drawen theron by the hande of the paynter, euen soo these naked and simple people, doo soone receaue the customes of owre Religion, and by conuersation with owre men, shake of theyr fierce and natiue barbarousnes."[4] The mention of the nakedness of the Indians is typical; to a ruling class obsessed with the symbolism of dress, the Indians' physical appearance was a token of a cultural void. In the eyes of the Europeans, the Indians were culturally naked.

This illusion that the inhabitants of the New World are essentially without a culture of their own is both early and remarkably persistent, even in the face of overwhelming contradictory evidence. In his journal entry for the day of days, 12 October 1492, Columbus expresses the thought that the Indians ought to make good servants, "for I see that they repeat very quickly whatever was said to them." He thinks, too, that they would easily be converted to Christianity, "because it seemed to me that they belonged to no religion." And he continues: "I, please Our Lord, will carry off six of them at my departure to Your Highnesses, that they may learn to speak." The first of the endless series of kidnappings, then, was plotted in order to secure interpreters; the primal crime in the New World was committed in the interest of language. But the actual phrase of the journal merits close attention: "that they may learn to speak" (*para que aprendan a hablar*).[5] We are dealing, of course, with an idiom: Columbus must have known, even in that first encounter, that the Indians could speak, and he argued from the beginning that they were rational human beings. But the idiom has a life of its own; it implies that the Indians had no language at all.

This is, in part, an aspect of that linguistic colonialism we have already encountered in *Musophilus*: to speak is to speak one's own language, or at least a language with which one is familiar. "A man would be more cheerful with his dog for company," writes Saint Augustine, "than with a foreigner."[6] The unfamiliarity of their speech is a recurrent motif in the early accounts of the New World's inhabitants, and it is paraded forth in the company of all their other strange and often repellent qualities. The chronicler Robert Fabian writes of three savages presented to Henry VII that they "were clothed in beasts skins, & did eate raw flesh, and spake such speach that no man could understand them, and in their demeanour like to bruite beastes." Roy Harvey Pearce cites this as an example of the typical English view of the Indians as animals, but Fabian is far more ambiguous, for he continues: "Of the which upon two yeeres after, I saw two apparelled after the maner of Englishmen in Westminster pallace, which that time I could not discerne from Englishmen, til I was learned what they were, but as for speach, I heard none of them utter one word."[7] When he sees the natives again, are they still savages, now masked by their dress, or was his first impression misleading? And the seal of the ambiguity is the fact that he did not hear them utter a word, as if the real test of their conversion to civilization would be whether they had been able to master a language that "men" could understand.

In the 1570's the strangeness of Indian language can still be used in precisely the same way. In his first voyage to "Meta Incognita," as George Best reports, Frobisher captured a savage to take home with him as ". . . a sufficient witnesse of the captaines farre and tedious travell towards the unknowen parts of the world, as did well appeare by this strange infidell, whose like was never seene, read, nor heard of before, and whose language was neither knowen nor understood of any. . . ."[8] For Gregorio García, whose massive study of the origins of the Indians was published in 1607, there was something diabolical about the difficulty and variety of languages in the New World: Satan had helped the Indians to invent new tongues, thus impeding the labors of Christian missionaries.[9] And even the young John Milton, attacking the legal jargon of his time, can say in rhetorical outrage, "our speech is, I know not what, American, I suppose, or not even human!"[10]

Of course, there were many early attempts to treat Indian speech as something men could come to understand. According to John H. Parry, "all the early friars endeavoured to master Indian languages, usually Nahuatl, though some acquired other languages; the learned Andrés de Olmos, an early companion of Zumárraga, was credited with ten."[11] Traders and settlers also had an obvious interest in learning at least a few Indian words, and there are numerous word lists in the early accounts, facilitated as Peter Martyr points out by the fortuitous circumstance that "the languages of all the nations of these Ilandes, maye well be written with our Latine letters."[12] Such lists even suggested to one observer, Marc Lescarbot, the fact the Indian languages could change in time, just as French had changed from the age of Charlemagne. This, he explains, is why Cartier's dictionary of Indian words, compiled in the 1530's, is no longer of much use in the early seventeenth century.[13]

Indian languages even found some influential European admirers. In a famous passage, Montaigne approvingly quotes in translation several Indian songs, noting of one that "the invention hath no barbarism at all in it, but is altogether Anacreontic." In his judgment, "Their language is a kind of pleasant speech, and hath a pleasing sound and some affinity with the Greek terminations."[14] Raleigh, likewise, finds that the Tivitivas of Guiana have "the most manlie speech and most deliberate that euer I heard of what nation soeuer,"[15] while, in the next century, William Penn judges Indian speech "lofty" and full of words "of more sweetness or greatness" than most European tongues.[16] And the great Bartolomé de Las Casas, as he so often does, turns the tables on the Europeans:

> A man is apt to be called barbarous, in comparison with another, because he is strange in his manner of speech and mispronounces the language of the other. . . . According to Strabo, Book XIV, this was the chief reason the Greeks called other peoples barbarous, that is, because they were mispronouncing the Greek language. But from this point of view, there is no man or race which is not barbarous with respect to some other man or race. . . . Thus, just as we esteemed these peoples of these Indies barbarous, so they considered us, because of not understanding us.[17]

Simple and obvious as this point seems to us, it does not appear to have taken firm hold in the early years of conquest and settlement. Something of its spirit may be found in Oviedo's observation of an Indian interpreter failing to communicate with the members of another tribe: "[he] did not understand them better than Biscayan talking Basque could make himself intelligible to a person speaking German or Arabic, or any other strange language."[18] But the view that Indian speech was close to gibberish remained current in intellectual as well as popular circles at least into the seventeenth century.[19] Indeed it is precisely in educated, and particularly humanist, circles that the view proved most tenacious and extreme. The rough, illiterate sea dog, bartering for gold trinkets on a faraway beach, was far more likely than the scholar to understand that the natives had their own tongue. The captains or lieutenants whose accounts we read had stood on the same beach, but when they sat down to record their experiences, powerful cultural presuppositions asserted themselves almost irresistibly.

For long before men without the full command of language, which is to say without eloquence, were thought to have been discovered in the New World, Renaissance humanists *knew* that such men existed, rather as modern scientists knew from the periodic table of the necessary existence of elements yet undiscovered. Virtually every Renaissance schoolboy read in Cicero's *De oratore* that only eloquence had been powerful enough "to gather scattered mankind together in one place, to transplant human beings from a barbarous life in the wilderness to a civilized social system, to establish organized communities, to equip them with laws and judicial safeguards and civil rights."[20] These lines, and similar passages from Isocrates and Quintilian, are echoed again and again in the fifteenth and sixteenth centuries as the proudest boast of the *studium humanitatis.* Eloquence, wrote Andrea Ugo of Siena in 1421, led wandering humanity from a savage, bestial existence to civilized culture. Likewise, Andrea Brenta of Padua declared in 1480 that primitive men had led brutish and lawless lives in the fields until eloquence brought them together and converted barbaric violence into humanity and culture.[21] And more than a hundred years later, Puttenham can make the same claim, in the same terms, on behalf of poetry:

> Poesie was th'originall cause and occasion of their first assemblies, when before the people remained in the woods and mountains, vagrant and dipersed like the wild beasts, lawlesse and naked, or verie ill clad, and of all good and necessarie prouision for harbour or sustenance vtterly vnfurnished: so as they litle diffred for their maner of life, from the very brute beasts of the field.[22]

Curiously enough, a few pages later Puttenham cites the peoples of the New World as proof that poetry is more ancient than prose:

> This is proued by certificate of marchants & trauellers, who by late nauigations haue surueyed the whole world, and discouered large countries and strange peoples wild and sauage, affirming that the American, the Perusine & the very Canniball, do sing and also say, their highest and holiest matters in certaine riming versicles and not in prose.[23]

But it was more reasonable and logically consistent to conclude, as others did, that the savages of America were without eloquence or even without language. To validate one of their major tenets, humanists needed to reach such a conclusion, and they clung to it, in the face of all the evidence, with corresponding tenacity.

Moreover, both intellectual and popular culture in the Renaissance had kept alive the medieval figure of the Wild Man, one of whose common characteristics is the absence of speech. Thus when Spenser's Salvage Man, in Book VI of the *Faerie Queene,* wishes to express his compassion for a distressed damsel, he kisses his hands and crouches low to the ground,

> For other language had he none, nore speach,
> But a soft murmure, and confused sound
> Of senselesse words, which Nature did him teach.[24]

To be sure, the Wild Man of medieval and Renaissance literature often turns out to be of gentle blood, having been lost, as an infant, in the woods; his language problem, then, is a consequence of his condition, rather than, as in Cicero, its prime cause. But this view accorded perfectly with the various speculations about the origins of the Indians, whether they were seen as lost descendants of the Trojans, Hebrews, Carthaginians, or Chinese. Indian speech, that speech no man could understand, could be viewed as the tattered remnants of a lost language.[25]

It is only a slight exaggeration, I think, to suggest that Europeans had, for centuries, rehearsed their encounter with the peoples of the New World, acting out, in their response to the legendary Wild Man, their mingled attraction and revulsion, longing and hatred. In the Christian Middle Ages, according to a recent account, "the Wild Man is the distillation of the specific anxieties underlying the three securities supposedly provided by the specifically Christian institutions of civilized life: the securities of *sex* (as organized by the institution of the family), *sustenance* (as provided by the political, social, and economic institutions), and *salvation* (as provided by the Church)."[26] These are precisely the areas in which the Indians most disturb their early observers. They appear to some to have no stable family life and are given instead to wantonness and perversion.[27] Nor, according to others, are they capable of political organization or settled social life. Against the campaign to free the enslaved Indians, it was argued that once given their liberty, they would return to their old ways: "For being idle and slothfull, they wander vp & downe, and returne to their olde rites and ceremonies, and foule and mischieuous actes."[28] And everywhere we hear of their worship of idols which, in the eyes of the Europeans, strikingly resemble the images of devils in Christian art.[29]

Certainly the Indians were again and again identified as Wild Men, as wild, in the words of Francis Pretty, "as ever was a bucke or any other wilde beast."[30] "These men may very well and truely be called Wilde," writes Jacques Cartier, at once confirming and qualifying the popular name, "because there is no poorer people in the world."[31] Peter Martyr records tales of Wild Men in the New World, but he distinguishes them from the majority of the inhabitants:

> They say there are certeyne wyld men whiche lyue in the caues and dennes of the montaynes, contented onely with wilde fruites. These men neuer vsed the companye of any other: nor wyll by any meanes becoome tame. They lyue without any certaine dwellynge places, and with owte tyllage or culturynge of the grounde, as wee reade of them whiche in oulde tyme lyued in the golden age. They say also that these men are withowte any certaine language. They are sumtymes seene. But owre men haue yet layde handes on none of them.[32]

As Martyr's description suggests, Wild Men live beyond the pale of civilized life, outside all institutions, untouched by the long, slow development of human culture. If their existence is rude and repugnant, it also has, as Martyr's curious mention of the Golden Age suggests, a disturbing allure. The figure of the Wild Man, and the Indians identified as Wild Men, serve as a screen onto which Renaissance Europeans, bound by their institutions, project their darkest and yet most compelling fantasies. In the words of the earliest English tract on America:

> the people of this lande haue no kynge nor lorde nor theyr god. But all thinges is comune/this people goeth all naked. . . . These folke lyuen lyke bestes without any resonablenes and the wymen be also as comon. And the men hath conuersacyon tih with wymen/who that they ben or who they fyrst mete/is she his syster/his mother/his daughter/or any

> other kyndred. And the wymen be very hoote and dysposed to lecherdnes. And they ete also on[e] a nother. The man etethe his wyfe his chylderne. . . . And that lande is ryght full of folke/for they lyue commonly, iii. C. [300] yere and more as with sykenesse they dye nat.[33]

This bizarre description is, of course, an almost embarrassingly clinical delineation of the Freudian id. And the id, according to Freud, is without language.

At the furthest extreme, the Wild Man shades into the animal—one possible source of the medieval legend being European observation of the great ages.[34] Language is, after all, one of the crucial ways of distinguishing between men and beasts: "The one special advantage we enjoy over animals," writes Cicero, "is our power to speak with one another, to express our thoughts in words."[35] Not surprisingly, then, there was some early speculation that the Indians were subhuman and thus, among other things, incapable of receiving the true faith. One of the early advocates on their behalf, Bernadino de Minaya, recalls that, on his return to Spain from the New World,

> I went on foot, begging, to Valladolid, where I visited the cardinal and informed him that Friar Domingo [de Betanzos, an exponent of the theory that the Indians were beasts] knew neither the Indians' language nor their true nature. I told him of their ability and the right they had to become Christians. He replied that I was much deceived, for he understood that the Indians were no more than parrots, and he believed that Friar Domingo spoke with prophetic spirit. . . .[36]

The debate was dampened but by no means extinguished by Pope Paul III's condemnation, in the bull *Sublimis Deus* (1537), of the opinion that the Indians are "dumb brutes created for our service" and "incapable of receiving the Catholic faith."[37] Friar Domingo conceded in 1544 that the Indians had language but argued against training them for the clergy on the grounds that their language was defective, lacking the character and copiousness necessary to explain Christian doctrine without introducing great improprieties which could easily lead to great errors.[38] Similarly, Pierre Massée observes that the Brazilian Indians lack the letters F, L, and R, which they could only receive by divine inspiration, insofar as they have neither "Foy, Loy, ne Roy."[39] Ironically, it is here, in these virtual slanders, that we find some of the fullest acknowledgment of the enormous cultural gap between Europeans and Indians, and of the near impossibility of translating concepts like conversion, Incarnation, or the Trinity into native speech.[40]

Perhaps the profoundest literary exploration of these themes in the Renaissance is to be found in Shakespeare. In *The Tempest* the startling encounter between a lettered and an unlettered culture is heightened, almost parodied, in the relationship between a European whose entire source of power is his library and a savage who had no speech at all before the European's arrival. "Remember / First to possess his books," Caliban warns the lower-class and presumably illiterate Stephano and Trinculo,

> for without them
> He's but a sot, as I am, nor hath not
> One spirit to command: they all do hate him
> As rootedly as I. Burn but his books.[41]

This idea may well have had some historical analogue in the early years of conquest. In his *Thresor de l'histoire des langves de cest univers* (1607), Claude Duret reports that the Indians, fearing that their secrets would be recorded and revealed, would not approach certain trees whose leaves the Spanish used for paper, and Father Chaumonot writes in 1640 that the Hurons "were convinced that we were sorcerers, imposters come to take possession of their country, after having made them perish by our spells, which were shut up in our inkstands, in our books, etc.,—inasmuch that we dared not, without hiding ourselves, open a book or write anything."[42]

The link between *The Tempest* and the New World has often been noted, most recently by Terence Hawkes who suggests, in his book *Shakespeare's Talking Animals,* that in creating Prospero, the playwright's imagination was fired by the resemblance he perceived between himself and a colonist. "A colonist," writes Hawkes,

> acts essentially as a dramatist. He imposes the 'shape' of his own culture, *embodied in his speech,* on the new world, and makes that world recognizable, habitable, 'natural,' able to speak his language.[43]

Conversely,

> the dramatist is metaphorically a colonist. His art penetrates new areas of experience, his language expands the boundaries of our culture, and makes the new territory over in its own image. His 'raids on the inarticulate' open up new worlds for the imagination. (212)[44]

To read such glowing tribute, one would never know that there had been a single doubt whispered in the twentieth century about the virtues of European colonialism. More important, one would never know that Prospero and the other Europeans leave the island at the end of the play. If *The Tempest* is holding up a mirror to colonialism, Shakespeare is far more ambivalent than Terence Hawkes about the reflected image.

Caliban enters in Act I, cursing Prospero and protesting bitterly: "This island's mine, by Sycorax my mother, / Which thou tak'st from me" (I. ii. 333-334). When he first arrived, Prospero made much of Caliban, and Caliban, in turn, showed Prospero "all the qualities o'th'isle." But now, Caliban complains, "I am all the subjects that you have, / Which first was mine own King." Prospero replies angrily that he had treated Caliban "with human care" until he tried to rape Miranda, a charge Caliban does not deny. At this point, Miranda herself chimes in, with a speech Dryden and others have found disturbingly indelicate:

Abhorred slave,
Which any print of goodness wilt not take,
Being capable of all ill! I pitied thee,
Took pains to make thee speak, taught thee each hour
One thing or other: when thou didst not, savage,
Know thine own meaning, but wouldst gabble like
A thing most brutish, I endow'd thy purposes
With words that made them known. But thy vile race,
Though thou didst learn, had that in't which good natures
Could not abide to be with; therefore wast thou
Deservedly confin'd into this rock,
Who hadst deserv'd more than a prison.[45]

To this, Caliban replies:

You taught me language; and my profit on't
Is, I know how to curse. The red plague rid you
For learning me your language! (I. ii. 353-367)

Caliban's retort might be taken as self-indictment: even with the gift of language, his nature is so debased that he can only learn to curse. But the lines refuse to mean this; what we experience instead is a sense of their devastating justness. Ugly, rude, savage, Caliban nevertheless achieves for an instant an absolute, if intolerably bitter, moral victory. There is no reply; only Prospero's command: "Hag-seed, hence! / Fetch us in fuel," coupled with an ugly threat:

If thou neglect'st, or dost unwillingly
What I command, I'll rack thee with old cramps,
Fill all thy bones with aches, make thee roar,
That beasts shall tremble at thy din. (I. ii. 370-373)

What makes this exchange so powerful, I think, is that Caliban is anything but a Noble Savage. Shakespeare does not shrink from the darkest European fantasies about the Wild Man; indeed he exaggerates them: Caliban is deformed, lecherous, evil-smelling, idle, treacherous, naive, drunken, rebellious, violent, and devil-worshipping.[46] According to Prospero, he is not even human: a "born devil," "got by the devil himself / Upon thy wicked dam" (I. ii. 321-322). *The Tempest* utterly rejects the uniformitarian view of the human race, the view that would later triumph in the Enlightenment and prevail in the West to this day. All men, the play seems to suggest, are *not* alike; strip away the adornments of culture and you will *not* reach a single human essence. If anything, *The Tempest* seems closer in spirit to the attitude of the present-day inhabitants of Java who, according to Clifford Geertz, quite flatly say, "To be human is to be Javanese."[47]

And yet out of the midst of this attitude Caliban wins a momentary victory that is, quite simply, an assertion of inconsolable human pain and bitterness.

And out of the midst of this attitude Prospero comes, at the end of the play, to say of Caliban, "this thing of darkness I / Acknowledge mine" (V. i. 275–276). Like Caliban's earlier reply, Prospero's words are ambiguous; they might be taken as a bare statement that the strange "demi-devil" is one of Prospero's party as opposed to Alonso's, or even that Caliban is Prospero's slave. But again the lines refuse to mean this: they acknowledge a deep, if entirely unsentimental, bond. By no means is Caliban accepted into the family of man; rather, he is claimed as Philoctetes might claim his own festering wound. Perhaps, too, the word "acknowledge" implies some moral responsibility, as when the Lord, in the King James translation of Jeremiah, exhorts men to "acknowledge thine iniquity, that thou hast transgressed against the Lord thy God" (3:13). Certainly the Caliban of Act V is in a very real sense Prospero's creature, and the bitter justness of his retort early in the play still casts a shadow at its close. With Prospero restored to his dukedom, the match of Ferdinand and Miranda blessed, Ariel freed to the elements, and even the wind and tides of the return voyage settled, Shakespeare leaves Caliban's fate naggingly unclear. Prospero has acknowledged a bond; that is all.

Arrogant, blindly obstinate, and destructive as was the belief that the Indians had no language at all, the opposite conviction—that there was no significant language barrier between Europeans and savages—may have had consequences as bad or worse. Superficially, this latter view is the more sympathetic and seductive, in that it never needs to be stated. It is hard, after all, to resist the story of the *caciques* of the Cenú Indians who are reported by the Spanish captain to have rebutted the official claim to their land thus:

> what I said about the Pope being the Lord of all the universe in the place of God, and that he had given the land of the Indies to the King of Castille, the Pope must have been drunk when he did it, for he gave what was not his; also . . . the King, who asked for, or received, this gift, must be some madman, for that he asked to have that given him which belonged to others.[48]

It is considerably less hard to resist the account of the *caciques* of New Granada who declared in a memorial sent to the pope in 1553 that "if by chance Your Holiness has been told that we are bestial, you are to understand that this is true inasmuch as we follow devilish rites and ceremonies."[49] The principle in both cases is the same: whatever the natives may have actually thought and said has been altered out of recognition by being cast in European diction and syntax.

Again and again in the early accounts, Europeans and Indians, after looking on each other's faces for the first time, converse without the slightest difficulty; indeed the Indians often speak with as great a facility in English or Spanish as the Renaissance gentlemen themselves. There were interpreters, to be sure, but these are frequently credited with linguistic feats that challenge belief. Thus Las

Casas indignantly objects to the pretense that complex negotiations were conducted through the mediation of interpreters who, in actual fact, "communicate with a few phrases like 'Gimme bread,' 'Gimme food,' 'Take this, gimme that,' and otherwise carry on with gestures."[50] He argues that the narratives are intentionally falsified, to make the *conquistadores'* actions appear fairer and more deliberative than they actually were. There may have been such willful falsification, but there also seems to have been a great deal of what we may call "filling in the blanks." The Europeans and the interpreters themselves translated such fragments as they understood or thought they understood into a coherent story, and they came to believe quite easily that the story was what they had actually heard. There could be, and apparently were, murderous results.[51]

The savages in the early accounts of the New World may occasionally make strange noises—"Oh ho" or "bow-wow"[52]—but, once credited with intelligible speech, they employ our accents and are comfortable in our modes of thought. Thus the amorous daughter of a cruel *cacique,* we learn in *The Florida of the Inca,* saved the young Spanish captive with the following words:

> Lest you lose faith in me and despair of your life or doubt that I will do everything in my power to save you . . . I will assist you to escape and find refuge if you are a man and have the courage to flee. For tonight, if you will come at a certain hour to a certain place, you will find an Indian in whom I shall entrust both your welfare and mine.[53]

It may be objected that this is narrative convention: as in adventure movies, the natives look exotic but speak our language. But such conventions are almost never mere technical conveniences. If it was immensely difficult in sixteenth-century narratives to represent a language barrier, it is because embedded in the narrative convention of the period was a powerful, unspoken belief in the isomorphic relationship between language and reality. The denial of Indian language or of the language barrier grew out of the same soil that, in the mid-seventeenth century, would bring forth the search for a universal language. Many sixteenth-century observers of the Indians seem to have assumed that language—their language—represented the true, rational order of things in the world. Accordingly, Indians were frequently either found defective in speech, and hence pushed toward the zone of wild things, or granted essentially the same speech as the Europeans. Linguists in the seventeenth century brought the underlying assumption to the surface, not, of course, to claim that English, or Latin, or even Hebrew expressed the shape of reality, but to advocate the discovery or fashioning of a universal language that would do so.

Behind this project, and behind the narrative convention that foreshadowed it, lay the conviction that reality was one and universal, constituted identically for all men at all times and in all places. The ultimate grounds for this faith were theological and were many times explicitly voiced, as here by Raleigh in his *History of the World:*

> The same just God who liueth and gouerneth all thinges for euer, doeth in these our times giue victorie, courage, and discourage, raise, and throw downe Kinges, Estates, Cities, and Nations, for the same offenses which were committed of old, and are committed in the present.[54]

There is a single faith, a single text, a single reality.

This complex of convictions may illuminate that most startling document, the *Requerimiento,* which was drawn up in 1513 and put into effect the next year. The *Requerimiento* was to be read aloud to newly encountered peoples in the New World; it demands both obedience to the king and queen of Spain as rulers of the Indies by virtue of the donation of the pope, and permission for the religious fathers to preach the true faith. If these demands are promptly met, many benefits are promised, but if there should be refusal or malicious delay, the consequences are made perfectly clear:

> We shall take you and your wives and your children, and shall make slaves of them, and as such shall sell and dispose of them as their Highnesses may command; and we shall take away your goods, and shall do you all the mischief and damage that we can, as to vassals who do not obey, and refuse to receive their lord, and resist and contradict him; and we protest that the deaths and losses which shall accrue from this are your fault, and not that of their Highnesses or ours, nor of these cavaliers who come with us. And that we have said this to you and made this Requisition, we request the notary here present to give us his testimony in writing, and we ask the rest who are present that they should be witnesses of this Requisition.[55]

Las Casas writes that he doesn't know "whether to laugh or cry at the absurdity" of the *Requerimiento,* an absurdity born out in the stories of its actual use.[56] In our times, Madariaga calls it "quaint and naive," but neither adjective seems to me appropriate for what is a diabolical and, in its way, sophisticated document.[57]

A strange blend of ritual, cynicism, legal fiction, and perverse idealism, the *Requerimiento* contains at its core the conviction that there is no serious language barrier between the Indians and the Europeans. To be sure, there are one or two hints of uneasiness, but they are not allowed to disrupt the illusion of scrupulous and meaningful communication established from the beginning:

> On the part of the King, Don Fernando, and of Doña Juana, his daughter, Queen of Castille and Leon, subduers of the barbarous nations, we their servants notify and make known to you, as best we can, that the Lord our God, Living and Eternal, created the Heaven and the Earth, and one man and one woman, of whom you and we, and all the men of the world, were and are descendants, and all those who come after us.[58]

The proclamation that all men are brothers may seem an odd way to begin a document that ends with threats of enslavement and a denial of responsibility for all ensuing deaths and losses, but it is precisely this opening that justifies the close. That all human beings are descended from "one man and one woman" proves that there is a single human essence, a single reality. As such, all problems of communication are merely accidental. Indeed, the *Requerimiento* conveniently passes over in silence the biblical account of the variety of languages and the scattering of mankind. In Genesis 11, we are told that "the whole earth was of one language, and of one speech," until men began to build the tower of Babel:

> And the Lord said, Behold, the people is one, and they have all one language; and this they begin to do: and now nothing will be restrained from them, which they have imagined to do. Go to, let us go down, and there confound their language, that they may not understand one another's speech. So the Lord scattered them abroad from thence upon the face of all the earth: and they left off to build the city. (Gen. 11:6–8)

In place of this, the *Requerimiento* offers a demographic account of the dispersion of the human race:

> on account of the multitude which has sprung from this man and woman in the five thousand years since the world was created, it was necessary that some men should go one way and some another, and that they should be divided into many kingdoms and provinces, for in one alone they could not be sustained.[59]

The Babel story has to be omitted, for to acknowledge it here would be to undermine the basic linguistic premise of the whole document.

The *Requerimiento,* then, forces us to confront the dangers inherent in what most of us would consider the central liberal tenet, namely the basic unity of mankind. The belief that a shared essence lies beneath our particular customs, stories, and language turns out to be the cornerstone of the document's self-righteousness and arrogance. It certainly did not cause the horrors of the Conquest, but it made those horrors easier for those at home to live with. After all, the Indians had been warned. The king and queen had promised "joyfully and benignantly" to receive them as vassals. The *Requerimiento* even offered to let them see the "certain writings" wherein the pope made his donation of the Indies. If, after all this, the Indians obstinately refused to comply, they themselves would have to bear responsibility for the inevitable consequences.

The two beliefs that I have discussed in this paper—that Indian language was deficient or non-existent and that there was no serious language barrier—are not, of course, the only sixteenth-century attitudes toward American speech. I have already mentioned some of the Europeans, missionaries, and laymen who took native tongues seriously. There are, moreover, numerous practical acknowledgments of the language problem which do not simply reduce the native speech to gibberish. Thus René de Laudonnière reports that the Indians "every houre made us a 1000 discourses, being merveilous sory that we could not understand them." Instead of simply throwing up his hands, he proceeds to ask the Indian names for various objects and comes gradually to understand a part of what they are saying.[60]

But the theoretical positions on Indian speech that we have considered press in from either side on the Old World's experience of the New. Though they seem to be opposite extremes, both positions reflect a fundamental inability to sustain the simultaneous perception of likeness and difference, the very special perception we give to metaphor. Instead they either push the Indians toward utter difference—and thus silence—or toward utter likeness—and thus the collapse of their own, unique identity. Shakespeare, in *The Tempest*, experiments with an extreme version of this problem, placing Caliban at the outer limits of difference only to insist upon a mysterious measure of resemblance. It is as if he were testing our capacity to sustain metaphor. And in this instance only, the audience achieves a fullness of understanding before Prospero does, an understanding that Prospero is only groping toward at the play's close. In the poisoned relationship between master and slave, Caliban can only curse; but we know that Caliban's consciousness is not simply a warped negation of Prospero's:

> I prithee, let me bring thee where crabs grow;
> And I with my long nails will dig thee pig-nuts;
> Show thee a jay's nest, and instruct thee how
> To snare the nimble mamoset; I'll bring thee
> To clustering filberts, and sometimes I'll get thee
> Young scamels from the rock. (II. ii. 167–172)

The rich, irreducible concreteness of the verse compels us to acknowledge the independence and integrity of Caliban's construction of reality. We do not sentimentalize this construction—indeed the play insists that we judge it and that we prefer another—but we cannot make it vanish into silence. Caliban's world has what we may call *opacity,* and the perfect emblem of that opacity is the fact that we do not to this day know the meaning of the word "scamel."

But it is not until Vico's *New Science* (1725) that we find a genuine theoretical breakthrough, a radical shift from the philosophical assumptions that helped to determine European response to alien languages and cultures. Vico refuses to accept the position by then widely held that "in the vulgar languages meanings were fixed by convention," that "articulate human words have arbitrary significations." On the contrary, he insists, "because of their natural origins, they must have had natural significations."[61] Up to this point, he seems simply to be reverting to the old search for a universal character. But then he makes a momentous leap:

> There remains, however, the very great difficulty: How is it that there are as many different vulgar tongues as there are peoples? To solve it, we must here establish this great truth: that, as the peoples have certainly by diversity of climates acquired different natures, from which have sprung as many different customs, so from their different natures and customs as many different languages have arisen. (133)

For Vico, the key to the diversity of languages is not the arbitrary character of signs but the variety of human natures. Each language reflects and substantiates the specific character of the culture out of which it springs.

Vico, however, is far away from the first impact of the New World upon the Old, and, in truth, his insights have scarcely been fully explored in our own times. Europeans in the sixteenth century, like ourselves, find it difficult to credit another language with opacity. In other words, they render Indian language transparent, either by limiting or denying its existence or by dismissing its significance as an obstacle to communication between peoples. And as opacity is denied to native speech, so, by the same token, is it denied to native culture. For a specific language and a specific culture are not here, nor are they ever, entirely separable. To divorce them is to turn from the messy, confusing welter of details that characterize a particular society at a particular time to the cool realm of abstract principles. It is precisely to validate such high-sounding principles—"Eloquence brought men from barbarism to civility" or "All men are descended from one man and one woman"—that the Indian languages are peeled away and discarded like rubbish by so many of the early writers. But as we are now beginning fully to understand, reality for each society is constructed to a significant degree out of the *specific* qualities of its language and symbols. Discard the particular words and you have discarded the particular men. And so most of the people of the New World will never speak to us. That communication, with all that we might have learned, is lost to us forever.

NOTES

1. Samuel Daniel, *Poems and a Defence of Ryme,* ed. Arthur Colby Sprague (Cambridge 1930) 11. 957-962.
2. Peter Martyr, *The Decades of the Newe Worlde (De orbe novo),* trans. Richard Eden, Decade 3, Book 9, in *The First Three English Books on America,* ed. Edward Arber (Birmingham 1885) 177.
3. Antonio de Nebrija, *Gramática de la lengua castellana,* ed. Ig. González-Llubera (Oxford 1926) 3; Lewis Hanke, *Aristotle and the American Indians: A Study in Race Prejudice in the Modern World* (Chicago and London 1959) 8.
4. Martyr (n. 2 above) Decade 2, Book 1, p. 106.
5. Christopher Columbus, *Journals and Other Documents on the Life and Voyages of Christopher Columbus,* trans. and ed. Samuel Elio Morison (New York 1963) 65. For the Spanish, see Cristoforo Colombo, *Diario de Colón, libro de la primera navegación y descubrimiento de las Indias,* ed. Carlos Sanz López [fascimile of the

original transcript] (Madrid 1962) fol. 9b. There has been considerable debate about Columbus' journal, which survived only in Las Casas' transcription. But Las Casas indicates that he is quoting Columbus here, and the words are revealing, no matter who penned them.

6. Austine, *Concerning The City of God against the Pagans,* trans. Henry Bettenson, ed. David Knowles (Harmondsworth 1972) Book 19, Ch. 7, p. 861. The whole passage, with its reference to Roman linguistic colonialism, is interesting in this context:

   > . . . the diversity of languages separates man from man. For if two men meet, and are forced by some compelling reason not to pass on but to stay in company, then if neither knows the other's language, it is easier for dumb animals, even of different kinds, to associate together than these men, although both are human beings. For when men cannot communicate their thoughts to each other, simply because of difference of language, all the similarity of their common human nature is of no avail to unite them in fellowship. So true is this that a man would be more cheerful with his dog for company than with a foreigner. I shall be told that the Imperial City has been at pains to impose on conquered peoples not only her yoke but her language also, as a bond of peace and fellowship, so that there should be no lack of interpreters but even a profusion of them. True; but think of the cost of this achievement! Consider the scale of those wars, with all that slaughter of human beings, all the human blood that was shed!

   For a variation of the theme of linguistic isolation, see Shakespeare, *Richard II,* ed. Peter Ure (Cambridge, Mass. 1956) I. iii. 159–173.

7. Robert Fabian, in Richard Hakluyt, *The Principal Navigations, Voyages, Traffiques, and Discoveries of the English Nation* . . . (12 vols. Glasgow 1903–05) 7. 155. Roy Harvey Pearce, "Primitivistic Ideas in the *Faerie Queene,*" *Journal of English and Germanic Philology* 44 (1945) 149.
8. In Hakluyt (n. 7 above) 7. 282.
9. See Lee Eldridge Huddleston, *Origins of the American Indians; European Concepts, 1492–1729,* Latin American Monographs 11 (Austin, Tex. 1967) 66.
10. Milton, *Prolusiones,* ed. Donald Leman Clark, trans. Bromley Smith, in *Works,* ed. Frank Allen Peterson (18 vols. New York 1931–38) 12. 277.
11. John H. Parry, *The Spanish Seaborne Empire* (London and New York 1966) 163. Cf. France V. Scholes and Ralph L. Roys: "Although some of the friars, notably Fray Luis de Villalpando and Fray Diego de Landa, learned to speak and write Maya and gave instruction to the others, it is doubtful whether more than half of the clergy became proficient in the language." Quoted in *Landa's relación de las cosas de Yucatán,* trans. Alfred M. Tozzer, *Papers of the Peabody Museum of American Archaeology and Ethnology* 18 (1941) 70 n. 313.
12. Martyr (n. 2 above) Decade 1, Book 1, p. 67. See, in the same volume, Sebastian Münster, p. 29, and Martyr, Decade 2, Book 1, p. 138. For examples of word lists, see Martyr, Decade 3, Book 1, p. 45; Francisco López de Gómara, *The Pleasant Historie of the Conquest of the Weast India, now called New Spayne,* trans. T. N. (London 1578) 370 ff.; John Davis, in Hakluyt (n. 7 above) 7. 398–399; Sir Robert Dudley, in Hakluyt, 10. 211–212; William Strachey, *The Historie of Travell into Virginia Britania (1612),* ed. Louis B. Wright and Virginia Freund, Hakluyt Society, Ser. 2, 103 (London 1953) 174–207; James Rosier, "Extracts of a Virginian Voyage made An. 1605. by Captaine George Waymouth," in Samuel Purchas, *Hakluytus*

Posthumus, or Purchas his Pilgrimes, Hakluyt Society, Extra series (20 vols. Glasgow 1905-07; rpt. of 1625 ed.) 18. 359. The most delightful of the lists is Roger Williams, *A Key into the Language of America* (London 1643; rpt. Providence, R.I. 1936). There are also sample conversations in Indian languages; see Williams, *Key;* Jean de Léry, *Navigatio in Brasiliam Americae,* Ch. 19, in Theodor de Bry, *Americae tertia pars* (Frankfort 1592) 250 ff.; Martyr (n. 2 above) Decade 3, Book 8, p. 170.

13. Lescarbot, in Claude Duret, *Thresor de l'histoire des langves de cest univers* (Cologny 1613) 954-955. I am indebted for this reference and for many useful suggestions to Professor Natalie Zemon Davis.
14. Montaigne, *Selected Essays,* trans. John Florio, ed. Walter Kaiser (Boston 1964) 79. The possibility that Indian language has traces of Greek is explored by Sarmiento de Gamboa and Gregorio García (see Huddleston [n. 9 above] 30, 73), and by Thomas Morton, *New English Canaan,* in *Tracts and Other Papers Relating Principally to the Origin, Settlement, and Progress of the Colonies in North America,* comp. Peter Force (4 vols. Washington [c. 1836-47]; rpt. New York 1947 and Gloucester, Mass. 1963) 2. 15-18.
15. Raleigh, *The Discoverie of the large and bewtiful Empire of Guiana,* ed. V. T. Harlow (London 1928) 38.
16. Quoted in Gary B. Nash, "The Image of the Indian in the Southern Colonial Mind," in *The Wild Man Within: An Image in Western Thought from the Renaissance to Romanticism,* ed. Edward Dudley and Maximillian E. Novak (Pittsburgh 1972) 72. See, likewise, Cornelius J. Jaenen, "Amerindian Views of French Culture in the Seventeenth Century," *Canadian Historical Review* 55 (1974) 276-277.
17. Bartolomé de Las Casas, *A Selection of his Writings,* trans. and ed. George Sanderlin (New York 1971) 144. Thomas More makes the same point in the early sixteenth century to defend English: "For as for that our tong is called barbarous, is but a fantasye. For so is, as euery lerned man knoweth, euery strange langue to other." *Dialogue concerning Heresies,* quoted in J. L. Moore, *Tudor-Stuart Views on the Growth, Status, and Destiny of the English Language,* Studien zur Englischen Philologie 41 (Halle 1920) 19.
18. Oviedo, quoted in Sir Arthur Helps, *The Spanish Conquest of America and its Relation to the History of Slavery and to the Government of Colonies,* ed. M. Oppenheim (4 vols. London 1900-04; rpt. New York 1966) 1. 269.
19. For a nineteenth-century variation, see Daniel Webster's remark in a letter to Ticknor, 1 March 1826: "I ought to say that I am a total unbeliever in the new doctrines about the Indian languages. I believe them to be the rudest forms of speech; and I believe there is as little in the languages of the tribes as in their laws, manners, and customs, worth studying or worth knowing. All this is heresy, I know, but so I think"; see George Ticknor Curtis, *Life of Daniel Webster* (2 vols. New York 1872) 1. 260. By 1826, it should be noted, Webster is on the defensive. I owe this reference to Professor Larzer Ziff.
20. Cicero, *De oratore* I. viii. 33, in *On the Good Life,* trans. Michael Grant (Harmondsworth 1971) 247.
21. Andrea Ugo and Andrea Brenta, in Karl Müllner, *Reden und Brief Italienischer Humanisten* (Vienna 1899) 110-111, 75-76. See, likewise in the same volume, the orations of Lapo de Castiglionchio, Andrea Giuliano of Venice, Francesco Filelfo, Antonio da Rho, Tiphernas (Gregorio da Città di Castello), and Giovanni Toscanella.
22. George(?) Puttenham, *The Arte of English Poesie* (London 1589; Scolar Press facs. ed. Menston 1968) 3-4. The myth that Orpheus tamed wild beasts by his music is

intended to show, according to Puttenham, "how by his discreete and wholsome lessons vttered in harmonie and with melodious instruments, he brought the rude and sauage people to a more ciuill and orderly life, nothing, as it seemeth, more preuailing or fit to redresse and edifie the cruell and sturdie courage of man then it" (4). Without speech, according to Hobbes, "there had been amongst men, neither commonwealth, nor society, nor contract, nor peace, no more than amongst lions, bears, and wolves": *Leviathan,* ed. Michael Oakeshott (Oxford 1960) 18.

23. Puttenham (n. 22 above) 7. See also Sir Philip Sidney, *An Apologie for Poetrie,* in *English Literary Criticism: The Renaissance,* ed. O. B. Hardison, Jr. (New York 1963): "Euen among the most barbarous and simple Indians where no writing is, yet haue they their Poets, who make and sing songs, which they call *Areytos,* both of theyr Auncestors deedes and praises of theyr Gods: a sufficient probabilitie that if euer learning come among them, it must be by hauing theyr hard dull wits softned and sharpened with the sweete delights of Poetrie. For vntill they find a pleasure in the exercises of the minde, great promises of much knowledge will little perswade them that knowe not the fruites of knowledge" (102). On the Indian *Areytos,* see Martyr (n. 2 above) Decade 3, Book 7, pp. 166–167; likewise, Las Casas, *History of the Indies,* trans. and ed. Andrée Collard (New York 1971) 279–280. For a comparable phenomenon in the British Isles, see J. E. C. Hill, "Puritans and 'The Dark Corners of the Land'," *Royal Historical Society Transactions,* Ser. 5, 13 (1963) 82: "On Sundays and holy days, we are told of North Wales about 1600, 'the multitude of all sorts of men, women and children' used to meet to hear 'their harpers and crowthers sing them songs of the doings of their ancestors.'"
24. *The Faerie Queene,* VI. iv. 11, in *The Works of Edmund Spenser. A Variorum Edition,* ed. Edwin Greenlaw *et al.* (9 vols. Baltimore 1932–49). On Spenser's Wild Man, see Pearce (n. 7 above) and Donald Cheney, *Spenser's Image of Nature: Wild Man and Shepherd in "The Faerie Queene"* (New Haven 1966). On the figure of the Wild Man, see Dudley and Novak (n. 16 above); Richard Bernheimer, *Wild Men in the Middle Ages: A Study in Art, Sentiment, and Demonology* (Cambridge, Mass. 1952).
25. On the comparison of Indian and Old World words, see Huddleston (n. 9 above) esp. 23, 30, 37, 44, 91–92. The Indians were described by Cotton Mather as "the veriest *ruines of mankind,* which [were] to be found any where upon the face of the earth": quoted in Roy Harvey Pearce, *Savagism and Civilization: A Study of the Indian and the American Mind* (Baltimore 1965; rpt. 1967) 29.
26. Hayden White, "The Forms of Wildness: Archaeology of an Idea," in Dudley and Novak (n. 16 above) 21.
27. "Thei vse no lawful coniunction of mariage, but euery one hath as many women as him listeth, and leaueth them agayn at his pleasure," Sebastian Münster, *A Treatyse of the Newe 'India',* trans. Richard Eden, in Arber (n. 2 above) 37. See, likewise Martyr (n. 2 above) Decade 3, Book 1, p. 138; Martyr, trans. Michael Lok, in *A Selection of Curious, Rare, and Early Voyages and Histories of Interesting Discoveries chiefly published by Hakluyt . . .* (London 1812) Decade 8, Ch. 8, p. 673; Laudonnière, in Hakluyt (n. 7 above) 8. 453; Henry Hawks, in Hakluyt (n. 7 above) 9. 386; Bernal Díaz del Castillo, *The Conquest of New Spain,* trans. J. M. Cohen (Baltimore 1963) 19, 122, 124. On one of Frobisher's voyages, a native man and woman, captured separately, are brought together before the silent and eagerly expectant sailors. The observers are astonished at the "shamefastnes and chastity of those Savage captives" (in Hakluyt [n. 7 above] 7. 306).
28. Martyr, trans. Lok (n. 27 above) Decade 7, Ch. 4, p. 627. "Wandering up and down" seems almost as much of an offense as idolatry. There is a trace of this disapproval

and anxiety in Iago's description of Othello as an "erring barbarian," an "extravagant and wheeling stranger."

29. See for example, Martyr, trans. Lok (n. 27 above) Decade 4, Ch. 9, p. 539: "with such a countenance, as we use to paint hobgoblins or spirites which walke by night."
30. In Hakluyt (n. 7 above) 11. 1297. Note that Spenser uses the same metaphor for his Wild Man: "For he was swift as any bucke in chace" (*FQ,* VI, iv. 8).
31. In Hakluyt (n. 7 above) 8. 201-202.
32. Martyr, ed. Arber (n. 2 above) Decade 3, Book 8, p. 173.
33. *Of the newe landes,* in Arber (n. 2 above) p. xxvii; cf. Wilberforce Eames, "Description of a Wood Engraving Illustrating the South American Indians (1505)," *Bulletin of the New York Public Library* 26 (1922) 755-760.
34. Horst Woldemar Janson, *Apes and Ape Lore in the Middle Ages and the Renaissance* (London 1952).
35. Cicero, *De oratore* I. viii. 32, in *On the Good Life* (n. 20 above) 247.
36. Quoted in Lewis Hanke, "Pope Paul III and the American Indians," *Harvard Theological Review* 30 (1937) 84.
37. Quoted in Hanke (n. 36 above) 72; likewise in Hanke (n. 3 above) 19.
38. Quoted in Hanke (n. 36 above) 102. On his death-bed, Domingo de Betanzos recanted his denigration of the Indians.
39. Massée, in Duret (n. 13 above) 945.
40. For a more sympathetic grasp of the problem of translating religious concepts, see Las Casas (n. 23 above) 238-239; Marc Lescarbot, *History of New France,* trans. W. L. Grant (3 vols. Toronto 1907-14) 2. 179-180; José de Acosta, *The Natural and Moral History of the Indies,* trans. Edward Grimston [1604], ed. Clements R. Markham, Hakluyt Society 60-61 (2 vols. London 1880) 2. 301-302. Cornelius Jaenen (n. 16 above) suggests that the difficulty was more cultural than linguistic: "The natives saw some danger in divulging their religious vocabulary to the evangelists of the new religion, therefore they refused to cooperate extensively in the linguistic task of compiling dictionaries and grammars, and of translating religious books" (277).
41. *The Tempest,* ed. Frank Kermode (Cambridge, Mass. 1954) III. ii. 90-93.
42. Duret (n. 13 above) 935; Chaumonot, quoted in Jaenen (n. 16 above) 275-276.
43. Terence Hawkes, *Shakespeare's Talking Animals* (London 1973) 211. For a more sober appraisal of colonialism in *The Tempest,* see Dominique O. Mannoni, *Prospero and Caliban: The Psychology of Colonization,* trans. Pamela Powesland (New York 1956) 97-109.
44. "Raids on the inarticulate"—the quotation is from T. S. Eliot's *Four Quartets* and, as Hawkes uses it, suggests that the sixteenth-century fantasy that the Indians were without speech is alive in the 1970's.
45. The lines are sometimes attributed, without any textual authority, to Prospero. "Which any print of goodness wilt not take," it might be noted, plays on the *tabula rasa* theme.
46. Shakespeare even appeals to early seventeenth-century class fears by having Caliban form an alliance with the lower-class Stephano and Trinculo to overthrow the noble Prospero. On class-consciousness in the period, see Christopher Hill, "The Many-Headed Monster in Late Tudor and Early Stuart Political Thinking," in *From the Renaissance to the Counter-Reformation. Essays in Honor of Garrett Mattingly,* ed. Charles H. Carter (New York 1965) 296-324.
47. Clifford Geertz, "The Impact of the Concept of Culture on the Concept of Man," in his selected essays, *The Interpretation of Cultures* (New York 1973) 52. I am indebted throughout to this suggestive essay.

48. Enciso, *Suma de geographia,* quoted in Helps (n. 18 above) 1. 279-280.
49. Quoted in Hanke (n. 36 above) 95. It is not impossible that the *caciques* said something vaguely similar; see Las Casas (n. 23 above) 82: "what could we expect from these gentle and unprotected Indians suffering such torments, servitude and decimation but immense pusillanimity, profound discouragement and annihilation of their inner selves, to the point of doubting whether they were men or mere cats?"
50. Las Casas, (n. 23 above) 241.
51. *Ibid.,* 50-52, 130-131.
52. Both are in James Rosier (n. 12 above) 18. 342, 344.
53. Garcilaso de la Vega, *The Florida of the Inca,* trans. and ed. John Grier Varner and Jeannette Johnson Varner (Austin, Tex. 1951) 69-70; quoted by Howard Mumford Jones, *O Strange New World. American Culture: The Formative Years* (New York: 1964; Viking paperback ed. 1967) 25-26.
54. Sir Walter Raleigh, *The History of the World* (London 1614) II. xix. 3, pp. 508-509.
55. In Helps (n. 18 above) 1. 266-267.
56. Las Casas (n. 23 above) 196. For the actual use of the *Requerimiento,* see Lewis Hanke, *The Spanish Struggle for Justice in the Conquest of America* (Philadelphia 1949; rpt. Boston 1965) 34.
57. Salvador de Madariaga, *The Rise of the Spanish American Empire* (New York 1947) 12.
58. In Helps (n. 18 above) 1. 264.
59. *Ibid.*
60. In Hakluyt (n. 7 above) 8. 466.
61. Giambattista Vico, *The New Science,* trans. Thomas G. Bergin and Max H. Fisch (Ithaca 1948) 132.

Nymphs and Reapers Heavily Vanish: The Discursive Con-texts of *The Tempest*

Francis Barker
Peter Hulme

I

No one who has witnessed the phenomenon of midsummer tourism at Stratford-upon-Avon can fail to be aware of the way in which "Shakespeare" functions today in the construction of an English past: a past which is picturesque, familiar and untroubled. Modern scholarly editions of Shakespeare, amongst which the Arden is probably the most influential, have seemed to take their distance from such mythologizing by carefully locating the plays against their historical background. Unfortunately such a move always serves, paradoxically, only to highlight in the foregrounded text preoccupations and values which turn out to be not historical at all, but eternal. History is thus recognized and abolished at one and the same time. One of the aims of this essay is to give a closer account of this mystificatory negotiation of "history," along with an examination of the ways in which the relationship between text and historical context can be more adequately formulated. Particular reference will be made to the way in which, in recent years, traditional notions of the historicial sources of the text have been challenged by newer analyses which employ such terms as "intertextuality" and "discourse." To illustrate these, a brief exemplary reading will be offered of *The Tempest.* But to begin with, the new analyses themselves need setting in context.

II

The dominant approach within literary study has conceived of the text as autotelic, "an entity which always remains the same from one moment to the next" (Hirsch 1967, p. 46); in other words a text that is fixed in history and, at the same time, curiously free of historical limitation. The text is acknowledged as having been produced at a certain moment in history; but that history itself is reduced to being no more than a background from which the single and irreducible meaning of the text is isolated. The text is designated as the legitimate object of literary criticism, *over against* its contexts, whether they be arrived at through the literary-historical account of the development of particular traditions and genres or, as more frequently happens with Shakespeare's plays, the study of "sources." In either case the text has been separated from a surrounding ambit of other texts over which it is given a special pre-eminence.

In recent years, however, an alternative criticism, often referred to as "structuralist" and "post-structuralist," has sought to displace radically the primacy of the autotelic text by arguing that a text indeed "cannot be limited by or to . . . the originating moment of its production, anchored in the intentionality of its author."[1] For these kinds of criticism exclusive study of the moment of production is defined as narrowly "historicist" and replaced by attention to successive *inscriptions* of a text during the course of its history.[2] And the contextual background—which previously had served merely to highlight the profile of the individual text—gives way to the notion of *intertextuality,* according to which, in keeping with the Saussurean model of language, no text is intelligible except in its differential relations with other texts.[3]

The break with the moment of textual production can easily be presented as liberatory; certainly much work of importance has stemmed from the study of inscription. It has shown for example that texts can never simply be *encountered* but are, on the contrary, repeatedly constructed under definite conditions: *The Tempest* read by Sir Walter Raleigh in 1914 as the work of England's national poet is very different from *The Tempest* constructed with full textual apparatus by an editor/critic such as Frank Kermode, and from the "same" text inscribed institutionally in that major formation of "English Literature" which is the school or university syllabus and its supporting practices of teaching and examination.[4]

If the study of the inscription and reinscription of texts has led to important work of historical description, it has also led to the formulation of a political strategy in respect of literary texts, expressed here by Tony Bennett when he calls for texts to be "articulated with new texts, socially and politically mobilized in different ways within different class practices" (Bennett 1982, p. 224). This strategy also depends, therefore, on a form of intertextuality which identifies in all texts a potential for new linkages to be made and thus for new political meanings to be constructed. Rather than attempting to derive the text's significance from the moment of its production, this politicized intertextuality emphasizes the present *use* to which texts can now be put. This approach undercuts itself, however, when, in the passage from historical description to contemporary rearticulation, it claims for itself a radicalism which it cannot then deliver. Despite speaking of texts as always being "installed in a field of struggle" (Bennett 1982, p. 229), it denies to itself the very possibility of combating the dominant orthodoxies. For if, as the logic of Bennett's argument implies, "the text" were wholly dissolved into an indeterminate miscellany of inscriptions, then how could any confrontation between different but contemporaneous inscriptions take place: what would be the ground of such a contestation?[5] While a genuine difficulty in theorizing "the text" does exist, this should not lead inescapably to the point where the only option becomes the voluntaristic ascription to the text of meanings and articulations derived simply from one's own ideological preferences. This is a procedure only too vulnerable to pluralistic incorporation, a recipe for peaceful co-existence with the dominant readings, not for a contestation of those readings themselves. Struggle can only occur if two positions attempt to occupy the same space, to appropriate the "same" text; "alternative" readings condemn themselves to mere irrelevance.

Our criticism of this politicized intertextuality does not however seek to reinstate the autotelic text with its single fixed meaning. Texts are certainly not available for innocent, unhistorical readings. Any reading must be made *from* a particular position, but is not *reducible* to that position (not least because texts are not infinitely malleable or interpretable, but offer certain constraints and resistances to readings made of them). Rather, different readings struggle with each other on the site of the text, and all that can count, however provisionally, as knowledge of a text, is achieved through this discursive conflict. In other words, the onus on new readings, especially radical readings aware of their own theoretical and political positioning, should be to proceed by means of a *critique* of the dominant readings of a text.

We say critique rather than simply criticism, in reference to a powerful radical tradition which aims not merely to disagree with its rivals but to *read their readings:* that is, to identify their inadequacies and to explain why such readings come about and what ideological role they play.[6] Critique operates in a number of ways, adopting various strategies and lines of attack as it engages with the current ideological formations, but one aspect of its campaign is likely to have to remain constant. Capitalist societies have always presupposed the naturalness and universality of their own structures and modes of perception, so, at least for the foreseeable future, critiques will need to include an *historical* moment, countering capitalism's self-universalization by reasserting the rootedness of texts in the contingency of history. It is this particular ground that what we have been referring to as alternative criticism runs the risk of surrendering unnecessarily. As we emphasized earlier, the study of successive textual inscriptions continues to be genuinely important, but it must be recognized that attention to such inscriptions is not logically dependent on the frequent presupposition that *all* accounts of the moment of production are either crudely historicist or have recourse to claims concerning authorial intentionality. A *properly* political intertextuality would attend to successive inscriptions without abandoning that no longer privileged but still crucially important *first* inscription of the text. After all, only by maintaining our right to make statements that we can call "historical" can we avoid handing over the very notion of history to those people who are only too willing to tell us "what really happened."

III

In order to speak of the Shakespearean text as an historical utterance, it is necessary to read it with and within series of *con-texts.*[7] These con-texts are the precondition of the plays' historical and political signification, although literary criticism has operated systematically to close down that signification by a continual process of occlusion. This may seem a strange thing to say about the most notoriously bloated of all critical enterprises, but in fact "Shakespeare" has been force-fed behind a high wall called Literature, built out of the dismantled pieces of other seventeenth-century discourses. Two particular examples of the occlusive process might be noted here. First, the process of occlusion is accomplished in the production of critical meaning, as is well illustrated by the case of Caliban. The occlusion of his political claims—one of the subjects of the present essay—is achieved by installing him at the very centre of the play, but only as the ground of a nature/art confrontation, itself of undoubted importance of the Renaissance, but here, in Kermode's account, totally without the historical contextualization that would locate it among the early universalizing forms of incipient bourgeois hegemony (Shakespeare 1954, pp. xxxiv–lxiii). Secondly, source criticism, which might *seem* to militate against autotelic unity by relating the text in question to other texts, in fact only obscures such relationships. Kermode's paragraphs on "The New World" embody the hesitancy with which Shakespearean scholarship has approached the problem. Resemblances between the *language* of the Bermuda pamphlets and that of *The Tempest* are brought forward as evidence that Shakespeare "has these documents in mind" but, since this must remain "inference" rather than "fact," it can only have subsidiary importance, "of the greatest interest and usefulness," while clearly not "fundamental to [the play's] structure of ideas." Such "sources" are then reprinted in an appendix so "the reader may judge of the verbal parallels for himself," and the matter closed (Shakespeare 1964, pp. xxvii–xxviii).

And yet such closure proves premature since, strangely, source criticism comes to play an interestingly crucial role in Kermode's production of a site for *The Tempest*'s meaning. In general, the fullness of the play's unity needs protecting from con-textual contamination, so "sources" are kept at bay except for the odd verbal parallel. But occasionally, and on a strictly *singular* basis, that unity can only be protected by recourse to a notion of source as explanatory of a feature otherwise aberrant to that posited unity. One example of this would be Prospero's well-known irascibility, peculiarly at odds with Kermode's picture of a self-disciplined, reconciliatory white magician, and therefore to be "in the last analysis, explained by the fact that [he] descend[s] from a bad-tempered giant-magician" (Shakespeare 1964, p. lxiii). Another would be Prospero's strange perturbation which brings the celebratory masque of Act IV to such an abrupt conclusion, in one reading (as we will demonstrate shortly) the most important scene in the play, but here explained as "a point at which an oddly pedantic concern for classical structure causes it to force its way through the surface of the play (Shakespeare 1964, p. lxxv)." In other words the play's unity is constructed only by shearing off some of its "surface" complexities and explaining them away as irrelevant survivals or unfortunate academicisms.

Intertextuality, or con-textualization, differs most importantly from source criticism when it establishes the necessity of reading *The Tempest* alongside congruent texts, irrespective of Shakespeare's putative knowledge of them, and when it holds that such congruency will become apparent from the constitution of discursive networks to be traced independently of authorial "intentionality."

IV

Essential to the historic-political critique which we are proposing here are the analytic strategies made possible by the concept of *discourse*. Intertextuality has usefully directed attention to the relationship *between* texts: discourse moves us towards a clarification of just what kinds of relationship are involved.[8]

Traditionally *The Tempest* has been related to other texts by reference to a variety of notions: *source,* as we have seen, holds that Shakespeare was influenced by his reading of the Bermuda pamphlets. But the play is also described as belonging to the *genre* of pastoral romance and is seen as occupying a particular place in the *canon* of Shakespeare's works. Intertextuality has sought to displace work done within this earlier paradigm, but has itself been unable to break out of the practice of connecting text with text, of assuming that single texts are the ultimate objects of study and the principal units of meaning.[9] Discourse, on the other hand, refers to the *field* in and through which texts are produced. As a concept wider than "text" but narrower than language itself (Saussure's *langue*), it operates at the level of the enablement of texts. It is thus not an easy concept to grasp because discourses are never simply observable but only approachable through their effects just as, in a similar way, grammar can be said to be *at work* in particular sentences (even those that are ungrammatical), governing their construction but never fully present "in" them. The operation of discourse is implicit in the regulation of what statements can and cannot be made and the forms that they can legitimately take. Attention to discourse therefore moves the focus from the interpretative problem of meaning to questions of instrumentality and function. Instead of *having* meaning, statements should be seen as *performative* of meaning; not as possessing some portable and "universal" content but, rather, as instrumental in the organization and legitimation of power-relations—which of course involves, as one of its components, control over the constitution of meaning. As the author of one of the first modern grammars said, appropriately enough in 1492, "Language is the perfect instrument of empire."[10] Yet, unlike grammar, discourse functions effectively precisely because the question of codifying its rules and protocols can never arise: the utterances it silently governs speak what appears to be the "natural language of the age." Therefore, from within a given discursive formation no general rules for its operation will be drawn up except against the ideological grain; so the constitution of the discursive fields of the past will, to some degree, need comprehending through the excavatory work of historical study.

To initiate such excavation is of course to confront massive problems. According to what we have said above, each individual text, rather than a meaningful unit in itself, lies at the intersection of different discourses which are related to each other in a complex but ultimately hierarchical way. Strictly speaking, then, it would be meaningless to talk about the unity of any given text—supposedly the intrinsic quality of all "works of art." And yet, because literary texts *are* presented to us as characterized precisely by their unity, the text must still be taken as a point of purchase on the discursive field—but in order to demonstrate that, athwart its alleged unity, the text is in fact marked and fissured by the interplay of the discourses that constitute it.

V

The ensemble of fictional and lived practices, which for convenience we will simply refer to here as "English colonialism," provides *The Tempest*'s dominant discursive con-texts.[11] We have chosen here to concentrate specifically on the figure of usurpation as the nodal point of the play's imbrication into this discourse of colonialism. We shall look at the variety of forms under which usurpation appears in the text, and indicate briefly how it is active in organizing the text's actual diversity.[12]

Of course conventional criticism has no difficulty in recognizing the importance of the themes of legitimacy and usurpation for *The Tempest*. Indeed, during the storm-scene with which the play opens, the issue of legitimate authority is brought immediately to the fore. The boatswain's peremptory dismissal of the nobles to their cabins, while not, according to the custom of the sea, strictly a mutinous act, none the less represents a disturbance in the normal hierarchy of power relations. The play then proceeds to recount or display a series of actual or attempted usurpations of authority: from Antonio's successful palace revolution against his brother, Prospero, and Caliban's attempted violation of the honour of Prospero's daughter—accounts of which we hear retrospectively; to the conspiracy of Antonio and Sebastian against the life of Alonso and, finally, Caliban's insurrection, with Stephano and Trinculo, against Prospero's domination of the island. In fact it could be argued that this series *is* the play, in so far as

The Tempest is a dramatic action at all. However, these rebellions, treacheries, mutinies and conspiracies, referred to here collectively as usurpation, are not *simply* present in the text as extractable "Themes of the Play."[13] Rather, they are differentially embedded there, figural traces of the text's anxiety concerning the very matters of domination and resistance.

Take for example the play's famous *protasis,* Prospero's long exposition to Miranda of the significant events that predate the play. For Prospero, the real beginning of the story is his usurpation twelve years previously by Antonio, the opening scene of a drama which Prospero intends to play out during *The Tempest* as a comedy of restoration. Prospero's exposition seems unproblematically to take its place as the indispensable prologue to an understanding of the present moment of Act I, no more than a device for conveying essential information. But to see it simply as a neutral account of the play's prehistory would be to occlude the contestation that follows insistently throughout the rest of the first act, of Prospero's version of true beginnings. In this narration the crucial early days of the relationship between the Europeans and the island's inhabitants are covered by Prospero's laconic "Here in this island we arriv'd" (I.ii.171). And this is all we would have were it not for Ariel and Caliban. First Prospero is goaded by Ariel's demands for freedom into recounting at some length how his servitude began, when, at their first contact, Prospero freed him from the cloven pine in which he had earlier been confined by Sycorax. Caliban then offers his compelling and defiant counter to Prospero's single sentence when, in a powerful speech, he recalls the initial mutual trust which was broken by Prospero's assumption of the political control made possible by the power of his magic. Caliban, "which first was mine own King," now protests that "here you sty me / In this hard rock, whiles you do keep from me / The rest o'th'island" (I.ii.344–6).

It is remarkable that these contestations of "true beginnings" have been so commonly occluded by an uncritical willingness to identify Prospero's voice as direct and reliable authorial statement, and therefore to ignore the lengths to which the play goes to dramatize its problems with the proper beginning of its own story. Such identification hears, as it were, only Prospero's play, follows only his stage directions, not noticing that Prospero's play and *The Tempest* are not necessarily the same thing.[14]

But although different beginnings are offered by different voices in the play, Prospero has the effective power to impose his construction of events on the others. While Ariel gets a threatening but nevertheless expansive answer, Caliban provokes an entirely different reaction. Prospero's words refuse engagement with Caliban's claim to original sovereignty. ("This island's mine, by Sycorax my mother, / Which thou tak'st from me," I.ii.333–34). Yet Prospero is clearly disconcerted. His sole—somewhat hysterical—response consists of an indirect denial ("Thou most lying slave," I.ii.346) and a counter accusation of attempted rape ("Thou didst seek to violate / The honour of my child," I.ii.349–50), which together foreclose the exchange and serve in practice as Prospero's only justification for the arbitrary rule he exercises over the island and its inhabitants. At a stroke he erases from what we have called Prospero's play all trace of the moment of his reduction of Caliban to slavery and appropriation of his island. For, indeed, it could be argued that the series of usurpations listed earlier as constituting the dramatic action all belong to that play alone, which is systematically silent about Prospero's own act of usurpation: a silence which is curious, given his otherwise voluble preoccupation with the theme of legitimacy. But, despite his evasiveness, this moment ought to be of decisive *narrative* importance since it marks Prospero's self-installation as ruler, and his acquisition, through Caliban's enslavement, of the means of supplying the food and labour on which he and Miranda are completely dependent. "We cannot miss him: he does make our fire, / Fetch in our wood, and serves in offices / That profit us" (I.ii.313–5). Through its very occlusion of Caliban's version of proper beginnings, Prosper's disavowal is itself performative of the discourse of colonialism, since this particular reticulation of denial of dispossession with retrospective justification for it, is the characteristic trope by which European colonial regimes articulated their authority over land to which they could have no conceivable legitimate claim.[15]

The success of this trope is, as so often in these cases, proved by its subsequent invisibility. Caliban's "I'll show thee every fertile inch o'th'island" (II.ii.148) is for example glossed by Kermode with "The colonists were frequently received with this kindness, though treachery might follow," as if this were simply a "fact" whose relevance to *The Tempest* we might want to consider, without seeing that to speak of "treachery" is already to interpret, from the position of colonizing power, through a purported "description." A discursive analysis would indeed be alive to the use of the word "treachery" in a colonial context in the early seventeenth century, but would be aware of how it functioned for the English to explain to themselves the *change* in native behaviour (from friendliness to hostility) that was in fact a *reaction* to their increasingly disruptive presence. That this was an explanatory trope rather than a description of behaviour is nicely caught in Gabriel Archer's slightly bemused comment: "They are naturally given to treachery, howbeit we could not finde it in our travell up the river, but rather a most kind and loving people" (Archer 1979). Kermode's use of the word is of course by no means obviously contentious: its power to shape readings of the play stems from its continuity with the grain of unspoken colonialist assumptions.

So it is not just a matter of the occlusion of the play's initial colonial moment. Colonialist legitimation has always had then to go on to tell its own story, inevitably one of native violence: Prospero's play performs this task within *The Tempest.* The burden of Prospero's play is already deeply concerned with producing legitimacy. The purpose of Prospero's main plot is to secure recognition of his claim to the usurped duchy of Milan, a recognition scaled in the blessing given by Alonso to the prospective marriage of his own son to Prospero's daughter. As part of this, Prospero reduces Caliban to a role in the supporting sub-plot, as instigator of a mutiny that is programmed to fail, thereby forging an equivalence between Antonio's initial *putsch* and Caliban's revolt. This allows Prospero to annul the memory of his failure to prevent his expulsion from the dukedom, by repeating it as a mutiny that he will, this time, forestall. But, in addition, the playing out of the colonialist narrative is thereby completed:

Caliban's attempt—tarred with the brush of Antonio's supposedly self-evident viciousness—is produced as final and irrevocable confirmation of the natural treachery of savages.

Prospero can plausibly be seen as a playwright only because of the control over the other characters given him by his magic. He can freeze Ferdinand in mid-thrust, immobilize the court party at will, and conjure a pack of hounds to chase the conspirators. Through this physical control he seeks with considerable success to manipulate the mind of Alonso. Curiously though, while the main part of Prospero's play runs according to plan, the sub-plot provides the only real moment of drama when Prospero calls a sudden halt to the celebratory masque, explaining, aside:

> I had forgot that foul conspiracy
> Of the beast Caliban and his confederates
> Against my life: the minute of their plot
> Is almost come.
>
> (IV.i.139–42)

So while, on the face of it, Prospero has no difficulty in dealing with the various threats to his domination, Caliban's revolt proves uniquely disturbing to the smooth unfolding of Prospero's plot. The text is strangely emphatic about this moment of disturbance, insisting not only on Prospero's sudden vexation, but also on the "strange hollow, and confused noise" with which the Nymphs and Reapers—two lines earlier gracefully dancing—now "heavily vanish," and the apprehension voiced by Ferdinand and Miranda:

> FERDINAND: This is strange: your father's in some passion
> That works him strongly.
> MIRANDA: Never till this day
> Saw I him touch'd with anger, so distemper'd.
>
> (IV.i.143–5)

For the first and last time Ferdinand and Miranda speak at a distance from Prospero and from his play. Although this disturbance is immediately glossed over, the hesitation, occasioned by the sudden remembering of Caliban's conspiracy, remains available as a site of potential fracture.

The interrupted masque has certainly troubled scholarship, introducing a jarring note into the harmony of this supposedly most highly structured of Shakespeare's late plays. Kermode speaks of the "apparently inadequate motivation" for Prospero's perturbation (Shakespeare 1964, p. lxxv), since there is no obvious reason why he should so excite himself over an easily controllable insurrection.

What then is the meaning of this textual excess, this disproportion between apparent cause and effect? There are several possible answers, located at different levels of analysis. The excess obviously marks the recurrent difficulty that Caliban causes Prospero—a difficulty we have been concerned to trace in some detail. So, at the level of character, a psychoanalytic reading would want to suggest that Prospero's excessive reaction represents his disquiet at the irruption into consciousness of an unconscious anxiety concerning the grounding of his legitimacy, both as producer of his play and, *a fortiori,* as governor of the island. The by now urgent need for action forces upon Prospero the hitherto repressed contradiction between his dual roles as usurped and user. Of course the emergency is soon contained and the colonialist narrative quickly completed. But, none the less, if only for a moment, the effort invested in holding Prospero's play together as a unity is laid bare.

So, at the formal level, Prospero's difficulties in staging his play are themselves "staged" by the play that we are watching, this moment presenting for the first time the possibility of distinguishing between Prospero's play and *The Tempest* itself.

Perhaps it could be said that what is staged here in *The Tempest* is Prospero's anxious determination to keep the sub-plot of his play in its place. One way of distinguishing Prospero's play from *The Tempest* might be to claim that Prospero's carefully established relationship between main and sub-plot is reversed in *The Tempest*, whose *main* plot concerning Prospero's anxiety over his *sub*-plot. A formal analysis would seem to bear this out. The climax of Prospero's play is his revelation to Alonso of Miranda and Ferdinand playing chess. This is certainly a true *anagnorisis* for Alonso, but for us a merely theatrical rather than truly dramatic moment. *The Tempest*'s dramatic climax, in a way its only dramatic moment at all, is, after all, this sudden and strange disturbance of Prospero.

But to speak of Prospero's anxiety being staged by *The Tempest* would be, on its own, a recuperative move, preserving the text's unity by the familiar strategy of introducing an ironic distance between author and protagonist. After all, although Prospero's anxiety over his sub-plot may point up the *crucial* nature of that "sub" plot, a generic analysis would have no difficulty in showing that *The Tempest* is ultimately complicit with Prospero's play in treating Caliban's conspiracy in the fully comic mode. Even before it begins, Caliban's attempt to put his political claims into practice is arrested by its implication in the convention of clownish vulgarity represented by the "low-life" characters of Stephano and Trinculo, his conspiracy framed in a grotesquerie that ends with the dubiously amusing sight of the conspirators being hunted by dogs, a fate, incidentally, not unknown to natives of the New World. The shakiness of Prospero's position is indeed staged, but in the end his version of history remains *authoritative,* the larger play acceding as it were to the containment of the conspirators in the safely comic mode, Caliban allowed only his poignant and ultimately vain protests against the venality of his co-conspirators.

That this comic closure is necessary to enable the European "reconciliation" which follows hard on its heels—the patching up of a minor dynastic dispute within the Italian nobility—is, however, itself symptomatic of the text's own anxiety about the threat posed to its decorum by its New World materials. The lengths to which the play has to go to achieve a legitimate ending may then be read as the quelling of a fundamental disquiet concerning its own functions within the projects of colonialist discourse.

No adequate reading of the play could afford not to comprehend *both* the anxiety and the drive to closure it necessitates. Yet these aspects of the play's "rich complexity" have been signally ignored by European and North American critics, who have tended to listen exclusively to Prospero's voice: after all, he speaks their language. It has been left to those who have suffered colonial usurpation to discover and map the traces of that complexity by reading in full measure Caliban's refractory place in both Prospero's play and *The Tempest*.[16]

VI

We have tried to show, within the limits of a brief textual analysis, how an approach via a theory of discourse can recognize *The Tempest* as, in a significant sense, a play imbricated within the discourse of colonialism; and can, at the same time, offer an explanation of features of the play either ignored or occluded by critical practices that have often been complicit whether consciously or not, with a colonialist ideology.

Three points remain to be clarified. To identify dominant discursive networks and their mode of operation within particular texts should by no means be seen as the end of the story. A more exhaustive analysis would go on to establish the precise articulation of discourses within texts: we have argued for the discourse of colonialism as the articulatory *principle* of *The Tempest*'s diversity but have touched only briefly on what other discourses are articulated and where such linkages can be seen at work in the play.

Then again, each text is more than simply an *instance* of the operation of a discursive network. We have tried to show how much of *The Tempest*'s complexity comes from its *staging* of the distinctive moves and figures of colonialist discourse. Discourse is always performative, active rather than ever merely contemplative; and, of course, the mode of the theater will also inflect it in particular ways, tending, for example, through the inevitable (because structural) absence of any direct authorial comment, to create an effect of distantiation, which exists in a complex relationship with the countervailing (and equally structural) tendency for audiences to identify with characters presented—through the language and conventions of theatre—as heroes and heroines. Much work remains to be done on the articulation between discursive performance and mode of presentation.

Finally, we have been concerned to show how *The Tempest* has been severed from its discursive con-texts through being produced by criticism as an autotelic unity, and we have tried therefore to exemplify an approach that would engage with the fully dialectical relationship between the detail of the text and the larger discursive formations. But nor can theory and criticism be exempt from such relationships. Our essay too must engage in the discursive struggle that determines the history within which the Shakespearean texts will be located and read: it matters what kind of history that is.

NOTES

1. Bennett 1982, p. 227; drawing on the argument of Derrida 1977.
2. For the theory behind the concept of inscription see Balibar 1974 and 1983; Macherey and Balibar 1978; and Davies 1978. For an accessible collection of essays which put this theory to work on the corpus of English literature, see Widdowson 1982.
3. Intertextuality is a term coined by Julia Kristeva 1970, from her reading of the seminal work of Mikhail Bakhtin, 1968, 1973, 1981.
4. For Raleigh's *Tempest* see Hawkes, pp. 26–46; Kermode is editor of the Arden edition of *The Tempest* (Shakespeare 1964); on the formation of "English" see Davies 1978.
5. Stanley Fish (1980, p. 165), whose general argument is similar to Bennett's, admits that in the last analysis he is unable to answer the question: what are his interpretive acts interpretations *of?*
6. Marx's work was developed out of his critique of the concepts of classical political economy that had dominated economic thought in the middle of the nineteenth century. We choose here to offer a critique of Kermode's introduction to the Arden *Tempest* (Shakespeare 1964) because of the *strengths* of his highly regarded and influential work.
7. Con-texts with a hyphen, to signify a break from the inequality of the usual text/context relationship. Con-texts are themselves *texts* and must be *read with:* they do not simply make up a background.
8. MacCabe 1979 offers a helpful guide through some of discourse's many usages. The concept of discourse at work in the present essay draws on Michel Foucault's investigation of the discursive realm. A useful introduction to his theorization of discourse is provided by Foucault's essays, 1978 and 1981. His most extended theoretical text is *The Archaeology of Knowledge*, 1972. However, a less formal and in many ways more suggestive treatment of discourse is practiced and, to a certain extent theorized, in his early work on "madness" and in more recent studies of the prison and of sexuality, where discourse is linked with both the institutional locations in which it circulates and the power functions it performs: see Foucault 1967, 1977, 1979a. For a cognate approach to discourse see the theory of "utterance" developed by Valentin Vološinov, 1973.
9. On the weakness of Kristeva's own work in this respect see Culler 1981, pp. 105–7.
10. Antonio de Nebrija, quoted in Hanke 1959, p. 8.
11. In other words we would shift the emphasis from the futile search for the texts Shakespeare "had in mind" to the establishment of significant patterns within the larger discursive networks of the period. The notion of "English colonialism" can itself be focused in different ways. The widest focus would include present con-texts; the narrowest would concentrate on the con-texts associated with the initial period of English colonization of Virginia, say 1585 to 1622. In the first instance many of the relevant texts would be found in the contemporary collections of Hakluyt (1903–5) and Purchase (1905–7). For congruent approaches see J. Smith 1974; Frey 1979; Greenblatt 1980, chapter 4; and Hulme 1981.

12. See Macherey 1978. Macherey characterizes the literary text not as unified but as plural and diverse. Usurpation should then be regarded not as the centre of a unity but as the principle of a diversity.
13. Kermode's second heading (Shakespeare 1964, p. xxiv).
14. This is a weak form of the critical fallacy that, more chronically, reads Prospero as an autobiographical surrogate for Shakespeare himself. On some of the theoretical issues involved here see Foucault 1979b.
15. This trope is studied in more detail in Hulme (forthcoming) chapters 3 and 4. See also Jennings 1976.
16. See for example Lamming 1960 and Fernández Retamar 1973. Aimé Césaire's rewriting of the play, *Une Tempête,* 1969, has Caliban as explicit hero. For an account of how Caliban remains refractory for contemporary productions of *The Tempest* see Griffiths 1983.

REFERENCES

Archer, Gabriel (1979) "The description of the now discovered river and country of Virginia . . ." [1607], in Quinn, D. *et al.* (eds) *New American World,* vol. 5. London: Macmillan.

Bakhtin, Mikhail (1968) *Rabelais and His World.* Cambridge, Mass.: MIT Press.

——— (1973) *Problems of Dostoevsky's Poetics.* Ann Arbor, Mich.: Ardis.

——— (1981) *The Dialogic Imagination.* Austin: University of Texas Press.

Balibar, Renée (1974) *Les Français fictifs: le rapport des styles littéraires au français national.* Paris: Hachette.

Bennett, T. (1982) "Text and history," in Widdowson, Peter (ed.) *Re-Reading English.* London: Methuen, 223-36.

Césaire, Aimé (1969) *Une Tempête.* Paris: Seuil.

Culler, J. (1981) *The Pursuit of Signs.* London: Routledge & Kegan Paul. Davies, Tony (1978) "Education, ideology and literature," *Red Letters,* 7, 4-15.

Davies, Tony (1978) "Education, ideology and literature," *Red Letters,* 7, 4-15.

Derrida, Jacques (1977) "Signature event context," *Glyph,* I, 172-98.

Fernández Retamar, Roberto (1973) *Caliban: Apuntes sobre la Cultura de Nuestra América.* Buenos Aires: Editorial la Pleyade.

Fish, Stanley (1980) *Is There a Text in this Class?: The Authority of Interpretive Communities.* Cambridge, Mass.: Harvard University Press.

Foucault, Michel (1967) *Madness and Civilization: A History of Insanity in the Age of Reason.* London: Tavistock Publications.

——— (1972) *The Archaeology of Knowledge.* London: Tavistock Publications.

——— (1977) *Discipline and Punish: the Birth of the Prison.* London: Allen Lane.

——— (1978) "Politics and the study of discourse," *Ideology and Consciousness,* 3, 7-26.

——— (1979a) *The History of Sexuality,* vol. I. London: Allen Lane.

——— (1981) "The order of discourse," in Young, Robert (ed.) *Untying the Text: A Post-structuralist Reader.* London: Routledge & Kegan Paul, 48-78.

Frey, Charles (1979) "*The Tempest* and the New World," *Shakespeare Quarterly,* 30, 29-41.

Greenblatt, Stephen (1980) *Renaissance Self-Fashioning from More to Shakespeare.* Chicago: University of Chicago Press.

Griffiths, Trevor R. (1983) "'This island's mine': Caliban and colonialism," *The Yearbook of English Studies,* 13, 159-80.

Hakluyt, Richard (1903-5) *The Principle Navigations, Voyages Traffiques and Discoveries of the English Nation* [1589], 12 vols. Glasgow: James.

Hanke, Lewis (1959). *Aristotle and the American Indians.* Bloomington, Ind.: Indiana University Press.

Hawkes, Terence (1985) "Swisser-Swatter: Making a Man of English Letters." In *Alternative Shakespeares.* Ed. John Drakakis. London: Methuen, 1985.

Hirsch, Ed (1967) *Validity in Interpretation.* New Haven: Yale University Press.

Hulme, Peter (1981) "Hurricanes in the Caribbees: The constitution of the discourse of English colonialism," in Barker, F. *et al.* (eds) *1642: Literature and Power in the Seventeenth Century.* Colchester: University of Essex, 55-83.

——— "'*Of the caniballes': the discourse of European colonialism 1492-1797.*" London: Methuen, forthcoming.

Jennings, Francis (1976) *The Invasion of America: Indians, Colonialism and the Cant of Conquest.* New York: Norton.

Kristeva, Julia (1970) *Le Texte du roman.* The Hague: Mouton.

Lamming, George (1960) *The Pleasures of Exile.* London: Michael Joseph.

MacCabe, Colin (1979) "On discourse," *Economy and Society,* 8, 4, 279-307.

——— (1977) "An interview," *Red Letters,* 5, 3-9.

Macherey, P. (1978) *A Theory of Literary Production,* trans. Geoffrey Wall. Reprinted London: Routledge & Kegan Paul, 1980.

——— and Balibar, E. (1978) "On literature as an ideological form: Some Marxist propositions," *Oxford Literary Review,* 3, 4-12.

Purchas, Samuel (1905-7) *Purchase His Pilgrimes* [1625], 20 vols. Glasgow: James MacLehose.

Shakespeare, William (1954) *The Tempest*, ed. Frank Kermode. London: Methuen.

Smith, James (1974) "*The Tempest,*" in *Shakespearian and Other Essays.* Cambridge: Cambridge University Press, 159-261.

Vološinov, Valentin (1973) *Marxism and the Philosophy of Language.* New York: Seminar Press.

Widdowson, Peter (ed.) (1982) *Re-Reading English.* London: Methuen.

chapter 17

Essays on *Heart of Darkness*, by Joseph Conrad

Heart of Darkness: Geography as Apocalypse

Patrick Parrinder

Ex Africa semper aliquid novi. This motto from Pliny's *Natural History* may be taken to mark the beginning of what, following the example of Edward Said's "Orientalism," Christopher L. Miller calls the "Africanist" discourse of Europe. The word Africa, as Miller reminds us, was itself a European invention, acquired by the Romans from the Carthaginians, among whom it seems to have been merely an insignificant local place-name.[1] With hindsight we can find a latent apocalypticism in the progression from Carthaginian place-name to the signifier of a Roman military triumph (Scipio Africanus) and then to Pliny's proverb. It was not until 1899, however, that Conrad's anthropological horror-comic brought into focus the apocalyptic geography inherent in the European idea of Africa. For our present purposes we might venture a rough translation of *Ex Africa semper aliquid novi* as "There is always something new to be said about *Heart of Darkness*"—or so it seems, since *Heart of Darkness* is by far the most over-interpreted literary text of the last hundred years.

If, as I think would be generally agreed, *Heart of Darkness* is the prototypical modern "Africanist" narrative, then it stands *prima facie* accused of the charge of racism brought against it in Chinua Achebe's 1975 essay "An Image of Africa." "Can nobody see the preposterous and perverse arrogance in thus reducing Africa to the role of props for the break-up of one petty European mind?" Achebe asks, though the charge may be better directed against the trend of Anglo-American criticism of *Heart of Darkness* than against the text itself.[2] More recently, the widespread abandonment and disavowal of the universal symbolic meanings that a previous generation of New critics, Christian critics and myth-critics found in Conrad's tale have led commentators to return it to a discursive context which is, necessarily, that of the fin de siècle. In this chapter I shall suggest a few of the ways in which Conrad's experiences, his development as a novelist, contemporary fictional romance, contemporary ethnography, and the complex unfolding of the imperialist "scramble for Africa" led to this tale structured around the notion of a river journey connecting "the ends of the earth" to the "earliest beginnings of the world."

Conrad himself made his ill-fated journey up the Congo exactly a hundred years ago. He left London on 6 May 1890, calling at Tenerife, Freetown and Libreville, and landed at Boma at the mouth of the Congo River on 12 June. He travelled up-river on foot and by boat just as Marlow does, arriving at Stanley Falls, the "Inner Station" of *Heart of Darkness* and the scene of Marlow's meeting with Kurtz, on 1 September. On the return journey down the river he fell ill; he then gained a release from the three-year contract he had signed with the Upper Congo trading company, and by the end of December was back in London. The record of this journey is to be found in his letters, in the diary he kept from 13 June to 1 August, and in the so-called "Up-River Book" beginning on 3 August.[3] Foreshadowing this abortive episode is the moment in Conrad's schooldays—recorded in his essay "Geography and Some Explorers"—when, carried away by his fascination with the blank spaces in the atlas and with the explorers whom he called the "blessed of militant geography," Conrad put his finger on a spot in the middle of the "then white heart" of the map of Africa and declared, to the derision of his classmates, that one day he would go there. The fact that Marlow describes a similar boyhood dream is, in my view, one of the pieces of evidence compelling us to disregard the customary separation of author and fictive persona and to assert that, in many respects, *Heart of Darkness* is autobiographical and Marlow is Conrad.

However, the evidence points both ways. The editor of the splendidly informative Norton Critical Edition of *Heart of Darkness* (now in its third edition, which is markedly more New-Historicist than its predecessors) very curiously cuts Conrad's essay into two parts. The first ends with the schoolboy boast, followed by a characteristically gruff disclaimer ("My chums' chaffing as perfectly justifiable," Conrad writes), and the statement that "it is a fact that, about eighteen years afterwards, a wretched little stern-wheel steamboat I commanded lay moored to the bank of an African river." What could be stronger testimony to the autobiographical basis of *Heart of Darkness*? But now listen to the continuation of the same paragraph, which the Norton Critical Edition prints some forty pages later: "The subdued thundering mutter of the Stanley Falls hung in the heavy night air of the last navigable reach of the Upper Congo, while no more than ten miles away, in Reshid's camp just above the Falls, the yet unbroken power of the Congo Arabs slumbered uneasily. Their day was over."[4] Here we catch a glimpse of the actual history of the Congo, which what Conrad was to call the "foggishness" of *Heart of Darkness* is at such pains to suppress. For it turns out that what in Conrad's imaginative rewriting was to become the savage theatre of a "choice of nightmares" was, historically speaking, the setting for a clash of imperialisms.

The heart of Africa, in 1890, had already been opened up by Europeans. Conrad's "Up-River Book" records the passing of a number of mission stations on the way upstream from Kinshasa, the Central Station of *Heart of Darkness,* to Stanley Falls. Even more tellingly, Norman Sherry shows that the steamer in which Conrad made the up-river voyage was passed by a number of ships bound in the opposite direction.[5] It was not quite the pilgrimage into an untamed wilderness that Marlow describes. Might not the people in the villages on the banks of the Congo, however, have been as savage and primitive as Conrad or Marlow suppose? The answer is that, though the heart of Africa was lost in midnight darkness so far as Europeans were concerned, it was already known to Arab traders from the East coast, so that even the most remote Congolese villages must be supposed to have had some contact with Islamic civilisation. (This is a history which the opening section of V. S. Naipaul's Africanist novel *A Bend in the River* attempts to restore.)[6] The Arab involvement in the slave trade gave European imperialists, led by King Leopold of the Belgians, the perfect moral pretext for their own unscrupulous intervention.

King Leopold had been given the Congo as his personal property at the Berlin conference of 1884–5, a conference intended to settle differences between the colonising powers at which the United States as well as the major European nations were represented. Though Leopold never visited Africa, his agents were responsible for the bloodthirsty tyranny which, from 1895 onwards, became the subject of frequent exposures in the British press. Conrad was not unwilling for *Heart of Darkness* to be seen as a contribution to the British anti-Congo campaign of these years, but he does, of course, remove from the story any specific indications of how the situation it portrays had come about. In the Congo that Conrad knew, the explorer H. M. Stanley, acting with Leopold's authority, had made the Arab Tipu-Tipu "governor" of the Stanley Falls area in 1887. After 1890, however, there was open war between the Belgians and the Arabs. *Heart of Darkness* shows none of this, preferring to speak of the grotesque "civilising mission" practised by the agents of an anonymous company sent out from a "sepulchral city" to the heart of an unnamed continent. There are, however, at least two crucial textual elements in *Heart of Darkness* that recent critics have had to revalue in the light of the historical evidence.

The first is the ambush that Marlow and his companions run into just before reaching the Inner Station, and which is said by the Russian to have been plotted by Kurtz himself. Norman Sherry commented that any attack on a river steamer at this time could only have taken place as a result of orders from the Congolese Arab leadership.[7] In *Heart of Darkness* there is no mention of the Congolese Arabs and the attack seems inadequately motivated. The ambush is a lurid episode, typical of the imperialist fiction of the age, in which tribesmen armed with bows and arrows take on the colonists armed with rifles; the tribesmen, however, are overcome not by the power of European weaponry but by their awe of the ship's steam-whistle, which Marlow blows at the critical moment. Later the Russian tells Marlow that Kurtz had planned this attack on his fellow company members and former colleagues in the belief that "it would scare you away—that you would give up, thinking him dead."[8] Though it evinces the depths of Kurtz's moral depravity this is not the most convincing of Conrad's narrative inventions.

The second element which must be revalued is Marlow's notorious description of the cannibal crew—"Fine fellows—cannibals—in their place," and all that. The sensationalism of Marlow's intimate contact with primitive cannibals is enhanced by the fact, that, not only are they cannibals, but they are supposedly dying of hunger! When his helmsman is killed in the ambush, Marlow has to quickly shove his body overboard in order to prevent a cannibalistic orgy on board his ship. Up to this point, however, we are told that the starving crew have shown a miraculous restraint. Their only provisions were some rotting hippomeat and a supply of some "stuff like half-cooked dough" which did not seem to serve "any serious purpose of sustenance" (p. 42). This stuff has been identified as cassava (manioc), one of the staple foods of the Congolese at this time;—it had in fact been introduced to Africa from Brazil by the Portuguese. Conrad would have known that the explorer H. M. Stanley had alleged that his porters had been killed by a diet of pure cassava.[9] Stanley's testimony, however, is opposed by that of the pioneering English missionary W. Holman Bentley, who claimed that cassava dumplings were both portable and highly nutritious. He himself had lived on them in the Congo for years.[10]

Bentley is also a crucial witness in the controversy as to whether or not cannibalism was endemic amongst Congolese tribesmen in the late nineteenth century.[11] In *Conrad's Western World* Norman Sherry identified the cannibal crew in *Heart of Darkness* as members of the Bangala tribe, reputed to be the fiercest on the river. Sherry repeated Bentley's anecdotes of an old man who boasted of having killed and eaten seven of his wives, and of a Bangala chief's son who, when asked by the explorer George Grenfell if he ever ate human flesh, replied, "Ah! I wish that I could eat everybody on earth!"[12] Bentley ranges as far afield as Samoa in his selection of choice cannibal stories, but no amount of anecdotes such as these could constitute firm evidence of endemic cannibalism. More telling, perhaps, is another of Bentley's quotations from Grenfell (who traveled up the Congo in 1884–5):

> At the time I commenced this journey I could scarcely bring myself to believe the terrible stories which reached me from time to time. Since coming first to the Congo, the further I travelled the further cannibalism seemed to recede; everybody had it to say that their neighbours on beyond were bad, that they "eat men," till I began to grow skeptical; but here at Bangala I absolutely caught up with it, and was obliged to allow what I had hoped to be able to maintain as "not proven." I will not sicken you with the details of the preparations, as some of our boys

> gave them when they came to tell me, in the hope that I should be able to interfere, but before they reached the steamer the big drum's dum-dum announced the final act.
>
> From this point on the evidences of cannibalism were continually recurring, though the reluctant manner in which at some places the people acknowledged being "man-eaters," leads us to hope that a sentiment against it already exists.[13]

Actually, Grenfell's account has the classic features of the "cannibalistic" narratives anlaysed by William Arens in his controversial and important book *The Man-Eating Myth* (1979).[14] First, the author presents himself as an impeccably skeptical witness, as hard to convince as the proverbial Scottish jury.[15] He is aware that people tend to accuse the neighbouring tribes of being cannibalistic, though in the end it is precisely the uncorroborated testimony of non-Bangalas ("some of our boys") that he finds overwhelming. He does not witness the "final act" itself, but then no white man in his senses ever ventures that close to the cooking-pot.

A paragraph which begins by professing absolute skepticism ends by requiring us to invest an absolute faith in the hearsay evidence of the "boys," who might have been terrified out of their wits, or who might, for that matter, have been over-eager to please the white master whose interest in cannibalism was so blatantly displayed. Even if we decide that the balance of probability remains with Grenfell's account, his acknowledgement that a moral sentiment against cannibalism existed amongst the Bangala remains to be interpreted. We may, in fact, be dealing not with a socially approved custom but with deviant and quasi-criminal behaviour, felt to be shameful by some and passed off with bravado by others—like football hooliganism in late twentieth-century Britain.

Perhaps it is now impossible to separate slander from fact in the numerous allegations made against the tribe who provided the originals of Conrad's cannibal crewmen. In 1891 W. H. Stapleton reported of the "dreaded Bangala tribe" that "these people have long been the terror of the river. Any blood-curdling story is readily believed of these warlike people. Slaving and raiding are regarded as their favourite occupations, and it is always asserted that any victims killed and carried off are eaten by their captors."[16] Stapleton also records seeing "chopped up bits of mutilated bodies," as a result of which he and his companies suffered from nightmares and "found it difficult to eat our evening meal," but he adds that "needless to say, we did not visit the scene of the feast."[17] The most influential source of atrocity stories of this kind was H. M. Stanley, who of course was a newspaperman as well as an explorer. Stanley's evidence is now considered almost useless by historians. According to Henryk Zins, he "repeated every tale of cannibalism that he heard about and also invented many stories which were completely baseless."[18]

The European discovery of central Africa begins with the Portuguese in the fifteenth century. There was little interest in reports of African cannibalism, however, until the later nineteenth century, when the continent became the principal theatre of colonial expansion and imperialist power-struggle.[19] Africa grew dark, Patrick Brantlinger has said, as Victorian explorers, missionaries and scientists "flooded it with light."[20] The myth of the dark continent became a staple ingredient of late nineteenth-century popular fiction, a category to which (by virtue of its serialisation in *Blackwood's Magazine*) *Heart of Darkness* arguably belongs. There are at least three reasons why cannibalism was particularly stressed at this time. The first was the need to justify the human costs of the "civilising mission" in Africa. The young traders and missionaries who succumbed to fever and dysentery in such large numbers had to be shown to have sacrificed their lives in some urgent and noble cause. As Bentley writes at the end of one of his cannibalistic anecdotes, "Why do we tell these shocking stories? We have told how good men and true went out to the Congo one after the other only to die, and others again to take their places and die. This story needs some justification. . . . A great need exists, and men have gone to supply it."[21] The best evidence for this "need" was that, no sooner had the missions been established and the colonial power asserted its authority than cannibalism "in its grosser forms" became a thing of the past.[22] If, however, cannibalism was readily given up that would tend to suggest that it had not been a normal and integral element of the societies concerned.

Secondly, cannibalism was stressed because it was believed to be associated with primitiveness, with forms of humanity classified as low on the evolutionary scale. Cannibalism and civilisation were regularly opposed. Conrad manipulates, if he does not exactly endorse, this stereotype to the extent that cannibalism in *Heart of Darkness* takes on a symbolic dimension. Tony Tanner in a well-known article has elicited parallels between the cannibal helmsman and Kurtz, whose abandonment of all civilised restraints amounts to a kind of "cannibalism of consciousness": "Kurtz wants to eat everything," Tanner remarks. Symbolic cannibalism thus becomes the ultimate expression of a form of white imperial ideology.[23] Cannibalistic themes recur in other writers of the 1890s, notably in the scientific romances of H. G. Wells with their strongly primitivist and evolutionist emphasis. Wells adds the twist of a "cannibalism of the future"—the Morlocks and Martians are represented as post-human species which feed off *homo sapiens* or its descendants—where Conrad portrays in Kurtz the symbolic cannibalism of the super-civilised. Cannibalism in these texts becomes the sign not merely of savagery but also of decadence.

But (before we get too carried away) there is also a third reason for the fin-de-siècle emphasis on cannibalism in central Africa: cannibal acts clearly took place there. However exaggerated the travellers' tales may have been, they undoubtedly had some historical basis. It is here, however, that we need to distinguish between endemic cannibalism (as a sign of "natural" primitiveness and savagery) and epidemic cannibalism. There is no form of society in which outbreaks of cannibalism have not sometimes occurred among people driven to extremes, and nobody can say whether or not he or she might act cannibalistically in desperate circumstances. In the Congo the war between Leopold's forces and the Arab slave-traders led, in places, to complete social breakdown and, doubtless, starvation. George Grenfell, for one, had spoken of the need to stem the "Arab invasion" and to prevent further "Arab conquests";[24] this was done, though at a terrible cost which was to have repercussions throughout the period of colonial rule leading to the second catastrophic war which followed the Belgian withdrawal in 1960.[25] There is, as Brantlinger argues, inescapable evidence of cannibalistic incidents on both sides during the war of 1891–4. The Congolese atrocities were widely publicised in Britain during the years preceding *Heart of Darkness* and Conrad kept himself informed about them. We must, therefore, come back to the artistic and ideological consequences of the omission of the Arabs (and, therefore, of the possibility of a war between rival imperialisms) from *Heart of Darkness*. According to Brantlinger, "The omission has the effect of sharpening the light-and-dark dichotomies, the staple of racism. . . . Furthermore, because of the omission of the Arabs Conrad treats cannibalism not as a result of war but as an everyday custom of the Congolese."[26]

It seems to me that one crucial reason why Conrad omitted the Arabs must be that he had already dealt at length with the triangular relationship of European traders, Arab traders and native peoples in his Malayan novels. If we want to know why Conrad takes primitivism to such lengths in *Heart of Darkness* it is surely relevant that he had already used the Malay archipelago—scarcely, in the late nineteenth century, a blank space on the map—as a setting for a mode of pastoral romance dominated by the encounter between the European and the "savage mind." The peoples of what is now Indonesia are, of course, predominantly Moslem (remember the "Patna" in *Lord Jim* with its cargo of pilgrims bound for Mecca), but in *Almayer's Folly* (1895) and *An Outcast of the Islands* (1895) the Malay archipelago is a setting for the story of the white man who "goes native," trading his European integrity for the dark knowledge given to the pioneer who knows the savage mind intimately and who is worshipped, in consequence, as a kind of god. In particular, there are remarkable parallels between Willems in *An Outcast of the Islands* and Kurtz.

Willems, the former confidential clerk of Hudig and Co. in Macassar, has been found guilty of embezzlement and is sent to hide his shame at Almayer's remote trading-station in the bush. From Almayer's he moves to a native compound in order to live with Aïssa, a Malay woman. His estranged wife Joanna is also a Malay, but by contrast with her Aïssa is viewed as a kind of savage goddess, a barely human *femme fatale* whose embrace is as irresistible as it is horrifying. His love for Aïssa produces in Willems a virtually schizoid state of terror and self-hatred. "She found out something in me," he reflects. "She found it out, and I was lost."[27] From the European point of view Willems is "possessed of a devil" (p. 223), but Conrad's focus is on the psychology of the "lost man," the outlaw who surrenders his integrity to the lure of the primitive and yet remains fully conscious of what he has done. Though he chooses to live amongst Malays, Willems is in fact a thoroughgoing racist who becomes "carried away by the flood of hate, disgust, and contempt of a white man for that blood which is not his blood, for that race which is not his race; for the brown skins; for the hearts false like the sea, blacker than night" (p. 129). He seems on the verge of echoing Kurtz's expostulation of rage and despair, "Exterminate all the brutes." When he turns to violence, however, it is to lead an attack not against the Malays but against Almayer's station. The more Aïssa worships him, the more he is her prisoner, and the more he despises her as the cause of his degradation. Finally, in an anticipation of Kurtz's last words, he becomes haunted by the "horrible form" of the spirit of death (p. 268). When his lawful wife and savage mistress confront one another (a melodramatic flourish that we are mercifully spared in *Heart of Darkness*), Willems would like to murder both of them, but instead he is killed by Aïssa. There are still further parallels with *Heart of Darkness,* and *An Outcast* is undoubtedly a first sketch—cruder, more explicit and in some ways more unsparing—for the psychology of Kurtz.

In portraying the relatively civilised Malays, Conrad's rhetoric constantly evokes the extremes of savagery. "That woman was a complete savage. . . . He seemed to be surrendering to a wild creature the unstained purity of his life, of his race, of his civilization. He had a notion of being lost amongst shapeless things that were dangerous and ghastly," we are told of Willems (p. 72). There are similar effects in Conrad's portrayal of Eastern landscapes, as in the description in "The End of the Tether" (1902) of a secluded part of the Malay archipelago which "lay unchanged as on that day, four hundred years ago, when first beheld by Western eyes from the deck of a high-pooped caravel."[28] Moving his scene in 1899 from the Spice Islands to the Dark Continent, Conrad felt constrained to go beyond such routine primitivist effects to achieve a veritable orgy of primordialism.

Apart from the African setting, his principal structural innovations in *Heart of Darkness* are the invention of Marlow as narrator and the use of the river journey as a narrative framework. It is surely more than a coincidence that the three or four "classic" fictions based on river journeys in English—*Huckleberry Finn, Three Men in a Boat, News from Nowhere* and *Heart of Darkness*—were all produced within a few years of one another at the end of the nineteenth century. *Huckleberry Finn,* published in 1884, has some claim to be the prototype of the other books, two of which are set entirely on the Thames while one takes us from the Thames to the Congo. *Huckleberry Finn* and *Three Men in a Boat* are, by and large, episodic voyages in geographical space, though even Jerome K. Jerome invokes the "river of life" metaphor.[29] With *News from Nowhere* and *Heart of Darkness* however, the distance traversed in the river romance becomes at once a penetration to the heart of an alien social order and journey in symbolic, apocalyptic time. Both Morris and Conrad use the journey up-river as a means of establishing and exploring a mental chronology. When the nineteenth-century narrator of *News from Nowhere* wakes up in the Utopian future, he thinks at first that he might have gone back to the fourteenth century. A time-traveller from the present, he is full of curiosity about the new life, and he feels a growing ideological sympathy for it as the realisation of the socialist vision. Yet he dwells increasingly on his own memories once he reaches the familiar landscape of the Upper Thames, and his utopian guides come to recognise that he cannot wholeheartedly commit himself to their world. They feel only a mild sense of loss as his presence fades and he returns to the class society of the nineteenth century.[30]

If *News from Nowhere* questions the interrelationship of present and future, *Heart of Darkness* assumes our ready acceptance of the presence—up a great river such as the Congo—of the remote, prehistoric past. Characteristically, that estranged past can also be imaged as a future in which human explorers may land on a "virgin" planet:

> Going up that river was like travelling back to the earliest beginnings of the world, when vegetation rioted on the earth and the big trees were kings. An empty stream, a great silence, an impenetrable forest . . . There were moments when one's past came back to one, as it will sometimes when you have not a moment to spare to yourself; but it came in the shape of an unrestful and noisy dream remembered with wonder amongst the overwhelming realities of this strange world of plants and water and silence. . . . We penetrated deeper and deeper into the heart of darkness. . . . We were wanderers on a prehistoric earth, on an earth that wore the aspect of an unknown planet. (pp. 35-7)

Here Marlow's paradisal myth of a prehistoric vegetable world takes its place among the post-Darwinian attempts to imagine a wholly natural origin for humanity. The river is the image of life as a natural product following its inevitable and unalterable course; behind it, or above it, is only "the stillness of an implacable force brooding over an inscrutable intention" (p. 36). Marlow's narration is one that separates himself and his companions from the primordial spectacle unfolding before them. Yet there is no stable system of differences in *Heart of Darkness* and the beginning and end of the story, in particular, tend to cancel out the separateness of the observing consciousness. Here Marlow is seen by another narrator who refers to him in the third person while reinforcing and generalising the perspectives he has offered. The Thames and the Congo become indistinguishable. In the story's concluding words, a generic river, "the tranquil waterway" (literally the Thames, but identified with the Congo by poetic allusion) "leading to the uttermost ends of the earth flowed sombre under an overcast sky—seemed to lead into the heart of an immense darkness" (p. 76).

Conrad's invention of Marlow can, of course, be explained by his anxiety to make contact with the readers of *Blackwood's Magazine,* with which he had just signed a contract—these readers were to be found, or so Conrad thought, in every club, ship's cabin and officers' mess throughout the British Empire.[31] But in *Heart of Darkness* Marlow connects the Congo to the Thames and, since he tells the story on board the cruising yawl *Nellie* on which in 1890-92 Conrad and his friends used to sail in the Thames estuary, here is another piece of evidence linking Marlow and Conrad.[32] Marlow on his voyage up the Congo is at once the amateur ethnographer and the seeker after occult-knowledges; he attends to both surface and symbol. The savage dances on the shore reveal a picturesque animality but also something in the observer which acknowledges kinship with it. "The prehistoric man was cursing us, praying to us, welcoming us—who could tell?" (p. 37). After Conrad, the notion of the dance as elemental human expression linking the savage to the civilised state has a very considerable history, taking in not only the writers in the "poet and dancer" tradition but African ethnographers and Frantz Fanon's *The Wretched of the Earth*. Fanon wrote that "any study of the colonial world should take into consideration the phenomena of the dance and of possession. The native's relaxation takes precisely the form of a muscular orgy in which the most acute aggressivity and the most impelling violence are canalised, transformed and conjured away."[33] However, the choice of the dance as a "diagnostic" phenomenon embodying the whole essence of primitive cultures tends to reinforce the stereotypes and prejudices of post-Darwinian anthropology. Were we to judge Western society solely by its dance-forms we might reach some startling and subversive conclusions. Writers concerned to rescue native peoples from their pseudo-evolutionary categorisation as "primitive" or "prehistoric" almost invariably direct attention away from the dance to other social features such as technology, language, kinship structures or the plastic arts. Nadine Gordimer provides a representative example of late twentieth-century revisionist thinking in this area in her essay "The Congo River" (1960–1), describing a self-conscious retracing of Conrad's journey. "For myself," Gordimer writes, "I had not been many days on the river when I stopped thinking of the people around me as primitive, in terms of skills and aesthetics." She goes on to praise the design of Congolese boats, paddles and fishing spears—but not their dances.[34]

Beyond the dancing Africans we come to Kurtz, the severed heads, the horrors, the "unspeakable rites," the "abominable satisfactions." We are nowhere near to being given a ringside seat at Kurtz's orgies, a fact which Ian Watt for one seems to find regrettable.[35] Instead, our information about Kurtz is gathered from a Marlow who becomes increasingly sententious, repetitive and indirect. The evidence of Kurtz's "unspeakable rites" was, Marlow says, "reluctantly gathered from what I heard at various times" (p. 50). Kurtz's own monologues are for the most part reproduced in reported, not direct speech. We learn about him to a varying extent from the two acolytes whose appearance precedes his own discourses with Marlow: the Russian, that embodiment of the "pure . . . spirit of adventure" (p. 55) who has become a lost man under the influence of Kurtz's moral degradation, and the iconic black woman, "savage and superb, wild-eyed and magnificent," who lays claim to Kurtz although her "fecund and mysterious life" is portrayed as an emanation of the jungle itself (p. 60). Later, as befits one who was supposedly worshipped as a god, Kurtz's departure is marked by a religious ritual. The three tribal witch-doctors shout "strings of amazing words that resembled no sounds of human language," while shaking some sort of fetish—"a bunch of black feathers, a mangy skin with a pendent tail—something that looked like a dried gourd"—at the steamer which (in Marlow's account) appears as a "fierce river-demon" (p. 66). Marlow once again blows the steam-whistle, the terrified tribesmen scatter, and the white men make good their escape.

According to M. M. Mahood, "No African religion that has been put on record could accurately be described as devil worship."[36] But Marlow takes it for granted, time and again, that devil-worship is the key to the African psyche—how else could they have bowed down before Kurtz? The complexity of this theme stems from Marlow's recognition that devil-worship is not confined to Africans, and from his own complicity in such worship. At the start, he seems to be distanced from the idealogy of imperialism by virtue of his cynical reflectiveness—he is the experienced man who has seen through it all: "What redeems [imperialism] is the idea only. An idea at the back of it, not a sentimental pretence but an idea; and an unselfish belief in the idea—something you can set up, and bow down before, and offer a sacrifice to" (p. 10). But Marlow can also be touchy and defensive, and this can give a clue to the place in which he sets up his own altar: "I suppose it did not occur to him," Marlow says cuttingly of the Russian, "that Mr. Kurtz was no idol of mine" (p. 58).

It is here that Conrad reflects one of the double movements of the late nineteenth century, the coincidence of imperialism with its programme of cultural destruction and modernisation on the one hand, and the rise of anthropology on the other. While Kurtz is the author of a report for the International Society for the Suppression of Savage Customs, Marlow's thought is pervaded by the popular anthropology of his period. That is, he offers a kind of journalistic parody of real anthropological thinking.[37] Edward Tylor's monumental study of *Primitive Culture* (1871) argues that the key to the interpretation of primitive culture is primitive religion, and primitive religion is universally based on animism, the "doctrine of spirits," and fetishism in which the spirits are embodied in, or convey their influence through, material objects. Tylor anticipates J. G. Frazer in remarking on the extent to which animistic doctrines survive in civilised societies, so that animism and fetishism can truly be said to constitute a Key to all Mythologies, and Christianity itself is ultimately the most grotesque example of fetish-worship.[38] Fetish, derived from the Portuguese word for "charm," was almost universally used by writers on Africa from the seventeenth century to the twentieth, when Marcel Mauss dismissed it from the anthropological lexicon, describing fetishism as no more than a monument to the misunderstanding between European and African civilisation.[39]

When an object is defined as a fetish, according to Tylor, "a spirit is considered as embodied in it or acting through it or communicating by it, or at least . . . the people it belongs to do habitually think this of such objects; or it must be shown that the object is treated as having personal consciousness and power, is talked with, worshipped, prayed to, sacrificed to."[40] In *Heart of Darkness* Marlow does not use the word "fetish," preferring a moralised vocabulary of words such as "demon," "evil spirit," "fiend," "abomination," "powers of darkness," "idol," "idea." Marlow himself is initially compared to an "idol" (p. 7) and, as Mahood says, "the metaphor establishes its own sinister resonance."[41] Marlow begins by reminding his listeners of Britain's primitive past, thus establishing a broad evolutionary-anthropological framework for his tale. Following the clue supplied by the anthropologists, Marlow interprets the colonial world, African and European, as an arena of universal devil-worship. (Prudently, the most substantial European group left out of his tale of the dark continent are the Christian missionaries.)

To travel up the Congo is to become acquainted with the "flabby devil" of a "rapacious and pitiless folly" (p. 20, p. 24), while going among savages who make a "fiendish row" (p. 38) or chant a "satanic litany" (p. 66). Even the ship's boiler has a "sultry devil" in it (p. 39) and a shoe flung overboard is sacrificed to the "devil-god" of the river (p. 48). The geographical heart of darkness is a place where the most high-minded European can take his seat amongst the "devils of the land," since the "powers of darkness" have claimed him for their own (p. 49). Here the "fascination of the abomination" (p. 10) takes on a local habitation and a name.

Conrad's text is thus a story of the dark angel rampant in human affairs and an extraordinary exercise in fin-de-siècle satanism. In it, human origins and destiny are projected onto a geographical framework involving the ethnographical fallacy (and it is a fallacy) of equating "primitive" with "prehistoric" peoples. At the beginning of *Primitive Culture* Edward Tylor quotes with approval Samuel Johnson's observation that "one set of savages is much like another."[42] I take *Heart of Darkness* to endorse this viewpoint, with the addition that the worship of savage gods is widespread, perhaps universal, in Europe as well. Even Towson's *Inquiry into Some Points of Seamanship,* found by Marlow in the Russian's abandoned hut, may be viewed as a kind of fetish in the eyes of Marlow himself. Marlow's propensity for fetish-worship reaches its culmination, however, in the significance that he attaches to Kurtz's last words, spoken, so he believes, in a moment of "complete knowledge." When Marlow visits the Intended it is clear that she too has made a fetish of Kurtz, but also that Marlow views her more as a sort of tribal idol of the white races than as a fellow seeker after the knowledge of apocalypse. That it took an "Africanist" narrative, sensationally and unforgettably misrepresenting the history, geography and ethnography of the Congo, to set the scene for his vision of universal horror suggests that we now need to say (though we can only say it with Conradian irony) that *Heart of Darkness* is no idol of ours.

NOTES

1. Christopher L. Miller, *Blank Darkness: Africanist Discourse in French* (Chicago and London: University of Chicago Press, 1985) p. 5, p. 10.
2. Chinua Achebe, "An Image of Africa: Racism in Conrad's *Heart of Darkness*" in *Hopes and Impediments: Selected Essays 1965–1987* (Oxford Heinemann, 1988) pp. 1–13.
3. See Joseph Conrad, *Congo Diary and Other Uncollected Pieces,* ed. Zdzislaw Najder (Garden City, N.Y.: Doubleday, 1978).
4. Joseph Conrad, "Geography and Some Explorers" in *Heart of Darkness: An Authoritative Text, Backgrounds and Sources, Criticism,* ed. Robert Kimbrough, 3rd edn (New York and London: Norton, 1988) pp. 143–7, 186–7. Conrad's essay was first collected in *Last Essays,* ed. Richard Curle (1926).
5. Norman Sherry, *Conrad's Western World* (Cambridge: Cambridge University Press, 1971) p. 51.

6. V. S. Naipaul, *A Bend in the River* (New York: Knopf, 1979) esp. pp. 10-21. Naipaul's contemporary narrator journeys westwards from East Africa to the Upper Congo, following a route traditionally used by Arab traders and slavers.
7. Sherry, *Conrad's Western World,* p. 53.
8. Conrad, *Heart of Darkness,* ed. Kimbrough, p. 62. Subsequent page references in the text are to this edition.
9. M. M. Mahood, *The Colonial Encounter: A Reading of Six Novels* (London: Collins, 1977) p. 14.
10. Rev. W. Holman Bentley, *Pioneering on the Congo* (London: Religious Tract Society, 1900) I, p. 396.
11. For this controversy see *inter alia* Craig Raine, "Conrad and Prejudice," *London Review of Books* XI No. 12, 22 June 1989, pp. 16-18, with a reply by Patrick Parrinder, *London Review of Books* XI No. 17, 14 September 1989, p. 4; also Neal Ascherson, "Eating words about eating people," *Observer,* 15 November 1989.
12. Sherry, *Conrad's Western World,* pp. 59-60; see also Bentley, *Pioneering on the Congo,* II, pp. 210-13.
13. Bentley, *Pioneering on the Congo,* II, pp. 94-5.
14. W. Arens, *The Man-Eating Myth: Anthropology and Anthropophagy* (New York: Oxford University Press, 1979).
15. And also as hard to convince as David Livingstone had been in central Africa ten years earlier. Livingstone considered the evidence for cannibalism among one African group and concluded, "A Scotch jury would say, Not Proven." Quoted by Arens, *The Man-Eating Myth,* p. 85.
16. Bentley, *Pioneering on the Congo,* II, p. 254.
17. Ibid., p. 257.
18. Henry Zins, *Joseph Conrad and Africa* (Nairobi: Kenya Literature Bureau, 1982) p. 109. See also Arens, *The Man-Eating Myth,* pp. 85-7. Stanley's alleged "cannibals," like Stapleton's, were warriors feeding off their defeated enemies—not sufferers from protein deficiency like Marlow's "cannibals."
19. Ibid., *Joseph Conrad and Africa,* p. 109.
20. Patrick Brantlinger, *Rule of Darkness: British Literature and Imperialism 1830-1914* (Ithaca and London: Cornell University Press, 1988) p. 173.
21. Bentley, *Pioneering on the Congo,* II, p. 213.
22. Ibid., p. 258, p. 270.
23. Tony Tanner, "'Gnawed Bones' and 'Artless Tales'—Eating and Narrative in Conrad." In Norman Sherry, ed., *Joseph Conrad: A Commemoration* (London and Basingstoke: Macmillan, 1976) pp. 31-2.
24. Bentley, *Pioneering on the Congo,* II, p. 104.
25. See Colin Legum, *Congo Disaster* (Harmondsworth: Penguin, 1961).
26. Brantlinger, *Rule of Darkness,* p. 263.
27. Joseph Conrad, *An Outcast of the Islands* (Harmondsworth: Penguin, 1975) p. 221. Subsequent page references in the text are to this edition.
28. Joseph Conrad, *Youth, Heart of Darkness, The End of the Tether,* ed. Robert Kimbrough (Oxford: Oxford University Press, 1984) p. 242.
29. Jerome K. Jerome, *Three Men in a Boat (To Say Nothing of the Dog)* (Bristol: Arrowsmith, 1889) p. 37.
30. For a reading of Morris's *News from Nowhere* as a river romance see Patrick Parrinder, "News from the Land of No News," *Foundation* 51 (Spring 1991) pp. 29-37.
31. See Ian Watt, *Conrad in the Nineteenth Century* (London: Chatte & Windus, 1980) p. 131.

32. Ibid., p. 213.
33. Frantz Fanon, *The Wretched of the Earth,* trans. Constance Farrington (London: MacGibbon & Kee, 1965) p. 45. See also Geoffrey Gorer, *Africa Dances* (London: Faber, 1935) and, more generally, Havelock Ellis, *The Dance of Life* (London: Constable, 1923). Frank Kermode surveys the "poet and dancer" tradition in Chapter 4 of *Romantic Image* (London: Routledge, 1957). D. H. Lawrence's descriptions of native American dances, and Aldous Huxley's portrayal of the dance on the savage reservation in *Brave New World,* are well worth considering in this context.
34. Nadine Gordimer, "The Congo River" in *The Essential Gesture: Writing, Politics and Places,* ed. Stephen Clingman (London: Penguin, 1989) p. 166. An earlier draft of Gordimer's essay was titled "Towards the Heart of Darkness."
35. Watt, *Conrad in the Nineteenth Century,* p. 233.
36. Mahood, *The Colonial Encounter,* p. 27.
37. On the relationship between anthropology and popular fiction at this period see Brian V. Street, *The Savage in Literature: Representations of "Primitive" Society in English Fiction 1858-1920* (London and Boston: Routledge, 1975).
38. Edward B. Tylor, *Primitive Culture: Researches in the Development of Mythology, Philosophy, Religion, Language, Art, and Custom,* 4th edn (London: Murray, 1903) I, pp. 501-2. Tylor's assertion of an "unbroken line" between the "savage fetish-worshipper and the civilised Christian" receives a baroque elaboration in Frazer's *The Golden Bough* esp. its famous conclusion. Sir James George Frazer, *The Golden Bough: A Study in Magic and Religion* abridged edn (London: Macmillan, 1957) II, p. 934.
39. Miller, *Blank Darkness,* p. 49.
40. Tylor, *Primitive Culture,* 11, p. 145.
41. Mahood, *The Colonial Encounter,* p. 20.
42. Tylor, *Primitive Culture,* I, p. 6.

"Rebarbarizing Civilization": Conrad's African Fiction and Spencerian Sociology

BRIAN W. SHAFFER

To the memory of my father, Aaron B. Shaffer

Evidently, therefore, the conquest of one people over another has been, in the main, the conquest of the social man over the anti-social man; or, strictly speaking, of the more adapted over the less adapted.

Herbert Spencer, Social Statics

The conquest of the earth, which mostly means the taking it away from those who have a different complexion or slightly flatter noses than ourselves, is not a pretty thing when you look at it too much.

Joseph Conrad, Heart of Darkness

The text lives only by coming into contact with another text (with context). Only at the point of this contact between texts does a light flash, illuminating both the posterior and anterior, joining a given text to a dialogue.

Mikhail Bakhtin, "Speech Genres" and Other Late Essays

CONRAD AND SPENCER AT THE FIN DE SIÈCLE

One would have difficulty imagining a writer more important to his own day, yet more out of currency in our own, than Herbert Spencer (1820–1903). While Charles Darwin is typically viewed as the revolutionary scientist of late Victorian thought, it is nevertheless Spencer who first posits a process of cosmic evolution involving the survival of the fittest; and it is Spencer who provides, in Leo J. Henkin's words, "the ablest and most influential development of the argument from evolution to progress" (198). In *History of the Idea of Progress* Robert Nisbet maintains that "without question, Herbert Spencer is the supreme embodiment in the late nineteenth century of both liberal individualism and the idea of progress." No other name, he continues, is "more deeply respected . . . and more influential, in a score of spheres, than . . . Herbert Spencer" (229, 235). Indeed, from Alfred R. Wallace's assessment of Spencer as "the greatest all-round thinker and most illuminating reasoner of the Nineteenth Century" to Darwin's own view, that Spencer is "about a dozen times my superior" and "by far the greatest living philosopher in England; perhaps equal to any that have lived" (qtd. in Carneiro ix),[1] confirmations of Henkin's and Nisbet's later judgments are frequently encountered in British writing during the forty years spanning the turn of the century.

Immensely popular, available in inexpensive editions, and concerned with subjects ranging from social and cultural evolution to the function of art and trade, Spencer's works were at the height of their influence during the years in which Conrad's early fiction was taking shape.[2] The hypothesis that this fiction represents and challenges Spencerian ideas is therefore unlikely to be contested. Nevertheless, while it is a critical commonplace to acknowledge Conrad's debt to Darwinian and Huxleyan perspectives, the relevance of the Spencerian canon to the Conradian one has been virtually overlooked.[3] The only two critics to explore this connection in some detail are John E. Saveson, who notes the novelist's "use of Spencerian terms and concepts" and maintains that "Conrad's earliest assumptions are 'scientific' in the sense that they are Spencerian" (22, 18); and Allan Hunter, who argues that "Spencer explains his own approach to sociology in . . . terms that are similar to Conrad's" and that the novelist demonstrates "a certain familiarity with particular works" by Spencer (104, 86; see Saveson 17–36; Hunter, 86–91). But whereas Saveson focuses on Spencerian anthropology and psychology, contending that Conrad's moral treatment of character derives from a Spencerian standard of measurement, and Hunter concerns himself with Spencer's "evolutionary ethics" in Conrad's work, I seek to illuminate the ways in which the fiction appropriates and tests Spencer's influential "typology of civilization."

More specifically, I am interested in the positive and negative ways this typology informs Conrad's African fictions—*Heart of Darkness* (1899) and the short story that is in many ways its Ur-text, "An Outpost of Progress" (1897).[4] Positively, these fictions invoke Spencer's crucial distinction between "militant" and "industrial" societies and echo his perception that late-nineteenth-century

British civilization is on a "course of re-barbarization." Negatively, they ultimately undermine Spencerian resolutions: *Heart of Darkness* expunges the difference between militant and industrial societies, showing that, in Europe's expansion into the Congo, the two proclivities are mutually reinforcing rather than mutually exclusive; and "An Outpost of Progress" parodies the Spencerian faith in the "beneficent necessity" of progress. *Lord Jim* (1900) also merits brief discussion here, not only because Conrad repeatedly pleaded that this novel be considered together with *Heart of Darkness* but because it provides many interesting alternatives to and modified examples of Conrad's intersection with Spencerian ideas.[5] Thus, beyond Ian Watt's observation that "several aspects of evolutionary thought are present in *Heart of Darkness*" (153) and Cedric Watts's contention that the novella embodies "a critical summary of some important nineteenth-century preoccupations" (1), I seek to portray the complex "dialogic" posture—at once receptive and critical, reinforcing and subversive—that Conrad's Congo fictions assume toward the story of civilization embodied in Spencerian sociology. Gerald Graff, in a Bakhtinian moment, asserts "that no text is an island, that every work of literature is a rejoinder in a conversation or dialogue that it presupposes but may or may not mention explicitly" (10). It is in this sense, I believe, that we may view these fictions, which resolutely explore the relation between "civilization" and "jungle," as "rejoinders" to Spencer's typology of civilization. I advance this thesis fully recognizing that there is no explicit record of Conrad's having read Spencer and that Conrad was influenced by late-nineteenth-century evolutionary (and devolutionary) thinkers other than Spencer.

SPENCER'S "MILITANT-INDUSTRIAL" DISTINCTION IN *HEART OF DARKNESS*

Spencer's militant-industrial distinction, on which his typology of civilization rests, must be situated within his broader theory of universal progress. This theory holds that all phenomena—whether inorganic, organic, or "superorganic" (cultural)—necessarily evolve from indefinite, incoherent, and homogeneous states to definite, coherent, and heterogeneous ones (*First Principles* 380). Within this context takes shape Spencer's theory of the inevitable progress of civilization ("which could not have been other than it has been" [*Social Statics* 233]): the simple, repressive, corporate organization of militant society evolves into the complex, democratic, individualistic organization of industrial society. Spencer's fullest formulation of the militant-industrial distinction appears in his three-volume *Principles of Sociology* (1876, 1882, 1896), completed only three years before the publication of *Heart of Darkness* and considered the culmination of his "synthetic philosophy." This dichotomy pervades Spencer's entire corpus.

In *Principles of Sociology* the difference between these types of social organization centers on the difference between the society that lives by work in order to benefit individuals and the society that lives by war in order to benefit the state (1: 620).[6] Although this distinction between politically motivated "static-military" and economically motivated "dynamic-civil" societies dates back at least to Machiavelli (Rapoport 178), it is Spencer, the theory's leading Victorian exponent, who makes the distinction both the cornerstone of a teleological theory of social evolution and the primary factor in the rise of individualism. He characterizes militant society as centralized and totalitarian, industrial society as democratic and civil libertarian (1: 584).While he fluctuates in *Principles of Sociology* between the positions that these two forms of society are necessarily "mingled" and that they are necessarily "antagonistic" in a given civilization, he consistently exemplifies them "in a series of paired opposites: status vs. contract . . . subordination vs. equality, guilds and the command economy vs. the free market . . . and so forth" (Peel 207).

Before exploring the extent to which *Heart of Darkness* represents and criticizes these distinctions, I would like to glance briefly at an essay of Conrad's that illustrates how pertinent this use of Spencer becomes. For if there is one thing that might have attracted a person of Conrad's political disposition to the Spencerian story of civilization, it would have been Spencer's consignment of modern Russia to the militant camp rather than to the industrial one.[7] "Modern Dahomey [Africa] and Russia," Spencer writes, exemplify "that owning of the individual by the state in life, liberty, and goods, which is proper to a social system adapted for war" (2: 602). Moreover, he maintains that,

> of modern illustrations [of militant society], that furnished by Russia will suffice. Here again, with the wars which effected conquests and consolidations, came the development of the absolute ruler, who, if not divine by alleged origin, yet acquired something like divine *prestige.* (2: 584)

How familiar this sounds, not only when we think of Kurtz's godlike standing and his rule by tyranny within his African "tribe" but also when we consider Conrad's vitriolic essay of 1905, "Autocracy and War." There the Spencerian typology of civilization emerges as a means of distinguishing between a warlike and blindly absolutist Russia, which "lies outside the stream of progress" as a "despotism . . . utterly unEuropean," and a Europe wholly corrupt yet presumably aspiring to "peaceful . . . industrial and commercial competition" (97, 106). Conrad further chastises Russia's militancy by referring to the country as a "bottomless abyss that has swallowed up . . . every aspiration towards personal dignity, towards freedom" and "an autocracy whose only shadow of a title to existence [is] the invincible power of military conquest" (100, 110–11). I do not deny, however, that Conrad's earlier anti-Russian sentiment was fundamentally Polish.[8]

Likewise, although perhaps less obviously, the Spencerian distinction between militant and industrial societies is embedded metaphorically in *Heart of Darkness* (and invoked there for the benefit both of Marlow's audience within the tale and of Conrad's initial audience without) to counterpose Europe's self-image as a commercial and trading giant with Europe's image of Africa as the savage and warlike "dark continent." That this distinction, as I demonstrate below, dissolves into thin air when closely scrutinized does not invalidate the claim that a key register of meaning in the novella depends on the recognition of this distinction and on the view of civilized progress that underwrites it.

Focusing first on modern European industrial civilization, *Heart of Darkness* opens with images of London as an economically dynamic commercial and trading power, "the biggest, and the greatest, town on earth" (7). Barges, for the transport of goods and raw materials, appear on the Thames, just as steamboats, which Robert Kimbrough calls the "nineteenth-century symbol of Western civilization" (413), carry European traders into and out of the African jungle.[9] The motif of an industrial Europe is further emphasized when we learn, moments later, of the occupations of those aboard the *Nellie*—including an accountant, a lawyer, and a merchant seaman—each of whom has a stake in the commercial ventures of Europe and mirrors, as Hay notes (142), a European whom Marlow encounters in Africa. The accountant of the outer station, for example, tells Marlow that "when one has got to make correct entries one comes to hate those savages—hate them to the death" (22), a remark that suggests a Spencerian tension between the wealth orientation of industrial society and the presumed war orientation of "savagery," in which the bureaucratic keeping of business accounts has no place. Even the doctor who earlier examines Marlow is depicted as having a hand in his nation's industrial mission, though he functions primarily as a means for Conrad to ridicule the scientistic emphasis of psychological experimentation. Insisting that he leaves "mere wealth" to others, the doctor glorifies "the Company's business" and accepts the "interests of science" as his "share in the advantages [his] country shall reap" from its activity in the Congo (14–15). Further, Spencer's notions that industrial societies depend on trade and that trade is effected by free exchange resulting from a loss of economic autonomy (2: 614, 1:557) echo in the novella's repeated allusions to Europe's "trading mission" in Africa: "custom-house," "trade secrets," "trading places," "trading post," "business," "commerce," and so on. As Marlow explains, the "Trading Society" was "a Continental concern" (12). Like "An Output of Progress," which ironically assures us that "civilization follows trade" (116), *Heart of Darkness* clearly stresses the industrial basis of modern European social practice.

In *Principles of Sociology* Spencer also popularizes the assumption that the free trade and civil liberties of industrial civilization are organically related to the multiplicity "of associations, political, religious, commercial, professional, philanthropic and social" therein that encourage the "free-play of the sympathies" and that favor "the growth of altruistic sentiments and the resulting virtues" (qtd. in Wiltshire 250). *Heart of Darkness* makes the same connection between free trade and philanthropy, however ironically. The manager of the central station, for example, tells Marlow that "each station should be like a beacon on the road towards better things, a centre for *trade* of course but also for *humanising, improving, instructing*" (34; my emphasis). And the "brickmaker" at that outpost sees Kurtz's European mission as comprising "pity, and science, and progress" and deriving from "higher intelligence, wide sympathies, a singleness of purpose"

(28). At other points, too, the novella informs us that the "noble cause" of Europe is executed with "philanthropic desire."

Just as *Heart of Darkness* appears to invoke Spencer's industrial trope to characterize the way Europe would like to view itself, so it may allude to his militant schema to characterize the way Europe views Africa. Within Spencer's militant society the civil and the military heads are one, all productive forces are devoted to maintaining a strong military posture, and a rigid social hierarchy prevails. For Spencer, the militant society—whether composed of "a horde of savages, [a] band of brigands, or a mass of soldiers"—"tends to develop a despotism" and "a system of centralization"; for this reason it characteristically lacks commercial and philanthropic groups (1: 545; 2: 572, 577).

All these phenomena are evident in the organization of Kurtz's tribe. Indeed, the natives of his circle, as well as the organization of the circle itself, are equated with "savage(s)" or "savagery"—by definition militant (the novella has twenty-five such references [Bender 269–70]). Further, Kurtz's society is associated with the "savage clamour" of "dances ending with unspeakable rites" (43, 50), with "warlike yells" (47), with the "throb of drums" (65), and with the weaponry of battle—"spears, assegais, shields, knives" (27). Described "with spears in their hands, with bows, with shields, with wild glances and savage movements" (59) and as "a whirl of black limbs, a mass of hands clapping, of feet stamping, of bodies swaying, of eyes rolling" (37), Kurtz's men are depicted as implicitly trusting the authority of the civil and military leader who directs their raids on other tribes (56).[10] Even the "savage and superb, wild-eyed and magnificent" Congolese woman to whom Kurtz turns in the absence of his intended is depicted as donning "barbarous ornaments," her hair done in the shape of a "helmet" (60). Hence, whether or not the "certain attempts at ornamentation," those "heads on stakes" around Kurtz's house (57), derive from Spencer's account of the "organized criminality" of African Dahomey society, in which "wars are made to get skulls with which to decorate the royal palace" (2: 236), the novella suggests an appropriation of Spencer's militant-industrial opposition.

Lord Jim manifests a similar, if less ironic, appropriation of Spencer's typology of civilization. As Paul L. Wiley notes of the novel's Malaysian landscape, "[I]t is evident that the wilderness image has undergone changes relating it more closely to the almost surrealistic landscape of 'Heart of Darkness' than to the fecund jungle of *Almayer's Folly.*" Indeed, no matter how tentative or superficial the presentation of Spencer's distinction may be in the novel, numerous images and allusions contribute to a sense, as Wiley puts it, that Jim's "civilized background" and Patusan's "barbaric surroundings" are opposed (49). References to European (and particularly to Stein's) "commercial" and "trading" interests abound in the novel (134, 138–39, 151, 176, 181), as do suggestions that the "European mind" should possess "an unobscured vision, a tenacity of purpose, a touch of altruism" toward the pursuit of an "orderly" social fabric, a "peaceful life" (160, 227). Contrarily, groups indigenous to Patusan and environs are repeatedly associated with militancy: with "rifles" (179), "cannons" (161), "spears" (155, 184), and "armed men" (150). Doramin is called a "war comrade," and the Rajah

Allang is said to have "personal slaves" (142, 202). While Jim possesses "racial prestige" and the "power" and "virtues" of "races that never grow old, that have emerged from the gloom," native Malaysians are associated with "a tumult of warcries, the vibrating clang of gongs, the deep snoring of drums, [and] yells of rage" (220, 162, 218–19).

Commenting on Spencerian social evolution, David Wiltshire writes that "there is no way to the more congenial industrial type, but through the regimentation and violence of the militant stage" (249); and *Heart of Darkness* speaks to this point as well. While the evolutionary theory embedded in the novella is typically attributed to Darwin, one aspect points more in Spencer's direction: the notion that the relation between childhood and adulthood corresponds to that between savagery and civilization. Although this idea has ancient roots, Spencer popularized it for late-nineteenth-century audiences in his essay "Progress: Its Law and Cause," where he likens the "progress in intelligence seen during the growth of the child into the man" to the development from "savage" to "philosopher" (8). Further, as Sarah L. Milbury-Steen observes, Spencer forges an "analogy between the African tribesmen and children," recognizing similarities in the intellectual traits of uncivilized adults and civilized children. For Spencer,

> [c]hildren are ever dramatising the lives of adults: and savages, along with their other mimicries, similarly dramatise the actions of their civilised visitors. Want of power to discriminate between useless and useful facts, characterizes the juvenile mind, as it does the mind of primitive man. (Qtd. in Milbury-Steen 7)

Instances of this trope are also rife in *Heart of Darkness*. Marlow, for example, notes that the African "settlements," while "some centuries old," are "still no bigger than pin-heads" and that there is "something pathetically childish in the ruins of grass walls" (16, 23). Moreover, Marlow compares African natives to children when he maintains that these "big powerful men" possess "courage" and "strength," yet lack the "capacity to weigh the consequences" of their potential to take action to free themselves. He also views them as still belonging "to the beginnings of time—[as having] no inherited experience to teach them" (42–43). Even Kurtz, who "forgets" himself among these "simple" natives, is characterized as "contemptibly childish" and "not much heavier than a child" (67, 66). But although readers have noted that the Africans of *Heart of Darkness* are represented as "stuck in time, prior to time, and outside it, in a 'perpetual childhood'" (Miller, 179), to my knowledge no one has suggested that Conrad may be using Spencer's influential articulation of this all too common nineteenth-century Western myth about Africans. When we consider this metaphor from the perspective of Conrad's diatribe against Russia in "Autocracy and War," his deployment of Spencer's association of militancy and inarticulate childhood is even more explicit:[11]

> As [Russia's] boasted military force that, corrupt in its origin, has ever struck no other but faltering blows, so her soul, kept benumbed by her

> temporal and spiritual master with the poison of tyranny and superstition, will find itself on awakening possessed of no language, a monstrous full-grown child having first to learn the ways of living thought and articulate speech. (102)

Just as *Heart of Darkness* associates "strings of amazing words that resembled no sounds of human language" with the "monstrous passions" of African natives (66, 65), "Autocracy and War" illustrates the Spencerian analogy between the "organic" metamorphosis from militancy into industrialism and from childhood into adulthood. While Conrad seems not to have considered the ramifications of this use of Spencerian metaphors—and hence can be accused of bad anthropology here—these tropes, however deceptive their implications, undoubtedly struck him as awesome in their explanatory power.

SPENCER'S "REBARBARIZED" CIVILIZATION IN *HEART OF DARKNESS*

In *Civilization and Progress,* John Beattie Crozier writes that whether Spencer's theory of evolution is "to be regarded as true or false, will depend not so much on how far it will explain the illusory phenomena of the past, as [on] how far it will explain the phenomena that lie amongst us in the present" (40). This observation also applies to the orientation of *Heart of Darkness* toward Spencerian thought. For *Heart of Darkness* suggests implicitly what Spencer states explicitly of the Europe, and more particularly the Britain, of his time: that it is undergoing a "process of rebarbarization" (*Facts* 173). In other words, while maintaining the legitimacy of the militant-industrial distinction, the man Hannah Arendt calls "the first philosopher of evolution" (178) is also perhaps the first philosopher of "devolution," to the extent that he sees industrial Europe, at the end of the century, as sliding back into militancy. Indeed, Spencer observes in the Britain of his day a renewed interest in arming, regimentation, and the predatory spirit generally (1: 570). Further, he envisions militancy, imperialism, and slavery as interrelated aspects of a general retrogression accompanying rebarbarization (*Facts* 159, 196). Sounding like Conrad, who insists in "Autocracy and War" that "the true peace of the world . . . will be built on less perishable foundations than those of material interests" (107), Spencer writes of his loathing for "that conception of social progress which presents as its aim, increase of population, growth of wealth, spread of commerce." "Increase in the swarms of people whose existence is subordinated to material development," he continues, "is rather to be lamented than to be rejoiced over" (*Facts* 7). My suggestion here is simply that, beyond Conrad's firsthand experience of Africa in 1890, when he was employed by the Société Anonyme Belge pour le Commerce du Haut Congo,[12] his insight into European decadence is deepened and qualified by Spencer's theory of a rebarbarized civilization—a theory that anticipates Oswald Spengler's. While culminating in the rebarbarization chapter of *Facts and Comments,* which was not in currency until 1902 and hence postdates Conrad's

African fictions, Spencer's observations on Europe's latent savagery nevertheless date from as early as his first book, *Social Statics,* originally published in 1850 and revised in 1892. There, he writes that

> while the mere propensity to thieve, commonly known under some grandiloquent alias, has been the real prompter of colonizing invasions, from those of Cortez and Pizarro downwards, the ostensible purpose of them has been either the spread of religion or the extension of commerce. (190)

Maintaining that aggression has recently led colonists to perpetrate "atrocities that disgrace civilization," Spencer argues that all profitable trade with colonies must be abandoned if it does not come naturally (198, 193). In "The Morals of Trade" Spencer even asks how "in this civilized state of ours" there can be "so much that betrays the cunning selfishness of the savage" (143).

It is a truism of Conrad scholarship that *Heart of Darkness* attacks turn-of-the-century European imperialism and trading practices (see, e.g., Hawkins, "Conrad's Critique"); yet what has been overlooked is just how close this attack comes to Spencer's sense of a rebarbarized European civilization. Conrad's novella also uses the word *trade* as a euphemism for what is actually raiding and "grubbing" and emphasizes the connections among enslavement, imperialism, and militancy. Kurtz's possessiveness toward everything around him ("my ivory, my station, my river" [49]), for example, reflects the other Europeans' self-serving crimes in the name, as Spencer would say, of the "spread of religion or the extension of commerce" (*Social Statics* 190). Marlow encounters a "chain-gang" (19); disease and slow death, the apparent effects of "a massacre or a pestilence" (21); and the "glorious slaughter" of Africans (52)—all on behalf of an "outraged" and "farcical law," a "fantastic invasion" of Europeans. "It was just robbery with violence," Marlow affirms, suggesting Spencer's complaint about forced trade, "aggravated murder on a great scale" (10). Moreover, instead of representing only native Africans as militant, *Heart of Darkness* also depicts weapon-toting European "pilgrims" as warlike, "bloodthirsty" savages. Carrying the "absurd long staves" of the Africans (26), gratuitously "squirting lead into [the] bush" (46), and resembling "mean and greedy phantoms" (67) who mercilessly scapegoat and beat innocent victims in an "imbecile rapacity" for ivory (26), these Europeans represent imperialism and slavery as two sides of the same coin—as indicative of industrial Europe's regression toward militancy.

It is in the metaphorical linking of savagery and animal life, however, that *Heart of Darkness* most forcefully refigures Spencer's caveat about rebarbarization. Just as Spencer observes that "the forces at work exterminate such sections of mankind as stand in the way, with the same sternness that they exterminate beasts of prey and herds of useless ruminants" (*Social Statics* 238), so Kurtz in *Heart of Darkness*—after native Africans have been likened to "creatures," "brutes," hyenas, "bees," dogs, and "ants"—concludes his peroration for the International Society for the Suppression of Savage Customs with the postscriptum "Exterminate all the brutes!" (51). Even Marlow notes that the individual African native is of "no more account" to Europeans than is "a grain of sand in a black Sahara" (51),[13] a comparison that contradicts Europe's avowed religious mission, as articulated by Marlow's aunt: "weaning those ignorant millions from their horrid ways" (16).

A look at *Lord Jim* is instructive too, for we are witness there to the suggestion that the "lies of our civilisation" (172) render non-Westerners brutes (206), "hyaenas" (146), and "cattle" (10, 245). And what better emblem of this rebarbarization than the exploits of Gentleman Brown (who is every bit the "beetle" to Jim's "butterfly")? Like Kurtz (and Jim), Brown cannot succeed in Europe, and so he brings his "vulgar and greedy brutes" to Patusan (214). "Malicious," "lawless," "savage," and "revengeful," this "hollow sham" of a "buccaneer" and "ruffian," who ultimately proves to be Jim's nemesis, is little more than a "common robber" who brings "terror" to every situation in which he finds himself. One of the novel's most "civilized" characters, he is also, paradoxically, the most barbaric.

BEYOND SPENCER: THE MILITARY-INDUSTRIAL COMPLEX IN *HEART OF DARKNESS*

In his monumental study of Conrad, Watt maintains that "the greatest authors are rarely representative of the ideology of their period; they tend rather to expose its internal contradictions or the very partial nature of its capacity for dealing with the facts of experience" (147). This comment on the content and function of modern art aptly describes the representation of Spencerian ideology in *Heart of Darkness* as useful and suggestive but ultimately incapable of dealing with "the facts of experience." In this sense, as Watts writes of Conrad's relation to Darwinism, Conrad is both "Spencerian and anti-Spencerian," invoking Spencer's categories and absorbing his rubrics even if finally opposing his perceptions and undermining his conclusions. For while Spencer decries the West's loss of ground in its realization of the industrial ideal, he never doubts that the militant-industrial distinction is a legitimate means of characterizing the development of civilization. *Heart of Darkness,* in contrast, ultimately subverts this distinction altogether, for the novella represents not the mutual exclusivity of militant and industrial tendencies but their mutual reinforcement in what might be called a "military-industrial complex." Whereas this phrase, coined by Dwight D. Eisenhower sixty years after the publication of *Heart of Darkness,* has specific resonances not wholly germane to our discussion here, its more general meaning—an informal alliance among a nation's political, military, and commercial interests—aptly characterizes what the novella glimpses of European activity in Africa.[14] By suggesting that commercial and trading mastery depends on brute military force and that "foreign trade and modern war have always been one and the same thing" (John Seely, qtd. in Coit 123), *Heart of Darkness* disarms the rhetoric of "imperialist civilization." For such a discourse is predicated on the maintenance of opposition like Spencer's, which *Heart of Darkness* undermines by highlighting the similarity between economically and politically motivated societal organizations. Meaning accrues in the novella through the invocation and then the subversion of the militant-industrial distinction and other dualities. Conrad accomplishes this feat, as Hay points out, "through repeated reversals or inversions of normal patterns of imagery" (137).[15]

Indeed, *Heart of Darkness* at many points conflates the two sides of Spencer's distinction, manifesting the "merry dance of death and trade" in the image of a military-industrial complex (17). In "Autocracy and War," an essay in which Mark Conroy correctly observes a "wedding of arms and trade" (81), Conrad charges that "industrialism and commercialism . . . stand ready, almost eager, to appeal to the sword as soon as the globe of the earth has shrunk beneath our growing numbers by another ell or so" and that "*Il n'y a plus d'Europe*—there is only an armed and trading continent, the home of slowly maturing economical contests for life and death, and of loudly proclaimed world-wide ambitions" (107, 112). *Heart of Darkness* too depicts the militant "sword" and industrial "torch" as mutually reinforcing. The French steamer that brings Marlow to Africa, for example, visits ports for "the sole purpose of landing soldiers and custom-house officers," and the construction of a Congolese railway reminds him of the shelling of Africa by a French navy vessel: "Another report from the cliff made me think suddenly of that ship of war I had seen firing into a continent" (16, 19). Not only do European trading and military posts dot the land, but expeditions devoted to "exploring" the terrain in fact "tear treasure out of" its bowels "with no more moral purpose at the back of it than there is in burglars breaking into a safe" (32–33). Even the Thames and Congo rivers, the one a waterway of "civilized commerce" and the other of "savage mystery" ("resembling an immense snake uncoiled" [12]), are conflated at the end of the novella, when the Thames itself seems to lead "to the uttermost ends of the earth . . . into the heart of an immense darkness" (76).

It is Kurtz's society, however, that most forcefully stands as a microcosm of the military-industrial complex. According to Watt, "The romantic, anarchic, and psychopathic energies of Kurtz find their ultimate sanction in Western industrial supremacy, for Kurtz really asserts his claims to 'the rightness of God' through his monopoly of firearms" (165). Kurtz's wealth and power, both cut from the whole cloth of his "method" and "immense plans," are linked symbiotically; but his technique for bettering commercial interests, which consists less of trading and barter than of raiding and murder, tends to go beyond the militant (an "unsound method") to the genocidal ("Exterminate all the brutes!").[16] In commenting, after Kurtz's death, that "Kurtz's knowledge however extensive did not bear upon the problems of commerce or administration" (70), Marlow is telling the truth to the extent that Kurtz's "trade secrets" were exclusively military: the annihilation of rival dealers in ivory. This conflation of Spencerian categories is further underscored when the steamer that removes Kurtz from the inner station is characterized as a "grimy fragment of another world, the forerunner of change, of conquest, of trade, of massacres" and when Kurtz declares of the European administration, "You show them you have in you something that is really profitable, and then there will be no limits to the recognition of your ability"

(67). In this sense *Heart of Darkness* stands as a riposte to the Spencerian claim that nineteenth-century Britain is a "compromise between militancy and industrialism," suggesting instead that the two "antagonistic" tendencies collectively constitute an unmistakably civilized form of activity—one that becomes "an instrument of pure brute force" (Tessitore 39).

FROM PROGRESS TO PARODY: SPENCER'S "LAW" AND CONRAD'S "OUTPOST"

In discussing the sources of Conrad's African fictions, Norman Sherry calls "An Outpost of Progress" "an interesting tail-piece to *Heart of Darkness*"; and this comment holds true as well for our consideration of both the debt and the antipathy these works show to the Spencerian story of civilization. For when one considers Spencer's place as "the last of the eighteenth-century Encyclopedists masquerading as a prophet of nineteenth-century scientific progress" (Wiltshire 195), Sherry's claim that "the ironic treatment of the concept of 'progress'" pervades "An Outpost of Progress" takes on particular resonance (125). Indeed, the entire story can profitably be read as a parody of Spencer's best-known and most succinct presentation of this idea, his "Progress: Its Law and Cause" (1857).

There Spencer posits a deterministic and teleological notion of progress as neither "an accident" nor "a thing within human control, but a beneficent necessity" (60). Whereas Spencer deems the "cause" of progress "inscrutable" and "an impenetrable mystery" (61-62)—words that continually appear in Conrad's African fictions—he considers the "law" of progress organic, universal, and knowable:

> Whether it be in the development of the Earth, in the development of Life upon its surface, in the development of Society, of Government, of Manufacture, of Commerce, of Language, Literature, Science, Art, the same evolution of the simple into the complex, through successive differentiations, holds throughout. From the earliest traceable cosmical changes down to the latest results of civilization, we shall find that the transformation of the homogeneous, is that in which progress essentially consists. (10)

When this essay is situated in the context of Spencer's other thoughts linking civilization and progress, it becomes clear just how easily apologists for colonial expansion could appropriate his idea of progress. In *Social Statics,* for example, Spencer writes that "instead of civilization being artificial it is a part of nature," one that necessarily progresses to the point at which "evil and immorality disappear . . . and man become[s] perfect" (32). And in *Principles of Sociology* he writes, "[W]hat remains to be done, calls for no other agency than the quiet pressure of a spreading industrial civilization on a barbarism which slowly dwindles" (2: 664).

It is less Spencer himself, however, than a number of influential "social Spencerians" who use these arguments to justify imperialism and to whom "An Outpost of Progress" can be seen as a response.[17] In *Spencer and Spencerism,* for example, Hector MacPherson suggests that "the scramble in China, the race for territory in South Africa, the expansion of Britain in Egypt . . . are all . . . evidence of the fact that civilization is beginning to overflow its old boundaries, and is becoming world-wide in its aspirations." He then goes on to forecast a millennium:

> Human history, beginning with a sordid struggle for existence and an ethical code steeped in blood, ends with a harmonious civilization resting upon the all-embracing conception of human brotherhood. Man and society, no longer at war, are destined to form one harmonious whole on the basis of reciprocity of service. With the magic wands of Reason, Science, and Industry, man on the basis of an egoism which is gradually being transfigured by sympathy, will yet lay the foundation of a new social order, in which peace, not strife, shall reign. Above the din of conflicting interests and warring passions may be heard, by those who listen in the spirit of evolutionary science, the inspiring tones of the humanitarian evangel—Peace on earth, and good will among men. (185-87)

MacPherson's comments typify a prevalent appropriation of Spencerian progress as justifying the end for which the means is colonization.

Arthur Symons maintains that Conrad takes "his revenge upon science" by "borrowing its very terms, making them dance at the end of a string, derisively" (11); and in precisely this way the scathingly ironic "Outpost of Progress" takes its revenge on Spencerian scientific progress. In this short fiction, initially entitled "A Victim of Progress," Conrad incisively parodies "progress and civilization and all the virtues" by telling the story of a murder and suicide that result when two Europeans (of either French or Belgian extraction) who are left alone at an African trading station quarrel over a lump of sugar for afternoon coffee (116). Hence, I disagree with Watt's claim that "Outpost" "has very little of the subversive force of *Heart of Darkness*" (35). For it is reasonable to view this story and Conrad's essay "The Crime of Partition" (1919) as, among other things, trenchant critiques of Spencerian ideals. "Progress," Conrad writes in this essay, "leaves its dead by the way, for progress is only a great adventure[,] as its leaders and chiefs know very well in their hearts. It is a march into an undiscovered country; and in such an enterprise the victims do not count" (118). As in "Outpost," progress here is depicted as anything but a "beneficent necessity."

"An Outpost of Progress" takes us into the center of Africa, where Carlier and Kayerts, the Bouvard and Pécuchet of the jungle (Darras 53), earn profits by sitting still and gathering in "the ivory those savages . . . bring" (90). Reduced to comic caricatures rather than raised to the level of psychological dramatic characters, Carlier and Kayerts—respectively, a former commissioned officer of cavalry "in an army guaranteed from harm by several European powers" and a former telegraph administrator—are depicted as blind, useless, and ineffectual "children" in the employ of the "ruthless and efficient" director of the "Great Trading Company" (88, 89, 87). For these two "Pioneers of Progress" "the river, the forest, all the great land throbbing with life, [are] like a great emptiness" and the natives of "this dog of a country" are little more than funny and "ungrateful brutes" who try "civilized nerves" (92, 93, 103, 89).

This assault on Spencerian progress cuts in two directions: it challenges the belief that "industrial" Europe is more advanced than "militant" Africa, and it attacks the presumption that any "principle," as Conrad himself says in a letter, "can stand alone at the beginning of things and look confidently to the end" (*Collected Letters* 2: 348). Carlier and Kayerts, for example, capitalize on some Africans' misperception of them as gods, when all the while they enslave the natives whose lives they disrupt. In two uncharacteristically honest remarks Carlier admits to Kayerts that they are both slave dealers because "there's nothing but slave-dealers in this cursed country" and, presaging Kurtz, that they face "the necessity of exterminating all the niggers before the country [can] be made habitable" (110, 108). Further, the reality of their exploitative operations at the outpost clashes profoundly with the civilized rhetoric with which the European press surrounds their mission—"it spoke much of the rights and duties of civilization, of the sacredness of the civilizing work, and extolled the merits of those who went about bringing light, and faith and commerce to the dark places of the earth"—while they themselves reduce "civilization" to a materialistic fetish: "the storehouse was in every station called the fetish, perhaps because of the spirit of civilization it contained" (94-95, 93).[18]

More specifically, however, a parody of Spencerian progress is enacted in the sense that both the "law" of progress ("in a hundred years there will be perhaps a town here . . . warehouses and barracks . . . civilization, my boy, and virtue") and the "cause of progress" are invoked only to be devastated by the reality they know there (95, 100). Even Spencer's notion of the survival of the fittest arises here,[19] when Carlier and Kayerts are deemed "unfitted for such a struggle" with even purely material problems. They are "unfitted," in fact, because they are the products of "the high organization" of "the crowd that believes blindly in the irresistible force of its own institutions and of its morals, in the power of its police and its opinion." Further, civilization is said to forbid Carlier and Kayerts "all independent thought, all initiative, all departure from routine," rendering them little more than "machines" (89-91). This attack on a fetishized notion of civilization, not to mention on Spencerian progress, may be the most blatant in all of Conrad's fiction, for it moves beyond the critical suggestion, in *Heart of Darkness,* that civilization depends for its perpetuation on the moral complacency and blindness of those who conduct its business (such as Marlow's "excellent aunt" and his audience aboard the *Nellie*).[20]

In his book on Conrad, Ford Madox Ford writes that he and Conrad "agreed that the novel is absolutely the only vehicle for the thought of our day." "With the novel," he continues, "you can do anything: you can inquire into any department of life, you can explore every department of the world of thought" (222). It is in this sense, I believe, that Conrad's African fictions inquire into Spencer's typology of civilization, both incorporating and criticizing it, both absorbing its rubrics and parodying its resolutions. As Bakhtin affirms, in reality "any utterance, in addition to its own theme, always responds (in the broad sense of the word) in one form or another to others' utterances which precede it." "The speaker," he continues, "is not Adam, and therefore the subject of his speech itself inevitably becomes the arena where his opinions meet those of . . . other viewpoints, world views, trends, theories, and so forth" (94). It is in this sense too that Conrad's African fictions constitute an arena in which a dialogue with Spencerian sociology is enacted. Whereas Conrad's appropriation of Spencer might not equal Arnold Bennett's, for example (Bennett insists that "you can see [Spencer's] *First Principles* in nearly every line I write" [392]), it is clear that Spencer's typology, as a vital matrix of the discourse of civilization and progress during this period, seeped its way into Conrad's "transformative" African narratives. On the evidence suggested here, then, I would reject the claim that Conrad's work "transforms, subverts, and rescues the established norms, values, and myths of imperialist civilization" (Parry 7) and would suggest instead just the opposite: that the "subversive-conservative" novelist invokes, only to destroy, such norms, values, and myths—even those of one as skeptical of imperialist civilization as the philosopher-scientist Herbert Spencer.[21]

NOTES

1. Privately, however, Darwin was less enthusiastic about Spencer's achievement. Darwin's notebooks, for example, record that Spencer's "deductive manner of treating every subject is wholly opposed to my frame of mind" and that his "conclusions never convince me" (qtd. in Howard 94).
2. To get an idea of Spencer's significance in these years, see Will Durant, who devotes nearly ten percent of *The Story of Philosophy* to Spencer (381-434)—more space than allotted to Plato, Aristotle, Kant, or Nietzsche. And Hector MacPherson deems Spencer an "epoch-maker" of the caliber of "Descartes, Locke, Spinoza, Hume, Kant, Hegel" (v). For F. A. P. Barnard, Spencer is "not only the profoundest thinker of our time, but the most capacious and most powerful intellect of all time" (qtd. in Hofstadter 31). Allan Hunter, writing about Spencer's *Data of Ethics,* explains that "there was a cheap edition of this highly influential work in 1894, which would seem to indicate that Spencer was not only still well thought of, but also still in the mainstream of ethical discussion at the time" (87). And James G. Kennedy notes that sales of Spencer's books in the last quarter of the nineteenth century extended into the millions (119, 153).
3. Among those who have commented on Conrad's indebtedness to Darwin and Huxley are Hunter; Levine, "Novel"; Renner; Saveson; Watt; and Watts. The exceptional few who briefly mention a connection between Spencer and Conrad are Green; Hawkins, "Conrad"; Levine, *Realistic Imagination*; O'Hanlon; and Watt. And in his notes to Conrad's *"Congo Diary" and Other Uncollected Pieces,* Zdzislaw Najder contends that Conrad's "agnosticism seems to have owed something to Spencer" (73).

4. In a letter to William Blackwood on the last day of 1898, for example, Conrad writes of *Heart of Darkness* that "the subject is of our time distinctly. . . . It is a story as much as my *Outpost of Progress* [sic] was but, so to speak[,] 'takes in' more—is a little wider—is less concentrated upon individuals" (*Collected Letters* 3:140).
5. In a number of letters written between 1899 and 1902, for example, Conrad insists that *Heart of Darkness* and *Lord Jim* be read together. He originally intended, pace Flaubert's *Trois contes,* to publish the short story "Jim: A Sketch" in a volume with "Heart of Darkness" and "Youth," maintaining that "the three tales, each being inspired by a similar moral idea," will make "a homogenous book." Later, he writes that even the full-length *Jim* was "not . . . planned to stand alone. *H of D* was meant in my mind as a foil, and *Youth* was supposed to give the note" (2: 167, 231, 271). Determining precisely what Conrad meant here has kept scholars busy for years. Eloise Knapp Hay's interpretation, however, is for me the most convincing: "*Heart of Darkness* was a 'foil' for *Lord Jim* in the contrast it offered between the illusion of a man concerned with personal conduct and the illusion of a man obsessed by race superiority." Hay also notes that the Marlows of the two works are "dissimilar." While both will "lie" for their respective secret sharers (Kurtz and Jim), "the Marlow of *Lord Jim* believes that even dangerous knowledge is worthy of public examination, whereas the Marlow of *Heart of Darkness* believes the contrary: that dangerous knowledge must be suppressed" (177, 129). Similarly, Ian Watt maintains that if *Youth* was Conrad's "Song of Innocence" and *Heart of Darkness* his "Song of Experience," then perhaps *Lord Jim* can be seen as "a dialogue between the two Marlows, with Jim as the voice of his earlier innocence, and Marlow confronting him with the disenchanted voice of later experience" (269). For alternative positions on this issue, see Fleishman 107 and Winner 31.
6. All Spencer citations not otherwise identified are from *Principles of Sociology.*
7. Ford Madox Ford corroborates such an image of Conrad when he writes, in a personal remembrance, that Conrad favored England because of its readiness "to face Russia with fleet or purse when or wherever they should meet. The first English music-hall song that Conrad heard was: 'We don't want to fight but, by jingo if we do, / We've got the ships, we've got the men, we've got the money too. / We've fought the bear before and so we will again, / The Russians shall not have Constantinople. . . .' A Pole of last century—and above all things Conrad was a Pole of last century—could ask nothing better" (56–57; Ford's ellipsis).
8. Conrad's Polish anti-Russian sentiment clearly has roots in his father's "Poland and Muscovy" (1864). In this tract Apollo Korzeniowski judges Muscovite civilization to be "terrible, depraved, destructive." Calling Muscovy "the plague of humanity," he writes that "her civilization means envy and [the] negation of human progress" (77).
9. Compare Conrad's view of London here with the one in his 1906 memoir, *The Mirror of the Sea,* where the city is labeled "the oldest and the greatest of riverports" and its "growth . . . as a well-equipped port" is described as having "been slow, while not unworthy of a great centre of distribution" (96, 102). In *Heart of Darkness,* as in *Mirror*, the Thames conjures industrial associations: "Amongst the great commercial streams of these islands, the Thames is the only one I think open to romantic feeling" (91). Marlow at one point recalls that "there was a big concern, a Company for trade on that river. Dash it all, I thought to myself, they can't trade without using some kind of craft on that lot of fresh water—steamboats!" (12).
10. The absolutism of Kurtz's command is made clear when the Russian proudly tells Marlow of an encounter with Kurtz over a small quantity of ivory: "He declared he

would shoot me unless I gave him the ivory and then cleared out of the country because he could do so, and had a fancy for it, and there was nothing on earth to prevent him killing whom he jolly well pleased" (56).

11. Similarly, a passage on Russia in Spencer's *Facts and Comments* (1902) appears uncannily prophetic of events represented in Conrad's novel of nine years later, *Under Western Eyes:*

> Along with that unceasing subjugation of minor nationalities by which its imperialism is displayed, what do we see within its own organization? We have its vast army, to service in which everyone is actually or potentially liable; we have an enormous bureaucracy ramifying everywhere and rigidly controlling individual lives. . . . As a result of the pressure felt personally and pecuniarily, we have secret revolutionary societies, perpetual plots, chronic dread of social explosions; and while everyone is in danger of Siberia, we have the all-powerful head of this enslaved nation in constant fear for his life. Even when he goes to review his troops, rigorous precautions have to be taken by a supplementary army of soldiers, policemen, and spies . . . while similar precautions, which from time to time fail, have ever to be taken against assassination by explosion, during drives and railway-journeys. (164–65)

12. Writing years after this employment, Conrad observes that in the Belgian Congo, "created by the act of European powers[,] ruthless, systematic cruelty towards the blacks is the basis of administration, and bad faith towards all the other states the basis of commercial policy" (*Collected Letters* 3: 97).
13. Unsurprisingly, both Spencer and Conrad have been taken to task for depicting the "primitive" mind in stereotypical terms (see, e.g., Dewey; Street 159–60). Both Spencer, in *Principles of Sociology,* and Marlow, in *Heart of Darkness,* attempt to defuse such criticism. Spencer, for example, writes that "the words 'civilised' and 'savage' must have given to them meanings differing greatly from those which are current. That broad contrast usually drawn wholly to the advantage of the men who form large nations, and to the disadvantage of the men who form simple groups, a better knowledge obliges us profoundly to qualify" (2: 233). And Marlow suggests that we simply hate and fear what we do not understand, observing that in our "civilized" view of "the jungle," "the incomprehensible . . . is also detestable" (10).
14. Roger Scruton's 1982 *Dictionary of Political Thought* defines "Military-Industrial Complex" as "a pattern of relations sometimes thought to exist between high-ranking industrialists concerned in the manufacture of military technology, and military advisors, concerned in making themselves useful (perhaps even indispensable) to a government" (298).

    Writing in 1917 Stanton Coit sees a broader military-industrial alliance: "the facts of history prove that every great war during the last three centuries has been undertaken in the service of foreign traders, who call upon their government to back their claims" (122–23). In *The Decline of the West* Spengler goes so far as to claim that "Imperialism is Civilization unadulterated" (36).
15. The case can be made that *Heart of Darkness* defuses the West's claim to superiority over the non-West by subverting the oppositions on which the West bases its hegemony: godly/godforsaken, complex/simple, mind/body, language/gesture, logic/illogic, rational/irrational, good/evil, efficient/inefficient, order/chaos, sane/insane, day/night, light/dark, historic/prehistoric, culture/nature, and so forth.
16. Avrom Fleishman rightly points out that "Conrad's African tales, even more than his Asian ones, demonstrate that the contact of Europeans and natives encourages the

submerged barbarism of the superficially civilized whites to express itself by genocide. Not only are the natives stirred up by the rapacious policies of the imperialists, but the whites become more savage than the 'savages'" (90).

17. For two different interpretations of Spencer's role in the phenomenon of social Darwinism see Arendt 178–79 and Williams 86–102.
18. "Outpost," Patrick Brantlinger aptly notes, "clearly implies that between civilization and the savagery that worships fetishes and practices cannibalism there is little to choose" (138). In this connection Benita Parry maintains that "by revealing the disjunctions between high-sounding rhetoric and sordid ambitions and indicating the purposes and goals of a civilisation dedicated to global expansionism and hegemony, Conrad's writings engender a critique more destructive of imperialism's ideological premises than do the polemics of his contemporary opponents of empire" (10). And Eloise Knapp Hay correctly speaks of Conrad's "maturing effect on English letters," due to his ability to call attention to "the horror in certain political realities that were being overlooked by comfortable, law-abiding English citizens and politicians" (11).
19. This phrase improved on Darwin's appellation "natural selection," as Darwin himself came to see "the advantages of H. Spencer's excellent expression of the 'survival of the fittest'" (qtd. in Carneiro xx).
20. Although *Lord Jim* too alludes to the "stream of civilisation" and to the "laws and order of progress" (138, 206), it is clearly more idealistic and less ironic on this score than *Heart of Darkness*, even if a "privileged" member of Marlow's interlocutors doubts that Jim can remain faithful to his code: Jim lacks "a firm conviction in the truth of ideas racially our own, in whose name are established the order, the morality of an ethical progress" (206). Here Jim is shown to differ from Kurtz, who has no qualms about holding such a conviction.
21. I would like to acknowledge a debt of gratitude to several persons who have read and commented on various drafts of this essay: Keith Carabine, Gerald Graff, Hunt Hawkins, Eloise Knapp Hay, N. Katherine Hayles, Cheryl Herr, Henry Levinson, Margot Norris, Erik Parens, Daniel Schwarz, and Aaron Shaffer. I would also like to thank the National Endowment for the Humanities for providing me with time to revise this essay during Daniel Schwarz's 1990 Summer Seminar for College Teachers, at Cornell University.

WORKS CITED

Arendt, Hannah. *The Origins of Totalitarianism.* 1951. New York: Harcourt, 1973.

Bakhtin, M. M. *"Speech Genres" and Other Late Essays.* Austin: U of Texas P. 1986.

Bender, Todd K. *A Concordance to Conrad's* Heart of Darkness. New York: Garland, 1979.

Bennett, Arnold. *The Journal of Arnold Bennett.* New York: Viking, 1933.

Brantlinger, Patrick. *Bread and Circuses: Theories of Mass Culture as Social Decay.* Ithaca: Cornell UP, 1983.

Carneiro, Robert L. Introduction. *The Evolution of Society: Selections from Herbert Spencer's* Principles of Sociology. Chicago: U of Chicago P, 1967. ix–lvii.

Coit, Stanton. *Is Civilization a Disease?* Boston: Houghton, 1917.

Conrad, Joseph. "Autocracy and War." *Notes on Life and Letters.* Garden City: Doubleday, 1921. 83–114.

———. *The Collected Letters.* 3 vols. to date. Ed. Frederick R. Karl and Laurence Davies. Cambridge: Cambridge UP, 1983– .

———. "The Crime of Partition." *Notes on Life and Letters.* Garden City: Doubleday, 1921. 115-33.

———. *Heart of Darkness.* Ed. Robert Kimbrough. 3rd ed. New York: Norton, 1988.

———. *Lord Jim.* Ed. Thomas C. Moser. New York: Norton, 1968.

———. *The Mirror of the Sea.* 1906. Marlboro: Marlboro, 1988.

———. "An Outpost of Progress." *Tales of Unrest.* Garden City: Doubleday, 1925. 86-117.

Conroy, Mark. *Modernism and Authority: Strategies of Legitimation in Flaubert and Conrad.* Baltimore: Johns Hopkins UP, 1985.

Crozier, John Beattie. *Civilization and Progress.* 4th ed. London: Longmans, 1898.

Darras, Jacques. *Conrad and the West: Signs of Empire.* London: Macmillan, 1982.

Dewey, John. "Interpretation of the Savage Mind." *Philosophy and Civilization.* Gloucester: Smith, 1968. 173-87.

Durant, Will. *The Story of Philosophy.* 1926. New York: Simon, 1933.

Fleishman, Avrom. *Conrad's Politics: Community and Anarchy in the Fiction of Joseph Conrad.* Baltimore: Johns Hopkins UP, 1967.

Ford, Ford Madox. *Joseph Conrad: A Personal Remembrance.* Boston: Little, 1924.

Graff, Gerald. *Professing Literature: An Institutional History.* Chicago: U of Chicago P, 1987.

Green, Martin. *Dreams of Adventure, Deeds of Empire.* New York: Basic, 1979.

Hawkins, Hunt. "Conrad and the Psychology of Colonialism." *Conrad Revisited: Essays for the Eighties.* Ed. Ross C. Murfin. University: U of Alabama P, 1985. 71-87.

———. "Conrad's Critique of Imperialism in *Heart of Darkness.*" *PMLA* 94 (1979): 286-99.

Hay, Eloise Knapp. *The Political Novels of Joseph Conrad: A Critical Study.* 1963. Chicago: U of Chicago P, 1981.

Henkin, Leo J. *Darwinism in the English Novel, 1860-1910: The Impact of Evolution on Victorian Fiction.* New York: Corporate, 1940.

Hofstadter, Richard. "The Vogue of Spencer." *Social Darwinism in American Thought.* 1944. New York: Braziller, 1965. 31-50.

Howard, Jonathan. *Darwin.* Oxford: Oxford UP, 1982.

Hunter, Allan. *Joseph Conrad and the Ethics of Darwinism: The Challenges of Science.* London: Croom Helm, 1983.

Kennedy, James G. *Herbert Spencer.* Boston: Twayne, 1978.

Kimbrough, Robert. "Conrad's *Youth* (1902): An Introduction." Conrad, *Heart* 406-18.

Korzeniowski, Apollo. "Poland and Muscovy." *Conrad under Familial Eyes.* Ed Zdzislaw Najder. Cambridge: Cambridge UP, 1983. 75-88.

Levine, George. "The Novel as Scientific Discourse: The Example of Conrad." *Novel* 21 (1988): 220-27.

———. *The Realistic Imagination: English Fiction from Frankenstein to Lady Chatterly.* Chicago: U of Chicago P, 1981.

MacPherson, Hector. *Spencer and Spencerism.* New York: Doubleday, 1900.

Milbury-Steen, Sarah L. *European and African Stereotypes in Twentieth-Century Fiction.* New York: New York UP, 1981.

Miller, Christopher. *Blank Darkness: Africanist Discourse in French.* Chicago: U of Chicago P, 1985.

Najder, Zdzislaw, ed. *"Congo Diary" and Other Uncollected Pieces.* By Joseph Conrad. Garden City: Doubleday, 1978.

Nisbet, Robert. *History of the Idea of Progress.* New York: Basic, 1980.

O'Hanlon, Redmond. *Joseph Conrad and Charles Darwin: The Influence of Scientific Thought on Conrad's Fiction.* Edinburgh: Salamander, 1984.

Parry, Benita. *Conrad and Imperialism: Ideological Boundaries and Visionary Frontiers.* London: Macmillan, 1983.
Peel, J. D. Y. *Herbert Spencer: The Evolution of a Sociologist.* London: Heinemann, 1971.
Rapoport, David C. "Military and Civil Societies: The Contemporary Significance of a Traditional Subject in Political Thought." *Political Studies* 12 (1964): 178-201.
Renner, Stanley. "The Garden of Civilization: Conrad, Huxley, and the Ethics of Evolution." *Conradiana* 7 (1975): 109-20.
Saveson, John E. *Joseph Conrad: The Making of a Moralist.* Amsterdam: Rodopi, 1972.
Scruton, Roger. *A Dictionary of Political Thought.* London: Macmillan, 1982.
Sherry, Norman. *Conrad's Western World.* Cambridge: Cambridge UP, 1971.
Spencer, Herbert. *Facts and Comments.* New York: Appleton, 1902.
———. *First Principles.* New York: Appleton, 1890.
———. "The Morals of Trade." *Essays: Scientific, Political, and Speculative.* Vol. 3. New York: Appleton, 1896. 113-51.
———. *Principles of Sociology.* 3 vols. 1904. Osnabruck: Zeller, 1966.
———. "Progress: Its Law and Cause." *Essays: Scientific, Political, and Speculative.* Vol. 1. New York: Appleton, 1896. 8-62.
———. Social Statics, *Together with* Man versus the State. 1892. New York: Appleton, 1913.
Spengler, Oswald. *The Decline of the West.* New York: Knopf, 1939.
Street, Brian V. *The Savage in Literature: Representations of "Primitive" Society in English Fiction, 1858-1920.* London: Routledge, 1975.
Symons, Arthur. *Notes on Joseph Conrad, with Some Unpublished Letters.* London: Meyers, 1925.
Tessitore, John. "Freud, Conrad, and *Heart of Darkness.*" *College Literature* 7 (1980): 30-40.
Watt, Ian. *Conrad in the Nineteenth Century.* Berkeley: U of California P, 1979.
Watts, Cedric. *Conrad's* Heart of Darkness*: A Critical and Contextual Discussion.* Milan: Mursia Intl., 1978.
Wiley, Paul L. "*Lord Jim* and the Loss of Eden." *Twentieth Century Interpretations of* Lord Jim. Ed. Robert E. Kuehn. Englewood Cliffs: Prentice, 1969. 46-52.
Williams, Raymond. "Social Darwinism." *Problems in Materialism and Culture: Selected Essays.* London: Verso, 1980. 86-102.
Wiltshire, David. *The Social and Political Thought of Herbert Spencer.* Oxford: Oxford UP, 1978.
Winner, Anthony. *Culture and Irony: Studies in Joseph Conrad's Major Novels.* Charlottesville: UP of Virginia, 1988.

chapter **18**

Essays on *Devil on the Cross*, by Ngugi wa Thiong'o

The Strength of the Rhetoric of Oral Tradition in Ngugi wa Thiong'o's *Devil on the Cross*

SAM A. ADEWOYE

One of the most meaningful ways of understanding and appreciating the artistic qualities of the African novel is to disorientate ourselves from the sentimental criticisms constantly levied against the novel. To many people,[1] the African novel is nothing but a forum for political pamphleteering, or an instrument for attacking the white man's unprecedented hegemony in Africa; indeed, many critics have exposed what they believed to be the political immaturity and socio-cultural imbalances of Africans. Consequently, then, more attention has been paid to what the African novelist says than to how he says it. This is really a contemptuous response to the African novel!

One of the surest means to disengage ourselves from this disdainful treatment is to concentrate on precise analysis of the literary qualities and components of the novel. We could look at it from the purview of Frye's discourse that literature is a "hypothetical verbal structure which exists for its own sake."[2] We should faithfully consider the novelist's techniques, the devices that he employs to mold, explore, and evaluate his materials.

The purpose of this paper, therefore, is to examine one of the richest literary devices that Ngugi uses in composing *Devil on the Cross*. The paper expounds the view that Ngugi uses the rhetoric of oral tradition in the novel in order to delve into the authenticity of the novelist's reflection on the experiences and life of his own people, demonstrating that the African novel is artistically rich because of the African materials embodied in the work and not necessarily because of the conflicts arising from the Africans' relationship with alien cultures. The conflicts which the African cultures have with the foreign cultures only serve as creative visions for the African novelist and they should not be seen as destructive conflicts as perceived in African history or sociology.

The paper concludes that the African tradition can serve as a source of inspiration for African novelists' creative vision. This is actually a challenge to the African folklorist who has hitherto monopolized this African heritage.

Devil on the Cross was originally written in the author's indigenous language, Gikuyu. This, according to the author, was to enable his message to reach a wider audience, comprising mostly illiterates in English. Also, according to Ngugi, the use of an indigenous language was "a way of affirming my faith in the possibilities of the languages of all the different Kenyan nationalities" (*Detained* 164). This affirmation of faith in the possibilities of the Kenyan language also applies to the possibilities of all other African indigenous languages, which Ngugi goes on to say have been "actively suppressed by the British Colonial Regime." In the use of Gikuyu language, Ngugi resolves to let his character determine the African world that his fiction explores:

> I would not avoid any subject—science, technology, philosophy, religion, music, political economy—provided it logically arose out of the development of character, plot, story and world view.

However, it must be noted that language performs more than a communicative function. It is also a means of identifying with a particular culture and tradition. Thus in the writing of his novel in Gikuyu, Ngugi consciously or unconsciously employs the cultural and traditional ingredients of the language. Ngugi is described as "the offspring of an all-pervasive oral tradition, of the genius of the village singer and the family story teller round the fire" (*Cook and Okenimkpe* 188). These elements of his background influence his style and consequent upon which he actively employs the rhetorics of oral tradition in his novel. As written in the blurb of *Devil on the Cross,* "The ancient rhythms of traditional story telling are used in counterpoint to written styles." It is therefore significant that although Ngugi employs the rhetoric of oral tradition, he has to put this oral tradition down in writing; thus his work could be called a written oral tradition. This, in effect, means that Ngugi blends two different literary styles; that of oral and the written fictional traditions to create a challenging novel. The concept of oral tradition in the novel is adequately summarized thus:

> Devil on the Cross's relationship with oral and literal tradition is embedded as much in its form and techniques as in its content. (*Cook and Okenimkpe* 128)

The novel takes the form of traditional story telling. We are first introduced to the narrator the "Gicaandi Player," a traditional village musician who refers to himself as Prophet of Justice. His audience are the people of Ilmorrog, who beg and plead with him to tell them the story and "reveal all that is hidden" (*Devil* 7). The story itself is the controversial tale of Jacinta Wariinga, which some people consider too disgraceful and shameful to be brought to light. Others consider the story one of sorrow that should not be told again, to avoid upwell of emotion. However, the Prophet of Justice proceeds to tell this story and this aspect of a story-teller and audience is the first rhetoric of oral tradition embedded in the form of Devil on the Cross.

Another rhetoric or oral tradition embedded in the general structure of the novel is the use of songs. The song first enters into the form as the story teller is about to begin his story and calls out to his audience:

> Come,
> Come. Let us reason together . . .
> Come let us reason together
> about Jacinta Wariinga. (*Devil* 13)

The song is gradually introduced into the prose structure and becomes an integral part as the story goes along. The characters speak and express original thoughts through song rather than speech. In narrating her plight to Muturi, Wariinga defends her suicide attempt:

> For today Kareendi has decided that she does not know the difference between / To straighten and to bend / To swallow and to spit out / To ascend and to descend / To go and to return. (*Devil* 25)

The rhetoric of songs also replaces normal conversational dialogues:

> Then they began to talk. It was not really a conversation. It was more a kind of incantation as if they were both taking part in a verse-chanting competition, citing verses remembered in dreams.
>
> GATUIRIA: Hail, our land!
> Hail, Mount Kenya!
> Hail, our land
> Never without water or food
> or green fields!
> WARIINGA: Hail, the splendor of this land!
> Hail, the land ringed round
> with deep lakes,
> Turkana to Naivasha
> Nam-Lowle to Mombassa!

> Hail, this necklace of blue
> waters!
>
> GATUIRIA: Hail, hail the shields of the land. (*Devil* 128)

Song, apart from its thematic function in story-telling, is also a means of easing boredom and monotony as narration builds up. Ngugi thus injects a bit of comic humor into the prose through the character of Mwaura the bus driver as he advertises his Matata Matamu Model T Ford:

> "I once heard a young man sing
> If God's Kingdom were near,
> It would take you whores to Court,
> Something given you free by the Lord
> You now sell for twenty shillings." (*Devil* 31)

This comic humor receives the generally expected reaction: "People were beside themselves with laughter and whistled loudly" (*Devil* 33).

In terms of the rhetoric of oral tradition in the techniques, Ngugi says that though he is writing in the Gikuyu language,

> I would use any and everything I had even learnt about the craft of fiction allegory, parable, satire, narrative description, reminiscence, flashback, interior monologue, stream of consciousness, dialogue, drama—provided it came naturally in the development of character, theme and story. (*Detained* 164)

And this he does successfully especially through myth, an element of oral tradition in Africa. Ngugi invokes biblical mythology "the complex mythology generally known to his and other East African societies" (*Cook and Okenimpke* 130).

Through his biblical mythology Ngugi is able to use allegory, parable and satire, which are some of the "crafts of fiction" known to him. In terms of allegory, Wariinga is given a mythical role and made the symbol of patience, purity and goodness. She is like Christ, who went through temptation but was able to resist and triumph over the devil. "Get thee behind me, Satan" (*Devil* 194), she cries when the voice tries to tempt her. Her Christ-like role is further heightened as she is portrayed in the manner of a savior. "But I shall save many other people, whose lives will not be ruined by words of honey and perfume" (*Devil* 253).

Biblical mythology contains a lot of parables and Ngugi adopts one of these into his writing as a method of artistic expression of the motif in his work. He re-interprets the parables of the talents in a very ironic and satirical way: "For the Kingdom of Heaven is as a man traveling into a far country, who called his own servants, and delivered unto them his goods. And unto one he gave five talents, to another one" (*Devil* 81). The man is the distant former colonial master. The talents are "capital" and the first two servants with five and two talents are the middle men and managers who conduct business on behalf of their forgotten master who comes to reap the profit made. The third servant, with just one talent, sees through the master's capitalist intentions and refuses to allow the master to reap where he has not sown. He does not invest the capital and so is considered a "member of a rebellious clan" (*Devil* 85) and thrown into jail. The other two, who invest profitably, are regarded in form of more capital and "back handers." Ngugi satirizes the concept of Christianity and this is very obvious in the substituted title of his novel where the devil, rather than Christ the saint, is placed on the cross. He satirizes the hypocritical and double standards of morality upheld by the so-called Christians. Gatuiria's father claims he cannot marry Wariinga as second wife because, in his words, "I am a man of the Church, I just want you to be mine, I'll find my own ways of coming to visit you" (*Devil* 253). This type of satire is very African indeed. It demonstrates the marginality of the African people's commitment to Christianity. They have always viewed the religion as alien to them.

The use of indigenous language is another technique employed by Ngugi:

> Clearly, his use of Gikuyu has released previously untapped aspects of his creative talent which may very well have been stirred by the way the language has been traditionally deployed. (*Cook and Okenimkpe* 123)

Proverbs are used in almost every speech because they are an integral part of Gikuyu and indeed all African languages. They are used to buttress points during discussions or arguments. At the same time, they add beauty to the language by making it evocative and colorful. The story-teller says Wariinga's problems started partly because she forgot the saying: "That which is born black can never be white" (*Devil* 11). Wariinga replies to the advice of her friends telling her to leave her penniless Kamoongonye with the proverb. "A restless child leaves home in search of meat just as a goat is being slaughtered" (*Devil* 21). At times, a cluster of different proverbs are used to express a single point. Mwaura leaves Wangari to act as she likes because, according to him:

> "The case of a fool remains unsettled. And again, if a wise man argues with a fool for too long, it is difficult to tell the difference between them. A person destined for ill-fortune cannot be diverted." (*Devil* 157)

This demonstrates the richness of the African proverbs; the proverbs which are a total embodiment of their communal life.

Apart from the use of proverbs, there is also a minor but significant aspect of oral tradition in the novel and this is riddling. This takes place between Muturi and Wangari inside the bus, on their way to Ilmorrog:

> "The children of us workers are fated to stay out in the sun, thirsty, hungry, naked, gazing at fruit ripening on trees which they can't pick even to quiet a demanding belly" . . . asking one another to guess the

> same riddle day by day: 'Oh, for a piece of one of those!'" Ripe bananas! Wangari replied, as if Muturi had asked a real riddle. (*Devil* 46)

The conduct, according to Ngugi, will determine the eventual form of *Devil on the Cross,* not language and technique. This content, he says, is: "The Kenyan people's struggle against the neo-colonial form and stage of imperialism." He makes this point as said before, in the interpretation of the parable of the talents narrated by the master of ceremonies. The theme of the parable is:

> For unto the man of property more will be given, but from the poor man will be taken even the little that he has kept in reserve. (*Devil* 85)

The competition is for the selection of "seven Experts in Modern Theft and Robbery." The American leader of the Foreign delegation from International Organization of Thieves and Robbers (IOTR) in his speech highlights the aims of the contest "to choose seven disciples. They will become the representatives of our representatives, thieves to teach other thieves, robbers to teach other robbers" (*Devil* 88). This exposure of imperialism and local exploitation of the poor masses is the main substance of Ngugi's work.

As in every traditional fable, there is always a major character around whom the theme and relevance of the story revolve. This character in *Devil on the Cross* is the person of Wariinga, who changes radically in the course of the story. Initially, we see Wariinga trying to commit suicide owing to external pressures. In her youth, she is corrupted and impregnated by the Rich Old Man after initially leading a good and disciplined life. She goes through a lot of emotional and physical hardships in the city and finally decides to return to her village. Wariinga later goes through a metamorphosis:

> This Wariinga is not the one who used to think that there was nothing she could do except type for others; the one who used to burn her body with Ambi and snow-fire to change the color of her skin to please the eyes of others, to satisfy their lust for white skin; the one who used to think that there was only one way of avoiding the pitfalls of life: suicide. (*Devil* 216)

She becomes an ideal young woman with a degree in auto-engineering. At the end of the story, her symbolic role is again brought out as she shoots the Rich Old Man, who, in the novel, represents the materialistic, licentious, arrogant and selfish hypocrites who rule over the society and who come in handy for powerful bashing in the novel. Wariinga is an exemplary character and is obviously what Ngugi's idea of a woman should be. The moral of her story is that a clean life of hard work and dedication attained by revolting against all that is corrupt is better than a dirty and cheap life of luxury. Clearly, Ngugi is an advocate of the need for a revolution by the masses like Wariinga against the materialists, like the Rich Old Man, for the attainment of a better Kenya.

The testimony given by each competitor is like a story told in the traditional way with the use of song, proverb, riddle and so on. Each competitor is the story teller while those in the den form the audience. Kihaahu describes his narration as "a song about myself. . . . Say yes, and I'll tell you a story full of wonder." Before he tells this story, he introduces himself by chanting appellations in traditional style.

> "I am the Cock that crows in the morning and silences all the others. I am the lion that roars in the forest, making elephants urinate. I am the eagle that flies in the sky, forcing hawks to seek refuge in their nests. I am the wind that stills all breezes. I am the lightning." (*Devil* 109)

The story teller then gives a detailed declaration of all his property, both legal and illegal. He gives a brief history of how he got into the art of modern theft, and rounds off by suggesting further ridiculous means of making money through the exploitation of the masses:

> While the competition to crown Kenyan's leading extortioner is satirically exaggerated, the assertive cocksure tone that emanates from the body of the meeting will be menacingly familiar to many readers. This unqualified satire gives the victims of neo-colonialism a rare opportunity of seeing their tormentor reduced to comic caricatures by being made to boast in public for their conscienceless excesses. (*Cook and Okenimpke* 123)

Ngugi's own words in the introduction to *Homecoming* best conclude this essay:

> The novelist is haunted by a sense of the past. His work is often an attempt to come to terms with "the thing that has been," a struggle, as it were, to sensitively register his encounter with history, his people's history. (39)

Ngugi is indeed haunted by "a sense of the past" and *Devil on the Cross* is an attempt to identify and link up with his Gikuyu history. He does this first by breaking away from normal literary norms and employing the historical literary rhetoric of oral tradition. This is enhanced by the use of Gikuyu language through which Ngugi demonstrates an impressive wealth of creative genius and imagination. He definitely succeeds in proving his faith in the literary possibilities of Kenyan languages in particular and African languages in general.

A remarkable development on the oral rhetorical framework which already emerged in *Grain of Wheat* and more forcefully in *Petals of Blood* and *Devil on the Cross* reveals the potential of the African novel to evolve rather totally distinct from the one we have inherited from the West. The collective aspiration of the African masses is also best given voice in the oral traditional rhetorical form which this novel utilizes.

NOTES

1. For example, in an article titled, "Cultural Diplomacy in African Writing," Mbella Sonne Dipoko states, "It is borne out of eternal conflicts, nurtured by subtle emotional crisis, complicated by political stress and all kinds of political involvements; it is a literature of revolt and compromise" in *The Writer in Modern Africa,* Ed. Per Wa Stberg (New York: Africa Publishing Company, 1969), p. 59.
2. Lewis Nkosi is one of the people who are fully aware of what constitutes the richness of the African Arts. Talking specifically about the works of Okigbo, Clark and Soyinka, he says:

   > Although they write about their country, and they have from time to time borrowed from their country's myths, these young writers' works are merely an extension of European traditions. But they are informed by freshness and strength that is often lacking in much of the writing of decadent Europe.

   "A Release of Energy: Nigeria, the Arts and Mbari" in *New Africa,* I, II (Nov. 1962), p. 11.

WORKS CITED

Cook, David, and Michael Okenimkpe. *Ngugi Wa Thiong'o: An Exploration of His Writings.* London: Heinemann Educational Books, 1983.

Frye, Northrop. *Anatomy of Criticism.* Princeton, New Jersey: Princeton University Press, 1957.

Thiong'o, Ngugi wa. *Detained: A Writer's Prison Diary.* London: Heinemann Educational Books, 1981.

———. *Devil on the Cross.* East Africa: Heinemann Educational Books, 1980.

———. "The Writer and His Past" in *Homecoming.* London: Heinemann, 1972.

Language, Oral Tradition, and Social Vision in Ngugi's *Devil on the Cross*

BAYO OGUNJIMI

> I was born in a large peasant family: father, four wives and about twenty-eight children. I also belonged as we all did, in those days, that is my generation, to a wider extended family and to community as a whole. We spoke Gikuyu as we worked in the fields. We spoke Gikuyu in and outside the home. I can vividly recall those evenings when we sat around the fireside and grown-ups and we, the children, would tell

> stories in turns. It was mostly the grown-ups telling the stories to us, the children, but everybody was interested and involved. . . . The stories with mostly animals as—the main characters were told in Gikuyu. Hare being small, weak, but full of innovative wit and cunning was our hero. We identified with him as he struggled against the brutes of prey like Lion, Leopard and Hyena.[1]

At the Second International Conference of African Literature in the English Language held at the University of Calabar in Nigeria in 1982, Ngugi restated the cultural background, linguistic and social vision that inform African oration in general. His last novel written in Gikuyu is an evolution of such literary tradition, a creative validation of the sources, didactic and aesthetic qualities of African aura-oral literature. The opening chapter of *Devil on the Cross,* which functions as a prologue, proves that the contemporary artist evolves from the historico-cultural generation of the Gicaandi Player or the Wandindi Player (the African traditional bard, minstrel and story-teller of old). The dialectical affinity between the two is reflected in Ngugi's invocation of the Muse, Gicaandi, at the beginning of the novel. The transposition of the utilitarian essence of the ancient art into the present is summed up in the remarks of Bahati, the old man of Nakuru—"All stories are old. All stories are new. All stories belong to tomorrow. And stories are not about ogres or animals or about men. All stories are about human beings."[2] The ritualistic invocation of the Muse, the communal essence of art in traditional societies, the creation of a new man of new sensibility in the age of imperialism and neo-colonialism, depict the epic potentialities of the novel form in modern society. This is an interesting point to note in that *Devil on the Cross* presents both the authentic and mock-heroic epic forms. The antithetical play of the opposites produces a fruitful synthesis, which is the commitment we find in the artist.

Devil on the Cross is a practical culmination of an important debate in African literature and in this guise it is an experimental novel. African writers and critics for quite a long time have been debating the issue of linguistic colonization and the need to write in national languages. Initial efforts directed towards this end are noted in the transliterative style and localization of fictional elements we find in writers like Achebe, Okara and Okot P'Bitek. Writing in the languages of the colonial powers provokes the tough question "who is the African writer writing for?" Linguistic acculturation in art and indeed in all spheres puts Europe in the position of "playing the role of primary audience and linguistic arbiter for the third world writing." An African artist that endeavors to break this historical advantage enjoyed by Europe is accused of committing "literary tribalism." Ngugi motivated by his ideological position writes:

> If our audience is composed of peasants and workers, then it seems to me that we must write in the languages of the peasants and workers of Africa. We cannot write in foreign languages unspoken and unknown by peasants and workers in our communities and pretend that we are

> writing for, and somehow communicating with, those peasants and workers, or pretend that we are writing a national literature.[3]

In South-East Asia and other third world nations, the issue of linguistic colonization is assuming its most critical phase. Responding to questions at a seminar on Indian writing in English, held at London's Commonwealth Institute, Nirad Chaudhuri, a popular Indian writer remarked, "So far as I write in English, I am not an Indian writer." The massive illiteracy in these affected regions poses a great problem for this experiment. However, its long time effect will not be less than the type of iconoclasm that accompanied the invention of printing during the Middle Ages and subsequent popularization of literature and radical consciousness. It is an historical reality that such development destroyed the monopoly of knowledge by the Papacy over Latin Christendom and produced the era of Lutheran Protestantism.

Language itself is a form of communicative aesthetics; such aesthetics is transformed into ideological essence in a materialist context. Ngugi identifies two working functions of language. To him "the verbal means of mutual apprehension" transposes into what Marx calls "the language of real life"[4] as daily manifested in the productive machinery in a communal or capitalist system. The manifestation is more pronounced in the latter because of the massive scale of specialization. Language thus becomes a dialectical realization of socio-culture—"The duality of language is in fact a dialectic unity."[5] An artistic synthesis of proverbs, folktales, folklores, myths and legends expressed in the wealthy Agikuyu language is a more objective programme towards an ideological conscientization. These materials are made relevant to provoke dynamic reality in the present situation. Of course, this paper examines how the artist has synthesized the sense of commitment with that of creativity—a synthesis that produces the type of Saint-Simonian spirit of avant-gardism in the novelist. The central thesis of the paper is that "art as a means of communication and an aspect of ideology . . . can help motivate men's minds in bringing about social change."[6]

AN ELEGY FOR THE HOMESTEAD

The theme of the destruction of the cultural homestead is recurrent and treated with deep concern in the novels, plays and critical works of Ngugi. Matters affecting national languages, arts, folktales, and lores and other essentials of the people's tradition, have always been considered with maximum interest. The traditional bards, minstrels and story-tellers that educate, enliven and inculcate discipline into the system are almost totally swept away by the tide of colonialism. Ngugi the artist is the offspring of the Gicaandi Player and his creativity is to fill the cultural vacuum created by colonialism. Gatuiria, the intellectual-artist embodies this concern of the novelist.

Ngugi is very critical about the permeation of every aspect of the contemporary social matrix by acculturation. He expresses this in the language understood by the people, the language of proverbs, fables and parables. Wariinga, a victim of acculturation is warned that "aping others cost the frog its buttocks." When we first meet Wariinga, she suffers from culture complex, behaving like Clementina, the new wife of Ocol in *The Song of Lawino.* In the P'Bitekian comic satirical mood, Ngugi flays the blacks who undergo the biological process of ecdysis. We are informed that Wariinga's "body was covered with light and dark spots like the guinea fowl. Her hair was splitting, and it had browned to the colour of moleskin because it had been straightened by red-hot iron combs." In short, Wariinga runs after a shadow and she is "in covetous pursuit of the beauty of other selves." This "masquerade motif" is a common strand in the novel as reflected by the "apemanship" of the intellectual class and the clientelism of the comprador class. The fable of the beautiful black girl and the man-eating foreign ogre is a further elucidation of this theme of culture complex. All these depict the anecdotal qualities of African proverbs. Proverbs are essential expressions of the inherent wisdom and resourcefulness of African culture. As Professor Obiechina rightly admits, they belong to the gnomic tradition of the people and express the profound functioning of their intellect. Blending proverbs with modern thematic, especially in a novel originally written in the vernacular language, affords the artist an ample chance of socializing his reader. The imagistic composition of the proverbs creates a strong rhythmical flow in the narrative rendition.

What Lindfors acclaims as the "diachronic" element in Ngugi's fiction extends to the dialectical usage of culture. A close link can be established between Ngugi's renaissance move of the homestead and his stance against the ethics of capitalist ideology. Culture in a kind of structuralist-functionalist framework is defined as a synthesis of the economic, the political, which produces the ideological. Ngugi's theory of organicism is however neither Althusserian nor Simonsian, in that he recognizes the supremacy of economic determinism. Further still, the philosophy behind this revival of the homestead transcends the Senghorian school of "Authenegraficanitus"[7] or Achebian concept of "nativism."[8] The absence of ideological dynamics in Achebe's cultural avant-gardism may justify Simonse's criticism of what he sees as cultural and thematic particularisms in Achebe's novels.[9] This to Simonse may constitute a problem for a more objective appraisal of African novel from the Marxist perspective of the modes of production approach. But even then, Simonse seems to underplay the role of cultural detraction in African Literature. What formulates the material culture on which Marxist literary criticism is based is the generic culture or the aggregation of life values that inform the essence and existence of any society in course of its growth. Such generic culture has duality of relationship both to the base and the superstructure; therefore it cannot be relegated to a tiny spectacle in [the] course of the growth of the society. Such "cultural concepts" brings the perpetual internal contradictions of the materialist culture of capitalist production. There is the fear of an historical omission if the discussion of the African novel is based on a materialist ideology that suppresses the culture contact between Africa and Europe. Ngugi's works make a cautious balance out of this complex dynamic.

Cultural nationalism to Ngugi means the enfranchisement of the people from a materialist culture which threatens their survival. The process of cultural reconstruction is the process of critical consciousness. Culture, history and materialist concept fuse to produce the reality we see in the Kamirithu Educational, Cultural and Community Centre in Limuru. The organizers of the Centre perceived integrated rural development as that of people's culture, economy and literacy. The artistic fruition of the Centre is the play *Ngaahika Ndenda* (I will marry when I want). The events associated with this play, logically are those that produced *Devil on the Cross* and *Ngugi Detained*. The cumulative radical values of a comprehensive art-piece produced from a synthesis of a familiar language, history and culture is stated by Chinweizu when he perceives such literature as

> an important medium for helping to shape national consciousness, for contributing to the historic projects of nation-building and development, and for moulding the world outlook and intellectual framework for national action. They are actually aware of literature's capacity to prepare people for life, and even on occasion to move them to action.[10]

Literature at this point ceases to be less particularistic, but tends to nurture "a revolutionary culture which is not narrowly confined by the limitations of tribal traditions or national boundaries, but is outward looking to Pan-Africa and the Third World and the needs of man." For Ngugi, the ultimate goal of such a universal force in art is to "be transformed into a socialist programme, or be doomed to sterility and death."[11]

A MOCK-EPIC OF CAPITALISM

Ousmane's protagonist in *The Money-Order* elucidates on what Marx identified as the effect of man's irreverent worship of money. In a letter to his cousin in Paris, Ibrahim Dieng advises:

> I beg you not to regard money as the essence of life. If you do, it will only lead you into a false path, where sooner or later you will be alone. Money gives no security. On the contrary it destroys all that is human in us.[12]

It is this absurd morality of bourgeois ideology that Ngugi castigates in his last novel. The virulent Swiftian satire and Brechtian comic-satirical dramatic elements fuse with the allegorical style of Bunyan, to produce the mock-heroic technique of Pope and Dryden. This tapestry of style strengthens the parabolic element for strong thematic effect.

The dramatic core of the novel is the Devil's Feast and basically it is about those whom Armah refers to as predators, askaris and zombies in *Two Thousand Seasons*. Very early in the novel, the passengers in the Matatu sensationally prepare us for this allegorical gathering. But more than the dramatic rendition of the allegory itself, the central character, the Devil figure is an archetype, the variants of which we find in D. O. Fagunwa and Amos Tutuota's folktales. The giant figure of the Devil is that of a monster and tormentor. Ngugi conjures such pictures as being synonymous with the destructive and parasitic role of those he calls "bourgeois compradors." Apart from the philosophical interpretation of the Feast as a conflicting drama between the forces of Good and Evil, the novelist metaphorically describes it as "dance of the hunter and the hunted"—"the joke between the leopard and goat."[13] The implied message is obvious: the oppressed can perceive the enormity of the crime of the ruling elites and prepare themselves for redress.

The setting in the Cave has the classic conventions of the epic tradition such as the invocation of the Muse, the introduction of the heroes, the descriptive list of subsidiary heroes, the competitive games and speeches, which are all imitation of a serious action. But all these present an empty façade and the novelist's mockery of neo-colonialism and capitalism in Africa. It is relevant to make reference to the setting in the Matatu, which is equally important stylistically and thematically. Though the two settings are somehow antithetical, they are complimentary in that they are calculated towards the same exposition. When the scene finally moves to the Cave, we are entertained and at the same time instructed with the aid of caricatures and burlesque figures. Ngugi uses his experiences as a dramatist to shape the fictional presentation of his characters and actions. This he effectively integrates with his ability to grapple with the various concepts and theories that strengthen capitalism as an oppressive ideology.

The feast is declared open by the Master of Ceremonies with the Biblical parody of the gospel parable:

> For the Kingdom of Earthly wiles can be likened into a ruler who foresaw that the day would come when he would be thrown out of a certain country by the masses and their guerilla freedom fighters. He was much troubled in his heart, trying to determine ways of protecting all property he had accumulated in that country and also ways of maintaining his rule over the natives by other means.[14]

The capitalist/client relationship at the heart of the parable defines what neo-colonialism is. Like the Master of Ceremonies, the foreign leader from the International Organization of Thieves and Robbers (IOTR), explains further the ideology of capitalism. Allegorical and satirical use of names is also effectively employed to match the mock-heroic setting. The foreign leader dabbles into an illogical tirade by saying, "No! You black people are incapable of planning and working out ways of cutting the ropes that tie you to your masters. You must have been misled by the Communists." The rationalization by capitalism which aims at the maximization of profits thereby widening the gap between the poor and the rich is reflected in his own Biblical allusion—"For unto the man of property more will be given, from the poor man will be taken." An attack on the politics of the Cartels and International monopoly capital is presented in the satirical war against their various institutions such as "World's Exploitation Banks; Money-Swallowing Insurance Schemes; Industrial Gobblers of Raw Materials: Cheap Manufacturers for Export Abroad, trades in Human Skins, Arms for Murder." The whole of Lenin's theory of imperialism and capitalism is rendered convincingly in a fictional mode to expose the inhumanity of an ideology that "wraps poison in leaves sugar." Other than using Biblical allusions for denouncing Christianity as a Colonial apparatus and "the opiate of the masses," Ngugi employs these Biblical elements for stylistic effects of parody and satire.

Ngugi's satire becomes more vitriolic when portraying the local allies of European Fetishism. The local competitors are all given satirical appellations and their popularity, an euphemism for notoriety is determined by their philistinism. It is of interest to note that the first speaker is a lumpen proletariat. Comically and pathetically, his own skill in theft does not qualify him for this ensemble of International Robbers. Of course, Ndaaya wa Kuhuria, the Napier-Grass-Son-of-Trembling is thrown out of the cave. This is a biting irony when we realize that the real "Caterpillars of Commonwealth" are exalted and exonerated. We are later introduced to Gitutu Gatuaguru, otherwise hailed as Rottenborough Groundflesh. An historical tragedy, his ancestors were traitors during the struggle against colonialism. His own Cathecism and code of conduct is "Reap where you never planted, eat for which you never shed a drop of blood." Kihaahu Gatheeca, whose foreign name is Lord Gabriel Bloodwell Stuart-Jones is another eminent competitor. The deceit and exploitation involved in his Modern-Day-Nursery, show how socio-economic programmes are used for profit motives by egocentric individuals.

Mukiraai, a very strategic character in the novel is encountered both in the Matatu and Cave. Such positioning is symbolic as an authentication of the dilemma of a petty-bourgeois, who aspires to the bourgeois class. Mukiraai is a University graduate with a chain of degrees in Economics, Business Administration and Commerce. An academic robot, he reduces all the radical and socializing themes of the debate in the Matatu to a campaign against Communism. A student of Social Darwinism, he believes that "people can never be equal like teeth. Human nature has rejected equality. Even universal nature herself has rejected any absurd nonsense about equality." As a competitor in the Devil's Feast, he defends the capitalist doctrine of Malthusianism. Of course, he is a member of the International Parenthood Association and as he tells us: "Children are our biggest enemy. Any increase in the population is contrary to our interest." But like the lumpen proletariat he is disqualified because "education is not property." Mukuraai becomes a stylistic device in the hand of the novelist. He later changes his ideological position and wages a war of calumny on the ideology of capitalism. We have no hope for a sane society through Mukiraai's type of intellectualism and more than Gatuiria, he illuminates the novelist's pessimism about the role of the petty-bourgeoisie as a revolutionary class.[15]

The more competitors want to display their expertise in the game to theft and robbery, the more incisive the novelist's satire becomes. The characterization of Nditika wa Ngunji and Kanyanju is particularly interesting in this regard. Nditika wa Ngunji's concept of Trinity is based on "Grabbing, Extortion and Confiscation." He displays all the vices of capitalist economy such as the exploitation of labour, smuggling, profiteering and hoarding. To him, "mass famine is jewellery of the wealthy." Ngunji manifests the illusory intellectualism that Swift satirizes in the Academy of Lagado. For the cupidity and egoism of the privileged class, he contemplates a pseudoscientifism "for manufacturing human parts." Therefore, "every man could have two mouths, two bellies, two cocks, two hearts and hence two lives. Our money would buy us immortality! We would leave death to the poor."[16] Kanyuanji contemplates a similar programme. Voice informs us that Kanyuanji wants to set up an experimental farm for milking the bodies of the workers. The company that will handle such a bogus project is "Kenyo-Saxon Exporters: Human Blood and Flesh." Ngugi carries the satirical aspects of Swift to a more serious level of reprobation and disgust. Ngugi's social philosophy and criticism of capitalism produce a kind of existentialism in him. His message is summed up in the poems "The Leveller" or "Elegy Written in a Country Churchyard."[17]

The use of Dream Vision allegory in the novel is a variant of the stream of consciousness technique common in his earlier novels. Voice carries the motif of Satanism but ironically, he is even holier than the "Devils" we find in the cave. Almost at every level of his utterances we seem to be hearing the voice of the novelist himself. Wariinga's dialogue with Voice can be perceived as a stylistic device of acquiring the psychological stamina Ngugi wants to see in the contemporary African woman.

ARTS FOR HEART'S SAKE

Ngugi writes for the oppressed, but he does not idealize their potentiality. Therefore when he warns them in the prologue/chapter of "the blindness of the heart" and "the deafness of the mind," he is only being realistic. This is an educative method of averting what Paulo Freire perceives as the chronic problem of the oppressed. More than any other of Ngugi's novels, *Devil on the Cross* works through diverse aesthetic patterns to effect the theory of mobilization.

The setting in the Matatu, like that of the Cave, is a forum for the education and socialization of the masses. The non-static claustrophobic setting is a panoramic condensation of the vast society, its social, economic and moral problems. We are provided with an image of a collapsing social system, symbolised by the ailing structure of the Matatu: "The engine moaned and screamed like several hundred dented axes being ground simultaneously. The car's body shook like a reed in the wind. The whole vehicle waddled along the road like a duck up a mountain. . . . The engine would growl, then cough as if a piece of metal were stuck in its throat, then it rasped as if it had asthma."[18] The implied metaphor is the correspondence between "the patient" and "the healer." For survival, the Kenyan body-politic deserves an urgent health service. "Healing is an implicit symbolism pervading the novel and it bears the revolutionary optimism of the novelist. The pattern of character-creation articulates this unhealthy contradiction and the need for panacea. The diviner and the tormented peasant, the unhealthy car that Wariinga the healthy mechanic puts back on road, are pointers to this symbolism. The whole syndrome is summed in a committed artist, the healer versus the uncommitted society, the patient.

Despite the perverse symbolism that Mwaura, the driver and his Matatu conveys, Ngugi's device is not meant to preach the pessimism of Armah in his first novel. The passengers in the Matatu are not somnambulists like Armah's characters in the rustic bus. Neither do they venture alone like "the man," for they realize that to venture alone is to perish alone without any concrete social change. Most of the passengers in the Matatu are conscious and critical of their societal crises, and they are willing to resign themselves to fate.

The programme of conscientization is discernable in the various fables told by Bahati, the Old Man of Nakuru. A custodian of oral tradition, he makes the relevant past flow into the conscious present. The fable of the peasant and the ogre and the Faustus-Mephistopheles story of Ndinguri have one thing in common, and that is the concept of violence. The diviner/artist warns the peasant, "Nothing good was ever born out of perfect conditions." Of course, he can only get rid of the ogre through violence. In *Ngugi Detained,* Ngugi indicates his interests in Blake and Hegel's theories of dialectics. Such theories perceive that revolution defies the law of inertia; it operates through the logic of antithesis at war with thesis to forge a synthesis. Logically, any literature organized to negate "the culture of silence" is a literature that advocates revolutionary violence. This Freirian-Fanonian circle is represented by Muturi, who re-affirms the belief of his creator in the use of violence when he says, "Even today guns like this should really be in the hands of workers so that they defend the unity and wealth and freedom of their country."[19] The conflict in the Cave confirms this novelist's attitude to social revolution.

The general philosophical debates in *Devil on the Cross* are based on the concept of Evil and Good. But Ngugi's philosophy is a characterization of the conflicts of the capitalist mode of production and ethics. Antithetical juxtapositions such as Heaven and Hell, God and Satan, Life and Death, Body and Heart are thematic syndromes for explaining such a materialist culture. Ngugi's strong logic about the natural and physical law governing the Body and the Heart is a way of depicting the social contradictions of our real world. Against the theological law in the book of Ecclesiastes 12, Ngugi defines human existence in terms of the atomic materialism of Lucretius[20] and Marxist theory of organicism. The body, the soul, the heart and the mind are functional parts of an organic structure. The death of one is the end of others and "the soul does not return to God who had created it." This is a form of atheistic existentialism in the novelist. One of his characters makes a comical reflection on this: "This Earth is my home. I am not passing through." Ngugi makes a parody of Jimmy Reeves's dream of a paradisal bloom in "This world is not my home I am just passing through," a re-affirmation of Jimmy Cliff's philosophy of "I want it right here on earth."

The concept of Evil and Good extends to the level of characterization. The novel makes a dramatic tabloid where characters act their virtues and vices. The guests and competitors at the Devil's Feast represent a level of sensibility which the novelist abhors. However, Wangari, Muturi, Wariinga, even the petty bourgeois Gatuiria articulate a genuine sensibility pointing to a new spirit of change. Wangari is an archetypal representation of Mumbi in the Agikuyu mythology. Her replicas in the previous novels of Ngugi are Mumbi, Nyankinyua and Wanja. Wangari epitomizes the historical contradiction of all generations and the novelist imbues her with a great sense of historical continuity. Her experiences in the Matatu make her lament the perversed spirit of heroism in Harambe. Ngugi illustrates this sense of failure in the songs of Wangari entitled "The Harambee of Money." An essential element of oral tradition profusely used by Ngugi is songs. In traditional societies songs have topical values and represent the contemporary social mood. Unemployment, the confiscation of her land by the "Kenya Economic Progress Bank" and her eventual arrest in Nairobi exacerbate her disillusionment. When we meet her in the Cave, she is involved in the revolutionary struggle against "the robbers" of her country. But ironically she is clamped down upon by the agents of reactionary violence. The fear Ngugi consistently expresses is the historical negation that relegates and replaces Kenyan Saints, martyrs and conquistadors with despots, who epitomize an historical fraud.

As for Wariinga, she embodies the contradictions of her own age. The purpose for which she is created is categorically stated by Ngugi himself in *Ngugi Detained.*[21] She becomes a complex character in terms of theme and style. Like Njoroge, her education suffers because of her class background, and she must have to strive for survival. Wariinga is sacked as an office typist for refusing the advances of her boss—the Manager of the Champion Construction Company. Deserted by her boyfriend and ejected out of her house by the hired thugs of the landlord, she attempts committing suicide but is rescued by Muturi. In a dramatic game and parable "of the hunter and the hunted" between her and the Rich Old Man of Nghorika, she becomes pregnant, and birthing a daughter called Wambui.

But for Wariinga, this is not the end of the road. Her remorseful mood and reflections and immediate sense of guilt signal a victory for her generation. The hidden symbolism of the patient and the healer re-surfaces. By the time we meet her in the Matatu, her moments of sombre reflections are over and she becomes more assertive and critical of the system. Her revolutionary optimism is strengthened by her rescuer, Muturi, who after listening to her story of woes asserts confidently: "But I don't agree with you that our children will never know laughter.

We must never despair. Despair is one sin that cannot be forgiven."[22] Muturi performs the historical role of Dedan Kimathi, Karega and other heroes of Agikuyu history and mythology. His role during the revolutionary onslaught in the Cave delineates further his revolutionary stance.

In an ironic tragi-comic plot device, Wariinga falls in love with Gatuiria, the son of the Rich Old Man of Nghorika, father of Wambui, her daughter. Such an affair gives another perspective of her virility of purpose. Gatuiria symbolises the contradictions of the petty bourgeois intellectual. In every episode we meet him, Ngugi convincingly presents him being caught between the anvil and hammer of ideology and class. This notwithstanding, he demonstrates the prospect of an intellectual who in the words of Amilcar Cabral is capable of "committing suicide, to be restored to life in the condition of a revolutionary worker."[23] In the melodramatic wedding episode, Wariinga becomes a stylistic device, a kind of "deux ex machina." Symbolically the destruction of the Old Man of Nghorika is a victory for womanhood and an assault on the bourgeois morality.

Most of Ngugi's female characters are usually dynamic with a strong sense of historical destiny and heroism. Wanja, Wangari and Wariinga are not comparable to the phoney female characters like Simi and Monica Faseyi in *The Interpreters* and Mrs. Koomson in *The Beautyful Ones Are Not Yet Born.* Even Soyinka's female character in *Season of Anomy* still lacks the potentiality of radical activism. Where Ngugi's female characters are embroiled in the decadent urban society, their immorality is the immorality of their general social order. But of course, they are not total victims of the complex formalized societies; they retrace their movements to the rural Ilmorog for assisting in social development. Stylistically, they become the artist's weapon. The holocaust in Wanja's house in *Petals of Blood* sees the extermination of the capitalist chiefs in the novel. Wariinga performs the same role, and her technical skill proves she is a force to be reckoned with in the society. But for Ngugi to make his central figure in *Devil on the Cross* a resourceful, productive and dynamic woman is to break the myth that the feminist anthropologist Joke Schrijvers condemns as "this discriminating tradition," which divides "people into two unequal sexes—strong and the weak, the dominant and the subordinated, the superior and the inferior, the active and passive, the powerful and the powerless (the male and female)."[24] Ngugi, however, does this within the confine of a culture and an economy rapidly undergoing modernization.

Ngugi's idea of social radicalism in art seems to be more comprehensive and realistic in terms of class involvement. Such idea is conveyed through an Agikuyu proverb: "A single finger cannot kill a louse, a single log cannot make a fire last through the night, a single man, however strong, cannot build a bridge across the river: and many hands can lift a weight however heavy." Ngugi advocates for the theory of class collectivity that embraces the workers, peasants, students, progressive intellectuals and others. What makes the novel more remarkable is the practical involvement of a class with a revolutionary potentiality, which has hitherto not assumed a distinct role in the African fiction, the students.

The ideological positioning of this budding fragment of the petty-bourgeoisie has always been reduced to a travesty of the Quixotic world order in many African novels. The inability of the petty-bourgeois intellectuals to operate as a coherent revolutionary force is partly accounted for by the elitist education devoid of rational ideological contents. A more comprehensive radical children's literature is a valuable asset to the course of the committed African artist in a socio-culture that still survives on conservative socialization process.

Students' participation in the revolutionary political process in Africa is proved by the cases of Ethiopia, Nigeria, Kenya and South Africa as depicted in *Devil on the Cross.* The coup in Kenya and the massive arrest and incarceration of students from the University of Nairobi attest to this. President Arap Moi during the Kenyatta Day on October 19th, 1983, reproached the University as "an institution which was brought into sorrowful disrepute by a student body which proved itself pathetically vulnerable to the crudest stupidities of dialectical subversion."[25] This type of outrageous outburst is expected from the boss of a neo-colonial capitalist state anywhere in Africa. In the novel, the solidarity movement of the students of Ilmorog with the workers will be regarded as subversive. The appearance of the "goatee beard" students' leader which recalls that of revolutionary Marxists like Castro and Guevara is enough to disorganize the state. Of course like Wangari and Muturi, the students' leader is arrested and detained.

Ngugi's sole aim is to put art to the service of the oppressed class. The various conflicts in the novel constitute "a struggle to replace capitalist society by socialist society, capitalist man by socialist man" to use the words of Professor Norman Rudich. More specifically his art moves in the direction of what Roger Garaudy defines as the ultimate vision of an avant-garde art:

> The work of art is thus not only a model of the relationship between man and the world in which he lives: it is also a design or a projection of a world which does not yet exist, a world in the process of being born. The true artist then has this "prophetic" function: he is pre-eminently the one who helps his contemporaries invent the future.[26]

Ngugi realizes the enormity of the ideological crisis in the African society. He does not idealize the situation; hence he only articulates his ideological position with series of symbols indicating a revolutionary optimism. The holocaust and the disorganization of the Devil's Feast, the melodramatic assassination of the Old Man of Nghorika cannot terminate a system deep-rooted in the society. But the novelist believes that with these symbolic gestures the masses can be oriented and organized towards a revolutionary consciousness that can change their lot. The Kenyan coup seemed to authenticate this view. Paradoxically, the state always underestimates the utilitarian values of art. But why censorship, why imprisonment and why the alienation of the committed artist?

NOTES

1. Ngugi wa Thiong'o "Language and Literature": A paper presented at the 2nd International Conference of African Literature and the English Language. University of Calabar, Nigeria, June 15-19, 1982, pp. 1-2.
2. Ngugi wa Thiong'o *Devil on the Cross.* Heinemann Educational Books Ltd., London, 1982, pp. 61-62.
3. Ngugi wa Thiong'o "The Making of a Rebel." *Index on Censorship* June 1980 Vol. 9 No. 3, p. 30.
4. See the article "Language and Literature," p. 5.
5. Ibid.
6. See D. D. Egbert *Social Radicalism and the Arts.* Alfred A. Knopf, New York, 1970, p. 88.
7. This is the new term that Sembene Ousmane gives to Negritude in his last novel, *The Last of the Empire.*
8. Professor E. N. Obiechina in an article "Cultural Nationalism in Modern African Creative Literature" employs this sociological concept to define Achebe's usage of culture. See *African Literature Today,* No. 1, 1968, p. 25.
9. See Simon Simonse "African Literature Between Nostalgia and Utopia: African Novels Since 1953 in the Light of the Modes of Production Approach" in *Research in African Literature,* Winter 1982, 13/4.
10. *South: The Third World Magazine.* January, 1983, p. 21.
11. Ngugi wa Thiong'o "Towards a National Culture," *East African Journal,* VII, 1971, p. 17.
12. Sembene Ousmane *The Money Order,* translated by Clive Wake. Heinemann Educational Books Ltd., London, 1972, p. 130.
13. In an article "The Robber and the Robbed: Two Antagonistic Images in Afro-American Literature and Thought," Ngugi gives the ideological interpretations of these metaphors. See Ngugi wa Thiong'o *Writers in Politics,* Heinemann Educational Books Ltd., London, 1981, pp. 123-138.
14. *Devil on the Cross,* p. 82.
15. Ngugi wa Thiong'o *Writers in Politics.* Heinemann Educational Books Ltd., London, 1981, p. 78.
16. *Devil on the Cross.*
17. These poems have existentialist perception about life. The poets' philosophy is about the inconsequentialness of life since "the paths of glory lead but the grave."
18. *Devil on the Cross,* p. 31.
19. Ibid.
20. In his book *De Rerum Natura* or *On the Nature of Things,* the Roman philosopher Lucretius Carus, based his natural law on the atomic materialism of Democritus and Epicurus. His attempt was to liberate mankind from religious fears by depicting that the soul is material and is born and dies with the body. This renders his philosophy to a kind of atheism.
21. Ngugi wa Thiong'o *Ngugi Detained.* Heinemann Educational Books Ltd., London, 1981, pp. 10-11.
22. *Devil on the Cross,* p. 27.
23. Amilcar Cabral *Unity and Struggle.* Heinemann Educational Books Ltd., London, 1980, p. 136.

24. "Viricentrism and Anthropology" by Joke Schrijvers in *The Politics of Anthropology: From Colonialism and Sexism Toward a View From Below,* ed. Gerrit Huizer and Bruce Mannheim. Maiton Publishers. The Hague, Paris, 1979.
25. Quoted from *The Weekly Review,* Nairobi, Kenya, October 22, 1982, p. 7.
26. Quoted from *Praxis and Ideology,* Part 2, p. 49.

chapter **19**

Essays on *The Handmaid's Tale*, by Margaret Atwood

The World as It Will Be? Female Satire and the Technology of Power in *The Handmaid's Tale*

Stephanie Barbé Hammer

Atwood's futurist novel of 1986 is an important book for many reasons. In particular, *The Handmaid's Tale* plays a significant role in the evolution of women's writing in so far as it represents one of the few commercially successful and critically recognized (if not universally acclaimed) contributions by a woman writer to a literary genre dominated by men—namely, satire.[1] Curiously however, despite its necessarily subversive status as a female invasion of male literary territory, *The Handmaid's Tale* possesses many formal and thematic features typical of traditional satire, as it is defined by contemporary literary theory. In fact, according to the understandings of satire put forth by accepted critics of the genre, Atwood's novel in many ways presents a satiric text-book case. The author employs a variety of themes and motifs commonly found in classical and modern satire: complex rhetorical devices such as formal disguise (a satire which masquerades as a novel which in turn masquerades as an autobiography) and irony,[2] a static or nonprogressive plot where very little actually seems to happen,[3] the character of a common-sense, average narrator who speaks in a seemingly straightforward manner, and the scene of a dystopic nightmare city.[4] Furthermore, *Handmaid* boasts what is perhaps the most crucial element of satiric writing, namely, the clear existence of a topical political target, which here is very obviously evangelical Christian fundamentalism.[5]

The presence of these features indicates that *Handmaid* is an excellent candidate for admittance to the canon of satiric literature—a state of affairs which, given the novel's subject matter, does not reassure, but rather unsettles and disturbs the female critic. After all, Atwood's narrative focuses specifically on men's domination of women by means of other women, and more generally portrays women's physical and mental imprisonment within a particularly sinister male regime. In this manner, the fact that *Handmaid* fits so well within a male literary canon raises potentially disturbing questions as to the true value of this novelist's achievement. In writing satire has Atwood indeed invaded a male literary bastion in order to produce a new female writing or is her writing itself penetrated by masculine assumptions as to what satire should be and do? Is *The Handmaid's Tale* a subversion of male writing or is this subversion itself already subverted by the regulations of an established male art form? Perhaps equally important is the question of aesthetic judgment; according to what standards should the quality of female satire be measured—should we base our assessment on traditional male conceptions of what satiric literature should be or upon an as yet undefined aesthetic of female satiric writing?

Mary McCarthy unwittingly raises these very issues in her review of the novel for the *New York Times.*[6] Tellingly, she compares *Handmaid* unfavorably to established male works of futurist satiric literature—*1984, Brave New World,* and *A Clockwork Orange*—and she remarks that Atwood's contribution to this subgenre lacks the ironic bite and linguistic imagination of the other three works.[7] And yet, should not female satire by definition make us redefine our traditional male notions as to what constitutes "good" satire? Barbara Ehrenreich's review for the *New Republic* (the most valuable essay written thus far on the novel)[8] is more sensitive to this problem. While she readily admits to her own impatience with what is for her a "fantasy of regression" on the part of a heroine who is a "sappy stand-in for Winston Smith," she also recognizes that the book concerns itself successfully with complex feminist issues.[9] In this way, Ehrenreich implies that the novel's very betrayal of certain aesthetic expectations is somehow linked to its satiric purpose.

How then, we might ask, does the challenge of writing female satire connect with *Handmaid's* atmosphere of male domination and with the author's ultimate satiric statement?

Such queries as to the value and function of female satire appear unnecessarily complicated when we first read Atwood's novel, for we discover that, on one level at least, *Handmaid's* satiric thrust is straightforward and unambiguous. Atwood's condemnation of Gilead's born again theocracy is never in doubt, because *Handmaid* relentlessly exposes the total hypocrisy of a regime which preaches biblical virtue but where vice reigns everywhere—from the brutal executions of dissidents to the institutionalized sexual promiscuity enjoyed by the commanders. The representatives of the new way are consistently monstrous. The sadistic aunts are frustrated older women who brutalize their younger, fertile charges out of jealousy and fear. The seemingly mild-mannered commander Fred cheats on his wife with alacrity and calmly justifies the oppressive regime which he partly masterminded with the observation that in the old society men felt they were no longer needed by women; he thereby suggests that women's liberation forced American men to take this drastic action; ergo the present regime is ultimately the women's "fault." And Atwood's most ironic portrait is certainly that of Fred's resentful and cruel wife Serena Joy. Neither serene nor joyous, this high-ranking wife is a former "total Woman" activist who is enraged and embittered by the existence which her successful advocacy now imposes upon her.

Within this demonic scheme even the victimized handmaids are forced into an existence which is no less hypocritical than that of their oppressors; in order to survive they and the narrator among them are constantly obliged to pretend to espouse a system of values which denigrates and threatens to annihilate them. In this manner, an allegedly profoundly Christian society ironically transforms every citizen into a sinner in so far as each person must become a liar and a hypocrite in order to exist within the system. This is, of course, the supreme irony of Atwood's fictional future world; this is a theocracy where not one person is devout and where such notions as faith and morality simply have no meaning.

Thus, on the level of topical satire, *Handmaid's* message unfolds with a cartoon-like clarity and is consequently not particularly surprising; American Christian fundamentalists are fanatical and dishonest, and therefore highly dangerous; they seek to erode the liberties which all Americans—and especially American women—cherish.

And yet, this topical satire represents only one very superficial layer of Atwood's critique in *The Handmaid's Tale;* simultaneously a far more complex critical process is unfolding here. This second satiric dimension lies embedded and partially concealed within Offred's own narrative procedure. Despite the heroine's apparent straightforwardness and despite her seeming fitness to give a true, woman-in-the-street report of a nightmare situation, Offred surreptitiously offers the reader a very different kind of narrative.

Significantly, the narrator reveals that she becomes Fred's mistress and that she later has secret erotic rendezvous with Nick, the strong and silent chauffeur who is possibly an agent of the secret police. A strange kind of love triangle now develops, a bedroom farce of multiple assignations under one roof, which would be comical if Offred's life did not depend on her successful juggling of these two sexual relationships. The plot as it now unfolds is weirdly reminiscent of popular gothic romance, for in such stories the heroine, like Offred, is often made a helpless prisoner by an evil and sexually desirous male force, until she is finally liberated by the romantic hero.

Offred's predicament recalls that of a romantic heroine in other ways as well. First, she is desired by and must eventually choose between two men who, second, embody an impressive combination of male stereotypes drawn from gothic romance and romantic comedy: on one hand, Fred, the older, paternal, established authority figure who connotes at once a lord of the manor and a seasoned military campaigner; and on the other hand, Nick, the ambiguous, delinquent, dangerous and therefore more sexually attractive younger man of inferior social position. The fact that Nick is a chauffeur is replete with erotic overtones from the movies, while the lower-class upper-class connection between him and Offred also recalls D. H. Lawrence's steamy love-affair in *Lady Chatterly's Lover.* Finally, Offred's choice of the younger man seems romantically validated by the novel's ending, in which Nick miraculously effects her escape from imprisonment in Commander Fred's household.

From the reader's point of view these fragments of romantic fiction are ironically jarring, to say the least; the grim realities of Offred's actual existence resemble those of a concentration camp inmate, far more than those of a gothic heroine. But while we read Offred's predicament as a grisly parody of a romantic conundrum, Offred herself is far less certain as to how to interpret her relationship with Fred and Nick. Despite herself, she takes pleasure in her status as Fred's mistress,[10] and although she recognizes the fallacy of reading romance into her affair with Nick, she is unwilling to regard him and her feelings for him in any other light:

> Being with him is safety; it's a cave, where we huddle together while the storm goes on outside. This is delusion of course. This room is one of the most dangerous places I could be. If I were caught there would be no quarter, but I'm beyond caring. . . . I dismiss these uneasy whispers, I talk too much. I tell him things I shouldn't. . . . I make of him an idol, a cardboard cutout. (*Handmaid,* pp. 269–70)

Offred's choice of metaphor is as important as it is sinister; the cave is the site of sexual pleasure for two of classical literature's tragically doomed love-affairs—that of Dido and Aeneas (where Dido fatally misunderstands Aeneas' intentions toward her) and that of Isolde and Tristan (who have fled briefly from society in order to consummate their love). Her use of this image under these circumstances is very revealing. With her reference to the cave Offred simultaneously demonstrates her cultural literacy (as a liberal arts college graduate), her as yet unspoken awareness of the disastrous implications of her relationship with Nick (a truth which she consciously recognizes an instant later, "This is delusion"), as well as her unconscious reliance on the romantic tropes of male literature in the ordering of her own erotic experience. Troublingly, it is the "truth" of male literary discourse which triumphs over Offred's common sense—those "uneasy whispers" which tell her that her relationship with Nick is not safety but danger. Thus, although Offred suspects that her feelings for Nick are unfounded she cannot help but choose to romanticize her predicament, to "idolize" the man into a hero of epic proportions, "a cardboard cutout."

Offred's conscious choice in favor of a romanticism which she herself acknowledges as mistaken becomes even more disturbing when we scrutinize her behavior throughout her story. When we do so, we cannot fail to notice that she reacts to her situation with a consistent passivity. She makes no effort to escape the Handmaid's training center although her best friend Moira is planning such a prison break and she rejects the overtures of the resistance underground. Even more surprisingly, Offred refuses to take advantage of her relationship with the commander, who clearly likes her and who, strangely enough, looks to her not for erotic pleasure, but primarily for companionship and for some kind of moral reassurance:

> Sometimes, after the games, he sits on the floor beside my chair, holding my hand. His head is a little below mine, so that when he looks up at me it's at a juvenile angle. It must amuse him, this fake subservience. . . . It's difficult for me to believe that I have power over him, of any sort, but I do; although it's of an equivocal kind. . . . There are things he wants to prove to me, gifts he wants to bestow, services he wants to render, tenderness he wants to inspire. (*Handmaid,* p. 210)

Comically but chillingly Offred responds to these opportunities with a request for hand-lotion and an indifferent question about current events; as already noted, she later simply surrenders her fate to the desirable but unreliable Nick.

Admittedly, Offred justifies her choice of non-action indirectly, by showing us that any form of self-assertion against this new society must fail. Significantly, the rebellious females of Offred's world are all defeated: Ofglen commits suicide in order to protect the May Day underground; Moira's escape attempt is thwarted and she is imprisoned in the city's brothel; Offred's own mother is glimpsed in a film-documentary about the dreaded toxic-waste colonies. To survive, Offred seems to suggest, one must surrender.

But despite this evidence, the description which Offred gives us of her own life prior to the Gileadian coup casts increasing doubt upon her apparently reliable narrative point of view. We learn, for example, that she was formerly the mistress of a married man, and the novel obliquely suggests that her husband Luke may have chosen her over his first wife for the same reasons that the commander favors her over his spouse—Offred is younger, more sexually attractive, and fertile (significantly, Luke seems to have had no children by his first marriage). More disturbingly, despite her intelligence and education, Offred seems to have exercised as little control over her former life as she does over her present existence. Uninspired by politics—a disinterest which her husband actively encouraged—Offred remained on the sidelines of political questions, just as she waited for Luke to make up his mind to marry her, and she worked, not as an explainer or analyzer but as a transcriber of books to disks in a predominantly female task force—an act which curiously prefigures her own present narrative recording. She is a woman who has, for the most part, lived by watching others do.

Seen from the point of view of her past, Offred's current existence begins to look less like a nonsensical metamorphosis and more like a horrible but nightmarishly appropriate extension of her former life; one might even argue that, in a larger sense, Offred has always been a handmaid—a woman who serves others, but never herself. Once the reader makes this connection, the apparently huge contrast between the idealized good old days and the bad new days shrinks considerably. We should keep in mind that, from the very beginning of the novel, Atwood ironizes the gap which Offred establishes between her seemingly golden past and her ghoulish present; early on we witness a confrontation between these false opposites when Offred encounters some curious Japanese tourists on the street:

> The skirts reach just below the knee and the legs come out from beneath them, nearly naked in their thin stockings, blatant, the high-heeled shoes with their straps attached to the feet like delicate instruments of torture. The women teeter on their spiked feet as if on stilts, but off balance; their backs arch at the waist, thrusting the buttocks out. Their heads are uncovered and their hair too is exposed in all its darkness and sexuality. They wear lipstick, red, outlining the damp cavities of their mouths, like scrawls on a washroom wall, of the time before. I stop walking. Ofglen stops beside me and I know that she too cannot take her eyes off these women. We are fascinated but also repelled. They seem undressed. It has taken so little time to change our minds about things like this. Then I think: I used to dress like that. That was freedom. (*Handmaid,* p. 28)

Offred makes an error here which is all the more troubling because of its familiarity; she mistakes the outward appearance of freedom for the thing itself. Her misguided equation of western fashion with feminine liberation—already signalled stylistically through Atwood's description of the high-heels, which emphasizes how very much this clothing imprisons rather than frees—is especially ironic given the fact that the person wearing it is not western but eastern, and is a representative of a culture notorious for its oppression of women, at least from a western point of view.

Here we arrive at the second level of Atwood's satiric message: this moment of inter-cultural confrontation suggests very clearly that *both* Offred and the Japanese tourist are prisoners of their societies. The only difference between them lies in the fact that Offred's culture has abolished the benevolent "western" toleration of women's hard-won but still relatively small and superficial prerogatives. But true personal freedom exists for neither woman in the world which Atwood is describing, which, by implication, reflects not a future reality but a present actuality. This is not the world as it will be, this is the world—symbolically at least—as it is.

In this manner Atwood employs her narrator-heroine to provoke two very contradictory reactions in the female reader. On one hand the very fact that Offred is not a revolutionary but an average, college-educated working mother makes her both recognizable and sympathetic to us. But at the same time Atwood turns our empathy for Offred against us, suggesting that her protagonist (and thus we too, in so far as we resemble her) acts or fails to act based on a dangerous amalgamation of gender assumptions which have governed women's behavior for centuries and which have guaranteed their oppression by men:[11] a vicious circle of passivity and helplessness—wherein passivity perpetuates impotence, which in turn justifies and excuses passivity; a dehabilitating narcissism which continually deflects the individual from her real self-interest and needs; a masochistic belief in salvation through erotic love no matter how unlikely and potentially dangerous to the individual. This last point is emphasized by the fact that we do not know whether Nick saves Offred or betrays her. Further, even though he does successfully effect her escape from the Republic of Gilead, his motives remain ambiguous; does he really love her, or does he simply resemble the other men of Gileadian society in that he becomes so enraptured at the thought of fathering a child that he decides to protect the vessel carrying it?[12] If the latter motive is indeed the case then Offred's relationship with Nick is not very different than her relationship with Fred. In both cases she is a breeder rather than a person in her own right.

But there remains yet another, more universal dimension to Atwood's satiric critique in *Handmaid.* One of the most striking features of this futurist novel is its lack of futuristic technological trappings—be they gismos, robots, or outlandish scientific theories, advances, or practices. This is in striking opposition to those futurist satiric novels touted by McCarthy—*1984, Brave New World, A Clockwork Orange,* or even *Fahrenheit 451.* These works all present worlds which are techno-nightmares—systems which dehumanize their citizens, forcing them to operate like machinery, rather than like individuals. Each boasts an especially demonic invention: the video-surveillance of Orwell, the quasi-poisoned test-tube babies of Huxley, the behaviorist Ludovico treatment of Burgess, and the insidiously efficient book-burning fire brigade of Bradbury. Correspondingly, these fictions propose a return to nature and to old-fashioned customs and values as a probably unattainable but certainly superior social ideal: Winston's and Julia's old fashioned love-affair in *1984,* the Shakespeare quoting Savage in *Brave,* the whiskey-drinking priest who affirms the centrality of free-will in *Clockwork,* and the hippylike book people living in pastoral harmony in *Fahrenheit.*

In *Handmaid* on the other hand, the exact opposite process seems to be at work. The Republic of Gilead strikes us, not as a techno-dystopia, but as a reactionary step backwards in time, to a kind of government and lifestyle that resembles that of the Middle Ages—based on one part biblical patriarchy, one part Islamic militantism, and one part Hindu caste system. Technology as we usually think of it—as the tools, mechanisms, machines and expertise that either make our lives easier or threaten to destroy them—seems to have been banished from this society with the exception of a few cars and a couple of computers. Perhaps the most chilling aspect of this technological banishment is Gileadian society's absurdly inefficient rejecting of any of the medical techniques for preventing and curing infertility—which seems to be this society's major problem.

Or is it? I cannot help but suspect that if infertility were really such a pressing concern this profoundly hypocritical society would find a way either to justify fertility technology or to at least provide it unofficially (as it does with sexual pleasure).[13]

I would suggest that, as is typical of Atwood's satiric strategy, this apparent technological absence in Gilead, is not what it appears to be. Instead, a very different kind of technology is at work here—insidious because it is at once invisible and all pervasive—and that is, very simply, the technology of power which Michel Foucault has called discipline:

> It is an important mechanism, for it automatizes and disindividualizes power. Power has its principle not so much in a person as in a certain connected distribution of bodies, surfaces, lights, gazes; in an arrangement whose internal mechanisms produce the relation in which individuals are caught up. . . . Consequently, it does not matter who exercises power. . . . Similarly, it does not matter what motive animates him. He who is subjected to a field of visibility, and who knows it, assumes responsibility for the constraints of power; he makes them play spontaneously upon himself; he inscribes in himself the power relation; in which he simultaneously plays both roles; he becomes the principle of his own subjection.[14]

This invisible, all-subjugating technology is exactly what drives Gileadian society. Significantly, we see no rulers in Atwood's fictional world,[15] but everyone in it from Commander Fred to his domestic servants, from the doctor who inspects Offred to Offred herself is caught up in a network of surveillance and counter-surveillance.[16] The novel constantly emphasizes the omnipresence of the scrutinizing gaze; the word "eye" is everywhere; the secret police are called "Eyes," and the farewell greeting "under his eye" refers to the divine gaze but also testifies to the fact that everyone is indeed under the eye of someone else. Aunt Lydia gives her "girls" better advice than she knows, when she tells them to be as invisible as possible, because "to be seen is to be penetrated" (p. 28). And even the apparently spontaneous, orgiastic group outlets for frustrated violence, such as the Salvaging, reveal themselves to be carefully orchestrated, closely supervised exercises in which the actors are painfully aware that they are being watched:

> It's a mistake to hang back too obviously in any group like this; it stamps you as lukewarm, lacking in zeal. (*Handmaid,* p. 278)

The constant monitoring of behavior of everyone by everyone (with an efficiency which makes a Big Brother unnecessary) coupled with the ever-present threat of clearly defined punishments represent the components of a technology of social control which is in no way medieval but which is rather radically modern.[17] Seen from this point of view Gilead's emphasis on child-bearing, the outlawing of reading for women, and the other bizarre rules and values which characterize this society reveal themselves to be the instruments which serve to make docile, not just women—although the bulk of these devices seem to be aimed at them, probably because they represent the most subversive threat—but a whole social body. It is total social control, the perfection of the exercise of power, that Gilead strives for; this is no theocracy, it is a world turned into a perpetual penitentiary.

Such a view of Gilead explains why for all its freakishness, the social order of *The Handmaid's Tale* seems weirdly familiar,[18] and in this familiarity lies the ultimate political thrust of Atwood's satiric argument. As was the case for Offred's apparent transformation from free mother to indentured surrogate, the social metamorphosis from democratic US of A to totalitarian Gilead is an ironic one, for this disciplined society of the future is a grotesque mirror image of our own—a society that controls our behavior so efficiently and discretely that we fail to notice the degree to which we are manipulated.[19]

With this ironic future portrait Atwood suggests that we are also Gileadians, constantly under scrutiny by the plethora of institutions with which we must have contact from the IRS audit to the university examination. And we are also the auditors and examiners who scrutinize the others.

In conclusion, I believe that *The Handmaid's Tale* is at once a text-book example of modern fictional satire and at the same time a clever appropriation of a predominantly male literature for feminist purposes. It subverts as it borrows from this literary canon, enabling us to admire it both as a satiric model *and* as a pioneering satiric effort. More importantly, the novel manifests satiric critique at its most complex; it offers itself as a satire for women and to a certain extent of them, while it simultaneously attacks both the insidious disciplinary mechanisms of contemporary society as well as our willful ignorance of them. Offred herself signals the importance of political self-recognition early on in the novel:

> We lived, as usual, by ignoring. Ignoring isn't the same as ignorance, you have to work at it. (*Handmaid,* p. 56)

And certainly, self-recognition is equally and dramatically absent from the academic conference assembled to discuss the Handmaid "document" in Atwood's parodistic "Historical Notes." Here the plenary speaker compounds the errors of the past with his pompous, unself-critical assumption of his own culture's superiority. Fittingly, his lecture is replete with both sexist jokes and an unwillingness to confront the moral questions posed by the past:

> Surely, we have learned by now that such judgments are of necessity culture-specific. Also, Gileadian society was under a good deal of pressure, demographic and otherwise, and was subject to factors from which we ourselves are happily more free. Our job is not to censure but to understand. (Applause). (*Handmaid,* p. 302)

By means of these negative exempla, Atwood urges us to recognize the flaws of our culture and to refuse passive acceptance of them. *Handmaid* is, above all, a book about responsibility, at once emotional, sexual, intellectual and civic.

Seen from this perspective, the satire in *The Handmaid's Tale* directs its criticism towards all of us—feminists and non-feminists, women and men. It warns us of the imperceptible technology of power, of the subtle domination of women by men, and of our unconscious imprisoning of each other and ourselves by ourselves.

NOTES

1. There can be no doubt that the history of satiric writing has been dominated by the "virile" irony of such writers as the Romans Horace and Juvenal, the 18th Century's Swift and Voltaire and such moderns as Orwell, Huxley, and Burgess. And even now, when we consider non-literary forms of satire such as the comic-strip, we see primarily the names of men, such as Gary Trudeau.
2. David Worcester argues that satire consists of precisely such a complex rhetorical infrastructure. See *The Art of Satire* (Cambridge: Harvard University Press, 1940; rpt. New York: Roosevelt Russell, 1966), p. 231.
3. In *The Plot of Satire* (New Haven: Yale University Press, 1965), Alvin Kernan uses Pope's *The Dunciad* to illustrate the regressive plot structure of satiric narrative, pp. 223 and following.
4. Kernan, *The Cankered Muse* (New Haven: Yale University Press, 1959), pp. 14–18.
5. Gilbert Highet goes so far as to maintain that satire is always essentially topical. See *The Anatomy of Satire* (Princeton: Princeton University Press, 1957), pp. 5-6.
6. "Breeders, Wives, and Unwomen," *New York Times Book Review,* February 9, 1986, p. 1.
7. McCarthy takes particular exception to Atwood's "inability to imagine a language to match the changed face of common life" ("Breeders," p. 35). But, she fails to take into account the linguistic deprivation which determines the lives of all Gileadians, but especially the Handmaids. These women have no access to the written word, very little access to even oral information, and only the most limited opportunity for speech. Since they are forbidden meaningful contact with any other person, they, and Offred among them, exist in a constant state of linguistic impoverishment—hence the thrill of playing Scrabble. Thus, what McCarthy ascribes to Atwood as a lack of imagination points instead to Offred's excruciating predicament—that of a person who is systematically being robbed of her language capability.
8. "Feminism's Phantoms," *The New Republic,* March 17, 1986, p. 33.
9. Ehrenreich, p. 34.
10. *The Handmaid's Tale* (Boston: Houghton Mifflin, 1986), pp. 162–3.
11. Ehrenreich argues that the book's "ultimate" satiric attack targets "a repressive tendency in feminism itself" and points to the insidious similarities between ideas of the anti-feminist right and those of the cultural feminist militants. See "Feminism's Phantoms." While this aspect of Atwood's satire is clearly an important one, I wonder if this *mise en question* of current feminist strains is not less crucial to the novel's critique than the attitude of the heroine herself—which typifies the female "yuppie"'s indifference to political issues, as Ehrenreich also notes. After all, Offred repeatedly reveals that it was the *average citizen's* renunciation of political activism which permitted the lunatic fringe to take over the country and transform it into Gilead:

    > There were stories in the newspapers, of course, corpses in ditches or the woods, bludgeoned to death or mutilated. . . . How awful we would say, and they were, but they were awful without being believable. . . . They were too melodramatic, they had a dimension that was not the dimension of our lives. (pp. 56–7)

Thus, while *Handmaid* admittedly expresses an indictment of extremist gender ideology of right and of left, it no less certainly damns the passive non-resistance exhibited by its anti-heroine.

12. Such an interpretation of Nick's motives are suggested by the ironic Historical Notes at the end of the novel, p. 311.
13. Again, the Historical Notes ironize the birthrate drop by noting that only Caucasian births were lessening, p. 304.
14. Michel Foucault, *Discipline and Punish* (New York: Vintage Books, 1979), p. 202. The cited section pertains to Foucault's description of Bentham's Panopticon, which the author sees as an idealization of the disciplinary mechanism. Such a model, according to Foucault, can be used "whenever one is dealing with a multiplicity of individuals on whom a task or a particular form of behavior must be imposed" (p. 205). Therefore, a regime of any political persuasion can and (in Foucault's opinion, necessarily *does*) use discipline to control the behavior of its citizens.
15. Aptly, Ehrenreich wonders why it is never clear in the novel, "who is in charge." See "Feminism's Phantoms."
16. The omnipresence of discipline helps explain why, as Joan L. Slonczewski remarks, so many of the characters in the novel strike us as passive. See "A Tale of Two Handmaids," *The Kenyon Review,* 6:4 (1986), p. 123.
17. Foucault notes that "the problem lies . . . in the steep rise in the use of these mechanisms of normalization and the wide-ranging powers which, throughout the proliferation of new disciplines, they bring with them," *Discipline,* p. 306.
18. Catherine R. Stimpson notes that Gilead's domesticated totalitarianism "become[s] even more frightening because its monstrosity seems . . . absurdly normal." See "Atwood Woman," *The Nation,* May 31st, 1986, p. 764. Given this state of affairs, again I disagree with Mary McCarthy's assessment, which claims that the element of recognition of our own society is missing from *Handmaid.* See "Breeders," p. 1.
19. Foucault comments on our contemporary society in the following manner: "We are neither in the amphitheatre, nor on stage, but in the panoptic machine, invested by its effects of power, which we bring to ourselves since we are part of its mechanism," *Discipline,* p. 217.

Margaret Atwood's *The Handmaid's Tale* and the Dystopian Tradition

AMIN MALAK

In *The History of Sexuality*, Michel Foucault impressively articulates the complex, formidably paradoxical relationship between sexuality and power, arguing how power dictates its law to sex:

> To deal with sex, power employs nothing more than a law of prohibition. Its objective: that sex renounce itself. Its instrument: the threat of a punishment that is nothing other than the suppression of sex. Renounce yourself or suffer the penalty of being suppressed; do not appear if you do not want to disappear. Your existence will be maintained only at the cost of your nullification. Power constrains sex only through a taboo that plays on the alternative between two nonexistences.[1]

Any reader of Margaret Atwood's *The Handmaid's Tale* needs to recall Foucault's observation to contextualize the agonies of the narrator-protatonist, Offred, the victim of such a prohibition ordinance. By focusing the narrative on one central character, Atwood reveals the indignity and terror of living under a futuristic regime controlled by Christian fundamentalists. The heroine is one of several "handmaids" who, because of their "viable ovaries," are confined to a prison-like compound in order to be available for periodically programmed sexual intercourse with their "Commanders of the Faith." This church-state regime, called Gilead, condones such an unorthodox practice out of necessity to overcome a fertility crisis amongst the dwindling Caucasian population; as one of the novel's epigrams suggests, the polygamy of the Old Testament provides the sanction. True to the precedent set in Genesis, the Commander's Wife arranges and supervises these sex sessions, in which the handmaid, desexed and dehumanized, is obliged to participate. The dire alternative for the handmaid is banishment to the Colonies, where women clean up radioactive waste as slave labourers. The dictates of state policy in Gilead thus relegate sex to a saleable commodity exchanged for mere minimal survival.

One of the novel's successful aspects concerns the skilful portrayal of a state that in theory claims to be founded on Christian principles, yet in practice miserably lacks spirituality and benevolence. The state in Gilead prescribes a pattern of life based on frugality, conformity, censorship, corruption, fear, and terror—in short, the usual terms of existence enforced by totalitarian states, instance of which can be found in such dystopian works as Zamyatin's *We,* Huxley's *Brave New World,* and Orwell's *1984.*

In order to situate Atwood's novel within the relevant context of dystopia, I wish to articulate the salient dystopian features those three classics reveal. The ensuing discussion will be an elaboration on Atwood's rendition and redefinition of those features.

1. *Power, Totalitarianism, War:* Dystopias essentially deal with power: power as the prohibition or perversion of human potential; power in its absolute form that, to quote from *1984,* tolerates no flaws in the pattern it imposes on society. Dystopias thus show, in extreme terms, power functioning efficiently and mercilessly to its optimal totalitarian limit. Interestingly, war or foreign threats often loom in the background, providing the pretext to join external tension with internal terror.
2. *Dream-Nightmare: Fantasy: Reality:* While dystopias may be fear-laden horror fiction (how the dream turns into a nightmare), the emphasis of the work is not on horror for its own sake, but on forewarning. Similarly, while dystopias contain elements of the fantastic with a "touch of excess" carrying the narrative "one step [or more] beyond our reality,"[2] the aim is neither to distort reality beyond recognition, nor to provide an escapist world for the reader, but "to allow certain tendencies in modern society to spin forward without the brake of sentiment and humaneness."[3]

3. *Binary Oppositions:* Dystopias dramatize the eternal conflict between individual choice and social necessity: the individual resenting the replacement of his private volition by compulsory uniformitarian decisions made by an impersonal bureaucratic machinery; Zamyatin's heroine poignantly sums up the conflict: "I do not want anyone to want for me. I want to want for myself."[4] The sphere of the binary opposition expands further to cover such dialectical dualities as emotion and reason, creative imagination and mathematical logic, intuition and science, tolerance and judgment, kindness and cruelty, spirituality and materialism, love and power, good and evil. The list can go on.
4. *Characterization:* Dystopias often tend to offer two-dimensional character types; this tendency is possibly due to the pressure of the metaphorical and ideological thrust of these works. Moreover, the nightmarish atmosphere of dystopias seems to preclude advancing positive, assertive characters that might provide the reader with consoling hope. If such positive characters do exist, they usually prove miserably ineffectual when contending with ruthless overwhelming powers.
5. *Change and Time:* Dystopian societies, consumed and controlled by regressive dogmas, appear constantly static: founded on coercion and rigid structures, the system resists change and becomes arrested in paralysis. Such a static life "shorn of dynamic possibility," becomes for the underprivileged members of society mediocre, monotonous and predictable: "a given and measured quantity that can neither rise to tragedy nor tumble to comedy."[5] Accordingly, dystopias are not associated with innovation and progress, but with fear of the future. They use, however, the present as an instructive referent, offering a tacit alternative to the dystopian configuration.
6. *Roman à These:* To varying degrees, dystopias are quintessentially ideological novels: they engage the reader in what Fredric Jameson calls a "theoretical discourse," whereby a range of thematic possibilities are posited and polarized against each other, yet the novels eventually reveal a definite philosophical and socio-political outlook for which fiction proves to be a convenient medium.

What distinguishes Atwood's novel from those dystopian classics is its obvious feminist focus. Gilead is openly misogynistic, in both its theocracy and practice. The state reduces the handmaids to the slavery status of being mere "breeders" (a term bearing Swift's satirical coinage):

> We are all for breeding purposes: We aren't concubines, geisha girls, courtesans. On the contrary: everything possible has been done to remove us from that category. There is supposed to be nothing entertaining about us. . . . We are two-legged wombs, that's all: sacred vessels, ambulatory chalices.[6]

In addition to the handmaids, Gilead offers its own state-sponsored brand of prostitutes called the Jezebels: dolled-up women whose sole function is to entertain foreign delegations. In order to erase the former identity of the handmaids, the state, moreover, cancels their original names and labels them according to the names of their Commanders, hence the names Offred, Ofglen, Ofwayne, Ofwarren. The women then become possessed articles, mere appendages to those men who exercise sexual mastery over them. The handmaid's situation lucidly illustrates Simone de Beauvior's assertion in *The Second Sex* about man defining woman not as an autonomous being but as simply what he decrees to be relative to him: "For him she is sex—absolute sex, no less. She is defined and differentiated with reference to man and not with reference to her; she is the incidental, as opposed to the essential. He is the Subject, he is the Absolute—she is the Other."[7] This view of man's marginalization of woman corroborates Foucault's earlier observation about the power-sex correlative; since man holds the sanctified reigns of power in society, he rules, assigns roles, and decrees after social, religious, and cosmic concepts convenient to his interests and desires.

However, not all the female characters in Atwood's novel are sympathetic, nor all the male ones demonic. The Aunts, a vicious élite of collaborators who conduct torture lectures, are among the church-state's staunchest supporters; these renegades turn into zealous converts, appropriating male values at the expense of their feminine instincts. One of them, Aunt Lydia, functions, ironically, as the spokesperson of antifeminism; she urges the handmaids to renounce themselves and become non-persons: "Modesty is invisibility, said Aunt Lydia. Never forget it. To be seen—to be *seen*—is to be—her voice trembled—penetrated. What you must be, girls, is impenetrable. She called us girls" (p. 39). On the other hand, Nick, the Commander's chauffeur, is involved with the underground network, of men and women, that aims at rescuing women and conducting sabotage. Besides, Atwood's heroine constantly yearns for her former marriage life with Luke, presently presumed dead. Accordingly, while Atwood poignantly condemns the misogynous mentality that can cause a heavy toll of human suffering, she refrains from convicting a gender in its entirety as the perpetrator of the nightmare that is Gilead. Indeed, we witness very few of the male characters acting with stark cruelty: the narrative reports most of the violent acts after the fact, sparing the reader gory scenes. Even the Commander appears more pathetic than sinister, baffled than manipulative, almost, at times, a Fool.

Some may interpret Atwood's position here as a non-feminist stance, approving of women's status-quo. In a review for the *Times Literary Supplement,* Lorna Sage describes *The Handmaid's Tale* as Atwood's "revisionist look at her more visionary self," and as "a novel in praise of the present, for which, perhaps, you have to have the perspective of dystopia."[8] It is really difficult to conceive Atwood's praising the present, because, like Orwell who in *1984* extrapolated specific ominous events and tendencies in twentieth-century politics, she tries to caution against right-wing fundamentalism, rigid dogmas, and misogynous theosophies that may be currently gaining a deceptive popularity. The novels' mimetic impulse then aims at wresting an imperfect present from a horror-ridden future: it appeals for vigilance, and an appreciation of the mature values of tolerance, compassion, and, above all, for women's unique identity.

The novel's thematics operate by positing polarized extremes: a decadent present, which Aunt Lydia cynically describes as "a society dying . . . of too much choice" (p. 35), and a totalitarian future that prohibits choice. Naturally, while rejecting the indulgent decadence and chaos of an anarchic society, the reader condemns the Gilead regime for its intolerant, prescriptive set of values that projects a tunnel vision on reality and eliminates human volition: "there is more than one kind of freedom, said Aunt Lydia. Freedom to and freedom from. In the days of anarchy, it was freedom to. Now you are being given freedom from. Don't underrate it" (p. 34). As illustrated by the fears and agonies that Offred endures, when human beings are not free to aspire toward whatever they wish, when choices become so severely constrained that, to quote from Dostoyevsky's *The Possessed,* "only the necessary is necessary," life turns into a painfully prolonged prison term. Interestingly, the victimization process does not involve Offred and the handmaids alone, but extends to the oppressors as well. Everyone ruled by the Gilead regime suffers the deprivation of having no choice, except what the church-state decrees; even the Commander is compelled to perform his sexual assignment with Offred as a matter of obligation: "This is no recreation, even for the Commander. This is serious business. The Commander, too, is doing his duty" (p. 105).

Since the inhabitants of Gilead lead the precarious existence befitting victims, most try in varied ways to cope, endure, and survive. This situation of being a victim and trying to survive dramatizes Atwood's major thesis in her critical work *Survival: A Thematic Guide to Canadian Literature,* in which she suggests that Canada, metaphorically still a colony or an oppressed minority, is "a collective victim,"[9] and that "the central symbol for Canada . . . is undoubtedly Survival, *la Survivance.*"[10] Atwood, furthermore, enumerates what she labels "basic victim positions," whereby a victim may choose any of four possible options, one of which is to acknowledge being a victim but refuse "to accept the assumption that the role is inevitable."[11] This position fully explains Offred's role as the protagonist-narrator of *The Handmaid's Tale.* Offred's progress as a maturing consciousness is indexed by an evolving awareness of herself as a victimized woman, and then a gradual development toward initiating risky but assertive schemes that break the slavery syndrome. Her double-crossing the Commander and his Wife, her choice to hazard a sexual affair with Nick, and her association with the underground network, all point to the shift from being a helpless victim to being a sly, subversive survivor. This impulse to survive, together with the occasional flashes of warmth and concern among the handmaids, transmits reassuring signs of hope and humanity in an otherwise chilling and depressing tale.

What makes Atwood's book such a moving tale is its clever technique in presenting the heroine initially as a voice, almost like a sleepwalker conceiving disjointed perceptions of its surroundings, as well as flashing reminiscences about a bygone life. As the scenes gather more details, the heroine's voice is steadily and imperceptively, yet convincingly, transfigured into a full-roundedness, that parallels her maturing comprehension of what is happening around her. Thus the victim, manipulated and coerced, is metamorphosed into a determined conniver who daringly violates the perverted canons of Gilead. Moreover, Atwood skillfully manipulates the time sequence between the heroine's past (pre-Gilead life) and the present: those shifting reminiscences offer glimpses of a life, though not ideal, still filled with energy, creativity, humaneness, and a sense of selfhood, a life that sharply contrasts with the alienation, slavery, and suffering under totalitarianism. By the end of the novel, the reader is effectively and conclusively shown how the misogynous regime functions on the basis of power, not choice; coercion, not volition; fear, not desire. In other words, Atwood administers in doses the assaulting shocks to our sensibilities of a grim dystopian nightmare: initially, the narrative voice, distant and almost diffidently void of any emotions, emphasizes those aspects of frugality and solemnity imposed by the state, then progressively tyranny and corruption begin to unfold piecemeal. As the novel concludes, as the horror reaches a climax, the narrative voice assumes a fully engaged emotional tone that cleverly keeps us in suspense about the heroine's fate. This method of measured, well-punctuated revelations about Gilead connects symbolically with the novel's central meaning: misogynous dogmas, no matter how seemingly innocuous and trustworthy they may appear at their initial conception, are bound, when allowed access to power, to reveal their ruthlessly tyrannical nature.

Regardless of the novel's dystopian essence, it nevertheless avoids being solemn; on the contrary, it sustains an ironic texture throughout. We do not find too many frightening images that may compare with Oceana's torture chambers: the few graphic horror scenes are crisply and snappily presented, sparing us a blood-curdling impact. (Some may criticize this restraint as undermining the novel's integrity and emotional validity.) As in all dystopias, Atwood's aim is to encourage the reader to adopt a rational stance that avoids *total* "suspension of disbelief." This rational stance dislocates full emotional involvement in order to create a Brechtian type of alienation that, in turn, generates an ironic charge. This rational stance too should not be total, because Atwood does want us to care sympathetically about her heroine's fate; hence the emotional distance between reader and character must allow for closeness, but up to a point. Furthermore, Atwood is equally keen on preserving the ironic flair intact. No wonder then that she concludes *The Handmaid's Tale* with a climatic moment of irony: she exposes, in a hilarious epilogue, the absurdity and futility of certain academic writings that engage in dull, clinically skeptic analysis of irrelevancies and inanities, yet miss the vital issues. "If I may be permitted an editorial aside," blabbers the keynote speaker at a twenty-second century anthropological conference,

> allow me to say that in my opinion we must be cautious about passing moral judgement upon the Gileadeans. Surely we have learned by now that such judgements are of necessity culture-specific. Also, Gileadean society was under a good deal of pressure, demographic and otherwise, and was subject to factors from which we ourselves are happily more free. Our job is not to censure but to understand. (Applause.) (pp. 314-15)

The entire "Historical Notes" at the end of the novel represents a satire on critics who spin out theories about literary or historical texts without genuinely recognizing or experiencing the pathos expressed in them: they circumvent issues, classify data, construct clever hypotheses garbed in ritualistic, fashionable jargon, but no spirited illumination ever comes out of their endeavours. Atwood soberly demonstrates that when a critic or scholar (and by extension a reader) avoids, under the guise of scholarly objectivity, taking a moral or political stand about an issue of crucial magnitude such as totalitarianism, he or she will necessarily become an apologist for evil; more significantly, the applause the speaker receives give us a further compelling glimpse into a distant future that still harbours strong misogynous tendencies.

While the major dystopian features can clearly be located in *The Handmaid's Tale,* the novel offers two distinct additional features: feminism and irony. Dramatizing the interrelationship between power and sex, the book's feminism, despite condemning male misogynous mentality, upholds and cherishes a man-woman axis; here, feminism functions inclusively rather than exclusively, poignantly rather than stridently, humanely rather than cynically. The novel's ironic tone, on the other hand, betokens a confident narrative strategy that aims at treating a depressing material gently and gradually, yet firmly, openly, and conclusively, thus skilfully succeeding in securing the reader's sympathy and interest. The novel shows Atwood's strengths both as an engaging story-teller and a creator of a sympathetic heroine, and as an articulate craftswoman of a theme that is both current and controversial. As the novel signifies a landmark in the maturing process of Atwood's creative career, her self-assured depiction of the grim dystopian world gives an energetic and meaningful impetus to the genre.

NOTES

1. Michel Foucault, *The History of Sexuality, Volume I: An Introduction,* trans. Robert Hurley (1978; rpt. New York: Vintage Books, 1980), p. 84.
2. Irving Howe in *1984 Revisited: Totalitarianism in Our Century,* ed. Irving Howe (New York: Harper and Row, 1983), p. 8.
3. Irving Howe, *Politics and the Novel* (New York: Horizon Press, 1957), p. 242.
4. Yevgeny Zamyatin, *We,* trans. Mirra Ginsberg (New York: Viking, 1972), p. v.
5. *Politics and the Novel,* p. 240.
6. Margaret Atwood, *The Handmaid's Tale* (Toronto: McClelland & Stewart, 1985), p. 146. All subsequent quotations will be followed parenthetically by the page number in this edition.
7. *The Second Sex,* trans. H. M. Parshley (1953; rpt. New York: Alfred A. Knopf, 1971), p. xvi.
8. Lorna Sage, "Projection from a Messy Present," *Times Literary Supplement* 4, no. 329 (21 March 1986), 307.
9. (Toronto: Anansi, 1972), p. 36.
10. *Ibid.,* p. 32.
11. *Ibid.,* p. 37.

chapter **20**

Essays on *Beloved*, by Toni Morrison

Giving Body to the Word: The Maternal Symbolic in Toni Morrison's *Beloved*

JEAN WYATT

In *Beloved* Toni Morrison puts into words three orders of experience that Western cultural narratives usually leave out: childbirth and nursing from a mother's perspective; the desires of preverbal infant; and the sufferings of those destroyed by slavery, including the Africans who died on the slave ships. The project of incorporating into a text subjects previously excluded from language causes a breakdown and restructuring of linguistic forms; to make room for the articulation of alternative desires, Morrison's textual practice flouts basic rules of normative discourse.

Through the device of the ghost story, Morrison gives a voice to the preverbal infant killed by a mother desperate to save her child from slavery: the dead baby, Beloved, comes back in the body of a nineteen-year-old, able to articulate infantile feelings that ordinarily remain unspoken. Her desire to regain the maternal closeness of a nursing baby powers a dialogue that fuses pronoun positions and abolishes punctuation, undoing all the marks of separation that usually stabilize language. Beloved also has a collective identity: she represents a whole lineage of people obliterated by slavery, beginning with the Africans who died on the Middle Passage, the "Sixty Million and more" of the novel's epigraph. She describes conditions on the slave ships in fragmented images without connective syntax or punctuation, capturing the loss of demarcation and differentiation of those caught in an "oceanic" space between cultural identities, between Africa and an unknown destination (Spillers 72).

The mother figure, Sethe, defines herself as a maternal body. Her insistence on her own physical presence and connection to her children precludes an easy acceptance of the separations and substitutions that govern language: she will not, for example, use signifiers to represent her nursing baby, so she cannot tell the story of the baby's murder. The novel's discourse also tends to resist substitution, "the very law of metaphoric operation" (Rose 38): when the narrative focuses on either the maternal body or the haunted house, metaphors abandon their symbolic dimension to adhere to a baseline of literal meaning. For instance, a figure of speech in which *weight* usually means "responsibility" turns out to describe only the physical weight of Sethe's breasts (18). A similar "literalization" of spatial metaphors mimics the materializations in the haunted house: the phrase "she moved him" indicates not that Beloved stirred Paul D's emotions but that she physically moved him, from one location to another (114).[1] The continual shift from the abstract to the concrete creates the illusion of words sliding back to a base in the material world, an effect congruent with Morrison's emphasis on embodiment—on both the physical processes of maternity and the concrete presence of the ghost: "Usually [slavery] is an abstract concept. . . . The purpose of making [the ghost] real is making history possible, making memory real—somebody walks in the door and sits down at the table, so you have to think about it" (qtd. in Darling 6).

Describing a child's entry into language as a move from maternal bodily connection to a register of abstract signifiers, Lacan inadvertently sums up the psychological prerequisites for belonging to a patriarchal symbolic order. I invoke his paradigm to point out Morrison's deviations from dominant language practices and from the psychological premises that underlie them; I use the term *maternal symbolic* to discuss not only an alternative language incorporating maternal and material values but also a system that, like Lacan's symbolic, locates subjects in relation to other subjects. While Sethe operates within her own "maternal symbolic" of presence and connection, it is Denver, Sethe's surviving daughter, who in the end finds a more inclusive replacement for Lacan's paternal symbolic: a social order that conflates oral and verbal pleasures, nurtures her with words, and teaches her that caring is "what language was made for" (252).[2]

THE MATERNAL BODY IN LANGUAGE: A DISCOURSE OF PRESENCE

The mother figure of *Beloved* occupies a contradictory position in discourse. On the other hand, Sethe's self-definition as maternal body enables Morrison to construct a new narrative form—a specifically female quest powered by the desire to get one's milk to one's baby—that features childbirth as high adventure. On the other hand, this same self-definition forecloses Sethe's full participation in language.

In presenting Sethe's journey from slavery in Kentucky to the free state of Ohio as a maternal quest, Morrison is elaborating the figure of the heroic slave mother that in many female slave narratives replaces the figure of the heroic male fugitive. Harriet Jacobs's *Incidents in the Life of a Slave Girl,* for example, turns the rhetoric of heroic resolve common to male slave narratives into a text of courage drawn from a mother's love for her children: "I was resolved that I would foil my master and save my children, or I would perish in the attempt"; "Every trial I endured, every sacrifice I made for [the children's] sakes, drew them closer to my heart, and gave me fresh courage" (84, 89-90). If Jacobs (and other female slave narrators, like Lucy Delaney) appropriates the conventions of male heroism for the celebration of motherhood,[3] Morrison in turn reconstructs the acts of maternal heroism as the reproductive feats of the maternal body. Both Sethe and Jacobs find the courage to escape because they want their children to be free—"It was more for my helpless children than for myself that I longed for freedom," writes Jacobs (89)—but Jacobs's spiritual and emotional commitment becomes in Sethe a physical connection to the nursing baby she has sent on ahead: "I had to get my milk to my baby girl" (16). Sethe, like Jacobs, experiences the wish to give up the fight for survival and die, but while Jacobs says she was "willing to bear on" "for the children's sakes" (127), the reason that Sethe gives for enduring is the physical presence of the baby in her womb: "[I]t didn't seem such a bad idea [to die], . . . but the thought of herself stretched out dead while the little antelope lived on . . . in her lifeless body grieved her so" that she persevered (31).

The central heroic feat of Sethe's journey is her giving birth in the face of seemingly insuperable obstacles. Alone in the wilderness in a sinking boat on the Ohio River, in a state of physical injury and exhaustion, Sethe has only Amy, a white runaway indentured servant, to help her. Breaking the silence that has surrounded birth in Western narrative, Morrison provides a physically detailed account of childbirth, and—also new in Western cultural discourse—she gives labor its due as good work: Sethe and Amy "did something together appropriately and well" (84).

When Sethe finally wins through to Ohio, the text celebrates not the achievement of freedom but togetherness; a confusion of prepositions reflects the multiplicity of connections between mother and children: "Sethe lay in bed under, around, over, among but especially with them all" (93). At the triumphant close of her maternal quest, Sethe reports, "I was big, Paul D, and deep and wide and when I stretched out my arms all my children could get in between. I was *that* wide"; "she had milk enough for all" (162, 100). Thus the "nurturing power of the slave mother" (Gates xxxi) celebrated in women's slave narratives becomes literal in Morrison's account: Sethe's monumental body and abundant milk give and sustain life. But in spite of its mythic dimensions, the maternal body seems to lack a subjective center. During the journey, Sethe experiences her own existence only in relation to her children's survival; she is "concerned" not for herself but "for the life of her children's mother." She thinks, "I believe this baby's ma'am is gonna die" and pictures herself as "a crawling graveyard for a six-month baby's last hours" (30, 31, 34).

Sethe maintains this roundabout self-definition through the many images of nursing that picture her as the sustaining ground of her children's existence; even after the children are weaned, her bond with them remains so strong that she continues to think of it as a nursing connection (100, 162, 200, 216). While celebrating the courage and determination that Sethe draws from this attachment, Morrison's narrative also dramatizes the problems of Sethe's maternal subjectivity, which is so embedded in her children that it both allows her to take the life of one of them and precludes putting that act into words.

When Sethe tries to explain her attempt to kill herself and her children to prevent their reenslavement, she finds speech blocked: "Sethe knew that the circle she was making around . . . the subject would remain one. That she could never close in, pin it down for anybody who had to ask."[4] A gap remains at the heart of her story, which the omniscient narrator subsequently fills in:

> [W]hen she saw [the slave owner] coming [to recapture them, she] collected every bit of life she had made, all the parts of her that were precious and fine and beautiful, and carried, pushed, dragged them through the veil, out, away, over there where no one could hurt them . . . where they would be safe. (163)

Sethe extends her rights over her own body—the right to use any means, including death, to protect herself from a return to slavery—to the "parts of her" that are her children, folding them back into the maternal body in order to enter death as a single unit (though she succeeded in killing only one of her daughters). The novel withholds judgment on Sethe's act and persuades the reader to do the same, presenting the infanticide as the ultimate contradiction of mothering under slavery. "It was absolutely the right thing to do, . . . but it's also the thing you have no right to do," Morrison commented in an interview (Rothstein).[5]

Sethe's sense of continuity with her children also makes it difficult for her to take the position of narrating subject and tell her story. Her troubled relation to language can be read as a carryover from a nursing mother's attitude toward separation. When she engineered her family's escape from slavery, Sethe had to send her nursing baby ahead of her to Ohio: "I told the women in the wagon . . . to put sugar water in cloth to suck from so when I got there in a few days [the baby] wouldn't have forgot me. The milk would be there and I would be there with it" (16). Sethe would not compromise with absence, overlooking the potentially life-threatening lack of food for her baby "for a few days" to insist on presence: the milk would be "there," and the mother would be "there with it." The standpoint of nursing mother precludes separation and the substitutions that any separation would require.

Sethe's embrace of a relational system of presence and connection, her reluctance to accept the principle of substitution, extends to her refusal to invest in words and helps explain the link between her failure to tell the story of her baby girl's death and that baby's embodiment in Beloved. Lacan's account of a child's entry into language opposes bodily connection and verbal exchange in a way that clarifies Sethe's choices. To move into a position in language and the social order, according to Lacan, an infant must sacrifice its imaginary sense of wholeness and continuity with the mother's body. (Sethe is of course in the mother's position rather than the child's, but her physical connection with her nursing baby resembles the infant's initial radical dependency on the mother's body.) Lacan later makes the repudiation of maternal continuity an oedipal event, when the social law of the father prohibits the child's access to the maternal body. In "The Function and Field of Speech and Language in Psychoanalysis," however, he borrows from Freud an unmediated mother-child anecdote, perhaps to focus more intensely on the either-or choice between bodily presence and abstract signifier. Freud's grandson Ernst becomes a speaking subject in the same moment that he acknowledges his mother's absence. Throwing a spool out of his crib and bringing it back to the accompaniment of sounds ("ooo! aaa!") that Freud interprets as "Fort! Da!" ("Gone! There!"), the baby assumes a symbolic mastery over what he cannot control in reality—his mother's presence and absence (Freud, *Pleasure* 8–10). Lacan adds that the child "thereby raises his desire to a second power," investing desire in language (103). By acknowledging that he must put a signifier there, where his mother's body used to be, the child both recognizes absence and accepts loss. The word "manifests itself first of all as the murder of the thing" (104), or in John Muller's gloss, "the word destroys the immediacy of objects and gives us distance from them" (29).[6] It is this distance, this loss, that Sethe rejects. Just as she declined any mediation between her body and her nursing baby, insisting on presence, she now refuses to replace that baby with a signifier, to accept the irrevocability of absence by putting the child's death into words. Her denial of loss is fundamentally antimetaphorical — that is, the refusal to displace libido onto words is a refusal to let one thing stand for another and so impedes the whole project of speech.[7] Sethe remains without a narrative but with the baby ghost—there, embodied, a concrete presence.

Through Sethe's reluctance to substitute words for things, not just Beloved but all the painful events of the past that Sethe has not transformed into narrative are left there, where those events first occurred. "[W]hat I did, or knew, or saw, is still out there. Right in the place where it happened," Sethe tells Denver (36). The plot reflects this spatialized time, as incidents from the past occupy the various rooms in which they originally took place. In the shed, the murder replays, at least for Beloved; in the keeping room, an injured and demoralized Sethe once more gets bathed "in sections" by loving hands; and a white man "coming into [Sethe's] yard" triggers a repeat of her murderous attack—with a saving difference (123–24, 272, 262). The plot—present time—cannot move forward because Sethe's space is crammed with the past:

> When she woke the house crowded in on her: there was the door where the soda crackers were lined up in a row; the white stairs her baby girl loved to climb; the corner where Baby Suggs mended shoes . . . the exact place on the stove where Denver burned her fingers. . . . There was no room for any other thing or body. (39)

There are no gaps in Sethe's world, no absences to be filled in with signifiers; everything is there, an oppressive plenitude.

Language reinforces the sense that materializations clog the haunted house: spatial images that usually function as figures of speech take shape as actions. For example, when Paul D, a former slave from the same plantation as Sethe, finds her again after an absence of eighteen years, he feels out his chances for establishing a relationship with her by asking if "there was some space" for him (45). While his expression seems natural in the circumstances, the situation in the house causes Paul D to make a space for himself more literally than any suitor in literature: "[H]olding the table by two legs, he bashed it about, wrecking everything, screaming back at the screaming house" (18). Evidently Morrison wants the opening statement of the novel—that "124 was spiteful. Full of a baby's venom" (3)—to be taken quite literally. Before the dead baby takes the shape of Beloved, her amorphous spirit haunts the house, filling it so completely with her spite that "[t]here was no room for any other thing or body until Paul D . . . broke up the place, making room, . . . then standing in the place he had made" (39).

After Paul D exorcises the ghost from the house and it returns in the shape of Beloved, spatial metaphors continue to reflect the materialization of things that belong by rights in a spiritual realm. The sentence "She moved him," for example, opens a chapter about Beloved's domestic relations with Paul D (114). Because the grammatical object of *moved* is a human being—*him* rather than *it*—the phrase seems at first glance to operate figuratively, as in "she affected him emotionally." But the spiritual meaning quickly gives way to physical actuality as it becomes clear that Paul D "was being moved" literally (126)—out of Sethe's bed, out of the living room, finally out of the house altogether—by Beloved's jealous desire to expel her rival.

Textual practice similarly seconds Sethe's emphasis on presence by rejecting metaphorical substitutions for the maternal body. In the opening scene, after Sethe has told Paul D about her quest to get her milk to her baby in Ohio, he cups her breasts from behind in a display of tenderness: "What she knew was that the responsibility for her breasts, at last, was in somebody else's hands" (18). The reader does a double take: the phrase "in somebody else's hands" usually functions as a metaphor meaning "someone else's responsibility"; here the hands are literally there, and what rests in them is not an abstract concept but flesh. The same slippage occurs in the next sentence, as Sethe imagines being "relieved of the weight of her breasts" (18). Because *weight* appears within the usually figurative phrase "relieved of the weight of," readers assume that it is a metaphor for care or responsibility, but the modifying phrase "of her breasts" gives *weight* back its literal meaning. When the maternal body becomes the locus of discourse, the metaphorical becomes the actual, a move that reinforces Sethe's definition of motherhood as an embodied responsibility: there are no substitutes, metaphorical or otherwise, for her breasts.

In the same passage, Paul D "reads" the story of slavery engraved on Sethe's back by a final savage beating. Because the scar tissue is without sensation—

"her back skin had been dead for years" (18)—Sethe's back is, in a sense, not her own; it has been appropriated and reified as a tablet on which the slave masters have inscribed their code. She cannot substitute for this discourse of violence her own version of the event, in spite of Paul D's insistence (over the space of three pages) that she tell him about it. Sethe refuses, repeating instead Amy Denver's description of the wound left by the whipping as "a whole tree . . . in bloom": "I got a tree on my back. . . . I've never seen it and never will. But that's what she said it looked like. A chokecherry tree. Trunk, branches, and even leaves" (79, 15-16). The metaphor masks suffering and puts it at the distance of a beautiful image—an act of poetic detachment appropriate, perhaps, to Amy's position of onlooker after the event but not to Sethe's subjective experience of pain.[8] Unable to seize the word and thus become master of her own experience, Sethe remains "a body whose flesh . . . bears . . . the marks of a cultural text" that inscribes her as slave (Spillers 67).[9] Sethe's problematic relation to language results from her position as body not only in a maternal order but also in a social order that systematically denied the subject position to those it defined as objects of exchange.[10]

In the absence of a speaking subject, Morrison makes the most of body language, as the passage I have been analyzing, quoted in full, shows:

> Behind her, bending down, his body an arc of kindness, he held her breasts in the palms of his hands. He rubbed his cheek on her back and learned that way her sorrow, the roots of it; its wide trunk and intricate branches. . . . [H]e would tolerate no peace until he had touched every ridge and leaf of it with his mouth, none of which Sethe could feel because her back skin had been dead for years. What she knew was that the responsibility for her breasts, at last, was in somebody else's hands.
>
> Would there be a little space, she wondered, a little time, some way to . . . just stand there a minute or two, . . . relieved of the weight of her breasts . . . and feel the hurt her back ought to. Trust things and remember things because the last of the Sweet Home men was there to catch her if she sank? (17-18)

On Sethe's back, the extreme of a patriarchal symbolic order "recast . . . in the terms of cultural domination" (Abel 187), a "hieroglyphics of the flesh" (Spillers 67); on her front, the locus of a maternal system of relations based on presence and connection: Paul D, flexible man, "reads" both stories through touch, quickly becoming a participant in Sethe's discourse of bodily connection. Implicit in the space Paul D's kind body protects is the possibility of yet a third relational system: Sethe thinks that with him there she might feel safe enough to "go inside," "feel the hurt her back ought to," and thus replace the outside language the slave owners imprinted on her body with an inner language of articulate memory; she might be able to tell her story (46, 18). But the potential for reclaiming her past along with its pain is not realized till Paul D re-creates this holding space in the last scene, enabling Sethe to move into the position of narrating subject from a base in physical intimacy. First she has to live out the unspeakable drama of the past that possesses the house—a symbiosis with her daughter that would only have been appropriate eighteen years before, when Beloved was a nursling in body as well as in spirit.

WHO IS BELOVED?

In part 2, Sethe lives out the dream of sustaining her ghostly daughter with her own substance—a nursing fantasy writ large. On the personal level, Beloved is the nursing baby that Sethe killed. But in the social dimension that always doubles the personal in *Beloved,* the ghost represents—as the generic name Beloved suggests—all the loved ones lost through slavery, beginning with the Africans who died on the slave ships. In one sense, then, the pain that haunts Sethe's house is nothing special: "Not a house in the country ain't packed to its rafters with some dead Negro's grief" (5). Accordingly, Beloved's message means one thing to those within the family circle and another thing altogether to those who listen from outside the house, from the vantage point of the community.[11] Morrison introduces the conversation of Sethe, Beloved, and Denver that takes up most of part 2 as "unspeakable thoughts, unspoken" (199): in its drive toward unity, the mother-daughter dialogue wipes out all the positions of separation necessary to language, and it is in this sense "unspeakable." But Stamp Paid, who listens from outside, from social ground, hears in Beloved's speech a whole chorus of "the black and angry dead," a communal "roaring" that is "unspeakable" because the accumulated sufferings under slavery overwhelm the expressive possibilities of ordinary discourse (198, 181, 199). What cannot be encompassed within the symbolic order continues to haunt it, hovering on the edge of language.

Beloved herself ends up outside social discourse, wandering, after the narrative's conclusion, in a limbo where she is "[d]isremembered and unaccounted for" (274). Her position in the epilogue is symmetrical with that of the "Sixty Million and more" of Morrison's epigraph. Having perished on the slave ships midway between a place in African history and a place in the history of American slavery, these lost souls never made it into any text. Lost still, they remain stranded in the epigraph, where their human features are erased beneath a number; they are quantified in death, as they had been in life by a property system that measured wealth in terms of a body count. Morrison's "and more" indicates the residue left over, left out, unaccounted for by any text—like Beloved at the end. Denver gestures toward the larger dimension of Beloved's identity when she responds to Paul D's question "You think [the ghost] sure 'nough your sister?" with an echo of the epigraph: "At times. At times I think she was—more" (266).

Morrison is unwilling, apparently, to leave the historical parallel at the level of suggestion. She links Beloved to the "Sixty Million and more" by joining her spirit to the body of a woman who died on one of the slave ships. But first, in a monologue that comes out of nowhere, Beloved gives an account of slave ship experience:

> I am always crouching the man on my face is dead . . . in the beginning the women are away from the men and the men are away from the women
>
> storms rock us and mix the men into the women and the women into the men that is when I begin to be on the back of the man for a long time I see only his neck and his wide shoulders above me . . . he locks his eyes and dies on my face . . . the others do not know that he is dead. (211-12)

Since Morrison does not identify these scattered perceptions as observations of life on a slave ship or tell how Beloved came to be there or give any coordinates of time and place, readers are baffled: they have no idea where they are. Their confusion thus imitates the disorientation of the Africans who were thrown into the slave ships without explanation, suspended without boundaries in time and space, "in movement across the Atlantic but . . . also nowhere at all . . . inasmuch as . . . the captive[s] . . . did not know where [they were]." The fragmented syntax and absence of punctuation rob the reader of known demarcations, creating a linguistic equivalent of the Africans' loss of differentiation in an "oceanic" space that "unmade" cultural identities and erased even the lines between male and female, living and dead (Spillers 72).

Readers who try to understand these unsettling images as metaphors for Beloved's passage from death to life can find a basis for doing so in the African American narrative tradition, which pictures the Middle Passage as a journey toward a horrific rebirth. (Robert Hayden calls the Middle Passage a "voyage through death to life upon these shores" [48, 54]; Richard Wright remarks, "We millions of black folk who live in this land were born into Western civilization of a weird and paradoxical birth" [12].) The nightmare collage of bodies piled on bodies in the slave ship, where it is hard to tell the living from the dead, would then figure Beloved's difficulty in discerning, in her transitional state, whether she is alive or dead, traveling toward death or toward life. But Morrison everywhere demands that readers confront the horrors of slavery "in the flesh" rather than at the comfortable distance of metaphor (qtd. in Darling 5). "I wanted that haunting not to be really a suggestion of being bedeviled by the past," she comments, "but to have it be incarnate" (qtd. in Rothstein). What at first appears symbolic becomes actual in a characteristic collapse of metaphor into literal reality—a slippage that accompanies the central materialization of the novel, Beloved's embodiment. Scattered through Beloved's monologue are fragments that form the following sequence. Beloved becomes attached to the face of a woman actually on the slave ships, follows the woman's body into the sea after the sailors throw it overboard, and "joins" with it: the woman's "face comes through the water . . . her face is mine . . . I have to have my face . . . she knows I want to join she chews and swallows me I am gone now I am her face" (211-13).[12] Beloved returns, then, in the body of one of the original "disappeared," and all her gestures are shadowed by a larger historical outline. Or, as she herself sees it, "All of it is now   it is always now": the unnumbered losses of slavery are collected in Beloved, in a temporal space outside the linear time of history (210).[13]

But Beloved is also the one-year-old baby that Sethe killed. Morrison skillfully exploits the parallels between a spirit in search of a body and a preoedipal child who desires a merger with her mother. To both, the boundaries between persons are permeable, permitting a "join," and both project this identity confusion as a dialectic of faces. As disembodied spirit, Beloved says, "I need to find a place to be," with the words "to be" taking on all the urgency of their literal meaning. Neither her language nor her need to find a support for her existence changes, however, when it is her mother's face that she needs: "I need to find a place to be . . . [Sethe's] smiling face is the place for me" (213). The ghost's insistence on becoming embodied blends, in Morrison's song of desire, with the preverbal child's dependence on the maternal face as a mirror of her own existence.[14]

Beloved wants from words the verbal equivalent of a face that reflects her exactly as she is, reassuring her of her own existence and of her identity with her mother. In the mother-daughter dialogue that follows her monologue, language bends to Beloved's desire. While a spoken dialogue (ideally) moves toward something new, with the difference voiced by one speaker moving the other speaker away from his or her original position, the dialogue among the three women imitates a mother-infant dialectic: it is motivated not by difference but by the desire to ascertain that the other is there and that the other is the same. It "moves" only toward the stasis of interreflecting mirrors, ending in identical statements wherein like mirrors like:

> You are mine
> You are mine
> You are mine. (217)

What happens to language here reflects what happens in the female family circle, as Sethe (and Denver, for a time) is persuaded by Beloved's preoedipal understanding that the mother is an extension of the self: "I am not separate from her   there is no place where I stop" (210). Punctuation disappears, leaving the sentence of each participant open to the sentence of the next speaker, and the personal pronouns *I* and *you* move toward each other, losing their difference first to become interchangeable and then to mesh in the possessive *mine*. Initially, some difference remains. Sethe and Denver say:

> You are my sister
> You are my daughter

to which Beloved responds:

> You are my face; you are me. (216)

In Sethe's and Denver's lines, normative language reflects normative family life. Separate pronouns correspond to the separate positions of family members who are connected only in the circumscribed ways authorized by conventional kinship structures. Beloved's statement, though, overthrows the classifications that locate persons in cultural space, insisting on a closer relationship than either language or family law allows: "you are me."

"You are my face; I am you. Why did you leave me who am you?" With this line, Beloved completes the limited and stubborn logic of the preoedipal: if I am you, there is no leeway for separation; you *cannot* leave me. In the lines

> I have your milk . . .
> I brought your milk

the nursing connection erodes the distinctions of the symbolic by making the boundary between "you" and "me" soluble (216). Is the milk that the baby drinks part of the baby or part of the mother? Does the "I" in "I have your milk" refer to Sethe, who might be saying that she "has" (is carrying) Beloved's milk, or to Beloved, who could just as well be the "I" who speaks, saying that she "has" Sethe's milk inside her? The dedifferentiation of possessive pronouns dramatizes the impossibility of separating what belongs to the one body from what belongs to the other when the two are joined by the nipple or, rather, by the milk that flows between them, blurring borders.

Nursing serves as a figure for the totality and exclusivity of mother-daughter fusion: "Nobody will ever get my milk no more except my own children," says Sethe, turning inward, and Beloved completes the circle, "lapping devotion like cream" (200, 243). Since Beloved has moved Paul D out and thus demolished the shadowy oedipal triangle ("the three shadows [who] held hands" [47, 49]) that threatened her hold on her mother, no father figure diverts Sethe's attention from her baby, and no "paternal signifier" points Beloved toward a larger symbolic order. She gets to live out the preoedipal wish "to be the exclusive desire of the mother" (Lacan, "Les formations" 14; qtd. in Rose 38).

The nursing paradigm does not work as the governing principle of family life, though. "Beloved . . . never got enough of anything: lullabies, new stitches, the bottom of the cake bowl, the top of the milk. . . . [W]hen Sethe ran out of things to give her, Beloved invented desire" (240). As preverbal infant, Beloved has not accepted the law of symbolic substitutions with which Freud's grandson made his peace, so no partial gift will do. She wants a total union with the mother, to have her and to be her. The text literalizes a nursing baby's fantasy of oral greed consuming the breast, the mother, and all (Klein 200–01): Sethe wastes away while Beloved becomes "bigger, plumper by the day" (239).[15] This drama of oral incorporation is also appropriate to Beloved's role as the past that sucks up all Sethe's energies, leaving nothing for "a life" with a present and future (46).

"You are mine" is of course what the slave owners said, and as in the larger social order, the disregard of the other as subject, the appropriation of the other to one's own desires, leads to violence. Although now Beloved's disregard of limits eats up Sethe's life, the logic of "You are mine" originally permitted Sethe to exercise life-or-death rights over the children she conceived as "parts of her" (163).

A MATERNAL SYMBOLIC

It is Denver, Sethe's surviving daughter, who in part 3 initiates the breakup of this self-consuming mother-child circle. Impelled by the need to get food for her starving mother, she moves into the larger community, but the search for food is aligned with her own "hunger" for learning. Denver joins a social order of language and exchange that both feeds her and teaches her to read. Morrison thus rewrites the entry into the symbolic in terms that retain the oral and maternal, challenging the orthodox psychoanalytic opposition between a maternal order of nurturing and a paternal order of abstract signification.

From the beginning, Denver's development reverses Lacan's maturational sequence: what Morrison explicitly calls Denver's "original hunger" is not for the mother's body but for words (118, 121). At the age of seven, after a year of reading lessons, Denver abandons language to avoid learning the truth about her mother's murder of her sister. She becomes deaf and dumb for two years, "cut off by an answer she could not bear to hear." Since the period of silence follows the period of verbal exchange, Denver's nostalgia focuses not on a past of mute connection with the mother's body but on a time of verbal *jouissance*—delight in "the capital *w*, the little *i*, the beauty of the letters in her name, the deeply mournful sentences from the Bible Lady Jones used as a textbook" (103, 102). Not for Denver the normal progress from oral to verbal, from the breast that fills the baby's mouth to verbal substitutes that never quite do so and always leave something to be desired. Instead, words give Denver the pleasures of the mouth, as the conflation of learning with eating implies: "sentences roll[ed] out like pie dough"; Lady Jones "watched her eat up a page, a rule, a figure" (121, 247).

What causes Denver to give up nourishing words for the hunger of not speaking? As a young girl, she lives out the unspeakable, as if to keep her mother's silence intact by locking it up in her body. Her empty ear and empty mouth reproduce in a corporeal language the empty place at the center of the text where her mother's story of the infanticide should be. In Freud's model of hysterical conversion, the symptom enacts the content of a repressed desire; here the paralysis of ear and throat represents not Denver's desire—her own primal hunger is for words—but her mother's wish that the story remain unspoken, the act unnamed, the memory repressed. Denver in effect closes herself up in her mother's silence. At the same time, she gives up her initial indifference to the ghost and begins to "fix [her concentration] on the baby ghost" (103). The complement of her mother's silence is the concrete presence of Beloved, the literalization of what Sethe refuses to abstract into words. When Denver goes "deaf rather than hear the answer, and [keeps] watch for the baby and [withdraws] from everything else" (105), she is retreating into her mother's world, making the rejection of speech and the obsession with the unnamed her own.

The paralysis of Denver's development shows how urgent is the need for a story that will make sense of the baby's death, mark the baby's disappearance, and lay her and the past she represents to rest. Even after Denver returns to speech and hearing, she lacks the narrative context to deal with the baby's death on a conscious level, so she processes it unconsciously in "monstrous and unmanageable dreams" about her mother: "She cut my head off every night" (103, 206). The unconscious, notorious for repetition without resolution, endlessly plays out dream derivatives of the repressed signifier. Meanwhile, the nonsignifying word *thing* marks the gap left by the signifier repressed from conscious thought: "Certain odd and terrifying feelings about her mother were collecting around the thing that leapt up inside her" in response to questions about her mother. Freud remarks that the unconscious operates by means of "thing presentation" rather than "word presentation" ("Unconscious" 201). In Denver's idiom the unconscious marker "thing" fills the gap where conscious significance fails. It represents something in her own unconscious: "The thing that leapt up *in her* . . . was a thing that had been lying there all along" (102; my emphasis). Sethe's inability to confront and articulate her action—she hears primary process noises rather than conscious sequential thought when she tries to tell Paul D about the baby's death—results in the unsignified "thing" being lodged like a lump, undigestible and unsignifiable, in her child's unconscious, where it generates the repeated dream of decapitation.[16]

When Denver tries to leave the haunted house to get food for her mother and Beloved, she finds herself imprisoned within her mother's time—a time that, clinging to places, is always happening again: "Out there . . . were places in which things so bad had happened that when you went near them it would happen again. . . . Denver stood on the porch . . . and couldn't leave it." She crosses the threshold into social discourse only when the voice of Baby Suggs, the ancestor, speaks out: "You mean I never told you . . . nothing about how come I walk the way I do and about your mother's feet, not to speak of her back? I never told you all that? Is that why you can't walk down the steps?" (243–44). To a child afraid to step out into the world, the particulars of how that world damaged her grandmother and mother are hardly comforting. It is the speech act itself, the voice of the grandmother putting the past where it belongs, into oral history, that frees Denver to enter the present.

After Denver leaves the closed family circle, she goes straight to the place of verbal nurturance, the house of Lady Jones, the woman who had taught her to read some ten years earlier. However belatedly (she is by now eighteen), she takes the crucial step from the imaginary of mother-daughter fusions to the symbolic order of language and society. But this step does not entail abandoning maternal intimacy. "Oh, baby," says Lady Jones when Denver tells her about her starving mother. "[I]t was the word 'baby,' said softly and with such kindness, that inaugurated her life in the world as a woman." Lady Jones's maternal language indicates that Denver is a child of the community, not just of her mother: "Everybody's child was in that face." She bakes raisin loaves for Denver while teaching her to read Bible verses, and "all through the spring, names appeared near or in gifts of food" (248, 246, 250, 249). Morrison thus confounds the distinction between words and good things to eat, between oral and verbal pleasures.

Denver moves into the symbolic by leaving one nurturing maternal circle for another, but there is a difference. The community, which operates as a network of mutual aid (originally, the network helped slaves escape), takes offense at Sethe's claim of maternal self-sufficiency—that "she had milk enough for all"—and demands instead a reciprocal nurturing. "To belong to a community of other free Negroes [is] to love and be loved by them, . . . [to] feed and be fed." Denver enters into this nurturing reciprocity, "pay[ing] a thank you for half a pie," "paying" for help by telling her story (100, 177, 252, 253).

Acts of maternal care also enable Sethe to move into an order of linguistic exchange. After the community of women intervenes and routs Beloved,[17] Sethe retreats into the keeping room in an imitation of Baby Suggs, who withdrew there to die. "I think I've lost my mother," Denver tells Paul D: the loss of Beloved entails the loss of Sethe, who is still attached to her baby (266). When Paul D offers to bathe her, taking the restorative maternal role once occupied by Baby Suggs (93, 98), Sethe can only protest that she is "nothing . . . now. . . . Nothing left to bathe." Then a consciousness of her body begins to emerge: "Will he [bathe her] in sections? First her face, then her hands, her thighs, her feet, her back? Ending with her exhausted breasts? And if he bathes her in sections, will the parts hold?" (272). Gone is her self-image as maternal lifegiver (her breasts are "exhausted" now, after the ordeal of sustaining Beloved); she puts herself together anew, imitating in her fear of fragmentation the first infantile self-image, the body in pieces, that precedes the cohesion of the mirror stage and motor control (Lacan, "Mirror Stage" 4). After the body, the spirit revives. Suddenly freed from the "serious work of beating back the past," Sethe lets all the losses she has repressed flood into her mind: "That she called, but Howard and Buglar walked on down the railroad track and couldn't hear her; that Amy was scared to stay with her because her . . . back looked so bad; that her ma'am had hurt her feelings and she couldn't find her hat anywhere." Having confronted her grief consciously, Sethe quickly moves to put loss into words: "She left me" (73, 272). The act of acknowledging absence and saying "she" slips Beloved off, detaches her from the maternal body that has held the nursing connection static, entombed, and puts a signifier there, where the child's body had been.

In thus shifting from a subjectivity embedded in maternal connection to a subjectivity based on the separate positions of the linguistic register (*she* and *me*), Sethe indeed follows the Lacanian schema, in which taking the position of speaking subject requires a repudiation of continuity with the mother's body (or, for Sethe, with the nursing infant's body). But Morrison revises Lacan here, too, softening his opposition between bodily communion and the abstractions of verbal exchange: "She was my best thing," Sethe says of her lost daughter. Paul D "leans over and takes her hand. With the other he touches her face. 'You your best thing, Sethe. You are.' His holding fingers are holding hers."

Sethe answers, "Me? Me?" expressing surprise and disbelief, perhaps, but also recognizing herself in the first-person singular (272-73).[18] Replacing Lacan's vision of the move into language—a move away from bodies touching to the compensations of abstract signifiers—Morrison makes physical contact the necessary support for Sethe's full acceptance of the separate subjectivity required by language systems.[19]

Though Paul D thus encircles Sethe physically, his intent is not to subsume her. The words "You are," standing alone, replace "You are mine," the hallmark of invasive identification in the mother-daughter dialogue. Paul D "wants to put his story next to hers"; the two stories may complement and complete each other (each person having lived out the missing fragment of the other's slave narrative), but they will lie "next to" each other—each whole, circumscribed, with its own beginning, middle, and end (273).[20] Difference can emerge within the space of relationship; a dialogue between self and other can replace the circular mother-daughter dialectic between same and same.

The hope at the end of the novel is that Sethe, having recognized herself as subject, will narrate the mother-daughter story and invent a language that can encompass the desperation of the slave mother who killed her daughter. Or will she? The heterosexual resolution, the enclosure of the mother in the symbolic, leaves out the preoedipal daughter, who wanders lost in the epilogue. She will not be remembered because "nobody anywhere knew her name"; she is "[d]isremembered and unaccounted for" because "they couldn't remember or repeat a single thing she said, and began to believe that . . . she hadn't said anything at all. So, in the end, they forgot her too." Outcast both as victim of slavery whose death is unspeakable and as preverbal infant who has not made her way into the symbolic order, Beloved remains outside language and therefore outside narrative memory. Her story is "not a story to pass on" (274-75). Of course, the sentence is ambiguous: Beloved's story, too terrible to find resolution in the logic of narrative, cannot be passed on from teller to teller, but it also cannot "pass on," or die (35). It continues to haunt the borders of a symbolic order that excludes it.[21]

NOTES

1. Margaret Homans's notion of literalization enabled me to see how Morrison's metaphors work. "Literalization," which "occurs when some piece of overtly figurative language, a similie or an extended or conspicuous metaphor, is translated into an actual event or circumstance," is in Homans's opinion a characteristic of women's writing (30). Homans uses Nancy Chodorow's theory to challenge Lacan: because men and women develop differently, women might not polarize body and word, signifier and absent referent, to the extent that men do; thus women writers are less likely to privilege the figurative over the literal and more likely to conceive of presence as commensurate with representation (14).
2. As a white middle-class feminist who practices psychoanalytic theory, I come to this project burdened not only by the usual guilt about my own implication in the racist

structures that Morrison uncovers but also by doubts about the suitability of psychoanalytic theory for analyzing an African American text. Psychoanalytic theory is, after all, based on assumptions about family and language grounded in Western European patriarchal culture, while Morrison's novel comes out of African and African American oral and written narrative traditions (see Christian, Holloway, Page, Sale, Sitter). Elizabeth Abel's essay "Race, Class, and Psychoanalysis?" performs an important service to feminist psychoanalysis by canvassing the difficulties of applying psychoanalysis to texts produced by other cultures and the possibilities for modifying object-relations theory and Lacanian theory to include "the roles of race and class in a diversified construction of subjectivity" (184). Reading Abel's essay both focused the limitations of my position as white middle-class female reader of an African American woman's text and gave me the courage to "[k]now it, and go on out the yard" (Morrison 244)—to go on in spite of recognizing the hazards of venturing into a cultural space not my own.

3. Hazel Carby points out that "slave narratives by women, about women, could mobilize the narrative forms of adventure and heroism normally constituted within ideologies of male sexuality" (38). Lucy Delaney, for instance, describes her mother's struggle to free her children in epic terms: "She had girded up her loins for the fight"; "others would have flinched before the obstacles which confronted her, but undauntedly she pursued her way, until my freedom was established" (35, 45). See also Claudia Tate's discussion of the idealized slave mother (the grandmother) in Jacobs's narrative (109–10).

4. Sethe may hesitate to tell her story in part because the language available to her—a language structured by the logic of bipolar oppositions—cannot readily encompass the contradictions of motherhood under slavery. Had she access to it, Sethe would find in the discourse of actual slave mothers a language better suited to a world where "safe" from slavery can only mean "dead." Harriet Jacobs, writing from within the paradoxes of "the peculiar institution," indeed conflates maternal love and infanticide: "I would rather see [my children] killed than have them given up to [the slaveholder's] power"; "death is better than slavery" (80, 62).

   Since Sethe cannot find a language of "motherlove" (132), her story remains in the rhetoric of the masters. As Mae Henderson points out, "The first [and, I would add, the only] full representation of the events surrounding the infanticide [is] figured from a collective white/male perspective, represented by schoolteacher and the sheriff" (78; see Morrison 149–51). Sethe's story is caught up in "the dominant metaphors of the master('s) narrative—wildness, cannibalism, animality, destructiveness" (Henderson 79).

5. Readers learn about the infanticide a bit at a time from different perspectives, a technique that prevents them from making simple judgments. Maggie Sale shows that Morrison's narrative strategy forces readers to see the event from multiple perspectives and to recognize that each version depends as much on the needs of the narrator and the listener as on the historical "facts." The lack of a single definitive account "challenges readers to examine their own responses" both to Sethe's act and to the circumstances that force her to it (44).

   Stephanie Demetrakopoulos, comparing Sethe and Beloved to mythic counterparts, remarks that "Sethe attempts to return the babies to perhaps a collective mother body, to devour them back into the security of womb/tomb death . . . as the ultimate act of protection" (52). Demetrakopoulos focuses on the destructive effects of Sethe's mothering, especially on her own growth as an individual.

6. Lacan returns to the *fort-da* anecdote in *Four Fundamental Concepts* only to contradict his earlier reading. Focusing on the spool instead of the accompanying words, Lacan says that it represents an *object petit a*—an object that is only ambiguously detached from the subject. Because Ernst holds the string that can pull back the spool, "it is a small part of the subject that detaches itself from him, while still remaining his, still retained" (62). In this later text, then, Lacan locates the *fort-da* episode in a zone intermediate between mother-child fusions and the clear-cut separations of the symbolic order instead of naming it, as he did earlier, "the moment . . . in which the child is born into language" ("Function" 104). Kaja Silverman and Elisabeth Bronfen read this second Lacanian interpretation as a parable for the eclipse the subject undergoes on entering language in *Four Fundamental Concepts* the spool stands for Ernst himself, and the game rehearses his absence; he plays out the fading of the subject as, entering the order of representation, he is replaced by a signifier (Silverman 168–71; Bronfen 27). Bronfen gives a comprehensive and valuable account of various theorists' uses of the *fort-da* episode (15–38), and she adds a new dimension to standard interpretations by considering all the implications of the game's enactment of death (including Freud's use of the anecdote to compensate for the death of Sophie—his daughter and Ernst's mother—during the writing of *Beyond the Pleasure Principle*).
7. Judith Butler helpfully summarizes the argument of Nicolas Abraham and Maria Torok, who distinguish between the work of mourning, which displaces libido onto words that "both signify and displace [the lost] object," and "incorporation," a refusal of loss in which one preserves the lost object as a (fantasized) part of one's own body (68). In *Black Sun* Julia Kristeva also identifies the melancholic's problem as a failure to transfer libido from the bodily connection with the mother to words; she or he maintains instead an undifferentiated sense of continuity with the maternal body.
8. Characteristically, Sethe can articulate only the part of the abuse connected with her maternal function: "[T]hey took my milk," she repeats (16, 17). In Anne Goldman's view, "Schoolteacher orders [Sethe's milk] to be appropriated" because, as the one product of her labor that doesn't belong to the masters, it is the "signifier of an identity, a subjectivity, independent of white authorities" (324). Mae Henderson understands "the theft of her 'mother's milk'" as "the expropriation of [Sethe's] future—her ability to nurture and ensure the survival of the future embodied in the next generation. . . . Sethe must discover some way of regaining control of her story, her body, her progeny, her milk, her ability to nurture the future" (71). Barbara Christian points out that the nephews "milk" Sethe at the behest of schoolteacher, who wants to make the experiment as part of his "scientific observation" of slaves. Christian aligns schoolteacher, who measures slaves' body parts and observes their bodily functions with "apparently neutral" scientific curiosity, with the nineteenth-century white American intellectuals who buttressed slavery with various "scientific" treatises on the physiology of African Americans (337–38).
9. Hortense Spillers's essay helped me understand slavery as a system of domination that mandated slaves' "absence from a subject position" while imprinting the terms of their subjugation on their bodies (67).

   By emphasizing the importance of language to a "used-to-be-slave woman," Morrison takes up a central theme of slave narratives (45). "[O]nly by grasping the word" could slaves, who were considered "silently laboring brutes," take part in speech acts that would help them achieve selfhood and give shape to their subjective reality (Baker 243, 245; see also Gates xxiii–xxxi).

Mae Henderson observes, "[B]ecause it is her back (symbolizing the *presence* of her *past*) that is marked, Sethe has only been able to read herself through the gaze of others. The challenge for Sethe is to learn to read herself—that is, to configure the history of her body's text. . . . Sethe must learn how to link these traces (marks of her passage through slavery) to the construction of a personal and historical discourse" (69).

10. Cathy Caruth summarizes theories of trauma and memory that can explain not only Sethe's inability to put the baby's death into narrative form but also the problems that other characters (notably Paul D and Baby Suggs) have in integrating the trauma of slavery. In the syndrome known was posttraumatic stress disorder, overwhelming events of the past "repeatedly possess, in intrusive images and thoughts, the one who has lived through them" (418). The original event escaped understanding even as it was happening because it could not "be placed within the schemes of prior knowledge. . . . Not having been fully integrated as it occurred, the event cannot become . . . a 'narrative memory' that is integrated into a completed story of the past" (418–19). Morrison's narrative form brilliantly recaptures traumatic memory: the past comes back in bits—a fragment here, a fragment there. Since the "truth" of the experience "may reside not only in its brutal facts, but also in the way that their occurrence defies simple comprehension," Morrison's text needs this pointillism, this fragmentation, to remain true both to the events and to "their affront to understanding" (Caruth 418–20). Philip Page shows how the circularity and fragmentation of Morrison's narrative structure parallel the indirect, piecemeal remembering of the characters. Gayle Greene also analyzes the way memory functions in *Beloved.*
11. For a summary of Beloved's multiple relations to language and for a different view of the female family circle, see my *Reconstructing Desire* (195–200).
12. Deborah Horvitz thinks that it is Sethe's mother who speaks in these passages, wanting to "join" with the body of her own mother (162–63). Others have speculated that the face Beloved claims as her own is that of Sethe's mother, who indeed came over on the slave ships (though she, of course, survived the voyage). These interpretations are useful in suggesting the range of what Beloved may represent: a whole line of daughters desperately wanting to "join" with the mothers wrenched away from them by slavery.
13. Linda Anderson describes Morrison's "exploration of history's absences, of how what is unwritten and unremembered can come back to haunt us" (137). Karla Holloway points out that these absences are not accidental, that "the victim's own chronicles of these events were systematically submerged, ignored, mistrusted, or superseded by 'historians' of the era. This novel positions the consequences of black invisibility in both the records of slavery and the record-keeping as a situation of primary spiritual significance" (516–17).
14. Morrison's account is true to a one-year-old's way of thinking, according to D. W. Winnicott. A baby looking into its mother's face imagines that it sees there the same thing its mother is looking at: its own face. The baby's still precarious sense of existence depends on the mother's mirroring face ("Mirror-Role" 112). Rebecca Ferguson also uses Winnicott's essay to explain Beloved's fixation on her mother's face (117–18). Barbara Mathieson cites Winnicott as support for her claim that Beloved's monologue mirrors the preoedipal child's conviction that its identity and its mother's identity "flow into one another as interchangeably as their faces" (2).
15. Barbara Schapiro discusses the novel's images of orality and the gaze in the context of slavery, pointing out that "the emotional hunger, the obsessive and terrifying

narcissistic fantasies" are not Beloved's alone; instead, they belong to all those denied both mothers and selves by a slave system that "either separates [a mother] from her child or so enervates and depletes her that she has no self with which to confer recognition" (194). Thus when Sethe complains, "There was no nursing milk to call my own," she expresses her own emotional starvation in the absence of her mother, and that emptiness in turn prevents her from adequately reflecting her own daughter Denver (200, 198).

16. Nicolas Abraham cites similar cases, in which an unarticulated secret passes directly from a parent's unconscious to a child's unconscious. The child does not consciously know what the secret is but nevertheless acts it out, driven by a thing lodged in its unconscious that fits in with neither its conscious wishes nor its unconscious fantasies. "What haunts are not the dead, but the gaps left within us by the secrets of others" (75).
17. Missy Dehn Kubitschek identifies yet another maternal discourse in *Beloved:* she reads the women's roar that casts Beloved out as an imitation of "the sounds accompanying birth" (174). Morrison's text replaces the biblical verse, "In the beginning was the Word, . . . and the Word was God" (John 1.1), with the line, "In the beginning there were no words. In the beginning was the sound, and they all knew what that sound sounded like" (259). The women's communal groan recalls women's creation of life, not God's, and overthrows the male authority of the word. Kubitschek's chapter on *Beloved* addresses Sethe's need to change the static conception of motherhood she developed under slavery.
18. As Marianne Hirsch writes, Sethe's "subjectivity . . . can only emerge in and through human interconnection" (198). I differ with Hirsch because she ignores the hiatus in the middle of Sethe's narrative and regards Sethe as a mother who tells her story throughout (6). But Hirsch also says that Sethe's "maternal voice and subjectivity" emerge only in the concluding scene, where her "Me? Me?" implies that "she questions, at least for a moment, the hierarchy of motherhood over selfhood on which her life had rested until that moment" (7).
19. Morrison may have D. W. Winnicott's maternal "holding environment" in mind. Like Morrison, Winnicott pictures development as a joint project of self and other (mother) rather than as a movement toward increasing separation. Only in the presence of the mother can the infant be truly "alone," in Winnicott's terms. That is, the mother's protective presence releases the infant from survival needs and enables it to claim its impulses as authentically its own—hence to catch the first glimpse of an ongoing subjectivity ("Capacity" 34). Just so, Paul D's holding guarantees a space in which Sethe can safely think any thought, feel any feeling, and finally take the leap into a different subjectivity, one grounded in language. Morrison's ideal of heterosexual relations fits the "holding fantasy" that Jessica Benjamin claims women retain from experiencing that early maternal presence: "the wish for a holding other whose presence does not violate one's space but permits the experience of one's own desire, who recognizes it when it emerges of itself" (96).
20. Deborah Sitter describes the dialogic relation between Paul D's story and Sethe's story, showing how Paul D comes to a new definition of manhood. Kate Cummings also traces Paul D's development from a definition of masculinity that enslaves him to the white slave master who named him to an identification with Sixo's different model of manhood—a shift that culminates in his "taking on the job of mothering" Sethe. Cummings lists mothering as one of three modes of resistance, along with menacing and naming: "Mothering provides the final and most fundamental opposition,

for through it the subject is reconstituted and the body reborn in the flesh" (563, 564).

21. I am grateful for the generous help of Elizabeth Abel in cutting this essay down to size; I also thank Frances Restuccia and John Swift for readings that enabled me to make new connections and Richard Yarborough for sharing his knowledge of Morrison's works.

WORKS CITED

Abel, Elizabeth. "Race, Class, and Psychoanalysis? Opening Questions." *Conflicts in Feminism.* Ed. Marianne Hirsch and Evelyn Fox Keller. New York: Routledge, 1990. 184-204.

Abraham, Nicolas. "Notes on the Phantom: A Complement to Freud's Metapsychology." *The Trial(s) of Psychoanalysis.* Ed. Françoise Meltzer. Chicago: U of Chicago P, 1987. 75-80.

Abraham, Nicolas, and Maria Torok. "Introjection—Incorporation: Mourning or Melancholia." *Psychoanalysis in France.* Ed. Serge Lebovici and Daniel Widlocher. New York: International UP, 1980. 3-16.

Anderson, Linda. "The Re-imagining of History in Contemporary Women's Fiction." *Plotting Change.* Ed. Anderson. London: Arnold, 1990. 129-41.

Baker, Houston A., Jr. "Autobiographical Acts and the Voice of the Southern Slave." Davis and Gates 242-61.

Benjamin, Jessica. "A Desire of One's Own: Psychoanalytic Feminism and Intersubjective Space." *Feminist Studies/Critical Studies.* Ed. Teresa de Lauretis. Bloomington: Indiana UP, 1986. 78-101.

Bronfen, Elisabeth. *Over Her Dead Body: Death, Femininity, and the Aesthetic.* New York: Routledge, 1992.

Butler, Judith. *Gender Trouble: Feminism and the Subversion of Identity.* London: Routledge, 1990.

Carby, Hazel. *Reconstructing Womanhood: The Emergence of the Afro-American Woman Novelist.* New York: Oxford UP, 1987.

Caruth, Cathy. Introduction. *Psychoanalysis, Culture and Trauma: II.* Spec. issue of *American Imago* 48 (1991): 417-24.

Christian, Barbara. "'Somebody Forgot to Tell Somebody Something': African-American Women's Historical Novels." *Wild Women in the Whirlwind: Afra-American Culture and the Contemporary Literary Renaissance.* Ed. Joanne M. Braxton and Andrée Nicola McLaughlin. New Brunswick: Rutgers UP, 1990. 326-41.

Cummings, Kate. "Reclaiming the Mother('s) Tongue: *Beloved, Ceremony, Mothers and Shadows.*" *College English* 52 (1990): 552-69.

Darling, Marsha. "In the Realm of Responsibility: A Conversation with Toni Morrison." *Womens' Review of Books* Mar. 1988: 5-6.

Davis, Charles T., and Henry Louis Gates, Jr., eds. *The Slave's Narrative.* New York: Oxford UP, 1985.

Delaney, Lucy. *From the Darkness Cometh the Light; or, Struggles for Freedom.* C. 1891. *Six Women's Slave Narratives.* Schomburg Library of Nineteenth-Century Black Women Writers. New York: Oxford UP, 1988. 1-64.

Demetrakopoulos, Stephanie. "Maternal Bonds as Devourers of Women's Individuation in Toni Morrison's *Beloved.*" *African American Review* 26.1 (1992): 51-60.

Ferguson, Rebecca. "History, Memory and Language in Toni Morrison's *Beloved*." *Feminist Criticism: Theory and Practice.* Toronto: U of Toronto P, 1991. 109-27.

Freud, Sigmund. *Beyond the Pleasure Principle.* Trans. James Strachey. New York: Norton, 1961.

———. "The Unconscious." 1915. *The Standard Edition of the Complete Psychological Works of Sigmund Freud.* Ed. and trans. James Strachey. Vol. 14. London: Hogarth, 1953-74. 159-215. 24 vols.

Gates, Henry Louis, Jr. "Introduction: The Language of Slavery." Davis and Gates xi-xxxiv.

Goldman, Anne. "'I Made the Ink': (Literary) Production and Reproduction in *Dessa Rose* and *Beloved*." *Feminist Studies* 16 (1990): 313-30.

Greene, Gayle. "Feminist Fictions and the Uses of Memory." *Signs* 16 (1990): 1-32.

Hayden, Robert. "Middle Passage." *Collected Works.* New York: Liveright, 1985. 48-54.

Henderson, Mae. "Toni Morrison's *Beloved*: Re-membering the Body as Historical Text." *Comparative American Identities: Race, Sex, and Nationality in the Modern Text.* Ed. Hortense Spillers. London: Routledge, 1991. 62-86.

Hirsch, Marianne. *The Mother-Daughter Plot: Narrative, Psychoanalysis, Feminism.* Bloomington: Indiana UP, 1989.

Holloway, Karla. "*Beloved:* A Spiritual." *Callaloo* 13 (1990): 516-25.

Homans, Margaret. *Bearing the Word: Language and Female Experience in Nineteenth-Century Women's Writing.* Chicago: U of Chicago P, 1986.

Horvitz, Deborah. "Nameless Ghosts: Possession and Dispossession in *Beloved*." *Studies in American Fiction* 17 (1989): 157-67.

Jacobs, Harriet. *Incidents in the Life of a Slave Girl.* Cambridge: Harvard UP, 1987.

Klein, Melanie. "Some Theoretical Conclusions regarding the Emotional Life of the Infant." *Developments in Psycho-analysis.* Ed. Klein et al. London: Hogarth, 1952. 198-236.

Kristeva, Julia. *Black Sun.* Trans. Leon Roudiez. New York: Columbia UP, 1989.

Kubitschek, Missy Dehn. *Claiming the Heritage: African-American Women Novelists and History.* Jackson: U of Mississippi P, 1991.

Lacan, Jacques. Ecrits: *A Selection.* Trans. Alan Sheridan. New York: Norton, 1981.

———. "Les formations de l'inconscient." *Bulletin de psychologie* 2 (1957-58): 1-15.

———. *The Four Fundamental Concepts of Psychoanalysis.* 1973. Trans. Alan Sheridan. New York: Norton, 1981.

———. "The Function and Field of Speech and Language in Psychoanalysis." 1953. Lacan, Ecrits 30-113.

———. "The Mirror Stage as Formative of the Function of the I." Lacan, Ecrits 1-7.

Mathieson, Barbara O. "Memory and Mother Love in Morrison's *Beloved*." *American Imago* 47 (1990): 1-21.

Morrison, Toni. *Beloved.* New York: Knopf, 1987.

Muller, John. "Language, Psychosis, and the Subject in Lacan." *Interpreting Lacan.* Ed. Joseph Smith and William Kerrigan. New Haven: Yale UP, 1983. 21-32.

Page, Philip. "Circularity in Toni Morrison's *Beloved*." *African American Review* 26.1 (1992): 31-40.

Rose, Jacqueline. "Introduction II." *Feminine Sexuality: Jacques Lacan and the Ecole Freudienne.* Ed. Juliet Mitchell and Rose. New York: Norton, 1982. 27-57.

Rothstein, Mervyn. "Toni Morrison, in Her New Novel, Defends Women." *New York Times* 26 Aug. 1987: C17.

Sale, Maggie. "Call and Response as Critical Method: African-American Oral Traditions and *Beloved*." *African American Review* 26.1 (1992): 41-50.

Schapiro, Barbara. "The Bonds of Love and the Boundaries of Self in Toni Morrison's *Beloved*." *Contemporary Literature* 32 (1991): 194-210.

Silverman, Kaja. *The Subject of Semiotics.* New York: Oxford UP, 1983.
Sitter, Deborah Ayer. "The Making of a Man: Dialogic Meaning in *Beloved.*" *African American Review* 26.1 (1992): 17-30.
Spillers, Hortense. "Mama's Baby, Papa's Maybe: An American Grammar Book." *Diacritics* 17 (1987): 65-81.
Tate, Claudia. "Allegories of Black Female Desire; or, Rereading Nineteenth-Century Sentimental Narratives of Black Female Authority." *Changing Our Own Words.* Ed. Cheryl A. Wall. New Brunswick: Rutgers UP, 1989. 98-126.
Winnicott, D. W. "The Capacity to Be Alone." *The Maturational Processes and the Facilitating Environment.* New York: International UP, 1965. 29-36.
———. "Mirror-Role of Mother and Family in Child Development." *Playing and Reality.* London: Tavistock, 1971. 111-18.
Wright, Richard. *Twelve Million Black Voices.* New York: Thunder's Mouth, 1988.
Wyatt, Jean. *Reconstructing Desire: The Role of the Unconscious in Women's Reading and Writing.* Chapel Hill: U of North Carolina P, 1990.

Daughters Signifyin(g) History: The Example of Toni Morrison's *Beloved*

Ashraf H. A. Rushdy

Despite the dangers of remembering the past, African American artists have insistently based a large part of their aesthetic ideal on precisely that activity. John Edgar Wideman prefaces his novel *Sent For You Yesterday* with this testament: "Past lives in us, through us. Each of us harbors the spirits of people who walked the earth before we did, and those spirits depend on us for continuing existence, just as we depend on their presence to live our lives to the fullest." This insistence on the interdependence of past and present is, moreover, a political act, for it advocates a revisioning of the past as it is filtered through the present. Wideman elsewhere has asked, "What is history except people's imaginary recreation?" Racial memories, he suggests, "exist in the imagination." They are in fact a record of "certain collective experiences" that "have been repeated generation after generation."[1]

As Toni Morrison has said, "If we don't keep in touch with the ancestor . . . we are, in fact, lost." Keeping in touch with the ancestor, she adds, is the work of a reconstructive memory: "Memory (the deliberate act of remembering) is a form of willed creation. It is not an effort to find out the way it really was—that is research. The point is to dwell on the way it appeared and why it appeared in that particular way." This concern with the appearance, with the ideology of transmission, is, though, only part of the overall trajectory of her revisionary project. Eventually her work, she states, must "bear witness and identify that which is useful from the past and that which ought to be discarded."[2] It must, that is, signify on the past and make it palatable for a present politic—eschewing that part of the past which has been constructed out of a denigrative ideology and reconstructing that part which will serve the present.

Morrison is both participant and theorist of this black aesthetic of remembering, and she has recently set out some of the mandates for establishing a form of literary theory that will truly accommodate African American literature—a theory based on an inherited culture, an inherited "history," and the understanding of the ways that any given artistic work negotiates between those cultural/historical worlds it inhabits. Moreover, not only does Morrison, following the line of Pauline Hopkins, delineate the "dormant inmost feelings in that history"; she takes up, delicately yet resolutely, the task of reviving the very figures of that history.[3]

By taking a historical personage—a daughter of a faintly famous African American victim of racist ideology—and constructing her as a hopeful presence in a contemporary setting, Morrison offers an introjection into the fields of revisionist historiography and fiction. She makes articulate a victim of a patriarchal order in order to criticize that order. Yet she portrays an unrelenting hopefulness in that critique. She does not inherit, as Deborah McDowell maintains some writers do, "the orthodoxy of victimage," nor does she reduce her narrative to anything resembling what Henry Louis Gates Jr. has called a "master plot of victim and victimizer."[4] She, like Ralph Ellison, returns to history not to find claims for reparation or reasons for despair, but to find "something subjective, willful, and complexly and compellingly human"—to find, that is, something for her art. She does so, moreover, by doing what Hortense Spillers claims Ishmael Reed does with the discursive field of slavery in his *Flight to Canada:* "construct[ing] and reconstruct[ing] repertoires of usage out of the most painful human/historical experience."[5] In articulating a reconstructive—critical and hopeful—feminist voice within the fields of revisionist historiography and contemporary fiction, what Morrison does is create daughters Signifyin(g) history.

RAISING *BELOVED*: A REQUIEM THAT IS A RESURRECTION

Morrison thought that her most recent book would be the least read of her novels because it would be perceived to be a work dealing with slavery, an institution that is willingly placed under erasure by what she calls a "national amnesia"; "I thought this has got to be the least read of all the books I'd written because it is about something the characters don't want to remember, I don't want to remember, black people don't want to remember, white people don't want to remember." But *Beloved* is not about slavery as an institution; it is "about those *anonymous* people called slaves."[6]

Morrison's sense of ambivalence, of wishing to forget and remember at the same time, is enacted in her attitude to the story and its characters. Speaking about the writing of *Beloved,* she declares her wish to invoke all those people who are "unburied, or at least unceremoniously buried," and go about "properly, artistically, burying them." However, this burial's purpose, it would appear, is to bring them back into "living life." This tension between needing to bury the past as well as needing to revive it, between a necessary remembering and an equally necessary forgetting, exists in both the author and her narrative. We might better understand that tension by attending to the author's construction of the scenes of inspiration leading her to write this novel.

Morrison has said that the idea of *Beloved* was inspired by "two or three little fragments of stories" that she had "heard from different places."[7] The first was the story of Margaret Garner, a slave who in January 1856 escaped from her owner Archibald K. Gaines of Kentucky, crossed the Ohio River, and attempted to find refuge in Cincinnati. She was pursued by Gaines and a posse of officers. They surrounded the house where she, her husband Robert, and their four children were harbored. When the posse battered down the door and rushed in, Robert shot at them and wounded one of the officers before being overpowered. According to Levi Coffen, "At this moment, Margaret Garner, seeing that their hopes of freedom were vain, seized a butcher knife that lay on the table, and with one stroke cut the throat of her little daughter, whom she probably loved the best. She then attempted to take the life of the other children and to kill herself, but she was overpowered and hampered before she could complete her desperate work."[8] Margaret Garner chose death for both herself and her most beloved rather than accept being forced to return to slavery and have her children suffer an institutionalized dehumanization. The story of Margaret Garner was eventually to become the historical analogue of the plot of *Beloved.*[9]

Morrison said that what this story made her realize was that "the best thing that is in us is also the thing that makes us sabotage ourselves" ("Conversation," 585). The story of Margaret Garner stayed with Morrison, representing, albeit unclearly, something about feminine selflessness. It took another story to clarify more precisely what Margaret Garner and her story meant.

Morrison found that story in Camille Billops's *The Harlem Book of the Dead*—an album featuring James Van Der Zee's photographs of Harlem funerals. These were photographs, Morrison has said, that had a "narrative quality." One photograph and its attendant story in particular caught her attention:

> In one picture, there was a young girl lying in a coffin, and he [Van Der Zee] says that she was eighteen years old and she had gone to a party and that she was dancing and suddenly she slumped and they noticed there was blood on her and they said, "What happened to you?" And she said, "I'll tell you tomorrow. I'll tell you tomorrow." That's all she would say. And apparently her ex-boyfriend or somebody who was jealous had come into the party with a gun and a silencer and shot her. And she kept saying, "I'll tell you tomorrow" because she wanted him to get away. And he did, I guess; anyway, she died. ("Conversation," 584)

After reading the narrative of Margaret Garner, Toni Morrison had thought she glimpsed an opaque truth that she had always known, somehow: "But that moment, that decision was a piece, a tail of something that was always around, and it didn't get clear for me until I was thinking of another story."

When Van Der Zee provided that next story, Morrison saw clearly what she'd glimpsed through a darker glass: "Now what made those stories connect, I can't explain, but I do know that, in both instances, something seemed clear to me. A woman loved something other than herself so much. She had placed all of the value of her life in something outside herself. That the woman who killed her children loved her children so much; they were the best part of her and she would not see them sullied" ("Conversation," 584). In 1978, nine years before the publication of *Beloved,* Morrison started attempting to formulate the terms of that tension between remembering and forgetting, burying and reviving. In the Foreword to *The Harlem Book of the Dead* she writes: "The narrative quality, the intimacy, the humanity of his photographs are stunning, and the proof, if any is needed, is in this collection of photographs devoted exclusively to the dead about which one can only say, 'How living are his portraits of the dead.' So living, so 'undead,' that the prestigious writer, Owen Dodson, is stirred to poetry in which life trembles in every metaphor."[10] One of Owen Dodson's "living" poems is on the page facing the picture of the young girl as she lies in her coffin.

If Van Der Zee's photographs give renewed life to the dead, so does Dodson's poetry give renewed voice. Across from a picture of a girl in a coffin resides her living voice, her expression of the safety of death. As early as 1973, Morrison had been concerned with making the dead articulate. When Sula dies, she feels her face smiling: "'Well, I'll be damned,' she thought, 'it didn't even hurt. Wait'll I tell Nell.'"[11]

In 1987, with *Beloved,* Morrison goes further in giving the dead voice, in remembering the forgotten. *Beloved* is, in effect, a requiem that is a resurrection. The most obvious example of this commemoration is Beloved herself, the ghost of Margaret Garner's unnamed child: "So I just imagined the life of a dead girl which was the girl that Margaret Garner killed, the baby girl that she killed. . . . And I call her Beloved so that I can filter all these confrontations and questions that she has in that situation" ("Conversation," 585). Beloved is more than just a character in the novel, though. She is the embodiment of the past that must be remembered in order to be forgotten; she symbolizes what must be reincarnated in order to be buried, properly: "Everybody knew what she was called, but nobody anywhere knew her name. Disremembered and unaccounted for, she cannot be lost because no one is looking for her."[12]

In the end, though, Beloved is not the most important character in Morrison's revisionist strategy. That character is Denver, the other daughter. Morrison's original intent in the novel, she said in 1985, was to develop the narrative of Beloved into the narrative of Denver. First she would imagine the life of the murdered child, "to extend her life, you know, her search, her quest, all the way through as long as I care to go, into the twenties where it switches to this other girl." This "other girl," Denver, is the site of hope in Morrison's novel. She is the daughter of history. Nonetheless, as Morrison emphasizes, even when Denver becomes the focus of the narrative's attention, "Beloved will be there also"

("Conversation," 585). Before turning to the novel, and determining how Morrison inscribes hope into a critical revision of history, let us return briefly to the narrative of Margaret Garner in order to see the history that she revises.

TOWARDS *BELOVED:* MARGARET GARNER

It was sometime in January 1856 that Margaret Garner attempted her escape and killed her daughter. The story and the ensuing court case were reported in the Cincinnati newspapers and reported again in *The Liberator* in March 1856. Another detailed narrative appeared in the *Annual Report of the American Anti-Slavery Society* in 1856.[13] The newspaper coverage may have been motivated by a variety of reasons, some of them, one intuits, having to do with the exoticism of the story. In much the same way, Jim Trueblood of Ralph Ellison's *Invisible Man* becomes the focus of white attention after he commits incest with his daughter:

> The white folks took up for me. And the white folks took to coming out here to see us and talk with us. Some of 'em was big white folks, too, from the big school way across the State. Asked me lots 'bout what I thought 'bout things, and 'bout my folks and the kids, and wrote it all down in a book. . . . That's what I don't understand. I done the worse thing a man could ever do in his family and instead of chasin' me out of the country, they gimme more help than they ever give any other colored man, no matter how good a nigguh he was.[14]

In *Beloved* Morrison has Paul D respond to the media attention Sethe gets for infanticide in much the same way as the "invisible man" responds to Trueblood's story:

> Because there was no way in hell a black man could appear in a newspaper if the story was about something anybody wanted to hear. A whip of fear broke through the heart chambers as soon as you saw a Negro's face in a paper, since the face was not there because the person had a healthy baby, or outran a street mob. Nor was it there because the person had been killed, or maimed or caught or burned or jailed or whipped or evicted or stomped or raped or cheated, since that could hardly qualify as news in a newspaper. It would have to be something out of the ordinary—something whitepeople would find interesting, truly different, worth a few minutes of teeth sucking if not gasps. And it must have been hard to find news about Negroes worth the breath catch of a white citizen of Cincinnati. (155–56)[15]

As Levi Coffin noted, the Margaret Garner case "attracted more attention and aroused deeper interest and sympathy" than any other he'd known (I'll return to the importance of this critique of print media later).

The case became a forum for "that noble anti-slavery lawyer" John Jolliffe, counsel for the defence, to argue that the 1850 Fugitive Slave Law was unconstitutional. Lucy Stone, who visited Garner in jail, spoke to the crowd outside her trial, describing Garner as a quintessentially American hero: "I thought the spirit she manifested was the same with that of our ancestors to whom we had erected a monument at Bunker Hill—the spirit that would rather let us all go back to God than back to slavery." A year and a half after her trial, Garner had become a symbol for what Frederick Douglass called his "philosophy of reform." Addressing an assembly celebrating the twenty-third anniversary of West Indian Emancipation, Douglass proclaimed:

> The whole history of the progress of human liberty shows that all concessions yet made to her august claims, have been born of earnest struggle. The conflict has been exciting, agitating, all-absorbing, and for the time being, putting all other tumults to silence. It must do this or it does nothing. If there is no struggle there is no progress. . . . This struggle may be a moral one, or it may be a physical one, but it must be a struggle. Power concedes nothing without a demand. It never did and it never will. Find out what any people will quietly submit to and you have found out the exact measure of injustice and wrong which will be imposed upon them. . . . The limits of tyrants are prescribed by the endurance of those whom they oppress. . . . If we ever get free from the oppressions and wrongs heaped upon us, we must pay for their removal. We must do this by labor, by suffering, by sacrifice, and if needs be, by our lives and the lives of others.
>
> Hence, my friends, every mother who, like Margaret Garner, plunges a knife into the bosom of her infant to save it from the hell of our Christian Slavery, should be held and honored as a benefactress.[16]

As late as 1892, the story of Margaret Garner could be used to signify the extreme measures a person would take to escape what the lawyer Jolliffe called the "seething hell of American slavery" and Douglass the "hell of our Christian Slavery."

In Frances E. W. Harper's *Iola Leroy,* Margaret Garner's case symbolized in the heroine's life what the author calls "school-girl notions." Iola is the daughter of the slaveowner Eugene Leroy and his wife Marie, who has "negro blood in her veins"; Iola, when she attends school in the North, does not yet know her maternal racial background. In discussion with her fellow school-girls in the Northern school, Iola defends the institution of slavery, claiming that their slaves are "content." One of her schoolfriends disagrees: "'I don't know,' was the response of her friend, 'but I do not think that the slave mother who took her four children, crossed the Ohio River on the ice, killed one of the children and attempted the lives of the other two, was a contented slave.'"[17] Significantly, when Iola does discover her racial heritage she begins a mission of education, the biggest part of which is the paper she reads to the Council Meeting at Mr. Stillman's house, a paper entitled "Education of Mothers." Nameless now, Margaret Garner had become a political symbol for discontent. By 1948, Herbert Aptheker would cite the Margaret Garner case to argue why "the Negro woman so often urged haste in slave plottings." By 1981, Angela Y. Davis would echo him in arguing that the Margaret Garner case demonstrated not only the willingness of slave women to organize insurrections, but also the unique desperation of the slave mother.[18]

By 1987, Margaret Garner's story would inspire a Pulitzer Prize-winning novel. Morrison has said that she does not know what eventually happened to Margaret Garner.[19] There are conflicting reports. According to Coffin and *The Liberator*, while Garner was being shipped back to Kentucky she jumped overboard with her baby; she was saved but her baby drowned. According to a report in the Cincinnati *Chronicle* and the Philadelphia *Press*, Margaret and her husband Robert worked in New Orleans and then on Judge Bonham's plantation in Mississippi until Margaret died of typhoid fever in 1858.[20] Whatever her fate, at Morrison's hands she has been buried in order to be resurrected into a new life, and she has been remembered in order that the institution she suffered may be forgotten.

SIGNIFYIN(G) ON HISTORY

Beloved, according to Stanley Crouch, one of its harshest reviewers, "means to prove that Afro-Americans are the result of a cruel determinism."[21] This criticism is a good place to start our discussion of the novel, not because Crouch has hit upon some truth regarding *Beloved* or Morrison (he has not) but because he demonstrates the sort of conclusion a reader may reach if unburdened by knowledge of the historical place of *Beloved*'s writing, its historical analogue, and its critical position in the African American aesthetic and politics of remembering history.

Beloved is the product of and a contribution to a historical moment in which African American historiography is in a state of fervid revision. The debate currently rages between those who argue that slavery led to the "infantilization" of adult Africans because the most significant relationship in any slave's life was that between the slave and the master, and those who argue that slaves formed viable internal communities, family structures, and protective personae that allowed them to live rich, coherent lives within their own system of values.[22] One premise underlying this debate is the question of whether slaves were acquiescent or resistant to the institution, whether they conformed to the "Sambo" or "Mammy" stereotypes who accepted their stations or whether they were in perpetual opposition to them—both in daily resistance and in sensational insurrections.[23] It is within this revisionary fray that *Beloved* may profitably be examined. As I hope to demonstrate below, the novel both remembers the victimization of the ex-slaves who are its protagonists and asserts the healing and wholeness that those protagonists carry with them in their communal lives. Crouch, unfortunately, reads the novel as if it were a rendition only of victimization, only of determinism; in other words, he misreads it.

Morrison has on more than one occasion asserted that she writes from a double perspective of accusation and hope, of criticizing the past and caring for the future. She claims that this double perspective is the perspective of a "Black woman writer," that is, "one who look[s] at things in an unforgiving/loving way . . . writing to repossess, re-name, re-own." In *Beloved,* this perspective is described as "the glare of an outside thing that embraces while it accuses" (271). It is on precisely this issue of a dual vision that she marks the distinction between black men's writing and black women's: "What I found so lacking in most black writing by men that seems to be present in a lot of black women's writing is a sense of joy, in addition to oppression and being women or black or whatever."[24]

Morrison writes out of a dual perspective in order to re-possess, as I've suggested earlier, by remembering the ancestor, not only an aesthetic act but an act of historical recovery: "Roots are less a matter of geography than sense of shared history; less to do with place, than with inner space."[25] Each act of writing a novel is for her an act of discovering deep within herself some relationship to a "collective memory." Memory itself, write Mary Frances Berry and John Blassingame, is for African Americans "an instrument of survival." It is an instrument, writes Morrison, that can be traced back to an African heritage: "It's true what Africans say: 'The Ancestor lives as long as there are those who remember.'"[26]

In the novel this truth is expressed by Sethe's mother-in-law. Baby Suggs knows that "death was anything but forgetfulness" (4). That remembering is both a resurrection and a pain is testified to by Amy Denver, who assisted in the birthing of Sethe's daughter: "Anything dead coming back to life hurts." The daughter Amy delivered testifies to that: "A truth for all times, thought Denver" (35). Let us now turn our attention to the novel in which all the double perspectives of this black woman writer are expressed—remembering and forgetting, accusing and embracing, burying and reviving, joy and oppression.

READING *BELOVED*

The obvious place to begin a reading tracing Morrison's signifyin(g) on the story of Margaret Garner is the site of infanticide. One of the recurrent tropes of the African American novel of slavery is the possible response to an institution attempting to render meaningless the mother-child relationship. In William Wells Brown's *Clotelle,* the slave mother Isabella would rather commit suicide than face slavery for herself and her children. Hunted by a crowd of dogs and slavecatchers, Isabella leaps into the Potomac as an act symbolizing the "unconquerable love of liberty which the human heart may inherit." The chapter is entitled "Death Is Freedom."[27] In Zora Neale Hurston's *Moses, Man of the Mountain,* slavery is described as an institution in which only death can give freedom. As Amram tells Caleb, "You are up against a hard game when you got to die to beat it."[28] It is an even harder game, Morrison would add, when you have to kill what you love most.

Coffin explicitly states Margaret's motivation: "The slave mother . . . killed her child rather than see it taken back to slavery" (557). Like Harriet Jacobs, Margaret, in Coffins' reading of her history, sees death as a better alternative than slavery. "It seemed to me," writes Jacobs, "that I would rather see them [her children] killed than have them given up to his [the slaveowner's] power. . . . When I lay down beside my child, I felt how much easier it would be to see her die than to see her master beat her about."[29]

Sethe killed Beloved, according to Stamp Paid, because she "was trying to outhurt the hurters." "She love those children" (243). Loving as a slave, according to Paul D (whom Stamp Paid is trying to persuade with his assessment of Sethe's motivation), meant loving small, loving in an unobvious way so that whatever was loved did not become part of a technique of punishment. Paul D's advice, and his credo, was to "love just a little bit" so that when the slave owners took whatever or whoever the slave loved and "broke its back, or shoved it in a croaker sack, well, maybe you'd have a little love left over for the next one" (45). Ella, another ex-slave who was loved by no one and who considered "love a serious disability" (256), lived by the simple dictum "Don't love nothing" (92). When Paul D learns of Sethe's infanticide he tells her that her love is "too thick." She responds by telling him that "Love is or it ain't. Thin love ain't love at all" (164). Although Paul D lives by his philosophy of loving small as a protective measure, he knows what Sethe means. "He knew exactly what she meant: to get to a place where you could love anything you chose—not to need permission for desire—well now, *that* was freedom" (162). Although Paul D knows the conditions of freedom and Sethe knows the conditions of love, each has to learn to claim that freedom, to claim that love, and thereby to claim genuine community and begin the process of healing.

Sethe's process of healing occurs when she acknowledges her act and accepts her responsibility for it while also recognizing the reason for her cat within a framework larger than that of individual resolve. Here, perhaps, is Morrison's most powerful introjection into the Margaret Garner story—the establishing of a context for Sethe's act. Sethe's own mother kills all the children fathered by the whites who raped her. As Nan, Sethe's grandmother tells her, "She threw them all away but you. The one from the crew she threw away on the island. The others from more whites she also threw away. Without names, she threw them" (62). Another important person helping Sethe through the exorcising of her painful memories is Ella, who, it is hinted, has also committed infanticide. By placing such a frame around Sethe's story, Morrison insists on the impossibility of judging an action without reference to the terms of its enactment—the wrongness of assuming a transhistorical ethic outside a particular historical moment. Morrison is not justifying Sethe's actions; she is writing about them in the only way she knows how—through eyes that accuse and embrace, through a perspective that criticizes while it rejoices. Towards that end, she has constructed two daughterly presences in her novel who help Sethe remember and forget her personal history, who embody the dual perspective of critique and rejoicing.

Beloved, the incarnation of the ghost of the murdered daughter, is the most obvious revisionist construction in Morrison's novel. Through Beloved, she signifies on history by resurrecting one of its anonymous victims. When Beloved comes back to haunt Sethe for murdering her, Beloved becomes the incarnated memory of Sethe's guilt. Moreover, she is nothing but guilt, a symbol of an unrelenting criticism of the dehumanizing function of the institution of slavery. In this, she is the daughter representing a severe critique, demonstrating the determinism in slave history. She represents, however, only half of Morrison's work: the accusing glare, the unforgiving perspective, the need to forget—"It was not a story to pass on." There is another daughter in the novel, another daughter of history—representing the embracing glance, the loving view, the need to remember.

When Sethe first sees the reincarnated Beloved, her "bladder filled to capacity." She runs immediately to the outhouse, but does not make it: "Right in front of its door she had to lift her skirts, and the water she voided was endless. Like a horse, she thought, but as it went on and one she thought, No, more like flooding the boat when Denver was born. So much water Amy said, 'Hold on, Lu. You going to sink us you keep that up.' But there was no stopping water breaking from a breaking womb and there was no stopping now" (51). She would later, in a retrospective moment, remember this scene in trying to discover who Beloved could be (132). What is worth noticing, though, is that at that precise moment she does not remember the birth of Beloved but the birth of Denver. Denver is the fictional recreation of Margaret Garner's other daughter, the daughter who survives. Coffin describes Garner and this daughter in the courtroom: "The babe she held in her arms was a little girl, about nine months old, and was much lighter in color than herself, light enough to show a red tinge in its cheek" (562-63).[30] In *Beloved,* Denver becomes the daughter of hope.

Denver is the first to recognize that Beloved is the incarnation of the ghost that had haunted 124; and she is also the first who lives through that recognition and develops the understanding necessary for an affirmative return to life. Like everyone else in the novel, she must learn to confront the past in order to face the future. She, too, must deal with what she has been repressing for most of her life: "the hurt of the hurt world" (28). Denver begins, like her mother, by attempting to prevent the past from intruding upon her life: "She had her own set of questions which had nothing to do with the past. The present alone interested Denver" (119). Denver is not able to avoid the past for long, though, because the past becomes an immediate pain to her present life and an incipient danger to her future. What Denver must do is remember, and she must do so by revising her memory—her history and her mother's history—in a collective anamnesis.[31] Denver is pre-eminently in this novel the signifyin(g) daughter.

The first recognition Denver has of the danger Beloved represents to Sethe—the danger of the past's taking over the present—occurs in the Clearing. When Sethe goes to the Clearing to commune with her dead mother-in-law Baby Suggs, a spiritual force begins to choke her. Sethe reflects on the moment: "But one thing for sure, Baby Suggs had not choked her as first she thought. Denver was right, and walking in the dappled tree-light, clearer-headed now—away from the enchantment of the Clearing—Sethe remembered the touch of those fingers that she knew better than her own" (98). Denver will later accuse Beloved, who is the incarnated memory of her own murder, of choking her mother:

> "You did it, I saw you," said Denver.
> "What?"
> "I saw your face. You made her choke."
> "I didn't do it."
> "You told me you loved her."
> "I fixed it, didn't I? Didn't I fix her neck?"
> "After. After you choked her neck."
> "I kissed her neck. I didn't choke it. The circle of iron choked it."
> "I saw you." Denver grabbed Beloved's arm.
> "Look out, girl," said Beloved and, snatching her arm away, ran ahead as fast as she could along the stream that sang on the other side of the woods. (101)

For Denver, this is the first of her two crucial moments. She has not gone to the other side of the woods in years because she has willfully isolated herself in the house and the yard: "124 and the field behind it were all the world she knew or wanted." There had been a time when "she had known more and wanted to."

Reflecting on what she thinks she has just witnessed—Beloved's attempt to choke her mother—and looking out at Beloved's flight, Denver remembers the moment that caused her willful isolation. When she was seven she had wandered beyond the confines of the house and yard and entered the children's class Lady Jones conducted. For a full year, she learned to write and read: "She was so happy she didn't even know she was being avoided by her classmates—that they made excuses and altered their pace not to walk with her. It was Nelson Lord—the boy as smart as she was—who put a stop to it; who asked her the question about her mother that put chalk, the little *i* and all the rest those afternoons held, out of reach forever." Denver never went back to Lady Jones's, but she also did not ask anybody whether Nelson Lord's question was true. Reflecting now both on the latest incident in the Clearing and on the moment Nelson Lord had ended her adventurousness forever, Denver begins to confront questions regarding the ways the past shapes the present—she begins to ask herself whether she has a complicitous role in her mother's history: "Walking toward the stream, beyond her green bush house, she lets herself wonder what if Beloved really decided to choke her mother. Would she let it happen? Murder, Nelson Lord had said. 'Didn't your mother get locked away for murder? Wasn't you in there with her when she went?' " (104). It was "the second question that made it impossible for so long to ask Sethe about the first." Because Denver knows her mother's loving care, she finds it impossible to ask about the moment Sethe might have expressed her love murderously.

At age seven, Denver chose not to ask Sethe to explain; she preferred the comfort she received from the ghost haunting 124: "Now it held for her all the anger, love and fear she didn't know what to do with" (103). It is Denver who hears and identifies her dead sister's presence in the ghost. And by recognizing the ghost's identity, Denver begins the process of confronting the ramifications of the past: "The return of Denver's hearing, cut off by an answer she could not bear to hear, cut on by the sound of her dead sister trying to climb the stairs, signaled another shift in the fortunes of the people of 124. From then on the presence was full of spite" (103-04). For ten years, Denver prefers to live in the ambivalence wrought of suspicion without desiring any explanation.

At age fifteen, confronted with the incarnated memory of her mother's crime, Denver again chooses the ghost: "The display she witnessed at the Clearing shamed her because the choice between Sethe and Beloved was without conflict." Ironically, although Denver thinks that the present alone is what interests her, she luxuriates in the past, in dwelling in a shadowy history which she is unwilling to confront or confirm. Now, though, she has realized that she must make a choice—a choice she defers for now but must eventually make.

She makes an initial choice based on her fear for her own life: "I love my mother but I know she killed one of her own daughters, and tender as she is with me, I'm scared of her because of it" (205). Because of this, Denver feels the onus of protecting Beloved: "It's all on me, now, but she can count on me. I thought she was trying to kill her that day in the Clearing. Kill her back. But then she kissed her neck and I have to warn her about that. Don't love her too much. Don't. Maybe it's still in her the thing that makes it all right to kill her children. I have to tell her. I have to protect her" (206). There is only so long Denver can nurture this resentment; there is only so much the past can inform her living present. Beloved becomes demanding: "Anything she wanted she got, and when Sethe ran out of things to give her, Beloved invented desire" (240). It takes an act of seeing how this memory is literally consuming her mother for Denver to realize that her initial choice must be altered: "Then Sethe spit up something she had not eaten and it rocked Denver like gunshot. The job she started out with, protecting Beloved from Sethe, changed to protecting her mother from Beloved" (243).

This is the second crucial moment in Denver's life, when she must assume responsibility for having nurtured resentment, for having kept the past alive for selfish reasons. She will now have to leave 124 and face the larger community. She will have to stop dwelling on her mother's history and recognize the larger communal history of slavery's suffering. In doing so, she must understand her mother's act in light of a larger narrative. Beloved had responded to Denver's accusation of choking Sethe's neck by referring to an institution: "I didn't choke it. The circle of iron choked it." Slavery, Beloved is saying in a lower frequency, is the thing to blame. Denver will have to learn to listen to that lower frequency.

As she stands on the steps, Denver remembers her grandmother's final words: "Lay down your sword. This ain't a battle; it's a rout." Standing uneasily on the steps she has not left since Nelson Lord asked her that painful question, Denver is visited by Baby Suggs's ghost:

> Denver stood on the porch in the sun and couldn't leave it. Her throat itched; her heart kicked—and then Baby Suggs laughed, clear as anything. "You mean I never told you nothing about Carolina? About your daddy? You don't remember nothing about how come I walk the way I do and about your mother's feet, not to speak of her back? I never told you all that? Is that why you can't walk down the steps? My Jesus my."
>
> But you said there was no defense.
>
> "There ain't."
>
> Then what do I do?
>
> "Know it, and go on out the yard. Go on." (244)

"Know it": historical knowledge, if it isn't the defense, *is* at least the only way to integrity. It is a knowledge of the larger collective—of her father, her mother, her grandmother, Carolina, Sweet Home, slavery. It is understanding the forces of slavery that compelled her mother to do what she did. There is another story besides Beloved's, a larger narrative besides her family's, a deeper pain than suspicion and fear and spite. She follows her grandmother's advice and leaves the yard. By leaving the house, she enables herself to know.

She is first of all initiated into maturity and then understanding. The first place she goes is to Lady Jones's. When Lady Jones recognizes her and says, "Oh, baby . . . Oh, baby," Denver passes an indefinable threshold: "Denver looked up at her. She did not know it then, but it was the word 'baby,' said softly and with such kindness, that inaugurated her life in the world as a woman. The trail she followed to get to that sweet thorny place was made up of paper scraps containing the handwritten names of others" (248). Those paper scraps represent her place in history—both within the family as a literate daughter of an unlettered mother and within the culture as a remembering being.

A woman now, Denver begins to glean the inner meaning of a larger reality, to comprehend the dangers that dwelling on the past holds. Denver's discovery, though, occurs when she becomes imbricated into a story Sethe is telling Beloved. The passage in which Sethe's relationship to Beloved is delineated must be quoted in full:

> *Denver thought* she understood the connection between her mother and Beloved: Sethe was trying to make up for the handsaw; Beloved was making her pay for it. But there would never be an end to that, and seeing her mother diminished shamed and infuriated her. Yet she knew Sethe's greatest fear was *the same one Denver had in the beginning*—that Beloved might leave. That before Sethe could make her understand what it meant—what it took to drag the teeth of that saw under the little chin; to feel the baby blood pump like oil in her hands; to hold her face so her head would stay on; to squeeze her so she could

> absorb, still, the death spasms that shot through that adored body, plump and sweet with life—Beloved might leave. Leave before Sethe could make her realize that worse than that—far worse—was what Baby Suggs died of, what Ella knew, what Stamp saw and what made Paul D tremble. That anybody white could take your whole self for anything that came to mind. Not just work, kill, or maim you, but dirty you. Dirty you so bad you couldn't like yourself anymore. Dirty you so bad you forgot who you were and couldn't think it up. And though she and others lived through and got over it, she could never let it happen to her own. The best thing she was, was her children. Whites might dirty *her* all right, but not her best thing, her beautiful, magical best thing—the part of her that was clean. . . . This and much more, *Denver heard* her say from her corner chair, trying to persuade Beloved, *the one and only person she felt she had to convince,* that what she had done was right because it came from true love. (251, emphasis added)

This moment of understanding, the moment when Sethe articulates her recognition of the reasons she killed Beloved, is filtered through Denver's hearing and understanding; it begins with Denver's thinking and ends with her hearing. Although Sethe thinks she is attempting to convince only one daughter of her love, in reality she is convincing the other daughter too. Denver had, "in the beginning," wished Beloved to stay because Beloved represented the ambiguity she felt about her mother—because Beloved was an accusation always readily available. Denver has since understood that because of a larger communal history, her mother's deed might not be so heinous as she had at first thought. That is not to say that Morrison is trying to negate the guilt Sethe feels, or even attempting to palliate it by reference to an institutional context. Rather, by having both of the daughters listen to Sethe's realization, Morrison represents for us the ambivalent duality of what she considers primarily the black woman writer's way of looking at the world—as she puts it, "in an unforgiving/loving way." Each daughter in this novel represents one way. Beloved accuses while Denver embraces; Beloved is unforgiving while Denver is loving; Beloved will be "Disremembered and unaccounted for" while Denver is the source of remembering. Two things occur when Denver finally follows Baby Suggs's advice and steps out of 124—one that leads to a personal healing and another that leads to a communal.

First, she tells the community that Beloved, the murdered baby, has returned to punish Sethe. It is a story that must be narrated for it subjects to be cured: "Nobody was going to help her unless she told it—told all of it" (253). The community responds in three ways: "those that believed the worst; those that believed none of it; and those, like Ella, who thought it through" (255). It is Ella, finally, who initiates the exorcism of Beloved; and it is significant that Ella is the one to do this. First of all, Ella, like the matured Denver, has outgrown the need to dwell on the past: "Whatever Sethe had done, Ella didn't like the idea of past errors taking possession of the presence. Sethe's crime was staggering and her pride outstripped even that; but she could not countenance the possibility of sin moving on in the house, unleashed and sassy. Daily life took as much as she had. The future was sunset; the past something to leave behind. And if it didn't stay behind, well, you might have to stomp it out" (256). Moreover, Ella too has a place in the larger narrative of slavery. Her puberty was spent "in a house where she was shared by father and son, whom she called 'the lowest yet.' It was 'the lowest yet' who gave her a disgust for sex and against whom she measured all atrocities" (256). And Ella's personal history has hints of infanticide in it too: "Ella had been beaten every way but down. She remembered the bottom teeth she had lost to the brake and the scars from the bell were thick as rope around her waist. She had delivered, but would not nurse, a hairy white thing, fathered by 'the lowest yet.' It lived five days never making a sound. The idea of that pup coming back to whip her too set her jaw working" (258–59). By registering her narrative within a framework of determinism and forgiveness, Ella has learned how to free herself. She offers that possibility to Sethe. For twenty-eight days, Sethe had been free—the time between crossing the Ohio River and the time she killed her baby daughter. Sethe had known then that "freeing yourself was one thing; claiming ownership of that freed self was another" (95). In that twenty-eight days, she had claimed herself. After murdering Beloved, she lost that claim. Ella, by exorcising Beloved, by not allowing the past to consume the present, offers Sethe the opportunity to reclaim herself. In the end Sethe does, and does so by an act of community. In this her life is following the pattern established by her daughter Denver.

Denver's personal healing is attested to when she meets Nelson Lord for the first time since he had asked her the question that had deafened her. This is the second thing that happens when she leaves 124. She sees Nelson: "All he did was smile and say, 'Take care of yourself, Denver,' but she heard it as though it were what language was made for. The last time he spoke to her his words blocked up her ears. Now they opened her mind" (252). This encounter demonstrates Denver's growth. She knows now her shared history—her family's, her community's, her culture's. As much as Nelson's original question had been the closure of language for her, so now is his amiable comment a renewal of communication.

Sethe, after Denver, will make a successful return to life in the same way. When she told Paul D how she killed Beloved, he made a comment that caused a forest to spring up between them (165). It will take Paul D's own education, and Sethe's attempts to understand herself and make Beloved understand her actions, before they are able to reunite. Paul D finally realizes that he "wants to put his story next to hers." Not only is this an act of a shared narrative, but it is also an affirmation that Sethe has a claim to herself:

> "Sethe," he says, "me and you, we got more yesterday than anybody. We need some kind of tomorrow."
>
> He leans over and takes her hand. With the other he touches her face. "You your best thing, Sethe. You are." His holding fingers are holding hers.
>
> "Me? Me?" (273)

Like Denver, who finds the ability to discover herself in Nelson Lord's words, Sethe finds the ability to reclaim, to recover, herself in Paul D's. Before she told Paul about Beloved, she had thought that theirs was a shared narrative: "Her story was bearable because it was his as well—to tell, to refine, and tell again. The things neither knew about the other—the things neither had word shapes for—well, it would come in time" (99). The full story does come in time, but it is a product of extreme stress and pain, of the effort to remember what each desires to forget. It is a story told in a language that deafens while it enlightens: "This was not a story to pass on."

HEARING *BELOVED*

It is a story, however, that does get passed on—and it is passed on through the ear. While Sethe thinks she is trying to convince only Beloved of the reasons she committed murder, Denver is *listening.* As I suggested earlier, Denver is the filtering ear for Sethe's process of self-discovery: "This and much more Denver heard her say." It is important that Denver, the signifyin(g) daughter, *hears* what Sethe has to say. It alerts us to how this novel situates itself in the African American literary tradition. *Beloved* belongs to that class of novels Gates characterizes as "speakerly texts"—those texts "whose rhetorical strategy is designed to represent an oral literary tradition" and to produce the "illusion of oral narration."[32] Within the structure of the broadest frame of *Beloved*'s "speakerly text" there exists what we might call the "aural being." It is this being who represents our belonging to this novel, and this being is represented within the novel by the signifyin(g) daughter.

Peter Brooks has suggested that meaning in novels resides in the dialogical relationship between "tellers and listeners," in the transmission of the "'horror,' the taint of knowledge gained." The reader of narratives, that is, is "solicited not only to understand the story, but to complete it."[33] That reader—when constructed within the novel, that aural being—is, like Marlowe's auditor, a creation of the speakerly text. Moreover, and this is distinctly an aspect of the African American literary tradition, the voice of the speakerly text is a product of a generational memory. We may find the protocols for this sort of generational memory represented in at least two other novels written by African American women: Hurston's *Their Eyes Were Watching God* (1937)—the prototype, Gates tells us, of the speakerly text—and Sherley Anne Williams's *Dessa Roes* (1986).

Beloved is also a novel that constructs its ideal "listener." Denver will tell and re-tell the story that she now understands. Like Pheoby in *Their Eyes Were Watching God,* Denver uses the knowledge of "horror," transmitted to her aurally, to perform a healing narrative—orally. And, like Pheoby, Denver represents the implied community of ideal readers, the "aural being." What, finally, Denver is to *Beloved* is the space for hearing the tale of infanticide with a degree of understanding—both as sister of the murdered baby and as the living daughter of the loving mother. Denver, that is, is a site of participation.

Morrison has said on various occasions that she writes into her narratives the "places and spaces so that the reader can participate."[34] It is a dialogic form that she has suggested is akin to music and to black preaching. These are art forms which, she suggests, are part of the repertoire of "Black art," which is difficult to define but does have "major characteristics."

> One of which is the ability to be both print and oral literature: to combine those two aspects so that the stories can be read in silence, of course, but one should be able to hear them as well. It should try deliberately to make you stand up and make you feel something profoundly in the same way that a Black preacher requires his congregation to speak, to join him in the sermon, to behave in a certain way, to stand up and to weep and *to cry and to accede or to change and to modify*—to expand on the sermon that is being delivered. In the same way that a musician's music is enhanced when there is a response from the audience. Now in a book . . . I have to provide the places and spaces so that the reader can participate. (Emphasis added)[35]

She intends her novels to be healing, belonging to a form she calls "village literature"—literature that should "clarify the roles that have become obscured," literature that is able to "identify those things in the past that are useful and those things that are not," a literature, finally, that is able to "give nourishment."[36] The novel as a form of "Black art" works with history as its subject in order to criticize and to revise—to cry and to modify.

Morrison claims that it is precisely because the black oral historical tradition is now a thing of the past that the African American novel is so necessary: "The novel is needed by African Americans now in a way that it was not needed before. . . . We don't live in places where we can hear those stories anymore; parents don't sit around and tell their children those classical, mythological, archetypal stories that we heard years ago."[37] Those stories must have a place in African American culture, and they've found their place in the novel. The novel becomes for Morrison what Aunt Sue was for Langston Hughes—the site of an oral history passed from generation to generation.

Because all those ancestors, like Aunt Sue, are no longer available, there must evolve within the African American tradition an art form that gives them voice. *Beloved* is but one more novel in a tradition doing just that. But it also does one more thing: it situates itself not only theoretically, but also performatively, as an oral literature.

I noted earlier that Morrison provides a criticism of print media through Paul D's assessment of what newspapers will or will not write about black people. Like other novels in the tradition of African American letters, Morrison criticizes the ideological imperative of print media in order to establish the value of oral historical relation. This criticism of print media is very much part of the overall revisionist motive in criticizing the historiography of slavery. It is, after all, only when slave narratives and slave accounts began to be taken seriously as historical documents that the other side of slavery could be articulated. The contemporary novel of signifyin(g) history, or the speakerly text, represents this struggle for the validation of orality. In Williams's *Dessa Rose,* for instance, the slave Dessa is given two voices—one as the white pro-slavery polemicist Adam Nehemiah "reconstructs" her voice in his journal, and the other as she orally tells her story to her grandchildren in her own voice. Dessa, that is, can save herself only by telling a story different from the one she is written to fit, by refusing to be written and asserting herself in voice.[38] In *Beloved* it is schoolteacher who uses writing in a detrimental way. Schoolteacher attempts to read and write Sethe as a subhuman thing by listing what he calls her "animal" characteristics alongside her human ones. Sethe resolved that "no one, nobody on this earth, would list her daughter's characteristics on the animal side of the paper" (251). Like Dessa, Sethe refuses to allow the written to usurp her humanity, and she finds that her humanity is best represented by the spoken word. To discover how *Beloved* is constructed to represent its own orality, we must first of all delineate the variety of oral communities in the novel.

Paul D belongs to a chain gang that had its own language, signifying nothing to those who didn't belong to its community: "They sang it out and beat it up, garbling the words so they could not be understood; tricking the words so their syllables yielded up other meanings" (108). Like the chain gang described by Frederick Douglass, the slaves would sing songs that "to many would seem unmeaning jargon, but which, nevertheless, were full of meaning to themselves."[39] But when he enters the community of Sethe and her two daughters, Paul D finds himself unable to comprehend their language: "Hearing the three of them laughing at something he wasn't in on. The code they used among themselves that he could not break" (132). When Sethe first converses with Ella, after escaping from the Sweet Home plantation, what Sethe says yields up a surplus of meaning to Ella because of her ear for the silences: "She listened for the holes—the things the fugitives did not say; the questions they did not ask. Listened too for the unnamed, unmentioned people left behind" (92). When Ella initiates the exorcism with a holler, language becomes wholly oral: "In the beginning was the sound, and they all knew what that sound sounded like" (259).

Finally, though, the most important oral community in this novel is comprised of those able to understand the mode of discourse necessary to relating the crux of this story—the murder of Beloved:

> Sethe knew that the circle she was making around the room, him, the subject, would remain one. That she could never close in, pin it down for anybody who had to ask. If they didn't get it right off—she could never explain. Because the truth was simple, not a long drawn-out record of flowered shifts, tree cages, selfishness, ankle ropes and wells. Simple: she was squatting in the garden and when she saw them coming and recognized the schoolteacher's hat, she heard wings. Little hummingbirds stuck their needle beaks right through her headcloth into her hair and beat their wings. And if she thought anything, it was No. No.

> Nono. Nonono. Simple. She just flew. Collected every bit of life she had made, all the parts of her that were precious and fine and beautiful, and carried, pushed, dragged them through the veil, out, away, over there where no one could hurt them. Over there. Outside this place, where they would be safe. And the hummingbird wings beat on. (163)

Paul D has trouble understanding this discourse, just as he had trouble understanding the code existing between Sethe and her daughters. "At first he thought it was her spinning. Circling him the way she was circling the subject. . . . Then he thought, No, it's the sound of her voice; it's too near" (161). Eventually, Paul D understands only that Sethe murdered Beloved; he suggests that it was because her love was "too thick." It will take him the rest of the novel to understand that for Sethe "Love is or it ain't. Thin love ain't love at all" (164).

It takes memory and articulation for Sethe to understand her own action. What she had to remember is another oral community between her grandmother and herself; "she was remembering something she forgot she knew" (61):

> Nan was the one she knew best, who was around all day, who nursed babies, cooked, had one good arm and half of another. And who used different words. Words Sethe understood then but could neither recall nor repeat now. She believed that must be why she remembered so little before Sweet Home except singing and dancing and how crowded it was. What Nan told her she had forgotten, along with the language she told it in. The same language her ma'am spoke, and which would never come back. But the message—that was and had been there all along. Holding the damp white sheets against her chest, she was picking meaning out of a code she no longer understood. (62)

The story Nan tells her is that of Sethe's mother's killing those children fathered by whites. The story is remembered when Beloved returns and asks about Sethe's mother. It is a story that has a progressive effect on Sethe, exactly as the story of Sethe's murder of Beloved has on Denver: "As small girl Sethe, she was unimpressed. As grown-up woman Sethe she was angry, but not certain at what." Now, in remembering her own relationship to her two daughters, she is able to understand her mother's acts and her grandmother's code. By situating herself within a communal narrative of grandmother-mother-daughter relationships, Sethe is able to understand herself. The code becomes unlocked and available for her hearing.

I have suggested that part of the significance of Denver's "hearing" her mother explain to Beloved the reasons for her action is that she becomes the "aural being" of his speakerly text. Moreover, the act of hearing symbolizes Denver's overcoming her deafness—wrought, as it was, of her first hearing of her mother's act. For Sethe, telling her story allowed her to understand *her* mother's history. For Denver, telling her mother's story allows her to understand the communal history and her place in it. As we saw, Sethe's final healing occurs in imitation of Denver—as Denver places her story next to Nelson Lord's, Sethe places hers next to Paul D's. Denver is, then, in a very real sense, completing her mother's story. That, finally, is what an aural being is to the speakerly text's unfolding—both the space for the reader's participation and, as Brooks suggests, a symbol of the illusion of completeness, of closure.

It is worth noting the differences between aural beings and their roles in the novels we can designate as speakerly texts. *Their Eyes Were Watching God* gives us a framed story, with the hearer—Pheoby—being presented at the beginning and end of the relation. She is the gauge of our understanding of Janie's tale and the source of Janie's justification in the eyes of the community: "Nobody better not criticize yuh in mah hearin."[40] In Hurston's novel, then, the scene of the grandmother's relating her story to her granddaughter is part of the overall enactment of the telling of the tale. Much as Nanny attempted to justify her life in an oral story to her granddaughter, so does Janie—that very granddaughter—attempt to justify her life by telling it to her friend. In *Dessa Rose,* we find out only in the epilogue that the aural beings are Dessa's grandchildren. By exposing the fact that this is an enactment of the grandmother's oral narration at the very end, Williams forces us to reconsider our relation to textual history. "Afro-Americans," she writes in her prefatory note, "having survived by word of mouth—and made of that process a high art—remain at the mercy of literature and writing" (ix). In a bold gesture, Williams makes Dessa's orality the foundation of any textual record of her. The white Nehemiah's records become illegible and blank sheets; Dessa's story is recorded by her son and *said* back to her. The oral transmission, then, is the enactment of part of this novel's polemical trajectory: the establishing of the primacy of a told tale.

Beloved differs from these two means of organizing orality within the speakerly text in that it is based on a variety of discrete oral linguistic communities; and its story is about the establishment of a communal narrative. The critique of the newspaper's report and the condemnation of schoolteacher's racist anthropology attest to the ex-slaves' refusal to be written. They are, nonetheless, discrete individuals prevented by various deafnesses from *hearing* the communal story to which they belong. Paul D must learn to understand the community of mother and daughters, just as he must learn to hear Sethe's story of her infanticide (he had felt her *voice* was too close, we recall). Denver must understand Sethe's story, as well, because she is the one who must go out and tell it—tell it in order to save her mother. Likewise, Sethe learns to understand how to claim herself as her own best thing only after she is able to understand what her grandmother told her, only after she is able to understand her mother's actions as part of a larger framework of experience.

The scenes of hearing the mother's tongue, understanding the mother's code, knowing the mother's history—these are themselves the very enactment of an ongoing generational oral transmission. In themselves, they represent the organization of this novel's speakerliness. Unlike *Dessa Rose* and *Their Eyes Were Watching God,* each of which enacts a single scene of oral transmission of one person's story to her grandchildren or to her friend, *Beloved* is concerned with demonstrating the variety and continuousness of oral transmissions necessary for any person to understand her own story. In this, each of the major characters in the novel signifies on the story of each of her or his fellow characters in order to establish a communal narrative—*Beloved* itself. The best figure for this (internal) formal revision is Paul D's desire to place his story next to Sethe's. The novel is, finally, about putting stories together and putting them to rest.

Putting to rest, of course, for Morrison means giving renewed and energetic life. From this rest, she gives her characters resurrection. In the end, perhaps the greatest achievement of Morrison's novel is that she gives the murdered victim of history *voice;* she resurrects the unjustly killed and allows that daughter to have renewed historical life by criticizing the sort of history that has hitherto excluded her and her rebellious spirit. In the end, this impetus is best expressed in one of W. E. B. Du Bois's most lyrical moments, in a passage that can almost act as a commentary on the novel which would be published nearly eighty-five years later: "It is a hard thing to live haunted by the ghost of an untrue dream; to see the wide vision of empire fade into real ashes and dirt; to feel the pang of the conquered, and yet to know that with all the Bad that fell on one black day, something was vanquished that deserved to live, something killed that in justice had not dared to die."[41] In giving that "ghost" a renewed voice and life, Morrison not only criticizes the institution responsible for Beloved's death but also shows the healing knowledge that accrues to those attentive to the ghost's presence. What Morrison does in *Beloved* is to remember in order to revive, to survive, to rename, to re-possess. At the end of *The Color Purple,* Alice Walker, signing herself as author and medium, writes, "I thank everybody in this book for coming." In the preface to *Dessa Rose,* Williams claims to have the feeling of "owning" a summer in the nineteenth century. Resuscitating historical figures may indeed give one the feeling of belonging to a larger community, of being at one with the ancestors—in Walker's metaphor, of being in the temple of the familiar; in Morrison's metaphor, of burying the dead to revive them. Nothing serves more persuasively to delineate how an author feels when she has revised and revived history than Morrison's own commentary on her novel. At the end of her conversation with Gloria Naylor, Toni Morrison reflects on what her creative act continues to mean to her:

> It was a conversation. I can tell, because I said something I didn't know I knew. About the "dead girl." That bit by bit I had been rescuing her from the grave of time and inattention. Her fingernails maybe in the first book; face and legs, perhaps, the second time. Little by little bringing her back into living life. So that now she comes running when called—walks freely around the house, sits down in a chair; looks at me. . . . She is here now, alive. I have seen, named and claimed her—and oh what company she keeps.

NOTES

1. John Edgar Wideman, *Sent For You Yesterday* (1983; rpt., New York: Random House, 1988), prefatory half-page; Wideman, *Interviews With Black Writers,* ed. John O'Brien (New York: Liveright, 1973), 220–21.

2. Toni Morrison, "Rootedness: The Ancestor as Foundation," in *Black Women Writers (1950-1980): A Critical Evaluation,* ed. Mari Evans (New York: Doubleday, 1984), 339-45, esp. 344; Morrison, "Memory, Creation, and Writing," *Thought: A Review of Culture and Idea* 59 (December 1984): 385-90, esp. 385, 389. Cf. Morrison, "City Limits, Village Values: Concepts of the Neighborhood in Black Fiction," in *Literature and the Urban Experience: Essays on the City and Literature,* ed. Michael C. Jaye and Ann Chalmers Watt (New Brunswick: Rutgers Univ. Press, 1980), 35-43.
3. Toni Morrison, "Unspeakable Things Unspoken: The Afro-American Presence in American Literature," *Michigan Quarterly Review* 28 (Winter 1989): 1-34, esp. 11; cf. 25, where she describes how in the writing of *Tar Baby* she had to deal with "the nostalgia, the history, the nostalgia for the history; the violence done to it and the consequences of that violence." See Pauline Hopkins, *Contending Forces: A Romance Illustrative of Negro Life North and South* (Boston: The Colored Cooperative Publishing Co., 1900), 13-14.
4. Deborah E. McDowell, "Boundaries: Our Distant Relations and Close Kin," in *Afro-American Literary Study in the 1990s,* ed. Houston A. Baker Jr. and Patricia Redmond (Chicago: Univ. of Chicago Press, 1989), 51-70, esp. 70; Henry Louis Gates Jr., "Introduction," *Reading Black, Reading Feminist: A Critical Anthology,* ed. Gates (New York: Meridian, 1990), 1-17, esp. 16.
5. Hortense J. Spillers, "Changing the Letter: The Yokes, the Jokes of Discourse, or Mrs. Stowe, Mr. Reed," in *Slavery and the Literary Imagination,* ed. Deborah E. McDowell and Arnold Rampersad (Baltimore: Johns Hopkins Univ. Press, 1989), 25-61, esp. 52. See also Ralph Ellison, "A Very Stern Discipline," in *Going to the Territory* (New York: Random House, 1986), 275-307, esp. 276, 287-88. The term, theory, and typographical notation of "signifyin(g)" are all derived from the work of Henry Louis Gates Jr., from his two formative essays, "Literary Theory and the Black Tradition" and "The 'Blackness of Blackness': A Critique of the Sign and the Signifying Monkey," both in *Figures in Black: Words, Signs, and the "Racial" Self* (New York: Oxford Univ. Press, 1987), 3-58, 235-76, and especially from his consummate book, *The Signifying Monkey: A Theory of African-American Literary Criticism* (New York: Oxford Univ. Press, 1988).
6. Bonnie Angelo, "The Pain of Being Black" [An Interview with Toni Morrison], *Time* (22 May 1989): 68-70, esp. 68. Morrison also expressed the difficulty of her chosen subject matter in *Beloved* to Sandi Russell in March 1986; see Russell, "'It's OK to Say OK,'" *Women's Review* [London] 5 (March 1986): 22-24; reprinted in *Critical Essays on Toni Morrison,* ed. Nellie Y. McKay (Boston: G. K. Hall, 1988), 43-54, esp. 45: "It was an era I didn't want to get into—going back into and through grief."
7. Gloria Naylor and Toni Morrison, "A Conversation," *Southern Review* 21 (1985): 567-93, esp. 584-85. Hereafter I will cite all quotations from this article parenthetically in the body of the essay.
8. Levi Coffin, *Reminiscences of Levi Coffin* (Cincinnati: Western Tract Society, 1876), 557-67, esp. 559-60. Portions of Coffin's narrative have been reprinted in *Black Women in White America: A Documentary History,* ed. Gerda Lerner (New York: Random House, 1971), 60-63; and Charles L. Blockson, *The Underground Railroad* (New York: Berkley, 1987), 195-200.
9. The story of Margaret Garner's escape will seem familiar to some readers as a historical event replicating (four years after) the literary event of Eliza's escape in Harriet Beecher Stowe's *Uncle Tom's Cabin,* chaps. 7 and 8. Eliza, too, crosses the semi-frozen Ohio River from Kentucky to escape Shelby. For the sources of the Eliza

episode, see Stowe, *The Key to Uncle Tom's Cabin* (1853; rpt., Port Washington, N.Y.: Kennikat Press, 1968), 21-23.

10. Toni Morrison, Foreword, Camille Billops, *The Harlem Book of the Dead* (New York: Morgan & Morgan, 1978). The photographs are by James Van Der Zee, the poetry by Owen Dodson, and the text by Camille Billops.
11. Toni Morrison, *Sula* (New York: Knopf, 1973), 149.
12. Toni Morrison, *Beloved* (New York: Knopf, 1987), 274. Subsequent quotations from *Beloved* will be taken from this edition and will be cited parenthetically in the body of the essay.
13. The story was reported in *The Liberator* 26 (21 March 1856): 47, reprinted from the Cincinnati *Commercial;* see Lerner, *Black Women in White America,* 62-63. It was also reported in the Philadelphia *Press* (14 March 1870), reprinted from the Cincinnati *Chronicle*; see Blockson, *The Underground Railroad,* 199-200. For the *Annual Report of the American Anti-Slavery Society* (New York, 1856), 44-47, see Frederick Douglass, *The Life and Writings of Frederick Douglass,* 5 vols., ed. Philip S. Foner (New York: International Publishers, 1950-1975), 2:568 n. 30.
14. Ralph Ellison, *Invisible Man* (New York: Random House, 1952), 53, 67.
15. While hearing Trueblood relate this story to him and the white Mr. Norton, the "invisible man" thinks to himself, "How can he tell this to white men . . . when he knows they'll say that all Negroes do such things?" (57).
16. For Levi Coffin, John Jolliffe, and Lucy Stone, see Coffin, *Reminiscences,* 557, 548, 561-62, 564-65. Frederick Douglass, "WEST INDIA EMANCIPATION, speech delivered at Canandaigua, New York, 4 August 1857," *The Life and Writings,* 2:426-39, esp. 437.
17. Frances E. W. Harper, *Iola Leroy, or Shadows Uplifted* (1892; rpt., Boston: Beacon, 1987), 65, 98.
18. Herbert Aptheker, "The Negro Woman," *Masses and Mainstream* 11 (February 1948): 10-17, esp. 11-12; Angela Y. Davis, *Women, Race & Class* (New York: Random House, 1981), 21, 29, 205.
19. Naylor and Morrison, "A Conversation," 584: "I'm not even sure what the denouement is of her story." Cf. Barbara Christian, "'Somebody Forget to Tell Somebody Something': African-American Women's Historical Novels," in *Wild Women in the Whirlwind: Afra-American Culture and the Contemporary Literary Renaissance,* ed. Joanne M. Braxton and Andrée Nicola McLaughlin (New Brunswick: Rutgers Univ. Press, 1990), 326-41, esp. 336. Christian is quoting Morrison's "Distinguished University of California Regents' Lecture," Univ. of California, Berkeley, 13 October 1987.
20. See note 13 above; cf. Coffin, *Reminiscences,* 567.
21. Stanley Crouch, "Aunt Medea," *New Republic* (19 October 1987): 38-43, esp. 42.
22. See, for instance, Stanley M. Elkins, *Slavery: A Problem in American Institutional and Intellectual Life,* 3rd rev. ed. (1959: Chicago: Univ. of Chicago Press, 1976), esp. 223-310; and those who have responded to his arguments, especially John W. Blassingame, *The Slave Community: Plantation Life in the Antebellum South,* 2nd rev. ed. (1972: Oxford: Oxford Univ. Press, 1979); George P. Rawick, *From Sundown to Sunup: The Making of the Black Community* (Westport, Conn.: Westport Publishing Co., 1972); Willie Lee Rose, *Slavery and Freedom,* ed. William H. Freehling (Oxford: Oxford Univ. Press, 1982), esp. 188-200; Mary Frances Berry and John W. Blassingame, *Long Memory: The Black Experience in America* (Oxford: Oxford Univ. Press, 1982); Eugene D. Genovese, *Roll, Jordan, Roll: The World the Slaves Made* (New York: Random House, 1974): Herbert Gutman, *The Black Family in Slavery*

and Freedom, 1750-1925 (New York: Random House, 1976); and Lawrence W. Levine, *Black Culture and Black Consciousness: Afro-American Folk Thought from Slavery to Freedom* (Oxford: Oxford Univ. Press, 1977).

23. For the debate concerning Herbert Aptheker's *American Negro Slave Revolts,* 5th rev. ed. (1943; New York: International Publishers, 1987), see Rawick, *From Sundown to Sunup,* 53-75.
24. Robert B. Stepto, "'Intimate Things in Place': A Conversation with Toni Morrison," in *Chant of Saints: A Gathering of Afro-American Literature, Art, and Scholarship,* ed. Michael S. Harper and Robert B. Stepto (Urbana: Univ. of Illinois Press, 1979), 213-29, esp. 225.
25. Russell, "'It's OK to Say OK,'" *Critical Essays on Toni Morrison,* 43-47, esp. 46, 44.
26. Claudia Tate, "Toni Morrison [An Interview]," in *Black Women Writers at Work,* ed. Claudia Tate (New York: Continuum, 1984), 118-31, esp 130-31; Berry and Blassingame, *Long Memory,* x; Morrison, Foreword, *The Harlem Book of the Dead.*
27. Williams Wells Brown, *Clotelle: or, The Colored Heroine. A Tale of the Southern States* (Boston: Lee & Shepherd, 1867), 50-52. In the first edition of this novel, entitled *Clotel; or, The President's Daughter. A Narrative of Slave Life in the United States* (1853), Clotel herself jumps into the Potomac. This novel, too, it is worth mentioning, uses a historical daughter as its protagonist, Clotelle being (as legend has it) the mulatto daughter of Thomas Jefferson and his slave housekeeper Sally Hemings. For a discussion of the Jefferson legend in relation to Brown's novels, see Bernard W. Bell, *The Afro-American Novel and Its Traditions* (Amherst: Univ. of Massachusetts Press, 1987), 39-40, 354 nn. 1, 4. For a more recent treatment of the Jefferson connection, see Barbara Chase-Riboud's wonderful novel, *Sally Hemings* (1979; rpt., New York: Avon, 1980).
28. Zora Neale Hurston, *Moses, Man of the Mountain* (1939; rpt. Urbana: Univ. of Illinois Press, 1984), 16.
29. Harriet A. Jacobs, *Incidents in the Life of a Slave Girl, Written by Herself,* ed. Jean Fagan Yellin (Cambridge: Harvard Univ. Press, 1987), 80, 86; cf. 16, 31, 35, 47, 55-56, 61-62, 109, 141, 166, 173.
30. As I pointed out earlier, in one account, Margaret Garner's second daughter is drowned; in others, we know nothing of her future.
31. I have discussed the ways that collective anamnesis informs three of Morrison's novels in another paper, "'Rememory': Primal Scenes and Constructions in Toni Morrison's Novels," *Contemporary Literature* 31 (Fall 1990): 300-23.
32. Gates, *The Signifying Monkey,* 170-216, esp. 181; cf. 22. Gates suggests an analogy between the "speakerly text" and the Russian Formalist idea of *skaz;* see Victor Erlich, *Russian Formalism: History-Doctrine* (The Hague: Mouton, 1969), 238; cited in Gates, 276 n. 19; cf. 112.
33. Peter Brooks, *Reading for the Plot: Design and Intention in Narrative* (Oxford: Oxford Univ. Press, 1984), 260; cf. 236.
34. Morrison, "Rootedness," 341. Cf. Naylor and Morrison, "A Conversation," 582; and Tate, "Toni Morrison [An Interview]," 125.
35. Morrison, "Rootedness," 341. For her comparison of the black novel to music, see Russell, "'It's OK to Say OK,'" 46; and Robert B. Stepto, "'Intimate Things in Place': A Conversation with Toni Morrison," 228.
36. Thomas LeClair, "'The Language Must Not Sweat': A Conversation with Toni Morrison," *New Republic* (21 March 1981): 25-29, esp. 26.
37. Morrison, "Rootedness," 340.

38. Sherley Anne Williams, *Dessa Rose* (1986; New York; Berkley, 1987), 10, 250, 260. Much of my reading of *Dessa Rose* is indebted to two recent studies: Gwendolyn Mae Henderson, "Speaking in Tongues: Dialogics, Dialectics, and the Black Woman Writer's Literary Tradition," in *Changing Our Own Words: Essays on Criticism, Theory, and Writing by Black Women,* ed. Cheryl A. Wall (New Brunswick: Rutgers Univ. Press, 1989), 16–37, esp. 25–26, 32; and Deborah E. McDowell, "Negotiating Between Tenses," *Slavery and the Literary Imagination,* 144–63, esp. 150, 156–57.
39. Frederick Douglass, *Narrative of the Life of Frederick Douglass, An American Slave,* ed. Houston A. Baker Jr., rev. ed. (1845; Harmondsworth: Penguin, 1982), 57. On other slave songs that specifically were meant to exclude the slaveholding community from understanding their intent, see Levine, *Black Culture and Black Consciousness,* 11, 51.
40. Zora Neale Hurston, *Their Eyes Were Watching God* (1937; rpt., Urbana: Univ. of Illinois Press, 1978), 284.
41. W. E. B. Du Bois, *The Souls of Black Folk, W. E. B. Du Bois: Writings,* ed. Nathan Huggins (New York: Library of America, 1986), 357–547, esp. 415.

Glossary

abject. Dealing with aspects of life (often associated with death, excrement, or graphic violence) that are frequently repressed because they bear unpleasant reminders of human mortality.

Adamic language. A language (named for the biblical Adam) in which words have a natural and organic relationship to the things they represent. Modern linguists see the relationship between language and its objects of representation as being arbitrary, a mere matter of agreed convention.

aesthetics. Branch of philosophy dealing with perception by the human senses, usually in relation to beauty, especially to art. The formal study of aesthetics is a product of the bourgeois era, and Marxist critics often emphasize that bourgeois aesthetics tends to convey values that are in the interest of the bourgeoisie, even while seeking to portray those values as absolute and universal.

affective fallacy. The belief (considered fallacious by the New Critics) that the meaning of a work of literature resides primarily in the thoughts and feelings it provokes in the reader.

affective stylistics. Reader-response approach (developed by Stanley Fish) that emphasizes the sequential feelings of the reader as he or she reads through a text.

Agrarians. Early name for the group that eventually became the New Critics. In this phase their work consisted largely of writing poetry that presented agrarian (rural) life in the antebellum South as a superior alternative to the alienated conditions caused by modern industrial capitalism. Sometimes called the *Southern Agrarians.*

alienation. The process by which individuals become distanced and estranged from the products of their labor, from the world around them, from other people, and eventually from themselves. Considered by Marxist critics an inevitable consequence of life in capitalist societies.

alienation effect. The process by which certain works of art (especially the epic theater of Bertolt Brecht) seek to distance their audience emotionally, thus leading to intellectual, rather than emotional, response on the part of the audience. Somewhat similar to defamiliarization, though generally with more political implications. The Marxist critic Walter Benjamin valued Brecht's alienation effects for their ability to shatter the aura that had traditionally surrounded works of art, thus potentially making art a tool of authority. Critics sometimes use the German term, *Verfremdungseffekt.*

allegory. A literary form in which the persons or objects described in the text are intended to evoke another set (often of a more abstract or general nature) of persons or objects.

allusion. A reference in a literary work to another literary work, thereby invoking the context and implications of the early work in the one that alludes to it.

ambiguity. Uncertainty in meaning or interpretation. Privileged by the New Critics as a crucial property of the best literature.

archaeology. Style of historical research, pioneered by Michel Foucault, that focuses on detailed study of numerous texts (many of them relatively obscure) from a variety of disciplines. The results of archaeological research generally yield local knowledge about a given period in time and do not attempt to posit narratives of historical change, which is viewed as radically discontinuous, with the relationships between different periods of time being difficult or impossible to discern or describe accurately.

archetypes. Fundamental images and motifs that seem to be common to large numbers of individuals in widely differing societies. Associated by Carl Jung with the contents of the collective unconscious and often seen as providing powerful literary images.

Aristotelian logic. The tendency, based on a central philosophical premise of the Greek philosopher Aristotle, to think in terms of either-or oppositions, that is, to belief that a given object must either have a certain characteristic or not have that characteristic. Challenged by poststructuralist theorists as too simplistic to describe the complexities and ambiguities of language. Also known as either-or logic, binary thinking, or dualistic thinking. Similar to the Bakhtinian concept of *monologism.*

aura. The sense, described by the Marxist theorist Walter Benjamin, of quasi-religious wholeness that surrounds works of art, provoking awe and wonder in their viewers or readers. Benjamin was concerned that this kind of response to art resembled the blind admiration of many individuals for authority figures, especially of Germans for Adolf Hitler and the Nazis.

avant-garde. Radical artistic and literary movement of the early to mid-twentieth century. Avant-garde artists employed highly unconventional techniques in an attempt to mount a challenge to the tradition of bourgeois aesthetics, which they saw as aesthetically bankrupt and politically authoritarian.

base. In Marxist theory, the economic system of a society, as determined by the dominant mode of production. So-called vulgar Marxists tend to see the base as determining the character of the remainder of society, or the superstructure. Most Marxist critics see the base and superstructure as interrelated in more complex ways.

binary thinking. See *Aristotelian logic.*

bourgeois cultural revolution. In Marxist thought, the historical process (extending roughly from the fifteenth to the nineteenth century) through which the bourgeoisie gradually supplanted the aristocracy and the Catholic Church as the most powerful ruling forces in Europe, resulting in a shift from feudalism to capitalism as the dominant economic system.

bourgeoisie. In Marxist theory, the class in a capitalist society that owns the means of production and derives its wealth from exploitation of labor of the working class, or proletariat.

bourgeois subject. See *subjectivity.*

bricolage. In structuralist and poststructuralist criticism, the assembly of items from bits and pieces of materials collected from various sources. In literature, the assembly of texts as a patchwork of fragments from other texts.

capitalism. Economic system (typical of modern Western Europe and North America) in which the private capital or wealth is used to finance business activities, the profits from which then go to increase that wealth. Under capitalism, a relatively small number of individuals, or capitalists, own most of the means of production of wealth (for example, factories and stores), while most individuals are employed as workers who do not share in these profits but work for wages that must be set below the actual value of their labor in order for profits to be made.

carceral. Having to do with prisons. Used by Michel Foucault to describe the nature of modern bourgeois societies, in which he sees everyday life as controlled and administered to an unprecedented extent. See *carceral society.*

carceral society. For Foucault, a society that is based on fundamentally carceral practices; that is, on the control of the behavior of the population through carceral techniques. Also known as a "disciplinary society."

carnivalesque. Having to with images of exuberant transgression, rule breaking, and collapse of hierarchies. Associated with Mikhail Bakhtin's description of the work of François Rabelais and other writers.

chronotope. The fundamental attitude toward space and time (and the relationship between the two) that is prevalent in a given society at a given time. Coined by Mikhail Bakhtin, who emphasizes that literary genres tend to be characterized by specific chronotopes.

class. In Marxist theory, a group of people living under economic conditions that divide their mode of life, their interests, and their culture from those of the other classes and put them in hostile contrast to the latter. Under capitalism, the principal classes are the bourgeoisie and the proletariat.

class consciousness. According to Karl Marx, the sense of belonging to a class and of participating in the historical role of that class.

cliché. An expression or idea used so commonly that it has ceased to convey any substantial meaning but merely expresses habitual modes of speech or, at most, stereotypical ideas.

collective unconscious. A repository of unconscious primordial desires and impressions common to the entire human race. Associated with the psychoanalytic work of Carl Jung.

colonial discourse analysis. Field of study in which various European and North American texts (literary and otherwise) about the phenomena of colonialism and imperialism are analyzed in order to determine characteristic attitudes toward these phenomena and the role played by those attitudes in European and North American culture.

colonialism. A particular type of imperialism in which citizens of a ruling central state establish residence in foreign territories, or colonies, ruled by that state, usually in the interest of economic or political domination of the colony by the central state.

commodification. In Marxist thought, the process through which not only goods but also services, ideas, activities, and ultimately human beings are reduced to the status of commodities in a capitalist society. Somewhat similar to *reification.*

commodity. In Marxist terminology, a good produced for resale in a capitalist society. Commodities are aspects of the capitalist economy that are valued not for their use value but for their exchange value. Commodities are thus interchangeable and are not valued for any genuine properties of their own.

communism. Political and economic system (first envisioned by Karl Marx) based on common ownership of property, especially of the means of production. In such a system, each member works for the common benefit of all rather than for his or her own individual interests. Marx summarized the basis of communist society with his famous slogan "From each according to his ability, to each according to his need." Contrast *individualism.*

cultural materialism. The belief, associated especially with British Marxist thinkers such as Raymond Williams, that the development of culture is closely related to the historical development of material practices in a given society.

cultural studies. Field in which the techniques and concerns often applied to the study of literary texts are used to study culture as a whole. Cultural critics may continue to study literary texts, but they focus on the way these texts contribute to the workings of the larger culture that surrounds them. Such critics may also study film, television, advertizing, political speeches, and other "cultural texts" in order to try to gain an understanding of the workings of culture.

culture. Defined by Marxist critic Raymond Williams as the "lived experience of the people," culture in the general sense involves the entire range of social practices and customs through which a society defines itself and conducts its everyday activities. In the more restricted sense, culture usually means art, literature, and related aesthetic activities.

decentering. The process (common to much contemporary criticism) of attempting to shift attention from its traditional points of focus onto areas that have traditionally been ignored or unappreciated. In poststructuralist criticism, the term also implies an emphasis on the intertextual proliferation of meaning, leading to multiple interpretations that may differ substantially from the most obvious one.

defamiliarization. Literally, making strange. The process by which works of art or literature present new and unfamiliar perspectives on reality, causing individuals to understand reality in new and different ways. Believed by the Russian formalists to be the most important strategy for all works of art.

defense mechanisms. In psychoanalysis, strategies (generally unconscious) through which individuals avoid dealing with unpleasant psychic material by reconstituting it in different form, thus avoiding conflict or anxiety.

demystification. The critical act of revealing the hidden assumptions behind generally accepted attitudes or ideas.

diachronic. Having to do with the way attitudes, practices, and systems change over time.

dialectical. Technique of thought and analysis that relies on the careful consideration of opposing alternatives before the reaching of any final conclusions. First developed extensively by the German idealist philosopher G. W. F. Hegel, but now most often associated with the thought of Karl Marx.

dialectical materialism. Model of history, proposed by Karl Marx, that sees historical change as driven primarily by the resolution of opposition between forces whose material (economic) interests are at odds.

dialectical thought. Technique of thought in which conclusions are drawn only after careful consideration of opposing alternatives. Dialectical thought is particularly crucial to Marxism, though Marx himself derived it from the work of predecessors, especially the nineteenth-century German philosopher G. W. F. Hegel.

dialogic. The inherent ability of language to express multiple meanings simultaneously, especially because the same statement can mean different things in different contexts or to different readers or listeners. Associated primarily with the theories of Mikhail Bakhtin, for whom dialogism is a fundamental mode of thought that emphasizes multiple simultaneous perceptions of reality. For Bakhtin, dialogism finds its supreme literary expression in the novel.

disciplinary society. See *carceral society.*

discourse. In the most general sense, any use of language. Now most frequently used to refer to a body of texts or statements that are conditioned by a common set of assumptions, attitudes, and goals. This latter use is particularly associated with the work of Michel Foucault.

division of labor. The process by which different kinds of work are assigned to different individuals in a given society. Ultimately leads to the kind of intense specialization typical of modern capitalist societies and consequently (according to Karl Marx) to alienation of workers.

dualistic thinking. See *Aristotelian logic.*

dystopia. A society, originally envisioned as ideal, in which flaws in the original conception or abuses of the original system have caused the society to become oppressive to large numbers of its inhabitants. See *utopia.*

dystopian literature. Imaginative literary works that describe fictional dystopias, usually as a means of criticizing or warning against current or potential practices in the real world.

ego. Essentially equivalent, according to Sigmund Freud, to the conscious, thinking mind. The ego is also the principal interface between the psyche and the outside world and is a moderator between the authoritarian demands of the superego and the unmitigated desires of the id.

either-or logic. See *Aristotelian logic.*

Elizabethan. Relating to England during the reign of Elizabeth I (1558–1603).

Enlightenment. The historical period (roughly from the seventeenth through the nineteenth century) immediately after the Renaissance in which reason, rationality, and scientific inquiry became central values in European thought.

epic theater. Type of drama, associated mostly with the work of twentieth-century German dramatist Bertolt Brecht, that employs a number of unconventional techniques to call attention to its status as a work of fiction and to encourage its audience to react to the drama intellectually and critically rather than emotionally. See *alienation effect, metafiction.*

***episteme* (also *epistemé*).** The fundamental conditions determining the characteristic style in which knowledge is pursued and formulated in a given society in a given period. Associated with the work of Michel Foucault, especially in *The Order of Things*. In his later work, Foucault emphasized that different disciplines might behave according to different epistemes in the same historical period.

epistemology. The branch of philosophy that deals with knowledge about being or existence and the ways in which this knowledge is obtained.

essentialist. An attitude marked by a belief that certain characteristics are inherent to certain groups. Usually used in a negative sense to describe the overly simplistic way some thinkers attribute inherent qualities to individuals on the basis of race, gender, or other categories.

exchange value. The price commanded by a good or service in a capitalist economy. Determined, according to Karl Marx, by the total amount of human labor required to produce the item rather than by the actual value of the uses to which it can be put.

false consciousness. An inaccurate perception of the social world resulting from ideological practices that strives to conceal the true nature of social relations from individuals. See *ideology.*

feudalism. Economic system (typical of Europe in the Middle Ages) in which a hereditary aristocracy maintained political power and land ownership, while granting the use of land to individuals (serfs, or vassals) in return for obedience and service.

figurative language. Language that, through various formal or stylistic devices, expresses meanings that differ from the literal meaning of the language. Similar to *connotative language.*

formalism. Type of literary criticism that interprets literary works primarily through a focus on the form, structure, and language of those works. Formalist critics tend to place great emphasis on style and technique in the construction of literary works. Prominent formalist schools include Russian formalism in the early twentieth century and American New Criticism in the mid-twentieth century.

Frankfurt School. A group of twentieth-century German Marxist theorists (including Theodor Adorno, Max Horkheimer, Herbert Marcuse, and Jürgen Habermas) who have been associated with the Institute for Social Analysis in Frankfurt, Germany. While the thinkers in this group may differ significantly in their ideas, Frankfurt-School Marxists continue to place a great deal of importance on the economic system in a given society, even while often focusing on discussions of culture and literature.

genealogy. Type of historical research promulgated by Michel Foucault. Somewhat similar to archaeology, except that the results of genealogical research tend to emphasize similarities between different historical periods, though without suggesting specific narratives models of the process of historical development from one period to another. In *Madness and Civilization,* for example, Foucault demonstrates that certain attitudes toward madness in the eighteenth century already contained the seeds of nineteenth-century psychiatry, even though that psychiatry seemed to make earlier approaches to madness obsolete.

genre. A specific type of literary work, the members of which are connected through adherence to certain characteristic conventions or techniques. The term is used on a number of different levels by different critics. Some use it to mean fundamental literary modes such as comedy, romance, tragedy, and satire. Others use it to mean basic literary forms such as fiction, drama, and poetry. It may also be applied to subsets of these forms with varying levels of specificity. To some critics, for example, the novel is a genre, whereas to others specific types of novels (the bildungsroman, the historical novel) are genres. The most sophisticate recent theories of genre have been those by critics such as Mikhail Bakhtin and Fredric Jameson, who tend to emphasize the characteristic ideology that lies behind a given genre.

grotesque body. The aspects of the human body associated with activities such as sex, eating, and excrement in which the boundaries of the individual body are shown to be open and permeable, emphasizing the connection of human beings to other human beings and to the world around them. Associated by Mikhail Bakhtin with prominent images in the work of François Rabelais.

gynocritics. Criticism that focuses on the study of literature by women, particularly to emphasize the role of gender issues in such literature. Coined by the feminist critic Elaine Showalter. Also called gynocriticism.

hegemony. The process through which the bourgeoisie (though a minority) maintains its power in a capitalist society through processes of ideological domination that cause the proletariat to accept bourgeois ideology and therefore submit willingly to domination. Associated with the work of Antonio Gramsci, who argues that bourgeois power resides more in ideological techniques of persuasion than in direct techniques of coercion.

hermeneutic. Pertaining to interpretation. The science of hermeneutics deals with the phenomenon of interpretation, especially of texts. This science has its roots in the interpretation and study of sacred texts.

heteroglossia. Literally, multiple languages. Expresses the complex nature of modern societies, which are informed by an intricate mixture of different attitudes and modes of linguistic expression. For Mikhail Bakhtin, the interaction among the different attitudes and opinions of a society has a rich potential that finds its ultimate literary expression in the novel.

historicity. The characteristic of being related to the flow of history and of changing with history.

historiography. The discipline of the writing of history, or the study of different styles and theories of the writing of history.

humanism. Belief in the importance of human activity and of the ability of human beings to solve problems common to humanity through rational action. Often implies a devotion to studies promoting literature and culture as expressions of human concerns, especially within the context of the Renaissance.

hybridity. The property of being informed by differing social and cultural positions. Postcolonial critics such as Homi Bhabha have emphasized that the colonial encounter between European and non-European cultures resulted in a permanent modification and influence of each culture by the other.

id. According to Sigmund Freud, the portion of the human psyche that is the site of unconscious, natural drives; a dark area of seething passion that knows only desire and has no sense of moderation or limitation.

idealism. The belief (associated with bourgeois philosophers such as G. W. F. Hegel and Immanuel Kant) that certain universal abstract principles (like truth or beauty) provide a fundamental basis for human endeavor and the design of human societies. Compare *metaphysical*. Contrast *materialism*.

identity theme. Characteristic patterns of interpretation and perception that define the personal styles of individuals. According to Norman Holland, the meaning of a literary work for a given reader is largely determined by that reader's identity theme.

Ideological State Apparatus. In the Marxist philosophy of Louis Althusser, any one of numerous institutions and practices that act to convince the general population (especially the working class) to accept the ideology of the ruling class (especially the bourgeoisie). Examples include schools, churches, the family, and culture.

ideology. A particular view of the world, typically informed by a specific social and political position, though that position may or may not be openly expressed. In much traditional Marxist criticism, ideology (sometimes associated with "false consciousness") is seen as a distortion of reality that helps the bourgeoisie maintain dominance over the proletariat in capitalist society. Much recent Marxist criticism, however, recognizes that this opposition between ideology and reality is simplistic. Such critics, especially Louis Althusser, emphasize that all perceptions of reality are influenced by one or another kind of ideology.

Imaginary Order. In the psychoanalysis of Jacques Lacan, the area of the human psyche dominated by the preverbal infantile stage of joyful fusion with the mother's body. The primary locus of fantasies and images and thus of obvious importance for the study of literature.

imperialism. Political system in which a single central state rules a collection of other territories, usually comprising citizens of nationalities different from that of the ruling state. Generally believed by Marxist critics to be an inevitable consequence of the drive for new markets and new sources of labor and materials that is central to capitalism.

individualism. Belief in the importance and autonomy of individual human beings as opposed to the importance of the social group. Generally associated with bourgeois ideology and with capitalism. Marxist critics note that individualism leads to an emphasis on competition, rather than cooperation, between individuals, thus making it possible for a bourgeois minority to exploit a working-class majority.

inform. To make a substantive contribution to an idea or attitude, as when a desire for social and economic justice informs Karl Marx's critique of capitalism.

intentional fallacy. The belief (considered fallacious by the New Critics) that the meaning of a work of literature is determined by the original intention of the author.

interpellation. The "hailing of the subject" by dominant ideologies, that is, the process through which the identities of individuals are shaped and molded by the prevailing views of the society in which they live.

interpretive community. Groups of individuals that, because of shared training or experience, tend to employ similar interpretive strategies or to interpret texts in similar ways. Associated with the later work of Stanley Fish.

intersubjectivity. The process of interaction or communication between different individuals, or subjects. Many recent critics (including Mikhail Bakhtin and a number of Marxist and feminist critics) have emphasized the importance of intersubjectivity as the source of subjectivity, rather than the other way around.

intertextuality. Term (coined by Julia Kristeva in reference to Mikhail Bakhtin's theory of language) that indicates the complex network of interrelations that ultimately links all texts together. May include overt forms such as allusion, but may also include the more subtle ways in which the system of language itself creates links among texts.

irony. Complex phenomenon through which language in one way or another implies a meaning or meanings that differ from the literal meaning of that language. A form of figurative language distinguished by the way the implied meaning often mounts a direct challenge to the literal meaning. Privileged by the New Critics as a crucial property of the best literature.

Jacobean. Relating to England during the reign of King James I (1603–1625).

Kantian subject. See *subjectivity.*

langue. In structuralist criticism, the rules and conventions that determine the ways in which a language can be used or understood by its speakers or listeners.

l'écriture féminine. Literally, women's writing. Associated by Hélène Cixous with the fluid, melodic language that is a natural result of feminine thought processes and especially of a special feminine relationship to the body.

le parler femme. Literally, women's speech. Associated by Luce Irigaray with the kinds of language use produced by women to help overcome their traditional domination by men in patriarchal society.

liberal humanism. See *liberalism.*

liberalism. Humanist political philosophy, central to capitalism, focusing on a belief in individual liberty, free enterprise, and democratic government. Generally implies gradual social and political reform leading to improvement and progress for society and for individuals. Marxist critics see liberalism as an illusion intended to hide the economic exploitation that is the true heart of capitalism. Also known as liberal humanism.

literal language. Language that states its meaning in precise, direct, and unambiguous terms. Similar to *denotative language.*

local knowledge. See *thick descriptions.*

logocentric. The notion (derived from the monotheistic religions of the Judeo-Christian tradition) that there is an ultimate center and ground to philosophical truth. Poststructuralist theorists such as Jacques Derrida have argued that Western philosophy has traditionally been informed by this mode of thought, which is insufficient for the appreciation of certain complexities of language and reality. Similar to *metaphysical.*

magical realism. A literary mode (generally associated with third-world and especially Latin American literature) in which fantastic and magical events are described in a straightforward way that makes them seem unremarkable or unsurprising. The effect is to suggest that seemingly fantastic events occur in the third world on a routine basis. Leading practitioners of magical realism include Gabriel García Márquez, Isabelle Allende, Gunter Grass, Ben Okri, and Salman Rushdie.

Manichean. Type of binary thought that tends to view reality in terms of radically opposed pairs, each entirely alien to the other, such as good and evil. Postcolonial theorists have emphasized the tendency of European colonialist thinkers to view the opposition between Europeans and non-Europeans in these terms.

materialism. The belief that physical reality (not abstract concepts) should be the basis for all human endeavor. Generally implies a belief in the historicity of all human attitudes and values, especially in the work of Karl Marx. Contrast *idealism.*

material practice. Any activity that is ultimately related to the production and distribution of goods and services in a society.

means of production. In Marxist thought, the material resources through which goods and services are produced in a given society.

Menippean satire. Genre (named for the ancient Greek satirist Menippus) associated by Mikhail Bakhtin with carnivalesque qualities in literature. Menippean satires tend to explore both fundamental philosophical ideas and controversial current events. They combine naturalistic detail with fantastic images. And they tend to combine the formal features of numerous other genres.

metafiction. Fiction that is largely about fiction. Rather than relate a narrative that is intended to mirror reality, metafiction calls attention to its own status as fiction and to the strategies through which it was constructed by its author. In drama, known as *metadrama.*

metaphor. A form of figurative language in which two seemingly different ideas or images are directly linked without the use of a connecting term such as "like" or "as." This linkage invites a comparison between the characteristics of the two ideas or images that presumably produces a new and fresh insight. Thus, the metaphor "truth is beauty" links the concepts of truth and beauty in ways that provide a new perspective on both. Often, metaphors lose their power through overuse, and thus become clichés.

metaphysical. Associated with the belief that the truth of reality is determined by abstract concepts or forces that go beyond the physical world. Typically viewed by poststructuralist critics as a negative characteristic leading to logocentric thought. Compare *idealism.*

metonymy. A form of figurative langage in which one word or image is substituted for another with which it has a close and natural connection. In particular, metonymy often involves the substitution of a characteristic of a thing for the thing itself. For example, to say that one lives "by the sweat of his brow" is a use of metonymy in which sweat, a characteristic result of hard work, substitutes for hard work itself.

mimesis. The process by which art or literature represents reality. The fictional world of mimetic art is generally expected to resemble the real world.

minor literature. Term coined by the French poststructuralist philosophers Gilles Deleuze and Félix Guattari to refer to literature written in a major European language by an author whose nationality is different from that implied by the language. Franz Kafka (a Czech Jew who wrote in German) is their central example, though Irish writers in English (James Joyce, Samuel Beckett) would also be good examples. Sometimes used now in the context of postcolonial literature written in the language of the formal imperial rulers.

mirror stage. In the psychoanalysis of Jacques Lacan, the stage (at about six to eighteen months of age) during which the infant begins to gain a sense of her own existence as a separate entity and to establish an awareness of the boundaries of her own body through its literal mirror image or through outside objects—notably the mother.

mode of production. The system by which production of goods and services is organized in a given society. Examples include the feudal mode of production of the Middle Ages and the capitalist mode of production of the modern era.

modernism. Important European and American artistic movement associated largely with the early twentieth century. Modernist works tend to be marked by intense focus on style and technique, which are often highly experimental. Modernist art is also informed by an intense sense of cultural and historical crisis, though different modernist writers (showing a wide range of political and aesthetic attitudes) react to this sense in very different ways. Leading modernist writers include James Joyce, Franz Kafka, Virginia Woolf, T. S. Eliot, and William Faulkner.

modernity. The historical phenomenon associated with the coming of the modern world, usually beginning in the early decades of the twentieth century. Modernity tends to be marked by a radical alienation in which individuals must strive to find a stable identity in a world wrought by radical change and the destruction of tradition. See *modernism.*

monologism. A style of thought based on a belief that there is one correct vision of the world. Associated by Mikhail Bakhtin with certain shortcomings of the Western philosophical tradition, with implications that it is linked to political oppression as well. Informed by Aristotelian logic. Somewhat similar to *logocentric* or *metaphysical* thought.

naturalism. Literary and artistic movement of the late nineteenth and early twentieth centuries. Naturalist literature is marked by an intense focus on detailed, almost scientific, representation of very specific aspects of life. It often deals with the more negative aspects of human existence and tends to see human life as determined by social and biological conditions beyond individual control. Naturalist literature is often highly critical of the economic exploitation central to capitalism. Leading naturalist writers include Émile Zola, Upton Sinclair, Frank Norris, and Theodore Dreiser.

Oedipal drama. The crucial process during which, according to Sigmund Freud, the young child must come to grips with the fact that his (and to an extent her) natural desires are limited by social reality. In particular, the child must come to realize that his or her erotic desire for the mother cannot be fulfilled because of the forbidding presence of the father.

ontology. The branch of philosophy that deals with the nature or essence of being or existence.

organic unity. The ability of all of the parts of a well-structured literary work to combine together to create a single, harmonious effect or impression. The term is derived from the way in which the various parts of a plant work together to create a coherent, living whole. Associated by the New Critics with the best works of literature, but often challenged by poststructuralist critics as a fallacious criterion.

Orientalism. The discourse, or body of texts and statement, by which Europeans in the eighteenth and nineteenth centuries developed stereotypical views of non-Europeans that acted to produce an image of Europeans as superior, especially in terms of rationality and responsibility. Derived from Edward Said's description of negative European stereotypes of Middle Eastern Arabs.

Panopticon. A prison design, first proposed by the British thinker Jeremy Bentham and important to nineteenth-century penal reform, in which the cells of prisoners are arranged in a circle around a central observation tower. All prisoners can thus be kept under surveillance at all times. Used metaphorically by Michel Foucault to describe the ability of modern governments efficiently to keep track of the movements of their citizens in the world at large.

parole. In structuralist criticism, the collection of actual uses of language that constitute the everyday life of a language.

patriarchy. Literally, rule by the father. The tendency, prevalent in most of the world, for societies to be dominated not only by men but also by masculine values and ideas.

phenomenology. The branch of knowledge, growing from the work of such twentieth-century philosophers as Edmund Husserl and Martin Heidegger, that deals with events as they are registered by the human consciousness in the flow of time. Phenomenological criticism is thus concerned with the ways works of literature are perceived by their readers.

pleasure principle. In psychoanalysis, the concept that, especially in infants, the fulfillment of individual desire (of a primarily erotic variety, though the erotic for Sigmund Freud goes well beyond conventional notions of the sexual) is the ultimate goal of life.

polyphony. The process through which multiple voices (generally representing different social positions and attitudes) interact in a literary text. Coined by Mikhail Bakhtin to describe the novels of Fyodor Dostoevsky.

positivism. Philosophical system that recognizes only positive facts and observable phenomenon, usually emphasizing that the only valid facts are those that can be verified by scientific observation.

postcolonial literature. Literature produced by writers from emerging nations that had previously been colonized by European imperial powers such as Great Britain and France. Leading postcolonial writers include Indian writers Salman Rushdie and Anita Desai; African writers Ngugi wa Thiong'o, Chinua Achebe, Wole Soyinka, and Buchi Emecheta; and Caribbean writers Derek Walcott and Michael Thelwell.

postmodernism. Artistic and literary movement of the latter half of the twentieth century marked by an extension of the formal experimentation of modernism but by an ironic and skeptical sense that differs strongly from the respect for the power of art typically found in modernist writers. Postmodernist literature tends to be playful and parodic and incorporates elements from popular culture as well as the tradition of "high" art. Leading postmodernist writers include E. L. Doctorow, Gabriel García Márquez, Thomas Pynchon, and Salman Rushdie.

poststructuralism. General term for a variety of approaches to literature, philosophy, and other disciplines that arose in the late 1960s, largely as a reaction to what was perceived as the overly rigid techniques of structuralism. Poststructuralism is marked by a radical skepticism toward the metaphysical tradition of Western philosophy and by a strong belief in the capacity of language to generate multiple meanings. Poststructuralist critics thus often focus on the language in a text and on its inherent ambiguities; but poststructuralist thought can be applied to any number of fields or disciplines.

privilege. To place special value on something for specific theoretical reasons. Sometimes associated by poststructuralist critics with the way in which Western philosophy tends to view reality by dividing it into dual oppositions, then privileging one term in the opposition over the other.

proletariat. According to the Marxist view of capitalism, the working class, whose interests are diametrically opposed to those of its bourgeois employers.

Real Order. In the psychoanalysis of Jacques Lacan, the deepest and most inaccessible part of the human psyche. It is concerned with fundamental and emotionally powerful experiences such as death and sexuality and is available to consciousness only in extremely brief and fleeting moments of joy and terror that Lacan describes as *jouissance*.

realism. Artistic and literary movement in which works are presumed to embody the fundamental characteristics of reality. Realistic works tend to focus on typical individuals in typical situations, though they may at the same time imply larger themes and historical processes. Marxist critics such as Georg Lukács have emphasized the importance of realism as a dominant mode of European art and literature during the nineteenth century when the bourgeoisie were at the height of its historical power. Leading bourgeois realist writers include Honoré de Balzac, Gustave Flaubert, George Eliot, and Thomas Mann. Socialist writers in the twentieth century have attempted to adapt realism to the expression of a socialist message, especially in the movement known as *socialist realism.*

reality principle. In psychoanalysis, the concept (which must gradually be grasped by the maturing child) that individual desires are limited by social reality.

reception aesthetics. An approach to literature (associated primarily with the work of the German critics Jauss and Iser) that places its emphasis on the aesthetic experience of readers while reading and interpreting a literary work.

reflexivity. See *self-referentiality.*

reification. The process through which not only goods but also services, ideas, activities, and ultimately human beings are reduced to the status of objects (stripped of all mystery or spiritual significance) in a capitalist society. In particular, all traces of the human labor involved in the production of goods are removed, making the goods seem self-sufficient. Leads, according to Marxist theorist Georg Lukács, to the fragmentation of different aspects of capitalist society into separate realms and to the loss of any sense of wholeness in life.

Renaissance. Literally, rebirth. The historical period, encompassing roughly the fourteenth to the eighteenth century (especially as described in modern historical accounts originating in the nineteenth century) in which the world view characteristic of Europe in the Middle Ages was supplanted by a new spirit of humanism and artistic creativity. Contemporary scholars often prefer the term *early modern period* to the term *Renaissance,* which seems to imply that Western culture was dead during the Middle Ages.

representation. The process through which meaning is expressed in a literary text. In traditional philosophy, representation is the process through which language conveys some preexisting meaning or reality. In recent criticism, especially poststructuralist criticism, there is much emphasis on the way in which meaning is actually generated in the process of representation.

repression. In psychoanalysis, the process through which unpleasant or unacceptable thoughts or desires are forced out of conscious awareness and relocated in the unconscious mind. Also often used in a political sense to indicate the process by which authoritarian governments forbid opposition to their policies.

Repressive State Apparatus. In the Marxist philosophy of Louis Althusser, any institution that employs techniques of repression to coerce the general population (especially the working class) into obedience to the commands of the ruling class (especially the bourgeoisie). Principal examples include the police and the military.

self-referentiality. Characteristic of works that call attention to their status as art and that represent the process of artistic creation rather than exterior reality. Similar to *reflexivity.* See *metafiction.*

semiotic language. In the work of Julia Kristeva, language that relies not on the direct expression of preexisting meaning, but on the creation of emotional impressions and effects through sound, rhythm, and related techniques. Kristeva associates this kind of language with poetry, music, and feminine thought.

sign. A unit (usually of language) in which some preexisting concept or thing is represented. For the structuralist Ferdinand de Saussure, the sign has two parts: The *signifier* is the written or spoken symbol itself, whereas the *signified* is the concept or meaning that the symbol represents. In turn, the signified is generally seen as an abstract concept that stands in for the physical item, or *referent,* being represented.

signification. The process of expressing meaning through signs, usually language.

socialism. A political and economic system in which the good of the community as a whole is valued over the desires of specific individuals. Generally implies community, rather than individual, ownership of the means of production. Generally associated with the thought of Karl Marx (for whom socialism is a transitional state between capitalism and communism), though there are many different socialist traditions.

socialist realism. A type of realism (generally associated with the literature of the Soviet Union) that attempts to convey an accurate representation of reality informed by a strong sense of the historical movement beyond capitalism to socialism. Socialist realist works are generally also expected to be accessible to ordinary readers and therefore to eschew experimental stylistic strategies. Leading socialist realist writers include Maxim Gorky, Mikhail Sholokhov, Valentin Kataev, and Fyodor Gladkov.

speech genres. Characteristic types of speech governed by specific conventions and expectations, much like literary genres. Mikhail Bakhtin emphasizes that all language use, including everyday speech, is governed by genre conventions of one kind or another.

stream of consciousness. A literary technique (usually associated with modernism) in which the inner thoughts and feelings of a character are represented in such a way as to create the impression that the reader is viewing these thoughts and feelings as they might occur to the character herself.

structuralism. A technique of thought that was extremely influential in Europe in the middle part of the twentieth century. Structuralist techniques basically rely on the insight that languages obey certain basic structural principles and that other human practices and institutions, being largely the products of language, obey similar principles. Structuralism builds upon the linguistic theories of Ferdinand de Saussure and came to be applied to virtually all areas of intellectual endeavor: Lacan applied structuralist methods to psychoanalysis; Althusser applied structuralism to Marxist analysis; and Lévi-Struauss applied structuralism to anthropology. Critics like Barthes and Todorov applied structuralism to literary criticism.

subaltern. Term coined by Italian Marxist Antonio Gramsci to refer to groups or classes in a society other than those that are politically dominant. The proletariat is the most important subaltern class in Europe, though the term is now widely used in connection with colonial and postcolonial peoples, especially in the work of a group of Indian historians who publish the journal *Subaltern Studies.*

subjectivity. Existence as an individual human being. In traditional bourgeois thought, the subject is an autonomous, fully formed entity, typically referred to in criticism as the bourgeois subject, the Kantian subject, or the transcendental subject. For poststructuralist critics, the subject is an unstable product of language that is continually in the process of creation. For Mikhail Bakhtin and for many Marxist and feminist critics, the subject is the product of ongoing social interactions with other subjects.

sublimation. In psychoanalysis, the process through which unconscious (usually repressed) material reemerges in the conscious mind in a modified (and therefore more acceptable) form.

superego. According to Sigmund Freud, the portion of the unconscious mind that acts as a sort of internalized representation of the authority of the father and of society, authority that establishes strict limitations on the fulfillment of the unrestrained desires residing in the id.

superstructure. In Marxist theory, the part of society that includes culture, politics, religion, education, and various other practices and institutions that go beyond the economic sphere. Marxist theorists such as Antonio Gramsci and Louis Althusser have emphasized the importance of the superstructure as the focus of bourgeois control over society as a whole.

surrealism. An avant-garde artistic movement of the early twentieth century. Surrealist art strives to tap into the unconscious mind and to achieve striking effects through the combination of seemingly incongruous images.

symbol. A form of figurative language in which a specific, concrete image, or thing is used to represent a larger and more complex set of associations and ideas. For example, the well-known hammer and sickle emblem involves two simple material objects, but their combination creates a symbol that evokes an entire range of ideas and principles that are central to Communism, such as a belief in the value of labor and the dignity and humanity of workers.

symbolic language. In the work of Julia Kristeva, language associated primarily with the direct expression of preexisting meaning. Kristeva associates this kind of language with masculine thought.

Symbolic Order. In the psychoanalysis of Jacques Lacan, the area of the human psyche (mostly in the conscious mind) that is primarily concerned with language and symbolic representation.

synchronic. Having to do with the nature of practices or attitudes prevalent at a given point in time.

technologies of the self. The process, described by Michel Foucault in his later work, through which individuals develop their own identities in relationship to the structure of power in the society around them.

teleological. Relating to or tending toward a specific final goal or conclusion.

text. In traditional criticism, the actual words of a given work. In poststructuralist criticism, a replacement for the notion of a "work" to indicate the belief that works are not autonomous, self-contained artifacts, but always engage in extensive relationships with other works, if only because they consist of language, as do the other texts.

textuality. In poststructuralist criticism, describes the dynamic relationship between literary works and the system of language. Suggests the existence of the work in dynamic tension with other works and with the activities of the reader or critic.

thick descriptions. Detailed descriptions of a limited aspect of the ideas and practices of a given society at a given time. Associated with the anthropology of Clifford Geertz and adapted for use by new historicist literary critics. Similar to *local knowledge.*

totalizing. Having to do with a mode of thought that attempts to encompass a broad range of phenomena within a single systematic theory. Used in a negative sense by poststructuralist critics, who believe all totalizing theories to be simplistic. Used in a positive sense by Marxist critics such as Georg Lukács and Fredric Jameson to indicate the power of Marxist thought to explain and describe a broad range of social and cultural phenomena in coherent and consistent ways.

transcendental subject. See *subjectivity.*

typicality. In the Marxist philosophy of Georg Lukács, the property of being representative of large historical forces in a given society at a given time.

use value. The actual value of the uses to which a good or service can be put. Relatively unrelated, according to Karl Marx, to the market value of the item in a capitalist economy.

utopia. An ideal society. Now often associated with unreasonably idealistic visions of such a society, but believed by many Marxist critics (especially Fredric Jameson) to be a necessary element of any genuine vision of political change. See *dystopia.*

vernacular. The everyday language used by the common people of a given society.

woman's sentence. Term coined by Virginia Woolf to indicate her belief that women writers should develop their own characteristic styles of expression rather than being forced to employ styles that have been developed in the course of a literary tradition dominated by men.

Index

Abject imagery, 115, 121, 279, 292, 293, 298, 302, 473
Adamic language, 57, 112, 123, 473
Adewoye, Sam, 231, 235, 254, 387-394
Adorno, Theodor, 78, 79, 81, 86, 127, 281, 303, 304, 479
Aesthetics, 15, 18, 19, 20, 23, 24, 44, 52, 69, 72, 75, 77-79, 84-86, 128, 129, 131, 133, 139, 144, 152, 160, 169, 172, 175, 194, 237, 241, 474, 476, 483, 486
Affective fallacy, 14, 25, 41, 473
Affective stylistics, 41-45, 49, 230, 473
Agrarians, 15, 16, 473
Alienation, 15, 73, 74, 77, 163, 204, 239, 286, 299-302, 304, 306, 314, 473, 474, 477, 478, 483
Allegory, 31, 76, 155-157, 190, 210, 238, 244, 271, 288, 289, 296, 298, 300, 302, 303, 307, 474
Althusser, Louis, 57, 82-84, 86, 124, 126, 131, 157, 240, 264, 268, 304, 480, 486, 487, 488
Ambiguity, 20, 21, 31, 56, 66, 169, 172, 183, 314, 474
Archaeology, 120, 124, 125, 131, 132, 282, 474, 479
Archetypes, 34, 39, 200, 474
Aristotelian logic, 2, 59, 474, 475, 477, 478, 483
Atwood, Margaret, 10, 257-283, 409-426
Aura, 77, 265, 278, 474
Avant-garde art, 3, 79, 95, 157, 474, 488
Baker, Houston, 152, 160, 161
Bakhtin, Mikhail, 9, 93, 98, 103-117, 139, 146, 205-209, 211, 269-276, 282, 313, 475, 477, 479, 481-483, 485, 487
  The Dialogic Imagination, 103, 110, 111, 114, 115, 270, 275
  Problems of Dostoevsky's Poetics, 16, 29, 43, 47, 49, 79, 103, 111-113, 115, 150, 162, 168, 195, 233, 259, 273, 293, 298, 305, 480
  Rabelais and His World, 103, 105-108, 110, 113, 115, 116, 269, 274-276, 475, 479
Balogun, F. Odun, 238, 242, 254
Barker, Francis, 68, 193, 338-351
Barthes, Roland, 58, 63, 67, 104, 120, 138, 487
Base, 71, 74, 75, 474
Beardsley, Monroe, 14, 25, 41
Beavis and Butt-head, 2
Beckett, Samuel, 45, 52, 234, 483
Benjamin, Jessica, 294, 297
Benjamin, Walter, 76-79, 81, 84, 86, 116, 156, 157, 281, 302, 474
Bhabha, Homi, 154, 155, 157, 158, 160, 480
Bildungsroman, 256, 479
Binary thinking, 474, 475
Blackmur, R. P., 16
Bloom, Harold, 32, 38, 66, 67, 291, 313
Booker, M. Keith, 106, 108, 112, 114, 115, 126, 131, 262, 263, 281
Bourgeois cultural revolution, 81, 475

Bourgeoisie, 23, 72, 74-76, 80-82, 84, 85, 109, 120, 129, 130, 154, 203, 207, 227, 232, 233, 242, 244, 302, 473-475, 479-481, 485, 487, 488
Brecht, Bertolt, 86, 232, 237, 241, 242, 254, 474, 478
Bricolage, 64, 268, 475
Brooks, Cleanth, 14-18, 20-25, 207, 211, 286, 287, 290, 291
Burke, Kenneth, 16

Canon (literature), 95, 96, 98, 110, 138, 145, 151-153, 159, 161, 174, 181, 189, 193, 194, 199, 218, 221, 225, 313, 314
Capitalism, 15, 16, 23, 57, 72-76, 79-81, 86, 87, 94, 139, 153, 162, 216, 229, 230, 236-240, 242, 244, 246-248, 250, 254, 272, 286, 289, 290, 298, 299, 301, 302, 304, 305, 313, 473, 475-482, 484, 485, 486, 487, 489
Carby, Hazel, 100, 161, 299, 304, 308, 311
Carceral society, 125, 126, 250, 251, 253, 276, 279, 281, 475, 477
Carnivalesque images, 104-110, 113-116, 269, 273-275, 300, 475, 482
Castration, 28, 36, 37, 90-93, 100, 265, 293-296
Chatterjee, Partha, 155
Chronotope, 114, 115, 208, 475
Cixous, Hélène, 90-96, 99, 100, 282, 306, 307, 311, 481
Clark, Katerina, 103, 104, 110, 114-116, 271, 275
Class, 33, 49, 51, 61, 72, 74, 75, 81, 83, 84, 86, 87, 98, 99, 107, 139, 154, 161, 162, 174-176, 189, 199, 226, 229, 239, 243, 244, 250, 254, 256, 298, 305, 313, 337, 405, 475, 480, 481, 485-487
Class consciousness, 74, 75, 84, 87, 162, 305, 313, 475
Cold War, 17, 22, 23, 25, 35, 81, 199, 200
Collective unconscious, 34, 39, 204, 474, 476
Colonialism, 139, 144, 150, 151, 153-163, 167, 169, 171, 173, 174, 180-183, 190-199, 210, 213, 220, 221, 222, 225, 226, 227, 229, 233, 238, 240, 242-253, 290, 305, 312, 343-348, 476, 480, 487. *See also* Imperialism
Commodification, 73-75, 80, 84, 237-239, 258, 279, 299, 301, 304, 308, 476
Communism, 72, 75, 476, 487, 488
Condensation, 30, 31
Conrad, Joseph, 10, 33, 38, 39, 112, 116, 117, 143, 151, 157, 160, 187, 188, 193, 199-212, 215-228, 353-385
Culler, Jonathan, 44, 52, 67

de Beauvoir, Simone, 95, 96, 100
Decentering, 123, 149, 476
Deconstruction, 52, 55-69, 143, 157, 158, 167, 174-180, 257, 263-268
Defamiliarization, 15, 240, 288, 474, 477
Degeneration, 215-218, 373-375
Deleuze, Gilles, 131, 153, 161, 483
de Man, Paul, 66, 67, 69, 104, 116, 136
Demystification, 171, 477
Derrida, Jacques, 39, 56, 57, 59-69, 79, 90, 104, 120, 131-133, 138, 175, 176, 265-268, 296, 297, 482
Diachronic approaches, 122, 477
Dialectical thought, 72, 86, 305, 477
Dialogism, 100, 103-105, 108-115, 206-211, 269-274, 477
Disciplinary society, 120, 126, 475, 477
Displacement, 30, 31, 129
Division of labor, 36, 59, 72, 73, 266, 477
Dreams, 27, 30-33, 38, 48, 202-204, 206, 241, 313, 314
Dualistic thought, 59, 60, 66, 141, 265, 474, 477
Dystopian thought, 126, 131, 237, 257, 258, 262-264, 266, 269-272, 279-283, 419-425, 477

Eagleton, Terry, 9, 16, 24, 62, 68, 73, 78, 84-86, 107, 109, 116, 120, 129-131
Ego, 29, 33, 38, 47, 48, 200, 310, 478
Eliot, T. S., 15, 17, 24, 69, 108, 143, 483
Ellmann, Mary, 96, 100
Emerson, Caryl, 103, 104, 108, 110, 111, 113, 115, 116, 275
Enkrateia, 128
Enlightenment, 6, 56, 78, 79, 86, 87, 121, 122, 127, 156, 188, 220, 303, 304, 478
Epic theater, 237, 474, 478
Episteme, 122-124, 478
Epistemology, 99, 101, 104, 131-133, 175, 202, 259, 283, 478
Essentialism, 91, 95, 478
Exchange value, 60, 73, 76, 84, 92, 138, 141, 201, 296, 299, 476, 478
Extrinsic approaches, 3, 4, 19, 138, 258, 259

False consciousness, 82, 478, 480
Fanon, Frantz, 153-155, 158, 160, 161, 163, 236, 242, 254, 362
The Wretched of the Earth, 154, 160, 236, 242, 362
Feminist criticism, 8, 37, 84, 89-102, 108, 112, 130, 144, 151, 154, 242-248, 305-312
Feudalism, 72, 73, 81, 478, 483
Figurative language, 31, 258, 267, 288, 290, 478, 481-483, 488. *See also* Metaphor, Metonymy
Fish, Stanley, 41-47, 49-52, 169-171, 174, 230, 233, 473, 481
Formalism, 14, 15, 17, 19, 23-25, 42, 53, 56, 60, 111, 115, 138, 144, 170, 263, 286, 478

Foucault, Michel, 9, 50, 56, 58, 67, 68, 79, 84, 98-101, 119-133, 136-139, 141, 146, 155, 167, 175, 193, 248-254, 275-281, 283, 296, 349, 416, 419, 474, 475, 477-479, 484, 488
The Archaeology of Knowledge, 124, 125, 131, 281
The Birth of the Clinic, 121, 122, 131, 136, 146, 254
The Care of the Self, 31, 129, 131, 281
Discipline and Punish, 125-127, 131, 136, 146, 248, 250, 254
The History of Sexuality, 98, 100, 126, 127, 129, 131, 132, 136, 250, 276, 277, 281, 419
Madness and Civilization, 121, 126, 132, 136, 296, 479
The Order of Things, 122-124, 132, 136, 478
The Use of Pleasure, 127, 129, 132
Frankfurt School, 78, 80, 479
Freud, Sigmund, 27-40, 48, 61, 80, 94, 111, 125-127, 200, 202-204, 233, 276, 292-297, 307, 313, 431, 478, 480, 484, 488

Gates, Henry Louis, Jr., 158-161, 191, 469
Gautier, Xaviére, 90, 100
Geertz, Clifford, 137, 138, 146, 327, 488
Gender, 36, 37, 91, 93, 95, 96, 98-101, 130, 141, 176, 179, 180, 182, 199, 216, 229, 243-245, 248, 257, 258, 266, 293, 296, 297, 304, 305, 307, 478, 479
Genealogy, 59, 120, 121, 125, 131, 479
Genre, 77, 104, 109-112, 114, 160, 195, 196, 204, 232, 257, 268-273, 313, 479, 482, 487
Gilbert, Sandra, 97-100
Graff, Gerald, 16, 24, 66, 120, 221, 225
Gramsci, Antonio, 74, 81, 82, 85, 86, 133, 150, 155, 479, 487, 488
Greenblatt, Stephen, 68, 136, 139-146, 167, 169, 170, 174, 181, 183-186, 191-193, 195, 319-338
Renaissance Self-Fashioning, 139-141, 145, 146
Shakespearean Negotiations, 140, 141, 146, 167, 174, 184, 186, 195
Grotesque body, 106, 479
Gubar, Susan, 97-100
Guha, Ranajit, 155, 161
Gynocritics, 96, 99, 479

Habermas, Jürgen, 78-80, 86, 87, 479
Hammer, Stephanie Barbé, 277, 282, 283, 409-419
Hartman, Geoffrey, 66, 68, 297
Hawkins, Hunt, 219, 222-226
Hegel, G. W. F., 71, 213, 214, 218, 268, 477, 480
Hegemony, 81, 82, 107, 153, 176, 479
Heresy of paraphrase, 14
Hermeneutics, 58, 259, 284, 479
Heteroglossia, 106, 110, 211, 479
Hirsch, E. D., 66
Holland, Norman, 33, 47-52, 172, 174, 233, 480
Holquist, Michael, 103-105, 107, 110, 112, 114-116, 271, 275
Horkheimer, Max, 78, 79, 86, 127, 303, 304, 479
Hulme, Peter, 169-171, 174, 183, 186, 193, 195
Humanism, 24, 85, 97, 98, 120, 236, 255, 480-482, 486
Hybridity, 153, 158, 194, 215, 269, 480

Id, 29, 30, 33, 200, 201, 226, 478, 480, 488
Idealism, 62, 71, 228, 477, 480, 482, 483
Identity theme, 47-50, 172, 233, 480
Ideological state apparatus, 82, 240, 480
Ideology, 21, 23, 57, 62, 74, 76, 78, 80-86, 105, 110, 111, 116, 121, 126, 130, 131, 139, 143, 145, 151, 157, 160, 162, 172, 182, 183, 192, 194, 212, 215, 217, 218, 227, 238, 240, 258, 267, 270, 272, 290, 291, 302-304, 478-481
Imaginary order, 35, 37, 91-93, 201, 294-296, 306, 307, 480
Imperialism, 8, 61, 62, 129, 150-163, 180-182, 186-189, 194, 195, 199, 203, 205, 207, 210-212, 216, 218-220, 223-229, 233, 234, 236, 237, 240-242, 291, 353-366, 476, 480. *See also* Colonialism
Implied reader, 44, 46, 52
Individualism, 80, 124, 129, 130, 253, 302, 476, 481
Ingarden, Roman, 44, 52
Intentional fallacy, 14, 25, 481
Interpellation, 82, 83, 264, 304, 481
Interpretive communities, 50, 51, 170, 172-174, 233, 481
Intersubjectivity, 111, 129, 310, 481
Intertextuality, 58, 63, 64, 104, 112, 138, 193, 207, 339-341, 476, 481
Intrinsic approaches, 19, 105, 114, 138, 261
Irigaray, Luce, 90, 94, 100, 481
Irony, 20, 21, 56, 100, 209, 225, 227, 259, 261, 290, 481
Iser, Wolfgang, 44-47, 51, 52, 172, 232, 233, 486

Jameson, Fredric, 80, 81, 84, 86, 87, 109, 154-157, 160, 162, 206, 212, 218, 298, 301, 302, 303, 305, 479, 489
JanMohamed, Abdul, 154, 158, 160
Jauss, Hans Robert, 44, 52, 486
Johnson, Barbara, 60, 66-68

Jones, Ann Rosalind, 91, 100
Jones, Ernest, 28, 29, 39
Joyce, James, 18, 32, 37, 38, 49, 61, 75, 76, 91, 96, 104, 108, 112, 115, 116, 143, 146, 153, 234, 235, 483
Jung, Carl, 32, 34, 39, 200, 204, 474, 476
Juraga, Dubravka, 106, 108, 112, 114, 115

Kafka, Franz, 75, 76, 153, 161, 204, 483
Kershner, R. B., Jr., 52, 104, 112, 116, 143, 146, 215, 218
Klein, Melanie, 33, 34, 39, 294
Kristeva, Julia, 64, 90, 91, 93, 94, 96, 99, 101, 104, 116, 306, 307, 313, 481, 486, 488

Lacan, Jacques, 8, 35-39, 57, 85, 90, 91, 93, 98, 154, 201, 264, 265, 269, 294-297, 307, 315, 437-441, 480, 483, 485, 487, 488
Langue, 57, 137, 342, 481
Le parler femme, 90, 91, 481
Liberalism, 97, 98, 109, 120, 157, 236, 255, 481, 482
Lichtenstein, Heinz, 47, 52
Literal language, 289, 290, 482
Local knowledge, 137, 146, 474, 482, 488
Logocentric thought, 57, 65, 66, 264, 267, 268, 482, 483. *See also* Metaphysics
Lombroso, Césare, 215, 216

Macherey, Pierre, 83, 86, 87
Magical realism, 232, 482
Malak, Amin, 275, 276, 281, 283, 419-425
Manichean oppositions, 160, 482
Marcuse, Herbert, 479
Marx, Karl, 8, 57, 71-74, 77, 78, 80, 85-87, 125, 131, 136, 236, 239, 279, 301, 476-478, 481, 482, 487, 489
Marxism, 8, 9, 15, 23, 62, 69, 71-87, 98, 103, 109-111, 115-117, 120, 129, 132, 133, 144, 146, 153, 154, 160-162, 204, 226, 229, 236-242, 244, 253, 254, 266, 285, 297-305, 397-400
Mau Mau, 187, 244, 245, 247-249, 251, 252, 254
Means of production, 28, 35, 76, 80, 92, 96, 128, 137, 207, 209, 261, 271, 273, 278, 280, 292, 297, 313, 475-477, 482, 487
Medvedev, Pavel, 103, 115
Menippean satire, 108-110, 116, 269, 273, 482
Metafiction, 478, 482, 486. *See also* Reflexivity
Metaphor, 18-20, 31, 33, 55, 60, 61, 182, 191, 200, 202, 221, 237, 239, 241, 243, 256, 259, 288, 292, 293, 301, 308, 482. *See also* Figurative language
Metaphysics, 18, 57, 59, 62-64, 66, 176, 226, 480, 482, 483, 485. *See also* Logocentric thought
Metonymy, 31, 483. *See also* Figurative language
Miller, J. Hillis, 56, 66, 68, 214, 218
Miller, Perry, 280, 283
Millett, Kate, 96, 101
Milton, John, 41-43, 321
Minor literature, 153, 161, 483
Mirror stage, 36, 85, 93, 483
Mode of production, 132, 474, 483
Modernism, 17, 18, 20, 23, 32, 75, 76, 78-80, 84, 86, 108, 109, 160, 202, 204, 212, 218, 287, 302, 483, 485, 487
Moi, Toril, 94, 99
Monologism, 105, 108, 109, 110, 207, 267, 271, 474, 483
Montrose, Louis, 136, 138, 143, 145-147
Morrison, Toni, 9, 149, 162, 285-315, 427-472
Morson, Gary Saul, 103, 104, 108, 110, 112, 113, 115, 116
Mudimbe, V. Y., 160, 162, 213, 217, 218, 236, 242
Myth, 19, 27, 34, 35, 58, 78, 95, 228, 231, 273, 305, 308, 312, 314, 390, 391

Naturalism, 75, 143, 146, 206, 484
New criticism, 1, 3-6, 8, 13-25, 34, 41, 42, 47, 56, 65-67, 98, 119, 137, 138, 144, 257-263, 285-291, 478
Nietzsche, Friedrich, 55, 56, 59-61, 67, 68, 78, 79, 121, 123, 124, 132, 136, 204
Nkrumah, Kwame, 162, 212, 236, 251, 298, 305
Nordau, Max, 215, 216

Object-relations psychology, 33, 294
Oedipal drama, 27-29, 32, 33, 36, 37, 92, 202, 226, 293, 294, 484
Ogunjimi, Bayo, 231, 235, 255, 394-407
Omolade, Barbara, 301, 305
Organic unity, 19-21, 56, 84, 484
Orientalism, 130, 133, 151, 156, 157, 160, 224, 225, 353, 484

Panopticon, 125, 126, 484
Paradox, 21, 56, 100, 144, 208
Parole, 57, 137, 484
Parrinder, Patrick, 216, 218, 222, 223, 225, 227, 353-366
Parry, Benita, 155, 158, 162, 210, 212, 218, 227
Patriarchal society, 89, 91, 94-97, 177, 189, 212, 228, 243, 255-257, 264, 265, 267, 272, 274, 294, 305, 307, 309, 314, 481, 484
Phenomenology, 44, 484
Pleasure principle, 28, 35, 38, 295-297, 484
Polyphony, 105, 112, 205, 206, 241, 485
Postcolonial literature, 150, 153, 155, 157, 229-256, 387-407, 483, 485
Postmodernism, 25, 80, 84, 86, 87, 108, 109, 112, 125, 161, 282, 312, 485
Poststructuralism, 55-69, 83, 119-133, 144, 145, 154-158, 162, 485, 474-476, 482-489

Proletariat, 72, 74, 75, 475, 479, 480, 485, 487
Psychoanalytic criticism, 27-40, 47, 48, 51, 52, 57, 111, 127, 200-205, 291-297
Pynchon, Thomas, 108, 485

Ransom, John Crowe, 13, 15-18, 22-24
Readerly text, 58
Reader-response criticism, 41-53, 167-174, 230-236
Real order, 35, 37, 485
Realism, 17, 75, 76, 87, 114, 202, 218, 232, 237, 482, 485-487
Reality principle, 28, 35, 486
Reception aesthetics, 44, 486
Reflexivity, 486. *See also* Metafiction
Reification, 74, 75, 77, 78, 302, 476, 486
Repression, 29-31, 60, 74, 175, 262, 276, 292, 293, 313, 486
Repressive state apparatus, 82, 240, 486
Richards, I. A., 15, 16, 24, 46-48, 53
Rorty, Richard, 65, 69, 259
Rushdie, Salman, 108, 152, 160, 163, 234, 235, 482, 485
Rushdy, Ashraf, 288, 291, 314, 448-472
Russian formalism, 15, 24, 25, 478

Said, Edward, 13, 16, 37, 55, 64, 108, 114, 130, 133, 151, 154-158, 160, 163, 208, 211, 224, 225, 305, 306, 353, 484
Saussure, Ferdinand de, 57, 61, 62, 69, 137, 342, 486, 487
Science, 5, 16-18, 21, 24, 29, 42, 44, 78, 79, 83, 120-122, 125, 127, 137, 151, 152, 211, 215, 228, 241, 259-261, 272, 284, 289, 290, 303, 304, 479
Sedgwick, Eve Kosofsky, 99, 101, 130, 133
Semiotic language, 91, 93, 94, 307, 313, 486
Sexuality, 27-35, 38, 39, 86, 91, 95-101, 106, 126-132, 136, 139, 175, 182, 205, 238, 247, 250, 258-262, 266, 273, 275-281, 283, 297, 299, 301, 305, 307, 308, 309, 312, 479, 485
Shaffer, Brian, 216, 219, 228, 366-385
Shakespeare, William, 10, 14, 21, 29, 32, 48, 135, 139-144, 146, 151, 161, 167-197, 251, 314, 319-351
Showalter, Elaine, 96-101, 479
Signification, 62, 123, 155, 265, 487
Socialism, 17, 72, 75, 78, 83, 85, 114, 232, 236, 245, 249, 254, 255, 405, 485-487
Socialist realism, 17, 114, 232, 486, 487
Speech genres, 103, 115, 487
Spencer, Herbert, 215, 216, 228, 366-385
Spivak, Gayatri Chakravorty, 64, 67, 69, 98, 99, 101, 154, 155, 158, 161, 163
Stream of consciousness, 202, 401, 487
Structuralism, 34, 35, 36, 52, 53, 57-61, 63, 65, 67-69, 82, 83, 86, 103, 122-124, 131, 133, 137, 475, 481, 484-487
Subalternity, 150, 151, 153, 155, 161, 170, 487
Subjectivity, 35, 50, 51, 53, 84, 111, 265, 266, 310, 311, 475, 481, 487, 489
Sublimation, 30, 31, 488
Superego, 29, 33, 200, 478, 488
Superstructure, 71, 74, 75, 474, 488
Surrealism, 79, 488
Symbolic language, 58, 86, 93, 94, 200-202, 244, 313, 488
Symbolic order, 35-37, 90-93, 201, 265, 294-296, 488
Symbols, 18-20, 27, 29, 31, 34, 137, 200, 201, 202, 237, 238, 240, 254, 279, 306, 488
Synchronic approaches, 122, 488

Takaki, Ronald, 174, 175, 180, 196
Tate, Allen, 15-17, 22
Teleological thought, 206, 217, 218, 488
Textuality, 64, 103, 135, 136, 488
Thick descriptions, 145, 482, 488
Thiong'o Ngugi wa, 10, 152-154, 162, 187, 188, 191, 193, 194, 219, 229-256, 387-407, 485
Todorov, Tzvetan, 58, 104, 109, 116, 487
Transcendental subject, 57, 155, 487, 489
Turner, Victor, 137
Typicality, 76, 221, 489

Understanding Poetry, 18, 24
Unity, 19-21, 47, 48, 52, 56, 58, 65, 84, 170, 214, 300, 484
Use value, 73, 476, 489
Utopian thought, 78, 81, 87, 92, 95, 108, 142, 146, 153, 175, 184, 185, 187, 264, 271-273, 281-283, 289, 300, 489

Voloshinov, V. N., 103, 111, 116, 273
Freudianism, 103, 111, 116
Marxism and the Philosophy of Language, 103, 111, 116

Warren, Austin, 18-20, 25
Warren, Robert Penn, 15, 17, 18, 20, 21, 23, 24, 286, 287, 290, 291
Wellek, René, 18-20, 24, 25
Williams, Raymond, 83-87, 109, 117, 136, 298, 305, 476
Williams, William Carlos, 5-8
Wimsatt, W. K., Jr., 14, 25, 41, 195
Winnicott, D. W., 33, 34, 39, 40, 294, 295
Winters, Yvor, 16
Wittig, Monique, 94, 95, 98, 101, 102
Woman's sentence, 90, 489
Woolf, Virginia, 89, 90, 99, 100, 112, 143, 287, 483, 489
Writerly text, 58
Wyatt, Jean, 40, 53, 102, 289, 291, 295-297, 303, 305, 306, 312, 315, 427-448